FIRST CLASS CRICKET
A COMPLETE RECORD 1939

FIRST CLASS CRICKET

A COMPLETE RECORD 1939

Edited by Jim Ledbetter
with Peter Wynne-Thomas
Researched by
The Association of Cricket Statisticians

Breedon Books Sport

First published in Great Britain by
The Breedon Books Publishing Company Limited
44 Friar Gate, Derby, DE1 1DA.
1991

ISBN 0 907969 72 0

Printed and bound in Great Britain by Butler and Tanner Limited,
Frome and London.
Jacket printed by Arkle Print Limited of Northampton.

CONTENTS

Acknowledgements

THE compilation of these scores would not have been possible without the help and co-operation of many individuals and organizations. We would like to acknowledge the assistance of the following in either providing the facilities for our research or contributing valuable match details: Essex County Cricket Club, Leicestershire County Cricket Club, Northamptonshire County Cricket Club, Nottinghamshire County Cricket Club, Warwickshire County Cricket Club, Worcestershire County Cricket Club, The British Library Newspaper Library, The Nottingham Central Library, Leicestershire County Record Office, Nottingham Polytechnic Library, The Army Cricket Association, Colonel N.J.Wilson of the Free Foresters Cricket Club, David Armstrong of the Minor Counties Cricket Association, J.A.Hunt of Oxford University Cricket Club, N.J.Leitch of the Scottish Cricket Union and county historians and statisticians Don Ambrose, Bert Avery, Philip Bailey, Andrew Hignell, Michael Hill, Richard V.Isaacs, Malcolm Lorimer, Howard Milton, H.A.Osborne, Frank Peach, Andrew Radd.

Introduction

THIS volume contains details of all the matches played in 1938-39, which have been recognized by the Association of Cricket Statisticians as having first-class status. The total of 363 matches consists of 288 games played in the British Isles, 17 in Australia, 17 in South Africa, seven in New Zealand, 25 in India and nine in the West Indies.

Details of matches played in the first-class counties in England have been taken, whenever possible, from the scorebooks of the individual counties. In the few instances where this was not possible, owing to the scorebook having been lost or destroyed, it has been necessary to consult other sources such as contemporary local and national newspapers. A number of county handbooks have also provided additional information. The data gathered has supplemented the scores taken from *Wisden* and *The Cricketer* and in a considerable number of instances has amended and corrected details in these publications.

The first-class matches in the British Isles involving non-county sides have posed greater difficulties. The absence of scorebooks for the Universities, the Army and the Free Foresters has unfortunately made it impossible to give comprehensive coverage of certain matches, especially those between two non-county sides. Newspaper accounts have been used for close-of-play scores but are less reliable, for example, on the fall of wickets and changes in second innings batting orders. There must always remain a doubt as to the absolute accuracy of information gathered from this type of evidence, unless substantiated by a number of other sources.

There was, however, no difficulty with any of the first-class games played in South Africa, as the South African authorities cancelled all first-class domestic cricket in 1938-39 to accommodate the MCC tour. W.Ferguson's immaculate scorebook of that tour, including even the duration of many of the longer innings, was a highly valuable source of information.

The Association's own publication *A Guide to First-Class Matches played in New Zealand 1863 to 1980* compiled by Brian Croudy (1981) provided full details of all the seven first-class games played in that country in 1938-39, supplemented by additional information from New Zealand newspapers.

Details of the 17 first-class matches in Australia have been drawn from a number of sources, apart from *Wisden* and *The Cricketer*. The yearly publications of the Victorian and New South Wales Cricket Associations contained useful information, whilst the ACS's *Guide to First-Class Matches played in Australia* compiled by Ken Williams (2nd edition 1983) included full details of Victoria's games against Tasmania and Western Australia.

First-class cricket matches in the West Indies received detailed coverage from the many island newspapers. The recent publication, *Statistics of West Indies Cricket 1865-1989* by J.Richards and M.Wong (Heinemann 1990) was also helpful in corroborating the information gleaned from the newspaper reports.

Reliable information about the first-class game in India proved more difficult to collect. The match details in both *Wisden* and *The Cricketer* were not comprehensive. The ACS's publication *A Guide to First-Class Cricket Matches played in India* compiled by Philip Bailey (1986) covers three of the 25 games, whilst S.K.Roy's *Bombay Pentangular* (1945) and *Twelve Years of the Ranji Trophy 1934-45* by S.K.Gurunathan (1946) were helpful in adding further information. Most of the remaining details were obtained from the *Times of India* which, unfortunately, was highly selective in its treatment of the various games played in 1938-39. The Bombay Pentangular Tournament was given extensive coverage but several of the Ranji Trophy matches contained only the barest details.

The First-Class Season in England, 1939

DESPITE the background of growing international tension and the abrupt end to the season, resulting in the cancellation of a number of Championship fixtures, the traditional cricket festivals at Scarborough and Folkestone and the early departure of the West Indian touring party, there was much to be savoured in the cricket played in 1939. Even the miserable weather in the early part of the season and the wet July was compensated for in the final weeks of August, when lovely weather saw out the season.

The three-match Test series against the West Indies resulted, as expected, in success for the stronger England side, always clear favourites to win the series. The winning margin was a narrow one, a solitary victory in the First Test followed by two draws, the first largely the consequence of time lost through rain and bad light, the second a high-scoring game in which England's opponents gave their best batting performance of the series, albeit against a weakened England attack. However, set against the winning of the series was the failure of the selectors to unearth new talent and to solve some of the current problems in the England side. Little new had been learnt in a series, which was considered by many critics to be a useful preparation for the more difficult series against South Africa in 1940 and Australia in the winter of 1940-41.

The selectors had been given the opportunity to try out new players in key positions as a consequence of the unavailability of three members of the successful side which had toured South Africa during the winter, P.A.Gibb, L.E.G.Ames and K.Farnes. The initial selections for these vacant places in the team for the First Test were both popular and sensible, both in terms of producing a match-winning side and giving players in form an opportunity at Test level.

Gimblett, after an excellent start to the season, was given another chance as a Test opener. Wood came in for Ames, who was not keeping wicket due to a back injury, whilst the Derbyshire fast bowler, Copson, made his first Test appearance. The side was also strengthened by the return of three absentees from the South African tour, Hardstaff and Compton as middle-order

September 1939 and a bust of W.G.Grace is removed from the Lord's pavilion upon the outbreak of war. It was one of many cricketing artefacts put into storage to protect them from German bombing in the years ahead.

batsmen, and Bowes, hopefully refreshed after his winter break, joining Copson in a new-look opening attack. With Hammond, Hutton, Paynter, Verity and Wright retaining their places, the team appeared well-balanced and powerful.

This side did all that could be expected of it, securing a comfortable victory by eight wickets, but the two changes for the Old Trafford Test seemed inexplicable, with Goddard replacing Verity and Fagg coming in for Gimblett. The final Test saw further changes to the side, although a number of changes were forced on the selectors through injury. Keeton became the third opening batsman to be tried as a partner to Hutton. Oldfield of Lancashire was given his Test chance, replacing his more experienced teammate Paynter. Perks came in for the injured Bowes, with the 35-year-old Nichols, still the best all-rounder in English cricket, was selected as his opening bowling partner.

The series confirmed that England possessed a highly talented and essentially youthful batting side with Hutton, Compton and Hardstaff all hopefully looking forward to long and fruitful Test careers. All were to score over 2,000 runs during the 1939 season. Hammond still remained a great Test batsman, although Paynter had an indifferent series. It was ironic that Edrich, after being given more chances than most at Test level before making his epic double century at Durban, failed to secure a place in the side after also scoring over 2,000 runs.

The outstanding batting problem of finding an opening partner for Hutton was not resolved by the end of the series. Gimblett, Fagg and Keeton were all tried in successive Tests without quite fitting the bill, although Gimblett was unfortunate to be discarded after the First Test. However, he did have the consolation of being chosen for the winter tour of India, subsequently cancelled on the outbreak of war. John Langridge also chosen for the tour, must have been on the selector's immediate shortlist for this position. With a number of young batsmen, such as Robertson, Avery and Dollery, showing promise and players of Test experience such as Edrich, Barnett, Gimblett and Ames also capable of forcing their way back into the England side, there appeared to be no difficulties for the selectors in this department. Gibb, who missed all of the 1939 season, but who played a key part in England's success in South Africa, should also not be forgotten.

Bowling presented greater problems for the future, with several of the current England attack moving towards the end of their Test careers. Bowes (31) and Farnes (28), were still a Test match opening attack, Perks had shown potential in the two Tests in which he appeared, whilst Copson also showed himself a hostile fast bowler, capable of performing at this level. However, both players were in their late 20s. Nichols at 35, could only be considered as a short-term solution, his selection although merited, exposing a dearth of high-class all-rounders in the game. His closest rival was James Langridge of Sussex, only two years his junior, although F.R.Brown of Surrey and the Popes of Derbyshire might also come into contention in the future. G.H.Pope was selected for the aborted winter tour of India.

The manner in which the makeshift England attack was savaged in the Third Test still showed the necessity of Verity being in the England side, for although Goddard and Wright had excellent seasons with their counties, neither had achieved anything like the same success at Test level. Wright, at 25, had apparently time on his side, but Goddard, 14 years his senior, would soon need to be replaced by a younger off-spinner. E.P.Robinson of Yorkshire was a possible successor for this position in the England side. Wilkinson of Lancashire, who had promised much both in the 1938 season and on the MCC tour of South Africa, had a mediocre season and for the moment appeared to have fallen out of the reckoning. It would have been interesting to see how the Essex leg-spinner, T.B.P.Smith, would have fared on the MCC tour of India.

The two prestige matches at Lord's were in sharp contrast to each other. The Varsity match produced one of the most exciting finishes for years and, according to some writers, was one of the best games ever played between the two Universities, Cambridge, set 430 to win after having had the worst of the match on the first two days, were eight wickets down for 249 at one stage of their second innings, but a courageous fight-back by the lower-order batsmen left them only 45 short at the end, having made the largest score in the fourth innings in this series of games between Oxford and Cambridge. This was for the most part the consequence of a magnificent century from P.J.Dickinson, ably supported by J.Webster. Even after Dickinson's dismissal, Webster and Downes, the last man,

contrived to add another 40 runs for the tenth wicket before Webster was dismissed just after seven o'clock.

However, the Gentlemen v Players match was a disappointing affair, the stronger Players side winning fairly comfortably by 160 runs, miserable weather not helping matters. The rain and the winning of the toss also assisted the Players, with their fast bowlers, Bowes and Copson, giving the Gentlemen an uncomfortable time in both innings. Set 315 to win and already without the injured Stephenson, they also lost Wyatt retired hurt and never appeared to have any chance of winning the game. The later batsmen threw caution to the winds, allowing Wright, despite being expensive, to win the match for the Players.

THE COUNTY CHAMPIONSHIP

THIS season saw the introduction on a two-year experimental basis of the eight-ball over into first-class cricket at both Test and county level. In some quarters it was estimated the change could save over 90 minutes in the course of a three-day match, a calculation disputed by others. Few observations were made during the season on this change, probably due to the necessity of waiting until the end of the two-year period before making any final judgement.

Far more heated discussion arose over the points system, employed in the County Championship. An article in the Spring Edition of *The Cricketer* by E.M.Roberts had warned that a side near the top of the table could be tempted, in some instances, to play for a 'no result' rather than for the first-innings points. Whilst the latter would give a side four points, if its average happened to be above this number, its average and possibly its position in the table would be worsened. A 'no result', on the other hand, would simply not be counted as a match in the table, thus retaining a county's average and position.

Three games during the season high-lighted this problem. In the July fixture between Yorkshire and Nottinghamshire, the Yorkshire batsmen deliberately batted at a slow rate to avoid taking a first-innings lead, even suffering barracking from their own supporters to achieve their objective. On the same day, Middlesex, another contender for the title, made no effort to declare against Lancashire until they were certain neither side could achieve first-innings points. Subsequently, Middlesex were to adopt another tactic as a means of securing a 'no result' against Sussex, resting all their regular bowlers to avoid bowling out their opponents, who stood no chance in the time available of passing the Middlesex first-innings total. It was clear that some further thought needed to be given to this aspect of awarding points in the future.

Although the Championship was not finally decided until the final week in August, Yorkshire, the favourites, retained the title after heading the table for most of the season. Once again ably led by Brian Sellers, who chalked up his fifth title in seven years, Yorkshire, even when depleted by Test calls and injury, could still call on a pool of talented players, having an impressive staff of 13 capped players when the season began.

Yorskhire's Len Hutton, scored over 2,000 runs for the County Champions, including nine centuries.

It was hard to pin-point a weakness in the side. The batting maintained a high level of consistency, with Hutton having an outstanding season, scoring over 2,000 runs, including nine hundreds, for his county. His opening partner, Sutcliffe, at 45, still scored over a 1,000 runs and had the distinction of making four consecutive centuries. Solid support was always forthcoming from the dependable trio of Leyland, Barber and Mitchell, although Yardley did not quite live up to the promise shown in the MCC tour of South Africa, failing to make 1,000 runs. The bowling was also of a high standard. The decision of the England selectors to omit Verity after the First Test was Yorkshire's gain, for the slow left-armer headed the first-class bowling averages, taking 165 wickets for Yorkshire. Despite criticisms in some quarters that he was a negative bowler, he was still a match-winner on responsive wickets. Bowes and Robinson were also in

Medium-pacer Tom Smailes took 10-47 in an innings for Yorkshire against Derbyshire at Bramall Lane.

fine form, each claiming over 100 wickets. No other county could call upon such a talented trio of bowlers, who bore the brunt of the Yorkshire attack. T.F.Smailes was less effective than in previous years, but still managed to achieve all ten wickets in an innings against Derbyshire. Even unknown and untried bowlers responded to the call. J.Smurthwaite, on his first Championship appearance, helped Smailes bowl out Derbyshire for 20, the lowest score of the season, Smurthwaite having the remarkable analysis of five wickets for seven runs.

Yorkshire were worthy winners of their 21st Championship. Despite their reputation of being a tough side, who gave no quarter, they were the only team to continue playing after 31 August to give James Parks all three days play in his benefit match. Unfortunately for Sussex, Verity, in one of the finest performances of his career, was to take seven for nine as Sussex were bowled out for 33.

Middlesex were again runners up for the fourth successive year. Led by a new captain, the enthusiastic I.A.R.Peebles, their success was built around the outstanding batting of Compton and Edrich, both of whom scored almost 2,000 runs in Championship matches. J.D.B.Robertson was also a major run contributor, continuing to maintain his previous season's progress. Sadly for Middlesex, these three attractive stroke-makers, who between them scored 16 of the county's 17 centuries, and were the only batsmen to make over 1,000 runs, received little consistent support from the remaining batsmen. Only one other player made over 500 runs. The bowling too was a little thin, G.O.Allen and R.W.V.Robins being clearly missed and most of the remaining bowlers having disappointing returns. The exception was Sims, who had an excellent season and was the only bowler to claim 100 wickets. That they ran Yorkshire so close was in the main due to the contribution of individual match-winners in the side.

Gloucestershire were one of the most improved sides in 1939, not only moving up from tenth position to fill the third slot in the table but also having the distinction of beating the champions on both occasions. Of course, they possessed in Hammond, the best batsman in the country. He scored over 2,000 runs for Gloucestershire, including a triple-hundred against Glamorgan and six other hundreds. He received solid support from Crapp and Emmett, although more could have been forthcoming from the

Jack Robertson of Middlesex, seen here on his way to 154 against Warwickshire with a century before lunch.

talented Barnett. Goddard had a magnificent season, claiming 181 wickets at a cost of 14.66. At times he was virtually unplayable on the Bristol wicket, which had the reputation of taking spin from the first over. He captured 84 wickets for eight runs apiece in seven games there, including 30 in a week against Kent and Yorkshire, equalling the world record of 17 wickets in a day against the former. He claimed nine wickets in an innings on three occasions. The bowling was, however, not just a one-man band, for Goddard was well supported by Scott, a very promising fast-medium bowler, who took 100 wickets for the first time in only his second season and Lambert, another fine young prospect. With a number of young players, all looking capable of improvement, added to the experience of such players capable of again mounting a serious challenge to Yorkshire in the future.

Essex, although being led by three different captains, had their best season since 1897, rising two places to finish in fourth position. It was even more commendable as Farnes was not to make an appearance for the county until August, when he achieved his first ever hat-trick. Much of the credit for the county's successful season must go to Nichols, who was once again the first player to achieve the double for the fifth successive year, an undoubted factor in his deserved recall to the England side. The other bowlers gave consistent support, with R.Smith being described in some quarters as the most improved all-round player in the country.

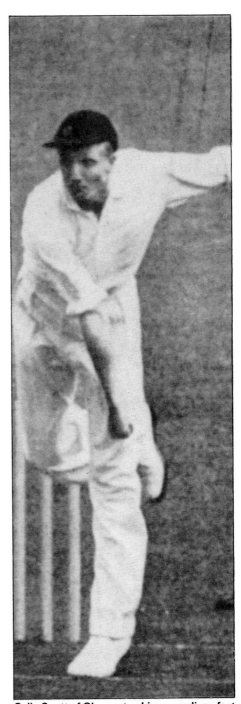

Colin Scott of Gloucestershire, a medium-fast bowler who took 100 wickets in only his second season of first-class cricket. Scott, who was also a hard-hitting lower order batsman, went on to make 235 appearances for Gloucester before retiring in 1954.

Captain J.W.A.Stephenson of Essex was one of the most interesting characters in the game. An all-rounder, he made his first-class debut for the Army in 1931 and his last appearance for the South of England in 1948. He made 61 appearances for Essex before the war, his military career preventing him from being a regular.

Peter Smith also had a fine season and was chosen for the MCC tour to India in the winter, as was Nichols. O'Connor was again the county's leading run scorer, making over 1,000 runs for the 15th successive season, whilst much would be hoped of A.V.Avery, who emerged as a stylish and effective opening batsman.

Kent also achieved their highest position for five years, finishing fifth under the positive and enterprising leadership of F.G.H.Chalk. It was no coincidence that Kent were to draw only three of their 27 Championship matches. They were not only the best batting side in the country in terms of runs scored, they were also one of the most entertaining. If Ames was unable to keep wicket, his absence from the England side enabled him to score over 1,800 runs for Kent, in the process winning the Lawrence Trophy for the fastest century for the second time. A.E.Fagg also had another fine season as the county's opening batsman, being chosen for England in the Second Test, whilst B.H.Valentine, L.J.Todd and the captain all passed 1,000 runs for the county. It was no surprise that Kent were to make the highest total of the season, 580-9 against Sussex. The bowling had variety, with C.Lewis, A.E.Watt, N.W.Harding and L.J.Todd all taking over 50 wickets. Wright, despite his absences on Test duty, still managed to capture 131 wickets for his side. At times he was to prove almost unplayable, achieving career best figures of 9 for 47 against Gloucestershire, which included the fifth hat-trick of his career. He could almost be termed an all-rounder with an improvement in his batting producing an individual best score of 84*.

Unlike Kent, Lancashire who finished in sixth place, had no less than 16 of their 31 games producing no definite result, with ten having no decision on the first innings. The county was to suffer 13 blank days on account of the weather, which also badly affected the Second Test at Old Trafford. The batting once again proved the sides strong point, with Iddon, Paynter, Oldfield, who gained his first England cap and Washbrook all scoring over 1,500 runs for Lancashire. Place also looked a highly promising prospect, the highlight of his season being his chanceless 164 against the tourists. The bowling gave cause for concern. Wilkinson, after his highly successful 1938 season, which had earned him a place in the MCC side which toured South Africa, captured only 63 Championship wickets. Pollard and Phillipson, the

Kent skipper F.G.H.Chalk is bowled by Pollard of Lancashire in the second innings at Dover. At the outbreak of war, Chalk joined the RAF and was reported missing in 1943. In 1989, a French farmer discovered Chalk's mortal remains in the wreckage of his Spitfire in a field near Boulogne.

opening bowlers, both had successful seasons but there was little support forthcoming from the other bowlers.

Worcester could look back upon their results in the 1939 season with considerable satisfaction. Sadly, this was dampened by the tragic death in a motoring accident of their opening batsman, C.H.Bull, killed during the match against Essex. After beginning with a victory over the West Indian tourists, they went on to compete the second most successful season in their history, in terms of Championship victories, finishing seventh and winning 12 matches, having climbed five places in the table. They experienced an astonishing July, when a succession of matches went to extremely tight finishes, including a tie and two victories by one wicket. A key factor in the county's success was the performance of Martin and Howorth, whose all-round ability led to both players achieving the double. Perks, with 143 wickets to his credit, was the pick of the bowlers, having his best season to date and winning his second England cap. The main reason for Worcestershire's improvement lay in solid performances by the majority of the players. If Gibbons was the major run-getter, scoring his first Championship double-century as well as achieving the feat of two hundreds in a match, five other players scored over 900 runs, with six batsmen contributing 14 centuries. The bowling also benefited from consistent contributions. The most promising young player was C.H.Palmer, who at 20 years of age, began the season with two successive centuries and just missed his 1,000 runs for the county.

Surrey, down five places in eighth place, began extremely well under their new captain, H.M.Garland-Wells, winning seven of their first ten matches and ending strongly with four consecutive victories but having a very indifferent mid-season. L.B.Fishlock and R.J.Gregory proved a very reliable opening partnership, both scoring over 1,500 runs and were well supported by all the other recognized batsmen. J.F.Parker fully deserved his selection as a member of the MCC side to India, a tour which was subsequently abandoned. F.R.Brown, available for just over half the Championship matches, showed himself to be one of best all-rounders in the country with aggressive batting and attacking leg-spin. A.R.Gover and E.A.Watts were the mainstay of the attack. Gover claiming over 100 wickets, whilst Watts earned the distinction of becoming the third Surrey bowler to take all ten wickets in an innings, when he performed the feat against Warwickshire. G.S.Mobey, who replaced E.W.J.Brooks as wicketkeeper, was selected for the winter tour to India.

Derbyshire experienced a decline in their fortunes, for the first time in six years finding themselves out of the top six places. This was despite fielding practically the same side throughout the season. The major problem was the brittleness of the batting, only six hundreds being scored by the county batsmen, with only G.H.Pope and D.Smith averaging over 30. It was fortunate for the county that their bowling attack was one of the most dangerous in the country,

In Derbyshire's second innings at Lord's, fast bowler Bill Copson hit Jim Sims for six — something of an empty gesture for (*above*) Sims then bowled Copson.

especially on their helpful home wickets where visiting sides scored over 200 on only three occasions out of 21 completed innings. Copson was the most successful of the bowlers, taking over 100 wickets and achieving a hat-trick against Oxford University. He was well supported by G.H. and A.V.Pope and T.B.Mitchell, who all claimed over 75 wickets for the county. They were indebted for many of their wickets to Elliott's ability behind the stumps.

Sussex, who finished in tenth position, owed their position in the table to their sound batting, six of their batsmen scoring over 1,000 runs. Both the Langridges had excellent seasons, John scoring over 2,000 runs and James over 1,600 runs as well as taking 84 wickets. Bowling was more of a problem, Sussex relying essentially on three players, James Langridge, J.H.Parks and J.K.Nye, who captured 100 wickets for the first time. One pleasing aspect of the season was the excellent promise shown behind the stumps by S.C.Griffith, who took over from W.Cornford towards the end of the season.

Warwickshire in 11th position, had a

Sussex wicketkeeper S.C. 'Billy' Griffith and leg slip James Langridge.

dismal finish to the season, winning only one of their last eight Championship matches. Their batting was solid and sound with H.E.Dollery being the outstanding batsman, scoring four hundreds and heading the batting averages. He was regarded in some quarters as a possible future Test batsman. The county relied heavily on two bowlers, Hollies and Mayer, who took two-thirds of the wickets. Hollies, with 110 wickets, took five wickets on no less than 11 occasions, including 9-93 against Glamorgan.

Nottinghamshire remained in 12th position for the second successive season. The team relied far too heavily on too few players. Keeton, who made the highest individual score for Notts, an undefeated 312 against Middlesex, Hardstaff and Heane provided most of the runs with Keeton and Harris often providing a sound start. Butler had his best season to date, taking 100 wickets and performing his third hat-trick. Voce also had a good season, bowling over 700 overs, often resorting to slow spin. Although Jepson gave these two some support, there was little else to fall back on, especially in terms of slow bowling.

Glamorgan, in finishing 13th, advanced three places up the table, somewhat disappointing after promising to finish much higher earlier in the season. Their batting proved far stronger than their bowling, with Emrys Davies and A.H.Dyson one of the most consistent opening pairs in the country, well supported by the more aggressive Smart and Turnbull, the latter leading his side with panache. Glamorgan began the season with scores of over 500 in their first three home games, in the course of which they made their highest-ever total in a Championship match, with E.Davies hitting the highest score, 287*, by a Glamorgan player. Haydn Davies was also to claim a new county record with his 64 victims behind the stumps. The bowling was much less effective, no bowler getting near 100 wickets, with the acquisition from Middlesex, P.F.Judge, a rare example of an amateur turning professional, taking most wickets. The absence of A.D.G.Matthews until the latter part of the season was keenly felt. A stronger bowling side would have made Glamorgan a much formidable contender for a top place in the table.

Somerset suffered a decline in their fortunes, falling seven places to finish 14th. The crucial absence of Wellard for five games in August was an important factor

Umpire Robinson removes mud from the boot of Notts batsman Charlie Harris during the rain-swept game at The Oval in August.

over 900 runs in seven games. His early consistency and his positive approach made his England recall and subsequent selection for the winter tour to India a fully deserved one. If F.S.Lee was not as prolific as he was in 1938, he was still the county's second-highest run scorer, whilst Buse, at three, gave steady support. Unfortunately, none of the remaining batsmen showed anything like the same consistency as the first three and batting collapses were too frequent throughout the year. Four bowlers provided the mainstay of the attack with Wellard and Andrews both claiming 100 wickets with good support from the much improved Hazell and Buse, the latter having a fine all-round season with 78 wickets and over 1,000 runs.

Hampshire's season was highly disappointing, all the more so because they lost many games, which they appeared to have a good chance of winning. In 14 of their matches, they led on first innings, yet won only two of them, losing another eight. Despite five batsmen scoring over 1,000 runs, the batting, apart from Arnold and Bailey, lacked consistency, Creese being a good example of a player, beginning the season in brilliant form, only to fall away very badly. The side lacked a match-winning bowler, both Boyes and Heath being far less effective than the previous season. A mediocre bowling attack made it difficult to dismiss opponents twice in a game, although the bowling of the young leg-spinner, Dean, at the end of the season, including a hat-trick against Worcestershire gave hope for next season.

Finishing in 16th position, Northamptonshire could at least point to an improvement in their fortunes, vacating the last spot in the table for the first time in six years, as well as winning their first Championship match since 1935, when they defeated Leicestershire in May. R.P.Nelson always attempted to force wins by declarations, sometimes, however, being a little overgenerous to his opponents. J.E.Timms was the most successful batsman, becoming the first Northamptonshire player to make a hundred in each innings of a match. It was encouraging that several of the younger batsmen, such as D.Brookes and the Oxford captain E.J.H.Dixon, showed potential for the future. The bowling was always a problem with only J.R.Partridge and W.E.Meritt managing to take over 70 wickets.

Leicestershire experienced one of the worst season's in their history, securing only

in this decline. The county possessed one of the best opening pairs in the country in Gimblett and F.S.Lee. Gimblett had his best season to date, starting magnificently with five hundreds in successive matches and just

Yorkshire's opening pair Herbert Sutcliffe (left) and Len Hutton take the field. Hutton, as we have seen, had an outstanding season with 2,000 runs, but as remarkable was the continuing good form of 45-year-old Sutcliffe, who scored 1,000 runs and had the distinction of making four consecutive centuries for the County Champions.

one victory and filling the last position in the Championship table. The retirement of George Geary and the absence of J.E.Walsh, a fine left-arm bowler, and C.E.Dempster for a considerable number of matches made their task even more difficult. At times the county were forced to field an extremely youthful and inexperienced side. The most heartening feature of a miserable season was the magnificent keeping of Dawkes, seen by some as a possible England 'keeper. Armstrong was the most consistent batsman and Sperry made the most progress amongst the bowlers, playing an important role in the county's solitary victory against Hampshire. Consistently poor fielding was another key factor in a season best forgotten for Leicestershire.

Although they did not know it, first-class cricket was to be suspended for seven years. Yet these current and former Middlesex players were still a team at the end of September 1939, all of them now members of the wartime London Police Reserve. From left to right: W.H.Wignall, G.E.Hart, W.J.R.Harrington, A.W.Martin (groundsman), D.C.S Compton, T.Smith (staff), W.F.F.Price, L.H.Compton and A.W.Thompson.

COUNTY CHAMPIONSHIP TABLE 1939

	P	W	L	D	Tie	1st inns lead in match L	1st inns lead in match D	Pts	Ave
Points Awarded	12	-	-		6	4	4		
Yorkshire (1)	28	20	4	4	0	2	3	260	9.28
Middlesex (2)	22	†14	6	2	0	3	1	180	8.18
Gloucestershire (10)	26	15	7	4	0	1	3	196	7.53
Essex (6)	24	12	10	2	0	4	2	‡170	7.08
Kent (9)	26	14	9	3	0	2	1	180	6.92
Lancashire (4)	21	10	6	5	0	3	1	140	6.66
Worcestershire (11)	27	11	10	5	1	2	4	162	6.00
Surrey (3)	24	11	7	6	0	0	2	140	5.83
Derbyshire (5)	25	10	8	7	0	1	5	144	5.76
Sussex (8)	29	10	12	7	0	1	4	140	4.82
Warwickshire (13)	22	7	8	7	0	1	2	‡98	4.45
Nottinghamshire (12) ...	23	6	8	9	0	2	5	100	4.34
Glamorgan (16)	24	6	8	10	0	1	5	96	4.00
Somerset (7)	27	6	11	9	1	2	4	102	3.77
Hampshire (14)........	26	3	17	6	0	8	4	84	3.23
Northamptonshire (17)	22	1	12	9	0	3	3	36	1.63
Leicestershire (15)	20	1	14	5	0	1	0	16	0.80

†Includes one win in a match restricted to one day's play.
‡Includes two points for tie on the first innings in match lost.

Method of Scoring
12 points for a win.
6 points to each side for a tie.
4 points for a first innings lead in a match either lost or drawn.
2 points each if scores level on first innings in match lost or drawn.
8 points for a first innings lead in a match restricted to the final day's play.
The Champion County is the side with the highest average number of points, after its total points have been divided by the number of games played.
A match in which no decision is reached on the first innings, will not be included as a 'match played' in the table.

Notes
Figures in parentheses indicate the positions in the 1938 Championship table.
The following games have not been included in the final Championship table.
1. The Surrey v Lancashire match at Old Trafford, played on 30 August and 31, which was abandoned at the end of the second day, due to the deteriorating international situation.
2. Matches in which no result was reached on the first innings. Derbyshire v Lancashire; Derbyshire v Yorkshire; Essex v Lancashire; Essex v Kent; Glamorgan v Hampshire; Glamorgan v Leicestershire; Hampshire v Nottinghamshire; Hampshire v Glamorgan; Lancashire v Sussex; Lancashire v Northamptonshire; Lancashire v Gloucestershire; Lancashire v Warwickshire; Lancashire v Essex; Leicestershire v Northamptonshire; Middlesex v Lancashire; Nottinghamshire v Sussex; Somerset v Lancashire; Surrey v Glamorgan; Surrey v Nottinghamshire; Surrey v Hampshire; Sussex v Middlesex; Warwickshire v Middlesex; Worcestershire v Leicestershire; Worcestershire v Essex; Yorkshire v Nottinghamshire.
3. Matches which were not played because of the international situation. Middlesex v Kent; Gloucestershire v Nottinghamshire; Lancashire v Leicestershire.

FIRST-CLASS AVERAGES 1939

BATTING	Pld	In	NO	Runs	HS	Ave	100s
G.A.Headley (WIndies)	20	30	6	1745	*234	72.60	6
†W.R.Hammond (Glos)	28	46	7	2479	302	63.56	7
†L.Hutton (Yorks)	33	52	6	2883	*280	62.27	12
†D.C.S.Compton (Middx)	31	50	6	2468	*214	56.09	8
†J.Hardstaff Jun (Notts)	30	46	7	2129	159	54.58	5
H.Sutcliffe (Yorks)	21	29	3	1416	*234	54.46	6
†W.W.Keeton (Notts)	25	39	5	1765	*312	51.91	2
J.Iddon (Lancs)	31	45	11	1716	*217	50.47	4
W.J.Edrich (Middx)	29	45	1	2186	161	49.68	7
Jas.Langridge (Sussex)	27	42	8	1652	161	48.58	2
L.E.G.Ames (Kent)	25	46	6	1846	201	46.15	5
†N.Oldfield (Lancs)	33	48	5	1922	*147	44.69	4
†E.Paynter (Lancs)	31	50	4	1953	222	42.45	4
H.E.Dollery (War)	27	41	5	1519	177	42.19	4
A.V.Avery (Essex)	23	36	4	1335	161	41.71	2
John G.Langridge (Sussex)	31	51	0	2106	202	41.29	6
†A.E.Fagg (Kent)	27	51	6	1851	*169	41.13	5
†H.Gimblett (Som)	30	50	3	1922	129	40.89	5
J.D.B.Robertson (Middx)	28	44	1	1755	154	40.81	4
D.E.Davies (Glam)	28	45	3	1714	*287	40.80	3

BOWLING	Pld	Overs	Mds	Runs	Wkts	Ave
H.Verity (Yorks)	33	916.3	270	2509	191	13.13
C.W.S.Lubbock (Oxford U/ Northants)	6	73.4	8	271	19	14.26
†W.E.Bowes (Yorks)	28	712.3	151	1767	122	14.48
†T.W.J.Goddard (Glos)	29	819	139	2973	200	14.86
†W.H.Copson (Derby)	31	669.3	92	2238	146	15.36
J.C.Boucher (Ireland)	1	55	11	158	10	15.80
L.M.Cranfield (Glos)	3	56.4	5	231	14	16.50
†D.V.P.Wright (Kent)	26	571	64	2371	141	16.81
C.Lewis (Kent)	15	301.5	58	959	56	17.12
L.N.Constantine (WIndies)	22	488.4	67	1831	103	17.77
A.D.G.Matthews (Glam)	11	266.2	33	894	50	17.88
†L.Hutton (Yorks)	33	220.7	38	822	44	18.68
†M.S.Nichols (Essex)	29	666.5	90	2284	121	18.87
E.P.Robinson (Yorks)	30	659.5	130	2289	129	19.07
K.Farnes (Essex)	8	179.6	18	726	38	19.10
A.E.G.Rhodes (Derby)	28	123	14	479	25	19.16
†R.T.D.Perks (Worcs)	30	828	112	3057	159	19.22
G.H.Pope (Derby)	31	476.6	69	1640	83	19.75
A.V.Pope (Derby)	30	567.5	79	1862	94	19.80
S.Pether (Oxford U)	10	191.4	34	622	31	20.06

†Played for England but not featured above: A.Wood

THE COUNTY CHAMPIONSHIP

GLOUCESTERSHIRE v LANCASHIRE

Played at Gloucester, May 6, 8, 9, 1939.
Toss won by Lancashire.
Lancashire won by ten wickets.

GLOUCESTERSHIRE

C.J.Barnett	c Lister b Hopwood 120	c Farrimond Pollard	3
R.A.Sinfield	c Nutter b Hopwood.....18	b Phillipson	0
V.Hopkins	c Farrimond b Hopwood 0	c Nutter b Phillipson	1
*Mr W.R.Hammond	c Oldfield b Wilkinson 18	lbw b Pollard	22
W.L.Neale	c Nutter b Phillipson ...31	not out	21
J.F.Crapp	c & b Iddon 19	b Pollard	0
G.M.Emmett	b Phillipson 20	c Nutter b Phillipson	18
R.W.Haynes	c Farrimond b Nutter ...12	b Phillipson	0
†E.A.Wilson	c Farrimond b Phillipson 4	b Phillipson	4
T.W.J.Goddard	b Nutter 19	c Farrimond b Phillipson	7
C.J.Scott	not out 2	b Phillipson	2
Extras	(B 1, LB 2, NB 1) 4	(NB 1)	1
Total	**...........267**		**79**

Fall: 1st inns 1/61, 2/61, 3/126, 4/166, 5/200, 6/227, 7/242, 8/244, 9/249.
2nd inns 1/3, 2/3, 4/37, 5/37, 6/65, 7/65, 8/69, 9/77.

LANCASHIRE

C.Washbrook	c Wilson b Sinfield.......43	not out	17
E.Paynter	run out 17	not out	18
J.Iddon	c Crapp b Scott 7		
N.Oldfield	lbw b Goddard 12		
J.L.Hopwood	run out 30		
A.E.Nutter	c Hammond b Goddard 27		
W.E.Phillipson	c Crapp b Scott 9		
*Mr W.H.L.Lister	b Scott 61		
†W.Farrimond	c & b Sinfield 63		
R.Pollard	not out 26		
L.L.Wilkinson	run out 1		
Extras	(B 3, LB 9) 12	(LB 4)	4
Total	**...........308**	**(No wicket)**	**39**

Fall: 1st inns 1/50, 2/70, 3/70, 4/91, 5/142, 6/146, 7/157, 8/240, 9/303.

LANCASHIRE	O	M	R	W	O	M	R	W
Phillipson	17	2	42	3	11.6	4	18	7
Pollard	10	0	37	0	8	1	24	3
Hopwood	18	2	63	3				
Wilkinson	16	4	58	1				
Iddon	6	0	30	1				
Nutter	9	2	33	2	13	1	36	0

GLOUCESTERSHIRE	O	M	R	W	O	M	R	W
Scott	28	7	75	3	6.2	2	12	0
Barnett	8	1	31	0	3	0	17	0
Goddard	31	9	61	2				
Sinfield	38	5	109	2	3	0	6	0
Emmett	6	1	19	0				
Neale	1	0	1	0				

Umpires: G.Beet and J.A.Smart.

Close of play scores. First day: Lancashire 65/1 (C.Washbrook 42*, J.Iddon 3*). **Second day:** Gloucestershire 77/8 (W.L.Neale 21*, T.W.J.Goddard 7*).

Comments: Gloucestershire were put in to bat.
C.J.Barnett made 120 out of 166, hitting 13 4's.
It was the first championship century of the season.

KENT v ESSEX

Played at Gillingham, May 6, 8, 9, 1939.
Toss won by Kent.
Kent won by 116 runs.

KENT

A.E.Fagg	b Nichols 6	b Nichols	4
P.R.Sunnucks	b Taylor 51	c Taylor b Nichols	7
L.E.G.Ames	c Avery b Eastman 59	b Nichols	25
*Mr F.G.H.Chalk	b Nichols 62	b Stephenson	3
Mr B.H.Valentine	b Taylor 24	b R.Smith	7
Mr P.G.Foster	b Nichols 11	b R.Smith	21
L.J.Todd	b Nichols 4	b R.Smith	16
N.W.Harding	b Taylor 18	b R.Smith	2
D.V.P.Wright	b Taylor 4	c Wade b R.Smith	9
A.E.Watt	b Taylor 13	c & b P.Smith	4
†Mr W.H.V.Levett	not out 7	not out	23
Extras	(B 5, LB 5) 10	(B 7, LB 4)	11
Total	**...........269**		**132**

Fall: 1st inns 1/8, 2/115, 3/146, 4/194, 5/218, 6/222, 7/226, 8/246, 9/249.
2nd inns 1/10, 2/21, 3/42, 4/44, 5/70, 6/85, 7/92, 8/97, 9/102.

ESSEX

A.V.Avery	st Levett b Watt 29	run out	21
S.J.Cray	lbw b Todd 1	b Harding	0
R.M.Taylor	c Chalk b Todd 0	c Harding b Todd	5
J.O'Connor	b Watt 19	lbw b Watt	98
M.S.Nichols	c Harding b Watt 20	b Wright	19
Mr D.F.Cock	c Valentine b Watt 0	b Wright	0
*Capt.J.W.A.Stephenson	c Levett b Watt	0	b Watt	4
L.C.Eastman	b Watt 17	c Ames b Watt	9
T.P.B.Smith	not out 7	b Wright	1
†T.H.Wade	c Fagg b Wright 8	lbw b Wright	9
R.Smith	lbw b Wright 0	not out	0
Extras	(B 2, LB 6) 8	(B 2, LB 5, NB 3)	10
Total	**...........109**		**176**

Fall: 1st inns 1/2, 2/2, 3/45, 4/54, 5/56, 6/56, 7/93, 8/96, 9/109.
2nd inns 1/11, 2/18, 3/42, 4/111, 5/115, 6/120, 7/130, 8/130, 9/176.

ESSEX	O	M	R	W	O	M	R	W
Nichols	21	1	89	4	9	1	30	3
Stephenson	12	0	30	0	11	0	40	1
T.P.B.Smith	9	0	33	0	6	3	19	1
R.Smith	4	0	38	0	8.2	2	27	5
Eastman	7	0	19	1	3	0	3	0
Taylor	10.1	0	50	5	1	0	2	0

KENT	O	M	R	W	O	M	R	W
Harding	4	1	25	0	11	1	32	1
Todd	11	2	27	2	16	3	35	1
Watt	12	2	27	6	16	3	42	3
Wright	4.5	0	22	2	16.5	2	57	4

Umpires: H.G.Baldwin and F.Chester.

Close of play scores. First day: Essex 109 all out. **Second day:** Essex 159/8 (J.O'Connor 88*, T.H.Wade 2*).

Comments: L.E.G.Ames and P.R.Sunnucks added 107 for Kent's 2nd wicket.
F.G.H.Chalk did not enforce the follow-on.
Kent required only 30 minutes play on the third day to win the match.
R.Smith had career-best figures of 5 for 27 in Kent's 2nd innings.

SURREY v SOMERSET

Played at Kennington Oval, May 6, 8, 9, 1939.
Toss won by Somerset.
Surrey won by six wickets.

SOMERSET

F.S.Lee	c Gover b Berry 23	c Berry b Gover	59
H.Gimblett	b Gover 17	b Watts	53
Mr N.S.Mitchell-Innes	b Gover 0	c Squires b Watts	36
W.H.R.Andrews	c Brooks b Gover.........17	lbw b Gover	33
H.T.F.Buse	c Brooks b Berry 8	c Garland-Wells b Gover	30
Mr J.W.Seamer	c Barling b Gover..........8	b Berry	17
Mr H.D.Burrough	c Garland-Wells b Parker 29	b Berry	5
*Mr E.F.Longrigg	c Brooks b Gover........38	c Garland-Wells b Gregory	60
A.W.Wellard	b Gover 4	b Watts	26
†W.T.Luckes	c Brooks b Gover 1	not out	7
H.L.Hazell	not out 0		
Extras	(B 6, LB 6)............12	(B 1, LB 11, W 1)	13
Total	**157**	(9 wickets, declared)	**339**

Fall: 1st inns 1/38, 2/38, 3/44, 4/58, 5/75, 6/82, 7/134, 8/147, 9/154.
2nd inns 1/82, 2/145, 3/162, 4/218, 5/219, 6/240, 7/253, 8/317, 9/339.

SURREY

R.J.Gregory	b Andrews 8	b Andrews	34
L.B.Fishlock	c & b Hazell 90	st Luckes b Buse	101
H.S.Squires	b Andrews 0	c Luckes b Wellard	2
T.H.Barling	c Burrough b Wellard ...33	not out	21
†E.W.J.Brooks	c Longrigg b Wellard 1		
E.W.Whitfield	b Buse 18		
J.F.Parker	not out 111	not out	9
*Mr H.M.Garland-Wells	b Wellard 12	c Burrough b Wellard	23
F.Berry	c Mitchell-Innes b Andrews 11		
E.A.Watts	b Buse 1		
A.R.Gover	b Buse 3		
Extras	(B 7, LB 3, NB 2).........12	(B 4, LB 2, W 1, NB 1)	8
Total	**300**	(4 wickets)	**198**

Fall: 1st inns 1/25, 2/25, 3/97, 4/107, 5/137, 6/185, 7/218, 8/263, 9/278.
2nd inns 1/75, 2/78, 3/132, 4/187.

SURREY	O	M	R	W	O	M	R	W
Gover	16.2	5	38	7	23	1	78	3
Watts	11	0	37	0	22	1	88	3
Berry	14	5	20	2	16	1	71	2
Squires	3	0	14	0	2	0	7	0
Parker	8	2	26	1	8	0	51	0
Gregory	2	0	10	0	10.4	2	31	1

SOMERSET	O	M	R	W	O	M	R	W
Wellard	37	5	76	3	16.6	0	82	2
Andrews	28	4	93	3	8	0	64	1
Buse	19	2	67	3	9	0	44	1
Hazell	8	0	38	1				
Gimblett	4	0	14	0				

Umpires: C.N.Woolley and F.Walden.

Close of play scores. First day: Surrey 104/3 (L.B.Fishlock 60*, E.W.J.Brooks 1*). **Second day:** Somerset 152/2 (F.S.Lee 54*, W.H.R.Andrews 4*).

Comments: J.F.Parker hit 16 fours in his undefeated 111, made in 210 minutes. L.B.Fishlock hit 12 4's in his 101, made in about 135 minutes. He hit five boundaries off one over from W.H.R.Andrews.
Surrey scored 198 in 155 minutes to secure victory with five minutes to spare.

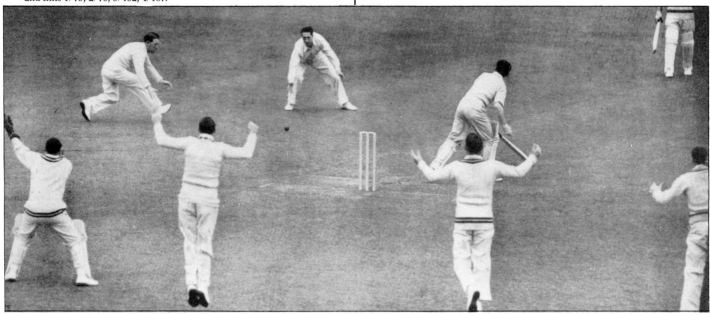

Surrey's behind-the-wicket fielders (from left) Brooks, Garland-Wells, Watts and Parker jump in anticipation as the ball drops towards Whitfield and Squires during the game against Somerset at The Oval.

SUSSEX v HAMPSHIRE

Played at Hove, May 6, 8, 9, 1939.
Toss won by Sussex.
Match drawn.

SUSSEX

John G. Langridge	lbw b Hill	140		
J.H.Parks	run out	75		
H.W.Parks	c Bailey b Knott	35		
Mr H.T.Bartlett	lbw b Bailey	49	(1) b Heath	4
Jas.Langridge	b Knott	71		
G.Cox	b Bailey	39	(2) c Pothecary b Knott	2
*Flt-Lt A.J.Holmes	c & b Heath	26		
C.Oakes	run out	8	(3) not out	6
†W.L.Cornford	c Creese b Knott	8		
D.J.Wood		0		
Extras	(B 5, LB 6)	11	(B 1)	1
Total	**(9 wickets, declared)**	**462**	**(2 wickets)**	**13**

Fall: 1st inns 1/112, 2/240, 3/297, 4/305, 5/371, 6/416, 7/440, 8/461, 9/462.
2nd inns 1/4, 2/13.   J.Cornford did not bat.

HAMPSHIRE

†N.T.McCorkell	lbw b J.Parks	11	c Holmes b John Langridge	88
J.Bailey	c Jas.Langridge b J.Cornford	28	b J.Cornford	58
G.Hill	c W.Cornford b Jas.Langridge	12	st W.Cornford b Jas.Langridge	4
W.L.C.Creese	c Wood b J.Parks	24	run out	25
Mr C.G.A.Paris	c John Langridge b Jas. Langridge	18	c John Langridge b J.Cornford	7
A.E.Pothecary	lbw b J.Parks	53	c J.Parks b John Langridge	10
D.F.Walker	c Jas.Langridge b Oakes	54	not out	107
G.S.Boyes	c J.Cornford b Oakes	23	b Jas.Langridge	24
*Mr G.R.Taylor	b Oakes	0	lbw b J.Parks	4
Mr C.J.Knott	c Cox b Oakes	1	lbw b J.Cornford	2
G.E.M.Heath	not out	1	c John Langridge b Jas.Langridge	4
Extras	(B 1, LB 2)	3	(B 14, LB 1, W 1)	16
Total		**228**		**349**

Fall: 1st inns 1/23, 2/39, 3/65, 4/77, 5/127, 6/161, 7/207, 8/207, 9/219.
2nd inns 1/149, 2/157, 3/157, 4/171, 5/191, 6/212, 7/263, 8/276, 9/285.

HAMPSHIRE	O	M	R	W	O	M	R	W
Heath	27	2	109	1	1.5	0	4	1
Knott	26.1	3	91	3	1	0	8	1
Hill	19	4	83	1				
Creese	14	2	51	0				
Bailey	27	1	117	2				

SUSSEX	O	M	R	W	O	M	R	W
J.Cornford	19	6	39	1	27	2	91	3
Wood	16	2	37	0	14	3	42	0
J.Parks	20	6	46	3	22	4	60	1
Jas.Langridge	17	1	67	2	28	4	65	3
Oakes	8	0	36	4	12	1	47	0
John Langridge	-				10	4	28	2

Umpires: C.W.L.Parker and H.W.Lee.

Close of play scores. First day: Sussex 416/6 (James Langridge 44*). **Second day:** Hampshire 48/0 (N.T.McCorkell 31*, J.Bailey 15*).
Comments: John G.Langridge made 140 in Sussex's 1st innings, hitting two 6's and 11 4's.
He and J.H.Parks put on 112 for the 1st Sussex wicket.
Langridge then added 128 with H.W.Parks for the 2nd wicket.
Hampshire followed on 234 runs behind.
N.T.McCorkell and J.Bailey put on 149 for Hampshire's 1st wicket in their 2nd innings. Hampshire's last-wicket pair, D.F.Walker and G.E.M.Heath, put on 64, which not only saved Hampshire from defeat, but allowed Walker to complete his century.

MIDDLESEX v ESSEX

Played at Lord's, May 10, 11, 12, 1939.
Toss won by Essex.
Middlesex won by two wickets.

ESSEX

A.V.Avery	c Price b Sims	121	b Smith	27
S.J.Cray	b Gray	7	b Smith	10
R.M.Taylor	b Edrich	9	c Thompson b Gray	10
J.O'Connor	c Price b Gray	128	lbw b Sims	14
M.S.Nichols	b Sims	45	c Price b Gray	41
L.C.Eastman	c & b Peebles	20	lbw b Peebles	36
T.P.B.Smith	b Peebles	1		
*Capt J.W.A.Stephenson	c Price b Smith	17	(7) b Gray	0
Mr D.F.Cock	b Sims	10		
†T.H.Wade	not out	16		
R.Smith	c & b Sims	12	(8) not out	26
Extras	(B 3, LB 11, W 2, NB 1)	17	(B 5, LB 4)	9
Total		**403**	**(7 wickets, declared)**	**173**

Fall: 1st inns 1/12, 2/28, 3/253, 4/288, 5/325, 6/327, 7/360, 8/369, 9/377.
2nd inns 1/27, 2/44, 3/60, 4/72, 5/133, 6/167, 7/173.

MIDDLESEX

J.D.B.Robertson	st Wade b Taylor	37	b Stephenson	7
S.M.Brown	b Nichols	12	c sub b Stephenson	58
W.J.Edrich	c Wade b Nichols	14	c Avery b Taylor	35
D.C.S.Compton	run out	181	(5) c R.Smith b Stephenson	15
J.H.A.Hulme	lbw b Nichols	6	(6) c O'Connor b Nichols	16
A.W.Thompson	b R.Smith	18	(7) c R.Smith b Nichols	10
†W.F.F.Price	c Taylor b Stephenson	18	(8) not out	21
J.M.Sims	c P.Smith b R.Smith	19	(9) run out	6
C.I.J.Smith	b Nichols	37	(4) b Stephenson	45
*Mr I.A.R.Peebles	c Stephenson b Nichols	7	not out	4
L.H.Gray	not out	1		
Extras	(LB 3)	3	(LB 5, W 2)	7
Total		**353**	**(8 wickets)**	**224**

Fall: 1st inns 1/20, 2/62, 3/68, 4/76, 5/105, 6/135, 7/189, 8/254, 9/274.
2nd inns 1/16, 2/86, 3/150, 4/159, 5/172, 6/181, 7/187, 8/206.

MIDDLESEX	O	M	R	W	O	M	R	W
Smith	29	6	66	1	16	0	56	2
Gray	19	1	76	2	15.1	0	54	3
Edrich	14	0	52	1				
Sims	28	5	101	4	10	2	38	1
Peebles	20	2	77	2	4	1	16	1
Thompson	4	1	14	0				

ESSEX	O	M	R	W	O	M	R	W
Nichols	24	2	82	5	11	0	81	2
Stephenson	13	2	67	1	11.6	0	94	4
Eastman	7	0	33	0				
R.Smith	11	1	56	2				
Taylor	12	1	56	1	4	0	42	1
P.Smith	14	3	56	0				

Umpires: F.I.Walden and C.N.Woolley.

Close of play scores. First day: Essex 356/6 (M.S.Nichols 42*, J.W.A.Stephenson 16*). **Second day:** Middlesex 353 all out.
Comments: A.V.Avery (121), J.O'Connor (128) added 225 in 210 minutes for the 3rd wicket.
J.O'Connor hit 128 in 210 minutes, scoring one 6 and nine 4's.
A.V.Avery scored 121, including nine 4's. He batted for 305 minutes.
D.C.S.Compton hit four 6's and 17 4's in his 181, his last 143 runs coming in less than two hours.
Middlesex 10th wicket partnership in the 1st innings realized 79, of which D.C.S.Compton contributed 78.
Middlesex won by two wickets in the last over after being set 130 minutes to score 224. Twenty minutes of this time was lost to rain.

NORTHAMPTONSHIRE v HAMPSHIRE

Played at Northampton, May 10, 11, 12, 1939.
Toss won by Hampshire.
Match drawn.

HAMPSHIRE

†N.T.McCorkell	lbw b Merritt	48
J.Bailey	c James b Buswell	19
G.Hill	c & b Merritt	21
W.L.C.Creese	c Herbert b Partridge	241
A.G.Holt	c Brookes b Merritt	25
A.E.Pothecary	c James b Partridge	40
D.F.Walker	b Herbert	21
*Mr C.G.A.Paris	c & b Partridge	17
G.S.Boyes	c O'Brien b Buswell	20
R.C.Court	not out	13
Extras	(B 23, LB 10, NB 2)	35
Total	(9 wickets, declared)	**500**

Fall: 1st inns 1/71, 2/75, 3/131, 4/178, 5/308, 6/372, 7/412, 8/452, 9/500.
G.E.M.Heath did not bat.

NORTHAMPTONSHIRE

Mr A.W.Snowden	c Creese b Heath	23	b Heath	6
H.W.Greenwood	b Court	7	lbw b Boyes	59
D.Brookes	c Boyes b Creese	50	c Boyes b Court	47
J.E.Timms	b Hill	114	c & b Heath	70
*Mr R.P.Nelson	b Heath	40	not out	79
†K.C.James	b Hill	2	c McCorkell b Heath	0
F.P.O'Brien	b Court	9	b Hill	8
W.E.Merritt	lbw b Heath	27	not out	4
R.J.Partridge	b Hill	6		
E.J.Herbert	not out	4		
J.E.Buswell	st McCorkell b Hill	7		
Extras	(B 1, LB 9)	10	(LB 7)	7
Total		**299**	(6 wickets)	**280**

Fall: 1st inns 1/16, 2/51, 3/130, 4/210, 5/215, 6/230, 7/258, 8/266, 9/290.
2nd inns 1/12, 2/109, 3/121, 4/242, 5/242, 6/264.

NORTHANTS	O	M	R	W
Buswell	22	4	87	2
Partridge	26.7	2	107	3
Timms	14	3	39	0
Herbert	17	4	70	1
Merritt	33	1	154	3
Nelson	3	1	8	0

HAMPSHIRE	O	M	R	W	O	M	R	W
Heath	24	2	83	3	21	2	80	3
Court	16	1	79	2	12	0	82	1
Boyes	8	0	25	0	14	3	43	1
Hill	18.4	4	50	4	17.1	3	38	1
Creese	5	0	30	1				
Bailey	3	0	22	0	9	2	30	0

Umpires: E.Cooke and E.Robinson.

Close of play scores. First day: Hampshire 441/7 (W.L.C.Creese 209*, G.S.Boyes 13*). **Second day:** Northants 46/1 (H.W.Greenwood 19*, D.Brookes 19*).

Comments: W.L.C.Creese made 241, the highest score of his career. It contained 37 4's, took 345 minutes and was his first double century.
He and A.E.Pothecary shared a 5th-wicket partnership of 130.
J.E.Timms scored his second consecutive century. His 114 included one 6 and 13 4's.
G.Hill took three wickets for four runs after tea on the second day.
Northants followed on 201 runs behind. On the third day, J.E.Timms and R.P.Nelson put on 121 for the 4th wicket.
Rain and bad light ended play at 4.30pm on the third day.

SURREY v WORCESTERSHIRE

Played at Kennington Oval, May 10, 11, 12, 1939.
Toss won by Surrey.
Surrey won by 249 runs.

SURREY

R.J.Gregory	c Bull b Lyttelton	46	not out	105
L.B.Fishlock	lbw b Lyttelton	56	not out	100
H.S.Squires	c Cooper b Howorth	101		
T.H.Barling	c Jenkins b Lyttelton	0		
E.W.Whitfield	c Buller b Howorth	12		
J.F.Parker	c Howorth b Perks	80		
*Mr H.M.Garland-Wells	c Martin b Howorth	9		
F.Berry	st Buller b Jenkins	14		
E.A.Watts	c Buller b Martin	22		
†E.W.J.Brooks	st Buller b Martin	36		
A.R.Gover	not out	3		
Extras	(B 10, LB 2, W 1, NB 4)	17	(LB 1, W 1, NB 4)	6
Total		**396**	(No wicket, declared)	**211**

Fall: 1st inns 1/73, 2/24, 3/41, 4/180, 5/261, 6/273, 7/320, 8/357, 9/367.

WORCESTERSHIRE

C.H.Bull	lbw b Watts	5	c Brooks b Gover	32
B.P.King	b Watts	2	b Watts	10
E.Cooper	c Garland-Wells b Berry	25	c Berry b Gover	7
H.H.I.Gibbons	b Gover	11	c Parker b Gover	56
S.H.Martin	c Brooks b Berry	0	c Brooks b Berry	16
Mr A.F.T.White	c Brooks b Gover	1	b Gover	0
*Hon C.J.Lyttelton	b Berry	2	c Barling b Squires	23
R.Howorth	c Brooks b Gover	58	lbw b Squires	2
†J.S.Buller	b Squires	14	not out	25
R.T.D.Perks	c Parker b Squires	21	st Brooks b Squires	10
R.O.Jenkins	not out	10	st Brooks b Squires	10
Extras	(B 4, LB 10)	14	(LB 4)	4
Total		**163**		**195**

Fall: 1st inns 1/7, 2/24, 3/41, 4/42, 5/47, 6/50, 7/59, 8/127, 9/133.
2nd inns 1/15, 2/24, 3/103, 4/112, 5/112, 6/139, 7/150, 8/150, 9/173.

WORCESTERSHIRE	O	M	R	W	O	M	R	W
Perks	22	3	82	1	10	1	53	0
Martin	20.5	2	100	2	13	0	79	0
Jenkins	13	0	84	1	3	0	30	0
Lyttelton	16	0	62	3				
Howorth	13	1	51	3	10	0	43	0

SURREY	O	M	R	W	O	M	R	W
Gover	13	0	55	3	17	3	56	4
Watts	9	0	32	2	13	1	57	1
Berry	6	0	26	3	7	2	22	1
Gregory	2	0	12	0				
Squires	3.3	0	24	2	6.7	1	38	4
Parker	-	-	-	-	4	0	8	0
Garland-Wells	-	-	-	-	2	0	10	0

Umpires: W.Reeves and F.J.Durston.

Close of play scores. First day: Surrey 396 all out. **Second day:** Worcestershire 14/0 (C.H.Bull 4*, B.P.King 10*).
Comments: H.S.Squires hit 11 fours in his 101, which took 190 minutes.
Surrey did not enforce the follow-on.
In Surrey's 2nd innings, L.B.Fishlock and R.J.Gregory put on an unbroken 1st wicket partnership of 211 in 150 minutes.
L.B.Fishlock hit ten 4's in his 100 and R.J.Gregory and six 4's and one 6, the latter boundary bringing him his century.
A.R.Gover dismissed C.H.Bull, H.H.I.Gibbons and A.F.T.White in 11 balls for three runs in Worcester's 2nd innings.

SUSSEX v SOMERSET

Played at Hove, May 10, 11, 1939.
Toss won by Sussex.
Somerset won by nine wickets.

SUSSEX

John G.Langridge...c Luckes b Wellard	17	c Mitchell-Innes b Buse	2
J.H.Parks ....c Luckes b Wellard	9	lbw b Andrews	31
H.W.Parks ....b Wellard	8	c Luckes b Buse	1
Mr H.T.Bartlett .....c Luckes b Wellard	49	b Wellard	48
Jas.Langridge........lbw b Andrews	13	c Gimblett b Wellard	30
G.Cox ....c Seamer b Buse	8	b Andrews	11
*Flt-Lt A.J.Holmes c & b Wellard	24	c Burrough b Wellard	6
C.Oakes ....not out	27	not out	20
†W.L.Cornford ......c Longrigg b Andrews	10	b Andrews	0
D.J.Wood ....c Longrigg b Andrews	0	c & b Andrews	2
J.H.Cornford ....c Hazell b Wellard	3	b Wellard	0
Extras.............(B 4, LB 1)	5	(B 1, LB 6)	7
Total	**173**		**158**

Fall: 1st inns 1/10, 2/30, 3/39, 4/83, 5/100, 6/112, 7/143, 8/158, 9/158.
2nd inns 1/10, 2/12, 3/52, 4/112, 5/125, 6/129, 7/134, 8/135, 9/151.

SOMERSET

F.S.Lee ....st W.Cornford b Jas.Langridge	75	c Jas.Langridge b J.Cornford	2
H.Gimblett ....c W.Cornford b J.Parks	43	not out	36
Mr N.S.Mitchell-Innes lbw b J.Parks	6	not out	44
W.H.R.Andrews .....c John Langridge b J.Cornford	6		
H.T.F.Buse ....b J.Cornford	0		
Mr J.W.Seamer ......b J.Cornford	3		
Mr H.D.Burrough ...b J.Parks	0		
*Mr E.F.Longrigg ...b Wood	51		
A.W.Wellard.........c John Langridge b J.Cornford	42		
†W.T.Luckes ....not out	15		
H.L.Hazell ....c W.Cornford b J.Cornford	4		
Extras.............(B 2, LB 3)	5		0
Total	**250**	(1 wicket)	**82**

Fall: 1st inns 1/63, 2/75, 3/82, 4/82, 5/90, 6/93, 7/185, 8/197, 9/246.
2nd inns 1/6.

SOMERSET	O	M	R	W	O	M	R	W
Wellard	20	3	67	6	16.6	1	63	4
Andrews	19	0	84	3	16	2	51	4
Buse	6	0	17	1	11	2	37	2

SUSSEX	O	M	R	W	O	M	R	W
J.Cornford	24	3	84	5	5	1	22	1
Wood	20	6	51	1	2	0	21	0
J.Parks	25	9	54	3	4	2	16	0
Jas.Langridge	11	0	56	1	1	0	12	0
Oakes	-	-	-	-	1.3	0	11	0

Umpires: J.A.Newman and J.Hardstaff.

Close of play scores. First day: Somerset 116/6 (F.S.Lee 51*, E.F.Longrigg 5*).

Comments: A bowler's match, in which only two batsmen scored over 50.
The game was completed in two days.

DERBYSHIRE v SURREY

Played at Queen's Park, Chesterfield, May 13, 15, 16, 1939.
Toss won by Derbyshire.
Match drawn.

DERBYSHIRE

D.Smith ....c Gover b Berry	20	not out	27
*Mr R.H.R.Buckston b Gover	4	b Gregory	15
T.S.Worthington ....lbw b Watts	71	not out	17
L.F.Townsend ....b Gregory	6		
A.E.Alderman ......b Gover	19		
G.H.Pope ....c Parker b Gregory	22		
A.E.G.Rhodes ....c Garland-Wells b Gregory	33		
A.V.Pope ....lbw b Gregory	4		
†H.Elliott ....c Squires b Gregory	13		
T.B.Mitchell ....run out	4		
W.H.Copson........not out	0		
Extras.............(B 11, LB 1, NB 1)	13	(B 4)	4
Total	**209**	(1 wicket)	**63**

Fall: 1st inns 1/19, 2/51, 3/70, 4/127, 5/140, 6/182, 7/188, 8/203, 9/209.
2nd inns 1/38.

SURREY

R.J.Gregory..........lbw b G.H.Pope	36
L.B.Fishlock ....c Elliott b Mitchell	22
H.S.Squires ....b Mitchell	3
T.H.Barling ....c A.V.Pope b Copson	52
E.W.Whitfield ....c Alderman b Copson	39
J.F.Parker ....b Copson	0
*Mr H.M.Garland-Wells ...run out	12
F.Berry ....c Elliott b Copson	2
E.A.Watts ....c A.V.Pope b G.H.Pope	4
†E.W.J.Brooks.......lbw b Copson	20
A.R.Gover ....not out	1
Extras.............(B 4, LB 4)	8
Total	**199**

Fall: 1st inns 1/42, 2/58, 3/64, 4/151, 5/157, 6/164, 7/168, 8/175, 9/180.

SURREY	O	M	R	W	O	M	R	W
Gover	14	0	46	2	4	0	17	0
Watts	8	0	24	1	3	0	12	0
Squires	11	1	29	0				
Berry	7	0	38	1	1	0	3	0
Gregory	15.5	2	46	5	5	0	15	1
Parker	3	0	10	0				
Garland-Wells	3	0	3	0				
Whitfield	-	-	-	-	4	0	12	0

DERBYSHIRE	O	M	R	W
Copson	17	4	47	5
A.V.Pope	9	0	29	0
G.H.Pope	12	1	57	2
Mitchell	13	2	51	2
Townsend	2	0	7	0

Umpires: A.Dolphin and E.Robinson.

Close of play scores. First day: Surrey 149/3 (H.T.Barling 52*, E.W.Whitfield 29*). **Second day:** No play.

Comments: Nearly a day and a half was lost through bad weather. After a blank second day, play began at 2.30pm on the third day.
W.H.Copson took four wickets for nine runs in four overs.

GLOUCESTERSHIRE v WORCESTERSHIRE

Played at Bristol, May 13, 15, 1939.
Toss won by Worcestershire.
Gloucestershire won by three wickets.

WORCESTERSHIRE

C.H.Bull	lbw b Goddard	21	c Crapp b Goddard	26
B.P.King	lbw b Goddard	20	(3) c Sinfield b Barnett	3
E.Cooper	b Goddard	7	(4) st Wilson b Goddard	28
H.H.I.Gibbons	b Goddard	15	(5) c Crapp b Goddard	4
S.H.Martin	run out	14	(6) c Haynes b Goddard	15
Mr A.F.T.White	b Goddard	1	(2) c Haynes b Lambert	3
*Hon C.J.Lyttelton	c Sinfield b Goddard	15	c Haynes b Goddard	2
R.Howorth	b Goddard	37	c Emmett b Sinfield	0
†J.S.Buller	lbw b Goddard	15	c Crapp b Goddard	4
R.T.D.Perks	not out	1	st Wilson b Goddard	16
R.O.Jenkins	c Wilson b Goddard	0	not out	1
Extras	(B 3)	3	(LB 2, NB 1)	3
Total		**149**		**105**

Fall: 1st inns 1/36, 2/50, 3/55, 4/73, 5/77, 6/92, 7/104, 8/134, 9/149.
2nd inns 1/8, 2/20, 3/48, 4/54, 5/74, 6/77, 7/77, 8/85, 9/88.

GLOUCESTERSHIRE

C.J.Barnett	st Buller b Martin	14	lbw b Perks	21
R.A.Sinfield	not out	69	b Perks	0
V.J.Hopkins	c & b Martin	7	b Perks	9
*Mr W.R.Hammond	b Howorth	44	c sub b Perks	4
W.L.Neale	lbw b Martin	0	b Perks	1
J.F.Crapp	c & b Howorth	6	b Martin	24
G.M.Emmett	b Martin	3	c King b Martin	19
R.W.Haynes	b Howorth	12	not out	9
†E.A.Wilson	lbw b Howorth	0	not out	2
T.W.J.Goddard	c Jenkins b Howorth	2		
G.E.E.Lambert	b Howorth	0		
Extras	(B 7, LB 1)	8	(LB 1)	1
Total		**165**	(7 wickets)	**90**

Fall: 1st inns 1/32, 2/48, 3/129, 4/130, 5/137, 6/143, 7/162, 8/162, 9/164.
2nd inns 1/0, 2/10, 3/18, 4/20, 5/39, 6/71, 8/87.

GLOUCESTERSHIRE	O	M	R	W	O	M	R	W
Lambert	6	0	24	0	5	0	13	1
Barnett	3	0	8	0	8	2	14	1
Sinfield	14	3	59	0	8	1	31	1
Goddard	14	2	55	9	12.2	2	44	7

WORCESTERSHIRE	O	M	R	W	O	M	R	W
Perks	9	0	46	0	12	0	44	5
Martin	23	8	44	4	9	3	22	2
Howorth	20.3	6	45	6	8.7	0	23	0
Jenkins	5	2	22	0				

Umpires: A.Skelding and H.Cruice.

Close of play scores. First day: Gloucestershire 165 all out.

Comments: Gloucestershire won in two days.
R.A.Sinfield carried his bat in Gloucestershire's 1st innings.
Gloucestershire, needing only 90 to win, lost five wickets for 39, R.T.D.Perks taking all five for 26, before eventually winning by three wickets.
T.W.J.Goddard dismissed all 11 Worcester players in the match. The one wicket which eluded him in Worcester's 1st innings was that of S.H.Martin, who was run out, whilst out of his crease backing up.

HAMPSHIRE v WARWICKSHIRE

Played at Portsmouth, May 13, 15, 16, 1939.
Toss won by Warwickshire.
Match drawn.

WARWICKSHIRE

A.J.W.Croom	lbw b Boyes	32	c Taylor b Boyes	80
W.A.Hill	b Steele	24	c Steele b Boyes	36
†J.Buckingham	b Steele	0	c Taylor b Creese	3
Mr R.E.S.Wyatt	c Walker b Steele	33	not out	22
H.E.Dollery	b Steele	12	c Steele b Boyes	4
J.S.Ord	lbw b Heath	10	c McCorkell b Boyes	1
F.R.Santall	lbw b Bailey	9	not out	4
*Mr P.Cranmer	b Heath	13		
K.Wilmot	not out	12		
J.H.Mayer	b Steele	7		
W.E.Hollies	c Walker b Steele	2		
Extras	(B 4, LB 5)	9	(B 2)	2
Total		**163**	(5 wickets)	**152**

Fall: 1st inns 1/44, 2/44, 3/92, 4/94, 5/106, 6/126, 7/128, 8/142, 9/161.
2nd inns 1/108, 2/117, 3/121, 4/133, 5/139.

HAMPSHIRE

†N.T.McCorkell	lbw b Mayer	17
J.Bailey	run out	0
G.Hill	c Hollies b Santall	15
W.L.C.Creese	c Mayer b Wilmot	104
J.Arnold	c Buckingham b Wilmot	50
D.F.Walker	b Mayer	4
A.G.Holt	not out	32
Revd J.W.J.Steele	not out	24
Extras	(B 7, LB 6)	13
Total	(6 wickets, declared)	**259**

Fall: 1st inns 1/0, 2/27, 3/57, 4/191, 5/202, 6/202.
*Mr G.R.Taylor, G.S.Boyes and G.E.M.Heath did not bat.

HAMPSHIRE	O	M	R	W	O	M	R	W
Heath	17	2	51	2	4	0	13	0
Steele	18.7	1	62	6	4	1	7	0
Hill	5	1	18	0	10	1	34	0
Boyes	10	5	18	1	18	2	85	4
Creese	-	-	-	-	9	3	11	1
Bailey	3	1	5	1				

WARWICKSHIRE	O	M	R	W
Mayer	17	6	63	2
Wilmot	14	1	60	2
Santall	11	0	45	1
Hollies	11.5	2	53	0
Croom	3	0	25	0

Umpires: D.Hendren and C.V.Tarbox.

Close of play scores. First day: Hampshire 168/3 (W.L.C.Creese 82*, J.Arnold 44*). **Second day:** Hampshire 259/6 (A.G.Holt 32*, Revd J.W.J.Steele 24*).

Comments: In a rain-affected match, there was only 80 minutes play on the second day, whilst play did not begin on the third day until 3.00pm. Revd J.W.J.Steele had career-best figures of six wickets for 62.
J.Bailey was run out off the first ball of the Hampshire innings.
J.Arnold and W.L.C.Creese put on 134 for Hampshire's 4th wicket.
W.L.C.Creese made his second successive century, his 104 including 15 4's and taking 140 minutes.
A.J.W.Croom and W.A.Hill put on 108 for Warwickshire's 1st wicket in their 2nd innings.

LANCASHIRE v SOMERSET

Played at Old Trafford, Manchester, May 13, 15, 16, 1939.
Toss won by Somerset.
Match drawn.

SOMERSET

F.S.Lee	not out	155
H.Gimblett	c Paynter b Iddon	108
Mr N.S.Mitchell-Innes	c Farrimond b Iddon	2
W.H.R.Andrews	b Pollard	8
H.T.F.Buse	c Farrimond b Phillipson	18
Mr J.W.Seamer	c Lister b Nutter	26
Mr H.D.Burrough	c Farrimond b Phillipson	46
Extras	(B 2, LB 4, W 1, NB 2)	9
Total	(6 wickets, declared)	**372**

Fall: 1st inns 1/184, 2/188, 3/205, 4/232, 5/304, 6/372.
*Mr E.F.Longrigg, A.W.Wellard, †W.T.Luckes and H.L.Hazell did not bat.

LANCASHIRE

C.Washbrook	c Luckes b Wellard	36	c Buse b Mitchell-Innes	36
E.Paynter	b Hazell	27	not out	76
J.Iddon	lbw b Hazell	59	not out	7
N.Oldfield	c Buse b Wellard	2		
J.L.Hopwood	c Mitchell-Innes b Hazell	2		
A.E.Nutter	b Hazell	0		
W.E.Phillipson	b Wellard	20		
*Mr W.H.L.Lister	c Gimblett b Hazell	15		
†W.Farrimond	c Mitchell-Innes b Hazell	5		
R.Pollard	c Burrough b Hazell	4		
Mr A.J.Birtwell	not out	1		
Extras	(B 2, LB 7, W 1)	10	(B 4, LB 8)	12
Total		**181**	(1 wicket)	**131**

Fall: 1st inns 1/64, 2/72, 3/74, 4/81, 5/81, 6/139, 7/166, 8/171, 9/177.
2nd inns 1/95.

LANCASHIRE	O	M	R	W
Phillipson	30	4	102	2
Pollard	21	1	60	1
Birtwell	15	0	60	0
Nutt	16	0	80	1
Hopwood	7	1	30	0
Iddon	9	0	31	2

SOMERSET	O	M	R	W	O	M	R	W
Wellard	29	9	68	3	9	3	23	0
Andrews	10	0	38	0	2	0	13	0
Hazell	23.4	6	65	7	7	0	33	0
Buse	-	-	-	-	5	1	21	0
Mitchell-Innes	-	-	-	-	3	0	17	1
Lee	-	-	-	-	2	0	6	0
Seamer	-	-	-	-	1	0	6	0

Umpires: W.Reeves and E.Cooke.

Close of play scores. First day: Somerset 372/6 (F.S.Lee 155*). **Second day:** Lancashire 15/0 (C.Washbrook 7*, E.Paynter 7*).

Comments: H.Gimblett and F.S.Lee put on 184 for Somerset's opening partnership.
H.R.Gimblett's 108 included one 6 and 12 4's. He reached his century in 150 minutes and his innings lasted 157 minutes.
F.S.Lee scored an undefeated 155 in 365 minutes.
Only 5 overs were bowled on the second day due to heavy rain.
Lancashire followed on 191 runs behind.

LEICESTERSHIRE v SUSSEX

Played at Grace Road, Leicester, May 13, 15, 16, 1939.
Toss won by Leicestershire.
Sussex won by seven wickets.

LEICESTERSHIRE

L.G.Berry	c Hammond b J.Cornford	43	c J.Parks b J.Cornford	32
*Mr C.S.Dempster	c Hammond b J.Cornford	13	c W.Cornford b Nye	3
N.F.Armstrong	lbw b Hammond	40	c J.Parks b Nye	29
F.T.Prentice	c John Langridge b Hammond	0	c & b Jas.Langridge	40
G.S.Watson	c John Langridge b Hammond	24	c John Langridge b Nye	52
M.Tompkin	st W.Cornford b Jas.Langridge	39	lbw b J.Cornford	18
†G.O.Dawkes	c J.Parks b Nye	39	c John Langridge b Jas.Langridge	1
G.Lester	c W.Cornford b Jas.Langridge	2	c Hammond b Jas.Langridge	2
Mr J.E.Walsh	c John Langridge b J.Cornford	4	c Nye b J.Cornford	11
H.A.Smith	b J.Cornford	11	c Jas.Langridge b Nye	0
W.H.Flamson	not out	1	not out	0
Extras	(B 7, LB 5, NB 1)	13	(B 18, LB 8, W 2)	28
Total		**229**		**216**

Fall: 1st inns 1/20, 2/89, 3/89, 4/106, 5/137, 6/202, 7/208, 8/212, 9/218.
2nd inns 1/4, 2/38, 3/114, 4/126, 5/165, 6/168, 7/176, 8/212, 9/216.

SUSSEX

John G.Langridge	c Dawkes b Flamson	30	c Lester b Smith	11
J.H.Parks	c Armstrong b Smith	1	c Watson b Smith	9
G.Cox	c Flamson b Smith	0	lbw b Walsh	5
*Flt-Lt A.J.Holmes	c Flamson b Walsh	12	not out	19
Jas.Langridge	c Dawkes b Flamson	84	not out	10
H.W.Parks	lbw b Flamson	141		
C.Oakes	c Flamson b Walsh	56		
H.E.Hammond	b Walsh	4		
†W.L.Cornford	c Watson b Flamson	40		
J.K.Nye	not out	7		
J.H.Cornford	not out			
Extras	(B 3, LB 8, W 2, NB 2)	15	(LB 1)	1
Total	(9 wickets, declared)	**391**	(3 wickets)	**55**

Fall: 1st inns 1/3, 2/3, 3/37, 4/66, 5/170, 6/257, 7/271, 8/374, 9/387.
2nd inns 1/14, 2/25, 3/27.

SUSSEX	O	M	R	W	O	M	R	W
J.Cornford	9.1	0	42	4	15.5	1	67	3
Nye	8	0	48	1	12	1	51	4
J.Parks	13	2	41	0				
Hammond	13	1	45	3	7	2	21	0
Jas.Langridge	9	1	29	2	20	4	49	3
Oakes	2	0	11	0				

LEICESTERSHIRE	O	M	R	W	O	M	R	W
Flamson	35	5	122	4	2	0	9	0
Smith	29	3	112	2	6.2	0	24	2
Walsh	21	1	92	3	5	0	21	1
Armstrong	5	0	15	0				
Lester	3	0	21	0				
Prentice	5	0	14	0				

Umpires: J.A.Smart and H.W.Lee.

Close of play scores. First day: Sussex 181/5 (H.W.Parks 43*, C.Oakes 4*). **Second day:** Sussex 391/9 (J.K.Nye 7*, J.H.Cornford 1*).

Comments: There were several interruptions for rain on the second day.
H.W.Parks hit 12 4's in his 141, which took 255 minutes. He was involved in two century partnerships. He added 104 for the 5th wicket with James Langridge and 103 with W.L.Cornford for the 8th. H.A.Smith took his 1,000th wicket for Leicestershire, when he dismissed J.H.Parks.

NOTTINGHAMSHIRE v GLAMORGAN

Played at Trent Bridge, Nottingham, May 13, 15, 16, 1939.
Toss won by Nottinghamshire.
Match drawn.

NOTTINGHAMSHIRE

C.B.Harris	run out	68
J.Knowles	b Mercer	47
*Mr G.F.H.Heane	c H.Davies b Smart	69
J.Hardstaff	c Dyson b Smart	67
G.V.Gunn	c Turnbull b E.Davies	119
W.Voce	c D.Davies b E.Davies	53
R.J.Giles	c D.Davies b Smart	10
†A.B.Wheat	not out	38
F.G.Woodhead	not out	2
Extras	(B 3, LB 11, W 1, NB 1)	16
Total	(7 wickets, declared)	**489**

Fall: 1st inns 1/117, 2/123, 3/252, 4/273, 5/396, 6/417, 7/484.
J.Bradley and H.J.Butler did not bat.

GLAMORGAN

A.H.Dyson	c Heane b Voce	20	lbw b Voce	44
D.E.Davies	c Bradley b Butler	34	b Butler	1
T.L.Brierley	c Voce b Bradley	14	c Wheat b Bradley	62
*Mr M.J.L.Turnbull	b Voce	3	c Butler b Bradley	9
D.Davies	c Hardstaff b Voce	1	not out	20
C.C.Smart	c Hardstaff b Voce	25	not out	19
E.C.Jones	lbw b Butler	8		
P.B.Clift	b Butler	0		
†H.G.Davies	c Harris b Butler	1		
A.J.Watkins	not out	14		
J.Mercer	c Giles b Butler	2		
Extras	(B 2, LB 3, NB 3)	8	(B 1, W 1)	2
Total		**130**	(4 wickets)	**157**

Fall: 1st inns 1/34, 2/55, 3/62, 4/64, 5/91, 6/111, 7/111, 8/112, 9/118.
2nd inns 1/7, 2/108, 3/118, 4/122.

GLAMORGAN	O	M	R	W
Mercer	21	1	82	1
Watkins	6	1	38	0
Jones	9	1	59	0
E.Davies	25	1	115	2
Smart	23	0	119	3
Clift	5	0	31	0
D.Davies	5	0	29	0

NOTTINGHAMSHIRE	O	M	R	W	O	M	R	W
Voce	22	6	43	4	8	0	38	1
Butler	14.1	2	48	5	9	0	50	1
Woodhead	2	2	0	0	8	4	12	0
Bradley	7	1	20	1	8	1	44	2
Heane	5	1	11	0				
Gunn	-	-	-	-	2	1	7	0
Giles	-	-	-	-	2	0	4	0

Umpires: C.W.L.Parker and F.Chester.

YORKSHIRE v KENT

Played at Headingley, Leeds, May 13, 15, 16, 1939.
Toss won by Yorkshire.
Yorkshire won by 101 runs.

YORKSHIRE

H.Sutcliffe	b Harding	9	c Ames b Todd	11
L.Hutton	c Levett b Watt	37	c Harding b Todd	66
A.Mitchell	b Todd	17	c Ames b Lewis	31
M.Leyland	b Watt	0	b Todd	0
C.Turner	c Levett b Harding	34	c Harding b Lewis	1
*Mr A.B.Sellers	b Wright	11	c Levett b Todd	14
T.F.Smailes	b Watt	1	run out	0
†A.Wood	b Harding	21	c Watt b Lewis	18
E.P.Robinson	run out	9	c Ames b Todd	19
H.Verity	not out	12	not out	9
W.E.Bowes	c Foster b Harding	6		
Extras	(B 4, LB 7, W 1)	12	(B 1, NB 1)	2
Total		**169**	(9 wickets, declared)	**171**

Fall: 1st inns 1/15, 2/67, 3/67, 4/69, 5/90, 6/91, 7/130, 8/143, 9/153.
2nd inns 1/33, 2/97, 3/99, 4/121, 5/126, 6/142, 7/143, 8/147, 9/171.

KENT

A.E.Fagg	b Bowes	8	lbw b Robinson	26
P.R.Sunnucks	b Bowes	6	c Turner b Verity	7
L.E.G.Ames	b Bowes	3	c Mitchell b Verity	38
*Mr F.G.H.Chalk	c Wood b Turner	4	b Robinson	7
L.J.Todd	c Turner b Verity	54	c Hutton b Verity	30
Mr P.G.Foster	c Mitchell b Bowes	5	b Robinson	0
N.W.Harding	b Turner	1	b Robinson	0
D.V.P.Wright	lbw b Verity	8	b Robinson	18
A.E.Watt	c Sellers b Verity	1	b Verity	4
†Mr W.H.V.Levett	not out	4	not out	0
C.Lewis	b Robinson	0	b Robinson	3
Extras	(B 4, LB 1, NB 1)	6	(B 3, LB 2, NB 1)	6
Total		**100**		**139**

Fall: 1st inns 1/12, 2/18, 3/19, 4/31, 5/36, 6/43, 7/90, 8/92, 9/100.
2nd inns 1/11, 2/73, 3/73, 4/99, 5/99, 6/99, 7/121, 8/135, 9/135.

KENT	O	M	R	W	O	M	R	W
Harding	10.1	1	48	4	3	0	12	0
Todd	10	1	39	1	14	2	56	5
Watt	12	1	51	3	7	0	34	0
Wright	4	0	19	1				
Lewis	-	-	-	-	11.1	0	67	3

YORKSHIRE	O	M	R	W	O	M	R	W
Bowes	13	4	28	4	2	0	7	0
Smailes	5	0	17	0	5	0	32	0
Turner	3	1	16	2				
Verity	8	1	32	3	12	1	52	4
Robinson	3	2	1	1	9.3	2	42	6

Umpires: E.J.Smith and G.M.Lee.

Close of play scores. First day: Nottinghamshire 489/7 (A.B.Wheat 38*, F.G.Woodhead 2*). **Second day:** Glamorgan 14/0 (A.H.Dyson 5*, D.E.Davies 8*).

Comments: There was only 30 minutes play on the second day.
There were three century partnerships in the Nottinghamshire 1st innings.
C.B.Harris and J.Knowles put on 117 for the 1st, G.F.H.Heane and J.Hardstaff scored 129 in 90 minutes for the 5th wicket.
G.V.Gunn hit one 6 and 14 4's in his 119, made in 160 minutes.
Glamorgan followed on 359 behind. In their 2nd innings, A.H.Dyson and T.L.Brierley put on 101 for the 2nd wicket.

Close of play scores. First day: Yorkshire 86/1 (L.Hutton 54*, A.Mitchell 20*). **Second day:** No play, (rain).

Comments: Twenty-one wickets fell for 355 runs on the first day.
Rain prevented any play on the second day.
Kent were set to make 241 in 240 minutes.
E.P.Robinson claimed a hat-trick, dismissing F.G.H.Chalk, P.G.Foster and N.W.Harding in Kent's 2nd innings.
The game finished at 2.45pm.

YORKSHIRE COUNTY CRICKET CLUB

Standing (left to right): A.Mitchell, A.Hayhurst (masseur), H.Verity, W.E.Bowes, T.F.Smailes, L.Hutton, Mr Ringrose (scorer), C.Turner. Seated: H.Sutcliffe, N.W.D.Yardley, A.B.Sellers (captain), M.Leyland. On ground: E.P.Robinson, A.Wood, W.Barber.

ESSEX v GLAMORGAN

Played at Ilford, May 17, 18, 19, 1939.
Toss won by Essex.
Glamorgan won by five wickets.

ESSEX

A.V.Avery	lbw b Mercer	1	c Dyson b Mercer	4
S.J.Cray	not out	6	c Turnbull b Mercer	6
R.M.Taylor	not out	2	c E.Davies b Dovey	37
J.O'Connor			c Brierley b Thomas	9
M.S.Nichols			lbw b Thomas	6
L.C.Eastman			lbw b Mercer	14
T.P.B.Smith			c H.Davies b Thomas	2
*Capt J.W.A.Stephenson			not out	22
R.Smith			lbw b Mercer	0
Mr D.F.Cock			c Dyson b Thomas	0
†T.H.Wade			b D.Davies	7
Extras		0	(B 1, LB 1)	2
Total	(1 wicket, declared)	**9**		**109**

Fall 1st inns 1/2.
2nd inns 1/7, 2/12, 3/51, 4/57, 5/63, 6/73, 7/85, 8/85, 9/86.

GLAMORGAN

A.H.Dyson			c Taylor b Nichols	0
D.E.Davies			b P.Smith	28
†H.G.Davies	not out	0	(did not bat)	
T.L.Brierley	not out	8	(3) c Eastman b Nichols	52
*Mr M.J.L.Turnbull			(4) c Taylor b P.Smith	4
D.Davies			(5) lbw b Nichols	2
C.C.Smart			(6) not out	14
E.C.Jones			(7) not out	5
Extras	(NB 1)	1	(B 5, LB 1, NB 2)	8
Total	(No wicket, declared)	**9**	(5 wickets)	**113**

Fall: 2nd inns 1/0, 2/82, 3/87, 4/94, 5/98.

A.J.Watkins, J.Mercer and D.Thomas did not bat in either innings.

GLAMORGAN	O	M	R	W	O	M	R	W
Mercer	5	3	2	1	17	5	41	4
Thomas	4	1	7	0	17	2	64	5
D.Davies	-	-	-	-	4	0	2	1

ESSEX	O	M	R	W	O	M	R	W
O'Connor	0.2	0	8	0				
Nichols	-	-	-	-	11.7	4	25	3
Eastman	-	-	-	-	7	1	29	0
T.P.B.Smith	-	-	-	-	10	0	37	2
Stephenson	-	-	-	-	2	0	14	0

Umpires: H.Elliott and J.Hardstaff.

Close of play scores. First day: No play. **Second day:** Essex 9/1 (S.J.Cray 6*, R.M.Taylor 2*).

Comments: Only 30 minutes play on the first two days contributed to the joint decisions of the two captains to declare their 1st innings' closed with only nine on the board in an attempt to provide a finish on the third day.
D.Thomas took 5 for 64 on his debut in first-class cricket.

KENT v WORCESTERSHIRE

Played at Gillingham, May 17, 18, 19, 1939.
Toss won by Worcestershire.
Worcestershire won by 83 runs.

WORCESTERSHIRE

C.H.Bull	c Levett b Todd	4	b Todd	4
Mr A.F.T.White	c Levett b Lewis	27	c Dovey b Lewis	29
B.P.King	c Foster b Dovey	21	c Foster b Todd	5
E.Cooper	c Levett b Lewis	1	lbw b Lewis	13
H.H.I.Gibbons	b Dovey	36	hit wkt b Watt	63
S.H.Martin	run out	25	b Lewis	0
*Hon C.J.Lyttelton	st Levett b Lewis	6	b Dovey	4
R.Howorth	st Levett b Lewis	20	c Ames b Lewis	1
†J.S.Buller	c Ames b Lewis	3	b Dovey	7
R.T.D.Perks	b Lewis	0	c Fagg b Lewis	29
P.F.Jackson	not out	1	not out	1
Extras	(LB 2)	2	(B 1, LB 1)	2
Total		**146**		**158**

Fall: 1st inns 1/6, 2/38, 3/41, 4/68, 5/112, 6/117, 7/134, 8/143, 9/143.
2nd inns 1/4, 2/18, 3/51, 4/60, 5/68, 6/87, 7/88, 8/100, 9/143.

KENT

A.E.Fagg	c & b Martin	1	lbw b Perks	1
P.R.Sunnucks	lbw b Howorth	5	c Lyttelton b Martin	1
L.E.G.Ames	c Buller b Martin	22	lbw b Martin	19
*Mr F.G.H.Chalk	c Bull b Howorth	26	c Buller b Perks	2
Mr B.H.Valentine	c Lyttelton b Martin	4	b Martin	48
L.J.Todd	c King b Martin	4	st Buller b Martin	28
Mr P.G.Foster	c Martin b Howorth	5	b Martin	4
†Mr W.H.V.Levett	c Perks b Martin	0	c White b Martin	2
A.E.Watt	b Howorth	0	c Howorth b Martin	34
C.Lewis	c Howorth b Martin	0	not out	3
R.R.Dovey	not out	0	b Martin	0
Extras	(B 4, LB 1)	5	(B 3, LB 3, NB 1)	7
Total		**72**		**149**

Fall: 1st inns 1/1, 2/27, 3/29, 4/45, 5/55, 6/65, 7/66, 8/67, 9/72.
2nd inns 1/2, 2/8, 3/11, 4/55, 5/78, 6/90, 7/94, 8/114, 9/149.

KENT	O	M	R	W	O	M	R	W
Todd	13	3	34	1	8	0	30	2
Watt	10	3	26	0	4	1	17	1
Lewis	16.3	4	46	6	14	3	57	5
Dovey	14	2	38	2	10	1	52	2

WORCESTERSHIRE	O	M	R	W	O	M	R	W
Perks	4	1	13	0	13	1	34	2
Martin	13	5	23	6	18	2	84	8
Howorth	9.2	1	31	4	1	0	5	0
Jackson	-	-	-	-	4	0	19	0

Umpires: F.J.Durston and J.A.Newman.

Close of play scores. First day: Worcestershire 143/9 (J.S.Buller 2*).
Second day: Kent 86/5 (L.J.Todd 6*, P.G.Foster 4*).

Comments: Only three and a quarter hours play was possible on the first day.
A.E.Watt hit S.H.Martin for three consecutive sixes in one over, 22 runs coming off the over.
S.H.Martin bowled unchanged throughout the match.

MIDDLESEX v NORTHAMPTONSHIRE

Played at Lord's, May 17, 18, 19, 1939.
Toss won by Northants.
Middlesex won by 118 runs.

MIDDLESEX

J.D.B.Robertson ..... b Lubbock 3	
S.M.Brown........... c James b Partridge 1	
W.J.Edrich.......... c Brookes b O'Brien......84	
D.C.S.Compton ..... c Buswell b O'Brien......94	
C.I.J.Smith .... b Lubbock 13	
Rev E.T.Killick ..... not out 13	
Mr N.S.Hotchkin.... not out 11	
Extras.............. (B 9, LB 4) 13	
Total .... (5 wickets, declared) 232	

Fall: 1st inns 1/4, 2/12, 3/191, 4/199, 5/205.

*Mr I.A.R.Peebles, †W.F.F.Price, J.M.Sims and L.H.Gray did not bat.

NORTHAMPTONSHIRE

Mr A.W.Snowden ...c Sims b Smith 19	
H.W.Greenwood .... c Edrich b Sims 20	
D.Brookes............ c Sims b Compton 22	
J.E.Timms .... st Price b Sims.............0	
*Mr R.P.Nelson ..... c Sims b Smith 5	
†K.C.James .... c & b Sims 23	
Mr C.W.S.Lubbock ... st Price b Sims.............0	
F.P.O'Brien.......... b Sims 15	
W.E.Merritt .... c Killick b Sims...........0	
J.E.Buswell .... c Killick b Sims...........0	
R.J.Partridge .... not out 2	
Extras.............. (LB 6, NB 2) 8	
Total 114	

Fall: 1st inns 1/37, 2/43, 3/44, 4/59, 5/91, 6/92, 7/103, 8/103, 9/114.

NORTHANTS	O	M	R	W
Lubbock 10	0	39	2
Partridge 16	1	45	1
Buswell 3	0	26	0
Merritt 4	0	17	0
Nelson 4	1	17	0
Timms 13	0	61	0
O'Brien 3	0	14	2

MIDDLESEX	O	M	R	W
Gray 6	1	21	0
Sims 12.7	1	43	7
Peebles...................2	0	12	0
Compton 5	1	10	1
Smith 12	3	20	2

Umpires: H.G.Baldwin and E.J.Smith.

Close of play scores. First day: No play. **Second day:** No play.

Comments: Middlesex were put in to bat.
Only one day's play was possible D.C.S.Compton and W.J.Edrich added 179 for the 3rd Middlesex wicket in 140 minutes.
J.M.Sims was involved in the dismissal of all the Northamptonshire batsmen, taking seven wickets and holding three catches.
Middlesex claimed eight points for a lead on 1st innings in a game restricted to one day, the first side to do so under the new points system.

SOMERSET v SUSSEX

Played at Taunton, May 17, 18, 19, 1939.
Toss won by Somerset.
Match drawn.

SOMERSET

F.S.Lee .... c John Langridge	c Nye b Hammond 43
	b Hammond 44	
H.Gimblett .... c H.Parks b Jas.Langridge 93	not out 103
H.T.F.Buse .... lbw b Hammond 52	b Nye 1
Mr J.W.Seamer ..... c Holmes b Jas.Langridge 6	b Nye 0
W.H.R.Andrews ..... b Nye 49	c J.Parks b John Langridge 15
*Mr E.F.Longrigg ... c J.Parks b Nye...........17	
Mr C.J.P.Barnwell c John Langridge b Nye 4	(6) not out 13
Mr G.M.Bennett ..... c J.Parks b Nye 0	
A.W.Wellard .... c & b Hammond...........1	
†W.T.Luckes .... not out 16	
H.L.Hazell.......... b Hammond 1	
Extras.............. (B 4, LB 8, W 2, NB 2) ..16	(B 7, W 1) 8
Total **299**	(4 wickets, declared)......**183**

Fall: 1st inns 1/116, 2/161, 3/181, 4/245, 5/267, 6/271, 7/271, 8/272, 9/277.
2nd inns 1/105, 2/106, 3/117, 4/153.

SUSSEX

John G.Langridge... c Longrigg b Andrews ...14	c Luckes b Buse 17
J.H.Parks .... c Longrigg b Andrews ...18	c Luckes b Wellard 10
G.Cox .... lbw b Wellard 15	not out 22
Mr H.T.Bartlett ..... c Seamer b Andrews 14	
Jas.Langridge........ c Seamer b Andrews 49	not out 2
H.W.Parks .... c Luckes b Buse 17	
*Flt-Lt A.J.Holmes c Seamer b Wellard 19	
C.Oakes .... lbw b Andrews 29	(4) lbw b Hazell 15
H.E.Hammond ...... c Lee b Andrews..........20	
†W.L.Cornford ...... not out 7	
J.K.Nye .... b Wellard 0	
Extras.............. (LB 8, NB 1) 9	(B 4, NB 1) 5
Total **211**	(3 wickets) **71**

Fall: 1st inns 1/23, 2/44, 3/66, 4/68, 5/110, 6/137, 7/159, 8/187, 9/210.
2nd inns 1/21, 2/45, 3/66.

SUSSEX	O	M	R	W	O	M	R	W
Nye 22	2	80	4	8	2	47	2
Hammond 22.3	3	71	4	8	0	63	1
J.Parks 11	1	41	0	3	0	11	0
Jas.Langridge 15	4	58	2	6	1	29	0
Oakes 5	0	33	0	1	0	10	0
John G.Langridge......-	-	-	-	3	0	15	1

SOMERSET	O	M	R	W	O	M	R	W
Wellard 18.7	5	69	3	7	2	19	1
Andrews...............22	3	75	6	4	0	25	0
Buse 13	3	36	1	5	1	18	1
Hazell................8	1	22	0	3	1	4	1

Umpires: C.W.L.Parker and H.Cruice.

Close of play scores. First day: Somerset 109/0 (F.S.Lee 38*, H.Gimblett 63*). **Second day:** Sussex 149/6 (Jas.Langridge 41*, C.Oakes 3*).

Comments. Play was severely curtailed on the first day, not beginning until 3pm and finishing at tea.
F.S.Lee and H.Gimblett made a century opening partnership in both innings, 116 in the 1st and 105 in the 2nd, the latter in 65 minutes. It was their third successive three-figure opening partnership. H.Gimblett hit 15 4's in his 2nd innings score of 103, which took 110 minutes.

YORKSHIRE v GLOUCESTERSHIRE

Played at Bradford, May 17, 18, 19, 1939.
Toss won by Yorkshire.
Gloucestershire won by six wickets.

YORKSHIRE

H..Sutcliffe	c Crapp b Goddard 18	c Crapp b Scott 0
L.Hutton	c Wilson b Scott 12	b Scott 42
A.Mitchell	c Neale b Scott 35	c Crapp b Scott 25
M.Leyland	c Emmett b Scott.......112	b Scott 36
W.Barber	b Scott 0	(7) not out 32
*Mr A.B.Sellers	b Goddard 9	(8) c Barnett b Scott........8
T.F.Smailes	c Wilson b Goddard 22	(6) st Wilson b Goddard....6
†A.Wood	c Hopkins b Goddard 4	(9) not out 3
E.P.Robinson	c Wilson b Goddard......4	(5) b Scott 7
H.Verity	not out 24	
W.E.Bowes	c Goddard b Scott 8	
Extras	(B 4, LB 1) 5	(LB 3) 3
Total	**253**	(7 wickets, declared)......**162**

Fall:1st inns 1/21, 2/37, 3/97, 4/97, 5/116, 6/166, 7/170, 8/176, 9/252.
2nd inns 1/0, 2/67, 3/69, 4/79, 5/90, 6/134, 7/158.

GLOUCESTERSHIRE

C.J.Barnett	b Bowes 34	c Mitchell b Robinson 90
R.A.Sinfield	c Hutton b Bowes 3	c Wood b Bowes 42
V.Hopkins	c Mitchell b Smailes 37	st Wood b Leyland 11
*Mr W.R.Hammond	lbw b Robinson 75	not out 29
W.L.Neale	c Verity b Smailes 4	
J.F.Crapp	lbw b Verity 18	not out 13
G.M.Emmett	c Sellers b Verity 8	(5) b Bowes 0
R.W.Haynes	b Robinson 6	
†E.A.Wilson	not out 8	
T.W.J.Goddard	c Robinson b Verity 1	
C.J.Scott	c Robinson b Verity 13	
Extras	(B 8, LB 9, NB 3).........20	(B 4, LB 1) 5
Total	**227**	(4 wickets) **190**

Fall: 1st inns 1/15, 2/53, 3/113, 4/121, 5/182, 6/187, 7/193, 8/201, 9/207.
2nd inns 1/128, 2/148, 3/160, 4/172.

GLOUCESTERSHIRE	O	M	R	W	O	M	R	W
Scott	18.7	3	91	5	11	0	87	6
Barnett	8	0	34	0	3	0	23	0
Goddard	22	4	76	5	7	0	49	1
Sinfield	12	2	47	0				

YORKSHIRE	O	M	R	W	O	M	R	W
Bowes	14	1	37	2	8.2	0	59	2
Smailes	10	3	36	2	3	0	19	0
Verity	23.3	6	74	4	3	0	33	0
Robinson	17	6	44	2	5	0	26	1
Leyland	7	1	16	0	7	1	48	1

Umpire: F.Chester and J.A.Smart.

Close of play scores. First day: No play, (rain). **Second day:** Gloucestershire 167/4 (W.R.Hammond 59*, J.F.Crapp 17*).

Comments: M.Leyland batted 165 minutes for his 112, which included one 6 and 16 4's.
Gloucestershire made 190 runs in 95 minutes to win the match. C.J.Barnett hit 90 in 60 minutes, striking four 6's and eight 4's out of 132 scored whilst he was at the wicket.

DERBYSHIRE v NORTHAMPTONSHIRE

Played at Derby, May 20, 22, 1939.
Toss won by Northamptonshire.
Derbyshire won by ten wickets.

NORTHAMPTONSHIRE

Mr A.W.Snowden	c Smith b G.H.Pope 9	absent ill 6
H.W.Greenwood	c Elliott b Copson 0	c Worthington b A.V.Pope 15
D.Brookes	b Copson 23	lbw b A.V.Pope 18
J.E.Timms	b G.H.Pope 18	lbw b G.H.Pope 4
*Mr R.P.Nelson	c Smith b Mitchell 20	not out 16
†K.C.James	b G.H.Pope 7	c Elliott b G.H.Pope 13
F.P.O'Brien	c G.H.Pope b Copson ...31	b Copson 4
P.Davis	b Mitchell 3	b Copson 3
W.E.Merritt	c Worthington b Mitchell 9	b G.H.Pope 3
R.J.Partridge	not out 0	b Copson 7
W.A.Buswell	c Buckston b Mitchell.....0	c Rhodes b Copson 0
Extras	(B 4, LB 3) 7	(LB 6) 6
Total	**124**	**95**

Fall: 1st inns 1/1, 2/29, 3/49, 4/52, 5/68, 6/102, 7/102, 8/124, 9/124.
2nd inns 1/37, 2/42, 3/48, 4/68, 5/73, 6/77, 7/80, 8/89, 9/95.

DERBYSHIRE

*Mr R.H.R.Buckston	b Merritt 17	not out 4
D.Smith	c Snowden b Buswell 10	not out 2
T.S.Worthington	b Buswell 16	
L.F.Townsend	b Timms 28	
A.E.Alderman	c Partridge b Buswell 17	
G.H.Pope	c James b Buswell........21	
A.E.G.Rhodes	b Timms 29	
A.V.Pope	b Nelson 46	
†H.Elliott	b Timms 5	
T.B.Mitchell	not out 4	
W.H.Copson	c Brookes b Nelson 8	
Extras	(B 8, LB 2, NB 3).........13	
Total	**214**	No wicket **6**

Fall: 1st inns 1/16, 2/42, 3/67, 4/83, 5/116, 6/131, 7/193, 8/197, 9/205.

DERBYSHIRE	O	M	R	W	O	M	R	W
Copson	13	2	41	3	12.5	2	34	4
A.V.Pope	12	1	25	0	8	2	15	2
G.H.Pope	7	2	21	3	15	4	40	3
Mitchell	7.6	2	30	4				

NORTHAMPTON	O	M	R	W	O	M	R	W
Buswell	13	2	54	4				
Partridge	9	1	42	0				
Merritt	9	1	44	1				
Timms	8	0	51	3				
Nelson	2.2	0	10	2				
James	-	-	-	-	1	0	6	0

Umpires: J.Hardstaff and E.Cooke.

Close of play scores. First day: Northamptonshire (2nd inns) 8/0. (A.W.Snowden 6*, H.W.Greenwood 1*).

Comments: Twenty wickets fell on the first day, The game finishing in two days.
A.W.Snowden did not continue his second innings owing to a motor accident at the weekend.
H.W.Greenwood kept wicket for Northants in Derbyshire's 2nd innings, which lasted eight balls, bowled by the regular wicketkeeper, K.C.James.

ESSEX v YORKSHIRE

Played at Ilford, May 20, 22, 23, 1939.
Toss won by Yorkshire.
Yorkshire won by seven wickets.

ESSEX

A.V.Avery	c Wood b Leyland	49	lbw b Verity	33
S.J.Cray	c Sellers b Smailes	8	lbw b Smailes	0
R.M.Taylor	b Smailes	3	(7) b Robinson	4
J.O'Connor	lbw b Leyland	15	c Barber b Robinson	45
M.S.Nichols	b Leyland	4	not out	31
Mr D.F.Cock	b Bowes	1	(9) lbw b Verity	12
*Capt J.W.A.Stephenson	c Hutton b Leyland	10	(8) st Wood b Verity	4
L.C.Eastman	lbw b Bowes	58	(6) b Robinson	0
T.P.B.Smith	c Hutton b Leyland	9	(10) b Verity	12
†T.H.Wade	lbw b Smailes	38	(3) st Wood b Verity	17
R.Smith	not out	0	c Verity b Leyland	6
Extras	(B 11, LB 2, NB 1)	14	(NB 1)	1
Total		**209**		**165**

Fall: 1st inns 1/26, 2/38, 3/80, 4/86, 5/87, 6/87, 7/100, 8/116, 9/209.
2nd inns 1/0, 2/35, 3/88, 4/98, 5/98, 6/102, 7/107, 8/126, 9/158.

YORKSHIRE

H.Sutcliffe	lbw b R.Smith	4	lbw b P.Smith	36
L.Hutton	b Nichols	0	st Wade b Taylor	35
A.Mitchell	c Wade b Taylor	29	not out	55
M.Leyland	c Taylor b P.Smith	31	c Avery b P.Smith	38
W.Barber	c Taylor b P.Smith	3	not out	49
*Mr A.B.Sellers	lbw b P.Smith	20		
T.F.Smailes	b Taylor	6		
†A.Wood	b Taylor	0		
E.P.Robinson	not out	21		
H.Verity	c Wade b P.Smith	4		
W.E.Bowes	c O'Connor b P.Smith	10		
Extras	(B 8, LB 3, NB 2)	13	(B 9, LB 13, NB 2)	24
Total		**141**	(3 wickets)	**237**

Fall: 1st inns 1/1, 2/17, 3/68, 4/77, 5/88, 6/103, 7/103, 8/115, 9/125.
2nd inns 1/77, 2/79, 3/139.

YORKSHIRE	O	M	R	W	O	M	R	W
Bowes	15	6	26	2	11	2	24	0
Verity	9	2	17	0	25	12	27	5
Smailes	9.2	3	31	3	7	1	22	1
Robinson	10	3	37	0	16	4	43	3
Leyland	18	3	74	5	9	0	42	1
Hutton	2	0	10	0	2	0	6	0

ESSEX	O	M	R	W	O	M	R	W
Nichols	10	3	19	1	8	0	38	0
R.Smith	6	2	11	1	3	0	10	0
Stephenson	6	1	17	0	8	0	39	0
Taylor	9	0	50	3	12	0	60	1
T.P.B.Smith	7.2	3	31	5	19	6	39	2
Eastman	-	-	-	-	7	1	27	0

Umpires: H.G.Baldwin and J.J.Hills.

Close of play scores. First day: Yorkshire 1/1 (H.Sutcliffe 1*, A.Mitchell 0*). **Second day:** Essex 110/7 (M.S.Nichols 4*, D.F.Cock 3*).

Comments: Essex were put into bat.
There was only three and a quarter hours play on the first day.
On the first day, L.Hutton was unfortunate to be bowled first ball, only for play to be suspended for the remainder of the day after only one more delivery.
The second day's play ended at 5.40pm owing to bad light.

LEICESTERSHIRE v SOMERSET

Played at Grace Road, Leicester, May 20, 22, 23, 1939.
Toss won by Somerset.
Somerset won by three wickets.

SOMERSET

F.S.Lee	lbw b Flamson	7	not out	42
H.Gimblett	c Smith b Astill	108	c Watson b Smith	23
H.T.F.Buse	c Tompkin b Flamson	75	c Sperry b Smith	3
W.H.R.Andrews	c Dawkes b Smith	1	c Tompkin b Smith	6
Mr J.W.Seamer	c Sperry b Smith	28	c Dawkes b Flamson	1
*Mr E.F.Longrigg	b Sperry	1	(7) b Smith	1
Mr C.J.P.Barnwell	lbw b Smith	14	(8) b Flamson	11
Mr G.M.Bennett	b Flamson	0		
A.W.Wellard	not out	32	(6) not out	8
†W.T.Luckes	c Flamson b Smith	7	c Berry b Flamson	7
H.L.Hazell	run out	0		
Extras	(B 2, LB 5, W 1)	8	(B 4)	4
Total		**281**	(7 wickets)	**106**

Fall: 1st inns 1/23, 2/184, 3/189, 4/204, 5/211, 6/240, 7/241, 8/247, 9/271.
2nd inns 1/43, 2/47, 3/53, 4/56, 5/66, 6/67, 7/86.

LEICESTERSHIRE

G.L.Berry	b Hazell	29	c Buse b Andrews	10
F.T.Prentice	c Gimblett b Wellard	6	(4) run out	34
N.F.Armstrong	c Wellard b Andrews	10	lbw b Andrews	73
G.S.Watson	c Luckes b Andrews	3	(2) c Longrigg b Buse	10
M.Tompkin	b Andrews	0	b Andrews	5
†G.O.Dawkes	lbw b Andrews	0	c Lee b Buse	81
G.Lester	b Buse	13	run out	36
*W.E.Astill	c & b Buse	0	b Buse	15
H.A.Smith	c Gimblett b Buse	12	b Wellard	1
W.H.Flamson	b Andrews	0	c Barnwell b Wellard	14
J.Sperry	not out	0	not out	12
Extras	(LB 7, NB 1)	8	(B 5, LB 7, NB 1)	13
Total		**81**		**304**

Fall: 1st inns 1/27, 2/44, 3/53, 4/54, 5/55, 6/55, 7/57, 8/80, 9/81.
2nd inns 1/15, 2/25, 3/118, 4/133, 5/139, 6/253, 7/259, 8/260, 9/279.

LEICESTERSHIRE	O	M	R	W	O	M	R	W
Flamson	25	1	114	3	17	3	59	3
Sperry	9	0	49	1	4	1	9	0
Smith	19	2	45	4	12.3	1	34	4
Prentice	10	2	20	0				
Lester	5	0	25	0				
Astill	7	1	20	1				

SOMERSET	O	M	R	W	O	M	R	W
Wellard	11	2	27	1	15.4	2	63	2
Andrews	17.4	7	41	4	23	0	111	3
Hazell	5	2	3	2	6	0	37	0
Buse	3	1	2	3	24	4	66	3
Gimblett	-	-	-	-	4	1	14	0

Umpires: G.M.Lee and C.V.Tarbox.

Close of play scores. First day: Leicestershire 55/6 (G.Lester 0*). **Second day:** Somerset 53/3 (F.S.Lee 21*).

Comments: W.E.Astill, having first played for Leicestershire in 1906, came out of retirement to captain the county at the age of 51.
H.Gimblett was making his third century in eight days. His 108, made in 165 minutes, included 13 4's.
H.Gimblett and H.T.F.Buse put on 161 for the 2nd wicket.
Leicestershire followed on 200 runs behind.
G.O.Dawkes and G.Lester added 114 for the 6th wicket in 80 minutes. Both made their highest scores for Leicestershire.

MIDDLESEX v GLOUCESTERSHIRE

Played at Lord's, May 20, 22, 23, 1939.
Toss won by Middlesex.
Gloucestershire won by three wickets.

MIDDLESEX

J.D.B.Robertson	c Wilson b Scott	47	b Goddard	32
S.M.Brown	c Haynes b Lambert	8	c Wilson b Scott	2
W.J.Edrich	lbw b Goddard	43	c Lambert b Goddard	12
D.C.S.Compton	b Goddard	44	c Hammond b Scott	46
J.H.A.Hulme	not out	62	lbw b Lambert	40
Mr N.S.Hotchkin	c Wilson b Scott	3	c Crapp b Goddard	21
†W.F.F.Price	b Barnett	18	b Goddard	20
J.M.Sims	c Scott b Goddard	3	c Crapp b Scott	5
C.I.J.Smith	b Goddard	0	c Barnett b Goddard	16
*Mr I.A.R.Peebles	b Goddard	0	b Goddard	5
L.H.Gray	b Scott	1	not out	1
Extras	(LB 6, W 1)	7	(LB 5, NB 2)	7
Total		**236**		**207**

Fall: 1st inns 1/22, 2/73, 3/142, 4/147, 5/154, 6/186, 7/196, 8/197, 9/207.
2nd inns 1/9, 2/38, 3/51, 4/126, 5/143, 6/174, 7/179, 8/199, 9/206.

GLOUCESTERSHIRE

C.J.Barnett	b Gray	0	c Robertson b Edrich	21
V.Hopkins	b Edrich	28	b Smith	4
G.M.Emmett	b Edrich	12	b Smith	19
*Mr W.R.Hammond	c Gray b Edrich	60	c Price b Sims	71
J.F.Crapp	st Price b Sims	5	lbw b Sims	22
W.L.Neale	c Peebles b Gray	5	c Edrich b Gray	34
R.W.Haynes	c Sims b Gray	5	b Gray	24
†E.A.Wilson	lbw b Smith	40	not out	23
C.J.Scott	c Sims b Gray	47	not out	5
T.W.J.Goddard	b Smith	0		
G.E.E.Lambert	not out	4		
Extras	(LB 1)	1	(B 4, LB 9, W 3)	16
Total		**207**	(7 wickets)	**239**

Fall: 1st inns 1/1, 2/37, 3/42, 4/55, 5/83, 6/101, 7/126, 8/199, 9/200.
2nd inns 1/9, 2/44, 3/67, 4/127, 5/160, 6/199, 7/217.

GLOUCESTERSHIRE	O	M	R	W	O	M	R	W
Scott	21	3	73	3	15	2	72	3
Barnett	5	0	10	1	6	0	23	0
Goddard	24	1	83	5	18.2	0	68	6
Lambert	11	1	40	1	10	1	37	1
Emmett	6	1	23	0				

MIDDLESEX	O	M	R	W	O	M	R	W
Smith	19.6	2	47	2	18	3	48	2
Gray	18	1	58	4	21	5	40	2
Edrich	12	1	33	3	11	1	41	1
Sims	10	0	50	1	15	2	63	2
Peebles	6	1	18	0	8	0	26	0
Compton	-	-	-	-	2	0	5	0

Umpires: F.Chester and W.Reeves.

Close of play scores. First day: Gloucestershire 71/4 (W.R.Hammond 22*, W.L.Neale 3*). **Second day:** Middlesex 207 all out.
Comments: J.D.B.Robertson had been awarded his county cap prior to the game. It was presented to him at lunch on the first day.

NOTTINGHAMSHIRE v KENT

Played at Trent Bridge, Nottingham, May 20, 22, 23, 1939.
Toss won by Nottinghamshire.
Kent won by nine wickets.

NOTTINGHAMSHIRE

W.W.Keeton	b Watt	17	b Watt	14
C.B.Harris	c Fagg b Watt	21	c Levett b Lewis	24
*Mr G.F.H.Heane	c Ames b Lewis	11	lbw b Lewis	68
J.Hardstaff	lbw b Lewis	14	b Todd	104
G.V.Gunn	st Levett b Dovey	1	lbw b Watt	9
J.Knowles	st Levett b Lewis	6	not out	93
W.Voce	b Dovey	0	c Fagg b Dovey	25
†A.B.Wheat	not out	1	c Todd b Lewis	1
F.G.Woodhead	b Lewis	0	c Chalk b Dovey	17
H.J.Butler	c Watt b Lewis	0	b Lewis	3
J.Bradley	lbw b Lewis	0	c Levett b Todd	7
Extras	(LB 7)	7	(LB 11)	11
Total		**78**		**376**

Fall: 1st inns 1/32, 2/49, 3/59, 4/70, 5/74, 6/75, 7/77, 8/77, 9/77.
2nd inns 1/31, 2/55, 3/180, 4/217, 5/229, 6/304, 7/305, 8/332, 9/337.

KENT

A.E.Fagg	b Butler	5	not out	35
P.R.Sunnucks	b Butler	8	c Keeton b Gunn	48
L.E.G.Ames	c Wheat b Woodhead	3	not out	0
*Mr F.G.H.Chalk	b Gunn	59		
Mr B.H.Valentine	c Harris b Woodhead	201		
L.J.Todd	c Wheat b Voce	6		
Mr P.G.Foster	not out	67		
†Mr .W.H.V.Levett	lbw b Gunn	5		
A.E.Watt	b Gunn	0		
C.Lewis	c Wheat b Gunn	5		
R.R.Dovey	not out	2		
Extras	(LB 5, NB 1)	6	(B 4, LB 1)	5
Total	(9 wickets, declared)	**367**	(1 wicket)	**88**

Fall: 1st inns 1/5, 2/14, 3/27, 4/189, 5/218, 6/316, 7/335, 8/335, 9/345.
2nd inns 1/83.

KENT	O	M	R	W	O	M	R	W
Todd	5	2	16	0	21.3	2	85	2
Watt	11	3	23	2	26	4	93	2
Lewis	12.3	6	18	6	36	5	106	4
Dovey	6	0	14	2	25	6	77	2
Valentine	-	-	-	-	1	0	4	0

NOTTINGHAMSHIRE	O	M	R	W	O	M	R	W
Voce	23	5	66	1	8	1	28	0
Butler	24	3	78	2	7	0	15	0
Woodhead	19	1	85	2	9.1	2	30	0
Heane	5	0	22	0				
Bradley	6	0	45	0				
Gunn	16	2	65	4	3	0	10	1

Umpires: A.Dolphin and H.Elliott.

Close of play scores. First day: Kent 252/5 (B.H.Valentine 158*, P.G.Foster 7*).
Second day: Nottinghamshire 249/5 (J.Knowles 13*, W.Voce 10*).

Comments: C.Lewis performed the hat-trick on the first day, his victims being J.Knowles, F.G.Woodhead and H.J.Butler. He claimed two wickets before lunch and took the third with his first ball after the interval. His last 22 deliveries earned him five wickets for two runs.
B.H.Valentine scored 201, including one 6 and 28 4's, out of 289, while he was at the wicket. His century came in 90 minutes and his double-century took 240 minutes.
F.G.H.Chalk and B.H.Valentine added 162 for Kent's 4th wicket.
J.Hardstaff hit 11 4's in his 104. He and G.F.H.Heane added 125 for the 3rd wicket.
It was Kent's first victory at Trent Bridge for 12 years.

NOTTINGHAMSHIRE COUNTY CRICKET CLUB

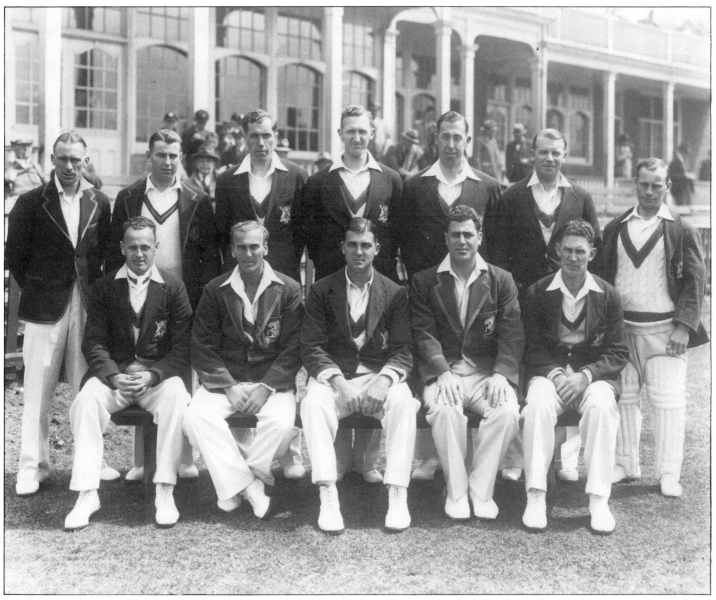

Standing (left to right): D.Jones, R.J.Giles, F.G.Woodhead, J.Knowles, H.J.Butler, G.V.Gunn, A.B.Wheat. **Seated:** W.W.Keeton, J.Hardstaff, G.F.H.Heane (captain), W.Voce, C.B.Harris.

SUSSEX v GLAMORGAN

Played at Hove, May 20, 22, 23, 1939.
Toss won by Glamorgan.
Sussex won by an innings and 79 runs.

GLAMORGAN

A.H.Dyson	c W.Cornford b Nye......1	lbw b J.Cornford	47
D.E.Davies	lbw b Hammond........24	c John Langridge b J.Parks	97
T.L.Brierley	c John Langridge b Hammond 21	lbw b Nye	13
D.Davies	c W.Cornford b Hammond............0	not out	49
*Mr M.J.L.Turnbull	lbw b J.Parks 0	(7) c J.Parks b Nye	6
C.C.Smart	b J.Parks 6	b J.Parks	5
E.C.Jones	not out 19	(5) c Hammond b Jas.Langridge	3
P.B.Clift	lbw b Nye............4	c W.Cornford b Nye	1
†H.G.Davies	b Hammond 1	b J.Cornford	21
A.J.Watkins	b Nye 3	b Nye	4
J.Mercer	c Jas.Langridge b Nye ...11	b J.Cornford	9
Extras	(LB 4) 4	(B 15, LB 6, NB 1)	22
Total	**94**		**277**

Fall: 1st inns 1/4, 2/45, 3/45, 4/50, 5/50, 6/59, 7/68, 8/70, 9/74.
2nd inns 1/140, 2/165, 3/191, 4/196, 5/213, 6/228, 7/230, 8/257, 9/262.

SUSSEX

John G.Langridge	st H.Davies b E.Davies	14
J.H.Parks	lbw b E.Davies	5
H.W.Parks	c D.Davies b E.Davies	161
C.Oakes	hit wkt b E.Davies	60
Jas.Langridge	c Smart b Clift	116
*Mr H.T.Bartlett	c Mercer b E.Davies	33
G.Cox	not out	18
H.E.Hammond	not out	27
Extras	(B 10, LB 6)	16
Total	(6 wickets, declared)	**450**

Fall: 1st inns 1/21, 2/28, 3/119, 4/322, 5/402, 6/402.
†W.L.Cornford, J.H.Cornford, and J.K.Nye did not bat.

SUSSEX	O	M	R	W	O	M	R	W
Nye	11.3	3	27	4	20	0	69	4
J.Cornford	8	3	22	0	22.5	1	78	3
Hammond	8	2	17	4	16	2	40	0
J.Parks	11	3	24	2	18	7	38	2
Oakes	-	-	-	-	5	2	16	0
Jas.Langridge	-	-	-	-	4	2	14	1

GLAMORGAN	O	M	R	W
Mercer	24	5	84	0
D.E.Davies	34	3	142	5
Smart	13	0	70	0
Jones	10	0	51	0
Watkins	11	1	39	0
D.Davies	2	0	12	0
Clift	9	1	36	1

Umpires: J.A.Newman and G.Beet.

Close of play scores. First day: Sussex 208/3 (J.H.Parks 82*, Jas.Langridge 40*).
Second day: Glamorgan 134/0 (A.H.Dyson 44*, D.E.Davies 82*).

Comments: Glamorgan lost their last eight 1st innings wickets for 49.
H.W.Parks and James Langridge added 203 for the 4th wicket in 165 minutes.
H.W.Parks was at the wicket 315 minutes for his 161.
A.H.Dyson and D.E.Davies scored 140 for the 1st wicket in Glamorgan's 2nd innings.

WARWICKSHIRE v LANCASHIRE

Played at Edgbaston, Birmingham, May 20, 22, 23, 1939.
Toss won by Lancashire.
Warwickshire won by seven wickets.

LANCASHIRE

E.Paynter	c Buckingham b Wilmot	3	b Mayer 42
C.Washbrook	c Buckingham b Wyatt	27	lbw b Hollies 44
J.Iddon	lbw b Wyatt	39	not out 74
N.Oldfield	c Santall b Hollies	141	not out 30
J.L.Hopwood	run out	51	
A.E.Nutter	b Mayer	22	
*Mr W.H.L.Lister	c Ord b Mayer	0	
R.H.Parkin	st Buckingham b Hollies	19	
W.E.Phillipson	b Mayer	40	
†W.Farrimond	not out	19	
R.Pollard	c Mayer b Wyatt	0	
Extras	(LB 1, NB 1)	2	(B 8, LB 2) 10
Total		**363**	(2 wickets, declared).....**200**

Fall: 1st inns 1/5, 2/48, 3/81, 4/189, 5/227, 6/227, 7/289, 8/310, 9/362.
2nd inns 1/58, 2/136.

WARWICKSHIRE

A.J.W.Croom	b Phillipson	21	c Farrimond b Phillipson 11
W.A.Hill	b Nutter	7	not out 99
F.R.Santall	c Washbrook b Nutter	77	c & b Phillipson 156
Mr R.E.S.Wyatt	lbw b Nutter	115	(5) not out.................2
J.S.Ord	c Nutter b Phillipson	21	
H.E.Dollery	b Nutter	30	
*Mr P.Cranmer	c Farrimond b Nutter	8	(4) c Washbrook b Pollard 2
†J.Buckingham	not out	2	
K.Wilmot	not out	0	
Extras	(B 1, LB 4, NB 3)	8	(B 2, LB 2, W 1, NB 2) 7
Total	(7 wickets, declared)	**289**	(3 wickets) **277**

Fall: 1st inns 1/30, 2/34, 3/163, 4/204, 5/272, 6/281, 7/287.
2nd inns 1/18, 2/262, 3/267.
J.H.Mayer and W.E.Hollies did not bat.

WARWICKSHIRE	O	M	R	W	O	M	R	W
Mayer	27	9	73	3	13	2	42	1
Wilmot	21	1	79	1	7	1	31	0
Santall	9	0	24	0	5	0	31	0
Wyatt	23.5	5	60	3	2	0	17	0
Hollies	23	3	87	2	12	0	69	1
Cranmer	1	0	13	0				
Croom	7	1	25	0				

LANCASHIRE	O	M	R	W	O	M	R	W
Phillipson	22	2	87	2	14.5	1	93	2
Pollard	19	2	71	0	12	1	75	1
Nutter	20	2	64	5	8	1	56	0
Parkin	7	1	25	0	9	1	46	0
Hopwood	2	0	18	0				
Iddon	4	1	16	0				

Umpires: F.I.Walden and C.N.Woolley.

Close of play scores. First day: Lancashire 316/8 (W.E.Phillipson 9*, W.Farrimond 3*). **Second day:** Warwickshire 289/7 (J.Buckingham 2*, K.Wilmot 0*).
Comments: N.Oldfield's 141, made in 255 minutes, was the highest score of his career. It included two 6's and 13 4's. It was the first century for Lancashire in 1939. He and J.L.Hopwood added 108 for the 4th wicket in 108 minutes.
F.R.Santall and R.E.S.Wyatt put on 129 for the 3rd wicket.
R.E.S.Wyatt hit 14 4's in his 115, made in 225 minutes.
Warwickshire were set 277 to make in 220 minutes, after Warwickshire had earlier declared, forfeiting 1st innings points in an attempt to engineer a finish.
F.R.Santall and W.A.Hill added 244 for the 2nd wicket in 145 minutes, Santall hitting Pollard for 23 in his 11th over. F.R.Santall made his 156 in 150 minutes. It included one 6 and 16 4's.
Warwickshire won with 20 minutes to spare, 185 runs being made in a 100 minutes after the tea interval. W.A.Hill hit the winning boundary to take his personal score to 99.

WORCESTERSHIRE v HAMPSHIRE

Played at Worcester, May 20, 22, 23, 1939.
Toss won by Hampshire.
Worcestershire won by six wickets.

HAMPSHIRE

†N.T.McCorkell	c Buller b Martin	7	b Perks	0
J.Bailey	b Martin	5	c Howorth b Perks	21
G.Hill	c White b Martin	3	b Perks	2
W.L.C.Creese	b Perks	11	c & b Jenkins	20
J.Arnold	not out	179	lbw b Perks	34
A.E.Pothecary	c Gibbons b Jenkins	25	b Perks	2
D.F.Walker	b Perks	1	b Howorth	62
A.G.Holt	st Buller b Howorth	28	c Buller b Perks	4
G.S.Boyes	b Howorth	47	c Bull b Perks	6
*Mr G.R.Taylor	b Jenkins	1	c Buller b Perks	27
G.E.M.Heath	c Martin b Jenkins	0	not out	3
Extras	(B 8, LB 1, NB 3)	12	(B 10, LB 3, W 1, NB 2)	16
Total		**319**		**197**

Fall: 1st inns 1/13, 2/17, 3/28, 4/28, 5/92, 6/101, 7/158, 8/298, 9/301.
2nd inns 1/0, 2/21, 3/25, 4/36, 5/53, 6/117, 7/117, 8/131, 9/183.

WORCESTERSHIRE

C.H.Bull	c McCorkell b Heath	0	c McCorkell b Heath	22
Mr A.F.T.White	c McCorkell b Heath	6	b Heath	9
B.P.King	c Arnold b Heath	16	lbw b Bailey	3
E.Cooper	lbw b Heath	8	lbw b Bailey	8
H.H.I.Gibbons	not out	111	not out	100
*Hon C.J.Lyttelton	c & b Bailey	5		
S.H.Martin	b Hill	39	(6) not out	102
R.Howorth	b Boyes	0		
†J.S.Buller	lbw b Creese	33		
R.T.D.Perks	b Boyes	35		
R.O.Jenkins	run out	0		
Extras	(B 3, LB 6)	9	(B 1, LB 11)	12
Total		**262**	(4 wickets)	**256**

Fall: 1st inns 1/0, 2/12, 3/21, 4/35, 5/39, 6/112, 7/189, 8/211, 9/253.
2nd inns 1/16, 2/38, 3/38, 4/49.

WORCESTERSHIRE	O	M	R	W	O	M	R	W
Perks	18	0	91	2	13.7	5	59	8
Martin	18	3	55	3				
Howorth	14	0	73	2	16	4	46	1
Lyttelton	8	1	48	0	4	1	10	0
Jenkins	10.4	0	40	3	17	3	66	1

HAMPSHIRE	O	M	R	W	O	M	R	W
Heath	29	1	86	4	21	2	104	2
Bailey	12	0	58	1	12.1	1	77	2
Hill	14.3	2	46	1	4	2	12	0
Boyes	13	1	45	2	10	1	40	0
Creese	3	0	18	1	5	1	11	0

Umpires: D.Hendren and H.Cruice.

Close of play scores. First day: Worcestershire 35/4 (H.H.I.Gibbons 4*, C.J.Lyttelton 1*). **Second day:** Hampshire 112/5 (J.Arnold 31*, D.F.Walker 26*).

Comments: J.Arnold with 179*, which included one 6 and 21 4's, made his highest score for seven years.
He and G.S.Boyes added 140 in 105 minutes for the 8th wicket in Hampshire's 1st innings.
Worcestershire had to make 255 in just over four hours to win. An unfinished 5th wicket stand of 208 by H.H.I.Gibbons and S.H.Martin won Worcestershire the match. H.H.I.Gibbons was the first Worcester batsman to score an undefeated century in both innings of the same match. H.H.I.Gibbons hit 14 4's in his 1st innings score of 111, the first by a Worcester batsman in 1939, and 12 4's in his 100 in the 2nd innings.
S.H.Martin, who had been unable to field or bowl in Hampshire's 2nd innings, batted with a torn thigh muscle. He reached his century and made the winning runs with the same stroke. His 102 included 14 4's.

GLOUCESTERSHIRE v WARWICKSHIRE

Played at Bristol, May 24, 25, 1939.
Toss won by Warwickshire.
Gloucestershire won by an innings and 16 runs.

WARWICKSHIRE

A.J.W.Croom	lbw b Scott	7	c Neale b Barnett	2
W.A.Hill	c Crapp b Goddard	38	lbw b Sinfield	29
F.R.Santall	c Hammond b Scott	29	b Goddard	34
Mr R.E.S.Wyatt	c Sinfield b Goddard	1	(5) c Scott b Sinfield	2
J.S.Ord	b Sinfield	1	(6) c Scott b Goddard	1
H.E.Dollery	lbw b Sinfield	2	(4) c Allen b Sinfield	14
†J.Buckingham	lbw b Sinfield	46	c Allen b Goddard	0
*Mr P.Cranmer	b Barnett	48	c Neale b Goddard	45
K.Wilmot	b Goddard	3	lbw b Goddard	10
J.H.Mayer	c Hammond b Sinfield	0	c Crapp b Goddard	4
W.E.Hollies	not out	2	not out	2
Extras	(B 4)	4	(B 11, NB 2)	13
Total		**181**		**156**

Fall: 1st inns 1/8, 2/50, 3/55, 4/61, 5/71, 6/87, 7/159, 8/179, 9/179.
2nd inns 1/5, 2/59, 3/73, 4/78, 5/82, 6/82, 7/115, 8/143, 9/150.

GLOUCESTERSHIRE

C.J.Barnett	c Dollery b Mayer	11
R.A.Sinfield	lbw b Hollies	18
Mr B.O.Allen	st Buckingham b Hollies	30
*Mr W.R.Hammond	not out	192
J.F.Crapp	lbw b Hollies	17
G.M.Emmett	run out	0
W.L.Neale	c Ord b Hollies	0
R.W.Haynes	c Cranmer b Mayer	30
†V.Hopkins	b Santall	41
C.J.Scott	c Croom b Santall	5
T.W.J.Goddard	b Santall	0
Extras	(B 2, LB 7)	9
Total		**353**

Fall: 1st inns 1/14, 2/50, 3/89, 4/164, 5/164, 6/164, 7/220, 8/313, 9/353.

GLOUCESTERSHIRE	O	M	R	W	O	M	R	W
Scott	12	2	54	2	3	0	17	0
Barnett	6	0	24	1	6	3	9	1
Goddard	17	1	62	3	13.5	0	66	6
Sinfield	11.4	0	37	4	11	1	51	3

WARWICKSHIRE	O	M	R	W
Mayer	15	2	91	2
Wilmot	9	2	24	0
Wyatt	11	1	56	0
Hollies	30	2	112	4
Croom	10	0	47	0
Santall	5.4	0	14	3

Umpires: A.Dolphin and H.Elliott.

Close of play scores. First day: Gloucestershire 206/6 (W.R.Hammond 101*, R.W.Haynes 22*).

Comments: Gloucestershire won in two days. The match finished at 5.20pm on the second day.
W.R.Hammond hit 24 4's in his 192*. It was his first 100 of the season.
J.F.Crapp, G.M.Emmett and W.L.Neale were dismissed in three consecutive deliveries in Hollies' 14th over but there was no hat-trick, Emmett being run out.
T.W.J.Goddard took his season's tally of wickets to 53 in this match.

LEICESTERSHIRE v LANCASHIRE

Played at Grace Road, Leicester, May 24, 25, 26, 1939.
Toss won by Lancashire.
Match drawn.

LANCASHIRE

C.Washbrook	c Tompkin b Armstrong	91	lbw b Flamson		8
E.Paynter	run out	159	c Armstrong b Flamson		21
J.Iddon	c Tompkin b Smith	7	c Armstrong b Lester		100
N.Oldfield	st Dawkes b Smith	1	c Lester b Smith		49
J.L.Hopwood	lbw b Smith	0	c Berry b Flamson		16
A.E.Nutter	c Flamson b Smith	86	not out		22
W.E.Phillipson	b Smith	12			
*Mr W.H.L.Lister	b Lester	12	(7) c Berry b Flamson		12
†W.Farrimond	not out	59			
R.G.Garlick	not out	15	(8) not out		7
Extras	(B 13, LB 6, W 1, NB 2)	22	(B 6, LB 1, NB 1)		8
Total	(8 wickets, declared)	464	(6 wickets, declared)		243

Fall: 1st inns 1/213, 2/252, 3/268, 4/268, 5/278, 6/309, 7/332, 8/443.
2nd inns 1/21, 2/46, 3/183, 4/187, 5/210, 6/229.
J.Briggs did not bat.

LEICESTERSHIRE

G.L.Berry	b Briggs	42	c & b Briggs		57
G.S.Watson	lbw b Briggs	57	lbw b Phillipson		21
N.F.Armstrong	c Oldfield b Garlick	97	c Phillipson b Nutter		79
F.T.Prentice	c Nutter b Phillipson	4	b Briggs		26
*Mr C.S.Dempster	c Farrimond b Nutter	51	b Iddon		12
M.Tompkin	b Phillipson	1	c Nutter b Phillipson		27
†G.O.Dawkes	c Washbrook b Phillipson	0	c sub b Phillipson		18
L.D.Thursting	c Farrimond b Phillipson	54	not out		33
G.Lester	lbw b Phillipson	15	st Farrimond b Briggs		6
H.A.Smith	b Briggs	28	not out		1
W.H.Flamson	not out	1			
Extras	(B 7, LB 2, NB 2)	11	(B 6, LB 6, W 1, NB 1)		14
Total		361	(8 wickets)		294

Fall: 1st inns 1/93, 2/121, 3/151, 4/254, 5/255, 6/255, 7/275, 8/326, 9/341.
2nd inns 1/72, 2/88, 3/160, 4/185, 5/228, 6/229, 7/270, 8/283.

LEICESTERSHIRE	O	M	R	W	O	M	R	W
Flamson	23	1	104	0	16	0	82	4
Smith	32	1	107	5	18	0	99	1
Prentice	7	0	37	0				
Lester	18	1	97	1	10	0	46	1
Armstrong	12	1	64	1	1	0	8	0
Thursting	5	0	33	0				

LANCASHIRE	O	M	R	W	O	M	R	W
Phillipson	30	3	139	5	21	2	87	3
Garlick	11	0	66	1				
Nutter	18	0	74	1	10	0	73	1
Briggs	16.1	1	71	3	22	1	97	3
Paynter	-	-	-	-	1	0	6	0
Hopwood	-	-	-	-	3	1	6	0
Iddon	-	-	-	-	3	0	11	1

Umpires: E.Robinson and H.W.Lee.

Close of play scores. First day: Lancashire 464/8 (W.Farrimond 59*, R.G.Garlick 15*). **Second day:** Lancashire 45/1 (E.Paynter 20*, J.Iddon 17*).

Comments: C.Washbrook and E.Paynter began the match with an opening partnership of 213. E.Paynter hit 18 4's in his 159, which took him 210 minutes. His 100 came in 160 minutes.
W.Farrimond and A.E.Nutter added 111 for the 8th wicket.
N.F.Armstrong and C.S.Dempster added 103 for Leicestershire's 4th wicket in 80 minutes.
J.Iddon made a 100 out of 165 in 105 minutes in Lancashire's 2nd innings. It included 12 4's. He and N.Oldfield added 137 for the 2nd wicket.
Leicestershire batted for four hours to save the game, being set a target of 347 at 80 an hour.

MIDDLESEX v HAMPSHIRE

Played at Lord's, May 24, 25, 26, 1939.
Toss won by Middlesex.
Middlesex won by nine wickets.

MIDDLESEX

J.D.B.Robertson	b Bailey	30			
S.M.Brown	c McCorkell b Bailey	53	(3) not out		1
W.J.Edrich	c & b Steele	30			
D.C.S.Compton	b Hill	143			
Rev E.T.Killick	c Boyes b Steele	53			
G.E.Hart	b Boyes	37			
†W.F.F.Price	c McCorkell b Boyes	1			
J.M.Sims	c Taylor b Bailey	15			
C.I.J.Smith	b Boyes	1			
*Mr I.A.R.Peebles	st McCorkell b Boyes	28	(1) not out		7
L.H.Gray	not out	1	(2) b Taylor		0
Extras	(LB 10)	10			
Total		402	(1 wicket)		8

Fall: 1st inns 1/58, 2/109, 3/137, 4/273, 5/349, 6/355, 7/356, 8/358, 9/396.
2nd inns 1/1.

HAMPSHIRE

†N.T.McCorkell	lbw b Edrich	15	lbw b Gray		36
J.Bailey	b Smith	38	b Gray		55
A.E.Pothecary	st Price b Sims	11	(6) not out		12
W.L.C.Creese	lbw b Smith	18	lbw b Sims		0
J.Arnold	b Smith	3	(7) lbw b Smith		62
D.F.Walker	c Peebles b Sims	26	(5) c Edrich b Sims		28
G.Hill	not out	33	(3) b Sims		13
Revd J.W.J.Steele	c & b Gray	1	c Price b Smith		5
G.S.Boyes	b Gray	0	c Price b Smith		0
*Mr G.R.Taylor	lbw b Peebles	34	b Gray		0
G.E.M.Heath	c Price b Edrich	0	c Price b Smith		1
Extras	(LB 4)	4	(B 7, LB 3, W 1, NB 1)		12
Total		183			224

Fall: 1st inns 1/27, 2/49, 3/74, 4/82, 5/97, 6/121, 7/122, 8/122, 9/182.
2nd inns 1/76, 2/91, 3/91, 4/123, 5/198, 6/214, 7/220, 8/220, 9/221.

HAMPSHIRE	O	M	R	W	O	M	R	W
Heath	17	1	72	0				
Steele	25	1	106	2				
Bailey	26.6	5	96	3				
Boyes	12	1	53	4				
Hill	9	0	54	1				
Creese	4	0	11	0				
Taylor	-	-	-	-	5	0	8	1

MIDDLESEX	O	M	R	W	O	M	R	W
Smith	13	3	29	3	16.6	2	50	4
Gray	9	3	26	2	17	2	57	3
Sims	22	1	84	2	14	1	66	3
Edrich	6.7	1	15	2	6	1	27	0
Peebles	7	2	25	1	7	0	12	0

Umpires: A.Skelding and C.W.L.Parker.

Close of play scores. First day: Hampshire 2/0 (N.T.McCorkell 2*, J.Bailey 0*). **Second day:** Hampshire 121/3 (J.Bailey 55*, J.Arnold 16*).

Comments: D.C.S.Compton hit two 6's and 14 4's in his 143. He reached his 100 in 120 minutes.
He and Revd E.T.Killick put on 136 for the 4th wicket.
Hampshire followed on 219 behind.

NORTHAMPTONSHIRE v GLAMORGAN

Played at Kettering, May 24, 25, 1939.
Toss won by Northamptonshire.
Glamorgan won by six wickets.

NORTHAMPTONSHIRE

H.W.Greenwood	st H.Davies b Judge 2	c Smart b Judge 27
P.Davis	c Dyson b Jones 32	c Smart b Mercer 13
D.Brookes	c Dyson b Judge.........11	(4) run out 49
J.E.Timms	retired hurt 35	(5) c Clift b Judge 4
*Mr R.P.Nelson	b E.Davies 2	(6) b E.Davies 1
†K.C.James	c H.Davies b Jones 0	(8) c Dyson b Judge........7
F.P.O'Brien	lbw b E.Davies 41	c Dyson b E.Davies 15
M.E.F.Dunkley	c Judge b E.Davies 6	(9) lbw b E.Davies 1
W.E.Merritt	c Dyson b Judge........28	(10) st H.Davies b E.Davies 8
R.J.Partridge	not out 7	(3) b Judge 9
J.E.Buswell	c Clift b E.Davies 10	not out 3
Extras	(B 9, LB 6, W 2) 17	(B 1) 1
Total	.............................**191**	...........................**138**

Fall: 1st inns 1/15, 2/37, 3/65, 4/72, 5/73, 6/136, 7/145, 8/178, 9/191.
2nd inns 1/28, 2/46, 3/51, 4/65, 5/66, 6/88, 7/99, 8/102, 9/124.

GLAMORGAN

A.H.Dyson	c James b Buswell 8	b Partridge.................26
D.E.Davies	st James b Merritt......23	c James b Buswell 26
T.L.Brierley	c Greenwood b Merritt...27	b Merritt 29
D.Davies	run out 0	c Brookes b Merritt 19
*Mr M.J.L.Turnbull	b Nelson 31	not out 51
C.C.Smart	b Buswell 48	not out 8
E.C.Jones	b Buswell 3	
†H.G.Davies	b Nelson 9	
P.B.Clift	b Buswell 0	
P.F.Judge	not out 2	
J.Mercer	b Buswell 1	
Extras	(B 9, LB 1) 10	(B 8, LB 3) 11
Total	.............................**162**	(4 wickets) **170**

Fall: 1st inns 1/16, 2/54, 3/58, 4/73, 5/142, 6/146, 7/159, 8/159, 9/160.
2nd inns 1/55, 2/67, 3/110, 4/117.

GLAMORGAN	O	M	R	W	O	M	R	W
Mercer	9	0	28	0	14.6	2	38	1
Judge	17	1	52	3	22	5	63	4
Jones	7	1	28	2				
E.Davies	12	2	49	4	13	3	30	4
Smart	5	0	17	0				
D.Davies	-	-	-		3	1	6	0

NORTHANTS	O	M	R	W	O	M	R	W
Buswell	8.2	0	38	5	13.3	3	54	1
Partridge	8	2	32	0	11	3	25	1
Merritt	8	1	52	2	11	2	40	2
Nelson	6	1	13	2	5	1	18	0
O'Brien	3	0	17	0	3	0	13	0
Timms	-	-	-	-	3	0	9	0

Umpires: J.Hardstaff and G.Beet.

Close of play scores. First day: Northamptonshire 32/1 (H.W.Greenwood 19*, R.J.Partridge 0*).

Comments: Glamorgan won in two days.
The former Middlesex player, P.F.Judge, made his debut for Glamorgan. His first two deliveries were both wides.
J.E.Timms retired in the 1st innings with a cut over the right eye.
M.J.L.Turnbull, the Glamorgan captain, finished the game with two consecutive 6's off J.E.Buswell, having scored 51*in 35 minutes.

SUSSEX v ESSEX

Played at Hove, May 24, 25, 26, 1939.
Toss won by Sussex.
Essex won by an innings and 13 runs.

SUSSEX

John G.Langridge	c Wade b Nichols 16	c Wade b Stephenson 70
J.H.Parks	b R.Smith 15	b P.Smith 48
H.W.Parks	lbw b P.Smith 20	lbw b Nichols 51
C.Oakes	c Wade b Nichols 3	c Wade b Nichols 0
Jas.Langridge	lbw b Stephenson 6	c Taylor b R.Smith 9
Mr H.T.Bartlett	c Wade b R.Smith 60	not out 31
*Flt-Lt A.J.Holmes	c R.Smith b Stephenson 2	b R.Smith 2
H.E.Hammond	b Stephenson 7	b R.Smith 2
†W.L.Cornford	c O'Connor b Nichols 3	c Wade b Nichols 5
J.K.Nye	b Stephenson 1	b Nichols....................1
J.H.Cornford	not out 9	c Taylor b Nichols 9
Extras	(B 1, LB 5, NB 1) 7	(B 6, LB 7, NB 3) 16
Total	.............................**149**	...........................**244**

Fall: 1st inns 1/23, 2/55, 3/55, 4/62, 5/72, 6/76, 7/90, 8/95, 9/96.
2nd inns 1/78, 2/174, 3/174, 4/186, 5/207, 6/213, 7/215, 8/220, 9/228.

ESSEX

A.V.Avery	c Holmes b J.Cornford....7
S.J.Cray	c J.Parks b Nye 6
†T.H.Wade	c Hammond b J.Parks ...24
J.O'Connor	c W.Cornford b Nye 23
M.S.Nichols	c John Langridge b Jas.Langridge......146
R.M.Taylor	lbw b Hammond.........62
*Capt J.W.A.Stephenson	lbw b Hammond.........29
L.C.Eastman	b Nye 3
Mr D.F.Cock	not out.....................78
T.P.B.Smith	b J.Parks 9
R.Smith	lbw b Nye 7
Extras	(B 2, LB 9, NB 1) 12
Total	.............................**406**

Fall: 1st inns 1/10, 2/28, 3/46, 4/68, 5/190, 6/275, 7/282, 8/319, 9/355.

ESSEX	O	M	R	W	O	M	R	W
Nichols	16	3	63	3	15.3	3	35	5
R.Smith	9.2	0	37	2	17	0	75	3
P.Smith	6	1	14	1	9	1	28	1
Stephenson	6	0	21	4	13	0	39	1
Taylor	2	0	7	0				
Eastman	-	-	-	-	11	2	29	0
O'Connor	-	-	-	-	2	0	22	0

SUSSEX	O	M	R	W
J.Cornford	23	3	88	1
Nye	31.6	2	110	4
J.Parks	9	4	39	2
Hammond	19	0	99	2
Jas.Langridge	12	1	40	1
Oakes	2	0	15	0
John Langridge	1	0	0	0
Holmes	1	0	3	0

Umpires: E.J.Smith and F.J.Durston.

Close of play scores. First day: Essex 142/4 (M.S.Nichols 37*, R.M.Taylor 43*).
Second day: Sussex 161/1 (J.G.Langridge 64*, H.W.Parks 39*).

Comments: It was Essex's first win of the season, after four successive defeats.
M.S.Nichols and R.M.Taylor added 122 for the 5th Essex wicket.
Nichol scored his first century of the season, his 146 being made in 270 minutes and including ten 4's.
Sussex, needing only 83 to avoid an innings defeat, lost their last eight 2nd-innings wickets for 70, Nine wickets fell for 83 runs before lunch on the third day.

ESSEX v WORCESTERSHIRE

Played at Chelmsford, May 27, 29, 30, 1939.
Toss won by Essex.
Essex won by 295 runs.

ESSEX

A.V.Avery	lbw b Jenkins	47	c White b Howorth	77
L.C.Eastman	st Buller b Jenkins	18	c Perks b Howorth	52
†T.H.Wade	c Buller b Jenkins	0	c & b Jenkins	0
J.O'Connor	c Whaite b Perks	4	not out	118
M.S.Nichols	not out	116	c Martin b Perks	4
R.M.Taylor	c Martin b Jenkins	9	b Perks	23
Mr D.F.Cock	b Jenkins	0		
*Capt J.W.A.Stephenson	lbw b Howorth	24		
T.P.B.Smith	b Jenkins	3	(7) not out	1
Mr J.N.Dennis	lbw b Jenkins	0		
R.Smith	c Howorth b Perks	35		
Extras	(B 6, LB 5, NB 4)	15	(B 3, LB 5, NB 2)	10
Total		**271**	(5 wickets, declared)	**285**

Fall: 1st inns 1/35, 2/35, 3/42, 4/82, 5/112, 6/112, 7/177, 8/188, 9/188.
2nd inns 1/99, 2/102, 3/200, 4/229, 5/275.

WORCESTERSHIRE

Mr A.F.T.White	b Nichols	9	c Dennis b R.Smith	9
B.P.King	b Nichols	54	c R.Smith b Stephenson	61
E.Cooper	b Nichols	20	c Wade b R.Smith	7
*H.H.I.Gibbons	b Nichols	0	b R.Smith	0
S.H.Martin	c P.Smith b Nichols	5	b R.Smith	7
J.M.H.Jewell	b P.Smith	2	c Wade b R.Smith	0
R.Howorth	not out	34	c R.Smith b Eastman	6
R.T.D.Perks	b P.Smith	23	b R.Smith	5
R.O.Jenkins	c Nichols b Taylor	2	not out	9
†J.S.Buller	(hurt in car crash)			
C.H.Bull	(killed in car crash)			
Extras	(B 1, LB 5)	6	(LB 1, W 1)	2
Total		**155**		**106**

Fall: 1st inns 1/19, 2/71, 3/71, 4/83, 5/92, 6/106, 7/144, 8/155.
2nd inns 1/16, 2/24, 3/24, 4/44, 5/44, 6/55, 7/64, 8/106.

WORCESTERSHIRE	O	M	R	W	O	M	R	W
Perks	25.6	6	74	2	17	2	80	2
Howorth	22	1	83	1	24	0	109	2
Jenkins	33	10	98	7	13	1	64	1
Gibbons	1	0	1	0	3	0	22	0

ESSEX	O	M	R	W	O	M	R	W
Nichols	12	0	64	5	7	1	18	0
R.Smith	5	0	40	0	13	1	46	6
T.P.B.Smith	8	0	35	2				
Taylor	2.2	0	10	1				
Eastman	-	-	-	-	7	0	32	1
Stephenson	-	-	-	-	4	0	8	1

Umpires: C.N.Woolley and A.Skelding.

Close of play scores. First day: Essex 271 all out. **Second day:** Essex 285/5 (J.O'Connor 118*, T.P.B.Smith 1*).
Comments: The game was marred by the tragic death of C.H.Bull of Worcestershire and a serious injury to J.S.Buller, sustained in a motor accident during the weekend.
On the first day M.S.Nicholls hit his second consecutive century. His undefeated 116 was made in about 270 minutes and included 11 4's. His 10th wicket partnership of 83 with R.Smith enabled Nichols, in his 70's, to reach his century. Nichols still needed 23 runs when Smith came in. Smith had to retire for a few minutes at 271/9, after being hit in the face by Perks and was dismissed without addition on his return. R.O.Jenkins with figures of 7 for 98 achieved the best bowling performance of his career.
H.H.I.Gibbons of Worcestershire followed up his feat in the previous game of two undefeated centuries with a pair in this match.
J.O'Connor hit two 6's and 19 4's in his undefeated 118 in the Essex 2nd innings.
H.Yarnold, the Worcestershire 12th man, was allowed to keep wicket in place of the injured Buller.

HAMPSHIRE v KENT

Played at Southampton, May 27, 29, 30, 1939.
Toss won by Kent.
Kent won by 179 runs.

KENT

A.E.Fagg	b Heath	12	c Boyes b Steele	149
P.R.Sunnucks	c Walker b Heath	5	c Walker b Steele	20
L.E.G.Ames	c Arnold b Bailey	18	c McCorkell b Steele	6
*Mr F.G.H.Chalk	b Heath	14	c Taylor b Steele	0
Mr B.H.Valentine	b Heath	44	c McCorkell b Steele	0
L.J.Todd	b Steele	7	c Creese	14
Mr P.G.Foster	lbw b Boyes	4	lbw b Heath	40
D.V.P.Wright	lbw b Heath	12	not out	84
†Mr W.H.V.Levett	c McCorkell b Boyes	1	c Boyes b Steele	9
A.E.Watt	not out	10	c Pothecary b Boyes	8
C.Lewis	b Boyes	1	c Walker b Heath	22
Extras	(LB 6)	6	(B 7, LB 4, NB 1)	12
Total		**134**		**364**

Fall: 1st inns 1/15, 2/20, 3/44, 4/64, 5/81, 6/98, 7/112, 8/113, 9/131.
2nd inns 1/52, 2/58, 3/58, 4/58, 5/115, 6/215, 7/255, 8/264, 9/280.

HAMPSHIRE

†N.T.McCorkell	c Levett b Todd	23	lbw b Watt	1
J.Bailey	c Valentine b Todd	2	b Todd	14
Mr R.H.Moore	b Watt	23	c Lewis b Watt	18
W.L.C.Creese	lbw b Watt	23	c Ames b Todd	7
J.Arnold	c Valentine b Watt	28	c Fagg b Wright	7
D.F.Walker	c Sunnucks b Todd	7	b Wright	8
A.E.Pothecary	lbw b Wright	36	c Watt b Todd	4
Rev J.W.J.Steele	run out	9	c Wright b Todd	27
*Mr G.R.Taylor	b Todd	0	c Foster b Wright	0
G.S.Boyes	not out	47	b Todd	8
G.E.M.Heath	c Valentine b Wright	9	not out	3
Extras	(LB 4)	4	(B 9, LB 1, W 1)	11
Total		**211**		**108**

Fall: 1st inns 1/21, 2/30, 3/60, 4/99, 5/100, 6/111, 7/129, 8/129, 9/158.
2nd inns 1/4, 2/35, 3/37, 4/44, 5/61, 6/66, 7/78, 8/80, 9/80.

HAMPSHIRE	O	M	R	W	O	M	R	W
Heath	16	0	48	5	21.5	1	94	2
Steele	9	0	31	1	32	3	121	6
Bailey	6	0	21	1	8	1	39	0
Boyes	10.1	3	28	3	19	3	62	1
Creese	-	-	-	-	12	3	36	1

KENT	O	M	R	W	O	M	R	W
Todd	17	3	52	4	19.4	5	40	5
Watt	23	1	86	3	11	2	20	2
Wright	11.2	0	58	2	11	3	37	3
Lewis	4	1	11	0				

Umpires: C.V.Tarbox and W.Reeves.

Close of play scores. First day: Hampshire 211/9 (G.S.Boyes 47*, G.E.M.Heath 9*). **Second day:** Hampshire 4/1 (J.Bailey 2*).

Comments: Hampshire with a 1st innings lead of 77, claimed four Kent 2nd innings wickets before their lead was passed. This was due to the Revd J.W.J.Steele dismissing L.E.G.Ames, F.G.H.Chalk and B.H.Valentine in four balls in Kent's 2nd innings.
Then A.E.Fagg and P.G.Foster added 100 for Kent's 6th wicket.
A.E.Fagg's 149 included 18 4's and was made in just under four hours.
D.V.P.Wright made 84*, his highest score for Kent. It included two 6's and nine 4's. He and C.Lewis put on 84 for Kent's 10th wicket. Hampshire, requiring 288 for victory with a full day's play to come, collapsed, losing by 179 runs.

LANCASHIRE v YORKSHIRE

Played at Old Trafford, Manchester, May 27, 29, 30, 1939.
Toss won by Lancashire.
Yorkshire won by an innings and 43 runs.

LANCASHIRE

C.Washbrook	lbw b Yardley	46	c Hutton b Turner	1
E.Paynter	b Bowes	13	c Sellers b Bowes	60
J.Iddon	c & b Yardley	1	c Wood b Bowes	9
N.Oldfield	b Yardley	27	b Bowes	66
J.L.Hopwood	b Verity	54	c Verity b Bowes	2
A.E.Nutter	b Hutton	85	c Hutton b Bowes	6
W.E.Phillipson	b Verity	7	c Turner b Verity	2
*Mr W.H.L.Lister	c Hutton b Robinson	0	b Verity	3
†W.Farrimond	c Barber b Verity	1	lbw b Bowes	8
R.Pollard	b Robinson	54	not out	9
L.L.Wilkinson	not out	4	c Wood b Hutton	12
Extras	(B 1, LB 7)	8	(B 6, LB 1)	7
Total		**300**		**185**

Fall: 1st inns 1/36, 2/49, 3/73, 4/112, 5/160, 6/182, 7/183, 8/188, 9/294.
2nd inns 1/8, 2/28, 3/131, 4/143, 5/144, 6/153, 7/153, 8/162, 9/168.

YORKSHIRE

H.Sutcliffe	b Phillipson	165
L.Hutton	b Wilkinson	13
A.Mitchell	c Phillipson b Nutter	136
Mr N.W.D.Yardley	b Nutter	0
W.Barber	b Wilkinson	34
C.Turner	c Pollard b Nutter	29
*Mr A.B.Sellers	not out	53
†A.Wood	b Wilkinson	65
E.P.Robinson	c Nutter b Wilkinson	11
H.Verity	not out	0
Extras	(B 6, LB 11, NB 5)	22
Total	(8 wickets, declared)	**528**

Fall: 1st inns 1/41, 2/329, 3/329, 4/329, 5/393, 6/395, 7/509, 8/523.
W.E.Bowes did not bat.

YORKSHIRE	O	M	R	W	O	M	R	W
Bowes	22	4	75	1	19	2	43	6
Turner	9	1	22	0	7	5	12	1
Yardley	15	3	52	3	5	0	14	0
Robinson	9.2	0	55	2	8	0	37	0
Verity	15	4	69	3	17	4	37	2
Hutton	5	0	19	1	4	0	35	1

LANCASHIRE	O	M	R	W
Phillipson	30	3	128	1
Pollard	23	3	103	0
Nutter	25	4	88	3
Wilkinson	36	2	168	4
Iddon	6	0	19	0

Umpires: G.M.Lee and J.A.Smart.

Close of play scores. First day: Yorkshire 67/1 (H.Sutcliffe 37*, A.Mitchell 15*). **Second day:** Yorkshire 528/8 (A.B.Sellers 53*, H.Verity 0*).

Comments: A.E.Nutter and R.Pollard added 106 in 80 minutes for Lancashire's 9th wicket.
H.Sutcliffe and A.Mitchell added 288 for Yorkshire's 2nd wicket.
Sutcliffe batted 340 minutes for his 165 (which included 16 4's), with his partner scoring 136. A.B.Sellers and A.Wood scored 114 for the 7th wicket.
W.E.Bowes took 5 for 21 in eight overs after lunch on the third day to win the match for his side.
E.Paynter and N.Oldfield delayed the end with a 3rd wicket partnership of 103.

MIDDLESEX v SUSSEX

Played at Lord's, May 27, 29, 30, 1939.
Toss won by Sussex.
Middlesex won by seven wickets.

SUSSEX

John G.Langridge	c Hulme b Smith	27	c Price b Sims	32
J.H.Parks	lbw b Smith	24	c Sims b Smith	19
H.W.Parks	c Killick b Gray	4	c Killick b Sims	42
C Oakes	c & b Sims	6	lbw b Sims	1
Jas.Langridge	lbw b Smith	22	(7) lbw b Smith	8
Mr H.T.Bartlett	c Price b Robins	44	(5) c Robertson b Sims	26
*Flt-Lt A.J.Holmes	c Edrich b Sims	18	(8) st Price b Sims	27
H.E.Hammond	c Price b Sims	21	(6) c Price b Smith	38
†W.L.Cornford	b Robins	4	c Gray b Robins	25
J.K.Nye	b Robins	0	c Price b Smith	3
D.J.Wood	not out	4	not out	5
Extras	(B 2, LB 2, W 3, NB 1)	8	(B 5, LB 4, W 1)	10
Total		**182**		**236**

Fall: 1st inns 1/29, 2/35, 3/51, 4/79, 5/96, 6/151, 7/152, 8/167, 9/167.
2nd inns 1/24, 2/86, 3/94, 4/99, 5/150, 6/171, 7/172, 8/208, 9/220.

MIDDLESEX

J.D.B.Robertson	c Hammond b Wood	22	c Hammond b J.Parks	16
S.M.Brown	c Holmes b Hammond	38	c Cornford b Hammond	28
W.J.Edrich	c Cornford b Nye	54	lbw b Hammond	43
D.C.S.Compton	c Nye b Hammond	81	not out	50
*Revd E.T.Killick	c John Langridge b Hammond	8	not out	13
J.H.A.Hulme	b J.Parks	28		
†W.F.F.Price	b Nye	6		
Mr R.W.V.Robins	c Cornford b Nye	15		
J.M.Sims	c Cornford b Wood	11		
C.I.J.Smith	c Hammond b J.Parks	0		
L.H.Gray	not out	0		
Extras	(B 1)	1	(B 4, LB 1)	5
Total		**264**	(3 wickets)	**155**

Fall: 1st inns 1/37, 2/91, 3/161, 4/195, 5/204, 6/215, 7/241, 8/264, 9/264.
2nd inns 1/37, 2/53, 3/130.

MIDDLESEX	O	M	R	W	O	M	R	W
Smith	19	6	44	3	20	8	48	4
Gray	14	4	35	1	11	3	28	0
Edrich	5	0	19	0	3	0	16	0
Sims	13.3	1	48	3	25.2	3	106	5
Robins	6	1	28	3	5	1	5	1
Robertson	-				6	0	23	0

SUSSEX	O	M	R	W	O	M	R	W
Nye	20	0	94	3	7	0	41	0
Hammond	12	1	67	3	11	0	57	2
Wood	12.1	1	56	2	3.6	0	27	0
J.Parks	6	1	17	2	7	0	25	1
Jas.Langridge	7	0	22	0				
Oakes	1	0	7	0				

Umpires: E.J.Smith and F.I.Walden.

Close of play scores. First day: Middlesex 161/3 (D.C.S.Compton 47*). **Second day:** Sussex 236 all out.

Comments: About 23,000 were present on Whit Monday for the second day's play. The match finished just before lunch on the third day.

NORTHAMPTONSHIRE v LEICESTERSHIRE

Played at Northampton, May 27, 29, 1939.
Toss won by Leicestershire.
Northamptonshire won by an innings and 193 runs.

LEICESTERSHIRE

G.L.Berry	b Buswell	3	b Buswell	31
G.S.Watson	b Partridge	1	st James b Merritt	56
N.F.Armstrong	b Partridge	1	lbw b Buswell	20
F.T.Prentice	lbw b Partridge	1	lbw b Buswell	1
*Mr C.S.Dempster	b Buswell	0	b Partridge	10
M.Tompkin	run out	32	st James b Merritt	13
†G.O.Dawkes	b Timms	16	c James b Merritt	1
G.Lester	not out	44	c Greenwood b Merritt	29
Mr J.E.Walsh	b Buswell	14	c Partridge b Merritt	4
H.A.Smith	b Nelson	13	st James b Merritt	8
W.H.Flamson	b Nelson	0	not out	10
Extras	(B 6, LB 3)	9	(B 7, LB 10, NB 3)	20
Total		134		183

Fall: 1st inns 1/2, 2/6, 3/6, 4/6, 5/8, 6/34, 7/73, 8/97, 9/134.
2nd inns 1/10, 2/100, 3/100, 4/103, 5/120, 6/121, 7/136, 8/152, 9/164.

NORTHAMPTONSHIRE

H.W.Greenwood	c Smith b Flamson	8
P.Davis	st Dempster b Walsh	84
D.Brookes	c Armstrong b Lester	187
J.E.Timms	c Tompkin b Flamson	55
*Mr R.P.Nelson	run out	44
F.P.O'Brien	b Walsh	10
†K.C.James	not out	42
M.E.F.Dunkley	c Smith b Flamson	12
W.E.Merritt	lbw b Flamson	7
R.J.Partridge	not out	20
Extras	(B 30, LB 11)	41
Total	(8 wickets, declared)	510

Fall: 1st inns 1/182, 2/194, 3/295, 4/387, 5/418, 6/421, 7/467, 8/477.
J.E.Buswell did not bat.

NORTHANTS	O	M	R	W	O	M	R	W
Buswell	14	2	43	3	12	2	47	3
Partridge	13	2	38	3	12	3	45	1
Merritt	6	0	21	0	10.7	0	56	6
Timms	5	0	22	1	6	2	15	0
Nelson	1.6	0	1	2	1	1	0	0

LEICESTERSHIRE	O	M	R	W
Flamson	27	2	125	4
Smith	31	1	99	0
Walsh	33	1	157	2
Lester	13	0	60	1
Armstrong	3	0	7	0
Prentice	4	0	21	0

Umpires: D.Hendren and E.Cooke.

Close of play scores. First day: Northants 280/2 (D.Brookes 120*, J.E.Timms 50*).
Comments: The match was completed in two days.
Leicestershire lost five wickets for eight runs in the first 30 minutes of the match.
D.Brookes' 187 was his highest individual score. He batted for 255 minutes and hit 24 4's. He and P.Davis put on 176 for the 2nd Northamptonshire wicket in just over 150 minutes. With J.E.Timms he then added 101 in 60 minutes for the 3rd wicket.
Leicestershire lost all their 2nd innings wickets after tea on the second day for 130 runs.
It was Northamptonshire's first home victory since defeating Warwickshire at Kettering in 1934. Their last win at Northampton was against Leicestershire in 1933. It was Northamptonshire's first victory in the County Championship since May 1935, against Somerset at Taunton, and at their 99th attempt.
C.S.Dempster kept wicket for Leicestershire after G.O.Dawkes had suffered a strain whilst batting.

NOTTINGHAMSHIRE v SURREY

Played at Trent Bridge, Nottingham, May 27, 29, 30, 1939.
Toss won by Surrey.
Nottinghamshire won by seven wickets.

SURREY

R.J.Gregory	b Butler	11	c Heane b Butler	4
L.B.Fishlock	c Heane b Woodhead	12	b Gunn	23
H.S.Squires	c Gunn b Butler	2	c Voce b Gunn	56
T.H.Barling	c Giles b Butler	4	c Maxwell b Butler	96
E.W.Whitfield	c Butler b Voce	7	b Butler	8
J.F.Parker	c & b Butler	25	b Butler	0
*Mr H.M.Garland-Wells	c Heane b Butler	40	c Hardstaff b Gunn	7
Mr F.R.Brown	c Woodhead b Butler	2	c Harris b Gunn	68
E.A.Watts	not out	77	c Butler b Voce	11
†E.W.J.Brooks	lbw b Voce	0	c Giles b Gunn	1
A.R.Gover	st Maxwell b Woodhead	22	not out	15
Extras	(LB 6)	6	(LB 6, NB 6)	12
Total		208		301

Fall: 1st inns 1/17, 2/19, 3/23, 4/34, 5/42, 6/83, 7/91, 8/136, 9/136.
2nd inns 1/12, 2/70, 3/95, 4/116, 5/120, 6/137, 7/266, 8/274, 9/276.

NOTTINGHAMSHIRE

W.W.Keeton	c Garland-Wells b Watts	79	c Garland-Wells b Watts	33
C.B.Harris	c Garland-Wells b Brown	44	lbw b Watts	13
*Mr G.F.H.Heane	lbw b Brown	24	lbw b Gover	1
J.Hardstaff	c Brooks b Gover	13	not out	114
G.V.Gunn	b Gover	0	not out	92
J.Knowles	b Gover	6		
†Mr C.R.N.Maxwell	c Brooks b Watts	10		
W.Voce	c Brooks b Squires	20		
R.J.Giles	not out	29		
F.G.Woodhead	b Brown	1		
H.J.Butler	lbw b Gover	5		
Extras	(B 7, LB 9, W 1, NB 5)	22	(B 4, LB 4, W 2, NB 1)	11
Total		247	(3 wickets)	264

Fall: 1st inns 1/82, 2/143, 3/164, 4/164, 5/167, 6/173, 7/191, 8/222, 9/235.
2nd inns 1/47, 2/48, 3/48.

NOTTINGHAMSHIRE	O	M	R	W	O	M	R	W
Voce	23	4	67	2	16.2	2	51	1
Butler	18	3	82	6	17	0	79	4
Woodhead	9.6	0	53	2	12	1	53	0
Gunn	-	-	-	-	16	0	98	5
Giles	-	-	-	-	4	0	8	0

SURREY	O	M	R	W	O	M	R	W
Gover	14	2	64	4	11	1	48	1
Watts	11	1	39	2	12	1	61	2
Brown	20	6	62	3	12	0	63	0
Parker	7	1	19	0	9	1	33	0
Squires	6	0	32	1	3	0	8	0
Gregory	4	1	9	0	4	0	16	0
Garland-Wells	-	-	-	-	1	0	8	0
Whitfield	-	-	-	-	3	0	16	0

Umpires: E.Robinson and G.Beet.

Close of play scores. First day: Nottinghamshire 155/2 (W.W.Keeton 70*, J.Hardstaff 10*). **Second day:** Nottinghamshire 2/0 (W.W.Keeton 1*, C.B.Harris 0*).

Comments: A.R.Gover and E.A.Watts put on 72 in 40 minutes for Surrey's 10th wicket.
In Surrey's 2nd innings, T.H.Barling and F.R.Brown added 129 for the 7th wicket.
J.Hardstaff and G.V.Gunn put on 216 in 155 minutes in an unbroken stand for the 4th wicket to win the game for Nottinghamshire.
J.Hardstaff's 114 included 13 4's.

SURREY COUNTY CRICKET CLUB

Standing (left to right): L.B.Fishlock, E.A.Watts, F.Berry, J.F.Parker, H.S.Squires, E.W.Whitfield, A.J.W.McIntyre. Seated: A.R.Gover, E.W.J.Brooks, H.M.Garland-Wells (captain), R.J.Gregory, T.H.Barling.

SOMERSET v GLOUCESTERSHIRE

Played at Taunton, May 27, 29, 30, 1939.
Toss won by Somerset.
Match drawn.

SOMERSET

F.S.Lee	c Crapp b Barnett	1	c Hammond b Scott	86
H.Gimblett	b Goddard	108	lbw b Goddard	57
H.T.F.Buse	b Scott	5	c Crapp b Goddard	42
W.H.R.Andrews	c Wilson b Lambert	4	(7) not out	7
Mr J.W.Seamer	b Scott	11	c Emmett b Goddard	20
†W.T.Luckes	c Wilson b Lambert	45		
Mr H.D.Burrough	c Scott b Lambert	13	(6) b Lambert	59
*Mr E.F.Longrigg	c Barnett b Scott	12	(4) c Hammond b Goddard	60
Mr C.J.P.Barnwell	c Crapp b Scott	18		
A.W.Wellard	lbw b Scott	25		
H.L.Hazell	not out	3		
Extras	(LB 2)	2	(B 6, LB 7)	13
Total		**247**	**(6 wickets, declared)**	**344**

Fall: 1st inns 1/1, 2/20, 3/35, 4/96, 5/160, 6/186, 7/194, 8/214, 9/242.
2nd inns 1/88, 2/154, 3/253, 4/255, 5/332, 6/344.

GLOUCESTERSHIRE

C.J.Barnett	c Hazell b Andrews	6	c Wellard b Andrews	4
R.A.Sinfield	c Luckes b Wellard	10	c Longrigg b Andrews	0
Mr B.O.Allen	c Wellard b Andrews	2	b Hazell	38
*Mr W.R.Hammond	c Wellard b Buse	91	c Luckes b Buse	19
G.M.Emmett	b Andrews	20	c Wellard b Hazell	29
J.F.Crapp	c Luckes b Andrews	15	not out	48
W.L.Neale	b Buse	31	not out	41
†E.A.Wilson	c Luckes b Wellard	39		
C.J.Scott	b Andrews	20		
G.E.E.Lambert	c Luckes b Wellard	5		
T.W.J.Goddard	not out	18		
Extras	(LB 7, NB 1)	8	(B 5, LB 6, W 1, NB 1)	13
Total		**265**	**(5 wickets)**	**192**

Fall: 1st inns 1/16, 2/18, 3/26, 4/77, 5/128, 6/164, 7/183, 8/219, 9/238.
2nd inns 1/4, 2/9, 3/49, 4/76, 5/101.

GLOUCESTERSHIRE	O	M	R	W	O	M	R	W
Scott	20.6	1	94	5	20	0	93	1
Barnett	5	2	25	1	3	1	8	0
Lambert	11	0	59	3	14	2	78	1
Goddard	21	8	43	1	19.6	2	110	4
Sinfield	11	2	24	0	17	7	42	0

SOMERSET	O	M	R	W	O	M	R	W
Wellard	28	5	86	3	23	2	67	0
Andrews	35	4	99	5	11	3	33	2
Buse	16	3	57	2	7	1	26	1
Hazell	5	2	15	0	17	4	39	2
Seamer	-	-	-	-	2	0	12	0
Gimblett	-	-	-	-	1	0	2	0

Umpires: J.A.Newman and J.J.Hills.

Close of play scores. First day: Gloucestershire 126/4 (W.R.Hammond 73*, J.F.Crapp 13*). **Second day:** Somerset 201/2 (F.S.Lee 61*, E.F.Longrigg 34*).

Comments: H.Gimblett made 108 in 165 minutes, hitting 17 4's.

WARWICKSHIRE v DERBYSHIRE

Played at Edgbaston, Birmingham, May 27, 29, 30, 1939.
Toss won by Warwickshire.
Warwickshire won by 71 runs.

WARWICKSHIRE

A.J.W.Croom	c Smith b Copson	10	c Elliott b A.V.Pope	8
W.A.Hill	b Copson	6	c A.V.Pope b Copson	0
F.R.Santall	c Alderman b Copson	11	c G.H.Pope b Mitchell	23
Mr R.E.S.Wyatt	c Elliott b Mitchell	21	st Elliott b Mitchell	27
H.E.Dollery	c Elliott b Copson	3	run out	177
J.S.Ord	c Alderman b Mitchell	20	c Elliott b Copson	8
†J.Buckingham	c Elliott b Mitchell	39	lbw b Mitchell	49
*Mr P.Cranmer	b Copson	13	c Smith b Copson	20
K.Wilmot	not out	11	c G.H.Pope b Mitchell	54
J.H.Mayer	b A.V.Pope	0	lbw b Mitchell	0
W.E.Hollies	c & b A.V.Pope	0	not out	2
Extras	(LB 7)	7	(LB 3, W 1)	4
Total		**141**		**372**

Fall: 1st inns 1/15, 2/27, 3/30, 4/38, 5/71, 6/94, 7/121, 8/138, 9/139.
2nd inns 1/1, 2/17, 3/54, 4/66, 5/81, 6/186, 7/210, 8/368, 9/368.

DERBYSHIRE

D.Smith	c Santall b Mayer	0	b Mayer	0
*Mr R.H.R.Buckston	c Croom b Wilmot	13	lbw b Hollies	19
T.S.Worthington	b Mayer	68	absent ill	0
L.F.Townsend	c Buckingham b Hollies	63	c Buckingham b Hollies	55
A.E.Alderman	c Ord b Hollies	4	(3) b Mayer	16
G.H.Pope	b Hollies	13	(5) c Dollery b Hollies	45
A.E.G.Rhodes	b Mayer	13	(6) c Dollery b Santall	8
A.V.Pope	lbw b Hollies	34	(7) not out	31
†H.Elliott	not out	4	(8) c Buckingham b Hollies	17
T.B.Mitchell	c Hill b Hollies	10	(9) st Buckingham b Hollies	4
W.H.Copson	c Buckingham b Hollies	4	(10) b Mayer	4
Extras	(B 8)	8	(B 8, LB 1)	9
Total		**234**		**208**

Fall: 1st inns 1/0, 2/51, 3/102, 4/107, 5/133, 6/158, 7/211, 8/216, 9/227.
2nd inns 1/0, 2/30, 3/40, 4/134, 5/149, 6/149, 7/170, 8/189, 9/208.

DERBYSHIRE	O	M	R	W	O	M	R	W
Copson	14	2	47	5	24	3	95	3
A.V.Pope	12.5	4	23	2	17	1	65	1
G.H.Pope	16	2	34	0	23	4	60	0
Mitchell	11	1	30	3	23.1	1	112	5
Rhodes	-	-	-	-	1	0	10	0
Townsend	-	-	-	-	7	0	26	0

WARWICKSHIRE	O	M	R	W	O	M	R	W
Mayer	18	3	79	3	13.2	2	52	3
Wilmot	16	2	53	1	8	0	37	0
Santall	6	1	25	0	8	0	23	1
Hollies	14.7	2	48	6	22	2	79	5
Wyatt	4	0	21	0				
Croom	-	-	-	-	4	0	8	0

Umpires: H.G.Baldwin and H.Cruice.

Close of play scores. First day: Derbyshire 137/5 (L.F.Townsend 30*, A.E.G.Rhodes 1*). **Second day:** Warwickshire 302/7 (H.E.Dollery 133*, K.Wilmot 30*).

Comments: D.Smith was dismissed by the first ball of Derbyshire's 1st innings and the fourth ball of the 2nd.

H.E.Dollery 177, made the highest score of his career, hitting 20 4's in a stay of 270 minutes.

He and J.Buckingham added 105 for the 6th wicket in Warwickshire's 2nd innings and with K.Wilmot he then put on 158 for the 8th wicket. Warwickshire, after being 12 runs behind the Derbyshire 1st innings score with only five 2nd innings wickets in hand, won by the comfortable margin of 71 runs.

T.S.Worthington was absent ill in Derbyshire's 2nd innings.

Derbyshire leg spinner Tommy Mitchell, took eight wickets against Warwickshire at Edgbaston.

England pace bowler Bill Copson, helped Derbyshire to victory over Kent at Ilkeston with 9-69 in the match.

DERBYSHIRE v KENT

Played at Ilkeston, May 31, June 1, 1939.
Toss won by Kent.
Derbyshire won by five wickets.

KENT

A.E.Fagg	run out 11	c Elliott b G.H.Pope 30
P.R.Sunnucks	b A.V.Pope 5	c A.V.Pope b G.H.Pope...10
L.E.G.Ames	c Elliott b Copson 14	c A.V.Pope b Copson 27
*Mr F.G.H.Chalk	c Alderman b Copson....17	c A.F.Townsend b G.H.Pope 0
Mr B.H.Valentine	c A.V.Pope b G.H.Pope 20	c Elliott b Copson 4
L.J.Todd	b G.H.Pope..............0	(7) c A.V.Pope b Copson ...8
Mr P.G.Foster	c Rhodes b Copson 24	(8) c G.H.Pope b Copson 6
D.V.P.Wright	c G.H.Pope b Copson ...17	(9) not out..................2
N.W.Harding	b Copson 18	(10) b A.V.Pope 0
A.E.Watt	b G.H.Pope..............9	(11) c G.H.Pope b A.V.Pope...................2
†Mr W.H.V.Levett	not out 3	(6) run out 5
Extras	(B 1, LB 3, W 1) 5	(B 1, LB 3, NB 1) 5
Total	**143**	**99**

Fall: 1st inns 1/16, 2/17, 3/48, 5/77, 6/101, 7/122, 8/123, 9/133.
2nd inns 1/17, 2/58, 3/58, 4/70, 5/77, 6/85, 7/95, 8/97, 9/97.

DERBYSHIRE

D.Smith	not out...................57	b Todd 6
*Mr R.H.R.Buckston	b Todd 2	
A.E.Alderman	c Levett b Harding 1	(2) not out 40
L.F.Townsend	b Todd 1	b Todd 21
G.H.Pope	c Levett b Wright 21	b Todd 0
A.E.G.Rhodes	c Levett b Watt 0	c & b Harding 46
A.F.Townsend	c Levett b Watt 0	(3) b Todd................0
A.V.Pope	c Valentine b Harding ...17	(7) not out 15
†H.Elliott	b Todd 0	
T.B.Mitchell	run out 2	
W.H.Copson	b Todd 4	
Extras	(B 3, LB 2, NB 2) 7	(B 2, LB 4) 6
Total	**112**	**(5 wickets)** **134**

Fall: 1st inns 1/24, 2/25, 3/26, 4/67, 5/68, 6/68, 7/95, 8/101, 9/106.
2nd inns 1/9, 2/9, 3/49, 4/51, 5/108.

DERBYSHIRE	O	M	R	W	O	M	R	W
Copson	13	2	39	5	12	2	30	4
A.V.Pope	8	1	28	1	10.6	1	34	2
G.H.Pope	13.4	1	71	3	8	1	30	3

KENT	O	M	R	W	O	M	R	W
Todd	7.3	2	29	4	15.2	1	61	4
Harding	6	0	29	2	8	1	38	1
Watt	5	0	23	2	6	0	18	0
Wright	4	0	24	1	1	0	11	0

Umpires: J.A.Smart and E.Robinson.

Close of play scores. First day: Kent 74/4 (B.H.Valentine 2*, W.H.V.Levett 2*).

Comments: On the first day 24 wickets fell for 329 runs. The game finished by 3.30pm on the second day.
D.Smith carried his bat for 57 in an innings which lasted 105 minutes.
A.F.Townsend was dismissed second ball in both innings.

GLAMORGAN v GLOUCESTERSHIRE

Played at Newport, May 31, June 1, 2, 1939.
Toss won by Glamorgan.
Match drawn.

GLAMORGAN

A.H.Dyson	not out ...99	c Wilson b Lambert ...120
D.E.Davies	lbw b Goddard ...34	not out ...287
T.L.Brierley	b Scott ...9	c Hammond b Goddard ...5
*Mr M.J.L.Turnbull	c Wilson b Lambert ...18	st Wilson b Emmett ...77
D.Davies	c Wilson b Scott ...1	c Lambert b Sinfield ...48
C.C.Smart	b Scott ...10	not out ...23
Mr W.Wooller	b Goddard ...18	
E.C.Jones	c Wilson b Sinfield ...0	
†H.G.Davies	c Wilson b Sinfield ...0	
P.F.Judge	c Neale b Goddard ...3	
J.Mercer	b Goddard ...0	
Extras	(B 1, LB 2, NB 1) ...4	(LB 17) ...17
Total	**196**	**(4 wickets) ...577**

Fall: 1st inns 1/65, 2/74, 3/104, 4/114, 5/132, 6/180, 7/181, 8/181, 9/196.
2nd inns 1/255, 2/265, 3/403, 4/527.

GLOUCESTERSHIRE

C.J.Barnett	c E.Davies b Mercer ...15
R.A.Sinfield	b E.Davies ...41
V.Hopkins	c Turnbull b Judge ...13
*Mr W.R.Hammond	c H.Davies b E.Davies 302
G.M.Emmett	st H.Davies b Jones ...53
J.F.Crapp	not out ...60
W.L.Neale	not out ...5
Extras	(B 12, LB 4) ...16
Total	**(5 wickets) ...505**

Fall: 1st inns 1/24, 2/52, 3/117, 4/285, 5/499.
†E.A.Wilson, C.J.Scott, G.E.E.Lambert and T.W.J.Goddard did not bat.

GLOUCESTERSHIRE	O	M	R	W	O	M	R	W
Scott	13	0	52	3	24	1	95	0
Barnett	4	0	18	0	5	0	32	0
Lambert	14	2	50	1	16	0	128	1
Goddard	22.6	7	45	4	38	7	123	1
Sinfield	10	3	16	2	36	5	116	1
Emmitt	2	0	6	0	7	0	51	0
Neale	1	0	5	0	1	0	11	0
Hammond	-	-	-	-	1	0	4	0

GLAMORGAN	O	M	R	W
Mercer	21	0	105	1
Judge	18	1	83	1
Wooller	23	1	124	0
Jones	9	0	41	1
E.Davies	21	2	91	2
D.Davies	2	0	9	0
Smart	6	1	36	0

Umpires: J.A.Newman and H.Cruice.

Close of play scores. First day: Gloucestershire 140/3 (W.R.Hammond 55*, G.M.Emmett 11*). **Second day:** Glamorgan 131/0 (A.H.Dyson 57*, D.E.Davies 69*).
Comments: In Glamorgan's first home fixture of the season, a batting feast by both sides created a number of new records. On the second day, 496 runs were scored for the loss of two wickets. On the last two days 922 runs were scored for the loss of only six wickets.
Glamorgan first innings: A.H.Dyson carried his bat for the sixth time in his career. The last two batsmen were dismissed in one over whilst he remained on 99. He was the second batsman to carry his bat for 99 and hit a century in the same match (C.B.Fry in 1907 against Worcestershire).
Gloucestershire first innings: W.R.Hammond hit the 150th century of his career. His 302 was his fourth triple hundred, his third for Gloucestershire and his second against Glamorgan, made in 5 hours, 40 minutes and including two 6's and 35 4's out of 447 whilst at the wicket. He equalled the highest score made against Glamorgan. W.R.Hammond and G.M.Emmett added 168 for the 4th wicket. W.R.Hammond and J.F.Crapp added 214 for the 5th wicket.
Glamorgan second innings: 577/4 was Glamorgan's highest score in first-class cricket and their highest 2nd innings total. It was also the fourth highest total for a 2nd innings in England. D.E.Davies scored his first double century, his highest ever score. His score of 287 is the highest individual score by a Glamorgan batsman. It took 450 minutes and included 25 4's. He and A.H.Dyson put on 255 for the first wicket, the second-highest opening partnership for Glamorgan. Davies was then involved in a 3rd wicket partnership of 138 in 80 minutes with M.J.L.Turnbull. E.A.Wilson did not concede a bye in Glamorgan's mammoth 2nd innings total. In the match he allowed only one bye whilst 773 runs were scored.

LANCASHIRE v HAMPSHIRE

Played at Old Trafford, Manchester, May 31, June 1, 2, 1939.
Toss won by Lancashire.
Lancashire won by an innings and 66 runs.

LANCASHIRE

C.Washbrook	b Heath ...35
E.Paynter	run out ...68
J.L.Hopwood	c Boyes b Hill ...45
N.Oldfield	c Walker b Court ...45
J.Iddon	not out ...141
A.E.Nutter	st McCorkell b Boyes ...55
*Mr W.H.L.Lister	c Walker b Hill ...19
W.E.Phillipson	not out ...62
Extras	(B 12, LB 4, NB 2) ...18
Total	**(6 wickets, declared) ...488**

Fall: 1st inns 1/80, 2/138, 3/180, 4/236, 5/340, 6/373.
†W.Farrimond, L.L.Wilkinson and R.Pollard did not bat.

HAMPSHIRE

†N.T.McCorkell	lbw b Wilkinson ...32	lbw b Wilkinson ...6
J.Bailey	b Pollard ...100	(4) b Wilkinson ...16
A.G.Holt	lbw b Wilkinson ...0	(2) c Iddon b Wilkinson ...32
W.L.C.Creese	c Washbrook b Iddon ...47	(5) c Iddon b Wilkinson ...0
J.Arnold	b Phillipson ...21	(6) c Washbrook b Wilkinson 34
D.F.Walker	b Pollard ...4	(7) b Phillipson ...8
G.Hill	b Wilkinson ...39	(8) c & b Wilkinson ...8
G.S.Boyes	b Phillipson ...5	(9) st Farrimond b Wilkinson 13
*Mr G.R.Taylor	c Lister b Wilkinson ...17	(10) not out ...0
R.C.Court	not out ...4	(11) lbw b Wilkinson ...0
G.E.M.Heath	b Pollard ...0	(3) c Farrimond b Phillipson 2
Extras	(B 11, LB 4, W 1, NB 5) ...21	(LB 12, W 1) ...13
Total	**290**	**132**

Fall: 1st inns 1/81, 2/81, 3/171, 4/209, 5/215, 6/217, 7/236, 8/278, 9/288.
2nd inns 1/13, 2/23, 3/55, 4/55, 5/68, 6/91, 7/108, 8/129, 9/132.

HAMPSHIRE	O	M	R	W
Heath	24	1	110	1
Court	19	2	104	1
Bailey	19	3	77	0
Boyes	19	4	61	1
Hill	15	0	99	2
Holt	2	0	19	0

LANCASHIRE	O	M	R	W	O	M	R	W
Phillipson	20	2	58	2	12	2	48	2
Pollard	20.3	2	45	3	7	3	10	0
Nutter	12	1	50	0	3	1	8	0
Wilkinson	24	1	108	4	17.5	2	53	8
Iddon	6	2	8	1				

Umpires: J.Hardstaff and E.Cooke.

Close of play scores. First day: Lancashire 488/6 (J.Iddon 141*, W.E.Phillipson 62*). **Second day:** Hampshire 17/1 (A.G.Holt 10*, G.E.M.Heath 0*).
Comments: J.Iddon hit 20 4's in his undefeated 141, made in 210 minutes. He was involved in a stand of 104 in 85 minutes with A.E.Nutter for the 5th wicket and an unbroken partnership of 115 in 65 minutes with W.E.Phillipson for the 7th Lancashire wicket. This century completed his set of centuries against all the 16 county opponents of Lancashire. His first century was against Surrey in 1927.
J.Bailey hit his first century in first-class cricket since 1933. He hit eight 4's and batted 250 minutes for his 100.
Hampshire followed on after losing their last seven wickets for 81.
L.L.Wilkinson, bowling unchanged for two hours and a quarter on the third morning of the match, took eight wickets for 53 runs, a career best.

LEICESTERSHIRE v NOTTINGHAMSHIRE

Played at Grace Road, Leicester, May 31, June 1, 2, 1939.
Toss won by Nottinghamshire.
Match drawn.

NOTTINGHAMSHIRE

W.W.Keeton	c Dawkes b Prentice	60	c Dawkes b Flamson 36
C.B.Harris	c Dempster b Prentice	15	c Lester b Smith 49
*Mr G.F.H.Heane	b Smith	39	not out 116
J.Hardstaff	b Flamson	36	not out 125
G.V.Gunn	c Armstrong b Smith	1	
J.Knowles	c Smith b Flamson	5	
W.Voce	b Flamson	6	
R.J.Giles	c Tompkin b Flamson	51	
†A.B.Wheat	c Lester b Armstrong	44	
F.G.Woodhead	c Dawkes b Flamson	24	
H.J.Butler	not out	0	
Extras	(B 4, LB 4, W 1)	9	(B 1, LB 6, NB 2) 9
Total		**290**	(2 wickets, declared)......**335**

Fall: 1st inns 1/39, 2/114, 3/117, 4/121, 5/146, 6/156, 7/167, 8/236, 9/290.
2nd inns 1/63, 2/114.

LEICESTERSHIRE

G.L.Berry	c Knowles b Woodhead	46	c Wheat b Gunn 70
G.S.Watson	c Heane b Butler	28	lbw b Butler 37
N.F.Armstrong	c Wheat b Voce	3	run out 52
G.Lester	c Butler b Woodhead	23	
F.T.Prentice	c Woodhead b Voce	40	not out 17
*Mr C.S.Dempster	c Woodhead b Voce	18	(4) not out 34
M.Tompkin	c Wheat b Woodhead	41	
†G.O.Dawkes	b Butler	16	
L.D.Thursting	not out	22	
H.A.Smith	b Woodhead	3	
W.H.Flamson	lbw b Woodhead	0	
Extras	(B 5, LB 5, NB 2)	12	(B 2, LB 5, NB 3) 10
Total		**252**	(3 wickets) **220**

Fall: 1st inns 1/43, 2/59, 3/97, 4/107, 5/139, 6/200, 7/215, 8/247, 9/252.
2nd inns 1/60, 2/169, 3/169.

LEICESTERSHIRE	O	M	R	W	O	M	R	W
Flamson	21.1	0	106	5	19	2	77	1
Smith	28	3	79	2	21	2	96	1
Prentice	21	3	58	2	20	2	97	0
Lester	7	1	38	0	5	0	34	0
Armstrong	1	1	0	1	4	0	22	0
Thursting	-	-	-	-	1	1	0	0

NOTTINGHAMSHIRE	O	M	R	W	O	M	R	W
Voce	22	3	74	3	10	1	46	0
Butler	21	2	62	2	8	1	22	1
Woodhead	18	5	51	5	11	0	54	0
Gunn	11	0	34	0	17	3	45	1
Giles	4	0	14	0	10	0	31	0
Heane	2	0	5	0	3	0	12	0

Umpires: F.J.Durston and H.G.Baldwin.

Close of play scores. First day: Leicestershire 66/2 (G.L.Berry 28*, G.Lester 6*). **Second day:** Nottinghamshire 126/2 (G.F.H.Heane 31*, J.Hardstaff 6*).

Comments: G.F.H.Heane and J.Hardstaff put on an unbroken 221 for the 3rd wicket in Nottinghamshire's 2nd innings in only 120 minutes.
J.Hardstaff hit one 6 and 15 4's in his unbeaten 125.
G.F.H.Heane hit eight 4's in his undefeated 116.
Leicestershire were set to make 374 in about four hours.
G.L.Berry and N.F.Armstrong added 109 in about even time for the 2nd wicket.

SURREY v SUSSEX

Played at Kennington Oval, May 31, June 1, 2, 1939.
Toss won by Surrey.
Surrey won by 388 runs.

SURREY

R.J.Gregory	c Nye b Hammond	4	lbw b Wood 57
L.B.Fishlock	b Hammond	4	run out 60
H.S.Squires	lbw b Hammond	97	not out 107
T.H.Barling	lbw b Hammond	48	(6) c C.Oakes b Nye 4
E.W.Whitfield	c Cornford b Nye	14	(7) lbw b Hammond 0
J.F.Parker	c Cornford b Nye	43	(8) not out 42
*Mr H.M.Garland-Wells	lbw b J.Parks	46	(5) c Cornford b Nye 28
Mr F.R.Brown	c Cornford b Nye	42	(4) c Cornford b Wood 7
E.A.Watts	not out	26	
A.R.Gover	run out	6	
†E.W.J.Brooks	lbw b Hammond	2	
Extras	(B 6, LB 5, W 2)	13	(B 5, LB 1, W 3) 9
Total		**345**	(6 wickets, declared)......**314**

Fall: 1st inns 1/9, 2/14, 3/117, 4/144, 5/208, 6/240, 7/294, 8/314, 9/329.
2nd inns 1/98, 2/164, 3/177, 4/236, 5/240, 6/241.

SUSSEX

John G.Langridge	c Squires b Watts	108	c Brooks b Gover 0
J.H.Parks	lbw b Gover	1	b Watts 16
H.W.Parks	b Brown	10	b Parker 14
G.Cox	b Parker	16	b Brown 10
*Mr H.T.Bartlett	c Garland-Wells b Gover	0	b Watts 8
C.Oakes	c Brown b Gover	31	c Squires b Brown 0
J.Y.Oakes	lbw b Gover	8	c & b Brown 5
H.E.Hammond	st Brooks b Parker	11	c Gover b Brown 0
†W.L.Cornford	c Barling b Gover	9	b Brown 5
J.K.Nye	c Parker b Gover	2	c Gover b Brown 0
D.J.Wood	not out	2	not out 1
Extras	(LB 6, W 2, NB 2)	10	(B 1, LB 1, W 1, NB 1) 4
Total		**208**	**63**

Fall: 1st inns 1/10, 2/38, 3/63, 4/67, 5/118, 6/136, 7/162, 8/184, 9/206.
2nd inns 1/1, 2/25, 3/42, 4/52, 5/52, 6/52, 7/55, 8/58, 9/62.

SUSSEX	O	M	R	W	O	M	R	W
Nye	20	1	124	3	14	0	73	3
Wood	5	0	34	0	10	0	69	2
Hammond	17.1	0	97	5	13	1	68	1
J.H.Parks	17	2	54	1	8	0	36	0
J.Y.Oakes	2	1	4	0	4	0	34	0
Langridge	3	0	19	0				
C.Oakes	-	-	-	-	5	0	25	0

SURREY	O	M	R	W	O	M	R	W
Gover	16.5	0	60	6	5	0	14	1
Watts	9	0	47	1	7	3	16	2
Brown	11	1	54	1	5.1	0	21	6
Parker	10	2	29	2	4	2	8	1
Gregory	3	1	8	0				

Umpires: F.Chester and C.W.L.Parker.

Close of play scores. First day: Sussex 75/4 (John G Langridge 40*, C.Oakes 4*). **Second day:** Surrey 314/6 (J.F.Parker 42*, H.S.Squires 107*).
Comments: H.S.Squires and T.H.Barling put on 103 for Surrey's 3rd wicket in their 1st innings. In the 2nd, Squires scored 107* in two hours, hitting 13 4's.
John Langridge scored over half the Sussex 1st innings total, being ninth out after opening the innings.
Sussex were dismissed for 63 in their 2nd innings in only 90 minutes. F.R.Brown, who finished with figures of six wickets for 21 runs, took all six wickets in a spell of 33 balls for 14 runs. The match was over before lunch on the third day.

WARWICKSHIRE v YORKSHIRE

Played at Edgbaston, Birmingham, May 31, June 1, 2, 1939.
Toss won by Yorkshire.
Yorkshire won by an innings and 54 runs.

WARWICKSHIRE

A.J.W.Croom	c Mitchell b Bowes	25	lbw b Verity	20
W.A.Hill	b Yardley	13	c Verity b Bowes	9
F.R.Santall	c Barber b Bowes	66	b Bowes	31
Mr R.E.S.Wyatt	c Smailes b Bowes	11	c Turner b Bowes	23
H.E.Dollery	b Bowes	47	c Verity b Bowes	30
J.S.Ord	lbw b Bowes	0	not out	14
†J.Buckingham	b Bowes	8	c Smailes b Bowes	8
*Mr P.Cranmer	c Wood b Bowes	4	c Mitchell b Verity	5
K.Wilmot	run out	0	c Mitchell b Verity	0
J.H.Mayer	c Hutton b Smailes	32	st Wood b Verity	0
W.E.Hollies	not out	1	c Wood b Verity	0
Extras	(B 6, LB 2, W 3, NB 1)	12	(B 1, LB 1, W 1, NB 1)	4
Total		**219**		**144**

Fall: 1st inns 1/42, 2/46, 3/118, 4/123, 5/131, 6/139, 7/143, 8/143, 9/216.
2nd inns 1/25, 2/40, 3/87, 4/94, 5/121, 6/137, 7/142, 8/142, 9/144.

YORKSHIRE

A.Mitchell	c Cranmer b Mayer	25
L.Hutton	b Wilmot	158
W.Barber	lbw b Santall	53
M.Leyland	c Wyatt b Santall	45
*Mr N.W.D.Yardley	c Dollery b Hollies	51
C.Turner	st Buckingham b Hollies	31
J.F.Smailes	st Buckingham b Hollies	7
†A.Wood	hit wkt b Wilmot	11
E.P.Robinson	c Buckingham b Hollies	2
H.Verity	not out	13
W.E.Bowes	st Buckingham b Hollies	11
Extras	(B 4, LB 5, NB 1)	10
Total		**417**

Fall: 1st inns 1/74, 2/179, 3/264, 4/335, 5/341, 6/373, 7/378, 8/380, 9/396.

YORKSHIRE	O	M	R	W	O	M	R	W
Bowes	20.5	3	50	7	20	6	46	5
Smailes	15	1	73	1	6	0	18	0
Turner	5	1	20	0				
Yardley	6	0	31	1				
Verity	14	5	25	0	16.4	4	38	5
Robinson	3	0	5	0	7	0	38	0
Leyland	1	0	3	0				

WARWICKSHIRE	O	M	R	W
Mayer	24	4	77	1
Wilmot	26	3	87	2
Wyatt	8	1	31	0
Hollies	36.5	3	131	5
Cranmere	1	0	3	0
Santall	13	0	71	2
Croom	1	0	7	0

Umpires: C.N.Woolley and J.J.Hills.

Close of play scores. First day: Yorkshire 64/0 (A.Mitchell 24*, L.Hutton 38*).
Second day: Warwickshire 19/0 (A.J.W.Croom 10*, W.A.Hill 6*).

Comments: Warwickshire were put in to bat.
L.Hutton made 158 in 310 minutes. He hit one 6 and ten 4's.
He and W.Barber put on 105 for the 2nd wicket.
Warwickshire's last six wickets fell in only 45 minutes to give Yorkshire an innings victory.
H.Verity finished the game by taking four wickets in 11 balls for one run.

GLAMORGAN v NOTTINGHAMSHIRE

Played at Swansea, June 3, 5, 1939.
Toss won by Glamorgan.
Glamorgan won by ten wickets.

GLAMORGAN

A.H.Dyson	c & b Jepson	22		
D.E.Davies	c Keeton b Gunn	134		
T.L.Brierley	c sub b Gunn	113		
*Mr M.J.L.Turnbull	c Jepson b Heane	56		
D.Davies	c Jepson b Gunn	4		
C.C.Smart	c Jepson b Gunn	60		
E.C.Jones	run out	54	(2) not out	0
†H.G.Davies	c sub b Butler	10	(1) not out	4
Mr J.C.Clay	not out	45		
J.Mercer	not out	2		
Extras	(NB 1)	1	(LB 4)	4
Total	(8 wickets, declared)	**501**	(No wicket)	**8**

Fall: 1st inns 1/58, 2/264, 3/271, 4/280, 5/391, 6/391, 7/415, 8/497.
P.F.Judge did not bat.

NOTTINGHAMSHIRE

W.W.Keeton	c & b Judge	63	lbw b Mercer	10
C.B.Harris	c Brierley b E.Davies	56	b Mercer	5
*Mr G.F.H.Heane	c H.Davies b Clay	22	c H.Davies b Jones	35
J.Hardstaff	st H.Davies b Clay	7	c & b Mercer	87
G.V.Gunn	not out	32	c Judge b Clay	21
J.Knowles	run out	7	c Smart b E.Davies	13
R.J.Giles	c Turnbull b Clay	1	b Judge	33
†A.B.Wheat	c Turnbull b Clay	1	not out	17
A.Jepson	c Dyson b E.Davies	4	b Mercer	1
H.J.Butler	c H.Davies b Clay	8	c H.Davies b Clay	62
W.Voce	absent ill	0	absent ill	0
Extras	(B 9, LB 6)	15	(B 5, LB 1)	6
Total		**216**		**290**

Fall: 1st inns 1/115, 2/143, 3/160, 4/163, 5/175, 6/177, 7/183, 8/198, 9/216.
2nd inns 1/13, 2/20, 3/74, 4/134, 5/153, 6/205, 7/217, 8/222, 9/290.

NOTTINGHAMSHIRE	O	M	R	W	O	M	R	W
Butler	19	2	92	1				
Voce	10	2	30	0				
Jepson	22	2	110	1				
Heane	21	2	96	1				
Gunn	23	1	142	4				
Giles	5	0	30	0				
Hardstaff	-	-	-	-	0.4	0	4	0

GLAMORGAN	O	M	R	W	O	M	R	W
Mercer	6	0	18	0	12	0	88	4
Judge	7	3	28	1	3	0	22	1
Clay	21.4	2	77	5	10.4	0	89	2
E.Davies	20	3	78	2	11	0	79	1
Jones	-	-	-	-	1	0	6	1

Umpires: E.J.Smith and H.Elliott.

Close of play scores. First day: Glamorgan 501/8 (J.C.Clay 45*, J.Mercer 2*).
Comments: The match finished in two days. Notts were handicapped on the first day by illness to W.Voce and H.J.Butler.
D.E.Davies and T.L.Brierley created a 2nd wicket record for Glamorgan by adding 206, made in 150 minutes.
M.J.L.Turnbull and C.C.Smart added 104 for the 5th wicket.
D.E.Davies hit four 6's in his 134. He hit three 6's and two 4's off one over bowled by G.V.Gunn.
T.L.Brierley's 113 included one 6 and 16 4's.
A.B.Wheat did not concede a bye in Glamorgan's total of 501/8.
W.W.Keeton and C.B.Harris put on 115 for Notts' 1st wicket.
Nottinghamshire followed on 285 behind.
J.Hardstaff hit four 6's and nine 4's in his 87 in Notts' 2nd innings. H.J.Butler hit 62 out of 68 in 30 minutes, hitting three 6's and six 4's. Notts scored over 500 runs on the second day and still lost the match with a day left for play.

KENT v SUSSEX

Played at Tonbridge, June 3, 5, 6, 1939.
Toss won by Sussex.
Kent won by an innings and 121 runs.

SUSSEX

John G.Langridge...c Levett b Watt 4	b Wright..................160
J.H.Parks ....c Levett b Harding 1	c Levett b Watt 2
H.W.Parks..........b Todd...................15	c Valentine b Wright....127
G.Cox..............b Watt...................15	b Wright 4
*Mr H.T.Bartlett ....b Todd..................5	b Wright...................0
C.Oakes............b harding.................13	b Wright..................34
J.Y.Oakes ....b Watt 0	c & b Wright 0
H.E.Hammond......b Todd....................17	st Levett b Wright 7
†W.L.Cornford ......lbw b Watt 0	c Fagg b Wright 4
J.K.Nye ....c Knott b Harding 14	run out 0
J.H.Cornford ....not out 3	not out 0
Extras.............(B 2, LB 4, W 1, NB 1) 8	(B 9, LB 11, NB 6)........26
Total **95**	......................**364**

Fall: 1st inns 1/2, 2/23, 3/31, 4/39, 5/45, 6/45, 7/70, 8/71, 9/77.

2nd inns 1/5, 2/312, 3/315, 4/315, 5/324, 6/324, 7/342, 8/346, 9/359.

KENT

A.E.Fagg ....lbw b C.Oakes...........91
*Mr F.G.H.Chalk ...c J.Oakes b C.Oakes 198
L.E.G.Ames..........lbw b C.Oakes...........11
Mr B.H.Valentine ...c Hammond b C.Oakes 50
Mr P.G.Foster ....b J.Cornford...............7
Mr C.H.Knott ....c Cox b C.Oakes...........9
L.J.Todd............c J.Oakes b C.Oakes 143
D.V.P.Wright........not out..................57
N.W.Harding ....b C.Oakes................6
A.E.Watt ....lbw b C.Oakes............0
Extras..............(B 4, LB 4) 8
Total ....(9 wickets, declared) ...**580**

Fall: 1st inns 1/171, 2/185, 3/301, 4/324, 5/337, 6/423, 7/571, 8/578, 9/580.
†Mr W.H.V.Levett did not bat.

KENT	O	M	R	W	O	M	R	W
Harding 6.1	1	16	3	18	3	67	0
Todd........................8	1	33	3	15	1	53	0
Watt 10	1	38	4	24	2	75	1
Wright ....-	-	-	-	22.7	2	84	8
Ames ....-	-	-	-	2	0	10	0
Valentine ....-	-	-	-	3	0	19	0
Knott ....-	-	-	-	2	0	23	0
Chalk ....-	-	-	-	1	0	7	0

SUSSEX	O	M	R	W
Nye 25	0	134	0
J.H.Cornford 30	4	126	1
Hammond 11	0	65	0
J.H.Parks 17	1	87	0
J.Y.Oakes 3	0	13	0
C.Oakes 21.3	1	147	8

Umpires: A.Skelding and F.J.Durston.

Close of play scores. First day: Kent 346/5 (F.G.H.Chalk 169*, L.J.Todd 2*).
Second day: Sussex 212/1 (John Langridge 106*, H.W.Parks 87*).
Comments: Sussex were dismissed before lunch on the first day. A.E.Fagg and F.G.H.Chalk began the Kent 1st innings with an opening partnership of 171 in 120 minutes. F.G.H.Chalk then added 116 with B.H.Valentine for the 3rd wicket in 60 minutes, F.G.H.Chalk achieved a career best of 198. He batted 290 minutes and hit 23 4's. L.J.Todd and D.V.P.Wright added 148 for the 7th wicket. L.J.Todd hit two 6's and 16 4's in his 143. Kent's 580/9 was to be the highest score made in the 1939 season. John Langridge and H.W.Parks added 307 for the 2nd wicket in the Sussex 2nd innings in 255 minutes. Langridge's 160 in 270 mins included 20 4's. Parks' 127 included 12 4's. D.V.P.Wright then ran through the Sussex side on a dusty wicket. Going on at 311, he took eight wickets for 31 in 63 balls. His first five wickets came in a mere 18 balls for only three runs.

Towards the end of Kent's long innings against Sussex at Tonbridge, Doug Wright pops the ball agonizingly over the head of a close fielder. Wright was undefeated on 57.

Kent skipper F.G.H.Chalk plays a rare false stroke during his magnificent innings of 198 at Tonbridge, but the Sussex first slip, Jim Hammond, spills the chance.

LANCASHIRE v DERBYSHIRE

Played at Old Trafford, Manchester, June 3, 5, 1939.
Toss won by Lancashire.
Lancashire won by an innings and 105 runs.

LANCASHIRE

C.Washbrook	c Elliott b A.V.Pope	2
J.L.Hopwood	c A.V.Pope b Copson	0
E.Paynter	lbw b A.V.Pope	222
N.Oldfield	c Alderman b Copson	44
J.Iddon	c Alderman b A.V.Pope	64
A.E.Nutter	c A.V.Pope b Copson	61
W.E.Phillipson	c Elliott b G.H.Pope	36
*Mr W.H.L.Lister	c G.H.Pope b Copson	3
†W.Farrimond	b G.H.Pope	23
L.L.Wilkinson	lbw b G.H.Pope	7
J.Briggs	not out	0
Extras	(B 15, LB 3, W 1, NB 2)	21
Total		**483**

Fall: 1st inns 1/0, 2/17, 3/122, 4/256, 5/407, 6/419, 7/426, 8/467, 9/477.

DERBYSHIRE

D.Smith	b Briggs	24	c Farrimond b Phillipson	0
*Mr R.H.R.Buckston	c Wilkinson b Nutter	10	c Farrimond b Phillipson	11
T.S.Worthington	c Phillipson b Briggs	14	c Wilkinson b Nutter	0
L.F.Townsend	c Lister b Wilkinson	8	c & b Nutter	2
A.E.Alderman	lbw b Wilkinson	39	b Phillipson	30
G.H.Pope	b Phillipson	35	b Nutter	68
A.E.G.Rhodes	not out	11	c Farrimond b Phillipson	8
A.V.Pope	c & b Wilkinson	0	c Farrimond b Phillipson	0
†H.Elliott	b Wilkinson	0	not out	23
T.B.Mitchell	st Farrimond b Briggs	11	c & b Wilkinson	6
W.H.Copson	c Oldfield b Briggs	26	c Washbrook b Nutter	22
Extras	(B 14, LB 9, NB 1)	24	(B 2, LB 2, W 1, NB 1)	6
Total		**202**		**176**

Fall: 1st inns 1/41, 2/51, 3/68, 4/70, 5/143, 6/153, 7/153, 8/157, 9/176.
2nd inns 1/0, 2/1, 3/13, 4/16, 5/93, 6/103, 7/103, 8/134, 9/151.

DERBYSHIRE	O	M	R	W
Copson	25	3	102	4
G.H.Pope	20.1	1	98	3
A.V.Pope	19	0	108	3
Mitchell	16	3	117	0
Townsend	4	0	21	0
Rhodes	3	0	16	0

LANCASHIRE	O	M	R	W	O	M	R	W
Phillipson	13	0	46	1	14	3	38	5
Nutter	8	1	20	1	7.5	0	28	4
Briggs	10.6	1	48	4	5	0	21	0
Wilkinson	18	2	64	4	13	1	79	1
Iddon	-	-	-	-	3	1	4	0

Umpires: J.Hardstaff and C.V.Tarbox.

Close of play scores. First day: Lancashire 483 all out.

Comments: The match was completed in two days, after Lancashire claimed the extra half-hour. Derbyshire followed on 281 behind.
E.Paynter's 222 was his seventh double century, made in 310 minutes and containing 26 4's. He was involved in three century stands with N.Oldfield, J.Iddon and A.E.Nutter.
With Oldfield, he added 105 for the 3rd wicket in 95 minutes; with Iddon 134 for the 4th in 90 minutes; with Nutter 151 for the fifth.

NORTHAMPTONSHIRE v ESSEX

Played at Peterborough, June 3, 5, 6, 1939.
Toss won by Northamptonshire.
Essex won by six wickets.

NORTHAMPTONSHIRE

H.W.Greenwood	lbw b P.Smith	30	c O'Connor b P.Smith	19
P.Davis	lbw b P.Smith	35	b Nichols	65
D.Brookes	b Stephenson	23	c Stephenson b Eastman	1
J.E.Timms	b P.Smith	1	c Wade b Stephenson	44
Mr A.W.Snowden	b Stephenson	7	c Wade b R.Smith	22
*Mr R.P.Nelson	c Avery b P.Smith	15	st Wade b P.Smith	41
F.P.O'Brien	b P.Smith	4	b Stephenson	11
†K.C.James	lbw b Eastman	13	run out	27
W.E.Merritt	c P.Smith b Eastman	26	b Stephenson	68
R.J.Partridge	not out	5	c Nichols b Stephenson	8
J.E.Buswell	b Eastman	9	not out	1
Extras	(B 14, LB 4)	18	(B 18, LB 10)	28
Total		**186**		**335**

Fall: 1st inns 1/57, 2/88, 3/94, 4/105, 5/108, 6/121, 7/136, 8/172, 9/176.
2nd inns 1/36, 2/37, 3/125, 4/149, 5/186, 6/205, 7/243, 8/280, 9/318.

ESSEX

L.C.Eastman	b Nelson	47	st James b Merritt	43
A.V.Avery	b O'Brien	62	lbw b Merritt	29
†T.H.Wade	c & b Merritt	66	c Merritt b Partridge	59
J.O'Connor	b Buswell	26	c Nelson b Buswell	21
H.S.Nichols	b Merritt	2	not out	48
R.M.Taylor	b Partridge	50	not out	17
T.P.B.Smith	c James b Partridge	8		
*Capt J.W.A.Stephenson	b Partridge	0		
Mr J.N.Dennis	b Merritt	14		
S.J.Cray	c James b Nelson	11		
R.Smith	not out	0		
Extras	(B 1, LB 8, W 1, NB 2)	12	(B 7, LB 3)	10
Total		**298**	(4 wickets)	**227**

Fall: 1st inns 1/69, 2/182, 3/182, 4/188, 5/235, 6/249, 7/251, 8/279, 9/297.
2nd inns 1/76, 2/114, 3/145, 4/189.

ESSEX	O	M	R	W	O	M	R	W
Nichols	9	1	30	0	11	2	31	1
R.Smith	6	0	30	0	11	1	39	1
P.Smith	25	4	64	5	26	2	117	2
Taylor	2	1	9	0	2	0	14	0
Stephenson	12	2	30	2	12.5	1	42	4
Eastman	2.7	0	5	3	19	5	64	1

NORTHANTS	O	M	R	W	O	M	R	W
Buswell	8	0	42	1	6	0	46	1
Partridge	11	2	69	3	7	0	26	1
Merritt	16	0	98	3	17	1	78	2
Nelson	16.7	3	43	2	6	0	26	0
Timms	7	1	24	0	4	0	22	0
O'Brien	4	0	10	1	3.6	0	19	0

Umpires: G.M.Lee and G.Beet.

Close of play scores. First day: Essex 235/4 (J.O'Connor 26*, R.M.Taylor 23*).
Second day: Northamptonshire 335 all out.

Comments: A.V.Avery and T.H.Wade put on 113 in 75 minutes for the 2nd Essex wicket in their 1st innings.
A.V.Avery retired hurt in the 2nd innings, returning at the fall of the 3rd wicket.

LANCASHIRE COUNTY CRICKET CLUB

Standing (left to right): R.H.Parkin, C.Washbrook, R.Pollard, W.E.Phillipson, N.Oldfield, A.E.Nutter, J.Briggs. **Seated:** W.Farrimond, J.Iddon, W.H.L.Lister (captain), J.L.Hopwood, E.Paynter.

SOMERSET v WORCESTERSHIRE

Played at Taunton, June 3, 5, 6, 1939.
Toss won by Worcestershire.
Somerset won by ten wickets.

WORCESTERSHIRE

*Hon C.J.Lyttelton	c Luckes b Wellard	0	(8) b Buse	34
R.Howorth	c Hazell b Andrews	24	(1) c Luckes b Andrews	24
B.P.King	b Wellard	0	(2) b Andrews	19
E.Cooper	b Gimblett	102	(3) c Luckes b Buse	12
H.H.I.Gibbons	c Wellard b Andrews	16	(4) b Andrews	4
S.H.Martin	c Buse b Andrews	1	(5) b Hazell	63
Mr G.E.B.Abell	c Mitchell-Innes b Buse	6	(6) b Hazell	44
Mr A.F.T.White	c & b Wellard	20	(7) c & b Andrews	15
R.T.D.Perks	c Mitchell-Innes b Wellard	40	b Wellard	16
R.O.Jenkins	not out	25	c Luckes b Wellard	14
†H.Yarnold	c Mitchell-Innes b Hazell	9	not out	5
Extras	(B 8, LB 2, NB 1)	11	(B 1, LB 2, NB 1)	4
Total		**254**		**254**

Fall: 1st inns 1/0, 2/0, 3/24, 4/57, 5/63, 6/82, 7/122, 8/187, 9/238.
2nd inns 1/42, 2/49, 3/53, 4/75, 5/167, 6/170, 7/186, 8/213, 9/249.

SOMERSET

F.S.Lee	run out	25	not out	35
H.Gimblett	c Perks b Jenkins	129	not out	27
H.T.F.Buse	c & b Martin	103		
Mr N.S.Mitchell-Innes	b Jenkins	60		
*Mr E.F.Longrigg	c Perks b Howorth	0		
Mr J.W.Seamer	lbw b Martin	27		
†W.T.Luckes	c Martin b Perks	0		
W.H.R.Andrews	not out	40		
Mr C.J.P.Barnwell	st Yarnold b Jenkins	19		
A.W.Wellard	run out	22		
H.L.Hazell	b Martin	7		
Extras	(B 3, LB 8)	11	(B 4, NB 3)	7
Total		**443**	(No wicket)	**69**

Fall: 1st inns 1/126, 2/175, 3/275, 4/284, 5/348, 6/353, 7/353, 8/394, 9/425.

SOMERSET	O	M	R	W	O	M	R	W
Wellard	18	4	74	4	17	1	81	2
Andrews	24	0	124	3	19	1	82	4
Buse	8	1	29	1	10.5	3	38	2
Gimblett	3	0	11	1	1	0	9	0
Hazell	1.4	0	5	1	11	3	40	2

WORCESTERSHIRE	O	M	R	W	O	M	R	W
Perks	26	0	152	1	4	0	13	0
Martin	22.1	1	94	3	5	1	18	0
Howorth	25	3	73	1	1	0	14	0
Jenkins	26	2	113	3	-	-	-	-
White	-	-	-	-	1	0	5	0
Gibbons	-	-	-	-	5	0	12	0

Umpires: W.Reeves and C.N.Woolley.

Close of play scores. First day: Somerset 179/2 (H.T.F.Buse 15*, N.S.Mitchell-Innes 4*). **Second day:** Worcestershire 167/5 (S.H.Martin 61*).

Comments: E.Cooper made 102 in about 225 minutes, hitting nine 4's. It was his first century of the season.
H.Gimblett hit his fifth century of the season in 105 minutes. His 129 included two 6's and 17 4's and was made in 155 minutes. It was the fifth successive match, in which Gimblett had made a century.
H.T.F.Buse made 103 in 230 minutes, hitting seven 4's.
H.Gimblett and F.S.Lee put on 126 for the 1st wicket. It was their fourth century opening stand of the season.
H.T.F.Buse and N.S.Mitchell-Innes added 100 for the 3rd wicket.

SURREY v WARWICKSHIRE

Played at Kennington Oval, June 3, 5, 6, 1939.
Toss won by Warwickshire.
Surrey won by three wickets.

WARWICKSHIRE

A.J.W.Croom	c Gregory b Gover	94	lbw b Brown	15
W.A.Hill	c Squires b Parker	91	b Brown	17
F.R.Santall	c Gover b Parker	0	c & b Brown	22
Mr R.E.S.Wyatt	b Parker	0	c Brooks b Brown	4
H.E.Dollery	b Watts	13	c Gregory b Parker	24
N.A.Shortland	c Gregory b Watts	6	b Brown	23
†J.Buckingham	lbw b Gover	1	b Watts	31
*Mr P.Cranmer	b Brown	18	c McIntyre b Brown	16
C.W.Grove	c & b Brown	3	c Brooks b Brown	2
J.H.Mayer	not out	7	c Gregory b Brown	9
W.E.Hollies	b Gover	0	not out	0
Extras	(LB 6, NB 6)	12	(B 1, LB 3)	4
Total		**245**		**165**

Fall: 1st inns 1/182, 2/182, 3/182, 4/209, 5/215, 6/215, 7/218, 8/235, 9/242.
2nd inns 1/24, 2/43, 3/58, 4/60, 5/106, 6/112, 7/138, 8/133, 9/165.

SURREY

R.J.Gregory	c Santall b Grove	37	c Mayer b Grove	10
L.B.Fishlock	c Buckingham b Mayer	0	lbw b Grove	8
H.S.Squires	lbw b Grove	69	b Hollies	9
T.H.Barling	c Croom b Grove	57	c Buckingham b Mayer	25
J.F.Parker	b Hollies	89	lbw b Hollies	20
A.J.W.McIntyre	c Santall b Mayer	14	st Buckingham b Hollies	14
*Mr H.M.Garland-Wells	run out	17	c Buckingham b Hollies	8
Mr F.R.Brown	b Santall	11	not out	4
E.A.Watts	lbw b Hollies	10	not out	0
A.R.Gover	st Buckingham b Hollies	1		
†E.W.J.Brooks	not out	0		
Extras	(LB 7, W1)	8	(W 1)	1
Total		**314**	(7 wickets)	**99**

Fall: 1st inns 1/1, 2/82, 3/119, 4/204, 5/223, 6/260, 7/281, 8/308, 9/313.
2nd inns 1/15, 2/22, 3/33, 4/59, 5/81, 6/93, 7/95.

SURREY	O	M	R	W	O	M	R	W
Gover	14.6	1	70	3	9	0	33	1
Watts	12	2	41	2	7.2	1	30	1
Parker	12	5	19	3	4	0	24	1
Brown	10	1	50	2	15	1	74	7
Squires	17	5	31	0				
Gregory	2	0	4	0				
Garland-Wells	5	0	18	0				

WARWICKSHIRE	O	M	R	W	O	M	R	W
Mayer	15	2	60	2	9	1	29	1
Grove	18	1	85	3	7	1	24	2
Santall	18	1	74	1				
Wyatt	4	1	9	0				
Hollies	18.6	0	72	3	7.2	0	45	4
Croom	1	0	6	0				

Umpires: D.Hendren and J.A.Newman.

Close of play scores. First day: Surrey 76/1 (R.J.Gregory 37*, H.S.Squires 38*). **Second day:** Warwickshire 165/9 (J.Buckingham 31*, W.E.Hollies 0*).

Comments: A.J.W.Croom and W.A.Hill put on 182 for Warwickshire's 1st wicket. The next nine 1st innings wickets fell for 63 in 100 minutes.
J.F.Parker began the collapse of dismissing A.J.W.Croom, F.R.Santall and R.E.S.Wyatt in his 9th over.

Warwickshire's Bob Wyatt is out to the first ball he received from Parker of Surrey in the match at The Oval. Warwickshire had 182 on the board before they lost a wicket but were all out for 245.

YORKSHIRE v HAMPSHIRE

Played at Bramall Lane, Sheffield, June 3, 5, 6, 1939.
Toss won by Hampshire.
Yorkshire won by an innings and 129 runs.

HAMPSHIRE

J.Bailey	c Yardley b Bowes	45	st Wood b Hutton	27
†N.T.McCorkell	c Verity b Turner	18	c Yardley b Turner	4
A.G.Holt	b Yardley	13	c Wood b Smailes	26
W.L.C.Creese	c Turner b Smailes	27	c Bowes b Turner	13
J.Arnold	b Turner	6	c Wood b Verity	52
D.F.Walker	lbw b Smailes	5	c Smailes b Turner	5
G.Hill	c & b Smailes	0	c Wood b Bowes	16
G.S.Boyes	c Wood b Bowes	22	c Smailes b Hutton	27
*Mr G.R.Taylor	c Smailes b Leyland	4	c Barber b Hutton	4
R.C.Court	b Smailes	9	c Sellers b Hutton	5
G.E.M.Heath	not out	15	not out	1
Extras	(B 1, LB 9)	10	(B 5, LB 4, NB 1)	10
Total		**174**		**190**

Fall: 1st inns 1/33, 2/59, 3/91, 4/98, 5/118, 6/118, 7/121, 8/126, 9/145.
2nd inns 1/21, 2/41, 3/55, 4/60, 5/98, 6/139, 7/170, 8/179, 9/185.

YORKSHIRE

H.Sutcliffe	b Heath	116
L.Hutton	not out	280
W.Barber	not out	91
Extras	(B 2, LB 4)	6
Total	(1 wicket, declared)	**493**

Fall: 1st inns 1/315.

*Mr A.B.Sellers, Mr N.W.D.Yardley, M.Leyland, †A.Wood, W.E.Bowes, H.Verity, T.F.Smailes and C.Turner did not bat.

YORKSHIRE	O	M	R	W	O	M	R	W
Bowes	19.4	5	35	2	15	2	38	1
Smailes	15	2	41	4	8	0	27	1
Turner	13	1	42	2	7	1	26	3
Yardley	6	1	14	1	2	0	5	0
Verity	4	2	5	0	8	3	14	1
Leyland	5	0	27	1	6	0	30	0
Hutton	-	-	-	-	9.1	0	40	4

HAMPSHIRE	O	M	R	W
Heath	28	2	131	1
Court	20	1	120	0
Bailey	5	1	17	0
Hill	20	1	70	0
Boyes	14	1	66	0
Creese	12	2	51	0
Arnold	3	0	32	0

Umpires: H.W.Lee and E.Cooke.

Close of play scores. First day: Yorkshire 122/0 (H.Sutcliffe 52*, L.Hutton 70*).
Second day: Hampshire 104/5 (J.Arnold 17*, W.A.Hill 3*).

Comments: L.Hutton made his highest score 280*) for Yorkshire, hitting 36 4's in his 375 minutes' stay at the wicket. It was his third 100 of the season and his second in succession.
L.Hutton and H.Sutcliffe put on 315 for the 1st wicket in 270 minutes.
H.Sutcliffe's 116 included 14 4's in a stay of 270 minutes. It was his third 100 of the season.
L.Hutton and W.Barber added 178 in 105 minutes in an unfinished 2nd wicket partnership.
The match finished early on the third morning after only 75 minutes' play.

DERBYSHIRE v WORCESTERSHIRE

Played at Queen's Park, Chesterfield, June 7, 8, 9, 1939.
Toss won by Derbyshire.
Derbyshire won by 315 runs.

DERBYSHIRE

D.Smith	c Jenkins b Perks	35	b Martin ... 123
*Mr R.H.R.Buckston	c Yarnold b Perks	15	c Jenkins b Perks ... 6
A.E.Alderman	b Jackson	1	lbw b Jackson ... 91
L.F.Townsend	b Perks	34	st Yarnbold b Jenkins ... 46
G.H.Pope	b Martin	53	c Abell b Howorth ... 50
A.E.G.Rhodes	b Howorth	5	c Abell b Jackson ... 15
Mr T.D.Hounsfield	c Abell b Howorth	0	run out ... 0
A.V.Pope	b Perks	1	lbw b Howorth ... 49
†H.Elliott	run out	2	not out ... 11
T.B.Mitchell	c Perks b Howorth	1	
W.H.Copson	not out	1	(10) b Jackson ... 2
Extras	(B 4, LB 4, NB 2)	10	(B 13, LB 13, W 1, NB 1) 28
Total		158	(9 wickets, declared) ... 421

Fall: 1st inns 1/50, 2/55, 3/55, 4/124, 5/137, 6/141, 7/143, 8/156, 9/156.
2nd inns 1/16, 2/129, 3/236, 4/322, 5/360, 6/409, 7/409, 8/414, 9/421.

WORCESTERSHIRE

R.Howorth	lbw b A.V.Pope	1	c Smith b Copson ... 25
B.P.King	c G.H.Pope b Copson	1	b A.V.Pope ... 2
E.Cooper	c Hounsfield b G.H.Pope	40	lbw b A.V.Pope ... 3
H.H.I.Gibbons	b G.H.Pope	26	c Elliott b Copson ... 6
S.H.Martin	run out	19	lbw b A.V.Pope ... 8
*Mr G.E.B.Abell	c Copson b G.H.Pope	47	c A.V.Pope b G.H.Pope ... 3
Mr A.F.T.White	b Mitchell	8	c Smith A.V.Pope ... 10
R.O.Jenkins	b Mitchell	6	c Alderman b A.V.Pope ... 12
R.T.D.Perks	b G.H.Pope	6	b Copson ... 15
†H.Yarnold	b Copson	0	not out ... 10
P.F.Jackson	not out	1	c Mitchell b A.V.Pope ... 1
Extras	(B 3, LB 3, NB 1)	7	(B 3, LB 2) ... 5
Total		162	102

Fall: 1st inns 1/2, 2/6, 3/66, 4/71, 5/104, 6/112, 7/130, 8/139, 9/140.
2nd inns 1/28, 2/32, 3/38, 4/39, 5/49, 6/59, 7/66, 8/83, 9/91.

WORCESTERSHIRE	O	M	R	W	O	M	R	W
Perks	14	3	62	4	18	1	70	1
Martin	10	3	12	1	17	0	79	1
Jackson	7	2	32	1	23.3	0	71	3
Jenkins	6	1	19	0	16	0	78	1
Howorth	6.4	1	23	3	16	0	95	2

DERBYSHIRE	O	M	R	W	O	M	R	W
Copson	12	0	56	2	10	1	45	3
A.V.Pope	11	2	42	1	10.2	1	47	6
G.H.Pope	8.1	2	30	4	2	1	1	1
Mitchell	4	0	27	2	1	0	4	0

Umpires: H.W.Lee and E.Cooke.

Close of play scores. First day: Derbyshire 26/1 (D.Smith 9*, A.V.Pope 5*).
Second day: Worcestershire 56/5 (S.H.Martin 8*, A.F.T.White 4*).

Comments: 21 wickets fell on the 1st day.
D.Smith scored Derbyshire's first century of the season. He hit 13 4's in his 123. He and A.V.Pope added 113 for the 2nd wicket in Derbyshire's 2nd innings.
A.E.Alderman and D.Smith put on 107 for the 3rd wicket.
Worcestershire were set to make 417 to win. On the third day, Derbyshire needed only 40 minutes to win the game.
T.B.Mitchell broke a finger, which was to keep him out of the game for the next two weeks.

GLOUCESTERSHIRE v SURREY

Played at Gloucester, June 7, 8, 9, 1939.
Toss won by Surrey.
Gloucestershire won by an innings and 57 runs.

SURREY

R.J.Gregory	c Goddard b Scott	83	c Wilson b Scott ... 49
L.B.Fishlock	lbw b Barnett	4	c Hopkins b Goddard ... 47
H.S.Squires	c Hopkins b Scott	2	c Wilson b Lambert ... 6
T.H.Barling	c Emmett b Lambert	18	c Goddard b Scott ... 1
J.F.Parker	b Barnett	72	lbw b Scott ... 18
A.J.W.McIntyre	b Goddard	1	lbw b Scott ... 0
*Mr H.M.Garland-Wells	c Emmett b Goddard	8	b Scott ... 13
Mr F.R.Brown	b Barnett	21	c Hopkins b Scott ... 11
E.A.Watts	c & b Barnett	14	c Crapp b Scott ... 9
A.R.Gover	not out	6	b Lambert ... 2
†E.W.J.Brooks	lbw b Scott	0	not out ... 9
Extras	(LB 7)	7	(B 4, LB 2) ... 6
Total		236	171

Fall: 1st inns 1/8, 2/17, 3/42, 4/153, 5/167, 6/181, 7/211, 8/224, 9/231.
2nd inns 1/98, 2/99, 3/118, 4/118, 5/134, 6/147, 7/148, 8/157, 9/161.

GLOUCESTERSHIRE

C.J.Barnett	b Gover	8
R.A.Sinfield	c Brown b Gover	72
V.Hopkins	c Gregory b Brown	23
*Mr W.R.Hammond	c Gregory b Parker	135
J.F.Crapp	lbw b Gover	52
G.M.Emmett	st Brooks b Squires	30
†E.A.Wilson	b Gover	62
W.L.Neale	lbw b Watts	20
G.E.E.Lambert	not out	15
C.J.Scott	b Gover	19
T.W.J.Goddard	c Squires b Watts	4
Extras	(B 13, LB 7, NB 4)	24
Total		464

Fall: 1st inns 1/11, 2/42, 3/203, 4/270, 5/314, 6/356, 7/425, 8/426, 9/453.

GLOUCESTERSHIRE	O	M	R	W	O	M	R	W
Scott	17	2	73	3	16	1	86	7
Barnett	9	0	29	4	3	0	13	0
Lambert	8	0	60	1	12	1	32	2
Sinfield	13	3	34	0	5	3	3	0
Goddard	10	2	33	2	10.7	2	31	1

SURREY	O	M	R	W
Gover	25	1	101	5
Watts	21	1	101	2
Brown	23	3	102	1
Parker	16	3	38	1
Garland-Wells	9	2	39	0
Squires	11	3	40	1
Gregory	9	1	19	0

Umpires: W.Reeves and E.J.Smith.

Close of play scores. First day: Gloucestershire 187/2 (R.A.Sinfield 65*, W.R.Hammond 83*). **Second day:** Surrey 91/0 (R.J.Gregory 42*, L.B.Fishlock 43*).

Comments: R.J.Gregory and J.F.Parker put on 111 for the 4th wicket.
R.A.Sinfield and W.R.Hammond added 161 for Gloucester's 3rd wicket in 150 minutes.
W.R.Hammond became the first batsman in 1939 to reach a 1,000 runs when he reached 73 in Gloucester's 1st innings. His 135 included 14 4's and was made in 190 minutes.
On the third day, Surrey lost all their 2nd innings wickets for 80 runs in just over an hour. C.J.Scott took 7 for 47 in 9 overs.

HAMPSHIRE v LANCASHIRE

Played at Southampton, June 7, 8, 9, 1939.
Toss won by Hampshire.
Lancashire won by six wickets.

HAMPSHIRE

†N.T.McCorkell	c Farrimond b Phillipson	53	lbw b Wilkinson	62
J.Bailey	c Phillipson b Nutter	97	c Lister b Nutter	9
A.G.Holt	b Phillipson	14	lbw b Wilkinson	21
Mr R.H.Moore	lbw b Wilkinson	13	c Briggs b Iddon	37
W.L.C.Creese	b Phillipson	48	b Iddon	8
J.Arnold	c Hopwood b Phillipson	28	c Nutter b Wilkinson	6
P.A.Mackenzie	c Farrimond b Nutter	76	(8) not out	20
G.S.Boyes	c Nutter b Phillipson	0	(9) b Wilkinson	23
*Mr G.R.Taylor	c Farrimond b Phillipson	41	(7) c Phillipson b Iddon	6
Mr C.H.Knott	b Phillipson	16	not out	3
G.E.M.Heath	not out	34		
Extras	(B 3, LB 9, NB 2)	14	(B 7, LB 3, NB 1)	11
Total		**434**	(8 wickets, declared)	**206**

Fall: 1st inns 1/91, 2/141, 3/161, 4/230, 5/234, 6/291, 7/291, 8/364, 9/388.
2nd inns 1/32, 2/76, 3/137, 4/140, 5/152, 6/160, 7/163, 8/201.

LANCASHIRE

C.Washbrook	c Boyes b Knott	4	c Boyes b Knott	45
E.Paynter	c McCorkell b Heath	26	lbw b Boyes	36
J.L.Hopwood	lbw b Heath	49	c Boyes b Knott	135
N.Oldfield	c Arnold b Knott	51	c Creese b Knott	32
J.Iddon	c Taylor b Knott	15	not out	102
A.E.Nutter	b Mackenzie	11	not out	26
*Mr W.H.L.Lister	c Creese b Knott	0		
W.E.Phillipson	c Boyes b Heath	36		
†W.Farrimond	run out	53		
L.L.Wilkinson	lbw b Boyes	3		
J.Briggs	not out	0		
Extras	(B 4, LB 3, W 1)	8	(B 1, LB 8)	9
Total		**256**	(4 wickets)	**385**

Fall: 1st inns 1/16, 2/56, 3/122, 4/138, 5/159, 6/159, 7/190, 8/222, 9/253.
2nd inns 1/69, 2/114, 3/160, 4/329.

LANCASHIRE	O	M	R	W	O	M	R	W
Phillipson	28	3	104	7	11	1	41	0
Nutter	17.2	3	76	2	5	0	25	1
Wilkinson	32	1	143	1	16	0	94	4
Briggs	14	0	97	0				
Paynter	-	-	-	-	1	0	1	0
Iddon	-	-	-	-	12	3	34	3

HAMPSHIRE	O	M	R	W	O	M	R	W
Heath	23	3	59	3	18	1	99	0
Knott	16	0	108	4	20.1	0	112	3
Mackenzie	12	1	49	1	4	0	18	0
Bailey	6	0	25	0	4	0	19	0
Boyes	5	1	7	1	16	1	74	1
Creese	-	-	-	-	11	0	44	0
Moore	-	-	-	-	2	0	10	0

Umpires: F.I.Walden and H.Cruice.

Close of play scores. First day: Hampshire 434 all out. **Second day:** Hampshire 166/7 (G.S.Boyes 0*).

Comments: G.R.Taylor decided not to enforce the follow-on. Lancashire were set to make 385 in just under five hours. J.L.Hopwood scored 135 including 18 4's. He and J.Iddon (102* including 12 4's) shared in a stand of 169 for the 4th wicket in 110 minutes. Lancashire won with 30 minutes to spare.

KENT v GLAMORGAN

Played at Tonbridge, June 7, 8, 9, 1939.
Toss won by Kent.
Match drawn.

KENT

A.E.Fagg	b Judge	10	not out	169
*Mr F.G.H.Chalk	lbw b Mercer	16	c H.Davies b Judge	1
L.E.G.Ames	c H.Davies b Mercer	177	c Dyson b Judge	20
Mr B.H.Valentine	st H.Davies b E.Davies	55	b Jones	38
Mr P.G.Foster	st H.Davies b E.Davies	7	run out	13
P.R.Sunnucks	b E.Davies	3	not out	54
L.J.Todd	not out	115		
D.V.P.Wright	b Mercer	0		
N.W.Harding	c Dyson b E.Davies	71		
A.E.Watt	b Judge	6		
†Mr W.H.V.Levett	st H.Davies b E.Davies	1		
Extras	(B 3, LB 6, W 1)	10	(B 2, LB 9)	11
Total		**471**	(4 wickets)	**306**

Fall: 1st inns 1/18, 2/44, 3/153, 4/165, 5/173, 6/351, 7/351, 8/455, 9/468.
2nd inns 1/2, 2/42, 3/104, 4/145.

GLAMORGAN

A.H.Dyson	st Levett b Wright	75
D.E.Davies	b Harding	11
T.L.Brierley	c Fagg b Wright	22
*Mr M.J.L.Turnbull	b Wright	102
D.Davies	c Todd b Wright	43
C.C.Smart	b Ames	50
E.C.Jones	not out	105
Mr W.E.Harris	lbw b Harding	25
†H.G.Davies	b Watt	12
J.Mercer	run out	3
P.F.Judge	b Harding	7
Extras	(B 15, LB 17, NB 5)	37
Total		**492**

Fall: 1st inns 1/36, 2/92, 3/170, 4/275, 5/282, 6/388, 7/446, 8/479, 9/484.

GLAMORGAN	O	M	R	W	O	M	R	W
Mercer	24	1	119	3	6	0	28	0
Judge	16	0	97	2	11	2	41	2
D.E.Davies	32.4	4	121	5	16	0	55	0
Jones	6	0	41	0	8	1	26	1
Smart	7	0	52	0	7	0	52	0
D.Davies	3	0	15	0				
Harris	3	1	16	0	5	0	27	0
Dyson	-	-	-	-	3	0	43	0
Brierley	-	-	-	-	3	0	11	0
Turnbull	-	-	-	-	1	0	12	0

KENT	O	M	R	W
Harding	21.5	2	87	3
Watt	29	5	113	1
Wright	31	3	136	4
Todd	24	5	95	0
Ames	7	2	24	1

Umpires: H.G.Baldwin and C.W.L.Parker.

Close of play scores. First day: Glamorgan 22/0 (A.H.Dyson 16*, D.E.Davies 2*). **Second day:** Glamorgan 479/8 (E.C.Jones 102*).

Comments: A batsman's match, in which a total of 1,269 runs were scored for the fall of only 24 wickets. L.E.G.Ames made 177, hitting 22 4's. He and B.H.Valentine added 109 for the 3rd wicket. Then, with L.J.Todd, Ames added a further 178 for the 6th wicket. L.J.Todd hit 15 4's in his undefeated 115. He and N.W.Harding put on 104 for the 8th wicket. M.J.L.Turnbull hit 102, including two 6's and 12 4's. It was his first century since 1937. E.C.Jones scored his first championship century, his undefeated 105 including 18 4's. A.E.Fagg, in Kent's 2nd innings, hit 20 4's in his 169*. He and P.R.Sunnucks added 161 in an unbroken 5th wicket partnership in 80 minutes.

NOTTINGHAMSHIRE v ESSEX

Played at Trent Bridge, Nottinghamshire, June 7, 8, 9, 1939.
Toss won by Essex.
Nottinghamshire won by eight wickets.

ESSEX

L.C.Eastman	c Harris b Butler 62	c & b Giles 17
A.V.Avery	c Wheat b Woodhead 29	
†T.H.Wade	b Butler 2	c Wheat b Giles 23
J.O'Connor	c Jepson b Butler 194	c Wheat b Gunn 33
M.S.Nichols	c Jepson b Butler 40	
R.M.Taylor	c Harris b Heane 70	c Jepson b Gunn 16
*Capt J.W.A.Stephenson	not out 61	c Heane b Gunn 18
Mr J.N.Dennis	b Woodhead 46	not out 1
S.J.Cray	not out 6	
R.Smith	(did not bat)	(2) b Butler 0
T.P.B.Smith	(did not bat)	(5) c Woodhead b Gunn 10
Extras	(B 7, LB 14) 21	(LB 6) 6
Total	(7 wickets, declared) **531**	(7 wickets, declared)......**124**

Fall: 1st inns 1/85, 2/89, 3/116, 4/323, 5/413, 6/416, 7/517.
2nd inns 1/0, 2/46, 3/49, 4/78, 5/98, 6/117, 7/124.

NOTTINGHAMSHIRE

W.W.Keeton	c Wade b Taylor 46	not out 93
C.B.Harris	b P.Smith 196	c Wade b Eastman 26
J.Knowles	c Eastman b Taylor 14	c R.Smith b Taylor 43
J.Hardstaff	lbw b Taylor 8	not out 67
G.V.Gunn	lbw b R.Smith 17	
*Mr G.F.H.Heane	c Stephenson b Eastman 48	
R.J.Giles	b P.Smith 41	
†A.B.Wheat	not out 13	
F.G.Woodhead	c R.Smith b P.Smith 6	
H.J.Butler	c O'Connor b Stephenson 7	
A.Jepson	b Stephenson 1	
Extras	(B 12, LB 9) 21	(LB 9) 9
Total	......**418**	(2 wickets) **238**

Fall: 1st inns 1/119, 2/173, 3/185, 4/252, 5/317, 6/366, 7/398, 8/406, 9/416.
2nd inns 1/67, 2/152.

NOTTINGHAMSHIRE	O	M	R	W	O	M	R	W
Butler	29	1	137	4	7	1	32	1
Woodhead	29	4	96	2	2	0	24	0
Jepson	15	0	74	0				
Gunn	20	1	104	0	9.4	1	30	4
Giles	19	3	67	0	14	1	32	2
Heane	9	1	32	1				

ESSEX	O	M	R	W	O	M	R	W
R.Smith	10	2	45	1	3	0	14	0
Stephenson	12.6	2	45	2	5.5	0	39	0
Taylor	23	2	117	3	6	0	63	1
P.Smith	31	5	95	3	5	1	50	0
Eastman	24	7	95	1	9	0	63	1

Umpires: G.Beet and J.J.Hills.

Close of play scores. First day: Essex 423/6 (J.W.A.Stephenson 0*, J.N.Dennis 7*). **Second day:** Nottinghamshire 309/4 (C.B.Harris 192*, G.F.H.Heane 20*).

Comments: J.O'Connor's 194 included three 6's and 26 4's. His third century of the season took 300 minutes. He and R.M.Taylor added 207 for the 4th wicket.
Capt J.W.A.Stephenson and J.N.Dennis added 101 for the 7th wicket. In reply W.W.Keeton and C.B.Harris put on 119 for the 1st wicket. C.B.Harris in a stay of 270 minutes, hit 32 4's in his 196. Nottinghamshire were eventually set a target of 238 in 130 minutes and won with 30 minutes to spare. J.Hardstaff hit two 6's and ten 4's in his undefeated 67, made in 30 minutes.
Essex were handicapped by the absence of A.V.Avery and M.S.Nichols. The latter broke a toe on the first day and was unable to bowl in the match.

SOMERSET v MIDDLESEX

Played at Frome, June 7, 8, 9, 1939.
Toss won by Somerset.
Middlesex won by five wickets.

SOMERSET

F.S.Lee	b Sims 151	c Edrich b Smith 0
H.Gimblett	c Gray b Sims 32	lbw b Gray 9
H.T.F.Buse	c Peebles b Sims 4	b Sims 29
Mr N.S.Mitchell-Innes	c Gray b Sims 0	lbw b Smith 18
*Mr E.F.Longrigg	b Sims 41	c Hulme b Sims 22
†W.T.Luckes	run out 0	c Smith b Sims 13
W.H.R.Andrews	lbw b Smith 34	lbw b Sims 4
Mr C.J.P.Barnwell	b Smith 16	lbw b Smith 14
Mr G.M.Bennett	c Peebles b Sims 12	b Sims 1
A.W.Wellard	c Killick b Peebles 39	c Robertson b Sims 7
H.L.Hazell	not out 0	not out 0
Extras	(B 17, LB 3, W 3, NB 2) 25	(B 10, LB 6, W 4, NB 2) ...22
Total	......**354**	......**139**

Fall: 1st inns 1/38, 2/44, 3/44, 4/144, 5/144, 6/202, 7/236, 8/263, 9/353.
2nd inns 1/0, 2/15, 3/52, 4/61, 5/105, 6/113, 7/126, 8/127, 9/137.

MIDDLESEX

J.D.B.Robertson	b Buse 48	c Longrigg b Wellard 16
S.M.Brown	c Luckes b Andrews 20	lbw b Wellard 12
W.J.Edrich	c Hazell b Buse 71	c Mitchell-Innes b Wellard 0
D.C.S.Compton	b Buse 30	not out 103
Revd E.T.Killick	c & b Andrews 0	b Andrews 12
J.H.A.Hulme	b Andrews 42	lbw b Hazell 0
†W.F.F.Price	b Buse 17	not out 21
J.M.Sims	not out 53	
C.I.J.Smith	c Buse b Andrews 1	
*Mr I.A.R.Peebles	c Hazell b Buse 12	
L.H.Gray	c Bue b Andrews 4	
Extras	(B 7, W 4, NB 3) 14	(B 13, LB 5, NB 2) 20
Total	......**312**	(5 wickets) **184**

Fall: 1st inns 1/30, 2/120, 3/172, 4/173, 5/177, 6/234, 7/248, 8/251, 9/305.
2nd inns 1/20, 2/21, 3/76, 4/136, 5/137.

MIDDLESEX	O	M	R	W	O	M	R	W
Smith	20	3	84	2	16	5	35	3
Gray	16	3	55	0	4	0	22	1
Sims	23.2	1	119	6	16.5	2	53	6
Peebles	15	7	33	1	3	1	4	0
Edrich	5	0	38	0	2	1	3	0

SOMERSET	O	M	R	W	O	M	R	W
Wellard	23	5	81	0	15	3	71	3
Andrews	23.6	2	105	5	13	2	33	1
Buse	23	4	75	5	7.7	2	30	0
Gimblett	4	0	28	0				
Hazell	2	0	9	0	6	0	30	1

Umpires: J.A.Smart and H.Elliott.

Close of play scores. First day: Middlesex 40/1 (J.D.M.Robertson 12*, W.J.Edrich 2*). **Second day:** Somerset 88/4 (E.F.Longrigg 10*, W.T.Luckes 8*).

Comments: F.S.Lee was dismissed twice in consecutive balls. He opened the Somerset 1st innings and was the last batsman to be dismissed. He was then out to the first ball of the 2nd innings.
His 151 in the 1st innings was made in 315 minutes and included 20 4's.
He and E.F.Longrigg put on 100 for the 4th wicket.
D.C.S.Compton hit his fourth century of the season. His 2nd innings of 103* was made in 150 minutes and included 16 4's.
S.M.Brown retired after the fall of the 2nd wicket in the 2nd innings and resumed his innings at the fall of the 3rd wicket.

MIDDLESEX COUNTY CRICKET CLUB

Standing (left to right): J.D.B.Robertson, J.M.Sims, C.I.J.Smith, J.W.Edwards (masseur), L.H.Compton, L.H.Gray, D.C.S.Compton. Seated: W.J.Edrich, G.O.B.Allen, I.A.R.Peebles (captain), W.F.F.Price, F.G.Mann. On ground: S.M.Brown.

SUSSEX v WARWICKSHIRE

Played at Horsham, June 7, 8, 9, 1939.
Toss won by Warwickshire.
Sussex won by four wickets.

WARWICKSHIRE

A.J.W.Croom	lbw J.Cornford	14	b Nye	3
W.A.Hill	c John Langridge b J.Parks	53	b J.Cornford	4
F.R.Santall	lbw J.Parks	22	(10) not out	1
Mr R.E.S.Wyatt	c W.Cornford b Jas.Langridge	25	(9) retired hurt	0
H.E.Dollery	c W.Cornford b J.Parks	0	(4) c Bartlett b Hammond	41
N.A.Shortland	c W.Cornford b Jas.Langridge	34	(5) b J.Parks	26
†J.Buckingham	b Jas.Langridge	26	(3) c & b J.Cornford	27
*Mr P.Cranmer	not out	14	(6) b Jas.Langridge	33
C.W.Grove	c Hammond b Jas.Langridge	0	(7) c Bartlett b Jas.Langridge	1
J.H.Mayer	c Hammond b Nye	17	(8) c W.Cornford b Jas.Langridge	24
W.E.Hollies	st W.Cornford b Jas.Langridge	0	c J.Parks b Nye	1
Extras	(B 5, LB 6, NB 1)	12	(B 6)	6
Total		**217**		**167**

Fall: 1st inns 1/38, 2/86, 3/107, 4/107, 5/179, 6/182, 7/191, 8/191, 9/216.
2nd inns 1/6, 2/14, 3/48, 4/98, 5/118, 6/129, 7/159, 8/166, 9/167.

SUSSEX

John G.Langridge	b Mayer	0	c Croom b Mayer	6
J.H.Parks	c Croom b Grove	9	c Buckingham b Grove	5
H.W.Parks	lbw b Mayer	0	lbw b Hollies	19
*Mr H.T.Bartlett	b Mayer	74	b Mayer	6
Jas.Langridge	c Buckingham b Grove	1	not out	87
C.Oakes	lbw b Mayer	47	c Dollery b Grove	52
J.Y.Oakes	b Mayer	11	c Shortland b Cranmer	21
H.E.Hammond	b Mayer	15	not out	5
†W.L.Cornford	c Buckingham b Hollies	7		
J.K.Nye	c Cranmer b Hollies	6		
J.H.Cornford	not out	1		
Extras	(B 1, LB 6, NB 1)	8	(LB 5)	5
Total		**179**	(6 wickets)	**206**

Fall: 1st inns 1/1, 2/1, 3/21, 4/27, 5/126, 6/149, 7/150, 8/163, 9/177.
2nd inns 1/5, 2/21, 3/33, 4/45, 5/155, 6/200.

SUSSEX	O	M	R	W	O	M	R	W
Nye	15	3	62	1	9.1	0	55	2
J.H.Cornford	11	0	42	1	8	0	40	2
Hammond	7	0	42	0	4	1	31	1
J.H.Parks	12	1	47	3	8	0	10	1
Jas.Langridge	4.2	1	12	5	5	0	25	3

WARWICKSHIRE	O	M	R	W	O	M	R	W
Mayer	20.3	3	70	6	21	3	62	2
Grove	18	4	52	2	9	0	44	2
Hollies	13	5	33	2	22	4	75	1
Cranmer	2	0	16	0	2	0	12	1
Santall		-		-	5	0	8	0

Umpires: F.J.Durston and A.Skelding.
Close of play scores. First day: Sussex 127/5 (H.T.Bartlett 64*, J.Y.Oakes 0*).
Second day: Sussex 154/4 (Jas.Langridge 63*, C.Oakes 52*).
Comments: Horsham cricket week.
James Langridge took five wickets for 12 runs in 34 balls after missing the two previous games through lumbago. In a spell of 18 balls, he took four wickets for four runs. John Langridge and H.W.Parks, having put on 307 together the previous day against Kent, both players making centuries, were dismissed in consecutive balls for nought in the first over of the 1st innings. R.E.S.Wyatt retired hurt after only eight minutes' batting in the 2nd innings, with Warwickshire 3/39. James Langridge and C.Oakes put on 110 for the 5th wicket in Sussex 2nd innings.

YORKSHIRE v LEICESTERSHIRE

Played at Hull, June 7, 8, 9, 1939.
Toss won by Leicestershire.
Yorkshire won by an innings and 30 runs.

LEICESTERSHIRE

G.L.Berry	c Robinson b Yardley	8	lbw b Verity	16
G.S.Watson	b Verity	80	run out	5
N.F.Armstrong	b Verity	20	c Mitchell b Verity	10
F.T.Prentice	lbw b Verity	10	(5) c Smailes b Verity	22
M.Tompkin	st Wood b Verity	2	(6) c sub b Verity	4
Mr C.S.Dempster	not out	165	(4) c Turner b Verity	29
*Mr M.St.J.Packe	st Wood b Leyland	16	c Robinson b Verity	2
L.D.Thursting	c Verity b Smailes	24	not out	4
†G.O.Dawkes	lbw b Smailes	0	lbw b Verity	0
H.A.Smith	b Barber	24	b Robinson	3
W.H.Flamson	b Barber	4	b Verity	1
Extras	(B 9, LB 2, NB 2)	13	(B 8)	8
Total		**366**		**104**

Fall: 1st inns 1/39, 2/76, 3/117, 4/122, 5/127, 6/197, 7/248, 8/248, 9/348.
2nd inns 1/14, 2/32, 3/33, 4/81, 5/86, 6/92, 7/92, 8/92, 9/99.

YORKSHIRE

H.Sutcliffe	not out	234
A.Mitchell	c Dawkes b Prentice	32
W.Barber	b Flamson	34
M.Leyland	c Tompkin b Smith	18
Mr N.W.D.Yardley	lbw b Smith	74
C.Turner	hit wkt b Thursting	38
*Mr A.B.Sellers	c Packe b Thursting	5
†A.Wood	c Dawkes b Packe	32
Extras	(B 15, LB 14, W 2, NB 2)	33
Total	(7 wickets, declared)	**500**

Fall: 1st inns 1/70, 2/153, 3/185, 4/343, 5/422, 6/434, 7/500.
H.Verity, T.F.Smailes and E.P.Robinson did not bat.

YORKSHIRE	O	M	R	W	O	M	R	W
Smailes	18	5	54	2	10	3	24	0
Turner	16	3	51	0	3	2	1	0
Yardley	10	1	46	1				
Verity	32	12	76	4	19.3	6	38	8
Robinson	14	2	40	0	12	4	31	1
Leyland	16	1	74	1	2	0	2	0
Barber	3.2	0	12	2				

LEICESTERSHIRE	O	M	R	W
Flamson	25	1	91	1
Smith	26	0	108	2
Prentice	28	2	113	1
Armstrong	10	0	51	0
Thursting	17	0	104	2
Packe	2	0	0	1

Umpires: G.M.Lee and C.V.Tarbox.

Close of play scores. First day: Yorkshire 20/0 (H.Sutcliffe 11*, A.Mitchell 8*).
Second day: Leicestershire 28/1 (G.L.Berry 15*, N.F.Armstrong 6*).

Comments: W.E.Bowes was rested for this match.
C.S.Dempster's 165* was the first century scored against Yorkshire in 1939. He batted for 210 minutes and hit 20 4's.
He and H.A.Smith added 100 for the 9th wicket.
H.Sutcliffe made his fourth century of the season. It was his 16th double century for Yorkshire. He hit 16 4's in a stay of 375 minutes. It was also his 147th century and his 3rd consecutive 100. He and N.W.D.Yardley put on 158 for the 4th wicket.
Leicester lost their remaining nine 2nd innings wickets in only 105 minutes on the third day. H.Verity taking 8 for 32 in 15 overs and 3 balls.
It was Yorkshire's fourth successive victory by an innings.

GLAMORGAN v SOMERSET

Played at Newport, June 10, 12, 13, 1939.
Toss won by Somerset.
Match drawn.

SOMERSET

F.S.Lee	run out	9
H.Gimblett	run out	46
H.F.T.Buse	c D.Davies b Judge	86
Mr C.J.P.Barnwell	lbw b Mercer	6
*Mr E.F.Longrigg	c H.Davies b Smart	33
Mr A.T.M.Jones	st H.Davies b Judge	52
W.H.R.Andrews	c Harris b Smart	57
A.W.Wellard	b Judge	13
Mr G.M.Bennett	b Mercer	19
†W.T.Luckes	not out	17
H.L.Hazell	c Turnbull b Mercer	19
Extras	(B 9, LB 16, W 3)	28
Total		**385**

Fall: 1st inns 1/28, 2/87, 3/113, 4/170, 5/213, 6/296, 7/319, 8/336, 9/356, 10/385.

GLAMORGAN

A.H.Dyson	c Barnwell b Andrews	3
D.E.Davies	c & b Jones	68
T.L.Brierley	c & b Andrews	6
D.Davies	st Luckes b Wellard	216
*Mr M.J.L.Turnbull	b Buse	62
C.C.Smart	b Andrews	141
E.C.Jones	not out	61
Mr W.E.Harris	c Jones b Wellard	4
†H.G.Davies	not out	11
Extras	(LB 1, NB 1)	2
Total	(7 wickets)	**574**

Fall: 1st inns 1/3, 2/9, 3/134, 4/249, 5/453, 6/533, 7/537.
J.Mercer and P.F.Judge did not bat.

GLAMORGAN	O	M	R	W
Mercer	33.5	10	89	3
Judge	35	7	82	3
D.E.Davies	26	4	97	0
Jones	9	1	24	0
Smart	18	4	65	2

SOMERSET	O	M	R	W
Wellard	47	9	161	2
Andrews	38	5	158	3
Buse	23	2	90	1
Hazell	27	6	84	0
Gimblett	7	0	40	0
Jones	1	0	3	1
Lee	1	0	2	0
Bennett	2	0	28	0
Barnwell	1	0	6	0

Umpires: W.Reeves and E.J.Smith.

Close of play scores. First day: Somerset 306/6 (A.M.T.Jones 42*, A.W.Wellard 5*). **Second day:** Glamorgan 219/3 (D.Davies 94*, M.J.L.Turnbull 45*).

Comments: Glamoran scored over 500 for the third successive time at home. Their total of 574 was only three runs short of their highest score, made earlier in the season against Gloucestershire.
D.Davies made the highest score of his career. His 216 (including 19 4's) took eight hours, 40 minutes and was the fifth highest score by a Glamorgan player.
E. and D.Davies put on 125 for the 3rd wicket.
D.Davies and M.J.Turnbull added 115 for the 4th wicket.
D.Davies and C.C.Smart put on 204 for the 5th wicket, a Glamorgan record for that wicket.
C.C.Smart made 141 in 160 minutes, hitting three 6's and 17 4's.
W.T.Luckes did not concede a bye in Glamorgan's 574.

GLOUCESTERSHIRE v ESSEX

Played at Gloucester, June 10, 12, 1939.
Toss won by Essex.
Gloucestershire won by an innings and 93 runs.

ESSEX

L.C.Eastman	c Hammond b Scott	28	b Scott	26
R.Smith	c Scott b Barnett	0	b Lambert	43
†T.H.Wade	c Hopkins b Scott	8	run out	17
J.O'Connor	lbw b Goddard	29	c Hammond b Lambert	5
R.M.Taylor	c Hopkins b Lambert	29	c Scott b Lambert	4
*Capt J.W.A.Stephenson	c Scott b Goddard	31	c Scott b Lambert	19
T.P.B.Smith	b Goddard	1	(11) c Hammond b Sinfield	5
Mr J.N.Dennis	c Hopkins b Lambert	10	b Sinfield	28
F.H.Rist	c Hopkins b Goddard	2	c Emmett b Goddard	18
S.J.Cray	b Lambert	0	not out	4
F.H.Vigar	not out	2	(7) b Lambert	9
Extras	(LB 10)	10	(LB 4)	4
Total		**150**		**182**

Fall: 1st inns 1/4, 2/17, 3/48, 4/93, 5/131, 6/136, 7/136, 8/138, 9/141.
2nd inns 1/72, 2/72, 3/77, 4/97, 5/104, 6/117, 7/134, 8/169, 9/174.

GLOUCESTERSHIRE

C.J.Barnett	st Wade b P.Smith	45
R.A.Sinfield	lbw b R.Smith	5
V.Hopkins	c Stephenson b Taylor	52
*Mr W.R.Hammond	c Dennis b Taylor	14
J.F.Crapp	st Wade b P.Smith	84
G.M.Emmett	b P.Smith	99
W.L.Neale	lbw b Taylor	37
†E.A.Wilson	c P.Smith b R.Smith	36
C.J.Scott	c Cray b Stephenson	21
G.E.E.Lambert	c & b Stephenson	12
T.W.J.Goddard	not out	1
Extras	(B 14, LB 5)	19
Total		**425**

Fall: 1st inns 1/15, 2/93, 3/117, 4/124, 5/271, 6/324, 7/362, 8/404, 9/423.

GLOUCESTERSHIRE	O	M	R	W	O	M	R	W
Scott	8	0	49	2	13	0	72	1
Barnett	3	1	9	1	3	0	19	0
Lambert	10.7	0	38	3	11	1	44	5
Goddard	13	4	30	4	8	1	31	1
Sinfield	5	3	14	0	2.4	0	12	2

ESSEX	O	M	R	W
Stephenson	19	1	87	2
R.Smith	22.2	2	92	2
P.Smith	26	5	102	3
Vigar	4	1	22	0
Taylor	16	2	74	3
Eastman	7	3	29	0

Umpires: H.Elliott and J.A.Smart.

Close of play scores. First day: Gloucestershire 280/5 (G.M.Emmett 67*, W.L.Neale 5*).

Comments: The match finished in two days.
W.R.Hammond lost his ninth successive toss.
J.F.Crapp and G.M.Emmett added 147 for the 5th wicket in 95 minutes.
Essex began well in the 2nd innings, 72 runs being added in only 40 minutes for the first wicket. A storm altered the state of the wicket and Essex were quickly bowled out to lose by an innings.
G.E.E.Lambert achieved best career bowling figures of 5 for 44 in the Essex 2nd innings.

57

LANCASHIRE v NOTTINGHAMSHIRE

Played at Old Trafford, Manchester, June 10, 12, 13, 1939.
Toss won by Lancashire.
Match drawn.

LANCASHIRE

C.Washbrook	b Butler	8	not out	56
E.Paynter	c Wheat b Butler	69	c & b Woodhead	19
J.L.Hopwood	b Jepson	35	c Woodhead b Butler	0
N.Oldfield	not out	147	c Wheat b Harris	50
J.Iddon	c Wheat b Jepson	21	lbw b Harris	2
A.E.Nutter	not out	109		
Extras	(B 4, LB 10)	14	(B 2, LB 7)	9
Total	**(4 wickets, declared)**	**403**	(4 wickets, declared)	**136**

Fall: 1st inns 1/25, 2/97, 3/140, 4/168.
2nd inns 1/31, 2/32, 3/130, 4/136.

*Mr W.H.L.Lister, W.E.Phillipson, †W.Farrimond, R.Pollard and L.L.Wilkinson did not bat.

NOTTINGHAMSHIRE

W.W.Keeton	c Farrimond b Phillipson	58	not out	7
C.B.Harris	c Nutter b Phillipson	67	not out	7
*Mr G.F.H.Heane	c Phillipson b Pollard	22		
J.Hardstaff	b Pollard	60		
G.V.Gunn	c & b Iddon	53		
J.Knowles	b Pollard	2		
R.J.Giles	b Pollard	10		
†A.B.Wheat	c Farrimond b Pollard	1		
F.G.Woodhead	c Farrimond b Phillipson	21		
H.J.Butler	b Phillipson	9		
A.Jepson	not out	0		
Extras	(LB 11, NB 1)	12	(B 4, LB 5)	9
Total		**316**	(No wicket)	**23**

Fall: 1st inns 1/117, 2/140, 3/171, 4/223, 5/229, 6/243, 7/245, 8/302, 9/315.

NOTTINGHAMSHIRE	O	M	R	W	O	M	R	W
Butler	23	2	93	2	10	0	46	1
Woodhead	15	1	62	0	7	1	19	1
Giles	19	1	74	0	5	0	21	0
Jepson	21	0	103	2	5	0	29	0
Gunn	9	1	41	0				
Harris	3	0	16	0	2.1	0	12	2

LANCASHIRE	O	M	R	W	O	M	R	W
Phillipson	22.5	5	78	4	2	0	2	0
Pollard	21	5	54	5				
Iddon	10	1	44	1				
Wilkinson	20	2	100	0				
Nutter	10	1	28	0	1	0	3	0
Paynter	-	-	-	-	4	2	3	0
Washbrook	-	-	-	-	2	0	6	0
Oldfield					1	1	0	0

Umpires: A.Dolphin and H.W.Lee.

LEICESTERSHIRE v KENT

Played at Grace Road, Leicester, June 10, 12, 13, 1939.
Toss won by Leicestershire.
Kent won by nine wickets.

LEICESTERSHIRE

G.L.Berry	c Harding b Todd	13	lbw b Watt	20
G.S.Watson	b Todd	1	b Harding	4
N.F.Armstrong	c Fagg b Dovey	63	c Ames b Harding	50
F.T.Prentice	lbw b Wright	119	b Wright	27
M.Tompkin	c Levett b Dovey	7	lbw b Wright	0
Mr C.S.Dempster	b Todd	29	(7) c Todd b Wright	55
*Mr M.St.J.Packe	b Harding	39	(6) b Wright	10
†G.O.Dawkes	lbw b Watt	4	not out	30
H.A.Smith	not out	6	c Foster b Wright	12
J.Sperry	c Foster b Wright	0	b Todd	4
W.H.Flamson	c Chalk b Wright	2	b Todd	0
Extras	(B 5, LB 3)	8	(B 7, LB 12)	19
Total		**291**		**231**

Fall: 1st inns 1/9, 2/36, 3/94, 4/119, 5/171, 6/246, 7/268, 8/289, 9/289.
2nd inns 1/6, 2/63, 3/109, 4/109, 5/119, 6/120, 7/209, 8/225, 9/229.

KENT

A.E.Fagg	c Dawkes b Sperry	90	c Packe b Flamson	0
*Mr F.G.H.Chalk	lbw b Sperry	10	not out	55
L.E.G.Ames	b Sperry	13	not out	79
†Mr W.H.V.Levett	c Dawkes b Sperry	7		
L.J.Todd	c Packe b Sperry	54		
Mr P.G.Foster	run out	107		
P.R.Sunnucks	c Dawkes b Prentice	16		
D.V.P.Wright	b Flamson	42		
N.W.Harding	b Prentice	7		
A.E.Watt	c & b Smith	22		
R.R.Dovey	not out	0		
Extras	(B 5, LB 11, W 1)	17	(B 2, LB 1, NB 1)	4
Total		**385**	(1 wicket)	**138**

Fall: 1st inns 1/23, 2/45, 3/57, 4/153, 5/198, 6/240, 7/312, 8/344, 9/367.
2nd inns 1/1.

KENT	O	M	R	W	O	M	R	W
Todd	17	3	58	3	9.4	2	22	2
Harding	15	2	60	1	14	1	66	2
Watt	17	2	69	1	13	2	44	1
Wright	12.7	0	63	3	14	0	65	5
Dovey	16	8	33	2	2	0	17	0

LEICESTERSHIRE	O	M	R	W	O	M	R	W
Sperry	29	0	143	5	5	1	43	0
Flamson	18	1	79	1	6.4	0	26	1
Smith	21	2	98	1	9	0	32	0
Prentice	10	1	40	2	7	1	33	0
Armstrong	3	0	8	0				

Umpires: J.A.Newman and G.Beet.

Close of play scores. First day: Lancashire 369/4 (N.Oldfield 129*, A.E.Nutter 94*). **Second day:** Nottinghamshire 235/5 (G.V.Gunn 13, R.J.Giles 5*).

Comments: Rain interrupted play on all three days.
A.E.Nutter made his first first-class century. His undefeated 109 included eight 4's. N.Oldfield made 147*, hitting 13 4's. It was the highest score of his career. A.Nutter and N.Oldfield put on an unbroken 235 for Lancashire's 5th wicket, a county record. W.W.Keeton and C.B.Harris put on 117 for the 1st wicket. On the third day, A.Dolphin, the umpire, standing at square leg, was forced to retire after being knocked-out by a shot from N.Oldfield. Notts were set an impossible target of 224 in 80 minutes.

Close of play scores. First day: Kent 50/2 (A.E.Fagg 14*, W.H.V.Levett 4*).
Second day: Leicestershire 43/1 (Berry 15*, Armstrong 21*).

Comments: H.A.Smith's benefit match.
F.T.Prentice made 119 in 240 minutes, hitting one 6 and 15 4's.
D.V.P.Wright finished off Leicester's 1st innings with three wickets in seven balls.
P.G.Foster made his first century for Kent. His 107 included one 6 and eight 4's in a stay of 165 minutes.
The match finished in heavy rain. L.E.G.Ames and F.G.H.Chalk won the game for their side with an unbroken partnership of 137 for the 2nd wicket.

MIDDLESEX v YORKSHIRE

Played at Lord's, June 10, 12, 1939.
Toss won by Yorkshire.
Yorkshire won by an innings and 246 runs.

YORKSHIRE

H.Sutcliffe	c & b Compton	175
L.Hutton	b Peebles	29
A.Mitchell	lbw b Gray	1
M.Leyland	not out	180
Mr N.W.D.Yardley	lbw b Edrich	7
*Mr A.B.Sellers	b Compton	14
T.F.Smailes	not out	7
Extras	(B 12, LB 5)	17
Total	(5 wickets, declared)	**430**

Fall: 1st inns 1/56, 2/57, 3/358, 4/377, 5/416.
†A.Wood, W.E.Bowes, H.Verity and E.P.Robinson did not bat.

MIDDLESEX

J.D.B.Robertson	c Robinson b Smailes	1	c Sutcliffe b Bowes ... 19
S.M.Brown	c sub b Bowes	17	c Wood b Bowes ... 3
W.J.Edrich	c Smailes b Bowes	1	c Wood b Bowes ... 9
D.C.S.Compton	lbw b Bowes	25	c & b Verity ... 18
Revd E.T.Killick	c Mitchell b Verity	6	lbw b Robinson ... 15
J.H.A.Hulme	c Sutcliffe b Bowes	0	c Smailes b Robinson ... 1
†W.F.F.Price	c Wood b Verity	2	c sub b Verity ... 10
J.M.Sims	st Wood b Verity	1	c Wood b Robinson ... 21
C.I.J.Smith	c Mitchell b Bowes	0	c Hutton b Verity ... 9
*Mr I.A.R.Peebles	c Hutton b Verity	2	not out ... 8
L.H.Gray	not out	0	c Wood b Verity ... 1
Extras	(B 5, LB 1, W 1)	7	(B 6, LB 2) ... 8
Total		**62**	**122**

Fall: 1st inns 1/3, 2/5, 3/31, 4/52, 5/52, 6/52, 7/57, 8/60, 9/62.
2nd inns 1/4, 2/30, 3/39, 4/65, 5/69, 6/78, 7/82, 8/100, 9/121.

MIDDLESEX	O	M	R	W
Smith	21	1	85	0
Gray	21	1	119	1
Edrich	10	5	37	1
Peebles	15	0	70	1
Sims	10	0	62	0
Compton	12	0	40	2

YORKSHIRE	O	M	R	W	O	M	R	W
Bowes	12	3	20	5	8	0	30	3
Smailes	2	0	3	1	5	1	9	0
Verity	9	5	17	4	9.4	5	36	4
Robinson	4	0	15	0	9	2	36	3
Yardley	-	-	-	-	5	0	19	0

Umpires: H.G.Baldwin and C.N.Woolley.

Close of play scores. First day: Yorkshire 430/5 (M.Leyland 180*, T.F.Smailes 7*).

Comments: The game finished at 5pm on the second day.
H.Sutcliffe and M.Leyland hit 301 in a 3rd-wicket partnership for Yorkshire, the second highest total for a Yorkshire 3rd wicket.
H.Sutcliffe, aged 44, became the oldest cricketer to hit four consecutive first-class centuries. His 175 included 17 4's.
M.Leyland in his undefeated 180, hit 20 4's.
Rain over the weekend made things extremely difficult for Middlesex. They were dismissed twice in 270 minutes, after following on 368 behind. In the 1st innings, D.C.S.Compton reached his 1,000 runs for the season.
It was Yorkshire's fifth consecutive victory by an innings.
There was a crowd of 24,000 on the first day.

SUSSEX v SURREY

Played at Horsham, June 10, 12, 13, 1939.
Toss won by Sussex.
Surrey won by nine wickets.

SUSSEX

John G.Langridge	b McIntyre	54	c Brookes b Watts ... 17
J.H.Parks	c Watts b Berry	27	c Brooks b Garland-Wells 52
H.W.Parks	c Fishlock b Gover	24	c Parker b Garland-Wells 76
G.Cox	hit wkt b Gover	14	c Squires b Watts ... 74
Jas.Langridge	not out	59	c Brooks b Gover ... 40
C.Oakes	c Berry b Gover	3	c Gregory b Garland-Wells 4
*Flt-Lt A.J.Holmes	c Brooks b Squires	37	c Gover b Watts ... 16
†Mr S.C.Griffith	b Watts	8	b Watts ... 0
J.Y.Oakes	c Garland-Wells b Squires	25	c Parker b Watts ... 0
J.K.Nye	c Brooks b Gover	0	not out ... 12
J.H.Cornford	lbw b Gover	0	c Garland-Wells b Watts 7
Extras	(B 5, LB 7, NB 2)	14	(B 5, LB 5, NB 1) ... 11
Total		**265**	**309**

Fall: 1st inns 1/53, 2/103, 3/118, 4/131, 5/135, 6/198, 7/215, 8/258, 9/265.
2nd inns 1/25, 2/137, 3/169, 4/197, 5/229, 6/284, 7/284, 8/284, 9/298.

SURREY

L.B.Fishlock	b J.Parks	51	not out ... 107
H.S.Squires	c Cornford b Jas.Langridge	54	c Griffith b Nye ... 18
T.H.Barling	b Cornford	11	not out ... 88
J.F.Parker	lbw b C.Oakes	11	
A.J.W.McIntyre	c Jas.Langridge b Nye	4	
†E.W.J.Brooks	c Holmes b Nye	42	
*Mr H.M.Garland-Wells	c Holmes b Nye	58	
R.J.Gregory	c Jas.Langridge b Cornford	16	
E.A.Watts	c Cornford b Nye	66	
F.Berry	not out	20	
A.R.Gover	b J.Parks	4	
Extras	(B 6, LB 9, W 1, NB 1)	17	(B 5, LB 3) ... 8
Total		**354**	(1 wicket) **221**

Fall: 1st inns 1/84, 2/123, 3/125, 4/139, 5/139, 6/244, 7/247, 8/270, 9/349.
2nd inns 1/43.

SURREY	O	M	R	W	O	M	R	W
Gover	17.2	1	75	5	17	1	96	2
Watts	10	0	42	1	16.2	0	88	5
Berry	16	1	56	1	9	0	35	0
Squires	8	2	24	2	5	0	29	0
Parker	5	0	23	0	4	1	15	0
McIntyre	3	0	18	1				
Garland-Wells	3	0	13	0	9	0	35	3

SUSSEX	O	M	R	W	O	M	R	W
Nye	22	1	103	4	13	1	63	1
Cornford	19	3	88	2	12	0	44	0
J.H.Parks	19	3	72	2	9	2	25	0
Jas.Langridge	11	3	50	1	3	0	23	0
C.Oakes	3	0	23	1	4	0	32	0
Holmes	1	0	1	0				
John Langridge	-	-	-	-	3	0	10	0
J.Y.Oakes	-	-	-	-	2.5	0	16	0

Umpires: F.Chester and H.Cruice.

Close of play scores. First day: Surrey 141/5 (E.W.J.Brooks 1*, H.M.Garland-Wells 1*). **Second day:** Sussex 282/5 (G.Cox 73*, Jas.Langridge 34*).

Comments: Second match of Horsham cricket week.
E.W.J.Brooks and H.M.Garland-Wells put on 105 for Surrey's 6th wicket. J.H. and H.W.Parks added 112 for the 2nd wicket in 90 minutes. Leading by 193 runs, Sussex lost their last five wickets for 27 on the third day. E.A.Watts took three wickets in his first over of the morning. Surrey hit 221 in 170 minutes to win by nine wickets. L.B.Fishlock made 107, including 15 4's. With T.H.Barling, he added an unbroken 178 for the 2nd wicket in 115 minutes.

WARWICKSHIRE v HAMPSHIRE

Played at Edgbaston, Birmingham, June 10, 12, 13, 1939.
Toss won by Hampshire.
Match drawn.

HAMPSHIRE

†N.T.McCorkell	lbw b Wilmot	12
J.Bailey	c Croom b Mayer	40
A.G.Holt	c Buckingham b Mayer	115
W.L.C.Creese	c Buckingham b Mayer	4
J.Arnold	b Mayer	109
P.A.Mackenzie	b Mayer	29
G.Hill	st Buckingham b Hollies	22
G.S.Boyes	c Mayer b Hollies	9
*Mr G.R.Taylor	c Dollery b Hollies	14
Mr C.J.Knott	c Mayer b Hollies	0
G.E.M.Heath	not out	3
Extras	(B 1, LB 3, W 1, NB 2)	7
Total		**364**

Fall: 1st inns 1/13, 2/99, 3/105, 4/242, 5/315, 6/330, 7/346, 8/347, 9/347.

WARWICKSHIRE

A.J.W.Croom	c Mackenzie b Heath	24	c Creece b Knott	69
W.A.Hill	c McCorkell b Knott	13	b Heath	49
†J.Buckingham	c Hill b Heath	4	lbw b Knott	33
H.E.Dollery	lbw b Mackenzie	25	c Boyes b Heath	170
J.S.Ord	c Arnold b Heath	0	not out	105
N.A.Shortland	c Knott b Heath	6	(7) not out	2
*Mr P.Cranmer	c Knott b Mackenzie	9	(6) c Boyes b Holt	42
W.E.Fantham	c McCorkell b Mackenzie	0		
K.Wilmot	not out	40		
J.H.Mayer	c Boyes b Mackenzie	0		
W.E.Hollies	b Knott	13		
Extras	(B 1, LB 5, W 1)	7	(B 10, LB 8, W 1, NB 1)	20
Total		**141**	(5 wickets, declared)	**490**

Fall: 1st inns 1/22, 2/31, 3/58, 4/60, 5/69, 6/84, 7/88, 8/89, 9/91.
2nd inns 1/119, 2/129, 3/200, 4/415, 5/484.

WARWICKSHIRE	O	M	R	W
Mayer	23	3	71	5
Wilmot	24	3	88	1
Hollies	19.6	3	85	4
Cranmer	12	0	59	0
Fantham	0	—	54	0

HAMPSHIRE	O	M	R	W	O	M	R	W
Heath	22	3	55	4	24	5	80	2
Knott	17	4	30	2	28	4	124	2
Hill	1	0	3	0	14	0	47	0
Mackenzie	7	0	34	4	14	1	73	0
Boyes	3	1	12	0	14	0	61	0
Bailey	-	-	-	-	9	3	15	0
Creese	-	-	-	-	7	1	33	0
Holt	-	-	-	-	2	0	24	1
Arnold	-	-	-	-	2	1	11	0
Taylor	-	-	-	-	1	0	2	0

Umpires: F.I.Walden and E.Cooke.

Close of play scores. First day: Warks 7/0 (A.J.W.Croom 1*, W.A.Hill 6*). **Second day:** Warks 96/0 (A.J.W.Croom 52*, W.A.Hill 39*).

Comments: J.Arnold and A.G.Holt added 137 for the 4th wicket in 95 minutes. J.Arnold made 109 hitting 12 4's. He reached his century in 185 minutes. A.G.Holt's 115, included 16 4's and took about 200 minutes. W.E.Hollies finished off the Hampshire 1st innings with 4 for 17 runs in 30 balls. Hollies then helped K.Wilmot to put on 50 for Warwickshire's 10th wicket. Warwickshire followed on 223 behind. A.J.W.Croom and W.A.Hill put on 119 for the 1st wicket. H.E.Dollery and J.S.Ord added 215 in 140 minutes for the 4th wicket. H.E.Dollery hit four 6's and 13 4's in his 170. It was made in 210 minutes, the final 70 runs coming in 35 minutes. J.S.Ord's undefeated 105 was his first century in county cricket. He hit 15 4's in a stay of 180 minutes. Hampshire used ten bowlers in Warwickshire's 2nd innings.

WORCESTERSHIRE v NORTHAMPTONSHIRE

Played at Dudley, June 10, 12, 13, 1939.
Toss won by Worcestershire.
Match drawn.

WORCESTERSHIRE

B.P.King	lbw b Timms	6
R.Howorth	c O'Brien b Merritt	54
E.Cooper	b Herbert	21
H.H.I.Gibbons	not out	212
S.H.Martin	c Nelson b Herbert	46
Mr C.H.Palmer	b Timms	132
*Hon.C.J.Lyttelton	b Herbert	54
Mr A.F.T.White	not out	10
Extras	(B 7, LB 4)	11
Total	(6 wickets, declared)	**546**

Fall: 1st inns 1/16, 2/64, 3/88, 4/192, 5/453, 6/527.
R.O.Jenkins, R.T.D.Perks and †H.Yarnold did not bat.

NORTHAMPTONSHIRE

H.W.Greenwood	b Perks	4	c Yarnold b Martin	7
P.Davis	c Yarnold b Martin	45	c Lyttelton b Perks	18
D.Brookes	b Perks	12	not out	111
J.E.Timms	c Martin b Howorth	51	b Perks	12
*Mr R.P.Nelson	c & b Howorth	10	(8) not out	15
†K.C.James	c Yarnold b Howorth	57	(5) b Perks	3
F.P.O'Brien	c & b Howorth	8	(7) c & b Jenkins	26
M.E.F.Dunkley	lbw b Howorth	10		
W.E.Merritt	lbw b Jenkins	71	(6) c Howorth b Jenkins	21
R.J.Partridge	not out	18		
E.J.Herbert	run out	7		
Extras	(B 2, LB 10, W 4, NB 2)	18	(LB 5)	5
Total		**311**	(6 wickets)	**218**

Fall: 1st inns 1/10, 2/47, 3/71, 4/122, 5/130, 6/145, 7/182, 8/254, 9/296.
2nd inns 1/23, 2/25, 3/40, 4/44, 5/93, 6/178.

NORTHANTS	O	M	R	W
Partridge	19	0	104	0
Timms	15	0	85	2
Herbert	27	6	101	3
Merritt	15	0	114	1
Nelson	18	1	82	0
O'Brien	4	0	28	0
Davis	4	0	21	0

WORCESTERSHIRE	O	M	R	W	O	M	R	W
Perks	22	3	71	2	14	0	64	3
Martin	18	3	44	1	11	2	30	1
Jenkins	13	2	41	1	16	1	62	2
Palmer	4	0	24	0	2	0	8	0
Howorth	18.2	1	79	5	10	1	33	0
Lyttelton	4	0	34	0	2	0	16	0

Umpires: J.Hardstaff and E.P.Robinson.

Close of play scores. First day: Worcestershire 546/6 (H.H.I.Gibbons 212*, A.F.T.White 10*). **Second day:** Northamptonshire 183/7 (K.C.James 32*, W.E.Merritt 1*).

Comments: H.H.I.Gibbons and S.H.Martin put on 104 for the 4th wicket. Then H.H.I.Gibbons and C.H.Palmer put on 261 in 150 minutes for Worcestershire's 5th wicket.
C.H.Palmer made his first century in county cricket in only 110 minutes on his first appearance of the season. He hit 19 4's in his 132.
H.H.I.Gibbons 212* was the highest score of his career. He hit 23 4's. It was his maiden double century.
The second day was interrupted by rain.
Northamptonshire followed on 235 behind.
D.Brookes made his third century of the season. His 111* included 12 4's and took 185 minutes.

HAMPSHIRE COUNTY CRICKET CLUB

Standing (left to right): G.Hill, J.Bailey, A.G.Holt, N.T.McCorkell, G.E.M.Heath, L.Harrison, D.F.Walker. Seated: A.E.Pothecary, G.S.Boyes, G.R.Taylor (captain), J.Arnold, W.L.C.Creese.

GLAMORGAN v WORCESTERSHIRE

Played at Cardiff, June 14, 15, 16, 1939.
Toss won by Worcestershire.
Match drawn.

GLAMORGAN

A.H.Dyson .... b Perks 2	st Yarnold b Jenkins 67
D.E.Davies .... lbw b Jenkins 42	lbw b Perks 0
T.L.Brierley .... b Perks 1	b Martin 21
D.Davies .... b Howorth 45	c Cooper b Jenkins 53
*Mr M.J.L.Turnbull b Perks 13	b Howorth 5
C.C.Smart .... c Jenkins b Howorth ...12	b Perks 37
Mr W.Wooller .... c Lyttelton b Howorth...31	c & b Perks 23
E.C.Jones .... st Yarnold b Howorth ...0	lbw b Perks 8
†H.G.Davies .... b Perks 3	b Howorth 4
J.Mercer .... not out 4	not out 45
P.F.Judge .... b Perks 1	not out 3
Extras .... (LB 5, NB 2) 7	(B 8, LB 4, NB 3) 15
Total **161**	**(9 wickets)** **281**

Fall: 1st inns 1/2, 2/6, 3/85, 4/101, 5/121, 6/122, 7/122, 8/129, 9/158.
2nd inns 1/1, 2/30, 3/117, 4/135, 5/173 6/212, 7/226, 8/233, 9/237.

WORCESTERSHIRE

B.P.King .... b Judge 0
R.Howorth .... c & b Wooller 56
E.Cooper............ c H.Davies b Mercer 41
H.H.I.Gibbons ...... lbw b Smart 34
S.H.Martin.......... b Mercer 8
Mr C.H.Palmer ...... b Judge 128
*Hon C.J.Lyttelton b Smart 0
†H.Yarnold .... b Wooller 40
Mr A.F.T.White ..... b Smart 47
R.O.Jenkins .... not out 5
R.T.D.Perks .... lbw b Judge 7
Extras .... (B 14, LB 6, W 2) 22
Total **388**

Fall: 1st inns 1/6, 2/107, 3/109, 4/138, 5/183, 6/183, 7/284, 8/365, 9/381.

WORCESTERSHIRE	O	M	R	W	O	M	R	W
Perks	18.2	4	65	5	16	0	72	4
Martin	6	3	11	0	21	6	49	1
Howorth	17	1	68	4	20	4	100	2
Jenkins	5	1	10	1	11	0	45	2

GLAMORGAN	O	M	R	W
Mercer	23	1	86	2
Judge	17	2	84	3
E.Davies	7	1	19	0
Wooller	30	0	123	2
Smart	10	1	38	3
Jones	3	0	16	0

Umpires: A.Dolphin and E.P.Robinson.

Close of play scores. First day: Worcestershire 189/6 (C.H.Palmer 27*, H.Yarnold 2*). **Second day:** Worcestershire 388 all out.

Comments: C.H.Palmer scored his second consecutive century. His 128 included 17 4's.
R.Howarth and E.Cooper put on 101 for the 2nd wicket. C.H.Palmer and H.Yarnold added 101 for the 7th wicket.
Rain curtailed the second day's play and also prevented play beginning until 1.15pm on the third day.
The Glamorgan last pair, J.Mercer and P.F.Judge came together with their side only 10 runs ahead and with 30 minutes play remaining. They hit 44 runs in 10 minutes to save the game for their side.
J.Mercer hit 31 off a Howorth over, (6, 2, 4, 6, 0, 6, 6, 1), making 41 out of the last 44 scored in a mere ten minutes.

HAMPSHIRE v NOTTINGHAMSHIRE

Played at Portsmouth, June 14, 15, 16, 1939.
Toss won by Nottinghamshire.
Match drawn.

NOTTINGHAMSHIRE

W.W.Keeton .... c Mackenzie b Boyes 77
C.B.Harris .... c Boyes b Heath 43
*Mr G.F.H.Heane ... c & b Hill 138
J.Hardstaff .... c McCorkell b Steele 37
G.V.Gunn .... not out 100
R.J.Giles .... c Creese b Boyes 18
W.Voce.............. c Hill b Steele 1
J.Knowles .... not out...................14
Extras............. (B 5, LB 12, W 1)........18
Total .... **(6 wickets, declared)** **446**

Fall: 1st inns 1/95, 2/186, 3/251, 4/370, 5/418, 6/421.

A.Jepson, †A.B.Wheat and H.J.Butler did not bat.

HAMPSHIRE

†N.T.McCorkell ..... c Voce b Jepson 25
A.G.Holt .... c Voce b Butler 10
A.E.Pothecary ...... b Butler 73
J.Arnold .... lbw b Voce 81
W.L.C.Creese .... not out 4
P.A.Mackenzie ...... not out 0
Extras............. (B 2, LB 8, W 1, NB 2) ...13
Total .... **(4 wickets)** **206**

Fall: 1st inns 1/12, 2/70, 3/190, 4/205.

*Mr G.R.Taylor, Revd J.W.J.Steele, G.S.Boyes, G.Hill and G.E.M.Heath did not bat.

HAMPSHIRE	O	M	R	W
Heath	23	3	63	1
Steele	34	1	155	2
Hill	29	2	98	1
Mackenzie	4	0	26	0
Boyes	14	1	57	2
Creese	3	0	29	0

NOTTINGHAMSHIRE	O	M	R	W
Voce	14	2	62	1
Butler	16	2	57	2
Harris	1	0	1	0
Jepson	8	1	17	1
Giles	12	1	32	0
Gunn	7	1	24	0

Umpires: F.J.Durston and F.Chester.

Close of play scores. First day: Nottinghamshire 300/3 (G.F.H.Heane 101*, G.V.Gunn 29*). **Second day:** Hampshire 206/4 (W.L.C.Creese 4*, P.A.Mackenzie 0*).

Comments: There was no play on the third day.
It was G.F.H.Heane's second century of the season. His 138 included ten 4's.
G.V.Gunn made an undefeated 100, which included a 6 and eight 4's.
G.F.H.Heane and G.V.Gunn added 119 for the 4th wicket.
J.Arnold and A.E.Pothecary added 120 runs for Hampshire's 3rd wicket in 90 minutes.

LANCASHIRE v SUSSEX

Played at Liverpool, June 14, 15, 16, 1939.
Toss won by Lancashire.
No result.

LANCASHIRE
*Mr W.H.L.Lister, J.Iddon, E.Paynter, J.L.Hopwood, C.Washbrook, N.Oldfield, A.E.Nutter, †W.Farrimond, L.L.Wilkinson, W.E.Phillipson and R.Pollard.

SUSSEX
*Flt-Lt A.J.Holmes, John Langridge, James Langridge, J.H.Parks, H.W.Parks, G.Cox, †W.L.Cornford, J.H.Cornford, C.Oakes, J.Oakes and J.K.Nye.

Umpires: G.M.Lee and F.Walden.

Comments: No play was possible in this match owing to rain.

Although he won his first England cap in 1939, for batsman Norman Oldfield, the outbreak of war meant the end of his Lancashire career after 151 appearances. After the war, however, Oldfield reappeared for Northants, for whom he made 159 appearances before becoming a first-class umpire.

SURREY v DERBYSHIRE

Played at Guildford, June 14, 15, 1939.
Toss won by Derbyshire.
Derbyshire won by an innings and 43 runs.

DERBYSHIRE
D.Smith	c & b Berry	34
A.E.Alderman	c Brooks b Gover	49
T.S.Worthington	c Berry b Parker	37
L.F.Townsend	b Parker	12
G.H.Pope	c Watts b Parker	24
A.E.G.Rhodes	b Parker	0
*T.D.Hounsfield	c Fishlock b Parker	4
A.V.Pope	b Brown	41
†H.Elliott	c Gover b Parker	5
T.R.Armstrong	not out	8
W.H.Copson	c McIntyre b Gover	25
Extras	(B 3, LB 3, NB 2)	8
Total		**247**

Fall: 1st inns 1/76, 2/100, 3/138, 4/145, 5/149, 6/157, 7/172, 8/198, 9/214.

SURREY
L.B.Fishlock	c Armstrong b A.V.Pope	8	b Copson	0
J.S.Squires	c G.H.Pope b Copson	5	c Alderman b G.H.Pope	7
T.H.Barling	c Worthington b Copson	7	c Elliott b Rhodes	29
J.F.Parker	b Copson	5	c Elliott b Rhodes	5
A.J.W.McIntyre	lbw b Copson	0	b G.H.Pope	17
*Mr H.M.Garland-Wells	c Rhodes b A.V.Pope	15	c Elliott b Rhodes	0
Mr F.R.Brown	c Armstrong b A.V.Pope	26	b G.H.Pope	12
E.A.Watts	c G.H.Pope b A.V.Pope	1	b G.H.Pope	7
F.Berry	c Copson b A.V.Pope	4	b G.H.Pope	0
†E.W.J.Brooks	c Alderman b A.V.Pope	0	c G.H.Pope b Copson	27
A.R.Gover	not out	3	not out	12
Extras	(LB 3)	3	(LB 10, NB 1)	11
Total		**77**		**127**

Fall: 1st inns 1/9, 2/13, 3/23, 4/23, 5/38, 6/50, 7/59, 8/74, 9/74.
2nd inns 1/4, 2/17, 3/22, 4/68, 5/68, 6/68, 7/81, 8/81, 9/94.

SURREY	O	M	R	W
Gover	10.1	0	48	2
Watts	8	0	44	0
Brown	10	0	67	1
Berry	7	0	26	1
Garland-Wells	2	0	14	0
Parker	15	3	34	6
Squires	2	0	6	0

DERBYSHIRE	O	M	R	W	O	M	R	W
Copson	11	1	30	4	7.1	1	12	2
A.V.Pope	10.3	2	44	6	10	3	23	0
G.H.Pope	-	-	-	-	11	3	46	5
Rhodes	-	-	-	-	8	1	35	3

Umpires: J.J.Hills and H.Cruice.

Close of play scores. First day: Surrey 38/4 (J.F.Parker 5*, H.M.Garland-Wells 10*).

Comments: The match was over by 3.45pm on the second day.
Play on the first day was interrupted by rain and bad light.
J.F.Parker had a spell of five wickets for ten runs on the first day.
A.V.Pope and W.H.Copson bowled unchanged in Surrey's 1st innings, Surrey followed on 170 behind.

YORKSHIRE v NORTHAMPTONSHIRE

Played at Headingley, Leeds, June 14, 15, 16, 1939.
Toss won by Northamptonshire.
Match drawn.

NORTHAMPTONSHIRE

P.Davis	c Verity b Bowes	7
H.W.Greenwood	b Bowes	0
D.Brookes	b Bowes	31
J.E.Timms	c Smailes b Robinson	92
*Mr R.P.Nelson	c Hutton b Verity	14
†K.C.James	lbw b Robinson	4
F.P.O'Brien	c Wood b Smailes	4
W.E.Merritt	b Bowes	9
M.E.F.Dunkley	b Bowes	5
R.J.Partridge	b Bowes	0
E.J.Herbert	not out	9
Extras	(B 1, LB 4)	5
Total		**180**

Fall: 1st inns 1/0, 2/20, 3/68, 4/97, 5/101, 6/130, 7/143, 8/153, 9/153.

YORKSHIRE

H.Sutcliffe	c James b Timms	5
L.Hutton	c Merritt b Partridge	3
A.Mitchell	not out	102
W.Barber	b Partridge	5
Mr N.W.D.Yardley	c Greenwood b Partridge	4
*Mr A.B.Sellers	c James b Merritt	27
T.F.Smailes	c Herbert b Timms	27
†A.Wood	c O'Brien b Herbert	19
E.P.Robinson	b Merritt	6
Extras	(B 4, LB 5)	9
Total	(8 wickets)	**207**

Fall: 1st inns 1/8, 2/14, 3/23, 4/47, 5/110, 6/178, 7/201, 8/207.

H.Verity and W.E.Bowes did not bat.

YORKSHIRE	O	M	R	W
Bowes	20	3	57	6
Smailes	15	2	46	1
Verity	18	3	47	1
Robinson	11.2	2	25	2

NORTHANTS	O	M	R	W
Partridge	17	3	48	3
Timms	12	2	44	2
Herbert	14	2	37	1
Merritt	9.3	1	59	2
Nelson	4	0	10	0

Umpires: J.Hardstaff and H.Elliott.

Close of play scores. First day: Yorkshire 5/0 (H.Sutcliffe 3*, L.Hutton 1*).
Second day: Yorkshire 207/8 (A.Mitchell 102*).

Comments: Bad weather constantly interrupted this match. Play finished early on the first day and did not begin on the second day until 3pm.
There was no play on the third day.
A.Mitchell hit 11 4's in his undefeated 102, made in just over three hours.

DERBYSHIRE v LANCASHIRE

Played at Buxton, June 17, 19, 20, 1939.
Toss won by Derbyshire.
Match drawn.

DERBYSHIRE

A.E.Alderman	b Pollard	20
D.Smith	c Wilkinson b Pollard	0
T.S.Worthington	c Farrimond b Paynter	101
L.F.Townsend	c Farrimond b Paynter	92
G.H.Pope	b Nutter	22
A.E.G.Rhodes	b Pollard	72
*Mr T.D.Hounsfield	c Nutter b Wilkinson	23
A.V.Pope	b Wilkinson	17
†H.Elliott	run out	0
T.R.Armstrong	b Pollard	2
W.H.Copson	not out	1
Extras	(B 3, LB 2, W 1)	6
Total		**356**

Fall: 1st inns 1/1, 2/36, 3/181, 4/215, 5/294, 6/325, 7/349, 8/353, 9/354.

LANCASHIRE

C.Washbrook	c Elliott b G.H.Pope	31
E.Paynter	st Elliott b Townsend	98
J.L.Hopwood	lbw b Rhodes	0
N.Oldfield	c Alderman b A.V.Pope	59
J.Iddon	lbw b A.V.Pope	44
A.E.Nutter	not out	23
*Mr W.H.L.Lister	lbw b Rhodes	0
†W.Farrimond	lbw b Rhodes	4
R.Pollard	not out	4
Extras	(B 2, LB 2)	4
Total	(7 wickets)	**267**

Fall: 1st inns 1/90, 2/95, 3/149, 4/219, 5/254, 6/254, 7/262.

J.Briggs and L.L.Wilkinson did not bat.

LANCASHIRE	O	M	R	W
Pollard	27.2	4	80	4
Nutter	22	3	73	1
Briggs	15	1	57	0
Wilkinson	16	0	63	2
Iddon	13	1	57	0
Paynter	6	0	20	2

DERBYSHIRE	O	M	R	W
Copson	13	1	41	0
A.V.Pope	17	4	57	2
H.H.Pope	10	0	56	1
Rhodes	11	2	38	3
Armstrong	11	1	54	0
Townsend	10	1	17	1

Umpires: H.G.Baldwin and C.N.Woolley.

Close of play scores. First day: Derbyshire 294/5 (A.E.G.Rhodes 53*, T.D.Hounsfield 0*).

Comments: Rain prevented any play on the third day.
T.S.Worthington and L.F.Townsend added 145 for the 3rd Derbyshire wicket.
T.S.Worthington made 101 in 255 minutes, including one 6 and nine 4's.

GLAMORGAN v KENT

Played at Neath, June 17, 19, 1939.
Toss won by Glamorgan.
Kent won by nine wickets.

GLAMORGAN

A.H.Dyson	lbw b Todd	33	c Fagg b Todd 12
H.D.Davies	lbw b Wright	51	b Harding 4
T.L.Brierley	c Dovey b Todd	34	c Foster b Todd 6
D.Davies	c Levett b Wright	5	c Valentine b Wright 1
*Mr M.J.L.Turnbull	c Levett b Todd	5	(6) b Todd 5
C.C.Smart	c Levett b Wright	15	(5) b Wright 5
E.C.Jones	c Levett b Watt	1	not out 28
†H.G.Davies	b Wright	43	b Wright 10
Mr J.C.Clay	st Levett b Watt	4	b Todd 4
J.Mercer	b Watt	0	b Wright 4
P.F.Judge	not out	12	c Watt b Wright 27
Extras	(B 7, LB 6, NB 1)	14	(B 8, LB 3, NB 1) 12
Total		**217**	**118**

Fall: 1st inns 1/82, 2/126, 3/126, 4/137, 5/143, 6/154, 7/186, 8/201, 9/202.
2nd inns 1/12, 2/19, 3/28, 4/28, 5/39, 6/39, 7/49, 8/56, 9/61.

KENT

A.E.Fagg	b Mercer	82	not out 36
†Mr W.H.V.Levett	c Dyson c Mercer	25	st H.Davies b Clay........16
L.E.G.Ames	b Clay	12	not out 31
R.R.Dovey	lbw b Clay	0	
*Mr B.H.Valentine	b Mercer	17	
L.J.Todd	run out	15	
Mr P.G.Foster	b Mercer	57	
P.R.Spencer	c Dyson b E.Davies	18	
D.V.P.Wright	c H.Davies b Judge	2	
N.W.Harding	lbw b Judge	0	
A.E.Watt	not out	4	
Extras	(B 12, LB 4)	16	(B 4, LB 1) 5
Total		**248**	(1 wicket) **88**

Fall: 1st inns 1/90, 2/119, 3/121, 4/122, 5/150, 6/169, 7/225, 8/230, 9/230.
2nd inns 1/34.

KENT	O	M	R	W	O	M	R	W
Harding	4	3	5	0	7	2	17	1
Todd	18	6	46	3	13	1	32	4
Watt	11.3	2	25	4	4	1	6	0
Wright	23	3	85	3	12.5	1	51	5
Dovey	6	0	42	0				

GLAMORGAN	O	M	R	W	O	M	R	W
Mercer	20.5	3	75	4	5	1	15	0
Judge	11	1	29	2	7	1	11	0
E.Davies	17	4	48	1	4.2	0	19	0
Clay	21	4	60	2	5	0	24	1
Smart	4	0	17	0				
Jones	1	0	3	0	2	0	14	0

Umpires: J.Smart and H.Cruice.

Close of play scores. First day: Kent 122/4 (B.H.Valentine 1*).

Comments: The game was completed in two days.
W.H.V.Levett caught five batsmen in succession and stumped a sixth in Glamorgan's 1st innings. This equalled both the record for most dismissals in an innings against Glamorgan and the Kent wicketkeeping record for most dismissals in an innings.
H.G.Davies hit 43 out of 47 in 25 minutes in Glamorgan's 1st innings, striking two 6's and six 4's.
A.H.Dyson was recalled on two occasions in the 1st innings, after believing he had been dismissed.
P.F.Judge and E.C.Jones almost doubled their side's 2nd innings total with a last-wicket partnership of 57, after 9 wickets had fallen for 61.

NORTHAMPTONSHIRE v MIDDLESEX

Played at Northampton, June 17, 19, 20, 1939.
Toss won by Northamptonshire.
Middlesex won by seven wickets.

NORTHAMPTONSHIRE

H.W.Greenwood	lbw b Sims	11	lbw b Sims 24
P.Davis	c Price b Sims	74	c Price b Sims 80
D.Brookes	st Price b Sims	25	b Edrich 23
J.E.Timms	lbw b Sims	1	not out 120
*Mr R.P.Nelson	run out	2	c L.Compton b Sims 15
†K.C.James	c Price b Sims	12	b Gray 23
W.E.Merritt	c Edrich b D.Compton	59	c Price b Gray 5
M.E.F.Dunkley	st Price b Sims	14	b Sims 12
Mr S.M.Nasiruddin	b Sims	12	run out 0
R.J.Partridge	not out	1	c L.Compton b Sims 21
E.J.Herbert	lbw b Peebles	0	not out 3
Extras	(B 4, LB 6, NB 1)	11	(B 10, LB 6, NB 1) 17
Total		**222**	(9 wickets, declared)......**343**

Fall: 1st inns 1/24, 2/65, 3/69, 4/77, 5/107, 6/190, 7/190, 8/216, 9/221.
2nd inns 1/54, 2/90, 3/198, 4/226, 5/263, 6/273, 7/299, 8/306, 9/333.

MIDDLESEX

J.D.B.Robertson	run out	21	b Nelson 144
S.M.Brown	c Greenwood b Timms	9	b Nelson 24
W.J.Edrich	c Nelson b Timms	81	b Merritt 7
D.C.S.Compton	b Timms	47	not out 111
J.H.A.Hulme	b Partridge	3	not out 2
A.Thompson	c Herbert b Partridge	38	
†W.F.F.Price	b Partridge	6	
L.H.Compton	c Davis b Merritt	24	
J.M.Sims	c Greenwood b Herbert	24	
*Mr I.A.R.Peebles	c Partridge b Merritt	10	
L.H.Gray	not out	0	
Extras	(B 13, LB 3, NB 1)	17	
Total		**280**	(3 wickets) **288**

Fall: 1st inns 1/23, 2/41, 3/95, 4/98, 5/204, 6/215, 7/220, 8/270, 9/280.
2nd inns 1/89, 2/102, 3/282.

MIDDLESEX	O	M	R	W	O	M	R	W
Gray	10	0	47	0	20	2	66	2
Edrich	3	0	4	0	12	0	41	1
Sims	27	2	79	7	35	4	145	5
Peebles	11.5	2	27	1	17	4	47	0
D.Compton	17	6	32	1	12	2	27	0
Robertson	9	2	22	0				

NORTHANTS	O	M	R	W	O	M	R	W
Partridge	27	6	66	3	13	0	79	0
Timms	21	5	55	3	4.4	0	48	0
Nelson	13	1	51	0	8	1	56	2
Merritt	15	1	58	2	4	0	28	1
Herbert	14.5	5	33	1	12	0	77	0

Umpires: C.W.L.Parker and A.Skelding.

Close of Play Scores. First day: Middlesex 91/2 (W.J.Edrich 17*, D.C.S.Compton 43*). **Second day:** Northamptonshire 177/2 (P.Davis 76*, J.E.Timms 42*).
Comments: W.J.Edrich and A.Thompson added 106 for the Middlesex 5th wicket in their 1st innings.
In their 2nd innings, J.E.Timms and P.Davis added 108 for Northants 3rd wicket. J.E.TImms made 120* in 250 minutes, hitting six 4's.
Middlesex were set 286 to win in 180 minutes, winning with 20 minutes to spare.
J.D.B.Robertson hit his first championship century. It took only 95 minutes and contained 20 4's. His 144 took 155 minutes.
D.C.S.Compton's century was made in 82 minutes, at that time the quickest of the season. He hit R.J.Partridge for 22 in one over. His innings of 111 included 13 4's.
J.D.B.Robertson and D.C.S.Compton hit 180 in 90 minutes for the 3rd wicket.

NOTTINGHAMSHIRE v YORKSHIRE

Played at Trent Bridge, Nottingham, June 17, 19, 20, 1939.
Toss won by Yorkshire.
Match drawn.

YORKSHIRE

H.Sutcliffe	c & b Butler	71	b Jepson	15
L.Hutton	c Jepson b Giles	26	lbw b Butler	3
A.Mitchell	b Jepson	6	b Butler	20
M.Leyland	c & b Voce	15	lbw b Jepson	0
W.Barber	run out	72	c Gunn b Voce	17
Mr N.W.D.Yardley	lbw b Jepson	7	lbw b Butler	0
*Mr A.B.Sellers	c Wheat b Jepson	2	c Voce b Jepson	30
†A.Wood	b Voce	10	c Wheat b Jepson	13
T.F.Smailes	not out	14	c Keeton b Jepson	3
H.Verity	b Butler	10	c & b Jepson	1
W.E.Bowes	c Wheat b Butler	0	not out	1
Extras	(LB 9, NB 2)	11	(LB 4, NB 1)	5
Total		**244**		**108**

Fall: 1st inns 1/50, 2/63, 3/83, 4/152, 5/174, 6/180, 7/208, 8/219, 9/244.
2nd inns 1/6, 2/26, 3/26, 4/42, 5/42, 6/62, 7/99, 8/106, 9/107.

NOTTINGHAMSHIRE

W.W.Keeton	c Sellers b Smailes	10	lbw b Bowes	1
C.B.Harris	b Smailes	1	b Bowes	2
*Mr G.F.H.Heane	c Mitchell b Bowes	19	(5) not out	0
J.Hardstaff	run out	7	lbw b Smailes	0
G.V.Gunn	lbw b Bowes	8		
J.Knowles	b Smailes	8	(3) lbw b Bowes	0
R.J.Giles	b Bowes	18		
W.Voce	not out	37		
†A.B.Wheat	lbw b Bowes	1		
H.J.Butler	b Verity	4		
A.Jepson	b Bowes	2		
Extras	(B 1, LB 4)	5		
Total		**120**	(4 wickets)	**3**

Fall: 1st inns 1/9, 2/28, 3/34, 4/45, 5/50, 6/59, 7/80, 8/88, 9/97.
2nd inns 1/2, 2/2, 3/3, 4/3.

NOTTINGHAMSHIRE	O	M	R	W	O	M	R	W
Voce	22	6	50	2	8	1	30	1
Butler	22.4	5	55	3	13	3	33	3
Jepson	16	1	49	3	11	2	27	6
Giles	17	1	45	1	5	1	13	0
Gunn	12	2	34	0				

YORKSHIRE	O	M	R	W	O	M	R	W
Bowes	18.6	8	29	5	3.6	3	0	3
Yardley	9	2	15	0				
Smailes	8	1	28	3	3	1	3	1
Verity	9	3	37	1				
Hutton	1	0	6	0				

Umpires: D.Hendren and F.I.Walden.

Close of play scores. First day: Nottinghamshire 9/0 (W.W.Keeton 6*, C.B.Harris 1*). **Second day:** Nottinghamshire 3/4 (G.F.H.Heane (0*).

Comments: W.Voce's benefit match. He was given the honour of tossing for innings. H.Sutcliffe reached his 1,000 runs for the season, when he had scored 41 in Yorkshire's 1st innings. He was the third player to do so in 1939, having achieved this target in every season since 1919. There was no play on the final day, due to rain. W.E.Bowes took three wickets for no runs in 30 balls in Nottinghamshire's 2nd innings.
Yorkshire became the first county to field nine Test players in their side.

SURREY v ESSEX

Played at Kennington Oval, June 17, 19, 20, 1939.
Toss won by Surrey.
Match drawn.

ESSEX

L.C.Eastman	c Watts b Gover	2	(2) lbw b Watts	11
A.V.Avery	retired hurt	11	absent hurt	0
†T.H.Wade	lbw b Gover	8	c Watts b Gover	4
J.O'Connor	c Fishlock b Parker	8	b Gover	78
M.S.Nichols	not out	52	lbw b Gover	23
R.M.Taylor	c Garland-Wells b Squires	0	c Brooks b Gover	23
Mr A.B.Lavers	b Squires	18	b Watts	13
*Mr F.St.G.Unwin	b Gover	33	lbw b Watts	2
Capt J.W.A.Stephenson	b Gover	5	not out	25
R.Smith	c Berry b Watts	8	(1) b Watts	47
T.P.B.Smith	c Gregory b Watts	5	(10) st Brooks b Squires	14
Extras	(B 5, W 1)	6	(B 4, LB 2, NB 2)	8
Total		**156**		**248**

Fall: 1st inns 1/2, 2/18, 3/37, 4/38, 5/64, 6/131, 7/139, 8/150, 9/156.
2nd inns 1/15, 2/21, 3/105, 4/153, 5/168, 6/188, 7/196, 8/211, 9/248.

SURREY

R.J.Gregory	c Stephenson b R.Smith	18	c Nichols b P.Smith	37
L.B.Fishlock	c Eastman b R.Smith	6	c Unwin b Eastman	16
H.S.Squires	c Unwin b R.Smith	2	c R.Smith b P.Smith	0
T.H.Barling	c Unwin b R.Smith	19	lbw b P.Smith	34
J.F.Parker	c R.Smith b Nichols	49	(6) not out	17
A.J.W.McIntyre	lbw b Taylor	6	(7) not out	13
*Mr H.M.Garland-Wells	st Wade b P.Smith	4		
E.A.Watts	lbw b Taylor	3		
F.Berry	c O'Connor b Taylor	3		
†E.W.J.Brooks	lbw b Taylor	0	(5) c O'Connor b P.Smith	18
A.R.Gover	not out	0		
Extras		0	(B 5, LB 6)	11
Total		**110**	(5 wickets)	**146**

Fall: 1st inns 1/14, 2/20, 3/31, 4/50, 5/68, 6/75, 7/86, 8/100, 9/110.
2nd inns 1/46, 2/46, 3/54, 4/113, 5/116.

SURREY	O	M	R	W	O	M	R	W
Gover	13	0	38	4	16	1	85	4
Watts	6.4	0	26	2	16	2	51	4
Berry	4	1	5	0	6	1	15	0
Parker	9	3	18	1	10	0	35	0
Squires	15	1	39	2	12.2	0	45	1
Garland-Wells	6	1	13	0	3	1	9	0
Gregory	2	0	11	0				

ESSEX	O	M	R	W	O	M	R	W
Nichols	6.2	2	14	1	14	3	40	0
R.Smith	9	1	40	4	6	1	21	0
Stephenson	4	0	13	0	9	1	18	0
Taylor	7	1	28	4	2	0	9	0
P.Smith	6	0	15	1	13	3	40	4
Eastman	-	-	-	-	2	0	7	1

Umpires: C.V.Tarbox and F.J.Durston.

Close of play scores. First day: Surrey 110/9 (J.F.Parker 49*). **Second day:** Surrey 59/3 (T.H.Barling 4*).

Comments: Essex were put in on a wicket recovering from rain.
F.St.G.Unwin was captaining Essex for the first time.
A.V.Avery retired hurt with a broken finger, hit by a rising ball from Gover.
Rain stopped play early on the third day. There was no play after lunch.
R.M.Taylor was also injured and did not field on the third day.

ESSEX COUNTY CRICKET CLUB

Standing (left to right): Fletcher, T.P.B.Smith, L.C.Eastman, T.H.Wade, R.Smith, A.V.Avery, R.M.Taylor. Seated: M.S.Nichols, J.W.A.Stephenson, D.R.Wilcox, F.St.G.Unwin (captain), J.O'Connor.

SUSSEX v GLOUCESTERSHIRE

Played at Worthing, June 17, 19, 1939.
Toss won by Sussex.
Gloucestershire won by four wickets.

SUSSEX

John G.Langridge	c Crapp b Goddard	19	b Lambert	19
J.H.Parks	c Hopkins b Goddard	31	c Hammond b Goddard	23
H.W.Parks	hit wkt b Sinfield	17	lbw b Scott	16
G.Cox	c Hopkins b Scott	17	lbw b Goddard	11
Jas.Langridge	c Hammond b Sinfield	19	b Scott	0
H.T.Bartlett	b Scott	0	c Barnett b Goddard	30
C.Oakes	b Goddard	5	b Scott	0
*Flt-Lt A.J.Holmes	c Barnett b Scott	71	c Neale b Goddard	13
†W.L.Cornford	lbw b Goddard	2	c & b Goddard	2
J.K.Nye	b Barnett	23	b Scott	4
J.H.Cornford	not out	2	not out	2
Extras	(B 5, LB 11, NB 3)	19	(LB 2, NB 2)	4
Total		**225**		**124**

Fall: 1st inns 1/32, 2/66, 3/78, 4/98, 5/98, 6/105, 7/161, 8/164, 9/222.
2nd inns 1/42, 2/46, 3/69, 4/69, 5/73, 6/74, 7/107, 8/117, 9/122.

GLOUCESTERSHIRE

C.J.Barnett	c & b Jas.Langridge	24	c Nye b J.Cornford	14
R.A.Sinfield	c J.Cornford b Nye	1	c W.Cornford b Nye	5
V.Hopkins	lbw b J.Parks	13	not out	83
*Mr W.R.Hammond	c Cox b Nye	33	b Nye	8
J.F.Crapp	not out	89	b J.Parks	14
G.M.Emmett	c J.Parks b Nye	3	lbw b Jas.Langridge	12
W.L.Neale	c J.Cornford b J.Parks	2	c sub b Bartlett	15
†E.A.Wilson	b J.Parks	1	not out	4
C.J.Scott	b J.Parks	9		
G.E.E.Lambert	c J.Parks b J.Cornford	5		
T.W.J.Goddard	c Oakes b Jas.Langridge	3		
Extras	(B 6, LB 1, NB 1)	8	(B 1, LB 5, NB 1)	7
Total		**191**	(6 wickets)	**162**

Fall: 1st inns 1/9, 2/37, 3/41, 4/91, 5/110, 6/116, 7/118, 8/152, 9/176.
2nd inns 1/16, 2/32, 3/40, 4/65, 5/98, 6/158.

GLOUCESTERSHIRE	O	M	R	W	O	M	R	W
Scott	16	2	58	3	8	0	25	4
Barnett	7.2	1	14	1	3	1	6	0
Goddard	22	6	86	4	11.3	1	53	5
Sinfield	10	0	48	2				
Lambert	-	-	-	-	8	2	36	1

SUSSEX	O	M	R	W	O	M	R	W
J.Cornford	19	4	51	1	6	0	46	1
Nye	18	2	48	3	9	1	47	2
J.Parks	16	7	33	4	10	1	29	1
Jas.Langridge	13.1	1	44	2	8	2	28	1
Oakes	3	0	7	0				
Bartlett	-	-	-	-	4	0	5	1

Umpires: J.J.Hills and F.Chester.

Close of play scores. First day: Gloucestershire 110/5 (J.F.Crapp 33*).
Comments: The game finished inside two days.
V.Hopkins, 83*, made his highest score of the season.
A.J.Holmes, the Sussex captain, did not field in Gloucester's 2nd innings, having suffered a strain whilst batting.

WARWICKSHIRE v WORCESTERSHIRE

Played at Edgbaston, Birmingham, June 17, 19, 20, 1939.
Toss won by Worcestershire.
Match drawn.

WORCESTERSHIRE

R.Howorth	lbw b Mayer	20	c Hollies b Mayer	10
B.P.King	c Grove b Mayer	8	b Grove	16
E.Cooper	c Croom b Grove	48	lbw b Mayer	2
H.H.I.Gibbons	c Grove b Mayer	0	lbw b Mayer	2
S.H.Martin	c Ord b Grove	16	c Croom b Wilmot	28
Mr C.H.Palmer	b Mayer	62	b Mayer	15
*Hon C.J.Lyttelton	b Wilmot	81	(11) not out	6
Mr A.F.T.White	c Buckingham b Mayer	6	(7) b Hollies	17
†H.Yarnold	b Mayer	1	(8) c Croom b Mayer	19
R.T.D.Perks	c Buckingham b Wilmot	19	c Hollies b Grove	2
R.O.Jenkins	not out	7	(9) b Grove	30
Extras	(B 1, LB 2)	3	(B 4, LB 4)	8
Total		**271**		**153**

Fall: 1st inns 1/17, 2/40, 3/40, 4/67, 5/115, 6/200, 7/230, 8/236, 9/248.
2nd inns 1/13, 2/19, 3/19, 4/31, 5/60, 6/95, 7/97, 8/141, 9/145.

WARWICKSHIRE

A.J.W.Croom	run out	0	b Perks	17
W.A.Hill	c & b Martin	5	not out	35
†J.Buckingham	b Perks	32		
H.E.Dollery	b Martin	70	(3) not out	18
J.S.Ord	c Cooper b Martin	56		
N.A.Shortland	b Perks	3		
*Mr P.Cranmer	b Perks	1		
K.Wilmot	not out	52		
J.H.Mayer	c & b Perks	10		
C.W.Grove	b Perks	5		
W.E.Hollies	c Howorth b Perks	4		
Extras	(B 8, LB 3, NB 2)	13		0
Total		**246**	(1 wicket)	**70**

Fall: 1st inns 1/4, 2/9, 3/79, 4/154, 5/158, 6/160, 7/218, 8/239, 9/240.
2nd inns 1/42.

WARWICKSHIRE	O	M	R	W	O	M	R	W
Mayer	25	3	86	6	19	2	69	5
Grove	20	1	71	2	15	3	36	3
Wilmot	14.5	3	46	2	6	1	13	1
Hollies	16	1	58	0	9	1	27	1
Cranmer	2	1	7	0				

WORCESTERSHIRE	O	M	R	W	O	M	R	W
Perks	28	7	55	6	6	0	34	1
Martin	32	5	93	3	5	0	36	0
Lyttelton	1	0	5	0				
Howorth	16	1	58	0				
Jenkins	8	0	22	0				

Umpires: A.Dolphin and E.P.Robinson.

Close of play scores. First day: Warwickshire 27/2 (J.Buckingham 10*, H.E.Dollery 4*). **Second day:** Worcestershire 54/4 (S.H.Martin 11*, C.H.Palmer 15*).

Comments: Rain interfered with play on the third day with Warwickshire needing to make 179 in 120 minutes.

DERBYSHIRE v LEICESTERSHIRE

Played at Queen's Park, Chesterfield, June 21, 22, 23, 1939.
Toss won by Leicestershire.
Derbyshire won by nine wickets.

LEICESTERSHIRE

G.L.Berry	not out	58	lbw b Copson	4
G.S.Watson	b A.V.Pope	6	c Alderman b G.H.Pope	13
N.F.Armstrong	b G.H.Pope	15	lbw b G.H.Pope	15
F.T.Prentice	lbw b Copson	3	c G.H.Pope b Townsend	1
M.Tompkin	lbw b Copson	0	lbw b G.H.Pope	1
†G.O.Dawkes	b Copson	3	b Townsend	30
*Mr M.St J.Packe	lbw b G.H.Pope	15	not out	48
G.A.Knew	c & b G.H.Pope	0	lbw b Mitchell	1
G.Lester	st Elliott b Mitchell	6	c Worthington b Townsend	2
H.A.Smith	b G.H.Pope	0	c & b Townsend	0
J.Sperry	c Townsend b Mitchell	16	c Alderman b Townsend	2
Extras	(B 1, LB 3)	4	(B 4, LB 3)	7
Total		**126**		**124**

Fall: 1st inns 1/10, 2/39, 3/55, 4/57, 5/61, 6/81, 7/81, 8/104, 9/105.
2nd inns 1/8, 2/32, 3/33, 4/35, 5/36, 6/88, 7/78, 8/96, 9/104.

DERBYSHIRE

D.Smith	c Smith b Prentice	43	b Smith	13
*Mr R.H.R.Buckston	b Smith	4		
T.S.Worthington	c Watson b Sperry	20	not out	13
A.E.Alderman	lbw b Smith	37	(2) not out	27
L.F.Townsend	b Smith	1		
G.H.Pope	lbw b Prentice	4		
A.E.G.Rhodes	c & b Prentice	2		
A.V.Pope	b Smith	65		
†H.Elliott	lbw b Smith	6		
T.B.Mitchell	not out	1		
W.H.Copson	b Sperry	1		
Extras	(B 8, LB 1)	9	(W 1)	1
Total		**197**	(1 wicket)	**54**

Fall: 1st inns 1/7, 2/62, 3/80, 4/85, 5/94, 6/98, 7/140, 8/187, 9/192.
2nd inns 1/23.

DERBYSHIRE	O	M	R	W	O	M	R	W
Copson	10	1	28	3	8	0	24	1
A.V.Pope	13	0	45	1	4	0	12	0
G.H.Pope	8	4	14	4	8	1	19	3
Rhodes	3	0	13	0				
Townsend	1	1	0	0	10.4	0	45	5
Mitchell	3	0	22	2	3	0	17	1

LEICESTERSHIRE	O	M	R	W	O	M	R	W
Sperry	18.1	3	60	2				
Smith	17	3	64	5	7.1	0	25	1
Prentice	18	3	64	3	7	1	28	0

Umpires: C.W.L.Parker and J.Hardstaff.

Close of play scores. First day: Derbyshire 94/5 (A.E.Alderman 16*, A.E.G.Rhodes 0*). **Second day:** Derbyshire 51/1 (T.S.Worthington 13*, A.E.Alderman 24*).

Comments: There were several interruptions for rain and bad light on the first day. Play did not begin on the second day until 2.45pm.
Derbyshire needed only three runs to win on the third day, with nine wickets in hand, having failed to win the game in the extra half-hour on the 2nd day.
It required only one ball on the 3rd day for Derbyshire to win the match.
G.L.Berry carried his bat in Leicestershire's 1st innings with an undefeated 58 in just under 150 minutes.

ESSEX v HAMPSHIRE

Played at Brentwood, June 21, 22, 23, 1939.
Toss won by Hampshire.
Essex won by five wickets.

HAMPSHIRE

†N.T.McCorkell	b R.Smith	5	b R.Smith	10
J.Bailey	lbw b Nichols	6	b Nichols	5
A.G.Holt	c O'Connor b Stephenson	18	b R.Smith	3
J.Arnold	c G.Unwin b Vigar	58	c Wade b Stephenson	18
W.L.Creese	b Vigar	30	c Nichols b Stephenson	21
A.E.Pothecary	c & b Stephenson	75	not out	20
A.Mackenzie	st Wade b P.Smith	22	b R.Smith	0
G.Hill	c Vigar b Nichols	71	lbw b R.Smith	5
G.S.Boyes	st Wade b P.Smith	33	lbw b Nichols	2
*Mr G.R.Taylor	not out	0	b R.Smith	1
R.C.Court	lbw b P.Smith	0	c Stephenson b Nichols	1
Extras	(B 8, LB 3)	11	(B 3, LB 6, NB 1)	10
Total		**329**		**96**

Fall: 1st inns 1/9, 2/13, 3/51, 4/121, 5/122, 6/173, 7/252, 8/327, 9/329.
2nd inns 1/15, 2/17, 3/37, 4/65, 5/66, 6/67, 7/87, 8/92, 9/93.

ESSEX

L.C.Eastman	lbw b Hill	46	c Taylor b Hill	71
R.Smith	c McCorkell b Court	4	c Mackenzie b Court	1
†T.H.Wade	b Court	0	lbw b Court	13
J.O'Connor	lbw b Boyes	122	lbw b Court	0
M.S.Nichols	c McCorkell b Hill	20	not out	36
Mr E.J.Unwin	c McCorkell b Court	2	b Court	12
Mr F.St.G.Unwin	c Boyes b Hill	0	not out	17
Mr A.B.Lavers	c Pothecary b Mackenzie	29		
*Capt.J.W.A.Stephenson	c Taylor b Mackenzie	8		
F.H.Smith	st McCorkell b Boyes	19		
T.P.B.Vigar	not out	11		
Extras	(B 8, LB 3, NB 1)	12	(LB 5)	5
Total		**273**	(5 wickets)	**155**

Fall: 1st inns 1/19, 2/21, 3/57, 4/85, 5/102, 6/103, 7/147, 8/170, 9/234.
2nd inns 1/5, 2/85, 3/85, 4/89, 5/115.

ESSEX	O	M	R	W	O	M	R	W
Nichols	22	3	68	2	12.2	2	35	3
R.Smith	14	2	67	1	15	4	34	5
Stephenson	13	2	29	2	3	1	17	2
T.P.B.Smith	25	2	72	3				
Vigar	13	2	49	2				
Eastman	6	2	21	0				
Lavers	3	0	12	0				

HAMPSHIRE	O	M	R	W	O	M	R	W
Court	19	3	70	3	15.6	1	53	4
Bailey	24	7	56	0	6	1	47	0
Hill	20	5	52	3	8	0	32	1
Boyes	16	7	23	2	9	3	18	0
Mackenzie	14	0	60	2				

Umpires: F.Chester and J.J.Hills.

Close of play scores. First day: Hampshire 311/7 (G.Hill 66*, G.S.Boyes 21*). **Second day:** Essex 273 all out.

Comments: Brentwood cricket week.
J.O'Connor in making 122 in five hours, including 15 4's hit his 4th century of the season. It was his 72nd century for Essex, beating the previous best for the county of 71 centuries by A.C.Russell. He also passed his 1,000 runs for the season.
Essex needed to make 153 in 210 minutes to win.

SOMERSET v KENT

Played at Bath, June 21, 22, 23, 1939.
Toss won by Somerset.
Match drawn.

SOMERSET

F.S.Lee	c Watt b Wright	23	c Foster b Watt	29
H.Gimblett	c Harding b Wright	52	c Spencer b Todd	14
H.T.F.Buse	c Fagg b Wright	3	c Spencer b Wright	0
Mr C.J.P.Barnwell	st Levett b Wright	4	c Fagg b Wright	0
Mr H.D.Burrough	b Wright	25	c Todd b Wright	4
*Mr R.A.Ingle	b Wright	7	st Levett b Wright	3
†W.T.Luckes	c Fagg b Watt	0	c & b Wright	5
W.H.R.Andrews	c Harding b Wright	2	c Fagg b Wright	2
Mr G.M.Bennett	b Wright	0	st Levett b Wright	9
A.W.Wellard	b Wright	6	c Watt b Wright	48
H.L.Hazell	not out	10	not out	0
Extras	(B 3, LB 10)	13	(B 8, LB 7)	15
Total		**145**		**129**

Fall: 1st inns 1/66, 2/72, 3/76, 4/97, 5/120, 6/121, 7/126, 8/126, 9/133.
2nd inns 1/28, 2/29, 3/31, 4/41, 5/51, 6/59, 7/69, 8/73, 9/122.

KENT

A.E.Fagg	b Andrews	39	lbw b Wellard	6
*Mr F.G.H.Chalk	c Wellard b Andrews	23	c Buse b Wellard	3
Mr P.G.Foster	c Gimblett b Andrews	1	b Andrews	29
Mr B.H.Valentine	b Andrews	4	c Luckes b Andrews	4
L.J.Todd	lbw b Andrews	15	not out	8
T.W.Spencer	c Wellard b Buse	33	b Wellard	0
D.V.P.Wright	c Gimblett b Andrews	7	not out	4
N.W.Harding	c Bennett b Andrews	12	run out	4
†Mr W.H.V.Levett	b Buse	23		
A.E.Watt	not out	11	c Lee b Andrews	10
C.Lewis	c Gimblett b Buse	0		
Extras	(LB 8)	8	(B 2, LB 2)	4
Total		**176**	(7 wickets)	**72**

Fall: 1st inns 1/49, 2/51, 3/74, 4/77, 5/108, 6/116, 7/134, 8/159, 9/176.
2nd inns 1/4, 2/9, 3/15, 4/34, 5/46, 6/51, 7/68.

KENT	O	M	R	W	O	M	R	W
Harding	4	0	22	0	3	0	10	0
Watt	11.6	0	45	2	11	1	28	1
Wright	11	3	35	8	17.4	6	45	8

SOMERSET	O	M	R	W	O	M	R	W
Wellard	22	3	53	0	8	1	32	3
Andrews	31	7	56	7	8	1	36	3
Buse	16.6	1	46	3				
Hazell	4	0	13	0				

Umpires: H.Smith and H.Cruice.

Close of play scores. First day: Kent 102/4 (L.J.Todd 14*, P.R.Spencer 13*).
Second day: Somerset 129 all out.

Comments

D.V.P.Wright had career best match figures of 16 for 80. A.W.Wellard, who made 48 in Somerset's 2nd innings, was dropped five times off Wright, four times in the space of five balls, whilst in the 20's. Kent needed 99 to win on the last day but were unable to reach their target with rain reducing play to 75 minutes.
Kent's 2nd innings batting order was altered considerably.

SUSSEX v NOTTINGHAMSHIRE

Played at Worthing, June 21, 22, 23, 1939.
Toss won by Sussex.
Match drawn.

SUSSEX

John G.Langridge	lbw b Butler	1
J.H.Parks	c Wheat b Butler	41
H.W.Parks	b Jepson	11
G.Cox	c Voce b Butler	15
Jas.Langridge	lbw b Jepson	96
*Mr H.T.Bartlett	b Voce	114
Mr R.A.A.Holt	b Butler	8
C.Oakes	c Giles b Butler	75
A.G.Tuppin	lbw b Voce	3
†W.L.Cornford	not out	31
J.K.Nye	lbw b Butler	1
Extras	(B 10, LB 6, W 1)	17
Total		**413**

Fall: 1st inns 1/3, 2/24, 3/45, 4/117, 5/223, 6/238, 7/346, 8/358, 9/411.

NOTTINGHAMSHIRE

W.W.Keeton	c J.Parks b Tuppin	3	not out	96
C.B.Harris	c John Langridge b J.Parks	100	c Bartlett b Tuppin	36
*Mr G.F.H.Heane	lbw b Tuppin	7	c Bartlett b J.Parks	4
J.Hardstaff	c Cornford b Tuppin	6	c Holt b J.Parks	25
G.V.Gunn	c Tuppin b Jas.Langridge	30	c & b Jas.Langridge	61
J.Knowles	lbw b Tuppin	16	run out	21
R.J.Giles	lbw b Tuppin	0	c John Langridge b Nye	0
W.Voce	c John Langridge b Jas.Langridge	15	not out	4
†A.B.Wheat	not out	11		
H.J.Butler	b J.Parks	5		
A.Jepson	c Tuppin b J.Parks	3		
Extras	(LB 1, NB 1)	2	(B 6, LB 1)	7
Total		**198**	(6 wickets)	**254**

Fall: 1st inns 1/3, 2/21, 3/27, 4/80, 5/136, 6/136, 7/179, 8/179, 9/194.
2nd inns 1/53, 2/59, 3/104, 4/202, 5/243, 6/245.

NOTTINGHAMSHIRE	O	M	R	W
Voce	31	6	85	2
Butler	25	4	97	6
Jepson	27	2	84	2
Giles	23	1	97	0
Gunn	7	1	33	0

SUSSEX	O	M	R	W	O	M	R	W
Nye	12	2	42	0	18	3	56	1
Tuppin	19	1	72	5	6	1	29	1
J.Parks	15.7	2	53	3	20	4	59	2
Jas.Langridge	4	0	14	2	21	3	59	1
Oakes	4	0	15	0	8	0	24	0
John Langridge	1	1	0	0	4	1	15	0
Cox	-	-	-	-	2	0	5	0

Umpires: G.Beet and C.V.Tarbox.

Close of play scores. First day: Sussex 346/6 (H.T.Bartlett 114*, C.Oakes 46*).
Second day: Nottinghamshire 74/2 (W.W.Keeton 22*, J.Hardstaff 8*).

Comments

Worthing cricket week.
James Langridge and H.T.Bartlett added 106 for the 5th wicket.
H.T.Bartlett hit 12 4's in his 114 having batted nearly 180 minutes. He reached his century in 175 minutes.
C.B.Harris made exactly 100, which included one 6 and ten 4's. Nottinghamshire followed on 215 behind.
There was no play before lunch on the third day, enabling the visitors to escape with a draw.

WORCESTERSHIRE v LANCASHIRE

Played at Worcester, June 21, 22, 23, 1939.
Toss won by Worcestershire.
Lancashire won by seven wickets.

WORCESTERSHIRE

R.Howorth	b Phillipson 0	c Phillipson b Pollard 24	
B.P.King	c Nutter b Phillipson 10	c Iddon b Nutter 14	
E.Cooper	c Wilkinson b Pollard 0	c Wilkinson b Phillipson 56	
H.H.I.Gibbons	b Phillipson 4	c Farrimond b Pollard......9	
S.H.Martin	c Farrimond b Phillipson 6	c Pollard b Phillipson 31	
Mr C.H.Palmer	c Pollard b Phillipson 1	c Nutter b Phillipson 14	
*Mr A.F.T.White	b Phillipson 12	lbw b Wilkinson 31	
R.O.Jenkins	c Washbrook b Pollard ...9	run out..................11	
†H.Yarnold	b Phillipson 8	b Pollard 2	
R.T.D.Perks	c Iddon b Pollard 11	c Farrimond b Pollard......4	
P.F.Jackson	not out....................5	not out 2	
Extras	(LB 2, NB 1) 3	(B 4, LB 6, W 2) 12	
Total	**69**	**210**	

Fall: 1st inns 1/1, 2/10, 3/16, 4/16, 5/18, 6/26, 7/43, 8/47, 9/53.
2nd inns 1/38, 2/40, 3/59, 4/121, 5/156, 6/161, 7/201, 8/201, 9/205.

LANCASHIRE

C.Washbrook	lbw b Perks 36	not out 19	
E.Paynter	c Gibbons b Jackson 42	lbw b Jackson..............6	
J.L.Hopwood	c Yarnold b Perks 1	run out 6	
N.Oldfield	c Yarnold b Jenkins 6	lbw b Perks 3	
J.Iddon	lbw b Howorth 41	not out 7	
A.E.Nutter	c Yarnold b Jackson.......4		
*Mr W.H.L.Lister	b Martin 20		
W.E.Phillipson	c Jackson b Perks 27		
†W.Farrimond	not out....................24		
R.Pollard	c King b Jackson 13		
Extras	(B 14 LB 7, NB 1) ..22	(B 3, NB 1) 4	
Total	(9 wickets, declared) **236**	(3 wickets) **45**	

Fall: 1st inns 1/84, 2/96, 3/96, 4/113, 5/120, 6/162, 7/183, 8/214, 9/236.
2nd inns 1/7, 2/21, 3/29.

L.L.Wilkinson did not bat.

LANCASHIRE	O	M	R	W	O	M	R	W
Phillipson	10	3	26	7	20	4	63	3
Pollard	9.4	1	40	3	14.4	2	43	4
Nutter	-	-	-	-	10	2	29	1
Wilkinson	-	-	-	-	19	2	42	1
Iddon	-	-	-	-	3	0	18	0
Paynter	-	-	-	-	1	0	3	0

WORCESTERSHIRE	O	M	R	W	O	M	R	W
Perks	22	1	76	3	6.6	2	17	1
Martin	11	1	46	1				
Jackson	15.2	2	50	3	6	0	24	1
Jenkins	6	1	19	1				
Howorth	6	0	23	1				

Umpires: H.W.Lee and C.N.Woolley.

Close of play scores. First day: Lancashire 236/9 (W.Farrimond 24*). **Second day:** Worcestershire 138/4 (E.Cooper 51*, C.H.Palmer 0*).

Comments: W.E.Phillipson and R.Pollard bowled unchanged in Worcester's 1st innings, which lasted only 90 minutes.
There was no play on the second day until after 3pm.
Lancashire won soon after lunch on the third day.

YORKSHIRE v GLAMORGAN

Played at Bradford, June 21, 22, 1939.
Toss won by Glamorgan.
Yorkshire won by an innings and 95 runs.

GLAMORGAN

A.H.Dyson	c Robinson b Verity......59	c Mitchell b Bowes 8	
D.E.Davies	c Sutcliffe b Robinson ...13	b Verity 4	
T.L.Brierley	c Robinson b Verity......17	lbw b Verity 15	
D.Davies	c Yardley b Verity.......5	c Barber b Verity...........0	
*Mr M.J.L.Turnbull	c Mitchell b Verity 0	st Wood b Verity 10	
C.C.Smart	st Wood b Robinson 20	c Hutton b Verity 12	
E.C.Jones	lbw b Verity 11	c Barber b Verity...........0	
†H.G.Davies	run out....................4	st Wood b Verity 4	
D.Thomas	not out....................14	b Robinson 0	
P.F.Judge	c Sutcliffe b Verity 4	st Wood b Robinson 5	
J.Mercer	b Verity 10	not out 3	
Extras	(B 8, LB 3) 11	(LB 4) 4	
Total	**168**	**65**	

Fall: 1st inns 1/24, 2/71, 3/79, 4/85, 5/108, 6/128, 7/134, 8/137, 9/151.
2nd inns 1/8, 2/27, 3/27, 4/27, 5/46, 6/49, 7/49, 8/53, 9/57.

YORKSHIRE

H.Sutcliffe	c Smart b Judge 11
L.Hutton	b Judge 144
A.Mitchell	c D.Davies b Judge 3
M.Leyland	c Dyson b Judge 6
W.Barber	c Judge b E.Davies 37
Mr N.W.D.Yardley	c Thomas b Judge 6
*Mr A.B.Sellers	c & b Judge 30
†A.Wood	b E.Davies 9
E.P.Robinson	c Brierley b Judge 48
H.Verity	c Turnbull b Judge 4
W.E.Bowes	not out 16
Extras	(B 8, LB 5, W 1) 14
Total	**328**

Fall: 1st inns 1/23, 2/29, 3/43, 4/133, 5/140, 6/198, 7/225, 8/290, 9/303.

YORKSHIRE	O	M	R	W	O	M	R	W
Bowes	11	21	27	0	10	2	32	1
Yardley	4	2	9	0				
Robinson	14	2	73	2	3.4	1	9	2
Verity	16.3	3	48	7	12	6	20	7

GLAMORGAN	O	M	R	W
Mercer	10	0	62	0
Judge	25.4	0	75	8
E.Davies	23	3	106	2
Thomas	6	1	28	0
Jones	4	0	32	0
Smart	2	0	11	0

Umpires: H.G.Baldwin and D.Hendren.

Close of play scores. First day: Yorkshire 153/5 (L.Hutton 76*, A.B.Sellers 4*).

Comments: The match was finished by 3.30pm on the second day.
L.Hutton made his fourth century of the season. His 144 made in 270 minutes, included one 6 and 11 4's. He was last out.
H.Verity had match figures of 14 for 68.
Glamorgan's 2nd innings of 65 lasted 100 minutes.

HAMPSHIRE v MIDDLESEX

Played at Newport, (Isle of Wight), June 24, 26, 27, 1939.
Toss won by Middlesex.
Middlesex won by an innings and 25 runs.

MIDDLESEX

J.D.B.Robertson	b Boyes	97
S.M.Brown	c Arnold b Baring	1
W.J.Edrich	c Arnold b Boyes	118
J.J.Hulme	b Hill	1
L.H.Compton	c Arnold b Boyes	5
†W.F.F.Price	b Boyes	0
J.M.Sims	b Bailey	8
C.I.J.Smith	b Baring	7
*Mr I.A.R.Peebles	c Hill b Bailey	10
L.H.Gray	not out	2
Mr D.R.Hayward	st McCorkell b Boyes	2
Extras	(B 1, LB 2, NB 7)	10
Total		**261**

Fall: 1st inns 1/2, 2/175, 3/176, 4/198, 5/204, 6/232, 7/243, 8/257, 9/257.

HAMPSHIRE

†N.T.McCorkell	c Price b Sims	15	b Sims		24
J.Bailey	lbw b Gray	1	run out		37
A.G.Holt	lbw b Smith	1	lbw b Edrich		2
J.Arnold	b Smith	3	c Peebles b Edrich		3
W.L.C.Creese	c Compton b Gray	30	c Price b Robertson		34
A.E.Pothecary	lbw b Sims	14	lbw b Peebles		3
P.A.Mackenzie	b Smith	10	lbw b Peebles		9
G.Hill	not out	5	c Sims b Peebles		0
G.S.Boyes	b Smith	1	c Robertson b Hayward		16
*Mr G.R.Taylor	b Smith	7	b Peebles		3
Mr A.E.G.Baring	b Smith	0	not out		0
Extras	(B 4, LB 1, NB 1)	6	(B 10, LB 2)		12
Total		**93**			**143**

Fall: 1st inns 1/4, 2/10, 3/20, 4/38, 5/63, 6/80, 7/80, 8/81, 9/93.
2nd inns 1/45, 2/48, 3/58, 4/95, 5/100, 6/116, 7/116, 8/131, 9/143.

HAMPSHIRE	O	M	R	W
Baring	13	0	44	2
Bailey	6	0	26	2
Hill	26	4	81	1
Boyes	17.5	5	45	5
Creese	10	0	32	0
Mackenzie	4	0	23	0

MIDDLESEX	O	M	R	W	O	M	R	W
Smith	17.5	5	23	6	3	0	8	0
Gray	4	1	4	2	4	1	13	0
Sims	18	3	53	2	4	0	29	1
Peebles	3	1	5	0	9	1	23	4
Robertson	2	1	2	0	9	4	12	1
Edrich	-	-	-	-	9	0	41	2
Hayward	-	-	-	-	3.1	0	5	1

Umpires: W.Reeves and F.Chester.

Close of play scores. First day: Middlesex 41/1 (J.D.B.Robertson 28*, W.J.Edrich 7*). **Second day:** Hampshire 69/5 (A.E.Pothecary 11*, P.A.Mackenzie 2*).
Comments: Only one hour's play was possible on the first day.
W.J.Edrich and J.D.B.Robertson put on 173 for the 2nd wicket.
W.J.Edrich made 118 in 300 minutes. It was his first century of the season and came in 270 minutes with 15 4's.
The nine remaining Middlesex batsmen made only 36 between them.
J.D.B.Robertson and W.J.Edrich were the only batsmen in the match to score over 40 runs in an innings.
On the 3rd day, Hampshire needing only 43 to avoid the follow-on, lost their remaining five wickets for 24 runs.

KENT v NOTTINGHAMSHIRE

Played at Tunbridge Wells, June 24, 26, 27, 1939.
Toss won by Nottinghamshire.
Nottinghamshire won by 13 runs.

NOTTINGHAMSHIRE

W.W.Keeton	c Chalk b Watt	80	c Valentine b Todd		10
C.B.Harris	c & b Lewis	18	c Sunnucks b Watt		17
*Mr G.F.H.Heane	c & b Watt	53	b Todd		88
G.V.Gunn	b Todd	0	b Watt		9
J.Knowles	b Watt	13	c Valentine b Watt		32
F.H.Winrow	c Fagg b Todd	1	b Watt		0
R.J.Giles	b Watt	7	b Martin		27
W.Voce	c Fagg b Martin	0	c Valentine b Watt		4
†A.B.Wheat	c Levett b Martin	6	c Spencer b Watt		8
H.J.Butler	not out	34	c Valentine b Martin		5
A.Jepson	b Watt	1	not out		0
Extras	(LB 9)	9	(B 3, LB 4)		7
Total		**222**			**207**

Fall: 1st inns 1/42, 2/141, 3/146, 4/167, 5/168, 6/172, 7/173, 8/175, 9/211.
2nd inns 1/11, 2/49, 3/78, 4/161, 5/161, 6/161, 7/174, 8/202, 9/207.

KENT

A.E.Fagg	lbw b Voce	1	c Butler b Voce		7
*Mr F.G.H.Chalk	lbw b Voce	13	b Butler		5
P.R.Sunnucks	c Harris b Jepson	4	b Voce		4
Mr B.H.Valentine	c Harris b Voce	39	b Jepson		90
L.J.Todd	b Butler	81	b Butler		3
Mr P.G.Foster	b Jepson	3	b Jepson		68
T.W.Spencer	lbw b Voce	22	b Butler		9
†Mr W.H.V.Levett	c Heane b Butler	1	lbw b Voce		10
A.E.Watt	not out	1	b Butler		4
Mr J.W.Martin	c Wheat b Butler	1	b Butler		20
C.Lewis	b Butler	0	not out		5
Extras	(LB 9, W 1)	10	(B 5, LB 10)		15
Total		**176**			**240**

Fall: 1st inns 1/4, 2/9, 3/53, 4/78, 5/85, 6/172, 7/172, 8/174, 9/176.
2nd inns 1/13, 2/13, 3/24, 4/29, 5/181, 6/186, 7/196, 8/202, 9/228.

KENT	O	M	R	W	O	M	R	W
Todd	15	3	46	2	15	0	56	2
Martin	21	8	81	2	12.2	0	48	2
Watt	19.3	3	50	5	21	2	67	6
Lewis	16	6	36	1	10	1	29	0

NOTTINGHAMSHIRE	O	M	R	W	O	M	R	W
Voce	26	1	65	4	16.5	2	66	3
Butler	12.4	3	25	4	20	3	87	5
Jepson	13	2	35	2	11	1	48	2
Gunn	5	0	22	0	1	0	4	0
Giles	5	1	14	0	4	0	12	0
Heane	2	0	5	0	2	0	8	0

Umpires: C.V.Tarbox and J.A.Newman.

Close of play scores. First day: Kent 52/2 (F.G.H.Chalk 13*, B.H.Valentine 29*). **Second day:** Nottinghamshire 119/3 (G.F.H.Heane 63*, J.Knowles 17*).
Comments: Turnbridge Wells cricket week.
Kent lost their last five 1st innings wickets for four runs.
Kent needed 254 to win and after losing four for 29, came back into the match when B.H.Valentine and P.G.Foster added 152 for the 5th wicket in less than two hours. In a close finish, after the extra half-hour had been claimed, Nottinghamshire won with only ten minutes of the match remaining.
J.W.Martin made his debut for Kent.

KENT COUNTY CRICKET CLUB

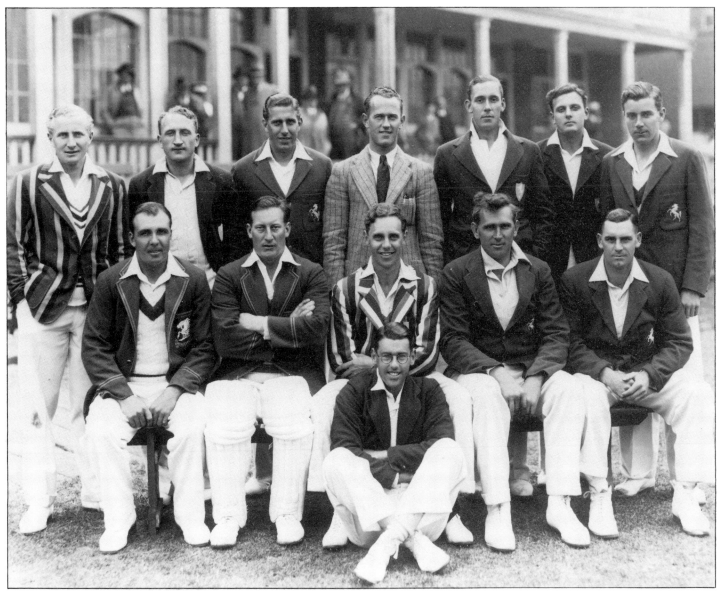

Standing: P.G.Foster, T.W.Spencer, A.E.Fagg, A.Wilson (masseur), N.W.Harding, R.R.Dovey, C.Lewis. Seated: L.E.G.Ames, W.H.V.Levett, F.G.H.Chalk (captain), A.E.Watt, L.J.Todd. On ground: P.R.Sunnucks.

LANCASHIRE v SURREY

Played at Old Trafford, Manchester, June 24, 26, 27, 1939.
Toss won by Surrey.
Surrey won by 14 runs.

SURREY

I.B.Fishlock	lbw b Phillipson 62	c Washbrook b Pollard....13
R.J.Gregory	lbw b Nutter 29	lbw b Phillipson 15
H.S.Squires	b Pollard 14	b Wilkinson 68
T.H.Baring	lbw b Pollard 1	lbw b Wilkinson 22
E.W.Whitfield	b Wilkinson 47	lbw b Wilkinson 2
J.F.Parker	lbw b Pollard 19	not out 88
A.J.W.McIntyre	lbw b Wilkinson 39	(8) c Farrimond b Pollard 0
*Mr H.M.Garland-Wells	b Phillipson 7	(7) c Iddon b Pollard 17
E.A.Watts	b Pollard 16	c Wilkinson b Pollard 5
†E.W.J.Brooks	c Nutter b Pollard......16	b Pollard 1
A.R.Gover	not out 13	
Extras	(B 4, LB 8, w 2, NB 1) ...15	(B 3, LB 5, NB 1) 9
Total	**278**	**(9 wickets, declared).....240**

Fall: 1st inns 1/55, 2/104, 3/112, 4/121, 5/157, 6/204, 7/227, 8/249, 9/249.
2nd inns 1/20, 2/32, 3/71, 4/83, 5/187, 6/218, 7/219, 8/237, 9/240.

LANCASHIRE

*Mr W.H.L.Lister	c Gover b Watts 6	(7) c Brooks b Gover 0
†W.Farrimond	c Garland-Wells b Squires 55	(9) run out 0
C.Washbrook	run out 35	(1) lbw b Watts 4
W.Place	b Watts 46	(2) c Brooks b Watts 15
J.L.Hopwood	c Gover b Watts 11	(3) c Parker b Garland-Wells 32
N.Oldfield	b Parker 13	(4) b Gover 131
J.Iddon	c Watts b Gregory 4	(5) b Watts 68
A.E.Nutter	b Squires 10	(6) c Watts b Gover 5
W.E.Phillipson	not out 8	(8) b Parker 10
R.Pollard	b Gover 0	not out 14
L.L.Wilkinson	b Gover 1	b Gover 10
Extras	(B 5, LB 3, NB 2) 10	(B 3, LB 11, NB 2) 16
Total	**199**	**305**

Fall: 1st inns 1/13, 2/91, 3/10, 4/122, 5/156, 6/173, 7/181, 8/194, 9/197.
2nd inns 1/16, 2/21, 3/83, 4/223, 5/228, 6/228, 7/279, 8/280, 9/280.

LANCASHIRE	O	M	R	W	O	M	R	W
Phillipson	20	1	77	2	12	0	74	1
Pollard	19.1	3	61	5	14	0	63	5
Wilkinson	16	0	73	2	11	0	43	3
Nutter	17	4	52	1	7	0	44	0
Hopwood	-	-	-	-	4	0	7	0

SURREY	O	M	R	W	O	M	R	W
Gover	16	0	60	2	16	0	87	4
Watts	13	2	32	3	14	1	65	3
Garland-Wells	2	0	9	0	9	0	48	1
Gregory	10	2	21	1	3	0	13	0
Parker	11	0	35	1	9	0	57	1
Squires	14	1	32	2	4	2	19	0

Umpires: A.Skelding and J.A.Smart.

Close of play scores. First day: Lancashire 6/0 (W.H.L.Lister 5*, W.Farrimond 1*). **Second day:** Surrey 105/4 (H.S.Squires 32*, J.F.Parker 15*).

Comments: Play delayed on the first day. J.F.Parker and H.S.Squires made 104 in 70 minutes for the 5th wicket in Surrey's 2nd innings. Lancashire were set to make 320 to win in 240 minutes. N.Oldfield and J.Iddon scored 140 in 90 minutes for the Lancashire 4th wicket in the 2nd innings. N.Oldfield made 131 in 205 minutes, hitting eight 4's. It was his third century of the season and he also reached his 1,000 runs in 1939. Surrey won with only ten minutes of the game remaining.

SOMERSET v LEICESTERSHIRE

Played at Bath, June 24, 26, 27, 1939
Toss won by Somerset.
Somerset won by nine wickets.

SOMERSET

F.S.Lee	lbw b Prentice 10	lbw b Smith......5
Mr R.J.O.Meyer	b Sperry 11	not out 61
H.T.F.Buse	c Smith b Walsh 79	not out 22
Mr C.J.P.Barnwell	st Dawkes b Walsh 9	
*Mr E.F.Longrigg	c Berry b Smith 56	
Mr F.M.McRae	b Walsh 18	
†W.T.Luckes	c Walsh b Sperry 2	
W.H.R.Andrews	lbw b Walsh 4	
Mr G.M.Bennett	not out 8	
A.W.Wellard	c Thursting b Walsh 6	
H.L.Hazell	b Walsh 0	
Extras	(B 7, LB 11, W 1, NB 1) 20	(W 1) 1
Total	**223**	**(1 wicket) 89**

Fall: 1st inns 1/15, 2/49, 3/68, 4/172, 5/201, 6/204, 7/208, 8/212, 9/223.
2nd inns 1/15.

LEICESTERSHIRE

G.L.Berry	c Luckes b Wellard......10	lbw b Andrews 2
G.S.Watson	b Meyer 53	b Meyer 30
N.F.Armstrong	lbw b Wellard 4	b Wellard 2
F.T.Prentice	c Andrews b Wellard 1	b Wellard 29
M.Tompkin	b Wellard 5	c Buse b Hazell 16
*Mr M.St.J.Packe	b Wellard 0	c Luckes b Wellard 10
†G.O.Dawkes	b Meyer 0	lbw b Wellard 36
L.D.Thursting	c Luckes b Meyer 1	lbw b Meyer 20
Mr J.E.Walsh	c Longrigg b Buse 23	not out 18
H.A.Smith	not out 18	c Luckes b Meyer 0
J.Sperry	run out 0	c Luckes b Buse 14
Extras	(B 1, LB 2, NB 1) 4	(B 8, LB 6, NB 1) 15
Total	**119**	**192**

Fall: 1st inns 1/29, 2/38, 3/42, 4/62, 5/62, 6/69, 7/74, 8/87, 9/117.
2nd inns 1/3, 2/10, 3/50, 4/86, 5/88, 6/115, 7/160, 8/160, 9/160.

LEICESTERSHIRE	O	M	R	W	O	M	R	W
Sperry	20	7	36	2	10	1	35	0
Smith	17	3	53	1	5	0	19	1
Walsh	19.7	4	72	6	5	0	28	0
Prentice	14	3	42	1				
Packe	-	-	-	-	4	0	6	0

SOMERSET	O	M	R	W	O	M	R	W
Wellard	10	1	46	5	18	6	49	4
Andrews	8	0	34	0	12	1	35	1
Meyer	4	0	28	3	9	1	47	3
Buse	2.4	0	7	1	6	0	14	1
Hazell	-	-	-	-	14	3	32	1

Umpires: G.M.Lee and F.J.Durston.

Close of play scores. First day: No play. **Second day:** Leicestershire (2nd innings) 12/2 (G.S.Watson 4*, F.T.Prentice 1*).

Comments: E.F.Longrigg and H.T.F.Buse added 104 for the 4th wicket in 80 minutes. Leicestershire followed on 104 behind under two-day match regulations. Somerset hit off the 89 runs required in 70 minutes.

WARWICKSHIRE v NORTHAMPTONSHIRE

Played at Edgbaston, Birmingham, June 24, 26, 27, 1939.
Toss won by Warwickshire.
Match drawn.

WARWICKSHIRE

A.J.W.Croom	c Merritt b Partridge 11	not out 53
W.A.Hill	b Partridge 21	lbw b Nelson 29
F.R.Santall	c Merritt b Buswell......66	c Brookes b Robinson 6
H.E.Dollery	b Partridge.........117	c Nelson b Robinson 20
J.S.Ord	c Merritt b Partridge 20	not out 27
†J.Buckingham	lbw b Merritt 50	
*Mr P.Cranmer	c Nelson b Partridge 55	
C.W.Grove	c Robinson b Partridge 0	
K.Wilmot	c Partridge b Merritt 27	
J.H.Mayer	not out 11	
W.E.Hollies	not out 1	
Extras	(B 1, LB 8, W 1, NB 1) ...11	(LB 3) 3
Total	(9 wickets, declared) 390	(3 wickets, declared)......138

Fall: 1st inns 1/32, 2/33, 3/170, 4/208, 5/257, 6/351, 7/351, 8/351, 9/389.
    2nd inns 1/52, 2/64, 3/108.

NORTHAMPTONSHIRE

P.Davis	b Wilmot	43
R.J.Partridge	b Mayer	4
D.Brookes	lbw b Wilmot	12
J.E.Timms	c Buckingham b Hollies	47
†K.C.James	b Grove	40
*Mr R.P.Nelson	c Buckingham b Hollies	74
H.W.Greenwood	c Hill b Hollies	94
W.E.Merritt	c Hill b Mayer	29
M.E.F.Dunkley	b Hollies	16
J.E.Buswell	b Hollies	4
A.G.Robinson	not out	0
Extras	(LB 15)	15
Total		378

Fall: 1st inns 1/17, 2/47, 3/63, 4/145, 5/166, 6/318, 7/331, 8/374, 9/378.

NORTHANTS	O	M	R	W	O	M	R	W
Partridge	25	1	126	6	4	1	13	0
Timms	6	0	34	0				
Buswell	18	0	103	1	9	1	45	0
Robinson	5	0	49	0	15	2	45	2
Merritt	10	1	53	2	4	0	32	0
Nelson	5	2	14	0	2	2	0	1

WARWICKSHIRE	O	M	R	W
Mayer	25.1	2	79	2
Grove	23	3	80	1
Wilmot	27	4	66	2
Hollies	39	3	130	5
Santall	3	0	8	0

Umpires: G.Beet and H.W.Lee.

Close of play scores. First day: Warwickshire 312/5 (J.Buckingham 28*, P.Cranmer 38*). **Second day:** Northamptonshire 231/5 (R.P.Nelson 41*, H.W.Greenwood 32*).

Comments: There was only four hours play on the first day.
H.E.Dollery and F.R.Santall put on 137 in 90 minutes for the 3rd wicket.
H.E.Dollery hit 13 4's in his 117. He reached his third century of the season in 160 minutes.
R.P.Nelson and H.W.Greenwood added 152 for the Northants 6th wicket.

WORCESTERSHIRE v GLOUCESTERSHIRE

Played at Worcester, June 24, 26, 27, 1939.
Toss won by Gloucestershire.
Worcestershire won by five wickets.

GLOUCESTERSHIRE

C.J.Barnett	b Perks.........25	c Howorth b Martin.......14
R.A.Sinfield	b Perks.........21	(6) c Yarnold b Martin 23
*Mr B.O.Allen	lbw b Martin 1	(2) lbw b Martin 19
V.Hopkins	c White b Martin 26	(3) b Perks 6
G.M.Emmett	c Yarnold b Perks 27	(4) c Palmer b Perks.....61
W.L.Neale	not out 70	(5) c White b Perks........59
R.W.Haynes	c King b Jenkins 8	c Jenkins b Martin 0
†E.A.Wilson	b Howorth 4	b Perks 16
C.J.Scott	lbw b Perks 6	(11) lbw b Martin 4
G.E.E.Lambert	c King b Martin 16	(9) c Howorth b Perks 6
T.W.J.Goddard	b Martin 3	(10) not out 7
Extras	(B 12, LB 15, W 1, NB 1) 29	(B 4, LB 2, NB 5) 11
Total	236	226

Fall: 1st inns 1/30, 2/31, 3/67, 4/114, 5/129, 6/148, 7/167, 8/195, 9/230.
    2nd inns 1/34, 2/35, 3/58, 4/126, 5/171, 6/173, 7/191, 8/203, 9/217.

WORCESTERSHIRE

R.Howorth	c Allen b Scott.........15	c Emmett b Lambert 1
E.Cooper	b Scott.........46	lbw b Lambert 2
H.Yarnold	b Scott 5	
B.P.King	lbw b Goddard 106	(3) b Lambert 35
H.H.I.Gibbons	lbw b Barnett 104	(4) b Lambert 12
S.H.Martin	c Haynes b Goddard 13	(5) b Lambert 4
Mr C.H.Palmer	run out 4	(6) not out 18
*†Mr G.E.B.Abell	b Lambert 23	
Mr A.F.T.White	not out 31	(7) not out 4
R.O.Jenkins	c Lambert b Goddard 28	
R.T.D.Perks	c Lambert b Goddard 4	
Extras	(LB 7) 7	(B 3) 3
Total	386	(5 wickets) 79

Fall: 1st inns 1/26, 2/39, 3/89, 4/227, 5/245, 6/256, 7/319, 8/321, 9/377.
    2nd inns 1/3, 2/4, 3/28, 4/32, 5/75.

WORCESTERSHIRE	O	M	R	W	O	M	R	W
Perks	26	3	94	4	19	1	99	5
Martin	30.5	7	66	4	18.4	2	60	5
Howorth	11	3	21	1	5	0	16	0
Jenkins	6	0	26	1	7	2	40	0

GLOUCESTERSHIRE	O	M	R	W	O	M	R	W
Scott	17	1	83	3				
Barnett	9	0	32	1	11	2	30	0
Lambert	19	4	83	1	11.3	1	46	5
Goddard	27.6	4	133	4				
Sinfield	16	2	48	0				

Umpires: E.Cooke and A.Dolphin.

Close of play scores. First day: Worc 39/2 (E.Cooper 19*). **Second day:** 83/3 (G.M.Emmett 34*, W.L.Neale 8*).

Comments: B.P.King and H.H.I.Gibbons added 138 for the 4th wicket.
B.P.King's 106 was his first century of the season. It took 140 minutes and included 15 4's.
H.H.I.Gibbons' 104 was his fourth hundred in 1939. He hit 11 4's in a stay of 180 minutes.
S.F.Martin bowled unchanged for 30 overs and five balls in Gloucestershires 1st innings.
Both G.E.B.Abell and H.Yarnold kept wicket for Worcestershire.
Hon C.J.Lyttelton, the usual Worcester captain, was away at Territorial camp.

YORKSHIRE v DERBYSHIRE

Played at Bramall Lane, Sheffield, June 24, 26, 27, 1939.
Toss won by Yorkshire.
Yorkshire won by 276 runs.

YORKSHIRE

H.Sutcliffe	c Worthington b A.V.Pope 9	b G.H.Pope	18
A.Mitchell	c Rhodes b G.H.Pope 14	c Smith b A.V.Pope	40
W.Barber	c Elliott b A.V.Pope 2	c Smith b A.V.Pope	100
M.Leyland	c G.H.Pope 0	c Elliott b G.H.Pope	1
Mr N.W.D.Yardley	c Gladwin b A.V.Pope 21	c & b Rhodes	34
Mr G.A.Wilson	b A.V.Pope 0	b Mitchell	21
*Mr A.B.Sellers	c Elliott b G.H.Pope 31	run out	43
T.F.Smailes	c A.V.Pope b G.H.Pope 4	c A.V.Pope	8
E.P.Robinson	b G.H.Pope 0	c Hounsfield b G.H.Pope	23
J.Smurthwaite	b G.H.Pope 0	b A.V.Pope	1
†K.Fiddling	not out 0	not out	5
Extras	(LB 2) 2	(B 8, LB 8)	16
Total	**83**		**310**

Fall: 1st inns 1/20, 2/26, 3/26, 4/31, 5/32, 6/63, 7/70, 8/70, 9/70.
2nd inns 1/45, 2/76, 3/77, 4/140, 5/189, 6/260, 7/281, 8/284, 9/290.

DERBYSHIRE

D.Smith	b Smurthwaite 5	b Smailes	8
A.E.Alderman	c Fidding b Smailes 1	c Smurthwaite b Smailes	0
T.S.Worthington	run out 0	c Mitchell b Smailes	32
L.F.Townsend	c Robinson b Smurthwaite 2	b Smailes	0
G.H.Pope	c Robinson b Smailes 0	lbw b Smailes	1
A.E.G.Rhodes	c Robinson b Smurthwaite 0	b Smailes	18
*Mr T.D.Hounsfield	c Sutcliffe b Smailes 2	not out	21
A.V.Pope	b Smurthwaite 6	b Smailes	4
C.Gladwin	c Smailes b Smurthwaite 0	b Smailes	0
†H.Elliott	not out 2	b Smailes	6
T.B.Mitchell	c Leyland b Smailes 0	st Fidding b Smailes	6
Extras	(LB 2) 2	(B 1)	1
Total	**20**		**97**

Fall: 1st inns 1/2, 2/2, 3/7, 4/8, 5/10, 6/10, 7/13, 8/14, 9/19.
2nd inns 1/0, 2/19, 3/19, 4/21, 5/56, 6/61, 7/71, 8/71, 9/79.

DERBYSHIRE	O	M	R	W	O	M	R	W
A.V.Pope	18	4	37	4	25	5	72	4
G.H.Pope	17.3	2	44	6	24.5	3	90	3
Mitchell	-	-	-	-	9	0	52	1
Gladwin	-	-	-	-	8	2	36	0
Rhodes	-	-	-	-	4	0	16	1
Townsend	-	-	-	-	5	0	28	0

YORKSHIRE	O	M	R	W	O	M	R	W
Smailes	4.3	0	11	4	17.1	5	47	10
Smurthwaite	4	2	7	5	14	5	43	0
Yardley	-	-	-	-	2	0	5	0
Robinson	-	-	-	-	1	0	1	0

Umpires: H.G.Baldwin and H.Elliott.

Close of play scores. First day: Yorkshire 13/0 (H.Sutcliffe 6*, A.Mitchell 6*). **Second day:** Derbyshire 31/4 (T.S.Worthington 16*, A.E.G.Rhodes 6*).
Comments: Play did not commence until 2.30pm on the first day, due to rain. Then, in under three and three quarter hours, 20 wickets fell for 103 runs. Yorkshire's 1st innings total of 83 was their lowest since they scored 56 against Gloucestershire in 1936. T.F.Smailes took ten wickets for the first time in his career. He was the fourth Yorkshireman to achieve this feat and the first bowler to achieve this feat since T.W.J.Goddard in 1937. His match figures of 14 wickets for 58 runs was a career-best performance. He also dismissed all 11 Derbyshire players in the match, bowling unchanged throughout the game. Twenty was Derbyshire's second-lowest score in their history, beaten only by their 16 against Notts in 1879. It was also the lowest county score for 17 years. Hampshire making only 15 in 1922. The innings lasted only 44 minutes and 67 balls. On the same day, four bowlers were unchanged in consecutive innings, the two Popes for Derbyshire and T.F.Smailes and J.Smurthwaite for Yorkshire. Smurthwaite was opening the Yorkshire bowling for the first time, taking five wickets for seven runs. It was also the first time he had bowled in a championship game. W.Barber hit 14 4's in his 100, his first century of the season.

DERBYSHIRE v SUSSEX

Played at Derby, June 28, 29, 30, 1939.
Toss won by Sussex.
Sussex won by 13 runs.

SUSSEX

John G.Langridge	c Smith b Copson 85	c Worthington b Mitchell	39
J.H.Parks	b Copson 15	lbw b A.V.Pope	3
H.W.Parks	c Elliott b A.V.Pope 10	c Worthington b Copson	4
G.Cox	b Copson 0	c & b A.V.Pope	5
Jas.Langridge	lbw b Copson 0	lbw b G.H.Pope	27
*Mr H.T.Bartlett	c Elliott b Rhodes 93	c & b Mitchell	39
Mr R.A.A.Holt	b Rhodes 0	b G.H.Pope	9
C.Oakes	lbw b Rhodes 8	b G.H.Pope	0
†W.L.Cornford	c Worthington b Copson 5	lbw b Mitchell	0
J.Duffield	c Elliott b Copson 33	not out	20
J.K.Nye	not out 1	b Mitchell	0
Extras	(B 5, LB 3) 8	(LB 1)	1
Total	**258**		**147**

Fall: 1st inns 1/20, 2/35, 3/36, 4/36, 5/181, 6/181, 7/193, 8/204, 9/245.
2nd inns 1/3, 2/12, 3/19, 4/66, 5/108, 6/117, 7/117, 8/118, 9/147.

DERBYSHIRE

A.E.Alderman	c Cornford b Nye 15	c Cornford b Duffield	30
D.Smith	b Nye 81	c Cornford b Duffield	0
T.S.Worthington	b Nye 0	c Cornford b Jas.Langridge	119
L.F.Townsend	c H.Parks b J.Parks 29	c Cornford b Nye	28
G.H.Pope	lbw b Duffield 37	c J.Parks b Jas.Langridge	1
A.E.G.Rhodes	c Nye b Jas.Langridge 8	c John Langridge b Jas.Langridge	0
*Mr T.D.Hounsfield	b Duffield 12	c J.Parks b Jas.Langridge	0
A.V.Pope	lbw b Duffield 0	c Cornford b Jas.Langride	0
†H.Elliott	lbw b Duffield 0	not out	0
T.B.Mitchell	not out 0	b Nye	0
W.H.Copson	b Duffield 0	b Nye	0
Extras	(B 2, LB 14) 16	(B 12, LB 2, W 1, NB 1)	16
Total	**198**		**194**

Fall: 1st inns 1/54, 2/58, 3/117, 4/161, 5/176, 6/191, 7/191, 8/191, 9/198.
2nd inns 1/6, 2/112, 3/185, 4/191, 5/191, 6/191, 7/191, 8/194, 9/194.

DERBYSHIRE	O	M	R	W	O	M	R	W
Copson	20.4	4	64	6	7	2	16	1
A.V.Pope	18	2	71	1	6	1	19	2
G.H.Pope	12	0	55	0	12	1	49	3
Mitchell	4	0	22	0	9	1	45	4
Rhodes	10	0	38	3	4	0	17	0

SUSSEX	O	M	R	W	O	M	R	W
Nye	16	0	73	3	15	1	69	3
Duffield	10.5	1	38	5	14	0	78	2
J.Parks	16	7	33	1	5	0	28	0
Jas.Langridge	9	1	36	1	3	1	3	5
Cox	1	0	2	0				

Umpires: A.Dolphin and H.Elliott.

Close of play scores. First day: Derbyshire 24/0 (A.E.Alderman 7*, D.Smith 11*). **Second day:** Sussex 147 all out.
Comments: Bad light and rain caused five interruptions on the first day, 70 minutes being lost.
John G.Langridge and H.T.Bartlett put on 145 for the Sussex 5th wicket in 120 minutes. J.Duffield took five wickets for no runs in an 11-ball spell to end Derbyshire's 1st innings, as 20 wickets fell on the second day. T.S.Worthington made 119 in 130 minutes, including one 6 and 14 4's. He and A.E.Alderman added 106 in 85 minutes for the 3rd wicket. On the third day, Derbyshire, needing 208 to win, wanted only 23 runs to secure victory after losing their third wicket with the score on 185. However the last 7 wickets fell for 9 runs in 25 minutes to give the visitors an unexpected win. James Langridge took his maiden hat-trick, the batsmen being A.E.G.Rhodes, T.D.Hounsfield and A.V.Pope, in a spell of 5 wickets for no runs in 11 balls. J.K.Nye then took Derbyshire's last three wickets in five balls. As soon as the final wicket fell, a thunderstorm broke out.

DERBYSHIRE COUNTY CRICKET CLUB

Standing (left to right): W.H.Copson, A.V.Pope, G.H.Pope, D.Smith, T.S.Worthington, A.E.Alderman. Seated: A.E.G.Rhodes, L.F.Townsend, R.H.R.Buckston (captain), H.Elliott, T.B.Mitchell.

GLAMORGAN v LANCASHIRE

Played at Cardiff, June 28, 29, 30, 1939.
Toss won by Lancashire.
Match drawn.

LANCASHIRE

C.Washbrook	lbw b Judge	16	run out	23
E.Paynter	lbw b Judge	27	b Judge	140
J.L.Hopwood	c Wooller b Judge	20	lbw b Wooller	30
N.Oldfield	lbw b Judge	11	lbw b Smart	19
J.Iddon	c Wooller b Mercer	32	c E.Davies b Judge	27
A.E.Nutter	lbw b Wooller	1	c H.Davies b E.Davies	19
W.E.Phillipson	c H.Davies b Mercer	61	(8) c Turnbull b Judge	2
*Mr W.H.L.Lister	c Dyson b E.Davies	3	(7) c Jones b Judge	5
†W.Farrimond	c Turnbull b E.Davies	50	not out	8
R.Pollard	b Mercer	4	b E.Davies	1
L.L.Wilkinson	not out	8	not out	5
Extras	(B 6, LB 8, W 1, NB 1)	16	(B 7, LB 5)	12
Total		249	(9 wickets, declared)	291

Fall: 1st inns 1/34, 2/59, 3/72, 4/83, 5/90, 6/140, 7/145, 8/214, 9/218.
2nd inns 1/58, 2/125, 3/174, 4/251, 5/252, 6/268, 7/277, 8/277, 9/278.

GLAMORGAN

A.H.Dyson	c Farrimond b Phillipson	44	c Washbrook b Hopwood	68
D.E.Davies	b Pollard	25	c Farrimond b Phillipson	12
T.L.Brierley	b Pollard	7	b Phillipson	0
D.Davies	b Wilkinson	8	(7) not out	10
*Mr M.J.L.Turnbull	b Phillipson	33	(6) not out	40
C.C.Smart	b Wilkinson	24	(5) run out	0
Mr W.Wooller	b Phillipson	67	(4) b Nutter	57
E.C.Jones	lbw b Wilkinson	43		
†H.G.Davies	lbw b Wilkinson	0		
P.F.Judge	b Phillipson	3		
J.Mercer	not out	0		
Extras	(B 11, NB 3)	14	(B 1 LB 2, NB 1)	4
Total		268	(5 wickets)	191

Fall: 1st inns 1/53, 2/62, 3/79, 4/95, 5/143, 6/149, 7/252, 8/252, 9/267.
2nd inns 1/32, 2/32, 3/134, 4/134, 5/173.

GLAMORGAN	O	M	R	W	O	M	R	W
Mercer	20	1	48	3	12	2	42	0
Judge	26	2	75	4	19	1	91	4
Wooller	19	1	78	1	14	0	68	1
D.E.Davies	9.1	1	28	2	9	1	48	2
Smart	2	1	4	0	6	0	30	1

LANCASHIRE	O	M	R	W	O	M	R	W
Phillipson	21.2	1	81	4	7	0	36	2
Pollard	22	5	66	2	9	0	58	0
Wilkinson	21	2	63	4	12	2	43	0
Nutter	13	3	37	0	9	1	24	1
Hopwood	1	0	7	0	5	0	26	1

Umpires: G.M.Lee and E.Cooke.

Close of play scores. First day: Glamorgan 31/0 (A.H.Dyson 18*, D.E.Davies 13*). **Second day:** Lancashire 56/0 (C.Washbrook 22*, E.Paynter 31*).

Comments: W.Wooller and E.C.Jones added 103 in 90 minutes for Glamorgan's 7th wicket.
E.Paynter hit 140 in 210 minutes with one 6 and 12 4's. He reached his century in 170 minutes.
Glamorgan were set to make 273 in 195 minutes.
A.H.Dyson and W.Wooller put on 102 in 90 minutes for the 3rd wicket in the 2nd innings.
W.Wooller captained Glamorgan in Lancashire's 2nd innings, M.J.L.Turnbull having suffered a strain.

GLOUCESTERSHIRE v YORKSHIRE

Played at Bristol, June 28, 29, 30, 1939.
Toss won by Yorkshire.
Gloucestershire won by seven wickets.

YORKSHIRE

H.Sutcliffe	b Goddard	34	lbw b Goddard	16
L.Hutton	b Lambert	12	lbw b Goddard	13
A.Mitchell	c Lambert b Goddard	1	b Barnett	0
M.Leyland	c Wilson b Lambert	49	b Sinfield	19
W.Barber	lbw b Lambert	14	b Goddard	11
Mr N.W.D.Yardley	b Goddard	12	b Goddard	6
*Mr A.B.Sellers	b Goddard	20	lbw b Goddard	11
T.F.Smailes	b Lambert	15	b Goddard	0
†A.Wood	st Wilson b Goddard	12	b Goddard	6
H.Verity	not out	5	not out	7
W.E.Bowes	b Goddard	0	b Lambert	13
Extras	(B 1, LB 1)	2	(B 2, LB 1)	3
Total		176		105

Fall: 1st inns 1/34, 2/37, 3/54, 4/75, 5/118, 6/128, 7/150, 8/168, 9/176.
2nd inns 1/23, 2/24, 3/42, 4/56, 5/64, 6/72, 7/76, 8/85, 9/86.

GLOUCESTERSHIRE

C.J.Barnett	c Smailes b Bowes	25	c Sellers b Bowes	11
R.A.Sinfield	c Mitchell b Verity	41	c Wood b Leyland	15
Mr B.O.Allen	b Smailes	17	c Yardley b Verity	56
*Mr W.R.Hammond	b Bowes	30	not out	16
J.F.Crapp	c Mitchell b Verity	33	not out	14
V.Hopkins	c Sellers b Verity	1		
G.M.Emmett	b Verity	0		
W.L.Neale	st Wood b Verity	1		
†E.A.Wilson	not out	3		
G.E.E.Lambert	c Mitchell b Verity	1		
T.W.J.Goddard	c Bowes b Verity	0		
Extras	(B 12, LB 4)	16	(LB 2)	2
Total		168	(3 wickets)	114

Fall: 1st inns 1/36, 2/75, 3/127, 4/129, 5/139, 6/139, 7/145, 8/166, 9/168.
2nd inns 1/13, 2/64, 3/92.

GLOUCESTERSHIRE	O	M	R	W	O	M	R	W
Barnett	11	1	35	0	7	1	16	1
Lambert	23	2	58	4	3	0	5	1
Goddard	28	6	61	6	18	6	38	7
Sinfield	7	1	20	0	12	3	43	1

YORKSHIRE	O	M	R	W	O	M	R	W
Bowes	23	5	53	2	14	0	46	1
Smailes	16	2	37	1	1	1	0	0
Yardley	5	2	11	0				
Verity	21.4	8	47	7	15.3	3	51	1
Barber	1	0	4	0				
Leyland	-	-	-	-	3	1	14	1

Umpires: F.J.Durston and J.J.Hills.

Close of play scores. First day: Gloucestershire 71/1 (R.A.Sinfield 20*, B.O.Allen 17*). **Second day:** Gloucestershire 31/1 (R.A.Sinfield 10*, B.O.Allen 10*).

Comments: B.O.Allen was the only batsman to score over 50 in this low-scoring game.
Gloucestershire completed the double over Yorkshire for the second time in five years.
T.W.J.Goddard had match figures of 13 wickets for 99 runs.
H.Verity had one spell of seven wickets for 21 runs in 52 balls on the second day.
T.F.Smailes was unable to bowl on the final day, owing to a strain.

HAMPSHIRE v ESSEX

Played at Southampton, June 28, 29, 30, 1939.
Toss won by Essex.
Essex won by 37 runs.

ESSEX

S.J.Cray	c Walker b Boyes 44	c Boyes b Bailey 28
R.Smith	run out 3	(9) not out 65
R.M.Taylor	b Hill 31	lbw b Bailey 26
J.O'Connor	c Court b Boyes 38	c Court b Boyes 65
M.S.Nichols	c Walker b Hill 7	lbw b Creese 1
Mr D.F.Cock	b Creese 27	c Pothecary b Creese.......6
*Mr F.St.G.Unwin	c Arnold b Boyes 0	b Hill 7
Mr A.B.Lavers	c Arnold b Boyes 25	c Pothecary b Hill 0
T.P.B,Smith	c Arnold b Boyes 1	not out 14
†T.H.Wade	c & b Boyes 0	b Boyes 3
F.H.Vigar	not out 2	c Taylor b Bailey 14
Extras	(LB 3) 3	(B 8, LB 3, NB 1) 12
Total	**181**	**(9 wickets, declared).....241**

Fall: 1st inns 1/15, 2/59, 3/110, 4/121, 5/134, 6/149, 7/153, 8/158, 9/158.
2nd inns 1/37, 2/62, 3/73, 4/74, 5/82, 6/115, 7/115, 8/197, 9/207.

HAMPSHIRE

†N.T.McCorkell	lbw b Taylor 22	b R.Smith 0
J.Bailey	b R.Smith 1	not out 11
A.E.Pothecary	c Vigar b Nichols 10	b Nichols 11
J.Arnold	c Taylor b P.Smith 30	c R.Smith b Taylor 50
W.L.C.Creese	b Nichols 8	c Nichols b Taylor 8
D.F.Walker	c Wade b P.Smith 29	c Cray b P.Smith 4
G.Hill	b Taylor 26	c Unwin b P.Smith 17
G.S.Boyes	not out 53	c Nichols b P.Smith 37
*Mr G.R.Taylor	b Taylor 6	c Unwin b P.Smith 1
R.C.Court	c Nicholas b P.Smith ...32	c Wade b Nichols 7
Mr I.N.R.Shield	c Taylor b Nichols 4	b P.Smith 0
Extras	(B 4, LB 3, NB 1) 8	(B 6, LB 4) 10
Total	**229**	**156**

Fall: 1st inns 1/10, 2/32, 3/34, 4/56, 5/86, 6/121, 7/135, 8/141, 9/193.
2nd inns 1/3, 2/18, 3/87, 4/92, 5/100, 6/125, 7/136, 8/147, 9/154.

HAMPSHIRE	O	M	R	W	O	M	R	W
Court	9	0	44	0	7	0	21	0
Shield	13	2	30	0	5	2	13	0
Hill	18	4	40	2	11	2	34	2
Boyes	18.5	7	45	6	21	4	58	2
Creese	4	0	19	1	18	5	48	2
Bailey	-	-	-	-	21	6	55	3

ESSEX	O	M	R	W	O	M	R	W
Nichols	16.5	1	58	3	9	2	34	2
R.Smith	6	1	29	1	4	0	26	1
Taylor	11	0	66	3	8	0	48	2
P.Smith	15	0	56	3	9.7	1	38	5
Vigar	4	0	12	0				

Umpires: F.Chester and C.V.Tarbox.

Close of play scores. First day: Essex 181 all out. **Second day:** Essex 136/7 (J.O'Connor 35*, R.Smith 7*).

Comments: The first day was interrupted by frequent showers. Hampshire were set to make 194 at 80 an hour to win. I.N.R.Shield was making his debut for Hampshire. There were several other changes in the Essex 2nd innings.

KENT v LEICESTERSHIRE

Played at Tunbridge Wells, June 28, 29, 30, 1939.
Toss won by Kent.
Kent won by 161 runs.

KENT

A.E.Fagg	lbw b Smith 64	c Prentice b Sperry 131
*Mr F.G.H.Chalk	c & b Flamson 24	b Sperry 1
L.E.G.Ames	b Smith 10	c Dawkes b Sperry 10
Mr B.H.Valentine	c Dawkes b Sperry 8	b Smith 24
L.J.Todd	c Flamson b Smith 25	c Packe b Prentice 13
T.W.Spencer	c Dawkes b Sperry 10	not out 33
D.V.P.Wright	c Dawkes b Flamson 1	
N.W.Harding	c Armstrong b Sperry ...11	(7) not out 5
†Mr W.H.V.Levett	c Armstrong b Smith 11	
Mr J.W.Martin	b Smith 9	
C.Lewis	not out 1	
Extras	(B 9, LB 7) 16	(LB 5) 5
Total	**190**	**(5 wickets, declared).....222**

Fall:
1st inns 1/44, 2/79, 3/88, 4/124, 5/140, 6/141, 7/161, 8/170, 9/181.
2nd inns 1/5, 2/37, 3/97, 4/138, 5/213.

LEICESTERSHIRE

G.L.Berry	c Fagg b Lewis 30	c Martin b Harding 42
G.S.Watson	c Fagg b harding 15	c Spencer b Martin 0
N.F.Armstrong	c Levett b Harding 6	st Levett b Todd 2
F.T.Prentice	c Levett b Harding 58	lbw b Todd 0
M.Tompkin	c Chalk b Harding 23	b Harding 14
*Mr M.St J Packe	c Todd b Lewis 0	c Levett b Martin 15
†G.O.Dawkes	c Levett b Martin 12	c Levett b Harding 5
L.D.Thursting	b Harding 0	c Chalk b Wright 0
H.A.Smith	lbw b Wright 7	c Fagg b Wright 0
J.Sperry	b Martin 2	not out 2
W.H.Flamson	not out 4	c Lewis b Harding 2
Extras	(LB 7, NB 2) 9	(B 2, NB 1) 3
Total	**166**	**85**

Fall:
1st inns 1/23, 2/39, 3/76, 4/140, 5/141, 6/143, 7/145, 8/157, 9/161.
2nd inns 1/1, 2/6, 3/6, 4/42, 5/64, 6/78, 7/81, 8/83, 9/83.

LEICESTERSHIRE	O	M	R	W	O	M	R	W
Sperry	21	4	77	3	10	1	51	3
Flamson	24	8	31	2	11	0	52	0
Smith	20.3	3	52	5	11	0	47	1
Prentice	1	0	14	0	8	0	54	1
Thursting	-	-	-	-	1	0	13	0

KENT	O	M	R	W	O	M	R	W
Martin	13.1	3	35	2	10	1	30	2
Todd	9	2	25	0	5	2	4	2
Harding	9	1	31	5	6.7	0	16	4
Wright	11	2	45	1	6	1	25	2
Lewis	12	3	21	2	5	2	7	0

Umpires: W.Reeves and E.J.Smith.

Close of play scores. First day: Kent 97/3 (A.E.Fagg 45*, L.J.Todd 7*).
Second day: Kent 2/0 (A.E.Fagg 1*, F.G.H.Chalk 1*).

Comments: Rain badly affected the first day's play, there being less than two hours play possible.
A.E.Fagg made 131 out of 213 in Kent's 2nd innings in 130 minutes. He hit 19 4's.
N.W.Harding achieved his best bowling figures in county cricket with match figures of 9 for 47.

NOTTINGHAMSHIRE v WORCESTERSHIRE

Played at Trent Bridge, Nottingham, June 28, 29, 30, 1939.
Toss won by Worcestershire.
Match drawn.

WORCESTERSHIRE

E.Cooper	b Voce	42	(3) c Voce b Knowles	97
R.Howorth	b Voce	0	(1) b Jepson	30
B.P.King	b Jepson	29	(2) c Harris b Voce	33
H.H.I.Gibbons	c Heane b Voce	53	c Jepson b Voce	23
S.H.Martin	st Wheat b Giles	28	not out	52
Mr C.H.Palmer	b Voce	110	b Hardstaff	4
*Mr A.F.T.White	c Harris b Jepson	25		
R.O.Jenkins	c Wheat b Voce	13	(7) not out	6
†H.Yarnold	c Voce b Butler	1		
R.T.D.Perks	c Voce b Butler	0		
P.F.Jackson	not out	5		
Extras	(B 1, LB 3)	4	(B 4, LB 4, W 1)	9
Total		**310**	(5 wickets)	**254**

Fall: 1st inns 1/0, 2/51, 3/115, 4/130, 5/182, 6/226, 7/269, 8/274, 9/286.
2nd inns 1/63, 2/65, 3/110, 4/243, 5/248.

NOTTINGHAMSHIRE

W.W.Keeton	b Jackson	42
C.B.Harris	c Howorth b Perks	9
*Mr G.F.H.Heane	c Cooper b Jenkins	82
J.Hardstaff	b Jackson	23
G.V.Gunn	lbw b Jackson	11
J.Knowles	lbw b Perks	45
R.J.Giles	b Martin	24
W.Voce	b Perks	34
†A.B.Wheat	run out	13
H.J.Butler	not out	46
A.Jepson	lbw b Jenkins	0
Extras	(B 17, LB 8, NB 3)	28
Total		**357**

Fall: 1st inns 1/27, 2/64, 3/110, 4/150, 5/200, 6/241, 7/290, 8/301, 9/357.

NOTTINGHAMSHIRE	O	M	R	W	O	M	R	W
Voce	21.6	3	72	5	16	1	65	2
Butler	12	1	71	2				
Jepson	22	2	90	2	12	1	54	1
Gunn	12	1	35	0	9	3	17	0
Giles	15	5	38	1	8	1	24	0
Heane	-	-	-	-	5	0	37	0
Harris	-	-	-	-	3	0	9	0
Hardstaff	-	-	-	-	4	1	31	1
Knowles	-	-	-	-	2	0	8	1

WORCESTERSHIRE	O	M	R	W
Perks	22	2	98	3
Martin	21	2	71	1
Howorth	18	1	82	0
Jackson	19	1	46	3
Palmer	1	0	3	0
Jenkins	3.3	0	29	2

Umpires: A.Skelding and J.A.Smart.

Close of play scores. First day: Worcestershire 310 all out. **Second day:** Worcestershire 38/0 (R.Howorth 17*, B.P.King 21*).

Comments: C.H.Palmer scored his third century in only his ninth innings for Worcestershire. His 110 included 14 4's.
E.Cooper and S.H.Martin added 122 for the 4th wicket in Worcester's 2nd innings. Bad light and rain brought the game to an early finish on the last day.

DERBYSHIRE v ESSEX

Played at Queen's Park, Chesterfield, July 1, 3, 1939.
Toss won by Essex.
Derbyshire won by ten wickets.

ESSEX

S.J.Cray	c Smith b Copson	0	c G.H.Pope b Copson	2
F.H.Vigar	b A.V.Pope	7	b A.V.Pope	0
R.M.Taylor	lbw b Copson	2	c Hounsfield b Copson	2
J.O'Connor	b Copson	6	b A.V.Pope	1
M.S.Nichols	lbw b Copson	67	lbw B G.H.Pope	53
R.Smith	lbw b A.V.Pope	45	c A.V.Pope b Copson	9
*Mr F.St.G.Unwin	c Elliott b Copson	1	c Elliott b A.V.Pope	3
Capt J.W.A.Stephenson	c Elliott b A.V.Pope	1	c Elliott b Copson	2
Mr D.F.Cock	b A.V.Pope	1	b G.H.Pope	36
†T.H.Wade	c Smith b Copson	11	(11) not out	3
T.P.B.Smith	not out	0	(10) st Elliott b Mitchell	1
Extras	(LB 2)		(LB 5)	
Total		**143**		**117**

Fall: 1st inns 1/0, 2/2, 3/14, 4/16, 5/101, 6/112, 7/113, 8/115, 9/134.
2nd inns 1/0, 2/4, 3/5, 4/5, 5/33, 6/38, 7/41, 8/110, 9/113.

DERBYSHIRE

A.E.Alderman	c Wade b R.Smith	10	not out	19
D.Smith	b Stephenson	26	not out	20
T.S.Worthington	c Wade b Nichols	32		
L.F.Townsend	b Nichols	1		
G.H.Pope	b Stephenson	82		
A.E.G.Rhodes	b Nichols	2		
*Mr T.D.Hounsfield	b Stephenson	11		
A.V.Pope	b Stephenson	1		
†H.Elliott	b Stephenson	24		
T.B.Mitchell	not out	13		
W.H.Copson	b Stephenson	5		
Extras	(B 1, LB 6)	7	(B 8)	8
Total		**214**	(No wicket)	**47**

Fall: 1st inns 1/21, 2/66, 3/68, 4/73, 5/77, 6/98, 7/102, 8/183, 9/208.

DERBYSHIRE	O	M	R	W	O	M	R	W
Copson	17.1	3	57	6	14	3	21	4
A.V.Pope	15	1	62	4	16	4	48	3
Rhodes	3	0	20	0				
G.H.Pope	3	1	2	0	6	0	27	2
Mitchell	-	-	-	-	3.2	0	16	1

ESSEX	O	M	R	W	O	M	R	W
Nichols	23	1	95	3				
R.Smith	4	0	27	1	5.6	2	14	0
Stephenson	19.7	8	41	6	5	1	25	0
T.P.B.Smith	5	0	23	0				
Taylor	2	0	21	0				
Vigar	1	1	0	0				

Umpires: F.I.Walden and E.Robinson.

Close of play scores. First day: Derbyshire 173/7 (G.H.Pope 63*, H.Elliott 22*).

Comments: Derbyshire won in two days.
W.H.Copson had match figures of 10 for 78.

GLOUCESTERSHIRE v KENT

Played at Bristol, July 1, 3, 4, 1939.
Toss won by Gloucestershire.
Gloucestershire won by an innings and 40 runs.

GLOUCESTERSHIRE

C.J.Barnett	lbw b Wright	66
R.A.Sinfield	c & b Longfield	15
V.Hopkins	c & b Wright	2
*Mr W.R.Hammond	not out	153
J.F.Crapp	c Levett b Wright	4
G.M.Emmett	lbw b Wright	0
W.L.Neale	lbw b Wright	0
†E.A.Wilson	b Wright	10
R.W.Haynes	b Wright	16
G.E.E.Lambert	b Wright	0
T.W.J.Goddard	lbw b Wright	0
Extras	(B 7, LB 10, NB 1)	18
Total		**284**

Fall: 1st inns 1/36, 2/43, 3/168, 4/180, 5/180, 6/180, 7/212, 8/284, 9/284.

KENT

A.E.Fagg	b Goddard	8	(3) c Hammond b Goddard	33
*Mr F.G.H.Chalk	c Neale b Goddard	40	lbw b Sinfield	21
L.E.G.Ames	lbw b Lambert	12	(1) c Haynes b Goddard	16
Mr B.H.Valentine	c Crapp b Goddard	14	c Hopkins b Sinfield	0
L.J.Todd	b Goddard	15	c Barnett b Goddard	2
T.W.Spencer	b Goddard	0	lbw b Goddard	15
Mr T.C.Longfield	b Goddard	0	c Emmett b Goddard	14
D.V.P.Wright	b Goddard	0	st Wilson b Goddard	2
N.W.Harding	not out	19	c Emmett b Goddard	13
†Mr W.H.V.Levett	b Goddard	8	not out	3
C.Lewis	b Goddard	0	c Haynes b Goddard	5
Extras	(B 2, LB 2)	4		0
Total		**120**		**124**

Fall: 1st inns 1/30, 2/53, 3/73, 4/77, 5/77, 6/87, 7/87, 8/96, 9/120.
2nd inns 1/21, 2/38, 3/46, 4/53, 5/73, 6/93, 7/103, 8/116, 9/117.

KENT	O	M	R	W				
Harding	12	3	39	0				
Todd	25	2	111	0				
Longfield	14	3	40	1				
Wright	21.5	8	47	9				
Lewis	8	0	29	0				

GLOUCESTERSHIRE	O	M	R	W	O	M	R	W
Barnett	2	0	9	0	1	0	6	0
Lambert	8	1	40	1	6	1	19	0
Goddard	15.4	2	38	9	16.2	1	68	8
Sinfield	9	2	29	0	12	3	31	2

Umpires: H.G.Baldwin and H.Cruice.

Close of play scores. First day: Gloucestershire 284 all out.
Comments: The match was completed in two days.
W.R.Hammond won the toss for the first time for Gloucestershire this season after 13 attempts.
D.V.P.Wright, taking nine wickets for 47 on the first day, a career-best analysis, finished off the Gloucestershire innings with the fifth hat-trick of his career, his victims being R.W.Haynes, G.E.E.Lambert and T.W.J.Goddard. He also claimed the wickets of J.F.Crapp, G.M.Emmett and W.L.Neale in one over. Wright's figures of 9 for 47 should be seen in the context of W.R.Hammond's innings, who made 153* of 241 whilst at the wicket. He made over half his side's total. He hit one six and 19 4's, batting for 290 minutes. It was his fourth 100 of the season. He added 125 with C.J.Barnett for the 3rd wicket in 150 minutes T.W.J.Goddard took 17 wickets on the second day. This equalled the world record of most wickets taken in one day by an individual bowler, held by H.Verity and C.Blythe but he was the first right-handed bowler to achieve this feat. He had taken 30 wickets for 205 runs in six days. He became the first bowler to take 100 wickets in 1939, during Kent's 2nd innings. Goddard dismissed all 11 Kent men in the match.

Gloucestershire skipper Wally Hammond, missed several games for the county as he led England against the West Indies in 1939.

Middlesex's Bill Edrich cuts Phillipson of Lancashire on his way to 102 at Old Trafford.

LANCASHIRE v MIDDLESEX

Played at Old Trafford, Manchester, July 1, 3, 4, 1939.
Toss won by Middlesex.
Middlesex won by 123 runs.

MIDDLESEX

J.D.B.Robertson	st Farrimond b Wilkinson	32	c Nutter b Wilkinson	10
S.M.Brown	c Nutter b Pollard	7	lbw b Wilkinson	31
W.J.Edrich	c Farrimond b Pollard	102	lbw b Wilkinson	13
D.C.S.Compton	c Lister b Pollard	7	c Nutter b Pollard	115
L.H.Compton	b Phillipson	17	(6) lbw b Wilkinson	1
G.E.Hart	c Farrimond b Nutter	39	(7) c Hopwood b Wilkinson	9
†W.F.F.Price	c Wilkinson b Phillipson	19	(8) c Paynter b Phillipson	1
J.M.Sims	lbw b Pollard	17	(9) run out	4
C.I.J.Smith	c Paynter b Nutter	52	(5) c Farrimond b Phillipson	1
*Mr I.A.R.Peebles	c & b Pollard	10	lbw b Pollard	13
L.H.Gray	not out	0	not out	1
Extras	(B 10, LB 4, NB 1)	15	(B 9, LB 6, NB 3)	18
Total		**317**		**217**

Fall: 1st inns 1/20, 2/67, 3/76, 4/112, 5/183, 6/219, 7/235, 8/305, 9/308.
2nd inns 1/32, 2/51, 3/72, 4/90, 5/99, 6/122, 7/123, 8/150, 9/206.

LANCASHIRE

C.Washbrook	hit wkt b Sims	42	c Peebles b Smith	82
E.Paynter	run out	16	c Price b Gray	12
J.L.Hopwood	c & b D.Compton	71	b Smith	5
N.Oldfield	b Smith	3	b Smith	9
J.Iddon	c Sims b Gray	11	st Price b Sims	39
A.E.Nutter	c Smith b D.Compton	13	c Gray b Smith	4
W.E.Phillipson	c Robertson b Smith	6	c Peebles b Smith	0
*Mr W.H.L.Lister	c Gray b Edrich	29	b Smith	0
†W.Farrimond	run out	9	not out	5
R.Pollard	run out	25	b Smith	4
L.L.Wilkinson	not out	8	st Price b Sims	1
Extras	(B 1, LB 5, W 1, NB 5)	12	(B 4, LB 1)	5
Total		**245**		**166**

Fall: 1st inns 1/33, 2/84, 3/99, 4/125, 5/153, 6/170, 7/171, 8/199, 9/218.
2nd inns 1/15, 2/26, 3/36, 4/129, 5/142, 6/142, 7/142, 8/161, 9/161.

LANCASHIRE	O	M	R	W	O	M	R	W
Phillipson	17	1	73	2	15	1	67	2
Pollard	17.4	1	78	5	13.7	4	41	2
Wilkinson	15	0	61	1	22	4	73	5
Nutter	13	0	69	2	5	0	18	0
Hopwood	2	0	11	0				
Paynter	2	0	10	0				

MIDDLESEX	O	M	R	W	O	M	R	W
Smith	23	3	72	2	19	5	55	7
Gray	12	2	46	1	7	0	27	1
Edrich	5.7	1	16	1	3	0	15	0
Sims	16	2	72	1	11.1	0	49	2
Peebles	1	0	6	0	4	2	8	0
D.C.S.Compton	4	0	21	2	3	0	7	0

Umpires: A.Dolphin and G.M.Lee.

Close of play scores. First day: Lancashire 69/1 (C.Washbrook 32*, J.L.Hopwood 19*). **Second day:** Middlesex 188/8 (D.C.S.Compton 105*, I.A.R.Peebles 3*).
Comments: W.Farrimond's benefit match. He had only one full season as Lancashire's wicketkeeper, despite having played for England and having first played for Lancashire in 1924.
W.J.Edrich made 102 in the 1st innings. He hit 13 4's and batted for about 200 minutes. D.C.S.Compton made 115 in just over 150 minutes in the 2nd innings. It included 17 4's.
Lancashire needed 290 to win in 300 minutes.
Lancashire lost their last five 2nd innings wickets for 14.
C.I.J.Smith performed the hat-trick (his first) in Lancashire's 2nd innings. His victims were A.E.Nutter, W.E.Phillipson and W.H.L.Lister.

Denis Compton, scored 115 in the second innings against Lancashire.

LEICESTERSHIRE v WORCESTERSHIRE

Played at Grace Road, Leicester, July 1, 3, 4, 1939.
Toss won by Worcestershire.
Worcestershire won by 24 runs.

WORCESTERSHIRE

R.Howorth	b Smith 41	c Dawkes b Sperry 13
B.P.King	c Berry b Sperry 10	(3) c & b Sperry 6
E.Cooper	c Smith b Thursting 17	(2) not out 184
H.H.I.Gibbons	lbw b Smith 33	lbw b Flamson............97
S.H.Martin	c Dawkes b Sperry 10	lbw b Smith 12
Mr C.H.Palmer	st Dawkes b Smith 53	b Flamson.................3
*Mr A.F.T.White	c Armstrong b Sperry 13	
R.O.Jenkins	c Smith b Flamson.......21	not out 23
Mr E.G.Bayliss	c Sperry b Smith 0	(7) b Flamson 0
R.T.D.Perks	b Smith 14	
†H.Yarnold	not out 4	
Extras	(B 4, LB 5) 9	(B 8, LB 9, NB 2) 19
Total	**225**	(6 wickets, declared).....**357**

Fall: 1st inns 1/35, 2/59, 3/84, 4/118, 5/118, 6/151, 7/197, 8/197, 9/215.
2nd inns 1/21, 2/37, 3/257 4/312.

LEICESTERSHIRE

G.L.Berry	c King b Perks............79	st King b Howorth 42
G.S.Watson	b Perks.................7	c King b Perks 2
N.F.Armstrong	b Perks.................3	(6) c Jenkins b Howorth 4
F.T.Prentice	c Gibbons b Martin 31	(3) st King b Howorth......39
M.Tompkin	c King b Howorth 14	(4) lbw b Jenkins 82
*Mr M.St.J.Packe	c Palmer b Jenkins 11	(5) c Palmer b Jenkins 56
†G.O.Dawkes	c & b Howorth 4	b Howorth 9
L.D.Thursting	c King b Perks 3	c King b Martin 71
H.A.Smith	not out 15	run out 22
J.Sperry	b Perks.................11	b Howorth 6
W.H.Flamson	c Cooper b Martin 6	not out 6
Extras	(B 8, LB 1, NB 4) 13	(B 16, LB 5, NB 1) 22
Total	**197**	**361**

Fall: 1st inns 1/27, 2/28, 3/112, 4/132, 5/157, 6/157, 7/163, 8/167, 9/190.
2nd inns 1/3, 2/74, 3/103, 4/194, 5/198, 6/214, 7/296, 8/349, 9/349.

LEICESTERSHIRE	O	M	R	W	O	M	R	W
Sperry	14	0	77	3	16	1	117	2
Flamson	12	1	39	1	18	1	81	3
Smith	16.2	2	52	5	16	0	66	1
Prentice	11	2	26	0	9	0	51	0
Thursting	3	0	22	1	4	0	23	0

WORCESTERSHIRE	O	M	R	W	O	M	R	W
Perks	25	2	75	5	21	2	104	1
Martin	20.5	5	66	2	15	2	71	1
Howorth	11	1	29	2	26	2	103	5
Jenkins	6	1	14	1	14	1	61	2

Umpires: C.N.Woolley and C.W.L.Parker.

Close of play scores. First day: Leicestershire 77/2 (G.L.Berry 42*, F.T.Prentice 16*). Second day: Worcestershire 298/4 (E.Cooper 153*, C.H.Palmer 0*).

Comments: H.Yarnold was struck on the eye whilst batting in Worcestershire's 1st innings and played no further part. B.P.King took over as wicketkeeper. N.F.Armstrong was also forced to go to hospital after a blow to the mouth, the ball falling on to his wicket and bowling him. The Worcestershire captain, A.F.T.White, became ill on the Sunday, H.H.I.Gibbons deputizing as captain on the last two days.
E.Cooper and H.H.I.Gibbons added 220 for the 3rd wicket in Worcester's 2nd innings.
E.Cooper batted 240 minutes for his undefeated 184, hitting 20 4's. Leicestershire lost in the extra half-hour on the third day, only 24 short of the required 385 runs.
On the first day, when the game was held up for bad light, a spectator ran on to the field and uprooted one set of stumps.

NORTHAMPTONSHIRE v SUSSEX

Played at Kettering, July 1, 3, 4, 1939.
Toss won by Northamptonshire.
Sussex won by five wickets.

NORTHAMPTONSHIRE

H.W.Greenwood	c Jas.Langridge b J.Parks 16	b Nye...................94
P.Davis	lbw b J.Parks.............12	c H.Parks b J.Parks.....5
D.Brookes	run out 0	lbw b Oakes 67
J.E.Timms	c Jas.Langridge b J.Parks 101	not out 114
F.P.O'Brien	c Nye b Cox 40	
*Mr R.P.Nelson	c Bartlett b Jas.Langridge 7	c H.Parks b Oakes 11
W.E.Merritt	c Bartlett b J.Parks 8	c J.Parks b Duffield 87
†W.Kemmey	c Cornford b Jas.Langridge 3	not out 8
M.E.F.Dunkley	b J.Parks 8	
R.J.Partridge	not out 0	
A.G.Robinson	run out 0	
Extras	(LB 3, NB 2) 5	(B 4, LB 8, NB 1) 13
Total	**200**	(6 wickets, declared).....**399**

Fall: 1st inns 1/31, 2/31, 3/39, 4/130, 5/171, 6/187, 7/190, 8/200, 9/200.
2nd inns 1/14, 2/150, 3/222, 4/222, 5/265, 6/383.

SUSSEX

John G.Langridge	b Partridge 4	b Nelson 93
J.H.Parks	c Kemmey b Partridge 13	(6) not out 50
H.W.Parks	b Nelson 25	c Kemmey b Partridge......8
G.Cox	c Merritt b Partridge 58	st Kemmey b Merritt 232
Jas.Langridge	lbw b Merritt 6	c Dunkley b Nelson 4
*Mr H.T.Bartlett	c Greenwood b Partridge 3	(7) not out 14
†W.L.Cornford	not out 41	
Mr R.A.A.Holt	b Robinson 4	
C.Oakes	c Dunkley b Merritt 0	(2) lbw b Robinson 9
J.Duffield	b Nelson 7	
J.K.Nye	c Merritt b Nelson 2	
Extras	(B 4, LB 4, W 1) 9	(B 16, LB 2) 18
Total	**172**	(5 wickets) **428**

Fall: 1st inns 1/20, 2/25, 3/82, 4/95, 5/106, 6/119, 7/138, 8/139, 9/168.
2nd inns 1/9, 2/40, 3/259, 4/295, 5/399.

SUSSEX	O	M	R	W	O	M	R	W
Nye	16	1	55	0	24	0	116	2
Duffield	6	0	14	0	16	0	76	1
J.Parks	19.6	1	55	5	22	6	78	1
Jas.Langridge	12	1	48	2	3	0	16	0
Cox	6	0	23	1	3	0	16	0
John Langridge	-	-	-	-	5	0	16	0
Oakes	-	-	-	-	9	1	68	2

NORTHANTS	O	M	R	W	O	M	R	W
Partridge	16	0	51	4	18	2	84	1
Timms	4	0	27	0	13	0	88	0
Robinson	11	1	32	1	16	0	77	1
Nelson	6.4	3	7	3	17	2	79	2
Merritt	10	1	46	2	10	0	75	1
O'Brien	-	-	-	-	2	0	7	0

Umpires: F.Chester and H.W.Lee.

Close of play scores. First day: Sussex 118/5 (G.Cox 58*, W.L.Cornford 3*). Second day: Northants 359/5 (J.E.Timms 102*, W.E.Merritt 67*).

Comments: H.W.Greenwood and D.Brookes put on 136 for the 2nd wicket in Northants 2nd innings. J.E.Timms became the first Northamptonshire batsman to make two centuries in a match when he scored his 4th and 5th of the season. His 101 was made in 150 minutes and included one 6 and 11 4's. His undefeated 114 included 17 4's. He also passed his 1,000 runs for the season. He and W.E.Merritt added 117 for the 6th wicket. W.E.Merritt hit C.Oakes for 28 in one over (two 6's and four 4's) in the 2nd innings. His 87, made in 57 minutes and including three 6's and ten 4's was on target for the quickest century of the season, made in 82 minutes. Sussex were set to make 428 in 315 minutes and won with 25 minutes to spare. It was the fourth highest winning innings total in England. The Sussex score of 428/5 had only been surpassed by the 502/6 scored by Middlesex against Notts in 1925 in a County Championship match. John G.Langridge and G.Cox put on 219 in 120 minutes for the 3rd wicket. Cox made his century in 87 minutes and his 232 in 200 minutes. It included four 6's and 32 4's. It was his highest score in county cricket and the best score for Sussex in the last five seasons in championship matches. J.H.Parks and G.Cox added 104 in 70 minutes for the 5th wicket.

SOMERSET v HAMPSHIRE

Played at Taunton, July 1, 3, 4, 1939.
Toss won by Somerset.
Match drawn.

SOMERSET

F.S.Lee	c Walker b Bailey	28
H.Gimblett	c Boyes b Shield	9
H.T.F.Buse	c Creese b Mackenzie	24
Mr R.J.O.Meyer	c Court b Hill	86
Mr F.M.McRae	c Taylor b Mackenzie	107
Mr C.J.P.Barnwell	b Boyes	83
†W.T.Luckes	not out	42
A.W.Wellard	c Boyes b Court	87
W.H.R.Andrews	b Shield	5
*Mr G.M.Bennett	not out	6
Extras	(B 7, LB 6)	13
Total	(8 wickets, declared)	**490**

Fall: 1st inns 1/14, 2/59, 3/63, 4/181, 5/332, 6/354, 7/465, 8/478.

H.L.Hazell did not bat.

HAMPSHIRE

P.A.Mackenzie	b Meyer	66	c Luckes b Wellard	28
J.Bailey	c Gimblett b Wellard	48	c Bennett b Buse	13
A.E.Pothecary	st Luckes b Hazell	13	c McRae b Hazell	35
J.Arnold	b Hazell	5	b Wellard	0
W.L.C.Creese	c McRae b Hazell	9	not out	86
†D.F.Walker	b Hazell	54	not out	90
G.Hill	lbw b Hazell	18		
G.S.Boyes	c Wellard b Meyer	36		
*Mr G.R.Taylor	c Luckes b Meyer	19		
R.C.Court	not out	27		
Mr I.N.R.Shield	c Bennett b Meyer	6		
Extras	(B 17, LB 3)	20	(B 19, LB 6)	25
Total		**321**	(4 wickets)	**277**

Fall: 1st inns 1/84, 2/123, 3/135, 4/151, 5/159, 6/196, 7/265, 8/279, 9/303.
2nd inns 1/35, 2/82, 3/86, 4/100.

HAMPSHIRE	O	M	R	W
Court	19	1	63	1
Shield	16	1	96	2
Bailey	26	10	66	1
Hill	17	0	69	1
Boyes	17	3	73	1
Mackenzie	9	0	71	2
Creese	7	0	39	0

SOMERSET	O	M	R	W	O	M	R	W
Wellard	22	1	63	1	23	4	73	2
Andrews	10	0	36	0				
Buse	15	1	38	0	9	2	19	1
Meyer	25.4	4	99	4	12	2	37	0
Hazell	19	2	65	5	19	2	72	1
Gimblett	-	-	-	-	3	1	19	0
Lee	-	-	-	-	2	0	28	0
Barnwell	-	-	-	-	1	0	4	0

Umpires: E.Cooke and J.J.Hills.

Close of play scores. First day: Somerset 429/6 (W.T.Luckes 24*, A.W.Wellard 56*). **Second day:** Hampshire 303/9 (R.C.Court 15*, I.N.R.Shield 0*).

Comments: Somerset made their highest score of the season. F.M.McRae scored his first century for Somerset. His 107 was made in 240 minutes and included 11 4's. His previous highest score was 54. He and R.J.O.Meyer added 118 for the 4th wicket in 120 minutes. F.M.McRae then added 151 in just under two hours with C.J.P.Barnwell for the 5th wicket. A.E.Wellard hit seven 6's in his 87 made in 75 minutes. Hampshire followed on 169 behind. W.L.C.Creese and D.F.Walker saved Hampshire with an unbroken 177 in 130 minutes for the 5th wicket.

WARWICKSHIRE v GLAMORGAN

Played at Edgbaston, Birmingham, July 1, 3, 4 1939.
Toss won by Glamorgan.
Warwickshire won by an innings and 91 runs.

GLAMORGAN

A.H.Dyson	c Hill b Mayer	0	c Cranmer b Wilmot	6
D.E.Davies	c Hollies b Wyatt	0	lbw b Hollies	72
T.L.Brierley	b Wilmot	25	lbw b Hollies	17
*Mr M.J.L.Turnbull	lbw b Mayer	25	c Mayer b Hollies	53
D.Davies	c & b Mayer	20	c Cranmer b Hollies	20
C.C.Smart	lbw b Santall	3	(7) not out	23
E.C.Jones	st Buckingham b Hollies	21	(6) c Mayer b Hollies	5
†H.G.Davies	b Mayer	0	c & b Hollies	1
A.J.Watkins	not out	4	c & b Hollies	9
J.Mercer	c Ord b Hollies	3	c Wyatt b Hollies	12
P.F.Judge	c Croom b Hollies	0	c Croom b Hollies	0
Extras	(B 1)	1	(B 4, LB 2, NB 1)	7
Total		**102**		**225**

Fall: 1st inns 1/0, 2/0, 3/40, 4/55, 5/58, 6/95, 7/95, 8/95, 9/101.
2nd inns 1/31, 2/64, 3/123, 4/174, 5/174, 6/184, 7/190, 8/208, 9/222.

WARWICKSHIRE

A.J.W.Croom	c & b E.Davies	145
W.A.Hill	c Brierley b Mercer	17
F.R.Santall	lbw b E.Davies	14
Mr R.E.S.Wyatt	c H.Davies b E.Davies	27
H.E.Dollery	lbw b E.Davies	14
J.S.Ord	b E.Davies	77
†J.Buckingham	not out	45
*Mr P.Cranmer	c Dyson b E.Davies	15
K.Wilmot	not out	41
Extras	(B 8, LB 13, W 2)	23
Total	(7 wickets, declared)	**418**

Fall: 1st inns 1/30, 2/57, 3/112, 4/158, 5/292, 6/324, 7/340.

J.H.Mayer and W.E.Hollies did not bat.

WARWICKSHIRE	O	M	R	W	O	M	R	W
Mayer	11	3	34	4	15	2	42	0
Wyatt	8	1	30	1	3	0	12	0
Wilmot	5	3	5	1	13	2	38	1
Santall	4	1	20	1	10	4	32	0
Hollies	3.6	0	12	3	30.2	3	93	9
Croom	-	-	-	-	1	0	1	0

GLAMORGAN	O	M	R	W
Judge	30	6	97	0
Mercer	27	2	100	1
E.Davies	40	9	132	6
Smart	10	1	37	0
Watkins	12	3	29	0

Umpires: F.J.Durston and D.Hendren.

Close of play scores. First day: Warwickshire 190/4 (A.J.W.Croom 80*, J.S.Ord 23*). **Second day:** Glamorgan 128/3.

Comments: Glamorgan's 1st innings of 102 was completed in just over two hours. A.J.W.Croom made 145 in nearly 355 minutes. It was his first century for two seasons. He hit a 6 and eight 4's. He and J.S.Ord added 134 for the 5th wicket. On the third day W.E.Hollies achieved his best innings analysis, taking 9 for 93, becoming the 6th Warwickshire bowler to accomplish this feat and the first for 14 years. He took the last seven wickets in seven overs for 29 runs.

WARWICKSHIRE COUNTY CRICKET CLUB

Standing (left to right): J.S.Ord, K.Wilmot, W.A.Hill, H.E.Dollery, W.E.Hollies, N.A.Shortland, J.Buckingham. Seated: J.H.Mayer, R.E.S.Wyatt, P.Cranmer (captain), F.R.Santall, A.J.W.Croom.

YORKSHIRE v SURREY

Played at Headingley, Leeds, July 1, 3, 4, 1939.
Toss won by Yorkshire.
Yorkshire won by 177 runs.

YORKSHIRE

L.Hutton	c & b Gover	151	lbw b Brown	81
A.Mitchell	b Watts	3	c Squires b Gover	0
W.Barber	b Watts	0	c Brooks b Brown	27
M.Leyland	c Watts b Garland-Wells	95	not out	60
Mr N.W.D.Yardley	b Gover	1	(6) c Barling b Brown	8
Mr G.A.Wilson	b Gover	8	(7) hit wkt b Watts	16
*Mr A.B.Sellers	c Parker b Watts	63		
†A.Wood	b Watts	28		
E.P.Robinson	b Gover	7	(5) c Squires b Brown	2
H.Verity	not out	12		
W.E.Bowes	b Watts	17		
Extras	(B 12, LB 6, NB 3)	21	(B 1, LB 4)	5
Total		**406**	(6 wickets, declared)	**199**

Fall: 1st inns 1/3, 2/3, 3/243, 4/259, 5/273, 6/279, 7/367, 8/376, 9/376.
2nd inns 1/0, 2/85, 3/134, 4/138, 5/159, 6/199.

SURREY

L.B.Fishlock	c Wilson b Bowes	26	c Robinson b Verity	53
R.J.Gregory	lbw b Yardley	7	c Mitchell b Yardley	7
H.S.Squires	c Mitchell b Yardley	0	c Robinson b Bowes	0
T.H.Baring	c Wood b Bowes	10	c Hutton b Bowes	15
J.F.Parker	lbw b Verity	46	not out	41
A.J.W.McIntyre	lbw b Yardley	0	c Verity b Robinson	4
*Mr H.M.Garland-Wells	c Bowes b Verity	29	c Leyland b Verity	1
Mr F.R.Brown	c Hutton b Leyland	119	run out	6
E.A.Watts	c Yardley b Verity	46	c Bowes b Hutton	5
†E.W.J.Brooks	not out	1	c Mitchell b Verity	0
A.R.Gover	c Sellers b Verity	0	c & b Verity	0
Extras	(B 2, LB 4)	6	(LB 6)	6
Total		**290**		**138**

Fall: 1st inns 1/11, 2/11, 3/39, 4/48, 5/48, 6/94, 7/140, 8/288, 9/289.
2nd inns 1/17, 2/20, 3/64, 4/96, 5/103, 6/108, 7/125, 8/136, 9/138.

SURREY	O	M	R	W	O	M	R	W
Gover	24	0	96	4	11	1	67	1
Watts	17.1	1	70	5	7.6	0	47	1
Brown	13	1	78	0	7	0	56	4
Parker	7	0	48	0	3	0	24	0
Garland-Wells	15	2	58	1				
Squires	4	0	21	0				
Gregory	2	0	14	0				

YORKSHIRE	O	M	R	W	O	M	R	W
Bowes	19	2	72	2	9	1	29	2
Yardley	12	0	59	3	5	0	35	1
Verity	14.7	0	59	4	9.2	1	17	4
Robinson	6	0	44	0	9	3	30	1
Hutton	3	0	16	0	4	0	21	1
Leyland	3	0	34	1				

Umpires: A.Skelding and J.A.Smart.

Close of play scores. First day: Yorkshire 268/4 (L.Hutton 150*, G.A.Wilson 5*). **Second day:** Yorkshire 34/1 (L.Hutton 26, W.Barber 7*).

Comments: Rain interrupted play on the first day.
L.Hutton and M.Leyland added 240 for the 3rd wicket in 190 minutes.
L.Hutton's 151 included one 6 and 13 4's.
F.R.Brown's 119 came in 105 minutes, including three 6's and 15 4's. He reached his century in 100 minutes. With E.A.Watts he added 148 in an 8th wicket partnership, made in 80 minutes.
Surrey, set to make 316 in 195 minutes, were bowled out for 138.

ESSEX v SOMERSET

Played at Westcliff-on-Sea, July 5, 6, 1939.
Toss won by Somerset.
Essex won by an innings and 40 runs.

SOMERSET

F.S.Lee	c Taylor b Nichols	19	c O'Connor b R.Smith	36
H.T.F.Buse	c O'Connor b Nichols	0	(3) c Eastman b R.Smith	30
Mr F.M.McRae	c Cock b Nichols	21	(4) c O'Connor b P.Smith	27
Mr J.Priddy	c Cock b P.Smith	27	(5) b R.Smith	7
Mr A.J.P.Ling	c P.Smith b Taylor	1	(7) c Nichols b P.Smith	30
Mr C.J.P.Barnwell	b R.Smith	27	(2) c P.Smith b R.Smiht	25
†W.T.Luckes	c Vigar b R.Smith	3	absent hurt	
*Mr G.M.Bennett	c Cock b R.Smith	6	c Cock b P.Smith	13
A.W.Wellard	c Vigar b P.Smith	19	(6) lbw b P.Smith	4
Mr S.Weaver	not out	0	(11) b P.Smith	3
H.L.Hazell	b P.Smith	0	(10) not out	4
Extras	(B 3, LB 1)	4	(B 3, LB 5)	8
Total		**127**		**187**

Fall: 1st inns 1/5, 2/24, 3/53, 4/61, 5/73, 6/80, 7/98, 8/121, 9/127.
2nd inns 1/32, 2/91, 3/98, 4/106, 5/109, 6/154, 7/174, 8/180, 9/348.

ESSEX

L.C.Eastman	c & b Buse	4
S.J.Cray	c Buse b Wellard	11
R.M.Taylor	b Wellard	22
J.O'Connor	c Buse b Wellard	8
M.S.Nichols	lbw b Wellard	0
R.Smith	c Hazell b Priddy	66
†Mr D.F.Cock	c Lee b Wellard	98
*Mr F.St.G.Unwin	c Weaver b Hazell	42
F.H.Vigar	not out	44
F.H.Rist	c Ling b Hazell	32
T.P.B.Smith	c Bennett b Hazell	3
Extras	(B 16, LB 8)	24
Total		**354**

Fall: 1st inns 1/7, 2/36, 3/44, 4/44, 5/66, 6/132, 7/252, 8/278, 9/348.

ESSEX	O	M	R	W	O	M	R	W
Nichols	12	2	25	3	14	3	35	0
R.Smith	14	2	42	3	13	1	67	4
T.P.B.Smith	13.4	1	50	3	21.2	1	67	5
Taylor	2	1	6	1	3	1	10	0

SOMERSET	O	M	R	W	O	M	R	W
Wellard	31	6	119	5				
Buse	27	4	82	1				
Weaver	4	0	34	0				
Priddy	10	2	49	1				
Hazell	11.3	1	46	3				

Umpires: E.Robinson and H.W.Lee.

Close of play scores. First day: Essex 207/6 (D.F.Cock 70*, F.St.G.Unwin 20*).

Comments: The match finished in two days.
D.F.Cock was awarded his county cap, after making 98, his highest score for Essex.
He and F.St.G.Unwin added 120 in 100 minutes for the 7th wicket. S.Weaver, the Chelsea footballer, made his debut for Somerset.
W.T.Luckes was absent hurt with a split finger in Somerset's 2nd innings.

GLAMORGAN v HAMPSHIRE

Played at Swansea, July 5, 6, 7, 1939.
Toss won by Glamorgan.
Match drawn.

HAMPSHIRE

J.Bailey	not out	23
P.A.Mackenzie	c Smart b Clay	12
A.E.Pothecary	c & b Judge	5
J.Arnold	not out	10
Total	(2 wickets)	**50**

Fall: 1st inns 1/26, 2/33.

*Mr G.R.Taylor, Mr I.N.R.Shield, G.S.Boyes, W.L.C.Creese, G.Hill, R.C.Court and †D.F.Walker did not bat.

GLAMORGAN

*Mr M.J.L.Turnbull, Mr J.C.Clay, A.H.Dyson, D.E.Davies, T.L.Brierley, D.Davies, C.C.Smart, E.C.Jones, †H.G.Davies, J.Mercer and P.F.Judge.

GLAMORGAN	O	M	R	W
Judge	5	0	21	1
Mercer	5	2	8	0
Clay	8	3	11	1
D.E.Davies	4	1	10	0

Umpires: C.V.Tarbox and H.Cruice.

Close of play scores. First day: Hampshire 50/2 (J.Bailey 23*, J.Arnold 10*). **Second day:** No play.

Comments: Hampshire were put in to bat. There was only 85 minutes play in this match, all before lunch on the first day.

SUSSEX v LANCASHIRE

Played at Hove, July 5, 6, 7, 1939.
Toss won by Sussex.
Match drawn.

SUSSEX

John G.Langridge	run out	8
H.E.Hammond	lbw b Pollard	4
H.W.Parks	c Oldfield b Wilkinson	35
G.Cox	b Wilkinson	182
Jas.Langridge	c Nutter b Phillipson	161
J.H.Parks	lbw b Wilkinson	3
*Flt-Lt A.J.Holmes	not out	41
C.Oakes	b Pollard	1
†W.L.Cornford	not out	5
Extras	(B 5, LB 2, NB 2)	9
Total	(7 wickets, declared)	**449**

Fall: 1st inns 1/9, 2/26, 3/90, 4/356, 5/362, 6/432, 7/437.
J.H.Cornford and J.K.Nye did not bat.

LANCASHIRE

C.Washbrook	c John Langridge b Jas.Langridge	40	c Jas.Langridge b J.Parks	18	
W.Place	retired hurt	25			
J.L.Hopwood	c W.Cornford b Nye	18	(2) c Hammond b Nye	15	
N.Oldfield	c J.Parks b Nye	5	(3) c & b J.Cornford	68	
J.Iddon	c J.Parks b Nye	9	(4) not out	51	
A.E.Nutter	c W.Cornford b Nye	8	(5) not out	13	
A.E.Phillipson	c John Langridge b J.Cornford	8			
*Mr W.H.L.Lister	c J.Parks b Jas.Langridge	1			
†W.Farrimond	not out	17			
R.Pollard	st W.Cornford b J.Cornford	7			
L.L.Wilkinson	c John Langridge b Hammond	3			
Extras	(LB 5, W 2)	7	(B 4, LB 4)	8	
Total		**148**	(3 wickets)	**173**	

Fall: 1st inns 1/80, 2/86, 3/99, 4/107, 5/109, 6/127, 7/130, 8/143, 9/148.
2nd inns 1/24, 2/54, 3/136.

LANCASHIRE	O	M	R	W
Phillipson	21	4	103	1
Pollard	18	0	102	2
Nutter	16	1	84	0
Wilkinson	25	1	131	3
Hopwood	1	0	4	0
Iddon	2	0	16	0

SUSSEX	O	M	R	W	O	M	R	W
Nye	17	1	57	4	13	1	74	1
J.H.Cornford	10	1	35	2	8	0	32	1
J.H.Parks	9	2	27	0	7	3	16	1
Hammond	6.2	0	15	1	4	0	23	0
Jas.Langridge	4	1	7	2	4	0	11	0
Cox	-	-	-	-	2	0	2	0
H.W.Parks	-	-	-	-	1	0	7	0

Umpires: J.A.Newman and W.Reeves.

Close of play scores. First day: Sussex 449/7 (A.J.Holmes 41*, W.L.Cornford 5*). **Second day:** Lancashire 51/1 (C.Washbrook 16*, N.Oldfield 16*).
Comments: G.Cox and James Langridge added 266 in 180 minutes for the 4th Sussex wicket, the second highest Sussex score for this wicket. G.Cox made 182 in 230 minutes, hitting 24 4's. He reached his century in 120 minutes. James Langridge made 161, including one 6 and 17 4's. His innings lasted 240 minutes. W.Place retired hurt with the Lancashire score at 50 without loss, after being struck on the head from a fielder's return. Play was delayed on the third day until 1pm, allowing Lancashire, who had followed on 301 behind, to save the game.

WORCESTERSHIRE v SURREY

Played at Worcester, July 5, 6, 7, 1939.
Toss won by Worcestershire.
Worcestershire won by three wickets.

SURREY

R.J.Gregory	lbw b Howorth	25	lbw b Perks	0
L.B.Fishlock	c Palmer b Howorth	46	lbw b Howorth	32
E.W.Whitfield	st Abell b Howorth	53	c Perks b Jenkins	60
T.H.Baring	c Abell b Martin	24	c Cooper b Howorth	6
H.S.Squires	c Blakey b Howorth	15	c King b Howorth	1
J.F.Parker	lbw b Jackson	29	b Jackson	1
A.J.W.McIntyre	c Palmer b Jackson	6	st Abell b Jackson	2
*Mr H.M.Garland-Wells	c Perks b Jackson	3	b Jackson	62
E.A.Watts	c Abell b Howorth	13	c Abell b Jackson	1
†E.W.J.Brooks	lbw b Jackson	3	not out	1
A.R.Gover	not out	31		
Extras	(B 3, LB 4, NB 4)	11	(B 1, LB 5, NB 3)	9
Total		**259**	(9 wickets, declared)	**175**

Fall: 1st inns 1/61, 2/90, 3/151, 4/151, 5/194, 6/205, 7/210, 8/211, 9/216.
2nd inns 1/0, 2/48, 3/60, 4/64, 5/69, 6/77, 7/172, 8/174, 9/175.

WORCESTERSHIRE

R.Howorth	b Gover	11	c Fishlock b Gover	0
E.Cooper	lbw b Garland-Wells	46	c Fishlock b Watts	20
B.P.King	lbw b Gover	4	lbw b Parker	30
H.H.I.Gibbons	c & b Squires	6	run out	53
S.H.Martin	lbw b Gregory	9	lbw b Gover	31
Mr C.H.Palmer	c Parker b Gover	84	run out	5
*†Mr G.E.B.Abell	c Gover b Squires	26	b Gover	7
G.M.Blakey	c Brookes b Gover	42	(9) not out	1
R.O.Jenkins	not out	22		
R.T.D.Perks	c & b Gover	11	(8) not out	13
Extras	(B 4, LB 6, NB 1)	11	(LB 2, NB 1)	3
Total	(9 wickets, declared)	**272**	(7 wickets)	**163**

Fall: 1st inns 1/28, 2/38, 3/49, 4/85, 5/85, 6/130, 7/229, 8/244, 9/272.
2nd inns 1/2, 2/35, 3/79, 4/134, 5/141, 6/142, 7/160.

P.F.Jackson did not bat.

WORCESTERSHIRE	O	M	R	W	O	M	R	W
Perks	17	4	52	0	7	1	35	1
Jackson	20	4	52	4	12	0	50	4
Martin	16	0	46	1	5	0	20	0
Howorth	26.1	3	74	5	12	3	40	3
Jenkins	5	0	24	0	5	0	21	1

SURREY	O	M	R	W	O	M	R	W
Gover	21.4	2	94	5	10	0	78	3
Watts	16	1	63	0	8.3	0	43	1
Squires	11	0	29	2				
Parker	4	2	10	0	4	0	21	1
Garland-Wells	10	2	24	1	3	0	18	0
Gregory	10	1	41	1				

Umpires: J.J.Hills and D.Hendren.

Close of play scores. First day: Surrey 210/7 (H.M.Garland-Wells 3*). **Second day:** Worcestershire 226/6 (C.H.Palmer 82*, G.M.Blakey 31*).

Comments: Surrey were put in to bat.
Eighty minutes were lost through rain on the first day.
G.M.Blakey was making his debut for Worcestershire.
Worcestershire, set to score 163 in 105 minutes, won off the third ball of the last over in extra-time.

ESSEX v GLOUCESTERSHIRE

Played at Westcliff-on-Sea, July 8, 10, 11, 1939.
Toss won by Gloucestershire.
Gloucestershire won by 234 runs.

GLOUCESTERSHIRE

C.J.Barnett	c Vere Hodge b R.Smith	30	c Taylor b Nichols	9
R.A.Sinfield	run out	45	b Nichols	4
V.Hopkins	c P.Smith b Taylor	8	c P.Smith b Nichols	0
*Mr W.R.Hammond	c Rist b P.Smith	207	c P.Smith b Nichols	40
J.F.Crapp	c Taylor b Nichols	56	c Taylor b R.Smith	48
G.M.Emmett	b P.Smith	37	b Nichols	70
W.L.Neale	b Taylor	11	not out	39
†E.A.Wilson	lbw b Taylor	10	(9) not out	18
C.J.Scott	not out	11	(8) b Nichols	7
G.E.E.Lambert	b P.Smith	0		
T.W.J.Goddard	c Unwin b Taylor	6		
Extras	(B 4, LB 6, W 1)	11	(LB 6)	6
Total		**432**	(7 wickets, declared)	**241**

Fall: 1st inns 1/73, 2/85, 3/88, 4/237, 5/374, 6/405, 7/413, 8/420, 9/425.
2nd inns 1/12, 2/12, 3/17, 4/74, 5/124, 6/204, 7/214.

ESSEX

L.C.Eastman	c & b Scott	0	c Hammond b Lambert	14
S.J.Cray	b Lambert	12	c Crapp b Scott	6
R.M.Taylor	c Hammond b Lambert	5	b Scott	5
F.H.Vigar	c Scott b Goddard	121	(6) c Crapp b Goddard	1
J.O'Connor	c Goddard b Lambert	0	(4) run out	20
M.S.Nichols	lbw b Lambert	61	(5) c & b Scott	20
R.Smith	c Lambert b Scott	6	b Scott	20
Dr N.Vere Hodge	c Hammond b Scott	4	b Goddard	0
*Mr F.St.G.Unwin	c Hammond b Goddard	19	not out	28
†F.H.Rist	c Lambert b Goddard	53	b Scott	10
T.P.B.Smith	not out	8	c Neale b Goddard	4
Extras	(LB 8, NB 3)	11	(B 5, LB 4, NB 2)	11
Total		**300**		**139**

Fall: 1st inns 1/0, 2/5, 3/40, 4/40, 5/150, 6/163, 7/171, 8/206, 9/281.
2nd inns 1/18, 2/26, 3/47, 4/52, 5/73, 6/81, 7/81, 8/101, 9/134.

ESSEX	O	M	R	W	O	M	R	W
Nichols	20	5	63	1	21	3	83	6
R.Smith	17	1	80	1	13.3	1	73	1
T.P.B.Smith	25	3	131	3	11	3	51	0
Taylor	18.4	1	103	4	4	1	28	0
Vigar	4	0	25	0				
Eastman	4	0	19	0				

GLOUCESTERSHIRE	O	M	R	W	O	M	R	W
Scott	22	1	99	3	12	2	57	5
Lambert	18	0	65	4	6	0	39	1
Goddard	21	3	95	3	9	4	22	3
Sinfield	3	0	11	0				
Neale	4	0	19	0				
Barnett	-	-	-	-	3	0	10	0

Umpires: J.Hardstaff and J.A.Newman.

Close of play scores. First day: Essex 34/2 (S.J.Cray 12*, F.H.Vigar 10*). **Second day:** Gloucestershire 180/5 (G.M.Emmett 61*, W.L.Neale 13*).
Comments: On the first day, W.R.Hammond scored 207 out of 320 in 225 minutes. He reached his century, made out of 163 in just over two hours. His innings included four 6's and 25 4's. It was his fifth 100 of the season. He and J.F.Crapp put on 149 in 110 minutes for the 4th wicket and he then shared a 5th wicket partnership of 137 in 90 minutes with G.M.Emmett.
F.H.Vigar scored his first century in county cricket. He batted for almost four hours for his 121, hitting 11 4's.
Essex were set to score 374 in 260 minutes.
The game finished soon after lunch on the third day.

Much of Essex's success in 1939 was due to all-rounder Morris Nichols (*above*), who, for the fifth successive season, was the first player to achieve the double. Such form earned him a recall to the England side.

GLAMORGAN v SUSSEX

Played at Pontypridd, July 8, 10, 11, 1939.
Toss won by Glamorgan.
Match drawn.

GLAMORGAN

A.H.Dyson	run out	68	not out	30
D.E.Davies	b Jas.Langridge	102		
T.L.Brierley	c H.Parks b Jas.Langridge	3	lbw b John Langridge	33
*Mr M.J.L.Turnbull	c Cox b Jas.Langridge	35		
D.Davies	lbw b Jas.Langridge	18		
C.C.Smart	not out	30	(4) c J.Cornford b Bartlett	19
E.C.Jones	b Jas.Langridge	10		
†H.G.Davies	c Holmes b J.Parks	3		
Mr J.C.Clay	b J.Cornford	47	(2) c J.Parks b Duffield	1
P.F.Judge	not out	1		
Extras	(B 10, LB 3, NB 6)	19	(LB 5)	5
Total	(8 wickets, declared)	**336**	(3 wickets)	**88**

Fall: 1st inns 1/175, 2/180, 3/207, 4/234, 5/238, 6/251, 7/262, 8/331.
2nd inns 1/1, 2/61, 3/88.

J.Mercer did not bat.

SUSSEX

John G.Langridge	c Jones b Clay	67
J.H.Parks	b E.Davies	21
H.W.Parks	b E.Davies	0
G.Cox	lbw b Clay	13
Jas.Langridge	b Clay	77
Mr H.T.Bartlett	lbw b E.Davies	0
*Flt-Lt A.J.Holmes	lbw b Mercer	28
H.E.Hammond	b Mercer	0
†W.L.Cornford	not out	25
J.Duffield	st H.Davies b Clay	13
J.H.Cornford	st H.Davies b E.Davies	7
Extras	(B 3, LB 8)	11
Total		**262**

Fall: 1st inns 1/34, 2/34, 3/53, 4/152, 5/153, 6/208, 7/208, 8/221, 9/247.

SUSSEX	O	M	R	W	O	M	R	W
J.H.Cornford	11	1	38	1	5	3	4	0
Hammond	18	3	82	0				
Jas.Langridge	23	3	100	5	5	1	11	0
J.H.Parks	13	2	34	1				
Duffield	5	0	28	0	7	1	22	1
Cox	10	2	21	0	7	0	19	0
John Langridge	3	0	14	0	3	0	8	1
Bartlett	-	-	-	-	2.4	0	19	1

GLAMORGAN	O	M	R	W
Mercer	8	0	17	2
Judge	6	3	19	0
Clay	35	10	88	4
D.E.Davies	34.2	2	119	4
Smart	1	0	8	0

Umpires: C.V.Tarbox and D.Hendren.

Close of play scores. First day: No play. **Second day:** Sussex 109/3 (John G.Langridge 43*, Jas.Langridge 26*).

Comments: There was no play on the first day, the ground being under water. A.H.Dyson and D.E.Davies put on 175 for Glamorgan's 1st wicket at the start of the match. It was their third century opening partnership of the season and their 24th in all. D.E.Davies made 102 in 180 minutes which included five 4's.

HAMPSHIRE v NORTHAMPTONSHIRE

Played at Southampton, July 8, 10, 11, 1939.
Toss won by Northamptonshire.
Hampshire won by eight wickets.

NORTHAMPTONSHIRE

H.W.Greenwood	b Steele	0	b Bailey	1
P.Davis	b Hill	22	c Bailey b Hill	8
D.Brookes	c Arnold b Boyes	10	st McCorkell b Boyes	72
J.E.Timms	b Hill	13	c Creese b Mackenzie	23
F.P.O'Brien	c Mackenzie b Hill	60	b Bailey	27
*Mr R.P.Nelson	c Pothecary b Hill	15	b Boyes	0
W.E.Merritt	c Taylor b Boyes	9	b Bailey	5
†W.Kemmey	c Mackenzie b Hill	5	b Bailey	0
M.E.F.Dunkley	c & b Hill	6	not out	3
R.J.Partridge	not out	0	b Boyes	4
A.G.Robinson	st McCorkell b Boyes	1	lbw b Boyes	5
Extras	(LB 5)	5	(B 8, W 1)	9
Total		**146**		**157**

Fall: 1st inns 1/0, 2/32, 3/32, 4/51, 5/118, 6/129, 7/134, 8/144, 9/145.
2nd inns 1/8, 2/12, 3/62, 4/113, 5/124, 6/137, 7/145, 8/145, 9/151.

HAMPSHIRE

P.A.Mackenzie	lbw b Robinson	1	b Partridge	3
J.Bailey	c Robinson b Nelson	56	c Greenwood b Partridge	55
A.E.Pothecary	c Nelson b Merritt	18	not out	54
J.Arnold	b Nelson	28	not out	13
W.L.C.Creese	b Merritt	29		
D.F.Walker	st Kemmey b Merritt	3		
†N.T.McCorkell	c O'Brien b Partridge	7		
G.Hill	not out	9		
*Mr G.R.Taylor	c Kemmey b Merritt	8		
G.S.Boyes	c Kemmey b Merritt	0		
Revd J.W.J.Steele	absent hurt	0		
Extras	(B 5, LB 4, W 1)	10	(B 4, LB 6)	10
Total		**169**	(2 wickets)	**135**

Fall: 1st inns 1/3, 2/37, 3/109, 4/110, 5/133, 6/148, 7/152, 8/169, 9/169.
2nd inns 1/8, 2/109.

HAMPSHIRE	O	M	R	W	O	M	R	W
Steele	3	1	7	1				
Bailey	6	2	9	0	19	6	49	4
Hill	26	9	45	6	6	1	23	1
Boyes	17.3	6	52	3	9.6	1	31	4
Creese	6	0	28	0	4	1	8	0
Mackenzie	-	-	-	-	6	0	37	1

NORTHAMPTON	O	M	R	W	O	M	R	W
Partridge	19	2	58	1	13	1	36	2
Robinson	10	4	17	1	5	0	21	0
Merritt	19.5	3	56	5	6	1	24	0
Timms	6	2	15	0	5	1	8	0
Nelson	8	4	13	2	10	6	16	0
O'Brien	-	-	-	-	2	0	10	0
Brookes	-	-	-	-	.5	0	10	0

Umpires: W.Reeves and F.J.Durston.

Close of play scores. First day: Hampshire 51/2 (J.Bailey 25*, J.Arnold 6*).
Second day: Northants 157 all out.
Comments: It was Hampshire's first victory of the season.
Revd J.W.J.Steele, after bowling only three overs, was forced to retire with a strain, after slipping on the wet turf. He took no further part in the match.
D.Brookes became the second Northants batsman to complete his 1,000 runs for the season.
J.Bailey and A.E.Pothecary added 101 for Hampshire's 2nd wicket in their 2nd innings.

LEICESTERSHIRE v WARWICKSHIRE

Played at Ashby de la Zouch, July 8, 10, 11, 1939.
Toss won by Leicestershire.
Warwickshire won by six wickets.

LEICESTERSHIRE

G.L.Berry	lbw b Wilmot	6	b Mayer	21
F.T.Prentice	c Buckingham b Wilmot	4	b Wilmot	0
N.F.Armstrong	st Buckingham b Hollies	21	lbw b Mayer	8
G.S.Watson	c Wilmot b Hollies	24	b Mayer	8
M.Tompkin	c Croom b Hollies	1	st Buckingham b Hollies	1
*Mr M.St.J.Packe	c Wyatt b Hollies	6	not out	42
G.Lester	run out		run out	8
†G.O.Dawkes	c Dollery b Wilmot	2	c Wilmot b Hollies	9
Mr G.H.Palmer	b Wilmot	0	hit wkt b Hollies	3
H.A.Smith	st Buckingham b Hollies	4	lbw b Wilmot	1
J.Sperry	not out	6	b Wilmot	8
Extras	(B 7, LB 4, W 1)	12	(B 9, LB 2, NB 1)	12
Total		**86**		**121**

Fall: 1st inns 1/11, 2/24, 3/41, 4/60, 5/73, 6/74, 7/76, 8/76, 9/77.
2nd inns 1/0, 2/28, 3/29, 4/43, 5/51, 6/73, 7/88, 8/98, 9/107.

WARWICKSHIRE

A.J.W.Croom	lbw b Palmer	13	lbw b Smith	9
W.A.Hill	b Palmer	9	b Palmer	11
F.R.Santall	c Packe b Smith	39	b Smith	26
Mr R.E.S.Wyatt	c Prentice b Smith	0	c Tompkin b Smith	26
H.E.Dollery	not out	23	not out	20
J.S.Ord	hit wkt b Lester	1	not out	0
*Mr P.Cranmer	b Lester	0		
†J.Buckingham	b Smith	7		
K.Wilmot	b Smith	3		
J.H.Mayer	c Armstrong b Smith	0		
W.E.Hollies	c Watson b Palmer	1		
Extras	(B 7, LB 8)	15	(B 4, LB 4)	8
Total		**111**	(4 wickets)	**100**

Fall: 1st inns 1/14, 2/37, 3/62, 4/85, 5/91, 6/91, 7/98, 8/108, 9/110.
2nd inns 1/26, 2/28, 3/72, 4/85.

WARWICKSHIRE	O	M	R	W	O	M	R	W
Mayer	8	1	15	0	11	3	37	3
Wilmot	15	5	21	4	10.4	5	30	3
Santall	8	1	14	0				
Hollies	10.3	5	24	5	15	3	42	3

LEICESTERSHIRE	O	M	R	W	O	M	R	W
Sperry	8	3	19	0	3	1	8	0
Palmer	8.7	1	36	3	9	2	29	1
Smith	12	6	28	5	13.7	5	44	3
Lester	3	1	13	2				
Prentice	-	-	-	-	8	2	11	0

Umpires: G.Beet and E.Robinson.

Close of play scores. First day: No play (rain). **Second day:** Leicestershire 67/5 (M.St.J.Packe 17*, G.Lester 6*).

Comments: A bowler's match in which the highest individual score was 42* by the Leicestershire captain, M.St.J.Packe.
Twenty-five wickets fell on the second day for 264 runs.
F.R.Santall hit two 6's and four 4's in his top score of 39 for Warwickshire in the match.
H.E.Dollery completed his 1,000 runs for the season.
It was Leicestershire's 10th defeat of the season.
The match finished at 3.30pm.

LEICESTERSHIRE COUNTY CRICKET CLUB

Standing (left to right): G.Lester, M.Tompkin, H.A.Smith, Mr King (scorer), G.S.Watson, F.T.Prentice, N.F.Armstrong. Seated: G.L.Berry, J.E.Walsh, C.S.Dempster (captain), W.H.Flamson, G.O.Dawkes.

NOTTINGHAMSHIRE v DERBYSHIRE

Played at Trent Bridge, Nottingham, July 8, 10, 11, 1939.
Toss won by Nottinghamshire.
Match drawn.

NOTTINGHAMSHIRE

W.W.Keeton	b G.H.Pope	54
C.B.Harris	lbw b A.V.Pope	0
*Mr G.F.H.Heane	c Smith b Mitchell	30
J.Hardstaff	lbw b Rhodes	81
G.V.Gunn	b A.V.Pope	8
J.Knowles	b Mitchell	88
R.J.Giles	c Elliott b A.V.Pope	10
W.Voce	lbw b Mitchell	6
†A.B.Wheat	c Hounsfield b Mitchell	2
H.J.Butler	b Mitchell	22
A.Jepson	not out	0
Extras	(B 2, LB 10)	12
Total		**313**

Fall: 1st inns 1/8, 2/19, 3/89, 4/129, 5/249, 6/264, 7/275, 8/288, 9/303.

DERBYSHIRE

A.E.Alderman	lbw b Jepson	40	b Jepson	9
D.Smith	b Butler	15	lbw b Giles	27
T.S.Worthington	c Heane b Voce	0	c Harris b Gunn	42
L.F.Townsend	c Wheat b Jepson	12	not out	32
G.H.Pope	b Jepson	37	not out	9
A.E.G.Rhodes	c Giles b Butler	1		
*Mr T.D.Hounsfield	b Gunn	16		
A.V.Pope	b Butler	57		
†H.Elliott	c Wheat b Voce	13		
T.B.Mitchell	b Butler	12		
W.H.Copson	not out	2		
Extras	(LB 5)	5	(B 3, LB 2, NB 1)	6
Total		**210**	(3 wickets)	**125**

Fall: 1st inns 1/18, 2/19, 3/44, 4/89, 5/90, 6/121, 7/124, 8/183, 9/197.
2nd inns 1/25, 2/47, 3/105.

DERBYSHIRE	O	M	R	W
Copson	15	1	70	0
A.V.Pope	22	2	74	3
Rhodes	7	1	31	1
G.H.Pope	15	2	56	1
Mitchell	17.1	2	70	5

NOTTINGHAMSHIRE	O	M	R	W	O	M	R	W
Voce	22	2	96	2	4	1	9	0
Butler	18.2	2	41	4	5	1	17	0
Giles	5	1	13	0	9	0	39	1
Jepson	11	1	29	3	5	0	18	1
Gunn	5	0	26	1	6	0	19	1
Harris	-	-	-	-	6	1	14	0
Hardstaff	-	-	-	-	3	1	3	0

Umpires: C.W.L.Parker and C.N.Woolley.

Close of play scores. First day: No play (rain). **Second day:** Derbyshire 50/3 (A.E.Alderman 21*, G.H.Pope 2*).

Comments: J.Hardstaff and J.Knowles added 120 in 75 minutes for the 5th wicket. Derbyshire followed on 103 behind under two-day match regulations.

SURREY v KENT

Played at Kennington Oval, July 8, 10, 11, 1939.
Toss won by Surrey.
Kent won by seven wickets.

SURREY

R.J.Gregory	c Todd b Harding	14	lbw b Wright	38
L.B.Fishlock	b Longfield	39	b Lewis	120
E.W.Whitfield	b Todd	46	b Longfield	109
H.S.Squires	c & b Wright	1	c Fagg b Lewis	18
J.F.Parker	lbw b Todd	9	lbw b Todd	21
G.J.Whittaker	b Todd	0	not out	1
†G.S.Mobey	lbw b Wright	1	c Levet b Lewis	9
*Mr H.M.Garland-Wells	c Spencer b Harding	38	c Valentine b Longfield	19
F.Berry	not out	19		
E.A.Watts	b Harding	12		
A.R.Gover	c Spencer b Wright	0		
Extras	(B 6, LB 1)	7	(B 18, LB 5, NB 2)	25
Total		**186**	(7 wickets, declared)	**360**

Fall: 1st inns 1/22, 2/98, 3/99, 4/114, 5/114, 6/115, 7/117, 8/163, 9/185.
2nd inns 1/138, 2/215, 3/230, 4/286, 5/330, 6/354, 7/360

KENT

A.E.Fagg	c Mobey b Watts	1	c Mobey b Gover	9
*Mr F.G.H.Chalk	lbw b Garland-Wells	34	c & b Berry	32
L.E.G.Ames	c Mobey b Watts	72	not out	136
Mr B.H.Valentine	c Whittaker b Berry	37	c Watts b Berry	54
L.J.Todd	c Mobey b Watts	13		
T.W.Spencer	c Mobey b Gover	17		
Mr T.C.Longfield	b Gregory	2		
D.V.P.Wright	b Parker	0		
N.W.Harding	b Watts	54	(5) not out	0
†Mr W.H.V.Levett	not out	38		
C.Lewis	b Parker	27		
Extras	(B 1, LB 6, NB 5)	12	(LB 2, NB 1)	3
Total		**316**	(3 wickets)	**234**

Fall: 1st inns 1/2, 2/88, 3/139, 4/155, 5/165, 6/167, 7/191, 8/194, 9/264.
2nd inns 1/16, 2/99, 3/230.

KENT	O	M	R	W	O	M	R	W
Harding	8	0	28	3	9	1	43	0
Todd	14	1	43	3	17	2	69	1
Longfield	7	2	27	1	11.1	1	69	2
Wright	15.6	3	81	3	23	1	92	1
Lewis	-	-	-	-	20	4	62	3

SURREY	O	M	R	W	O	M	R	W
Gover	23	1	100	1	6	0	67	1
Watts	19	1	63	4	8	0	44	0
Berry	14	2	33	1	6	0	47	2
Squires	7	0	29	0				
Garland-Wells	7	0	44	1	4	0	32	0
Gregory	9	2	17	1	1	0	20	0
Parker	6	2	18	2	1.2	0	21	0

Umpires: A.Skelding and F.I.Walden.

Close of play scores. First day: Kent 114/2 (L.E.G.Ames 62*, B.H.Valentine 12*). **Second day:** Surrey 126/0 (R.J.Gregory 33*, L.B.Fishlock 73*).
Comments: R.J.Gregory and L.B.Fishlock put on 138 for the 1st wicket in Surrey's 2nd innings.
L.B.Fishlock made 120, reaching his century in 160 minutes.
Kent were set to make 231 in 145 minutes.
L.E.G.Ames and B.H.Valentine added 131 for the 3rd wicket in 55 minutes, enabling Kent to knock off the necessary runs in 118 minutes.
L.E.G.Ames hit the fastest century of the season in 67 minutes, after being dropped first ball. He hit 18 4's, including the winning boundary.

Through the gap. Watts, who with Garland-Wells retrieved Surrey's fortunes somewhat after the first-innings collapse against Kent at The Oval, squeezes a ball from Harding between wicketkeeper Levett and first slip.

WORCESTERSHIRE v SOMERSET

Played at Kidderminster, July 8, 10, 11, 1939.
Toss won by Worcestershire.
Match tied.

WORCESTERSHIRE

R.Howorth	c Luckes b Wellard......16	b Buse	45
E.Cooper	lbw b Wellard............69	c Hazell b Buse	21
†B.P.King	c Weaver b Buse..........3	lbw b Buse	17
H.H.I.Gibbons	c Priddy b Hazell........29	b Wellard	0
S.H.Martin	b Wellard................0	c Bennett b Hazell	25
Mr C.H.Palmer	b Wellard................2	c & b Hazell	11
Mr J.Stanning	c Priddy b Wellard........4	(9) b Hazell	0
*Hon C.J.Lyttelton	c Lee b Wellard............1	(7) c Gimblett b Hazell	0
Mr E.H.Perry	st Lee b Wellard..........0	(10) run out	1
R.O.Jenkins	not out 1	(11) not out	0
R.T.D.Perks	c Lee b Hazell............0	(8) c Gimblett b Hazell	16
Extras	(B 5)........................5	(B 5, LB 1)	6
Total	**130**		**142**

Fall: 1st inns 1/35, 2/35, 3/112, 4/112, 5/116, 6/124, 7/128, 8/128, 9/130.
2nd inns 1/68, 2/69, 3/71, 4/89, 5/116, 6/116, 7/131, 8/139, 9/142.

SOMERSET

F.S.Lee	b Perks................5	c Jenkins b Howorth	23
H.Gimblett	b Perks................0	b Perry	5
H.T.F.Buse	c King b Martin.......26	b Perks	11
Mr F.M.McRae	c King b Perry 1	st King b Jenkins	28
*Mr E.F.Longrigg	C Howorth b Martin.....13	c & b Howorth	1
Mr J.Priddy	c Perks b Palmer 15	b Jenkins	13
†W.T.Luckes	b Perks................24	c Perks b Howorth	22
Mr G.M.Bennett	b Perry................10	(9) c Martin b Perks	16
A.W.Wellard	b Perks................0	(8) b Perrey	12
Mr S.Weaver	b Jenkins................19	not out	3
H.L.Hazell	not out 13	b Howorth	4
Extras	(LB 2, NB 3)............5	(LB 3)	3
Total	**131**		**141**

Fall: 1st inns 1/0, 2/8, 3/15, 4/35, 5/58, 6/72, 7/97, 8/97, 9/97.
2nd inns 1/7, 2/24, 3/64, 4/67, 5/72, 6/98, 7/113, 9/136.

SOMERSET	O	M	R	W	O	M	R	W
Wellard	16	1	45	7	16	1	62	1
Weaver	3	0	16	0	1	0	13	0
Buse	10	2	24	1	21	5	55	3
Hazell	11.7	2	40	2	5.7	1	6	5

WORCESTERSHIRE	O	M	R	W	O	M	R	W
Perks	13	1	40	4	10	2	34	2
Perry	12	2	31	2	10	1	43	2
Martin	11	1	26	2				
Howorth	4	1	18	0	9.4	1	27	4
Palmer	1	0	6	1				
Jenkins	2.5	0	5	1	10	1	34	2

Umpires: J.A.Smart and E.Cooke.

Close of play scores. First day: No play (rain). **Second day:** Worcestershire 43/0 (R.Howorth 26*, E.Cooper 16*).
Comments: Twenty wickets fell on each of the two days' play.
F.S.Lee took over as Somerset 'keeper, after W.T.Luckes damaged a finger in dismissing R.O.Howorth, the first dismissal of the match.
In Worcester's 1st innings, the last seven wickets fell for 18.
H.L.Hazell took five Worcestershire 2nd innings wickets for six runs in 47 balls on the morning of the third day.
Somerset were left with 142 to win in 150 minutes. When the last pair came together six runs were still needed.
The game finished with the fourth ball of the last over of extra-time. It was the first championship tie since 1926. It was also the most even game played in the County Championship in terms of the totals of each side, with only one run separating each innings.
E.Cooper completed his 1,000 runs for the season.

YORKSHIRE v MIDDLESEX

Played at Bradford, July 8, 10, 11, 1939.
Toss won by Yorkshire.
Match drawn.

YORKSHIRE

H.Sutcliffe	lbw b Smith 4	b Sims 29
L.Hutton	c & b Edrich 72	c Robertson b Peebles 47
A.Mitchell	lbw b Sims 33	b Sims 18
M.Leyland	c Edrich b Smith 8	not out 35
W.Barber	lbw b Smith 7	c Price b Sims 11
Mr N.W.D.Yardley	b Sims 1	b Sims 7
*Mr A.B.Sellers	b Smith 20	not out 11
†A.Wood	c Edrich b Sims 1	
E.P.Robinson	c Smith b Sims 15	
H.Verity	c Mann b Smith 3	
W.E.Bowes	not out 0	
Extras	(B 1, LB 4, NB 2) 7	(B 2, LB 11, NB 1) 14
Total	**171**	**(5 wickets) 172**

Fall: 1st inns 1/21, 2/98, 3/119, 4/129, 5/129, 6/130, 7/136, 8/152, 9/164.
2nd inns 1/82, 2/90, 3/107, 4/129, 5/139.

MIDDLESEX

S.M.Brown	c Robinson b Verity 25
J.D.B.Robertson	b Verity 60
W.J.Edrich	b Robinson 69
D.C.S.Compton	b Yardley 40
Mr F.G.Mann	b Bowes 4
Mr G.O.B.Allen	b Bowes 44
L.H.Compton	c Mitchell b Bowes 11
†W.F.F.Price	c Barber b Robinson 18
C.I.J.Smith	c Robinson b Bowes 0
J.M.Sims	c Wood b Robinson 10
*Mr I.A.R.Peebles	not out 0
Extras	(B 2, LB 9) 11
Total	**292**

Fall: 1st inns 1/68, 2/93, 3/149, 4/167, 5/225, 6/256, 7/278, 8/278, 9/284.

MIDDLESEX	O	M	R	W	O	M	R	W
Allen	7	0	25	0	5	0	24	0
Smith	17.3	3	48	5	7	2	11	0
Sims	14	2	49	4	19	1	62	4
Edrich	4	0	27	1				
D.C.S.Compton	3	0	15	0	1	0	5	0
Peebles	-	-	-	-	15	1	55	1
Robertson	-	-	-	-	1	0	1	0

YORKSHIRE	O	M	R	W
Bowes	28	5	60	4
Verity	31	7	94	2
Robinson	21.7	5	79	3
Hutton	2	0	7	0
Leyland	1	0	10	0
Yardley	7	1	31	1

Umpires: H.G.Baldwin and G.M.Lee.

Close of play scores. First day: No play (rain). **Second day:** Middlesex 167/4 (W.J.Edrich 30*, F.G.Mann 4*).

Comments: A.Wood's benefit match. It realised £2,563. Despite no play on the first day, Yorkshire were in some danger of losing the game, being only 18 runs in front with five wickets left on the last afternoon.

DERBYSHIRE v MIDDLESEX

Played at Derby, July 12, 13, 1939.
Toss won by Middlesex.
Derbyshire won by six wickets.

MIDDLESEX

J.D.B.Robertson	b Rhodes 23	b A.V.Pope 0
S.M.Brown	b Copson 2	c Elliott b Copson 0
W.J.Edrich	c G.H.Pope b Copson 2	c Elliott b Copson 0
D.C.S.Compton	run out 80	c Worthington b Copson ...4
Mr F.G.Mann	lbw b Rhodes 2	c Smith b Copson 22
Mr G.O.B.Allen	c Elliott b Mitchell 15	lbw b Copson 0
†W.F.F.Price	b Mitchell 1	c G.H.Pope b A.V.Pope 2
J.M.Sims	c Rhodes b A.V.Pope 13	b Copson 24
C.I.J.Smith	b A.V.Pope 8	c Smith b Copson 0
*Mr I.A.R.Peebles	run out 2	b A.V.Pope 12
L.H.Gray	not out 1	not out 4
Extras	(B 2) 2	(B 6, LB 2) 8
Total	**151**	**76**

Fall: 1st inns 1/8, 2/12, 3/59, 4/61, 5/89, 6/91, 7/122, 8/130, 9/145.
2nd inns 1/1, 2/3, 3/5, 4/8, 5/12, 6/25, 7/59, 8/59, 9/60.

DERBYSHIRE

A.E.Alderman	b Allen 2	c Smith b Sims 23
D.Smith	c Price b Smith 7	lbw b Sims 33
T.S.Worthington	c Compton b Allen 8	not out 36
L.F.Townsend	b Smith 4	c Compton b Sims 4
G.H.Pope	c Smith b Sims 44	run out 24
A.E.G.Rhodes	c Price b Sims 14	
*Mr T.D.Hounsfield	b Smith 0	
A.V.Pope	c & b Sims 3	
†H.Elliott	run out 8	not out 1
T.B.Mitchell	c Compton b Sims 2	
W.H.Copson	not out 0	
Extras	(B 2) 2	(B 9, LB 5, NB 1) 15
Total	**94**	**(4 wickets) 136**

Fall: 1st inns 1/3, 2/17, 3/19, 4/27, 5/54, 6/55, 7/58, 8/86, 9/94.
2nd inns 1/60, 2/65, 3/71, 4/122.

DERBYSHIRE	O	M	R	W	O	M	R	W
Copson	12	1	49	2	11	2	39	7
A.V.Pope	9.4	0	38	2	10.6	2	29	3
Rhodes	5	0	17	2				
G.H.Pope	6	0	22	0				
Mitchell	5	0	23	2				

MIDDLESEX	O	M	R	W	O	M	R	W
Smith	15	2	33	3	7	1	28	0
Allen	5	0	15	2	4	1	19	0
Gray	3	0	17	0				
Sims	6.6	1	27	4	8	0	37	3
Edrich	-	-	-	-	3	0	12	0
Peebles	-	-	-	-	5.4	1	18	0
Compton	-	-	-	-	3	1	7	0

Umpires: E.Robinson and J.J.Hills.

Close of play scores. First day: Middlesex 27/6 (F.G.Mann 13*, J.M.Sims 2*).
Comments: The game was completed in two days.
On the first day 26 wickets fell for 272 runs. The match was finished by 3pm on the second day.
D.C.S.Compton made 80 out of the 139 scored whilst at the wicket. He was last out in the 1st innings and was the only batsman in the match to pass the 50 mark on a difficult wicket.
W.H.Copson took his 100th wicket of the season when he dismissed S.M.Brown in the 1st innings. The Middlesex score of 12/5 in the 2nd innings, included five extras.

SUSSEX COUNTY CRICKET CLUB

Standing (left to right): J.H.Cornford, G.Cox, John G.Langridge, Mr Killick (scorer), H.E.Hammond, J.K.Nye, C.Oakes. Seated: H.W.Parks, W.L.Cornford, A.J.Holmes (captain), J.H.Parks, James Langridge.

GLAMORGAN v ESSEX

Played at Cardiff, July 12, 13, 14, 1939.
Toss won by Essex.
Match drawn.

ESSEX

L.C.Eastman	st H.Davies b Mercer	87
A.V.Avery	b E.Davies	161
F.H.Vigar	b Wooller	5
J.O'Connor	b Jones	79
M.S.Nichols	run out	32
R.M.Taylor	lbw b Wooller	6
T.P.B.Smith	b Wooller	30
*Mr F.St.G.Unwin	c H.Davies b Wooller	22
Capt J.W.A.Stephenson	b Mercer	8
†T.H.Wade	lbw b E.Davies	14
R.Smith	not out	9
Extras	(B 16, LB 1, W 3, NB 1)	21
Total		**474**

Fall: 1st inns 1/133, 2/149, 3/329, 4/362, 5/377, 6/421, 7/422, 8/445, 9/455.

GLAMORGAN

A.H.Dyson	b Nichols	7	not out	14
D.E.Davies	b Taylor	40	not out	14
T.L.Brierley	b Nichols	53		
Mr W.Wooller	c Wade b Nichols	0		
*Mr M.J.L.Turnbull	c Nichols b Taylor	4		
C.C.Smart	b Taylor	71		
†H.G.Davies	c Wade b Nichols	9		
E.C.Jones	c & b Vigar	27		
Mr J.C.Clay	c Nichols b Stephenson	32		
P.F.Judge	b Taylor	12		
J.Mercer	not out	1		
Extras	(B 13, LB 4)	17	(LB 4)	4
Total		**273**	(No wicket)	**32**

Fall: 1st inns 1/16, 2/106, 3/106, 4/110, 5/110, 6/123, 7/185, 8/245, 9/271.

GLAMORGAN	O	M	R	W
Mercer	29	3	101	2
Judge	15	1	64	0
Wooller	26	0	107	4
Clay	11	1	46	0
D.E.Davies	23.1	3	80	2
Smart	4	0	23	0
Jones	6	0	32	1

ESSEX	O	M	R	W	O	M	R	W
Nichols	19	5	63	4	3	0	11	0
R.Smith	12	2	44	0	1	0	3	0
Taylor	16.2	2	66	4				
Stephenson	9	0	29	1	3	0	14	0
T.P.B.Smith	12	1	44	0				
Vigar	4	1	10	1				

Umpires: E.J.Smith and H.Elliott.

Close of play scores. First day: Essex 391/5 (M.S.Nichols 26*, R.Smith 6*).
Second day: Glamorgan 32/0 (A.H.Dyson 14*, D.E.Davies 14*).

Comments: A.V.Avery returned to the Essex side after an absence of several weeks. He began with an opening partnership of 133 in 100 minutes with L.C.Eastman, followed by a 3rd wicket partnership of 180 in 165 minutes with J.O'Connor. His 161 included seven 4's and took 330 minutes. It was his highest score of the season. M.S.Nichols took three wickets for four runs in one spell of 30 minutes in Glamorgan's 1st innings. Glamorgan followed on 201 behind, but there was no play on the third day due to rain.

HAMPSHIRE v SUSSEX

Played at Portsmouth, July 12, 13, 14, 1939.
Toss won by Hampshire.
Sussex won by six wickets.

HAMPSHIRE

J.Bailey	c Holmes b Nye	4	c Jas.Langridge b Nye	71
P.A.Mackenzie	lbw b Nye	13	c John Langridge b Jas.Langridge	14
Mr J.P.Blake	lbw b J.Parks	29	c Hammond b Jas.Langridge	0
J.Arnold	c Hammond b Nye	109	lbw b Jas.Langridge	20
†N.T.McCorkell	c John Langridge b J.Parks	1	c Bartlett b Jas.Langridge	17
W.L.C.Creese	c J.Parks b Hammond	20	c sub b John Langridge	31
D.F.Walker	b Nye	66	b Jas.Langridge	8
G.S.Boyes	b Hammond	30	lbw b Jas.Langridge	11
*Mr G.R.Taylor	not out	14	run out	15
R.C.Court	b Nye	0	c Cornford b Hammond	21
Mr I.N.R.Shield	run out	2	not out	4
Extras	(B 5, LB 7, W 1)	13	(LB 7, NB 2)	9
Total		**301**		**221**

Fall: 1st inns 1/20, 2/25, 3/88, 4/98, 5/123, 6/208, 7/272, 8/288, 9/288.
2nd inns 1/43, 2/43, 3/71, 4/92, 5/151, 6/168, 7/174, 8/183, 9/204.

SUSSEX

John G.Langridge	c McCorkell b Court	7	b Court	60
J.H.Parks	c Walker b Boyes	33	c Walker b Boyes	12
H.W.Parks	c McCorkell b Court	27	c Creese b Boyes	37
G.Cox	c Walker b Shield	18	lbw b Creese	41
Jas.Langridge	c Creese b Bailey	40	not out	26
Mr H.T.Bartlett	run out	15	not out	43
*Flt-Lt A.J.Holmes	c & b Boyes	80		
H.E.Hammond	c Creese b Shield	17		
†W.L.Cornford	c & b Mackenzie	17		
J.Duffield	b Mackenzie	5		
J.K.Nye	not out	0		
Extras	(B 10, LB 15, W 2)	27	(B 6, LB 12)	18
Total		**286**	(4 wickets)	**237**

Fall: 1st inns 1/21, 2/72, 3/74, 4/117, 5/160, 6/160, 7/206, 8/250, 9/260.
2nd inns 1/57, 2/79, 3/154, 4/158.

SUSSEX	O	M	R	W	O	M	R	W
Nye	19	1	100	5	21	2	74	1
Duffield	10	1	48	0	2	0	23	0
J.Parks	16	1	69	2	7	3	14	0
Hammond	15	0	71	2	6.3	1	19	1
Jas.Langridge	-	-	-	-	21	0	76	6
John Langridge	-	-	-	-	2	0	6	1

HAMPSHIRE	O	M	R	W	O	M	R	W
Court	20	0	86	2	9	0	46	1
Shield	20	1	91	2	12	1	44	0
Bailey	15	5	30	1	2	1	12	0
Boyes	13.1	5	30	2	17	2	53	2
Mackenzie	4	0	22	2	3	0	17	0
Creese	-	-	-	-	14.4	5	47	1

Umpires: F.I.Walden and H.W.Lee.

Close of play scores. First day: Sussex 101/3 (G.Cox 14*, Jas.Langridge 9*).
Second day: Hampshire 184/8 (G.R.Taylor 2*, R.C.Court 1*).
Comments: J.Arnold made 109, hitting 11 4's in 135 minutes. He was the first Hampshire batsman to reach a 1,000 runs for the season.
H.T.Bartlett and Jas.Langridge hit 67 in 33 minutes to win the game for Sussex, who were set to make 237 in 5 hours.
James Langridge completed his 1,000 runs for the season in the 1st innings.

KENT v SOMERSET

Played at Maidstone, July 12, 13, 1939.
Toss won by Somerset.
Kent won by eight wickets.

SOMERSET

F.S.Lee .... c Fagg b Todd 44	c Todd b Watt 1
H.Gimblett .... c Levett b Harding 68	c Levett b Todd 21
H.T.F.Buse .... b Todd 2	c Valentine b Watt 8
Mr J.Priddy .... b Harding 3	c Harding b Todd 6
*Mr E.F.Longrigg ... c Fagg b Todd 0	c Longfield b Watt 2
W.H.R.Andrews ..... b Todd 0	c Levett b Watt 0
†W.T.Luckes .... not out 10	c Harding b Watt 0
Mr A.J.P.Ling ...... c Harding b Todd 0	b Wright 25
Mr G.M.Bennett .... b Todd 0	c & b Todd 72
A.W.Wellard ...... b Harding 5	c Foster b Wright 21
H.L.Hazell .... c Longfield b Watt 15	not out 15
Extras .... (B 9, LB 4, NB 3) 16	(B 10, LB 4) 14
Total **163**	.... **185**

Fall: 1st inns 1/99, 2/115, 3/129, 4/130, 5/132, 6/132, 7/132, 8/132, 9/139.
2nd inns 1/20, 2/36, 3/36, 4/41, 5/41, 6/47, 7/47, 8/117, 9/143.

KENT

A.E.Fagg .... b Andrews 77	not out 29
*Mr F.G.H.Chalk ... c Luckes b Andrews 73	b Wellard 11
L.E.G.Ames .... c Lee b Wellard 52	c Longrigg b Wellard 7
Mr B.H.Valentine ... b Wellard 14	not out 7
Mr P.G.Foster ...... b Wellard 7	
L.J.Todd .... c Lee b Wellard 12	
Mr T.C.Longfield ... b Wellard 1	
N.W.Harding .... c sub b Andrews 1	
D.V.P.Wright .... c Longrigg b Wellard 23	
A.E.Watt .... not out 14	
†Mr W.H.V.Levett run out 1	
Extras .... (B 6, LB 9, NB 3) 18	(LB 2) 2
Total **293**	(2 wickets) **56**

Fall: 1st inns 1/105, 2/210, 3/227, 4/233, 5/249, 6/253, 7/254, 8/266, 9/288.
2nd inns 1/16, 2/44.

KENT	O	M	R	W	O	M	R	W
Harding 14	2	49	3	8	0	44	0
Todd 16	3	46	6	15.3	4	43	3
Watt 9.4	3	30	1	12	4	22	5
Wright 4	1	14	0	7	0	62	2
Longfield 3	0	8	0				

SOMERSET	O	M	R	W	O	M	R	W
Wellard 20.7	2	75	6	5	0	21	2
Andrews 22	1	121	4	3	0	21	0
Buse 13	0	46	0	2.6	0	12	0
Hazell 5	1	24	0				
Priddy 1	0	9	0				

Umpires: F.J.Durston and F.Chester.

Close of play scores. First day: Kent 195/1 (A.E.Fagg 68*, L.E.G.Ames 41*).

Comments: Maidstone cricket week.
The game was completed in two days.
After lunch on the first day, Somerset lost their last nine wickets for 51 in 85 minutes. L.J.Todd took five wickets for 2 runs in 30 balls.
In Kent's 1st innings A.Fagg put on 105 with F.G.H.Chalk for the 1st wicket. Fagg then added another 105 for the 2nd with L.E.G.Ames.
In Somerset's 2nd innings, A.E.Watt took five wickets for seven runs, including a spell of 33 balls in which he claimed four wickets for no runs.
A.W.Wellard hit three consecutive sixes off D.V.P.Wright in Somerset's 2nd innings.

LANCASHIRE v WORCESTERSHIRE

Played at Old Trafford, Manchester, July 12, 13, 14, 1939.
Toss won by Lancashire.
Lancashire won by nine wickets.

LANCASHIRE

C.Washbrook .... c Yarnold b Jackson 3	not out 21
W.Place .... c Jackson b Martin 5	c sub b Martin 12
J.L.Hopwood .... c Howorth b Martin 25	not out 20
N.Oldfield .... lbw b Jenkins 125	
J.Iddon .... not out 217	
A.E.Nutter .... lbw b Howorth 33	
W.E.Phillipson ...... not out 62	
Extras .... (B 11, LB 11, NB 1) 23	
Total .... (5 wickets, declared) **493**	(1 wicket) **53**

Fall: 1st inns 1/12, 2/16, 3/66, 4/288, 5/358.
2nd inns 1/22.

*Mr T.A.Higson, †W.Farrimond, R.Pollard and L.L.Wilkinson did not bat.

WORCESTERSHIRE

E.Cooper .... lbw b Nutter 17	not out 104
R.Howorth .... b Nutter 50	c Nutter b Phillipson 9
B.P.King .... lbw b Pollard 6	st Farrimond b Wilkinson 43
H.H.I.Gibbons ...... c Nutter b Wilkinson ... 43	c Washbrook b Pollard 36
S.H.Martin .... b Phillipson 57	b Phillipson 52
Mr C.H.Palmer .... retired hurt 65	absent hurt 0
*Mr A.F.T.White ... b Phillipson 0	(6) b Phillipson 2
G.W.Blakey .... b Pollard 3	(7) c Place b Phillipson ... 0
R.O.Jenkins .... c Higson b Wilkinson ... 13	(8) c Farrimond b Pollard 2
†H.Yarnold .... not out 6	(9) b Pollard 6
P.F.Jackson .... b Pollard 0	(10) c Farrimond b Pollard 9
Extras .... (B 1, LB 7, W 1, NB 3) .. 12	(B 3, LB 4, NB 3) 10
Total **272**	.... **273**

Fall: 1st inns 1/49 2/58, 3/87, 4/135, 5/216, 6/216, 7/225, 8/271, 9/272.
2nd inns 1/13, 2/111, 3/164, 4/236, 5/242, 6/248, 7/251, 8/273, 9/273.

WORCESTERSHIRE	O	M	R	W	O	M	R	W
Martin 32	4	90	2	7.1	1	28	1
Jackson 21	1	103	1	7	1	25	0
Howorth 20	0	95	1				
Jenkins 17	0	74	1				
Blakey 8	0	47	0				
Palmer 4	0	22	0				
Cooper 2	0	18	0				
White 1	0	21	0				

LANCASHIRE	O	M	R	W	O	M	R	W
Phillipson 14	0	86	2	19	2	71	4
Pollard 12.2	0	74	3	16.1	1	73	4
Nutter 11	0	45	2	7	1	29	0
Wilkinson 12	0	46	2	17	0	65	1
Iddon 3	0	9	0	5	0	14	0
Hopwood .... -	-	-	-	3	0	11	0

Umpires: G.Beet and H.G.Baldwin.

Close of play scores. First day: Lancashire 493/5 (J.Iddon 217*, W.E.Phillipson 62*). **Second day:** Worcestershire 152/2 (E.Cooper 67*, H.H.I.Gibbons 27*).
Comments: N.Oldfield and J.Iddon added 222 for the 4th wicket. Oldfield's 125 included eight 4's.
Iddon and W.E.Phillipson then added 135 in an unfinished 6th-wicket partnership, which took less than an hour. J.Iddon remained undefeated with 217 (which included 24 4's), five runs short of his highest score.
In Worcester's 1st innings, C.H.Palmer retired after being struck on the forehead and took no further part in the match. He was batting with a runner at the time.
Worcestershire followed on 221 behind.
E.Cooper carried his bat in the 2nd innings, his 104 taking 285 minutes and including one 6 and six 4's.
Worcester's last five wickets fell for 37 after the taking of the new ball.
Worcester were without R.T.D.Perks, who had asked to be rested.

NORTHAMPTONSHIRE v YORKSHIRE

Played at Northampton, July 12, 13, 14, 1939.
Toss won by Northamptonshire.
Yorkshire won by an innings and 98 runs.

NORTHAMPTONSHIRE

P.Davis	b Bowes	8	c Barber b Robinson 32
D.Brookes	b Yardley	6	c Sellers b Verity 61
*Mr R.P.Nelson	c Mitchell b Bowes	55	st Wood b Leyland 37
J.E.Timms	b Bowes	16	c & b Verity 5
F.P.O'Brien	b Bowes	34	b Robinson 34
J.E.Merritt	b Bowes	0	st Wood b Verity 3
R.J.Partridge	not out	67	c Robinson b Verity 3
M.E.F.Dunkley	b Verity	5	c Verity b Leyland 0
†W.Kemmey	lbw b Hutton	18	lbw b Verity 5
E.J.Herbert	c & b Hutton	12	not out 3
J.E.Buswell	c Verity b Hutton	14	c Leyland b Verity 0
Extras	(B 4, LB 10)	14	(LB 5) 5
Total		**216**	..........................**188**

Fall: 1st inns 1/16, 2/18, 3/59, 4/67, 5/73, 6/99, 7/106, 8/150, 9/196.
  2nd inns 1/90, 2/97, 3/103, 4/150, 5/172, 6/178, 7/178, 8/183, 9/188.

YORKSHIRE

Mr N.W.D.Yardley	c Herbert b Partridge	93
L.Hutton	lbw b O'Brien	65
A.Mitchell	c & b Nelson	59
M.Leyland	c Herbert b Partridge	19
H.Sutcliffe	not out	107
W.Barber	not out	128
Extras	(B 15, LB 14, NB 3)	31
	(4 wickets, declared)	....**502**

Fall: 1st inns 1/142, 2/182, 3/218, 4/257.

*Mr A.B.Sellers, †A.Wood, E.P.Robinson,
H.Verity and W.E.Bowes did not bat.

YORKSHIRE	O	M	R	W	O	M	R	W
Bowes	19	3	43	5	12	3	23	0
Yardley	6	1	21	1	4	1	5	0
Robinson	5	0	34	0	17	8	34	2
Verity	15	4	41	1	30.4	15	58	6
Hutton	8.3	2	23	3	6	0	20	0
Leyland	6	1	40	0	9	0	43	2

NORTHANTS	O	M	R	W
Partridge	21	2	79	2
Buswell	15	0	81	0
Timms	15	0	78	0
Nelson	18	3	67	1
Merritt	18	1	73	0
Herbert	14	2	59	0
O'Brien	8	0	34	1

Umpires: A.Skelding and C.W.L.Parker.

Close of play scores. First day: Yorkshire 203/2 (A.Mitchell 32*, M.Leyland 10*). **Second day:** Northamptonshire 118/3 (R.P.Nelson 4*, L.P.O'Brien 14*).

Comments: N.W.D.Yardley and L.Hutton put on 142 for the 1st wicket.
H.Sutcliffe and W.Barber put on 245 in 195 minutes in an unbroken 5th wicket stand.
W.Barber hit 16 4's in his 128, made in 155 minutes.
H.Sutcliffe's undefeated 107 took 195 minutes and included seven 4's. Due to rain, only four overs were bowled before lunch on the third day.

NOTTINGHAMSHIRE v LEICESTERSHIRE

Played at Worksop, July 12, 13, 14, 1939.
Toss won by Nottinghamshire.
Match drawn.

NOTTINGHAMSHIRE

W.W.Keeton	c & b Palmer	22	c Dawkes b Sperry 12
G.B.Harris	c Dawkes b Sperry	17	c Lester b Prentice 24
*Mr G.F.H.Heane	c & b Palmer	54	not out 94
J.Hardstaff	c Smith b Sperry	58	c Berry b Prentice 84
G.V.Gunn	c Dawkes b Palmer	53	c Prentice b Palmer 16
J.Knowles	c Dawkes b Smith	8	not out 31
R.J.Giles	b Smith	1	
W.Voce	c Dawkes b Prentice	3	
†A.B.Wheat	c Smith b Prentice	27	
H.J.Butler	c Dawkes b Sperry	5	
A.Jepson	not out	20	
Extras	(B 3, LB 2, W 5)	10	(B 1, LB 1) 2
Total		**278**	(4 wickets, declared) **263**

Fall: 1st inns 1/39, 2/41, 3/151, 4/169, 5/189, 6/193, 7/204, 8/232, 9/243.
  2nd inns 1/20, 2/59, 3/188, 4/213.

LEICESTERSHIRE

G.L.Berry	b Jepson	25	lbw b Voce 0
F.T.Prentice	c Harris b Voce	26	not out 5
N.F.Armstrong	lbw b Jepson	15	not out 17
G.S.Watson	c Heane b Butler	55	
*Mr M.St J.Packe	run out	41	
M.Tompkin	b Butler	34	
G.Lester	b Voce	7	
†G.O.Dawkes	c Wheat b Butler	18	
Mr G.H.Palmer	not out	14	
H.A.Smith	c Voce b Butler	5	
J.Sperry	c Harris b Jepson	1	
Extras	(B 1, LB 3, NB 1)	5	(B 4) 4
Total		**246**	(1 wicket) **26**

Fall: 1st inns 1/43, 2/55, 3/73, 4/143, 5/181, 6/201, 7/222, 8/231, 9/245.
  2nd inns 1/0.

LEICESTERSHIRE	O	M	R	W	O	M	R	W
Sperry	21	0	93	3	20	2	63	1
Palmer	19	3	69	3	18	1	71	1
Smith	17	2	43	2	16	1	61	0
Lester	4	0	23	0	2	0	15	0
Prentice	10	2	40	2	11	0	51	2

NOTTINGHAMSHIRE	O	M	R	W	O	M	R	W
Voce	27	5	87	2	2	0	10	1
Butler	23	4	69	4	3	1	2	0
Jepson	20.4	5	54	3	1.6	0	10	0
Giles	4	0	18	0				
Gunn	7	1	13	0				

Umpires: A.Dolphin and J.A.Smart.

Close of play scores. First day: Leicestershire 113/3 (G.S.Watson 31*, M.St.J.Packe 15*). **Second day:** Nottinghamshire 227/4 (G.F.H.Heane 81*, J.Knowles 8*).

Comments: Rain prevented any chance of a finish on the third day, less than an hour's play being possible. There was no play after 12.45pm. G.F.H.Heane and J.Hardstaff were involved in century partnerships for the 3rd wicket in both innings, 110 in the 1st and 129 in the 2nd. Heane hit a 6 into the adjoining canal.
G.O.Dawkes took five catches behind the wicket on the first day for the second time that season.

SURREY v GLOUCESTERSHIRE

Played at Kennington Oval, July 12, 13, 14, 1939.
Toss won by Gloucestershire.
Surrey won by seven wickets.

GLOUCESTERSHIRE

C.J.Barnett	c Whitfield b Gover	40	lbw b Parker	34
R.A.Sinfield	lbw b Watts	20	c Parker b Gover	89
*Mr B.O.Allen	c Whittaker b Brown	16	c & b Brown	16
V.Hopkins	c Whittaker b Brown	14	c Fishlock b Brown	11
J.F.Crapp	c Parker b Gregory	42	c & b Watts	19
G.M.Emmett	b Parker	50	c Squires b Brown	62
W.L.Neale	c Watts b Gover	11	c Garland-Wells b Watts	8
†E.A.Wilson	c Mobey b Parker	0	run out	70
C.J.Scott	lbw b Watts	10	c Garland-Wells b Brown	0
G.E.E.Lambert	c Fishlock b Watts	0	not out	8
T.W.J.Goddard	not out	0	not out	13
Extras	(B 4, LB 2, NB 1)	7	(B 5, LB 9, NB 5)	19
Total		**210**	(9 wickets, declared)	**349**

Fall: 1st inns 1/61, 2/65, 3/94, 4/105, 5/184, 6/190, 7/190, 8/206, 9/210.
2nd inns 1/58, 2/94, 3/122, 4/158, 5/213, 6/225, 7/322, 8/327, 9/328.

SURREY

R.J.Gregory	c Allen b Lambert	1	not out	137
L.B.Fishlock	lbw b Goddard	39	c Barnett b Sinfield	61
E.W.Whitfield	c Allen b Lambert	0	c Lambert b Sinfield	28
H.S.Squires	lbw b Goddard	46		
J.F.Parker	c Hopkins b Goddard	15		
G.J.Whittaker	run out	6		
*Mr H.M.Garland-Wells	c Lambert b Goddard	15	(4) b Goddard	18
Mr F.R.Brown	c Hopkins b Goddard	12	(5) not out	46
†G.S.Mobey	not out	66		
E.A.Watts	c Lambert b Goddard	18		
A.R.Gover	b Goddard	31		
Extras	(LB 8, NB 2)	10	(B 5, LB 4, NB 2)	11
Total		**259**	(3 wickets)	**301**

Fall: 1st inns 1/6, 2/6, 3/66, 4/104, 5/112, 6/115, 7/130, 8/149, 9/171.
2nd inns 1/96, 2/170, 3/207.

SURREY	O	M	R	W	O	M	R	W
Gover	12	1	65	2	18	2	87	1
Watts	13.1	2	44	3	12	1	64	2
Brown	13	4	51	2	27	4	83	4
Garland-Wells	4	1	11	0	3	1	12	0
Squires	3	1	3	0	2	1	19	0
Parker	10	2	11	2	10	0	48	1
Gregory	8	4	18	1	9	3	17	0
GLOUCESTERSHIRE	O	M	R	W	O	M	R	W
Scott	14	2	60	0	5	0	58	0
Lambert	20	0	97	2	5	0	64	0
Barnett	2	1	1	0	3.7	0	26	0
Goddard	20.2	5	91	7	18	1	86	1
Sinfield	-	-	-	-	13	1	56	2

Umpires: G.M.Lee and D.Hendren.

Close of play scores. First day: Surrey 95/3 (H.S.Squires 38*, J.F.Parker 14*).
Second day: Gloucs 222/5 (G.M.Emmett 34*, W.L.Neale 5*).
Comments: W.R.Hammond was absent owing to an attack of lumbago.
G.S.Mobey and A.R.Gover added 88 for Surrey's 10th wicket to give them a 1st innings lead.
Surrey were set to make 301 in 215 minutes.
Surrey won with 45 minutes to spare, R.J.Gregory and F.R.Brown hitting the final 94 runs in 30 minutes.
R.J.Gregory was undefeated with 137, made in 170 minutes. He hit 19 4's.

DERBYSHIRE v YORKSHIRE

Played at Queen's Park, Chesterfield, July 15, 17, 18, 1939.
Toss won by Yorkshire.
Match drawn.

DERBYSHIRE

A.E.Alderman	st Wood b Verity	26
D.Smith	c Wood b Bowes	31
T.S.Worthington	c Wood b Hutton	55
G.H.Pope	c Wood b Robinson	39
L.F.Townsend	b Robinson	22
A.E.G.Rhodes	not out	11
†H.Elliott	c Robinson b Leyland	1
*Mr T.D.Hounsfield	not out	8
Extras	(B 11, LB 4)	15
Total	(6 wickets)	**208**

Fall: 1st inns 1/50, 2/61, 3/144, 4/180, 5/189, 6/192.

A.V.Pope, T.B.Mitchell and W.H.Copson did not bat.

YORKSHIRE

*Mr A.B.Sellers, Mr N.W.D.Yardley, H.Sutcliffe, M.Leyland, A.Mitchell, †A.Wood, W.Barber, W.E.Bowes, H.Verity, L.Hutton and E.P.Robinson.

YORKSHIRE	O	M	R	W
Bowes	16	4	29	1
Yardley	13	3	34	0
Verity	12	3	24	1
Robinson	24	6	65	2
Hutton	7	1	17	1
Leyland	9	4	24	1

Umpires: E.Cooke and A.Skelding.
Close of play scores. First day: Derbyshire 61/2 (T.S.Worthington 1*, G.H.Pope 0*).

Comments: Derbyshire were put in to bat.
Rain badly affected all three days' play. There was only 100 minutes play on the first day and none on the second. Play began on the third day at 3pm.

Yorkshire's England wicketkeeper Arthur Wood helped dismiss the first four Derbyshire batsmen at Chesterfied, but rain meant that there was no chance of a result.

ESSEX v SURREY

Played at Colchester, July 15, 17, 18, 1939.
Toss won by Surrey.
Essex won by ten wickets.

SURREY

R.J.Gregory	c Stephenson b Nichols 30	st Wade b P.Smith 17
L.B.Fishlock	lbw b Nichols 0	b Nichols 15
E.W.Whitfield	b Nichols 2	b P.Smith 7
H.S.Squires	c Unwin b Nichols 0	c Eastman b P.Smith 0
†G.S.Mobey	b R.Smith 43	b P.Smith 0
J.F.Parker	lbw b P.Smith 21	c Vigar b P.Smith 16
G.J.Whittaker	b Nichols 66	c & b P.Smith 7
*Mr H.M.Garland-Wells	c Unwin b P.Smith 16	b P.Smith 13
Mr F.R.Brown	b Stephenson 51	c R.Smith b Nichols 3
E.A.Watts	not out 19	not out 14
A.R.Gover	b P.Smith 22	run out 3
Extras	(LB 12, W 1, NB 2) 15	(B 3, W 1, NB 1) 5
Total	**285**	**100**

Fall: 1st inns 1/0, 2/2, 3/12, 4/42, 5/97, 6/101, 7/130, 8/234, 9/256.
2nd inns 1/28, 2/38, 3/38, 4/38, 5/54, 6/65, 7/65, 8/73, 9/81.

ESSEX

L.C.Eastman	run out 99	not out 14
A.V.Avery	c & b Brown 28	not out 12
F.H.Vigar	lbw b Brown 2	
J.O'Connor	c Fishlock b Gover 51	
M.S.Nichols	lbw b Gregory 93	
R.Smith	lbw b Watts 8	
R.M.Taylor	b Watts 6	
*Mr F.St.G.Unwin	c Whitfield b Gregory 33	
Capt J.W.A.Stephenson	c Brown b Gregory 27	
†T.H.Wade	b Parker 0	
T.P.B.Smith	not out 0	
Extras	(B 5, LB 4, W 1, NB 4) 14	(NB 1) 1
Total	**361**	(No wicket) **27**

Fall: 1st inns 1/100, 2/125, 3/132, 4/224, 5/236, 6/244, 7/319, 8/360, 9/361.

ESSEX	O	M	R	W	O	M	R	W
Nichols	21	4	79	5	13	5	31	2
R.Smith	13	1	81	1	2	0	15	0
Stephenson	11	1	52	1	1	0	2	0
T.P.B.Smith	12.2	0	42	3	10.1	0	47	7
Taylor	4	0	16	0				

SURREY	O	M	R	W	O	M	R	W
Gover	18	1	89	1				
Watts	18	0	61	2				
Brown	23	1	91	2	3	1	9	0
Parker	6	0	27	1	2	0	5	0
Garland-Wells	3	0	18	0				
Squires	8	0	35	0				
Gregory	7.4	1	26	3	7	0	12	0

Umpires: H.W.Lee and C.V.Tarbox.

Close of play scores. First day: 131/2 (Eastman 98*, J.O'Connor 1*). **Second day:** Surrey 16/0 (R.J.Gregory 12*, L.B.Fishlock 3*).
Comments: M.S.Nichols began the match by taking three Surrey wickets for three runs.
G.J.Whittaker and F.R.Brown added 104 in 70 minutes for Surrey's 8th wicket.
L.C.Eastman and A.V.Avery put on 100 for the 1st wicket.
L.C.Eastman, who had dominated the early Essex batting, and had only required two runs for his century at close of play on the first day, was unfortunately run out next morning, still one short of his 100. T.P.B.Smith took three wickets for no runs in one spell on the final day. In 13 deliveries he took four wickets for three runs.
Surrey's 2nd innings lasted a mere 105 minutes.
Rain stopped play during the afternoon of the second day.

HAMPSHIRE v GLAMORGAN

Played at Southampton, July 15, 17, 18, 1939.
Toss won by Hampshire.
Match drawn.

GLAMORGAN

A.H.Dyson	lbw b Baring 4
D.E.Davies	run out 14
T.L.Brierley	b Creese 16
*Mr M.J.L.Turnbull	b Creese 25
Mr W.Wooller	c & b Hill 18
C.C.Smart	c Creese b Baring 6
Mr R.J.Parkhouse	c McCorkell b Baring 0
E.C.Jones	c McCorkell b Baring 21
†H.G.Davies	c McCorkell b Heath 36
P.F.Judge	not out 4
J.Mercer	b Baring 4
Extras	(B 2, LB 4, NB 3) 9
Total	**157**

Fall: 1st inns 1/10, 2/26, 3/43, 4/66, 5/80, 6/81, 7/104, 8/149, 9/153.

HAMPSHIRE

†N.T.McCorkell	lbw b Mercer 14
J.Bailey	not out 8
G.E.M.Heath	b Mercer 0
Total	(2 wickets) **22**

Fall: 1st inns 1/22, 2/22.
*Mr A.E.G.Baring, P.A.Mackenzie, J.Arnold, A.E.Pothecary, W.L.C.Creese, D.F.Walker, G.S.Boyes and G.Hill did not bat.

HAMPSHIRE	O	M	R	W
Baring	12.6	4	27	5
Heath	8	2	27	1
Boyes	5	1	18	0
Hill	10	1	36	1
Creese	13	3	40	2

GLAMORGAN	O	M	R	W
Judge	4	0	15	0
Wooller	4	2	7	0
Mercer	1	1	0	2

Umpires: D.Hendren and J.F.Parker.

Close of play scores. First day: Glamorgan 153/8 (E.C.Jones 21*, P.F.Judge 4*). **Second day:** Hampshire 22/2 (J.Bailey 8*).

Comments: Glamorgan were put in to bat.
The game was played on a newly prepared wicket, after heavy rain the previous day. There was only 135 minutes play on the first day, 60 minutes on the second and none on the third.

KENT v GLOUCESTERSHIRE

Played at Maidstone, July 15, 17, 1939.
Toss won by Kent.
Kent won by 98 runs.

KENT

A.E.Fagg	c Hammond b Scott	77	c Scott b Lambert	8
*Mr F.G.H.Chalk	c Eagar b Lambert	5	b Goddard	34
L.E.G.Ames	c Crapp b Goddard	6	c Lambert b Goddard	79
Mr B.H.Valentine	c Goddard b Scott	6	c & b Goddard	5
Mr P.G.Foster	b Scott	4	lbw b Sinfield	16
L.J.Todd	c Hammond b Goddard	10	b Goddard	13
Mr T.C.Longfield	c Hammond b Goddard	1	c Lambert b Sinfield	3
N.W.Harding	b Scott	0	c Hammond b Sinfield	3
D.V.P.Wright	not out	41	not out	12
A.E.Watt	b Scott	22	b Scott	10
†Mr W.H.V.Levett	c Eagar b Goddard	5	c Crapp b Sinfield	0
Extras	(B 4, LB 1)	5	(B 2, LB 2, W 2)	6
Total		**182**		**189**

Fall: 1st inns 1/18, 2/25, 3/45, 4/52, 5/68, 6/70, 7/87, 8/130, 9/165.
2nd inns 1/13, 2/124, 3/125, 4/130, 5/160, 6/163, 7/163, 8/170, 9/188.

GLOUCESTERSHIRE

C.J.Barnett	c & b Harding	22	c Todd b Harding	12
R.A.Sinfield	lbw b Watt	15	c Valentine b Todd	6
G.M.Emmett	lbw b Watt	9	c Todd b Wright	21
*Mr W.R.Hammond	b Watt	3	b Harding	14
J.F.Crapp	b Harding	8	c Levett b Wright	11
Mr E.D.R.Eagar	c Todd b Longfield	47	lbw b Wright	12
Mr A.H.Brodhurst	c Valentine b Harding	54	c Harding b Wright	0
†E.A.Wilson	b Wright	5	not out	10
C.J.Scott	b Harding	3	b Wright	0
G.E.E.Lambert	not out	0	st Levett b Wright	7
T.W.J.Goddard	b Wright	0	c Chalk b Harding	8
Extras	(B 1, LB 2, NB 1)	4	(B 1, NB 1)	2
Total		**170**		**103**

Fall: 1st inns 1/33, 2/39, 3/43, 4/50, 5/58, 6/155, 7/162, 8/170, 9/170.
2nd inns 1/13, 2/19, 3/37, 4/63, 5/73, 6/73, 7/78, 8/78, 9/86.

GLOUCESTERSHIRE	O	M	R	W	O	M	R	W
Scott	20	1	86	5	10	0	41	1
Lambert	5	0	19	1	8	0	54	1
Goddard	18.2	1	70	4	13	0	76	4
Sinfield	2	0	2	0	4.5	0	12	4

KENT	O	M	R	W	O	M	R	W
Harding	14	3	52	4	9.7	1	48	3
Todd	9	2	27	0	6	2	12	1
Watt	13	3	44	3	5	0	21	0
Wright	7.2	0	32	2	8	2	20	6
Longfield	4	1	11	1				

Umpires: W.Reeves and G.M.Lee.

Close of play scores. First day: Gloucestershire 170 all out.

Comments: Kent won in two days. The game finished soon after tea on the second day.
L.E.G.Ames scored 79, including three 6's and ten 4's, out of 111 in 54 minutes in Kent's 2nd innings.
He and F.G.H.Chalk added 111 for the 2nd wicket in Kent's 2nd innings.
A.H.Brodhurst was making his debut for Gloucestershire.

MIDDLESEX v NOTTINGHAMSHIRE

Played at Kennington Oval, July 15, 17, 18, 1939.
Toss won by Nottinghamshire.
Nottinghamshire won by an innings and 190 runs.

NOTTINGHAMSHIRE

W.W.Keeton	not out	312
C.B.Harris	c Sims b Peebles	33
*Mr G.F.H.Heane	lbw b Sims	88
J.Hardstaff	c Price b Edrich	30
G.V.Gunn	c Smith b Peebles	43
J.Knowles	c Gray b Peebles	3
R.J.Giles	b Smith	16
W.Voce	b Smith	0
†A.B.Wheat	lbw b Smith	1
H.J.Butler	c Peebles b Sims	10
A.Jepson	not out	15
Extras	(B 3, LB 4, W 2)	9
Total	(9 wickets, declared)	**560**

Fall: 1st inns 1/104, 2/271, 3/355, 4/427, 5/436, 6/486, 7/486, 8/496, 9/530.

MIDDLESEX

J.D.B.Robertson	c Wheat b Jepson	14	c Jepson b Voce	21
S.M.Brown	c Giles b Voce	37	lbw b Voce	5
W.J.Edrich	c Heane b Voce	5	c Wheat b Heane	51
D.C.S.Compton	c Heane b Voce	17	b Heane	65
Mr N.S.Hotchkin	c Knowles b Butler	0	not out	41
L.H.Compton	b Butler	2	b Jepson	4
J.M.Sims	c Hardstaff b Voce	7	c Jepson b Heane	0
C.I.J.Smith	c Keeton b Voce	25	c & b Voce	40
*Mr I.A.R.Peebles	c Harris b Voce	2	c Voce b Butler	4
†W.F.F.Price	not out	7	absent hurt	0
L.H.Gray	c Gunn b Voce	1	(10) run out	7
Extras	(B 2)	2	(B 4, LB 6, NB 3)	13
Total		**119**		**251**

Fall: 1st inns 1/29, 2/48, 3/73, 4/75, 5/75, 6/82, 7/84, 8/111, 9/111.
2nd inns 1/15, 2/55, 3/111, 4/171, 5/178, 6/179, 7/228, 8/240, 9/251.

MIDDLESEX	O	M	R	W
Smith	26	2	102	3
Gray	12	0	74	0
Edrich	16	0	74	1
Sims	18	0	116	2
Peebles	20	0	95	3
D.C.S.Compton	16	2	59	0
Robertson	6	0	31	0

NOTTINGHAMSHIRE	O	M	R	W	O	M	R	W
Voce	19.4	3	70	7	25	6	69	3
Butler	15	4	31	2	15	2	50	1
Jepson	4	0	16	1	16	1	55	1
Giles	-	-	-	-	3	0	9	0
Heane	-	-	-	-	8.1	1	55	3

Umpires: H.G.Baldwin and A.Dolphin.

Close of play scores. First day: Nottinghamshire 480/5 (W.W.Keeton 263*, R.J.Giles 15*). **Second day:** Middlesex 49/1 (J.D.M.Robertson 19*, W.J.Edrich 20*).

Comments: The match was played at The Oval as Lord's was to be used at the weekend for the Eton and Harrow match.
W.W.Keeton's 312* was the highest individual innings by a Nottinghamshire batsman. He batted for seven hours, 15 minutes and hit 28 4's. It was the highest score of the 1939 season. It was also Keeton's first century of the season.
He and C.B.Harris put on 104 in 100 minutes for the 1st wicket.
With G.F.H.Heane he added 167 for the 2nd wicket.
Middlesex followed on 441 behind.
C.I.J.Smith hit 22 off a Heane over in Middlesex's 2nd innings.

SOMERSET v LANCASHIRE

Played at Yeovil, July 15, 17, 18, 1939.
Toss won by Lancashire.
Match drawn.

LANCASHIRE

W.Place	not out	68
E.Paynter	c Luckes b Hazell	55
J.L.Hopwood	c Wellard b Hazell	0
N.Oldfield	not out	41
Extras	(B 13, LB 4)	17
Total	**(2 wickets)**	**181**

Fall: 1st inns 1/105, 2/105.

*Mr T.A.Higson, J.Iddon, A.E.Nutter, W.E.Phillipson, †W.Farrimond, R.Pollard and L.L.Wilkinson did not bat.

SOMERSET

*Mr E.F.Longrigg, Mr G.M.Bennett, Mr A.J.P.Ling, Mr J.Priddy, †W.T.Luckes, H.L.Hazell, A.W.Wellard, W.H.R.Andrews, F.S.Lee, H.Gimblett and H.T.F.Buse.

SOMERSET	O	M	R	W
Wellard	23	1	80	0
Andrews	9	0	29	0
Buse	2	0	13	0
Hazell	17	5	32	2
Priddy	6	1	10	0

Umpires: G.Beet and E.J.Smith.

Close of play scores. First day: Lancashire 133/2 (W.Place 41*, N.Oldfield 20*).
Second day: Lancashire 181/2 (W.Place 68*, N.Oldfield 41*).

Comments: Only 135 minutes' play was possible on the first day, 60 minutes on the second and none on the third day. E.Paynter and W.Place began the match with an opening partnership of 105.

SUSSEX v NORTHAMPTONSHIRE

Played at Hove, July 15, 17, 18, 1939.
Toss won by Northamptonshire.
Match drawn.

NORTHAMPTONSHIRE

P.Davis	b Nye	14	lbw b J.Cornford	1
H.W.Greenwood	b J.Parks	45	lbw b J.Parks	14
D.Brookes	c Jas.Langridge b Nye	3	c Cox b Hammond	26
J.E.Timms	b Nye	0	lbw b J.Parks	14
F.P.O'Brien	c Jas.Langridge b Hammond	10	not out	26
*Mr R.P.Nelson	not out	123	c John Langridge b Jas.Langridge	8
†K.C.James	lbw b Hammond	54	not out	6
J.E.Merritt	bw b J.Cornford	12		
R.J.Partridge	c H.Parks b Jas.Langridge	47		
W.Kemmey	lbw b Jas.Langridge	2		
E.J.Herbert	c Holmes b Hammond	2		
Extras	(B 7, LB 11, W 1, NB 3)	22	(B 6, LB 9)	15
Total		**334**	**(5 wickets)**	**110**

Fall: 1st inns 1/46, 2/50, 3/50, 4/80, 5/82, 6/178, 7/203, 8/323, 9/328.
2nd inns 1/2, 2/33, 3/63, 4/63, 5/98.

SUSSEX

John G.Langridge	b Herbert	4
J.H.Parks	b Herbert	7
†W.L.Cornford	b Timms	52
H.W.Parks	c James b Timms	38
G.Cox	b O'Brien	54
Jas.Langridge	c James b Herbert	1
Mr H.T.Bartlett	lbw b Timms	81
*Flt-Lt A.J.Holmes	b Timms	31
H.E.Hammond	not out	16
J.K.Nye	b Timms	5
J.H.Cornford	lbw b Timms	0
Extras	(B 13, LB 8)	21
Total		**310**

Fall: 1st inns 1/8, 2/25, 3/105, 4/132, 5/135, 6/232, 7/281, 8/294, 9/310.

SUSSEX	O	M	R	W	O	M	R	W
Nye	23	1	90	3	13.6	4	37	0
J.H.Cornford	16	0	57	1	6	1	18	1
J.H.Parks	24	5	53	1	9	1	17	2
Hammond	22	2	54	3	6	1	19	1
Jas.Langridge	12	2	35	2	2	0	4	1
John Langridge	8	3	23	0				

NORTHANTS	O	M	R	W
Partridge	23	4	80	0
Herbert	19	0	79	3
Timms	15.4	2	57	6
Merritt	8	1	51	0
Nelson	7	2	17	0
O'Brien	1	0	5	1

Umpires: F.J.Durston and F.Chester.

Close of play scores. First day: Sussex 10/1 (J.H.Parks 3*, W.L.Cornford 2*).
Second day: Northants 94/43 (L.P.O'Brien 17*, R.P.Nelson 7*).
Comments: R.P.Nelson hit an undefeated 123 in 315 minutes. It included nine 4's and was his first century of the season.
With R.J.Partridge he added 120 for the 8th wicket.
The game had to be abandoned on the third day after only 16 runs had been scored.

WORCESTERSHIRE v LEICESTERSHIRE

Played at Worcester, July 15, 17, 18, 1939.
Toss won by Leicestershire.
Match drawn.

LEICESTERSHIRE

G.L.Berry	not out	21
F.T.Prentice	st Yarnold b Howorth	8
N.F.Armstrong	not out	6
Extras	(LB 3, W 1)	4
Total	(1 wicket)	**39**

Fall: 1st inns 1/21.
*Mr M.St.J.Packe, Mr G.H.Palmer, H.A.Smith, G.S.Watson, †G.O.Dawkes, M.Tompkin, J.Sperry and G.Lester did not bat.

WORCESTERSHIRE

*Hon C.J.Lyttelton, Mr A.F.T.White, Mr J.Stanning, E.Cooper, R.Howorth, B.P.King, H.H.I.Gibbons, S.H.Martin, R.T.D.Perks, R.O.Jenkins and †H.Yarnold.

WORCESTERSHIRE	O	M	R	W
Perks	5	3	3	0
Martin	7	1	20	0
Lyttelton	1	0	2	0
Howorth	3.2	0	8	1
Jenkins	1	0	2	0

Umpires: H.Elliott and C.N.Woolley.

Close of play scores. First day: No play. **Second day:** Leicestershire 39/1 (G.L.Berry 21*, N.F.Armstrong 6*).

Comments: There was just over 60 minutes play on the second day in this game.

ESSEX v LANCASHIRE

Played at Colchester, July 19, 20, 21, 1939.
Toss won by Lancashire.
Match drawn.

LANCASHIRE

E.Paynter	b R.Smith	14
W.Place	c Taylor b P.Smith	59
J.L.Hopwood	lbw b Stephenson	26
N.Oldfield	c Wade b Nichols	34
C.Washbrook	not out	87
A.E.Nutter	b P.Smith	16
W.E.Phillipson	c Nichols b Stephenson	6
*Mr T.A.Higson	c Taylor b Smith	10
†W.Farrimond	lbw b P.Smith	9
R.Pollard	lbw b P.Smith	0
L.L.Wilkinson	lbw b R.Smith	1
Extras	(B 2, LB 2, W 1)	5
Total		**267**

Fall: 1/17, 2/68, 3/125, 4/147, 5/179, 6/198, 7/211, 8/251, 9/251.

ESSEX

L.C.Eastman	c Farrimond b Pollard	4
A.V.Avery	not out	35
F.H.Vigar	c Paynter b Nutter	5
J.O'Connor	c Pollard b Nutter	11
M.S.Nichols	lbw b Nutter	9
R.Smith	b Wilkinson	1
R.M.Taylor	not out	5
Extras	(B 5, LB 4, NB 1)	10
Total	(5 wickets)	**80**

Fall: 1st inns 1/9, 2/28, 3/49, 4/62, 5/69.

*Mr F.St.G.Unwin, Capt J.W.A.Stephenson, T.P.B.Smith and †T.H.Wade did not bat.

ESSEX	O	M	R	W
Nichols	17	0	50	1
R.Smith	4.3	1	13	2
T.P.B.Smith	33	6	87	5
Taylor	11	0	58	0
Stephenson	9	0	24	2
Eastman	3	1	13	0
Vigar	2	0	17	0

LANCASHIRE	O	M	R	W
Phillipson	5	2	9	0
Pollard	6	0	21	1
Nutter	6	1	19	3
Wilkinson	6	0	21	1

Umpires: J.A.Newman and J.Durston.

Close of play scores. First day: Lancashire 267 all out.
Second day: Essex 80/5 (A.V.Avery 35*, R.M.Taylor 5*).

Comments: Rain interfered with the first two days and there was no play on the third.

GLOUCESTERSHIRE v HAMPSHIRE

Played at Bristol, July 19, 20, 21, 1939.
Toss won by Hampshire.
Gloucestershire won by five wickets.

HAMPSHIRE

†N.T.McCorkell	c Scott b Goddard	6	b Goddard	11
J.Bailey	c Hopkins b Goddard	7	b Goddard	10
Mr J.P.Blake	c Crapp b Sinfield	28	b Goddard	5
J.Arnold	lbw b Scott	18	c Emmett b Goddard	20
D.F.Walker	b Scott	1	(8) lbw b Goddard	5
W.L.C.Creese	lbw b Sinfield	22	c Eagar b Sinfield	9
A.E.Pothecary	c Scott b Goddard	0	(9) st Wilson b Goddard	0
P.A.Mackenzie	not out	14	(10) lbw b Goddard	0
*Mr G.R.Taylor	b Scott	4	(5) c Haynes b Goddard	4
G.S.Boyes	b Scott	0	(7) c Goddard b Sinfield	2
G.E.M.Heath	b Goddard	3	not out	0
Extras		0		0
Total		**103**		**66**

Fall: 1st inns 1/7, 2/21, 3/50, 4/52, 5/79, 6/82, 7/82, 8/96, 9/96.
2nd inns 1/11, 2/25, 3/42, 4/49, 5/50, 6/54, 7/62, 8/66, 9/66.

GLOUCESTERSHIRE

R.A.Sinfield	c Mackenzie b Bailey	2		
V.Hopkins	b Heath	0	(1) lbw b Creese	16
G.M.Emmett	b Bailey	19	(5) c Creese b Boyes	7
*Mr W.R.Hammond	b Bailey	30	(3) b Creese	3
J.F.Crapp	c Blake b Heath	21	(6) not out	7
Mr E.D.R.Eagar	c Walker b Boyes	6	(4) c Pothecary b Boyes	8
C.J.Scott	not out	15	not out	5
W.L.Neale	not out	8		
R.W.Haynes	(did not bat)		(2) b Creese	12
Extras	(B 3)	3	(B 2, LB 6)	8
Total	(6 wickets, declared)	**104**	(5 wickets)	**66**

Fall: 1st inns 1/1, 2/11, 3/46, 4/55, 5/64, 6/90.
2nd inns 1/25, 2/31, 3/40, 4/48, 5/54.

†E.A.Wilson and T.W.J.Goddard did not bat.

GLOUCESTERSHIRE	O	M	R	W	O	M	R	W
Scott	11	3	18	4	6	0	22	0
Hammond	1	0	6	0				
Goddard	19.5	7	36	4	9	2	36	8
Sinfield	14	3	43	2	3.5	0	8	2

HAMPSHIRE	O	M	R	W	O	M	R	W
Heath	8.1	0	33	2	3	0	12	0
Bailey	11	1	36	3	4	1	11	0
Boyes	6	0	25	1	2	0	18	2
Creese	2	0	7	0	3.6	2	17	3

Umpires: H.Elliott and F.I.Walden.

Close of play scores. First day: Hampshire 48/2 (J.P.Blake 19*, J.Arnold 16*).
Second day: No play.

Comments: After one hour's cricket on the first two days, 29 wickets fell for 291 on the final day.
W.R.Hammond's 30 was the highest score of the match.
Hampshire's 2nd innings lasted 75 minutes.

NOTTINGHAMSHIRE v SOMERSET

Played at Trent Bridge, Nottingham, July 19, 20, 21, 1939.
Toss won by Somerset.
Match drawn.

SOMERSET

F.S.Lee	b Voce	6		
H.Gimblett	c Woodhead b Gunn	46		
H.T.F.Buse	b Voce	6	run out	13
Mr C.J.P.Barnwell	c Jepson b Gunn	0	(2) c Heane b Hardstaff	21
*Mr E.F.Longrigg	c Wheat b Gunn	0	(1) b Jones	28
†W.T.Luckes	b Voce	10		
Mr A.J.P.Ling	hit wkt b Gunn	8		
Mr G.M.Bennett	lbw b Gunn	7		
A.W.Wellard	c Jones b Voce	50		
W.H.R.Andrews	not out	31	(4) not out	18
H.L.Hazell	b Woodhead	17		
Extras	(B 2, LB 1, NB 2)	5	(B 7, LB 2, W 1)	10
Total		**186**	(3 wickets)	**90**

Fall: 1st inns 1/25, 2/48, 3/50, 4/54, 5/69, 6/81, 7/81, 8/136, 9/148.
2nd inns 1/56, 2/58, 3/90.

NOTTINGHAMSHIRE

W.W.Keeton	c Luckes b Wellard	8
J.Knowles	lbw b Wellard	1
*Mr G.F.H.Heane	b Andrews	3
J.Hardstaff	b Buse	48
G.V.Gunn	c Lee b Buse	61
D.Jones	b Hazell	19
R.J.Giles	b Hazell	0
W.Voce	b Hazell	2
F.G.Woodhead	b Wellard	4
†A.B.Wheat	not out	5
A.Jepson	c & b Wellard	0
Extras	(LB 14)	14
Total		**165**

Fall: 1st innings 1/7, 2/10, 3/20, 4/132, 5/137, 6/140, 7/81, 8/159, 9/165.

NOTTINGHAMSHIRE	O	M	R	W	O	M	R	W
Voce	28	8	72	4				
Woodhead	9.3	3	17	1	4	0	22	0
Jepson	4	3	2	0	3	1	11	0
Giles	4	0	5	0				
Gunn	22	7	85	5				
Hardstaff	-	-	-	-	5	0	36	1
Jones	-	-	-	-	3	0	7	1
Knowles	-	-	-	-	2	0	4	0
Keeton	-	-	-	-	0.1	0	0	0

SOMERSET	O	M	R	W
Wellard	14.7	2	57	4
Andrews	8	2	22	1
Hazell	14	3	38	3
Buse	10	0	34	2

Umpires: E.Robinson and J.J.Hills.

Close of play scores. First day: No play (rain). **Second day:** Somerset 148/9 (W.H.R.Andrews 10*).

Comments: Play commenced in this game at 2.45pm on the second day.
A.W.Wellard hit 50 out of the 55 added for Somerset's 8th wicket in less than 30 minutes, scoring four 6's and three 4's.
J.Hardstaff and G.V.Gunn added 112 for the 4th wicket.

SOMERSET COUNTY CRICKET CLUB

Standing (left to right): H.L.Hazell, H.Gimblett, A.W.Wellard, H.T.F.Buse, F.S.Lee, W.T.Luckes. Seated: S.Weaver, G.M.Bennett, E.F.Longrigg (captain), F.M.McCrae, J.Priddy.

SURREY v GLAMORGAN

Played at Kennington Oval, July 19, 20, 21, 1939.
Toss won by Surrey.
Match drawn.

SURREY

R.J.Gregory	st H.Davies b Mercer	23
L.B.Fishlock	c H.Davies b Wooller	8
E.W.Whitfield	lbw b Mercer	4
†G.S.Mobey	c H.Davies b Wooller	5
J.F.Parker	lbw b Mercer	1
G.J.Whittaker	run out	6
H.S.Squires	c Turnbull b Wooller	16
*Mr H.M.Garland-Wells	c H.Davies b Wooller	7
F.Berry	not out	33
E.A.Watts	lbw b Mercer	12
Extras	(B 1, LB 4, W 3)	8
Total	**(9 wickets)**	**123**

Fall: 1st inns 1/26, 2/33, 3/40, 4/41, 5/42, 6/49, 7/57, 8/92, 9/123.

A.R.Gover did not bat.

GLAMORGAN

*Mr M.J.L.Turnbull, Mr W.Wooller, Mr R.J.Parkhouse, N.H.Dyson, D.E.Davies, T.L.Brierley, C.C.Smart, E.C.Jones, †H.G.Davies, P.F.Judge and J.Mercer.

GLAMORGAN	O	M	R	W
Mercer	18	4	33	4
Judge	6	1	23	0
Wooller	16	4	47	4
D.E.Davies	4	0	12	0

Umpires: C.N.Woolley and W.Reeves.

Close of play scores. First day: Surrey 123/9 (F.Berry 33*). **Second day:** No play.

Comments: Play did not begin until 3.45pm on the first day and there was no play on the second and third days.

WARWICKSHIRE v MIDDLESEX

Played at Edgbaston, Birmingham, July 19, 20, 21, 1939.
Toss won by Warwickshire.
Match drawn.

WARWICKSHIRE

A.J.W.Croom	not out	25
Mr R.Sale	not out	26
Extras	(B 2, LB 1, NB 1)	4
Total	**(No wicket)**	**55**

*Mr P.Cranmer, Mr R.E.S.Wyatt, Mr J.R.Thompson, F.R.Santall, J.H.Mayer, W.E.Hollies, †J.Buckingham, H.E.Dollery and K.Wilmot did not bat.

MIDDLESEX

*Mr I.A.R.Peebles, Mr N.S.Hotchkin, J.D.B.Robertson, S.M.Brown, W.J.Edrich, D.C.S.Compton, J.H.A.Hulme, G.E.Hart, †L.H.Compton, J.M.Sims and C.I.J.Smith.

MIDDLESEX	O	M	R	W
Smith	4	1	7	0
Edrich	8	2	25	0
D.Compton	5.5	0	17	0
Sims	1	0	2	0

Umpires: C.V.Tarbox and E.Cooke.

Close of play scores. First day: No play. **Second day:** Warwickshire 55/0 (A.J.W.Croom 25*, R.Sale 26*).

Comments: Play was only possible on the second day for 60 minutes during the afternoon. R.Sale of Oxford University made his debut for Warwickshire.

Middlesex's Joe Hulme, perhaps better known as an England footballer. The 1939 season was Hulme's last in first-class cricket, he scored over 8,000 runs for Middlesex and took 89 wickets at a cost of 36.4.

WORCESTERSHIRE v DERBYSHIRE

Played at Dudley, July 19, 20, 21, 1939.
Toss won by Derbyshire.
Match drawn.

DERBYSHIRE

*Mr R.H.R.Buckston	lbw b Howorth	33
D.Smith	st King b Jenkins	132
A.E.Alderman	c King b Perks	5
T.S.Worthington	c Perks b Jenkins	47
G.H.Pope	b Perks	40
L.F.Townsend	not out	38
A.E.G.Rhodes	b Perks	2
A.V.Pope	c Lyttelton b Jenkins	12
†H.Elliott	b Howorth	16
T.B.Mitchell	not out	8
Extras	(B 1, LB 3, W 1)	5
Total	(8 wickets)	**338**

Fall: 1st inns 1/94, 2/101, 3/201, 4/226, 5/271, 6/273, 7/297, 8/323.
W.H.Copson did not bat.

WORCESTERSHIRE

*Hon C.J.Lyttelton, Mr A.F.T.White, Mr J.Stanning, E.Cooper, R.Howorth, †B.P.King, H.H.I.Gibbons, S.H.Martin, R.T.D.Perks, R.O.Jenkins and G.M.Blakey.

WORCESTERSHIRE	O	M	R	W
Perks	18	2	56	3
Martin	24	6	84	0
Jenkins	21	1	76	3
Howorth	16	1	77	2
Blakey	9	0	40	0

Umpires: E.J.Smith and A.Skelding.
Close of play scores. First day: Derbyshire 13/0 (R.H.R.Buckston 6*, D.Smith 7*). **Second day:** Derbyshire 338/8 (L.F.Townsend 38*, T.B.Mitchell 8*).
Comments: There was only 25 minutes play on the first day and none on the third. D.Smith and T.S.Worthington added 100 for the third wicket in 90 minutes. D.Smith made 132 in nearly four hours, hitting 11 4's.

Derbyshire's stylish left-hander Denis Smith made 132 against Worcestershire. By the time he had ended his long career in 1952, Smith had scored a county record 30 centuries.

YORKSHIRE v SUSSEX

Played at Scarborough, July 19, 20, 21, 1939.
Toss won by Sussex.
Yorkshire won by ten wickets.

SUSSEX

John G.Langridge	c Verity b Bowes	2	c Robinson b Hutton	43
J.H.Parks	b Bowes	0	b Robinson	30
H.W.Parks	lbw b Bowes	14	lbw b Verity	22
G.Cox	c Sutcliffe b Bowes	6	c Hutton b Robinson	60
Jas.Langridge	c Robinson b Verity	72	not out	71
Mr H.T.Bartlett	c Robinson b Bowes	7	c Leyland b Verity	52
*Flt-Lt A.J.Holmes	c Mitchell b Bowes	0	c Hutton b Robinson	0
H.E.Hammond	c Leyland b Robinson	2	c Robinson b Verity	1
†W.L.Cornford	c Mitchell b Hutton	8	b Hutton	26
J.K.Nye	c Leyland b Bowes	16	c Mitchell b Hutton	8
J.H.Cornford	not out	11	st Wood b Verity	3
Extras	(B 15, LB 3)	18	(LB 3)	3
Total		**156**		**319**

Fall: 1st inns 1/0, 2/7, 3/27, 4/32, 5/56, 6/58, 7/67, 8/91, 9/119.
2nd inns 1/39, 2/102, 3/129, 4/185, 5/331, 6/243, 7/244, 8/277, 9/305.

YORKSHIRE

H.Sutcliffe	c J.Parks b J.Cornford	31		
L.Hutton	c John Langridge b J.Cornford	177	(1) not out	57
A.Mitchell	c Holmes b Hammond	2	(2) not out	32
M.Leyland	b Nye	4		
W.Barber	c John Langridge b Nye	84		
Mr N.W.D.Yardley	c Cox b Nye	17		
*Mr A.B.Sellers	c John Langridge b Jas.Langridge	18		
†A.Wood	c Hammond b Nye	18		
E.P.Robinson	c & b Nye	14		
H.Verity	c J.Parks b Jas.Langridge	0		
W.E.Bowes	not out	1		
Extras	(B 11, LB 8, W 1)	20	(LB 1)	1
Total		**386**	(No wicket)	**90**

Fall: 1st inns 1/99, 2/102, 3/129, 4/304, 5/331, 6/336, 7/368, 8/368, 9/378.

YORKSHIRE	O	M	R	W	O	M	R	W
Bowes	20	4	54	7	10	3	24	0
Yardley	11	1	29	0	4	2	7	0
Robinson	5	1	15	1	22	2	86	3
Hutton	2	0	6	1	17	1	74	3
Verity	5.6	0	34	1	24.4	5	98	4
Sellers	-	-	-	-	1	0	1	0
Leyland					6	0	26	0

SUSSEX	O	M	R	W	O	M	R	W
Nye	20.1	0	100	5	8	0	31	0
Hammond	17	0	104	1	6.2	1	27	0
J.H.Cornford	16	0	93	2	4	0	16	0
J.H.Parks	9	1	38	0				
Jas.Langridge	7	1	31	2				
Bartlett					2	0	15	0

Umpires: J.Hardstaff and G.Beet.
Close of play scores. First day: Yorkshire 304/4 (W.Barber 75*). **Second day:** Yorkshire 38/0 (L.Hutton 21*, A.Mitchell 16*).

Comments: L.Hutton and W.Barber made 175 in 110 minutes for the 4th wicket. L.Hutton took 210 minutes to make his 177, hitting 25 4's.
H.Sutcliffe completed his 50,000th run in first-class cricket when he reached 16 in the 1st innings. He was the sixth cricketer to reach this target. He was unable to bat in Yorkshire's 2nd innings because of a shoulder strain.
H.T.Bartlett hit 52 in 23 minutes, 44 coming in boundaries (four 6's and five 4's)
L.Hutton and A.Mitchell hit the 90 required for victory in 60 minutes.
Yorkshire required only 30 minutes on the third day to win the match.

DERBYSHIRE v SOMERSET

Played at Derby, July 22, 24, 25, 1939.
Toss won by Derbyshire.
Match drawn.

DERBYSHIRE

D.Smith	b Buse	71	c Luckes b Wellard	0
*Mr R.H.R.Buckston	run out	7	b Andrews	8
A.E.Alderman	b Hazell	24	b Wellard	1
T.S.Worthington	c Wellard b Buse	7	c Luckes b Andrews	22
G.H.Pope	lbw b Wellard	15	c Bennett b Andrews	20
L.F.Townsend	b Buse	8	c Luckes b Andrews	3
A.E.G.Rhodes	c Wellard b Buse	0	b Andrews	3
Mr T.D.Hounsfield	lbw b Buse	14	not out	17
A.V.Pope	not out	37	run out	1
†H.Elliott	c Longrigg b Andrews	1	not out	0
T.B.Mitchell	b Andrews	2		
Extras	(B 13, LB 1, NB 1)	15	(B 1, LB 1)	2
Total		**201**	(8 wickets)	**77**

Fall: 1st inns 1/12, 2/71, 3/84, 4/123, 5/132, 6/134, 7/141, 8/198, 9/199.
2nd inns 1/3, 2/3, 3/4, 4/28, 5/31, 6/56, 7/70, 8/71.

SOMERSET

F.S.Lee	c Smith b G.H.Pope	41
H.Gimblett	c G.H.Pope b Mitchell	71
H.T.F.Buse	b G.H.Pope	2
Mr C.J.P.Barnwell	b G.H.Pope	0
*Mr E.F.Longrigg	b G.H.Pope	0
†W.T.Luckes	st Elliott b Mitchell	5
Mr A.J.P.Ling	b G.H.Pope	0
Mr G.M.Bennett	b Mitchell	29
A.W.Wellard	c Buckston b Mitchell	11
W.H.R.Andrews	c Rhodes b Mitchell	9
H.L.Hazell	not out	0
Extras	(B 2, NB 1)	3
Total		**171**

Fall: 1st inns 1/90, 2/94, 3/94, 4/114, 5/114, 6/114, 7/131, 8/151, 9/164.

SOMERSET	O	M	R	W	O	M	R	W
Wellard	21	2	62	1	12	3	30	2
Andrews	10.2	1	25	2	12	2	45	5
Buse	23	2	76	5				
Hazell	5	0	23	1				

DERBYSHIRE	O	M	R	W	O	M	R	W
Rhodes	3	1	14	0				
G.H.Pope	17	0	59	5				
A.V.Pope	6	1	22	0				
Townsend	3	1	7	0				
Mitchell	11.3	0	66	5				

Umpires: J.Hardstaff and H.W.Lee.

Close of play scores. First day: Derbyshire 162/7 (T.D.Hounsfield 6*, A.V.Pope 10*). **Second day:** No play.

Comments: There was only three hours, 15 minutes play on the first day, play ending at 3.40pm.

GLAMORGAN v WARWICKSHIRE

Played at Llanelli, July 22, 24, 25, 1939.
Toss won by Glamorgan.
Glamorgan won by three wickets.

WARWICKSHIRE

A.J.W.Croom	not out	23	b Clay	51
W.A.Hill	not out	24	b Mercer	7
F.R.Santall			lbw b E.Davies	41
Mr R.E.S.Wyatt			c H.Davies b Clay	10
H.E.Dollery			run out	18
*Mr P.Cranmer			not out	41
Mr R.Sale			lbw b Clay	0
†J.Buckingham			not out	8
Extras	(LB 1)	1	(B 13, LB 7, W 1)	21
Total	(No wicket, declared)	**48**	(6 wickets, declared)	**197**

Fall: 2nd inns 1/35, 2/113, 3/115, 4/142, 5/155, 6/156.

J.H.Mayer, W.E.Hollies and K.Wilmot did not bat.

GLAMORGAN

D.E.Davies	not out	18	(2) b Mayer	67
T.L.Brierley	c Croom b Mayer	6	(3) lbw b Hollies	30
D.Davies	not out	23	(4) c Hill b Wilmot	11
A.H.Dyson			(1) lbw b Wilmot	2
*Mr M.J.L.Turnbull			lbw b Wilmot	7
C.C.Smart			c Croom b Hollies	44
Mr J.C.Clay			b Wilmot	6
†H.G.Davies			not out	28
E.C.Jones			not out	0
Extras	(NB 1)	1	(B 4, LB 1)	5
Total	(1 wicket, declared)	**48**	(7 wickets)	**200**

Fall: 1st inns 1/10.
2nd inns 1/35, 2/77, 3/105, 4/107, 5/137, 6/156, 7/172.

J.Mercer and A.D.G.Matthews did not bat.

GLAMORGAN	O	M	R	W	O	M	R	W
Matthews	4	0	16	0	5	0	39	0
Mercer	5	0	17	0	9	0	33	1
Clay	4	1	11	0	16	3	59	3
D.E.Davies	3	0	3	0	12	3	45	1

WARWICKSHIRE	O	M	R	W	O	M	R	W
Mayer	4	0	11	1	8	1	59	1
Wyatt	5	3	3	0				
Cranmer	2.5	0	29	0				
Wilmot	1	9	4	0	12	1	75	4
Hollies	-	-	-	-	13.4	0	61	2

Umpires: F.I.Walden and F.G.Baldwin.

Close of play scores. First day: No play (rain). **Second day:** Warwickshire 43/1 (A.J.W.Croom 29*, F.R.Santall 4*).

Comments: Two freak declarations contributed to a result in a game severely restricted by the weather. Play did not begin until 4pm on the second day. Glamorgan were set to make 198 in 150 minutes and won with 15 minutes remaining. H.G.Davies hit all the remaining 27 runs needed for victory in ten minutes. Earlier D.E.Davies had made 67 out of the first 77 runs in 50 minutes. This game resulted in considerable discussion, as to whether the Glamorgan captain, M.J.L.Turnbull by his 1st innings declaration was in breach of law 54, which stipulated that no declaration should take place later than 100 minutes from the close.

GLOUCESTERSHIRE v SUSSEX

Played at Bristol, July 22, 24, 25, 1939.
Toss won by Gloucestershire.
Match drawn.

GLOUCESTERSHIRE

R.A.Sinfield .... c John Langridge b Jas.Langridge 31	(6) lbw b Jas.Langridge ...11		
V.Hopkins .... c W.Cornford b Jas.Langridge 9	c Hammond b Nye 0		
*Mr B.O.Allen .... c John Langridge b Jas. Langridge 1	(1) b Jas Langridge 13		
G.M.Emmett .... c J.Parks b Jas.Langridge 3	(3) lbw b Nye 6		
J.F.Crapp .... c John Langridge b J.Parkes 17	(4) lbw b Jas.Langridge 9		
Mr E.D.R.Eagar ... c W.Cornford b J.Parks ...3	(5) b J.Parks 45		
W.L.Neale .... not out 11	c Nye b J.Parks 0		
†E.A.Wilson .... b J.Parks 2	not out 16		
L.M.Cranfield ...... b J.Parks 0	not out 1		
C.J.Scott .... c & b J.Parks 0			
G.E.E.Lambert ..... c H.Parks b Jas.Langridge 15			
Extras.............(B 1, LB 1, W 1) 3	(B 4) 4		
Total **95**	**(7 wickets)** **105**		

Fall: 1st inns 1/25, 2/29, 3/43, 4/54, 5/61, 6/70, 7/76, 8/76, 9/78.
2nd inns 1/5, 2/13, 3/21, 4/47, 5/79, 6/79, 7/87.

SUSSEX

John G.Langridge... c Allen b Sinfield 35	
J.H.Parks .... lbw b Scott 21	
H.W.Parks .... c Scott b Sinfield 2	
G.Cox .... b Cranfield 3	
Jas.Langridge........ not out 59	
*Flt-Lt A.J.Holmes c Neale b Sinfield 12	
Sir W.F.W.Becher ... lbw b Sinfield 4	
H.E.Hammond ...... lbw b Sinfield 12	
Extras .... (LB 2) 2	
Total .... **(7 wickets, declared)** **150**	

Fall: 1st inns 1/52, 2/58, 3/61, 4/61, 5/88, 6/134, 7/150.

†W.L.Cornford, J.H.Cornford and J.K.Nye did not bat.

SUSSEX	O	M	R	W	O	M	R	W
Nye 3		0	13	0	4	0	20	2
J.H.Parks 18		5	27	5	12	3	15	2
Hammond 1		0	2	0				
Jas.Langridge 16		2	50	5	13	2	66	3

GLOUCESTERSHIRE	O	M	R	W
Scott 5		1	13	1
Lambert 2		0	14	0
Sinfield 13.6		1	60	5
Cranfield 11		0	61	1

Umpires: W.Reeves and E.Cooke.

Close of play scores. First day: Gloucestershire 11/0 (R.A.Sinfield 5*, V.Hopkins 5*).

Comments: Only 15 minutes play took place on the first day and none on the second.
J.H.Parks had a bowling spell of five wickets for eight runs on the third day.
Sussex claimed the extra half-hour in a vain attempt to secure victory.

KENT v SURREY

Played at Blackheath, July 22, 24, 25, 1939.
Toss won by Surrey.
Match drawn.

SURREY

R.J.Gregory.......... b Harding 4	not out 108		
L.B.Fishlock .... c Levett b Todd 7	c Foster b Lewis 4		
E.W.Whitfield ...... c Todd b Harding 0	c Todd b Lewis 10		
H.S.Squires .... c Lewis b Harding 64	c Dovey b Lewis 13		
J.F.Parker .... c Watt b Lewis 96	lbw b Todd 3		
G.J.Whittaker ...... c Levett b Watt 4	lbw b Lewis 1		
Mr P.J.Dickinson.... c Lewis b Watt 0	c Harding b Lewis 11		
*Mr H.M.Garland-Wells .... c Ames b Todd 32	lbw b Lewis 0		
†G.S.Mobey.......... not out 11	b Ames 9		
E.A.Watts .... b Todd 2	not out 25		
A.R.Gover .... c Levett b Todd 0			
Extras .... (B 8, LB 3) 11	(B 1, LB 2) 3		
Total **231**	**(8 wickets)** **187**		

Fall: 1st inns 1/7, 2/8, 3/21, 4/171, 5/180, 6/180, 7/206, 8/220, 9/225.
2nd inns 1/16, 2/37, 3/73, 4/88, 5/105, 6/109, 7/109, 8/135.

KENT

*Mr F.G.H.Chalk ... b Watts 18	
Mr P.G.Foster .... b Watts 24	
L.E.G.Ames.......... c Parker b Gover 43	
Mr B.H.Valentine ... b Watts 64	
L.J.Todd............. c Gregory b Gover.........0	
T.G.Evans .... c Fishlock b Gover 8	
N.W.Harding .... b Gover 4	
†Mr W.H.V.Levett c Mobey b Watts 17	
A.E.Watt .... not out 21	
C.Lewis .... b Gover 0	
R.R.Dovey .... b Gover 0	
Extras .... (LB 1, NB 2) 3	
Total **202**	

Fall: 1st inns 1/37, 2/52, 3/137, 4/143, 5/154, 6/163, 7/163, 8/191, 9/202.

KENT	O	M	R	W	O	M	R	W
Harding....................14		1	45	3	2	0	6	0
Todd.......................16		2	45	4	12	1	38	1
Watt.......................15		0	54	2	1	0	8	0
Lewis......................11		2	46	1	20	8	49	6
Dovey......................7		3	30	0	5	0	10	0
Ames	-	-	-	-	5	0	31	0
Valentine	-	-	-	-	2	0	7	0
Chalk	-	-	-	-	2	0	28	0
Foster	-	-	-	-	1	0	7	0

SURREY	O	M	R	W
Gover 19.6		1	93	6
Watts 13		0	56	4
Gregory 3		1	8	0
Parker 8		1	22	0
Squires 1		0	3	0
Garland-Wells...............3		0	17	0

Umpires: J.A.Newman and A.Dolphin.

Close of play scores. First day: Kent 18/0 (F.G.H.Chalk 2*, P.G.Foster 16*).
Second day: Kent 86/2 (L.E.G.Ames 22*, B.H.Valentine 21*).
Comments: Rain severely curtailed play on the second day, after delaying the start on the first.
J.F.Parker and J.F.Squires added 150 for Surrey's 4th wicket in 130 minutes.

LEICESTERSHIRE v HAMPSHIRE

Played at Aylestone Road, Leicester, July 22, 24, 25, 1939.
Toss won by Hampshire.
Leicestershire won by four wickets.

HAMPSHIRE

†N.T.McCorkell	c Watson b Palmer	3	c Sperry b Smith	22
J.Bailey	b Berry	2	(8) b Smith	11
Mr J.P.Blake	c Dawkes b Palmer	3	c Packe b Sperry	14
J.Arnold	c Dawkes b Palmer	44	c Tompkin b Sperry	12
D.F.Walker	run out	4	b Sperry	8
A.E.Pothecary	c Packe b Prentice	67	c Dawkes b Sperry	0
P.A.Mackenzie	c Dawkes b Sperry	14	(9) b Sperry	9
*Mr G.R.Taylor	b Prentice	26	(10) not out	0
G.S.Boyes	not out	16	(2) b Sperry	0
R.C.Court	lbw b Prentice	0	(7) b Sperry	0
G.E.M.Heath	c Dawkes b Sperry	0		
Extras	(B 9, LB 5)	14	(LB 1, NB 2)	3
Total		**193**	(9 wickets, declared)	**79**

Fall: 1st inns 1/5, 2/8, 3/12, 4/25, 5/101, 6/134, 7/170, 8/192, 9/192.
2nd inns 1/0, 2/35, 3/37, 4/54, 5/54, 6/54, 7/59, 8/79, 9/79.

LEICESTERSHIRE

Mr C.S.Dempster	b Boyes	38	c Court b Boyes	10
G.L.Berry	c Taylor b Heath	6	lbw b Bailey	22
N.F.Armstrong	not out	71	(7) not out	18
F.T.Prentice	c Boyes b Bailey	4	(8) not out	3
G.S.Watson	c Walker b Bailey	3	(3) c & b Bailey	2
*Mr M.St.J.Packe	b Boyes	1	(4) b Boyes	8
M.Tompkin	b Bailey	4	(5) b Boyes	39
†G.O.Dawkes	b Bailey	6	(6) c Court b Boyes	5
Mr G.H.Palmer	b Bailey	1		
H.A.Smith	c Arnold b Boyes	8		
J.Sperry	c Blake b Bailey	8		
Extras	(B 4, LB 3)	7	(B 7, LB 2)	9
Total		**157**	(6 wickets)	**116**

Fall: 1st inns 1/23, 2/71, 3/89, 4/93, 5/98, 6/113, 7/121, 8/131, 9/140.
2nd inns 1/22, 2/24, 3/47, 4/49, 5/61, 6/111.

LEICESTERSHIRE	O	M	R	W	O	M	R	W
Sperry	19.4	2	52	3	14.1	6	19	7
Palmer	17	7	42	3	1	0	10	0
Smith	14	4	43	0	13	2	33	2
Prentice	16	3	42	3	5	0	14	0

HAMPSHIRE	O	M	R	W	O	M	R	W
Heath	14	4	25	1	1	0	7	0
Bailey	29.7	6	72	6	12	0	40	2
Court	2	0	8	0				
Boyes	25	7	45	3	11.7	1	60	4

Umpires: G.Beet and G.M.Lee.

Close of play scores. First day: Leicestershire 28/1 (C.S.Dempster 16*, N.F.Armstrong 0*). **Second day:** Leicestershire 117/6 (N.F.Armstrong 51*, D.O.Dawkes 4*).

Comments: There was only two and a half hours play on the second day. Play was abandoned for the day soon after lunch.
Leicestershire were set to make 116 runs in 110 minutes. It was their first victory of the season.

MIDDLESEX v LANCASHIRE

Played at Lord's, July 22, 24, 25, 1939.
Toss won by Middlesex.
Match drawn.

MIDDLESEX

Mr B.D.Carris	c Phillipson b Pollard	19
J.D.B.Robertson	c & b Nutter	79
W.J.Edrich	c Wilkinson b Nutter	125
G.E.Hart	b Pollard	17
S.M.Brown	lbw b Nutter	1
J.H.A.Hulme	c & b Wilkinson	16
†W.F.F.Price	lbw b Wilkinson	6
L.H.Compton	c Farrimond b Higson	9
J.M.Sims	not out	42
C.I.J.Smith	c Farrimond b Nutter	10
Extras	(B 2, LB 2, W 2, NB 4)	10
Total	(9 wickets, declared)	**334**

Fall: 1st inns 1/48, 2/131, 3/174, 4/187, 5/224, 6/230, 7/251, 8/315, 9/334

*I.A.R.Peebles did not bat

LANCASHIRE

W.Place	c Carris b Smith	0
C.Washbrook	not out	34
J.L.Hopwood	c Robertson b Smith	0
N.Oldfield	b Robertson	9
J.Iddon	not out	26
Extras	(B 3, LB 2)	5
Total	(3 wickets)	**74**

Fall: 1st inns 1/0, 2/0, 3/22.

*Mr T.A.Higson, †W.Farrimond, A.E.Nutter, W.E.Phillipson, R.Pollard and L.L.Wilkinson did not bat.

LANCASHIRE	O	M	R	W
Phillipson	11	0	57	0
Pollard	23	5	52	2
Nutter	19.3	2	70	4
Wilkinson	9	0	53	2
Hopwood	13	1	36	0
Higson	10	2	45	1
Iddon	2	0	11	0

MIDDLESEX	O	M	R	W
Smith	8	3	9	2
Edrich	7	0	24	0
Robertson	6	2	14	1
Carris	4	1	11	0
Sims	2	0	11	0

Umpires: C.N.Woolley and E.Robinson.

Close of play scores. First day: Middlesex 181/3 (W.J.Edrich 60*, S.M.Brown 1*). **Second day:** Middlesex 238/6 (W.J.Edrich 87*, L.H.Compton 7*).

Comments: Play began late on the first day and only an hour was possible on the second. Play began at 1.30pm on the third day.
Middlesex continued batting on the third day with the purpose of preventing either side gaining a 1st innings lead, as this would have reduced their average in the Championship table.
W.J.Edrich made 125 in nearly five hours, hitting 14 4's.

NORTHAMPTONSHIRE v WORCESTERSHIRE

Played at Rushden, July 22, 24, 25, 1939.
Toss won by Northamptonshire.
Worcestershire won by one wicket.

NORTHAMPTONSHIRE

P.Davis	c Jenkins b Howorth 26	b Perks 5
H.W.Greenwood	lbw b Jenkins 31	c Perks b Martin 6
D.Brookes	c & b Howorth 2	lbw b Perks 3
J.E.Timms	c Palmer b Perks 26	c Perks b Martin 7
F.P.O'Brien	c & b Howorth 3	c Cooper b Martin 1
*Mr R.P.Nelson	b Perks 51	run out 4
†K.C.James	lbw b Martin 25	lbw b Martin 0
W.E.Merritt	c White b Martin........53	b Perks 28
R.J.Partridge	not out 26	b Perks 2
W.Kemmey	st King b Howorth 10	b Perks 4
E.J.Herbert	b Perks 1	not out 1
Extras	(B 2, LB 5) 5	(LB 5) 5
Total	**261**	**66**

Fall: 1st inns 1/59, 2/61, 3/63, 4/66, 5/96, 6/153, 7/204, 8/228, 9/249.
2nd inns 1/7, 2/15, 3/15, 4/18, 5/27, 6/27, 7/35, 8/47, 9/59.

WORCESTERSHIRE

E.Cooper	c Timms b Nelson 20	b Partridge 2
R.Howorth	c Merritt b Herbert......11	c O'Brien b Partridge.......1
†B.P.King	c O'Brien b Herbert 3	c James b Timms..........34
H.H.I.Gibbons	c Greenwood b Nelson 9	c James b Partridge 0
S.H.Martin	b Herbert 38	(6) b Herbert 4
Mr C.H.Palmer	c Brookes b Partridge ...23	(7) b Partridge 5
*Hon C.J.Lyttelton	c Timms b Partridge.....14	(5) c James b Timms 11
Mr J.Stanning	not out 56	b Partridge 0
Mr A.F.T.White	lbw b Partridge 0	not out 31
R.O.Jenkins	b Herbert 36	b Timms 4
R.T.D.Perks	b Partridge 1	not out 6
Extras	(B 6, LB 8, W 1, NB 1) ...16	(LB 4) 4
Total	**227**	**(9 wickets) 102**

Fall: 1st inns 1/20, 2/24, 3/35, 4/80, 5/98, 6/132, 7/133, 8/189, 9/226.
2nd inns 1/2, 2/13, 3/13, 4/36, 5/57, 6/58, 7/58, 8/58, 9/71.

WORCESTERSHIRE	O	M	R	W	O	M	R	W
Perks	17.6	4	48	3	7.6	1	25	5
Martin	27	7	86	2	9	2	36	4
Howorth	21	1	75	4				
Jenkins	16	6	43	1				
Palmer	1	0	2	0				

NORTHANTS	O	M	R	W	O	M	R	W
Partridge	14.3	3	39	4	12.7	4	32	5
Herbert	15	1	45	4	11	1	39	1
Nelson	17	3	75	2				
Merritt	5	0	48	0				
Timms	5	2	4	0	7	1	27	3

Umpires: A.Skelding and J.J.Hills.

Close of play scores. First day: Northamptonshire 258/9 (R.J.Partridge 23*, E.J.Herbert 1*). **Second day:** Worcestershire 36/4 (B.P.King 1*).

Comments: A.F.T.White and R.T.D.Perks scored an unbeaten 30 for Worcestershire's 10th wicket to win the match by the narrow margin of one wicket.

YORKSHIRE v NOTTINGHAMSHIRE

Played at Bramall Lane, Sheffield, July 22, 24, 25, 1939.
Match drawn.

NOTTINGHAMSHIRE

W.W.Keeton	c Sellers b Smailes 65
J.Knowles	c Mitchell b Yardley.......0
*Mr G.F.H.Heane	c Barber b Robinson 19
G.V.Gunn	c Yardley b Leyland 7
D.Jones	b Smailes 8
R.J.Giles	not out 34
F.H.Winrow	b Smailes 2
W.Voce	c Robinson b Smailes 38
†A.B.Wheat	c Smailes b Verity 4
H.J.Butler	c Yardley b Robinson 14
A.Jepson	st Fiddling b Verity 0
Extras	(B 6, W 1, NB 2) 9
Total	**200**

Fall: 1st inns 1/6, 2/65, 3/76, 4/98, 5/103, 6/109, 7/159, 8/176, 9/200.

YORKSHIRE

Mr N.W.D.Yardley	b Voce 6
A.Mitchell	c Wheat b Knowles 44
W.Barber	b Voce 10
M.Leyland	not out 25
Extras	(B 7, LB 2) 9
Total	**(3 wickets) 94**

Fall: 1st inns 1/9, 2/33, 3/93.

*Mr A.B.Sellers, H.Verity, E.P.Robinson, T.F.Smailes, C.Turner, †K.Fiddling and W.Watson did not bat.

YORKSHIRE	O	M	R	W
Smailes	21	1	79	4
Yardley	2	0	7	1
Turner	1	0	1	0
Verity	17.1	3	51	2
Robinson	10	3	39	2
Leyland	4	0	14	1

NOTTINGHAMSHIRE	O	M	R	W
Voce	28	13	28	2
Butler	13	5	9	0
Jepson	3	1	2	0
Gunn	16	6	24	0
Giles	5	2	7	0
Heane	6	3	6	0
Winrow	4	4	0	0
Knowles	2.1	0	6	1
Keeton	1	0	3	0

Umpires: C.V.Tarbox and J.A.Smart.

Close of play scores. First day: No play. **Second day:** Yorkshire 17/1 (A.Mitchell 6*, W.Barber 5*).

Comments: This fixture raised serious questions about the system of scoring in the County Championship. By the final afternoon, when play resumed leaving only four hours of play, Yorkshire could only achieve 1st innings points, which would have reduced their average in the Championship table. As a 'no result' would exclude the game from counting in the championship, Yorkshire batted extremely slowly to avoid taking a 1st innings lead. A.Mitchell batted four hours for 44 runs. In the 150 minutes between lunch and tea he scored a mere 11 runs. The Yorkshire batsmen were even barracked by their own supporters.
W.Watson made his debut for Yorkshire, although he did not bat.
In Nottinghamshire's 1st innings, W.Voce hit a 6 over the pavilion into the car-park.

GLAMORGAN v LEICESTERSHIRE

Played at Swansea, July 26, 27, 28, 1939.
Toss won by Leicestershire.
Match drawn.

LEICESTERSHIRE

G.L.Berry	c Smart b E.Davies	76
F.T.Prentice	b Mercer	3
N.F.Armstrong	c Smart b Mercer	49
G.S.Watson	b Mercer	3
*Mr M.St.J.Packe	b Clay	12
G.Lester	c H.Davies b E.Davies	14
L.D.Thursting	st H.Davies b Mercer	11
†G.O.Dawkes	b Mercer	26
H.A.Smith	b Mercer	6
J.Sperry	b Mercer	4
C.H.Drake	not out	0
Extras	(B 5, LB 4, W 1)	10
Total		**216**

Fall: 1st inns 1/8, 2/101, 3/116, 4/145, 5/153, 6/178, 7/186, 8/201, 9/205.

GLAMORGAN

A.H.Dyson	lbw b Lester	53
D.E.Davies	c Thursting b Smith	15
T.L.Brierley	not out	39
D.Davies	not out	4
Extras	(B 6, LB 2, W 1)	9
Total	(2 wickets)	**120**

Fall: 1st inns 1/44, 2/107.

*Mr M.J.L.Turnbull, Mr J.C.Clay, C.C.Smart, E.C.Jones, †H.G.Davies, J.Mercer and A.D.G.Matthews did not bat.

GLAMORGAN	O	M	R	W
Matthews	9	0	30	0
Mercer	15.2	0	67	7
Clay	23	4	55	1
D.E.Davies	17	1	51	2
Smart	4	1	3	0

LEICESTERSHIRE	O	M	R	W
Sperry	10	1	33	0
Drake	9	2	16	0
Smith	10	2	23	1
Prentice	8	2	29	0
Lester	2	0	10	1

Umpires: J.A.Newman and E.Cooke.

Close of play scores. First day: Glamorgan 120/2 (T.L.Brierley 39*, D.Davies 4*). **Second day:** No play.

Comments: No play took place on the last two days.

HAMPSHIRE v GLOUCESTERSHIRE

Played at Bournemouth, July 26, 27, 28, 1939.
Toss won by Gloucestershire.
Gloucestershire won by 43 runs.

GLOUCESTERSHIRE

R.A.Sinfield	b Bailey	20	c Bailey b Baring		11
V.Hopkins	c Boyes b Baring	21	c Blake b Baring		0
G.M.Emmett	c Arnold b Bailey	2	lbw b Heath		31
*Mr W.R.Hammond	b Creese	27	c Boyes b Heath		8
J.F.Crapp	c Taylor b Creese	64	c Taylor b Bailey		38
†E.A.Wilson	c Boyes b Creese	6			
Mr E.D.R.Eagar	b Creese	5	(6) not out		48
W.L.Neale	b Bailey	22			
C.J.Scott	c Taylor b Bailey	15	(7) b Creese		22
G.E.E.Lambert	b Creese	4			
T.W.J.Goddard	not out	18	(8) b Creese		2
Extras	(B 4, LB 4)	8			
Total		**212**	(7 wickets, declared)		**160**

Fall: 1st inns 1/36, 2/41, 3/48, 4/108, 5/124, 6/131, 7/168, 8/183, 9/188.
2nd inns 1/1, 2/11, 3/27, 4/55, 5/117, 6/158, 7/160.

HAMPSHIRE

Mr R.H.Moore	c Emmett b Goddard	11	b Goddard		11
J.Bailey	lbw b Goddard	25	c Crapp b Goddard		5
Mr J.P.Blake	b Goddard	9	lbw b Goddard		0
J.Arnold	b Scott	35	lbw b Hammond		8
W.L.C.Creese	c Crapp b Goddard	26	c Wilson b Hammond		68
†D.F.Walker	c Emmett b Goddard	45	c Scott b Sinfield		20
P.A.Mackenzie	c Hopkins b Goddard	3	c Hammond b Sinfield		19
*Mr G.R.Taylor	b Sinfield	4	b Hammond		12
G.S.Boyes	c Hammond b Sinfield	4	c Sinfield b Goddard		3
Mr A.E.G.Baring	c Hopkins b Goddard	0	c Eagar b Goddard		5
G.E.M.Heath	not out	0	not out		0
Extras	(B 1, LB 4)	5	(B 1, LB 10)		11
Total		**167**			**162**

Fall: 1st inns 1/18, 2/33, 3/66, 4/98, 5/116, 6/134, 7/149, 8/153, 9/164.
2nd inns 1/16, 2/16, 3/19, 4/33, 5/87, 6/127, 7/151, 8/156, 9/161.

HAMPSHIRE	O	M	R	W	O	M	R	W
Baring	16	4	42	1	9	1	53	2
Heath	4	1	9	0	9	1	39	2
Boyes	12	4	20	0				
Bailey	17.7	1	83	4	4	0	34	1
Creese	18	2	50	5	4	0	34	2

GLOUCESTERSHIRE	O	M	R	W	O	M	R	W
Scott	12	0	61	1	3	0	19	0
Lambert	1	0	2	0	3	0	15	0
Goddard	20.2	2	77	7	15.4	2	65	5
Sinfield	10	3	22	2	7	0	23	2
Hammond	-	-	-	-	7	1	29	3

Umpires: F.J.Durston and E.Robinson.

Close of play scores. First day: Gloucestershire 125/5 (J.F.Crapp 43*, E.D.R.Eagar 0*). **Second day:** Hampshire 108/4 (J.Arnold 34*, D.F.Walker 2*).

Comments: Play was delayed until 3pm on the first day due to a saturated pitch.
There was also a shortened second day's play because of rain.
Hampshire were set to make 206 to win in under three hours.
T.W.J.Goddard took 12 wickets in the match for the second time against Hampshire in 1939.
Gloucestershire won after claiming the extra half-hour.

LANCASHIRE v NORTHAMPTONSHIRE

Played at Blackpool, July 26, 27, 28, 1939.
Toss won by Northamptonshire
Match drawn.

NORTHAMPTONSHIRE

Mr E.J.H.Dixon	b Nutter	20
H.W.Greenwood	c Farrimond b Phillipson	0
D.Brookes	c Farrimond b Phillipson	55
J.E.Timms	lbw b Wilkinson	83
†K.C.James	c Farrimond b Iddon	55
*Mr R.P.Nelson	not out	76
P.Davis	b Nutter	2
F.P.O'Brien	c Phillipson b Pollard	44
W.E.Merritt	c Oldfield b Phillipson	1
R.J.Partridge	lbw b Phillipson	3
E.J.Herbert	lbw b Phillipson	7
Extras	(B 6, LB 12, NB 4)	22
Total		**368**

Fall: 1st inns 1/1, 2/65, 3/85, 4/200, 5/239, 6/242, 7/338, 8/340, 9/346.

LANCASHIRE

W.Place	b Partridge	11
E.Paynter	b Herbert	4
C.Washbrook	b Partridge	30
N.Oldfield	lbw b Partridge	6
J.Iddon	lbw b Partridge	69
A.E.Nutter	c Brookes b Partridge	0
W.E.Phillipson	c Dixon b Merritt	11
*Mr T.A.Higson	c James b Partridge	16
†W.Farrimond	not out	28
R.Pollard	c James b Partridge	12
L.L.Wilkinson	not out	0
Extras	(B 2, LB 8, W 1)	11
Total	(9 wickets)	**198**

Fall: 1st inns 1/15, 2/19, 3/31, 4/75, 5/75, 6/96, 7/126, 8/163, 9/191.

LANCASHIRE	O	M	R	W
Phillipson	23.7	5	68	5
Pollard	26	3	71	1
Nutter	14	1	59	2
Higson	4	1	18	0
Wilkinson	19	2	77	1
Paynter	9	0	35	0
Iddon	9	0	18	1

NORTHANTS	O	M	R	W
Partridge	21	7	49	7
Herbert	17	4	47	1
Timms	6	0	30	0
Nelson	7	1	18	0
Merritt	6	0	43	1

Umpires: J.Hardstaff and C.V.Tarbox.

Close of play scores. First day: Northamptonshire 332/6 (R.P.Nelson 56*, F.P.O'Brien 43*). **Second day:** Lancashire 189/9 (w.Farrimond 28*, L.L.Wilkinson 0*).

Comments: There was no play on the third day.
J.E.Timms and K.C.James put on 115 for the 4th wicket in Northants 1st innings.

MIDDLESEX v DERBYSHIRE

Played at Lord's, July 26, 27, 28, 1939.
Toss won by Derbyshire.
Middlesex won by an innings and 24 runs.

DERBYSHIRE

D.Smith	lbw b Smith	4	c Price b Compton	96
*Mr R.H.R.Buckston	c Price b Sims	14	c Peebles b Sims	19
A.E.Alderman	c Edrich b Sims	13	b Peebles	57
T.S.Worthington	c Price b Peebles	18	not out	79
G.H.Pope	st Price b Sims	3	c Edrich b Sims	0
L.F.Townsend	c Mann b Sims	13	c Price b Smith	26
A.V.Pope	c Peebles b Sims	21	c & b Sims	6
A.E.G.Rhodes	c & b Sims	4	c Hart b Sims	8
†H.Elliott	not out	6	c Peebles b Smith	1
T.B.Mitchell	c Carris b Sims	13	c Price b Smith	0
W.H.Copson	b Sims	0	b Sims	10
Extras	(B 1)	1	(B 6, NB 5)	11
Total		**110**		**313**

Fall: 1st inns 1/7, 2/27, 3/40, 4/46, 5/58, 6/87, 7/87, 8/92, 9/108.
2nd inns 1/64, 2/156, 3/197, 4/198, 5/264, 6/279, 7/299, 8/302, 9/302.

MIDDLESEX

J.D.B.Robertson	c Mitchell b Rhodes	43
Mr B.D.Carris	c & b A.V.Pope	17
W.J.Edrich	b Townsend	61
D.C.S.Compton	not out	214
Mr F.G.Mann	b A.V.Pope	10
S.M.Brown	c Elliott b A.V.Pope	13
G.E.Hart	lbw b Mitchell	29
†W.F.F.Price	c Copson b Rhodes	55
Extras	(B 3, LB 2)	5
Total	(7 wickets, declared)	**447**

Fall: 1st inns 1/49, 2/81, 3/170, 4/217, 5/263, 6/329, 7/447.

*Mr I.A.R.Peebles, J.M.Sims and C.I.J.Smith did not bat.

MIDDLESEX	O	M	R	W	O	M	R	W
Smith	8	0	25	1	22	2	72	3
Edrich	4	0	10	0	11	2	51	0
Sims	11.1	2	32	8	23.7	1	128	5
Peebles	8	0	42	1	9	1	23	1
Compton	-	-	-	-	4	0	19	1
Robertson	-	-	-	-	2	0	9	0

DERBYSHIRE	O	M	R	W
Copson	25	3	107	0
A.V.Pope	28	5	98	3
G.H.Pope	8	0	48	0
Mitchell	17	1	95	1
Rhodes	11.5	0	75	2
Townsend	5	1	19	1

Umpires: J.A.Smart and A.Dolphin.

Close of play scores. First day: Middlesex 228/4 (D.C.S.Compton 94*, S.M.Brown 3*). **Second day:** Derbyshire 222/4 (T.S.Worthington 30*, L.F.Townsend 11*).

Comments: J.M.Sims took three wickets in six balls in Derbyshire's 1st innings. He captured seven wickets before lunch.
D.C.S.Compton reached his 2,000 runs for the season whilst his 214* was his highest first-class score. He reached his century and 2,000th run with the same stroke. He hit one 6 and 26 4's.
He added 118 with W.F.F.Price for the 7th wicket.
Derbyshire lost their last six wickets in only 90 minutes on the third morning.

SOMERSET v ESSEX

Played at Wells, July 26, 27, 1939.
Toss won by Essex.
Essex won by 123 runs.

ESSEX

L.C.Eastman	run out 14	lbw b Andrews.............38
A.V.Avery	c Luckes b Andrews 2	b Wellard 20
F.H.Vigar	c Wellard b Andrews....11	lbw b Hazell 0
J.O'Connor	lbw b Wellard 0	lbw b Wellard 53
M.S.Nichols	lbw b Andrews 4	b Wellard 4
R.Smith	b Wellard 9	b Wellard 0
*Mr D.R.Wilcox	b Wellard.....15	lbw b Wellard 38
R.M.Taylor	c Gomm b Wellard......0	b Wellard 0
Capt J.W.A.Stephenson	b Wellard...8	not out 4
†T.H.Wade	c Wellard b Andrews 6	c Luckes b Hazell.........1
T.P.B.Smith	not out 0	b Wellard 8
Extras	(LB 1, NB 3) 3	(LB 7, NB 1) 8
Total	**72**	**174**

Fall: 1st inns 1/13, 2/19, 3/20, 4/31, 5/40, 6/50, 7/50, 8/61, 9/72.
2nd inns 1/48, 2/49, 3/81, 4/92, 5/92, 6/157, 7/157, 8/164, 9/165.

SOMERSET

F.S.Lee	c O'Connor b Nichols 7	c Taylor b Nichols 16
H.Gimblett	Wilcox b R.Smith.......7	c Wade b Nichols..........15
H.T.F.Buse	b Stephenson 9	b Taylor 1
Mr C.J.P.Barnwell	c Wilcox b R.Smith 1	(9) c Wilcox b Nichols.....9
*Mr E.F.Longrigg	c Wade b Stephenson ...19	run out 0
Mr G.M.Bennett	b Nichols 2	(7) lbw b Taylor 3
†W.T.Luckes	b Nichols 0	(8) lbw b Taylor 0
Mr B.A.Gomm	c Avery b Stephenson ...5	(4) c Wilcox b Nichols.....5
W.H.R.Andrews	b Stephenson 4	(6) b Taylor 4
A.W.Wellard	b Stephenson 1	c Vigar b Taylor...........12
H.L.Hazell	not out 1	not out 0
Extras	0	(B 5, LB 2) 7
Total	**51**	**72**

Fall: 1st inns 1/14, 2/16, 3/18, 4/40, 5/45, 6/45, 7/45, 8/47, 9/50.
2nd inns 1/31, 2/32, 3/41, 4/41, 5/45, 6/49, 7/50, 8/55, 9/67.

SOMERSET	O	M	R	W	O	M	R	W
Wellard	18	3	35	5	26	6	68	7
Andrews	17.1	5	34	4	8	1	27	1
Hazell	-	-	-	-	24	8	60	2
Buse					3	1	11	0

ESSEX	O	M	R	W	O	M	R	W
Nichols	11	0	30	3	13.4	2	33	4
R.Smith	6	0	17	2	4	1	3	0
Stephenson	4.4	1	4	5	2	1	2	0
P.Smith	-	-	-	-	3	1	4	0
Taylor					8	3	23	5

Umpires: H.Baldwin and H.Cruice.

Close of play scores. First day: Essex 75/2 (L.C.Eastman 36*, J.O'Connor 12*).

Comments: The match was completed in two days, the consequence of a 'sporting' wicket (*Wisden*). The heavy atmosphere also helped the bowlers to make use of a late swing. Both sides were dismissed for their lowest scores of the season. On the first day 22 wickets fell for 198 runs. A.E.Wellard and W.H.R.Andrews bowled unchanged in Essex 1st innings. J.W.A.Stephenson finished off the Somerset 1st innings with three wickets in five balls. Somerset lost seven wickets for 12 runs after tea on the first day. The highest partnership of the match was a hard hitting 65 by J.O'Connor and D.R.Wilcox for the 6th wicket of the Essex 2nd innings. O'Connor hit a 6 and seven 4's in his 53, the highest score of the match and D.R.Wilcox six 6's in his 38. J.O'Connor was the only batsman in the match to score over 50, whilst no Somerset batsman reached 20. R.M.Taylor achieved career best figures of 5 for 23 in Somerset's 2nd innings. B.A.Gomm was making his first-class debut.

WARWICKSHIRE v SUSSEX

Played at Edgbaston, Birmingham, July 26, 27, 28, 1939.
Toss won by Sussex.
Warwickshire won by eight wickets.

SUSSEX

J.H.Parks	c Buckingham b Mayer ...6	c Wyatt b Hollies..........23
John G.Langridge	c Buckingham b Mayer 12	lbw b Wyatt................0
H.W.Parks	st Buckingham b Hollies 39	b Wyatt....................73
G.Cox	c Buckingham b Mayer ...1	c Wyatt b Hollies..........8
Jas.Langridge	c Buckingham b Wilmot 62	b Wyatt....................20
*Flt-Lt A.J.Holmes	c Wyatt b Mayer.....21	c Wyatt b Hollies..........3
Mr R.G.Stainton	hit wkt b Meyer 52	c Buckingham b Hollies 5
Sir W.F.W.Becher	c Sale b Wilmot 5	b Wyatt....................19
H.E.Hammond	c Buckingham b Wilmot 32	not out 3
†W.L.Cornford	not out 6	c Ord b Hollies............0
J.K.Nye	b Mayer 0	b Wyatt....................1
Extras	(LB 1, NB 1) 2	(B 4, LB 2) 6
Total	**238**	**162**

Fall: 1st inns 1/17, 2/20, 3/22, 4/83, 5/136, 6/149, 7/163, 8/230, 9/238.
2nd inns 1/8, 2/57, 3/71, 4/124, 5/127, 6/129, 7/155, 8/161, 9/161.

WARWICKSHIRE

A.J.W.Croom	c John Langridge b Hammond 4	c Cornford b Nye 5
Mr R.Sale	c Jas.Langridge b Nye.....101	not out 35
F.R.Santall	c Cox b Hammond..........0	c Cox b J.Parks............4
Mr R.E.S.Wyatt	c Cornford b Hammond 2	not out 35
H.E.Dollery	lbw b J.Parks.............90	
J.S.Ord	b Nye 7	
†J.Buckingham	not out 30	
*Mr P.Cranmer	c Cox b Jas.Langridge 69	
K.Wilmot	st Cornford b Jas.Langridge 1	
Extras	(B 10, LB 2) 12	(B 5, LB 1) 6
Total	(8 wickets, declared) ...**316**	(2 wickets) **85**

Fall: 1st inns 1/15, 2/15, 3/21, 4/197, 5/208, 6/213, 7/310, 8/316.
2nd inns 1/8, 2/21.

W.E.Hollies and J.H.Mayer did not bat.

WARWICKSHIRE	O	M	R	W	O	M	R	W
Mayer	17.7	1	50	6	10	2	27	0
Wyatt	7	2	13	0	17.1	3	58	5
Wilmot	18	4	59	3	8	0	21	0
Hollies	29	3	79	1	20	4	50	5
Santall	4	0	16	0				
Croom	5	1	19	0				

SUSSEX	O	M	R	W	O	M	R	W
Nye	11	3	64	2	6	0	30	1
J.Parks	23	4	64	1	9	3	20	1
Hammond	16	2	54	3				
Jas.Langridge	14	2	67	2	4	0	21	0
Cox	4	0	24	0				
John Langridge	2	0	19	0				
Holmes	3	0	12	0				
Stainton	-	-	-	-	1	0	8	0

Umpires: G.Beet and W.Reeves.

Close of play scores. First day: Warwickshire 5/0 (A.J.W.Croom 1*, R.Sale 4*).
Second day: Sussex 47/1 (J.H.Parks 15*, H.W.Parks 30*).

Comments: J.Buckingham dismissed six Sussex batsmen in their 1st innings, five caught and one stumped. R.Sale's 101 was his maiden first-class century. His innings lasted 190 minutes and included nine 4's. He was the youngest player to achieve this feat for Warwickshire in the County Championship at 19 years 266 days. He participated in a stand of 176 in 130 minutes with H.E.Dollery for the 4th wicket. R.E.S.Wyatt was involved in the dismissal of the first seven of the Sussex batsmen in their 2nd innings, taking three catches and four wickets.

WORCESTERSHIRE v YORKSHIRE

Played at Stourbridge, July 26, 27, 1939.
Toss won by Worcestershire.
Worcestershire won by 16 runs.

WORCESTERSHIRE

E.Cooper	c Wood b Verity ...16	c Mitchell b Verity ...16
R.Howorth	c Hutton b Bowes ...5	c Hutton b Verity ...16
†B.P.King	lbw b Bowes ...2	st Wood b Robinson ...0
H.H.I.Gibbons	c Mitchell b Robinson ...5	b Robinson ...2
S.H.Martin	c Verity b Robinson ...19	lbw b Bowes ...4
Mr C.H.Palmer	b Verity ...1	b Bowes ...28
*Hon C.J.Lyttelton	not out ...17	b Bowes ...1
R.T.D.Perks	c Hutton b Verity ...6	c Turner b Verity ...36
Mr J.Stanning	b Robinson ...13	b Verity ...2
Mr A.F.T.White	b Robinson ...4	b Robinson ...0
P.F.Jackson	b Verity ...1	not out ...3
Extras	(B 8, LB 5) ...13	(B 8, LB 2) ...10
Total	**102**	**118**

Fall: 1st inns 1/7, 2/10, 3/37, 4/39, 5/57, 6/57, 7/63, 8/93, 9/101.
2nd inns 1/13, 2/13, 3/22, 4/30, 5/31, 6/39, 7/40, 8/71, 9/102.

YORKSHIRE

L.Hutton	b Perks ...7	c Jackson b Martin ...10
A.Mitchell	b Perks ...2	b Perks ...12
W.Barber	lbw b Perks ...9	lbw b Perks ...8
M.Leyland	b Perks ...10	c Stanning b Martin ...39
Mr N.W.D.Yardley	st King b Howorth ...18	b Martin ...7
C.Turner	not out ...29	lbw b Perks ...10
*Mr A.B.Sellers	c & b Howorth ...0	b Perks ...0
†A.Wood	run out ...0	c King b Jackson ...1
E.P.Robinson	c Lyttelton b Howorth ...5	b Perks ...13
H.Verity	lbw b Jackson ...0	c Palmer b Martin ...6
W.E.Bowes	b Jackson ...0	not out ...4
Extras	(B 10, NB 1) ...11	(LB 1, NB 2) ...3
Total	**91**	**113**

Fall: 1st inns 1/13, 2/14, 3/36, 4/39, 5/84, 6/84, 7/84, 8/91, 9/91.
2nd inns 1/14, 2/28, 3/40, 4/52, 5/68, 6/68, 7/69, 8/84, 9/102.

YORKSHIRE	O	M	R	W	O	M	R	W
Bowes	4	2	5	2	11	2	23	3
Robinson	13	2	51	4	12	4	36	3
Verity	9.2	2	33	4	10.7	2	40	4
Leyland	-	-	-	-	1	0	9	0

WORCESTERSHIRE	O	M	R	W	O	M	R	W
Perks	10	3	20	4	12	1	50	5
Martin	3	1	9	0	10.6	4	30	4
Jackson	12.3	4	31	2	11	4	30	1
Howorth	4	0	20	3				

Umpires: H.W.Lee and J.J.Hills.

Close of play scores. First day: Worcestershire 102/8 (C.H.Palmer 28*, R.T.D.Perks 23*).

Comments: The match was completed in two days. No batsman reached 40 in this bowlers match.
On the first day 28 wickets fell for 295 runs on a wicket affected by strong sun and rain.
Yorkshire lost their last five 1st innings wickets for seven runs. R.Howorth was unable to bowl in Yorkshire's 2nd innings, due to a fractured finger, sustained whilst fielding.

ESSEX v SUSSEX

Played at Chelmsford, July 29, 31, August 1, 1939.
Toss won by Sussex.
Sussex won by 76 runs.

SUSSEX

John G.Langridge	lbw b Stephenson ...71	lbw b R.Smith ...8
J.H.Parks	lbw b Taylor ...25	c Wade b Nichols ...11
H.W.Parks	c Taylor b Nichols ...29	not out ...133
G.Cox	c Wilcox b Nichols ...0	c Wilcox b Taylor ...44
Jas.Langridge	b R.Smith ...15	b Taylor ...96
Mr R.G.Stainton	b R.Smith ...38	not out ...17
*Flt-Lt A.J.Holmes	b R.Smith ...0	
H.E.Hammond	lbw b R.Smith ...3	
†W.L.Cornford	b Nichols ...4	
J.K.Nye	lbw R.Smith ...7	
J.H.Cornford	not out ...1	
Extras	(B 1, LB 3, W 1, NB 1) ...6	(B 11, LB 10, W 1, NB 1) 23
Total	**199**	**(4 wickets, declared) ...332**

Fall: 1st inns 1/73, 2/129, 3/129, 4/129, 5/154, 6/154, 7/158, 8/163, 9/176.
2nd inns 1/13, 2/37, 3/113, 4/292.

ESSEX

L.C.Eastman	b Nye ...22	c H.Parks b Hammond ...39
A.V.Avery	b J.Parks ...42	c J.Cornford b Hammond 20
T.P.B.Smith	lbw b J.Cornford ...55	c Hammond b Nye ...32
J.O'Connor	lbw b J.Cornford ...50	c Jas.Langridge b Nye ...28
M.S.Nichols	lbw b Nye ...4	lbw b Hammond ...40
R.Smith	b Nye ...1	b J.Parkes ...8
Mr D.R.Wilcox	c J.Cornford b Nye ...8	c J.Cornford b J.Parks ...19
F.H.Vigar	b Nye ...3	(9) c Hammond b Nye ...15
R.M.Taylor	b J.Cornford ...7	(10) lbw b J.Parks ...3
Capt J.W.A.Stephenson	not out ...12	(8) c Nye b Jas.Langridge 17
†T.H.Wade	c John Langridge b J.Cornford ...5	not out ...4
Extras	(B 4, LB 5, W 1, NB 1) ...11	(B 1, LB 8, W 1) ...10
Total	**220**	**235**

Fall: 1st inns 1/35, 2/88, 3/179, 4/180, 5/184, 6/189, 7/195, 8/200, 9/212.
2nd inns 1/60, 2/65, 3/120, 4/133, 5/163, 6/187, 7/211, 8/211, 9/228.

ESSEX	O	M	R	W	O	M	R	W
Nichols	17	1	70	3	17	1	57	1
R.Smith	7.6	1	47	5	13	2	43	1
Stephenson	12	3	40	1	8	0	46	0
Taylor	7	0	36	1	17	1	87	2
T.P.B.Smith	-	-	-	-	16	1	76	0

SUSSEX	O	M	R	W	O	M	R	W
Nye	22	1	79	5	16	2	89	3
J.Cornford	18.5	3	69	4	12	3	46	0
J.Parks	12	3	22	1	16.5	5	32	3
Hammond	5	0	18	0	11	4	38	3
Jas.Langridge	2	0	10	0	2	0	20	1
John Langridge	1	0	10	0				
Holmes	1	0	1	0				

Umpires: A.Skelding and H.W.Lee.

Close of play scores. First day: Essex 170/2 (T.P.B.Smith 50*, J.O'Connor 47*).
Second day: Sussex 130/3 (H.W.Parks 53*, Jas.Langridge 4*).

Comments: There were two interruptions for rain on the second day.
On the third day James Langridge and H.W.Parks added 179 for the 4th wicket.
H.W.Parks hit two 6's and ten 4's in his undefeated 133.
Essex were set to make 312 to win in 210 minutes. They were all out with ten minutes of the match remaining. Almost immediately a thunderstorm broke over the ground.

KENT v DERBYSHIRE

Played at Gravesend, July 29, 31, August 1, 1939.
Toss won by Kent.
Kent won by 171 runs.

KENT

A.E.Fagg	b Copson	17	run out	20
Mr P.G.Foster	c Elliott b G.H.Pope	21	b Mitchell	16
L.E.G.Ames	lbw b A.V.Pope	31	not out	159
*Mr B.H.Valentine	b A.V.Pope	70	(6) b L.F.Townsend	36
L.J.Todd	b A.V.Pope	0	(5) not out	106
Mr J.G.W.Davies	c Buckston b A.V.Pope	1		
†T.G.Evans	b G.H.Pope	0		
T.W.Spencer	c Elliott b Copson	2	(4) c A.Townsend b Copson	36
D.V.P.Wright	b Copson	0		
N.W.Harding	b Copson	0		
A.E.Watt	not out	16		
Extras	(LB 4)	4	(B 2, LB 2)	4
Total		**162**	(4 wickets, declared)	**377**

Fall: 1st inns 1/22, 2/65, 3/75, 4/75, 5/85, 6/86, 7/112, 8/114, 9/114.
2nd inns 1/36, 2/36, 3/1234, 4/182.

DERBYSHIRE

D.Smith	c Wright b Harding	16	b Harding	30
*Mr R.H.R.Buckston	c Evans b Harding	1	c Ames b Wright	9
A.E.Alderman	c Todd b Wright	46	c Fagg b Harding	0
T.S.Worthington	c Ames b Harding	3	c Harding b Davies	28
G.H.Pope	run out	7	not out	86
L.F.Townsend	c Todd b Wright	23	c Spencer b Wright	7
A.F.Townsend	lbw b Wright	18	b Harding	1
A.V.Pope	c Fagg b Wright	11	c Ames b Davies	26
†H.Elliott	b Harding	6	b Wright	2
T.B.Mitchell	not out	0	c & b Davies	27
W.H.Copson	c Spencer b Harding	0	c & b Davies	0
Extras	(B 4, NB 2)	6	(B 9, LB 2, W 1, NB 3)	15
Total		**137**		**231**

Fall: 1st inns 1/6, 2/21, 3/25, 4/43, 5/98, 6/105, 7/130, 8/137, 9/137.
2nd inns 1/30, 2/35, 3/52, 4/73, 5/77, 6/139, 7/178, 8/185, 9/229.

DERBYSHIRE	O	M	R	W	O	M	R	W
Copson	12	0	46	4	17	0	101	1
A.V.Pope	18	2	76	4	16	2	76	0
G.H.Pope	7	1	35	2	16	1	92	0
Mitchell	1	0	1	0	9	0	74	1
L.F.Townsend	-	-	-	-	8	1	30	1

KENT	O	M	R	W	O	M	R	W
Harding	12.3	0	56	5	10	0	48	3
Todd	10	0	34	0	2	0	12	0
Watt	2	0	5	0	4	0	28	0
Wright	10	1	36	4	15	0	77	3
Davies	-	-	-	-	11.4	2	51	4

Umpires: C.W.L.Parker and F.I.Walden.

Close of play scores. First day: Kent 43/2 (L.E.G.Ames 7*, T.W.Spencer 0*).
Second day: Derbyshire 48/2 (D.Smith 26*, T.S.Worthington 11*).

Comments: On the first day 22 wickets fell for 342 runs.
L.E.G.Ames and L.J.Todd had an unbroken 195 partnership for the 5th wicket, scored in under two hours in Kent's 2nd innings.
A.V.Pope was caught by Ames, who then fell into the crowd. Despite Ames signalling a six, after consultation, the batsman was given out.
T.S.Worthington was struck on the cheekbone and taken to hospital during the third day's play.

LANCASHIRE v GLOUCESTERSHIRE

Played at Old Trafford, Manchester, July 29, 31, August 1, 1939.
Toss won by Gloucestershire.
Match drawn.

GLOUCESTERSHIRE

R.A.Sinfield	not out	7
V.Hopkins	lbw b Phillipson	0
G.M.Emmett	not out	4
Extras	(B 2, NB 1)	3
Total	(1 wicket)	**14**

Fall: 1st inns 1/1.

*Mr W.R.Hammond, Mr E.D.R.Eagar W.L.Neale, J.F.Crapp, †E.A.Wilson, C.J.Scott, G.E.E.Lambert and T.W.J.Goddard did not bat.

LANCASHIRE

*Mr T.A.Higson, E.Paynter, J.Iddon, C.Washbrook, J.L.Hopwood, R.Pollard, †W.Farrimond, N.Oldfield, W.E.Phillipson, J.T.Ikin and S.F.Hird.

LANCASHIRE	O	M	R	W
Phillipson	3.3	1	7	1
Pollard	3	1	4	0

Umpires: J.Hardstaff and C.V.Tarbox.

Close of play scores. First day: No play. **Second day:** Gloucestershire 14/1 (R.A.Sinfield 7*, G.M.Emmett 4*).

Comments: There was no play on the first and third days and only 30 minutes on the second.

NORTHAMPTONSHIRE COUNTY CRICKET CLUB

Standing (left to right): M.E.F.Dunkley, F.P.O'Brien, E.J.Herbert, L.Bullimer (scorer), D.Brookes, P.Davis, H.W.Greenwood. Seated: W.E.Merritt, K.C.James, R.P.Nelson (captain), J.E.Timms, R.J.Partridge.

NORTHAMPTONSHIRE v SOMERSET

Played at Northampton, July 29, 31, August 1, 1939.
Toss won by Somerset.
Match drawn.

SOMERSET

F.S.Lee	c Greenwood b Partridge	0	lbw b Lubbock		81
H.Gimblett	lbw b Merritt	46	c Merritt b Partridge		1
H.T.F.Buse	c James b Partridge	37	c Brookes b Merritt		70
W.H.R.Andrews	c James b Merritt	5	(8) b Merritt		4
*Mr G.M.Bennett	c Merritt b Lubbock	15	b Lubbock		21
Mr C.J.P.Barnwell	c James b Lubbock	1	not out		56
Mr G.E.Fletcher	not out	19	(4) c Nelson b Lubbock		15
†W.T.Luckes	lbw b Merritt	19	(7) c Brookes b Merritt		15
Mr B.A.Gomm	b Merritt	2			
A.W.Wellard	c Nelson b Merritt	4	(9) b Lubbock		2
H.L.Hazell	c James b Herbert	0			
Extras	(B 6, LB 2, NB 1)	9	(B 14, LB 11)		25
Total		**157**	(8 wickets, declared)		**290**

Fall: 1st inns 1/0, 2/65, 3/81, 4/108, 5/110, 6/110, 7/149, 8/151, 9/157.
 2nd inns 1/2, 2/166, 3/183, 4/2306, 5/209, 6/272, 7/283, 8/290.

NORTHAMPTONSHIRE

Mr E.J.H.Dixon	c Gomm b Andrews	123	lbw b Andrews		22
H.W.Greenwood	b Wellard	2	lbw b Andrews		16
D.Brookes	lbw b Wellard	28	b Andrews		2
J.E.Timms	b Buse	27	c Fletcher b Wellard		10
†K.C.James	lbw b Wellard	14	(9) lbw b Wellard		2
*Mr R.P.Nelson	c Hazell b Wellard	0	(8) not out		18
F.P.O'Brien	b Wellard	15	(6) c & b Wellard		21
W.E.Merritt	c Luckes b Wellard	25	(5) lbw b Wellard		5
Mr C.W.S.Lubbock	b Wellard	5	(7) b Wellard		5
R.J.Partridge	lbw b Andrews	1	not out		0
E.J.Herbert	not out	3	lbw b Hazell		6
Extras	(LB 3)	3	(LB 3)		3
Total		**246**	(9 wickets)		**110**

Fall: 1st inns 1/12, 2/52, 3/118, 4/145, 5/149, 6/176, 7/231, 8/239, 9/242.
 2nd inns 1/37, 2/39, 3/44, 4/55, 5/56, 6/76, 7/89, 8/91, 9/106.

NORTHANTS	O	M	R	W	O	M	R	W
Partridge	11	3	23	2	12	0	43	1
Herbert	12.3	2	32	1	13	4	32	0
Lubbock	8	1	19	2	13.4	4	44	4
Timms	5	0	24	0	8	3	19	0
Merritt	14	5	42	5	30	4	117	3
Nelson	5	2	8	0	7	5	10	0

SOMERSET	O	M	R	W	O	M	R	W
Wellard	28	4	91	7	18	2	41	5
Andrews	13.6	4	37	2	13	2	61	3
Buse	17	4	63	1	3	1	3	0
Hazell	7	0	31	0	2	1	2	1
Gomm	3	0	21	0				

Umpires: G.M.Lee and H.Elliott.

Close of play scores. First day: Northamptonshire 149/4 (E.H.J.Dixon 76*, R.P.Nelson 0*). **Second day:** Somerset 118/1 (F.S.Lee 44*, H.T.F.Buse 55*).

Comments: F.S.Lee was out to the first ball of the game.
E.J.H.Dixon made 123 in 255 minutes, hitting 13 4's. It was his first appearance at Northampton.
The second day was interrupted by showers.
H.Gimblett and H.T.F.Buse added 164 for Somerset's 2nd wicket in their 2nd innings.
Northants were set to make 202 in 140 minutes but their last pair had to survive ten minutes to save the game.

NOTTINGHAMSHIRE v MIDDLESEX

Played at Trent Bridge, Nottingham, July 29, 31, August 1, 1939.
Toss won by Nottinghamshire.
Middlesex won by ten wickets.

NOTTINGHAMSHIRE

W.W.Keeton	lbw b Sims	28	c Smith b Peebles		100
D.Jones	b Sims	7	lbw b Sims		20
*Mr G.F.H.Heane	lbw b Smith	0	lbw b Robertson		38
J.Hardstaff	c Price b Sims	24	hit wkt b Peebles		65
G.V.Gunn	c Edrich b Sims	4	st Price b Sims		34
J.Knowles	c Carris b Sims	58	b Sims		0
R.J.Giles	b Peebles	35	b Sims		18
W.Voce	c & b Sims	12	c Hart b Sims		28
†A.B.Wheat	c Mann b Peebles	2	lbw b Peebles		9
H.J.Butler	not out	7	not out		10
A.Jepson	lbw b Peebles	1	lbw b Sims		0
Extras	(B 4, LB 9, W 2, NB 1)	16	(B 6, LB 7, NB 1)		14
Total		**194**			**336**

Fall: 1st inns 1/34, 2/35, 3/44, 4/58, 5/77, 6/156, 7/173, 8/182, 9/191.
 2nd inns 1/71, 2/150, 3/173, 4/263, 5/263, 6/263, 7/297, 8/320, 9/336.

MIDDLESEX

Mr B.D.Carris	b Voce	25	not out ...1
J.D.B.Robertson	b Jepson	89	not out ...18
W.J.Edrich	c & b Gunn	160	
D.C.S.Compton	b Jepson	11	
Mr F.G.Mann	c Voce b Butler	44	
S.M.Brown	c Jepson b Gunn	18	
G.E.Hart	not out	59	
C.I.J.Smith	b Jepson	72	
†W.F.F.Price	not out	17	
Extras	(B 1, LB 13, W 1, NB 2)	17	
Total	(7 wickets, declared)	**512**	(No wicket) ...**19**

Fall: 1st inns 1/44, 2/171, 3/183, 4/297, 5/343, 6/374, 7/479.
J.M.Sims and *Mr I.A.R.Peebles did not bat.

MIDDLESEX	O	M	R	W	O	M	R	W
Smith	9	1	31	1	8	1	43	0
Edrich	5	0	32	0	7	0	46	0
Sims	17	1	77	6	24.6	3	86	6
Peebles	15	2	30	3	23	4	90	3
Compton	1	0	8	0	5	0	21	0
Robertson	-	-	-	-	9	2	36	1

NOTTINGHAMSHIRE	O	M	R	W	O	M	R	W
Voce	38	4	151	1				
Butler	23	3	86	1				
Jepson	25	5	110	3				
Gunn	20	2	97	2				
Heane	12	2	44	0				
Giles	2	0	7	0	2	0	8	0
Hardstaff					1.5	0	11	0

Umpires: E.J.Smith and C.N.Woolley.

Close of play scores. First day: Middlesex 28/0 (B.D.Carris 10*, J.D.B.Robertson 13*). **Second day:** Middlesex 512/7 (G.E.Hart 59*, W.F.F.Price 17*).

Comments: A wet pitch delayed play until after lunch on the first day.
J.D.B.Robertson and W.J.Edrich added 127 for the 2nd wicket.
W.J.Edrich and F.G.Mann put on 114 for the 4th wicket.
C.I.J.Smith and G.E.Hart hit 105 for the 7th in only 40 minutes.
W.J.Edrich hit 160 in 300 minutes, hitting 21 4's.
W.W.Keeton made a 100 in 140 minutes. It included 12 4's.
The last seven Notts wickets fell for 73 runs in 55 minutes in their 2nd innings.
W.Voce hit 26 of his 28 in boundaries (three 6's and two 4's).

SURREY v YORKSHIRE

Played at Kennington Oval, July 29, 31, August 1, 1939.
Toss won by Yorkshire.
Match drawn.

YORKSHIRE

L.Hutton	b Parker	45
A.Mitchell	c Mobey b Gover	0
W.Barber	c Dickinson b Brown	141
M.Leyland	c Brown b Squires	114
Mr N.W.D.Yardley	c Fishlock b Squires	30
*Mr A.B.Sellers	b Parker	7
†A.Wood	b Gover	49
T.F.Smailes	b Parker	5
E.P.Robinson	b Gover	17
H.Verity	b Watts	5
W.E.Bowes	not out	0
Extras	(B 3, LB 7, NB 8)	18
Total		**431**

Fall: 1st inns 1/0, 2/60, 3/288, 4/322, 5/339, 6/357, 7/389, 8/417, 9/428.

SURREY

R.J.Gregory	c & b Hutton	45	run out	108
L.B.Fishlock	c Mitchell b Hutton	37	st Wood b Smailes	54
E.W.Whitfield	lbw b Verity	5	b Robinson	11
H.S.Squires	c Hutton b Robinson	44		
J.F.Parker	c Smailes b Robinson	26		
†G.S.Mobey	lbw b Verity	5		
Mr F.R.Brown	lbw b Hutton	26		
Mr P.J.Dickinson	c Bowes b Verity	5	not out	49
*Mr H.M.Garland-Wells	c Smailes b Robinson	14		
E.A.Watts	b Verity	0		
A.R.Gover	not out	0		
Extras	(B 7, LB 2, W 2, NB 1)	12	(B 3, LB 1, NB 1)	5
Total		**219**	(3 wickets)	**227**

Fall: 1st inns 1/85, 2/92, 3/99, 4/144, 5/153, 6/199, 7/210, 8/219, 9/219.
　　2nd inns 1/104, 2/133, 3/227.

SURREY	O	M	R	W
Gover	28	2	110	3
Watts	14	1	47	1
Brown	20	0	103	1
Parker	14	1	61	3
Squires	12	1	36	2
Gregory	6	1	29	0
Garland-Wells	2	1	7	0
Dickinson	9	1	20	0

YORKSHIRE	O	M	R	W	O	M	R	W
Bowes	12	2	29	0	5	2	10	0
Smailes	7	1	20	0	9	1	27	1
Verity	22.3	8	49	4	4	2	13	0
Robinson	17	1	73	3	8	1	37	1
Hutton	10	2	32	3	7	0	45	0
Yardley	2	0	4	0	3	0	17	0
Leyland	-	-	-	-	11	2	31	0
Barber	-	-	-	-	3	0	32	0
Sellers	-	-	-	-	2.2	0	10	0

Umpires: D.Hendren and J.A.Smart.

Close of play scores. First day: Yorkshire 371/6 (A.Wood 22*, T.F.Smailes 1*). **Second day:** Surrey 94/2 (E.W.Whitfield 2*, H.S.Squires 0*).

Comments: R.J.Gregory's benefit match. His 108 was the first century scored by a professional batsman against Yorkshire in 1939 and took around 160 minutes.
A.R.Gover dismissed A.Mitchell with the first ball of the match. It was his 100th wicket of the season.
W.Barber and M.Leyland put on 228 for the 3rd wicket.
There was only three hours play on the second day.
Surrey followed on 212 behind.
R.J.Gregory and L.B.Fishlock put on 104 for Surrey's 1st wicket in their 2nd innings.
Over the three days, 21,283 paid at the gate.

Surrey's Bob Gregory carves his way to a second-innings century during his benefit match at The Oval. It was the first 100 scored by a professional against Yorkshire that season.

WARWICKSHIRE v LEICESTERSHIRE

Played at Edgbaston, Birmingham, July 29, 31, August 1, 1939.
Toss won by Leicestershire.
Warwickshire won by nine wickets.

LEICESTERSHIRE

Mr C.S.Dempster	b Hollies	24	b Wilmot	2
G.L.Berry	c Wyatt b Hollies	27	c Buckingham b Mayer	9
N.F.Armstrong	st Buckingham b Wyatt	23	lbw b Wilmot	18
M.Tompkin	run out	23	lbw b Mayer	19
Mr C.L.Edgson	b Hollies	2	b Wilmot	1
*Mr M.St.J.Packe	b Hollies	0	b Hollies	17
Mr J.A.T.Sharp	lbw b Hollies	2	(8) c Wyatt b Hollies	3
†G.O.Dawkes	c Cranmer b Wyatt	14	(7) b Mayer	8
H.A.Smith	c Croom b Hollies	23	b Meyer	5
C.H.Drake	b Hollies	1	not out	1
J.Sperry	not out	0	b Mayer	0
Extras	(B 2, LB 5)	7	(LB 2, NB 1)	3
Total		**146**		**86**

Fall: 1st inns 1/44, 2/55, 3/97, 4/101, 5/104, 6/106, 7/108, 8/144, 9/146.
2nd inns 1/7, 2/23, 3/31, 4/35, 5/63, 6/69, 7/73, 8/85, 9/86.

WARWICKSHIRE

A.J.W.Croom	c Edgson b Sperry	2	not out	45
W.A.Hill	b Drake	0	run out	10
F.R.Santall	c Armstrong b Drake	0	not out	71
Mr R.E.S.Wyatt	not out	74		
H.E.Dollery	b Drake	0		
J.S.Ord	c Packe b Drake	1		
†J.Buckingham	lbw b Smith	8		
*Mr P.Cranmer	b Smith	6		
K.Wilmot	b Sharp	6		
J.H.Mayer	lbw b Sharp	0		
W.E.Hollies	c Dawkes b Drake	0		
Extras	(B 6, NB 2)	8	(LB 1, W 2)	3
Total		**105**	(1 wicket)	**129**

Fall: 1st inns 1/2, 2/2, 3/2, 4/6, 5/14, 6/32, 7/44, 8/65, 9/65.
2nd inns 1/19.

WARWICKSHIRE	O	M	R	W	O	M	R	W
Mayer	8	2	21	0	13	2	37	5
Wyatt	18	3	44	3				
Wilmot	6	1	18	0	8	1	17	3
Hollies	21.4	2	55	6	7	0	29	2
Cranmer	1	0	1	0				

LEICESTERSHIRE	O	M	R	W	O	M	R	W
Sperry	6	1	14	1	6	0	25	0
Drake	11.6	4	21	5	7	0	42	0
Smith	13	0	37	2	8	0	31	0
Sharp	8	1	25	2	8	3	20	0
Packe					6	0	8	0

Umpires: H.G.Baldwin and H.Cruice.

Close of play scores. First day: Leicestershire 77/2 (N.F.Armstrong 13*, M.Tompkin 10*). **Second day:** Leicestershire 54/4 (M.Tompkin 10*, M.St.J.Packe 13*).

Comments: Rain reduced play to only a 100 minutes on the first day. C.H.Drake, 17 years old, in only his second county game, took four wickets for two runs in a 44-ball spell. He began with four maidens, taking three wickets for no runs. R.E.S.Wyatt was the only Warwickshire player to reach double figures, the next highest score after his 74* being eight. He and W.E.Hollies added 40 for Warwickshire's last wicket, with Hollies making no contribution. R.E.S.Wyatt scored 74 of the 97 off the bat in Warwickshire's 1st innings, 77% of the runs scored. It was the first occasion in 1939 that Leicestershire obtained 1st innings points. In their 2nd innings, Leicestershire lost their remaining six wickets for only 32 in 50 minutes on the third day. J.H.Mayer took three wickets in the final over of the innings, bowling H.A.Smith, G.O.Dawkes and J.Sperry, all middle stump. A.J.W.Croom and F.R.Santall won the match with an unbroken partnership of 110 for the 2nd wicket. J.A.T.Sharp made his debut for Leicestershire.

WORCESTERSHIRE v GLAMORGAN

Played at Stourbridge, July 29, 31, August 1, 1939.
Toss won by Glamorgan.
Worcestershire won by one wicket.

GLAMORGAN

A.H.Dyson	b Perks	22	b Perks	0
D.E.Davies	c Jackson b Martin	27	b Perks	9
T.L.Brierley	lbw b Jackson	6	c Jenkins b Perks	16
D.Davies	c Stanning b Jackson	7	lbw b Perks	1
*Mr M.J.L.Turnbull	c Jenkins b Martin	7	(7) b White b Perks	0
C.C.Smart	lbw b Jackson	14	(5) b Perks	31
E.C.Jones	b Jackson	6	(6) c Jenkins b Jackson	11
†H.G.Davies	c Cooper b Jackson	2	b Perks	12
A.D.G.Matthews	c Perks b Martin	14	b Perks	5
J.Mercer	c Gibbons b Martin	14	b Perks	16
P.F.Judge	not out	8	not out	1
Extras	(B 1, LB 2)	3	(B 8, LB 5)	13
Total		**130**		**115**

Fall: 1st inns 1/30, 2/44, 3/62, 4/65, 5/84, 6/85, 7/87, 8/108, 9/114.
2nd inns 1/0, 2/16, 3/19, 4/21, 5/37, 6/53, 7/74, 8/89, 9/110.

WORCESTERSHIRE

B.P.King	b E.Davies	6	(3) c & b Mercer	4
E.Cooper	c Smart b E.Davies	13	b Matthews	19
H.H.I.Gibbons	c H.Davies b Judge	25	(1) c & b Mercer	12
S.H.Martin	lbw b E.Davies	27	lbw b Matthews	23
Mr C.H.Palmer	not out	10	run out	13
Mr J.Stanning	c H.Davies b E.Davies	0	c Mercer b Matthews	2
*Mr A.F.T.White	lbw b E.Davies	0	(8) c Brierley b Judge	6
R.T.D.Perks	b Judge	2	(7) st H.Davies b Judge	31
R.O.Jenkins	b E.Davies	1	not out	30
†H.Yarnold	b Mercer	5	b Matthews	0
P.F.Jackson	c H.Davies b Mercer	0	not out	1
Extras	(B 7)	7	(B 4, LB 2)	6
Total		**96**	(9 wickets)	**153**

Fall: 1st inns 1/12, 2/19, 3/67, 4/71, 5/71, 6/71, 7/74, 8/75, 9/96.
2nd inns 1/18, 2/22, 3/53, 4/68, 5/76, 6/87, 7/106, 8/118, 9/141.

WORCESTERSHIRE	O	M	R	W	O	M	R	W
Perks	9	1	22	1	14.2	3	40	9
Martin	19.2	7	55	4	6	0	35	0
Jackson	11	0	50	5	8	4	27	1

GLAMORGAN	O	M	R	W	O	M	R	W
Matthews	2	0	7	0	14	1	28	4
Mercer	4.7	1	24	2	12	2	42	2
E.Davies	13	3	40	6	15	1	62	0
Judge	10	5	18	2	4	0	15	2

Umpires: J.A.Newman and G.Beet.

Close of play scores. First day: Glamorgan 14/0 (A.H.Dyson 11*, D.E.Davies 2*). **Second day:** Glamorgan 22/4 (D.E.Davies 3*, E.C.Jones 0*).

Comments: There was only 30 minutes play on the first day.
Twenty-four wickets fell on the second day for 234 runs.
R.T.D.Perks had career-best figures of nine wickets for 40 runs in Glamorgan's 2nd innings. He took 4 for 2 runs in four overs in the final half-hour of the second day. It was the fourth-best bowling performance by a Worcestershire bowler.
Worcestershire needed 150 to win but still required 32 with only two wickets remaining.
R.O.Jenkins, scoring 30 out of the last 47 needed, was chaired off the field after making the winning hit.
The highest individual score in the match was 31.
This was Glamorgan's narrowest defeat.

DERBYSHIRE v GLOUCESTERSHIRE

Played at Queen's Park, Chesterfield, August 2, 3, 4, 1939.
Toss won by Derbyshire.
Match drawn.

DERBYSHIRE

D.Smith	b Lambert	20	lbw b Goddard	30
A.F.Townsend	b Scott	10	c Hammond b Sinfield	49
A.E.Alderman	c Wilson b Scott	19	not out	27
G.H.Pope	b Lambert	26	not out	12
L.F.Townsend	b Lambert	1		
A.E.G.Rhodes	c & b Scott	5		
*Mr T.D.Hounsfield	b Scott	0		
A.V.Pope	c Lambert b Scott	26		
†H.Elliott	b Scott	6		
T.B.Mitchell	not out	1		
W.H.Copson	c Lambert b Scott	1		
Extras	LB 4, NB 2	6	(B 2)	2
Total		**121**	(2 wickets)	**120**

Fall: 1st inns 1/32, 2/32, 3/63, 4/65, 5/75, 6/75, 7/112, 8/113, 9/119.
2nd inns 1/53, 2/93.

GLOUCESTERSHIRE

R.A.Sinfield	c Elliott b Copson	3
V.Hopkins	b Mithcell	59
G.M.Emmett	b A.V.Pope	10
*Mr W.R.Hammond	b Rhodes	62
J.F.Crapp	st Elliott b Mitchell	0
Mr E.D.R.Eagar	b Mitchell	7
†E.A.Wilson	st Elliott b Mitchell	19
W.L.Neale	c Elliott b Mitchell	0
C.J.Scott	c Rhodes b Mitchell	12
G.E.E.Lambert	b Copson	15
T.W.J.Goddard	not out	9
Extras	(LB 1, W 1)	2
Total		**198**

Fall: 1stinns 1/4, 2/21, 3/111, 4/112, 5/128, 6/162, 7/162, 8/174, 9/174.

GLOUCESTERSHIRE	O	M	R	W	O	M	R	W
Scott	16	1	53	7	6	0	41	0
Lambert	12	1	33	3	5	0	22	0
Goddard	10	1	29	0	12	2	37	1
Sinfield	-	-	-	-	5	2	18	1

DERBYSHIRE	O	M	R	W
Copson	15.4	1	65	2
A.V.Pope	12	2	34	1
Rhodes	5	1	11	1
Mitchell	16	1	71	6
L.F.Townsend	6	4	15	0

Umpires: E.J.Smith and J.Hardstaff.

Close of play scores. First day: Gloucestershire 136/5 (V.Hopkins 49, E.A.Wilson 3*). **Second day:** Derbyshire 120/2 (A.E.Alderman 27*, G.H.Pope 12*).

Comments: There was less than three hours play on the second day. Further rain led to an early abandonment of the game on the final day.
C.J.Scott achieved his best analysis in county cricket, taking 7 for 53 in Derbyshire's 1st innings.
G.H.Pope was unable to bowl because of knee trouble.

ESSEX v KENT

Played at Chelmsford, August 2, 3, 4, 1939.
Toss won by Essex.
Match drawn.

ESSEX

L.C.Eastman	c Chalk b Watt	9
A.V.Avery	b Wright	78
*Mr D.R.Wilcox	b Harding	2
J.O'Connor	b Watt	11
M.S.Nichols	lbw b Watt	8
T.P.B.Smith	c Todd b Davies	25
Capt J.W.A.Stephenson	lbw b Todd	1
R.M.Taylor	b Watt	16
R.Smith	c Wright b Watt	1
†T.H.Wade	not out	5
Mr K.Farnes	b Wright	5
Extras	(B 4, LB 4, W 1, NB 2)	11
Total		**172**

Fall: 1st inns 1/23, 2/26, 3/43, 4/57, 5/130, 6/133, 7/156, 8/160, 9/167.

KENT

A.E.Fagg	not out	26
*Mr F.G.H.Chalk	b Farnes	15
L.E.G.Ames	not out	8
Extras	(B 1, W 1)	2
Total	(1 wicket)	**51**

Fall: 1st inns 1/38.
Mr B.H.Valentine, †Mr W.H.V.Levett, Mr P.G.Foster, Mr J.G.W.Davies, L.J.Todd, A.E.Watt, D.V.P.Wright and N.W.Harding did not bat.

KENT	O	M	R	W
Harding	11	0	48	1
Todd	14	1	47	1
Watt	13	2	29	5
Wright	7.4	1	22	2
Davies	5	0	15	1

ESSEX	O	M	R	W
Farnes	7	0	24	1
Nichols	7	1	25	0

Umpires: F.I.Walden and D.Hendren.

Close of play scores. First day: Kent 51/2 (A.E.Fagg 26*, L.E.G.Ames 8*).

Comments: There was no play in this match after tea on the first day.
A.V.Avery passed a 1,000 runs in a season for the first time.

GLAMORGAN v YORKSHIRE

Played at Cardiff, August 2, 3, 4, 1939.
Toss won by Yorkshire.
Yorkshire won by 86 runs.

YORKSHIRE

L.Hutton	lbw b Wooller 18	c Brierley b Matthews 4
A.Mitchell	b Matthews 3	c Judge b Jones............42
W.Barber	c H.Davies b E.Davies...2	c Wooller b Jones 59
M.Leyland	b Matthews 19	(5) not out 37
C.Turner	c Turnbull b Judge 6	(7) c & b Jones 8
Mr N.W.D.Yardley	b Wooller 85	(8) not out 10
*Mr A.B.Sellers	b Wooller 22	
†A.Wood	c H.Davies b Matthews ...2	
T.F.Smailes	c Wooller b Matthews ...55	(6) st H.Davies b Jones 17
E.P.Robinson	run out 2	(4) b Jones 0
H.Verity	not out 9	
Extras	(B 6, LB 5)...............11	(B 4, LB 5) 9
Total	**234**	**(6 wickets, declared)......186**

Fall: 1st inns 1/12, 2/27, 3/33, 4/44, 5/80, 6/123, 7/142, 8/210, 9/212.
2nd inns 1/17, 2/108, 3/108, 4/121, 5/148, 6/160.

GLAMORGAN

A.H.Dyson	b Robinson................22	c Barber b Smailes 2
D.E.Davies	c Wood b Robinson......14	c Yardley b Robinson 52
T.L.Brierley	c Robinson b Hutton 33	b Robinson 10
D.Davies	c Hutton b Verity 1	(7) c Robinson b Verity ...21
*Mr M.J.L.Turnbull	b Smailes 56	(4) lbw b Verity 22
Mr W.Wooller	c Wood b Robinson......16	(5) c Mitchell b Verity 10
E.C.Jones	lbw b Verity 4	(8) c Sellers b Verity 1
P.B.Clift	c Wood b Verity 11	(9) not out 3
†H.G.Davies	c Yardley b Robinson....28	(6) c Yardley b Robinson...2
A.D.G.Matthews	not out 3	b Robinson 0
P.F.Judge	b Robinson 1	lbw b Robinson............0
Extras	(LB 4, W 1) 5	(B 14, LB 2, NB 1).........17
Total	**194**	**140**

Fall: 1st inns 1/27, 2/44, 3/47, 4/128, 5/130, 6/139, 7/157, 8/185, 9/191.
2nd inns 1/7, 2/30, 3/71, 4/93, 5/102, 6/126, 7/134, 8/139, 9/140.

GLAMORGAN	O	M	R	W	O	M	R	W
Matthews	21.4	1	76	4	7	1	34	1
Judge	20	4	43	1	6	0	34	0
Wooller	21	3	74	3	4	0	18	0
D.E.Davies	14	1	30	1	3	0	31	0
Jones	-	-	-	-	7	0	60	5

YORKSHIRE	O	M	R	W	O	M	R	W
Smailes	6	0	33	1	4	0	23	1
Turner	2	0	5	0				
Verity	21	5	61	3	18	5	40	4
Hutton	8	2	30	1				
Robinson	16.4	4	60	5	16.6	2	59	5
Yardley					1	0	1	0

Umpires: H.G.Baldwin and J.A.Smart.

Close of play scores. First day: Glamorgan 20/0 (A.H.Dyson 7*, D.E.Davies 12*). **Second day:** Glamorgan 194 all out.

Comments: A.H.Dyson's benefit match. He completed his 1,000 runs for the season with his first run of the match.
Glamorgan were set to make 227 to win at a rate of 70 runs an hour.
Yorkshire won with 45 minutes play remaining.

Glamorgan wicketkeeper Haydn Davies, a Llanelli man.

HAMPSHIRE v SURREY

Played at Portsmouth, August 2, 3, 4, 1939.
Toss won by Hampshire.
Match drawn.

HAMPSHIRE

J.Bailey	c Garland-Wells b Brown	13	not out	36
†N.T.McCorkell	c Gover b Brown	34	b Gover	17
A.G.Holt	b Brown	21	not out	35
J.Arnold	lbw b Watts	26		
W.L.C.Creese	b Watts	9		
D.F.Walker	not out	108		
Mr J.P.Blake	c Dickinson b Parker	39		
P.A.Mackenzie	c & b Brown	35		
*Mr G.R.Taylor	b Brown	0		
Mr C.H.Knott	lbw b Brown	0		
G.E.M.Heath	c Parker b Brown	9		
Extras	(B 1, LB 2, NB 4)	7	(B 4, LB 1, W 1)	6
Total		**301**	(1 wicket)	**94**

Fall: 1st inns 1/18, 2/52, 3/96, 4/98, 5/107, 6/164, 7/257, 8/259, 9/259.
2nd inns 1/17.

SURREY

R.J.Gregory	c McCorkell b Knott	44
L.B.Fishlock	c Bailey b Knott	38
Mr P.J.Dickinson	lbw b Knott	0
H.S.Squires	c & b Mackenzie	40
J.F.Parker	st McCorkell b Knott	0
E.W.Whitfield	lbw b Knott	31
Mr F.R.Brown	b Knott	61
*Mr H.M.Garland-Wells	lbw b Knott	6
†G.S.Mobey	not out	4
E.A.Watts	c Walker b Knott	8
A.R.Gover	st McCorkell b Bailey	7
Extras	(LB 1)	1
Total		**240**

Fall: 1/80, 2/80, 3/97, 4/97, 5/133, 6/202, 7/210, 8/221, 9/229.

SURREY	O	M	R	W	O	M	R	W
Gover	16	2	47	0	6	2	16	1
Watts	19	3	53	2	2	0	5	0
Brown	26.4	3	86	7	3	0	12	0
Parker	13	0	57	1				
Squires	3	1	6	0				
Gregory	6	1	15	0				
Garland-Wells	4	0	30	0	5	1	18	0
Dickinson	-	-	-	-	5	0	11	0
Fishlock	-	-	-	-	2.4	0	11	0
Whitfield	-	-	-	-	2	0	15	0

HAMPSHIRE	O	M	R	W
Heath	17	3	37	0
Bailey	20.4	3	71	1
Knott	24	3	85	8
Creese	7	2	16	0
Mackenzie	2	0	30	1

Umpires: C.W.L.Parker and H.W.Lee.

Close of play scores. First day: Hampshire 301 all out. **Second day:** Surrey 107/4 (H.S.Squires 25*, E.W.Whitfield 0*).

Comments: There were constant interruptions for rain in this match.
D.F.Walker's 108* included 12 4's and was scored in approximately 210 minutes.
C.H.Knott achieved his career best bowling figures (8 for 85) for Hampshire.
F.R.Brown made 61 out of 88 in 50 minutes, hitting 4 6's and 6 4's.

LANCASHIRE v WARWICKSHIRE

Played at Old Trafford, Manchester, August 2, 3, 4, 1939.
Toss won by Warwickshire.
Match drawn.

WARWICKSHIRE

A.J.W.Croom	c Ikin b Garlick	12
W.A.Hill	c Paynter b Pollard	14
F.R.Santall	c Hopwood b Garlick	7
Mr R.E.S.Wyatt	not out	59
H.E.Dollery	lbw b Garlick	3
J.S.Ord	c Iddon b Garlick	14
†J.Buckingham	lbw b Garlick	0
*Mr P.Cranmer	c Iddon b Ikin	1
C.W.Grove	c Ikin b Pollard	5
J.H.Mayer	c Higson b Pollard	12
W.E.Hollies	b Pollard	0
Extras	(B 4, LB 1, NB 3)	8
Total		**135**

Fall: 1st inns 1/28, 2/36, 3/39, 4/59, 5/95, 6/99, 7/100, 8/119, 9/135.

LANCASHIRE

C.Washbrook	c Hollies b Mayer	45
E.Paynter	lbw b Wyatt	22
J.L.Hopwood	c Ord b Wyatt	1
N.Oldfield	not out	25
J.Iddon	c Hill b Mayer	2
J.T.Ikin	not out	1
Extras	(LB 2)	2
Total	(4 wickets)	**98**

Fall: 1st inns 1/53, 2/55, 3/80, 4/95.

*Mr T.A.Higson, W.E.Phillipson, †W.Farrimond, R.Pollard and R.G.Garlick did not bat.

LANCASHIRE	O	M	R	W
Phillipson	5	0	17	0
Pollard	18.4	5	40	4
Garlick	20	6	44	5
Hopwood	3	1	6	0
Ikin	6	1	20	1

WARWICKSHIRE	O	M	R	W
Mayer	6	0	23	2
Grove	5	0	15	0
Hollies	7	3	24	0
Wyatt	8	1	34	2

Umpires: C.N.Woolley and E.Cooke.

Close of play scores. First day: Warwickshire 63/4 (R.E.S.Wyatt 21*, J.S.Ord 2*). **Second day:** No play.

Comments: There was only two hours play on the first day and 320 minutes in the whole match.

NOTTINGHAMSHIRE v SUSSEX

Played at Trent Bridge, Nottingham, August 2, 3, 4, 1939.
Toss won by Sussex.
Match drawn.

SUSSEX

J.H.Parks	c Wheat b Butler	13
John G.Langridge	c & b Gunn	158
H.W.Parks	c Voce b Butler	100
G.Cox	b Jepson	39
Jas.Langridge	b Jepson	8
C.Oakes	not out	7
*Mr H.T.Bartlett	not out	0
Extras	(B 6, LB 3, NB 1)	10
Total	(5 wickets)	**335**

Fall: 1st inns 1/19, 2/224, 3/305, 4/322, 5/333.
H.E.Hammond, J.K.Nye, †W.L.Cornford and J.H.Cornford did not bat.

NOTTINGHAMSHIRE

*Mr G.F.H.Heane, H.J.Butler, G.V.Gunn, J.Hardstaff, C.B.Harris, W.W.Keeton, J.Knowles, W.Voce, †A.B.Wheat, A.Jepson and R.J.Giles.

NOTTINGHAMSHIRE	O	M	R	W
Voce	19	5	69	0
Butler	20	2	88	2
Jepson	14	1	57	2
Gunn	16	0	56	1
Giles	14	3	46	0
Heane	3	0	9	0

Umpires: H.Elliott and A.Skelding.

Close of play scores. First day: Sussex 335/5 (C.Oakes 7*, H.T.Bartlett 0*). **Second day:** No play.

Comments: John G.Langridge and H.W.Parks added 205 for the 2nd wicket in 195 minutes.
John G.Langridge made his 158 in 270 minutes, hitting 22 4's. He was caught and bowled in an unusual manner, G.V.Gunn catching the ball, after the batsman's drive struck his batting partner.
H.W.Parks struck ten 4's in his 100.
There was no play on the second and third days.

DERBYSHIRE v WARWICKSHIRE

Played at Ind Coope & Allsops Ground, Burton upon Trent, August 5, 7, 8, 1939.
Match drawn.

DERBYSHIRE

*Mr R.H.R.Buckston	b Grove	2		
A.F.Townsend	c Dollery b Mayer	6	(1) not out	19
D.Smith	b Hollies	11	(2) not out	27
A.E.Alderman	b Grove	38		
G.H.Pope	c Bukingham b Mayer	26		
L.F.Townsend	c Buckingham b Grove	21		
A.E.G.Rhodes	c Hollies b Grove	46		
A.V.Pope	not out	37		
†H.Elliott	c & b Grove	3		
T.B.Mitchell	st Buckingham b Hollies	5		
W.H.Copson	c Cranmer b Mayer	17		
Extras	(LB 2)	2		
Total		**214**	(No wicket)	**46**

Fall: 1st inns 1/7, 2/9, 3/31, 4/74, 5/101, 6/112, 7/115, 8/161, 9/176.

WARWICKSHIRE

A.J.Croom	c Copson b G.H.Pope	2
Mr R.Sale	hit wkt b G.H.Pope	0
W.A.Hill	lbw b A.V.Pope	9
Mr R.E.S.Wyatt	st Elliott b Mitchell	20
H.E.Dollery	b Copson	7
F.R.Santall	b Copson	2
†J.Buckingham	c A.V.Pope b G.H.Pope	24
*Mr P.Cranmer	c Elliott b Mitchell	41
C.W.Grove	hit wkt b Mitchell	4
J.H.Mayer	b Mitchell	0
W.E.Hollies	not out	0
Extras	(LB 9)	9
Total		**118**

Fall: 1st inns 1/2, 2/5, 3/35, 4/37, 5/42, 6/51, 7/108, 8/112, 9/112.

WARWICKSHIRE	O	M	R	W	O	M	R	W
Mayer	16.6	3	37	3	4	0	22	0
Grove	21	1	78	5	3	0	20	0
Hollies	26	6	82	2	1	0	4	0
Wyatt	4	1	15	0				

DERBYSHIRE	O	M	R	W
Copson	11	3	30	2
G.H.Pope	9	2	35	3
A.V.Pope	2	0	3	1
Mitchell	9	0	41	4

Umpires: A.Dolphin and H.Elliott.

Close of play scores. First day: Derbyshire 28/2 (D.Smith 10*, A.E.Alderman 10*). **Second day:** Derbyshire 46/0 (A.F.Townsend 19*, D.Smith 27*).

Comments: There was only seven hours play over the first two days due to rain, with less than 60 minutes on the first day.
T.B.Mitchell claimed three wickets in his 9th over to end the Warwickshire innings.
There was no play on the final day.

GLOUCESTERSHIRE v SOMERSET

Played at Bristol, August 5, 7, 8, 1939.
Toss won by Gloucestershire.
Gloucester won by an innings and 109 runs.

GLOUCESTERSHIRE

R.A.Sinfield	c McRae b Hazell	29
G.M.Emmett	c Lee b Andrews	96
W.L.Neale	lbw b Buse	13
*Mr W.R.Hammond	c Gimblett b Buse	19
J.F.Crapp	lbw b Meyer	7
Mr E.D.R.Eagar	c Wellard b Andrews	21
Mr A.H.Brodhurst	c Wellard b Andrews	0
†E.A.Wilson	c Lee b Meyer	64
C.J.Scott	b Wellard	1
G.E.E.Lambert	b Andrews	0
T.W.J.Goddard	not out	56
Extras	(B 12, LB 7, NB 4)	23
Total		**329**

Fall: 1st inns 1/73, 2/119, 3/150, 4/161, 5/202, 6/202, 7/221, 8/227, 9/228.

SOMERSET

F.S.Lee	b Lambert	2	(3) c Emmett b Goddard	0
H.Gimblett	c Scott b Lambert	17	(1) c Wilson b Goddard	5
H.T.F.Buse	not out	30	(2) c Eagar b Goddard	24
Mr R.J.O.Meyer	b Scott	0	c Scott b Goddard	0
Mr H.D.Burrough	b Goddard	7	b Goddard	21
Mr F.M.McRae	c Hammond b Goddard	12	c Crapp b Sinfield	5
*Mr E.F.Longrigg	c Goddard	0	c Brodhurst b Goddard	3
†W.T.Luckes	b Sinfield	0	lbw b Goddard	27
W.H.R.Andrews	b Goddard	0	c Lambert b Goddard	0
A.W.Wellard	c & b Lambert	20	(11) not out	11
H.L.Hazell	c Sinfield b Goddard	1	(10) c Lambert b Goddard	17
Extras	(B 6, LB 9, NB 2)	17	(W 1)	1
Total		**106**		**114**

Fall: 1st inns 1/9, 2/34, 3/35, 4/46, 5/64, 6/64, 7/69, 8/72, 9/104.
2nd inns 1/17, 2/25, 3/25, 4/50, 5/51, 6/59, 7/59, 8/59, 9/100.

SOMERSET	O	M	R	W
Wellard	26	4	76	1
Andrews	20	5	75	4
Meyer	21.2	5	72	2
Hazell	17	5	22	1
Buse	18	3	54	2
Gimblett	2	0	7	0

GLOUCESTERSHIRE	O	M	R	W	O	M	R	W
Scott	14	3	37	1	9	1	23	0
Lambert	9	2	25	3	4	0	18	0
Goddard	10	3	15	5	13.5	4	44	9
Sinfield	5	0	12	1	9	2	28	1

Umpires: J.A.Newman and F.I.Walden.

Close of play scores. First day: Gloucestershire 71/0 (R.A.Sinfield 29*, G.M.Emmett 32*). **Second day:** Somerset 72/8 (H.T.F.Buse 20*).

Comments: There was little play on the 1st day.
T.W.J.Goddard enjoyed an excellent all-round match. In addition to his 14 wickets for 59, he participated with E.A.Wilson in a partnership of 101, made in only 70 minutes, for Gloucestershire's 10th wicket.
Somerset followed on 223 behind.
It was the third occasion that T.W.J.Goddard had taken nine wickets in an innings in 1939.

KENT v HAMPSHIRE

Played at Canterbury, August 5, 7, 8, 1939.
Toss won by Kent.
Hampshire won by seven wickets.

KENT

A.E.Fagg	c McCorkell b Heath	28	c Arnold b Baring	3
*Mr F.G.H.Chalk	b Bailey	20	b Heath	18
L.E.G.Ames	b Creese	51	b Knott	14
Mr B.H.Valentine	c Arnold b Heath	9	c Walker b Baring	1
L.J.Todd	c Creese b Baring	9	c Creese b Baring	5
Mr P.G.Foster	c Arnold b Baring	0	b Knott	12
Mr J.G.W.Davies	b Baring	5	(8) not out	13
D.V.P.Wright	b Creese	5	(9) b Baring	2
†Mr W.H.V.Levett	c Proud b Baring	11	(7) b Knott	9
A.E.Watt	b Baring	19	c Walker b Baring	3
C.Lewis	not out	0	b Knott	0
Extras	(LB 4)	4	(LB 1, NB 2)	3
Total		**161**		**83**

Fall: 1st inns 1/39, 2/85, 3/105, 4/114, 5/118, 6/119, 7/126, 8/136, 9/160.
2nd inns 1/13, 2/27, 3/28, 4/42, 5/42, 6/62, 7/64, 8/71, 9/82.

HAMPSHIRE

†N.T.McCorkell	lbw b Wright	34	not out	40
J.Bailey	lbw b Lewis	30	c Todd b Lewis	40
D.F.Walker	b Lewis	0	c Levett b Lewis	0
J.Arnold	b Wright	21	c Valentine b Lewis	7
W.L.C.Creese	c Davis b Lewis	4	not out	16
Mr J.P.Blake	lbw b Lewis	0		
Mr R.B.Proud	b Wright	0		
*Mr G.R.Taylor	run out	8		
Mr A.E.G.Baring	b Lewis	15		
Mr C.H.Knott	c Ames b Lewis	0		
G.E.M.Heath	not out	0		
Extras	(B 14, LB 4, NB 5)	23	(B 6, LB 1, NB 1)	8
Total		**135**	(3 wickets)	**111**

Fall: 1st inns 1/64, 2/66, 3/95, 4/104, 5/104, 6/104, 7/108, 8/135, 9/135.
2nd inns 1/83, 2/83, 3/91.

HAMPSHIRE	O	M	R	W	O	M	R	W
Baring	18.1	0	67	5	13	2	43	5
Heath	13	2	26	2	5	1	14	1
Bailey	5	0	19	1				
Knott	5	0	18	0	7.5	1	23	4
Creese	13	4	27	2				

KENT	O	M	R	W	O	M	R	W
Todd	12	1	21	0	5	0	7	0
Watt	6	2	15	0	2	0	13	0
Wright	10	2	30	3	11	3	30	0
Davies	4	2	8	0	6	0	13	0
Lewis	17.6	3	38	6	10	1	40	3

Umpires: D.Hendren and H.W.Lee.

Close of play scores. First day: Kent 148/8 (W.H.V.Levett 10*, A.E.Watt 7*).
Second day: Kent 43/5 (P.G.Foster 1*, W.H.V.Levett 0*).

Comments: First game of the Canterbury week.
Play did not commence on the first day until 2.45pm owing to the wet state of the ground.

LEICESTERSHIRE v NORTHAMPTONSHIRE

Played at Grace Road, Leicester, August 5, 7, 8, 1939.
Toss won by Northamptonshire.
Match drawn.

NORTHAMPTONSHIRE

Mr E.J.H.Dixon	b Drake	30
H.W.Greenwood	c Packe b Drake	68
D.Brookes	c Packe b Armstrong	43
J.E.Timms	c Drake b Sperry	26
W.E.Merritt	c Packe b Armstrong	24
*Mr R.P.Nelson	lbw b Smith	44
F.P.O'Brien	c Smith b Armstrong	19
†K.C.James	c Dawkes b Drake	14
P.Davis	c Armstrong b Smith	8
R.J.Partridge	b Smith	6
E.J.Herbert	not out	1
Extras	(B 10, LB 4, W 1, NB 2)	17
Total		**300**

Fall: 1st inns 1/74, 2/113, 3/159, 4/203, 5/203, 6/228, 7/251, 8/271, 9/229.

LEICESTERSHIRE

G.L.Berry	c Dixon b Partridge	16
G.Lester	hit wkt b Merritt	26
N.F.Armstrong	hit wkt b Merritt	20
F.T.Prentice	not out	8
G.S.Watson	not out	1
Extras	(B 5, LB 7)	12
Total	(3 wickets)	**83**

Fall: 1st inns 1/43, 2/55, 3/82.

*Mr M.St.J.Packe, H.A.Smith, †G.O.Dawkes, J.Sperry, M.Tompkin and C.H.Drake did not bat.

LEICESTERSHIRE	O	M	R	W
Sperry	18	6	64	1
Drake	26	7	58	3
Smith	22.5	7	62	3
Lester	3	0	24	0
Prentice	11	1	43	0
Armstrong	8	1	32	3

NORTHANTS	O	M	R	W
Partridge	12	1	27	1
Herbert	2	0	10	0
Timms	2	0	3	0
Merritt	10.5	2	27	2
Nelson	2	1	4	0

Umpires: F.J.Durston and C.V.Tarbox.

Close of play scores. First day: No play (rain). **Second day:** Leicestershire 27/0 (G.L.Berry 12*, G.Lester 10*).

Comments: There was only 70 minutes' play on the second day.

SURREY v NOTTINGHAMSHIRE

Played at Kennington Oval, August 5, 7, 8, 1939.
Toss won by Nottinghamshire.
Match drawn.

NOTTINGHAMSHIRE

W.W.Keeton	c Gover b Watts	80
C.B.Harris	b Gover	34
*Mr G.F.H.Heane	c Gover b Parker	13
J.Hardstaff	not out	79
G.V.Gunn	not out	24
Extras	(B 10, LB 3, NB 5)	18
Total	(3 wickets, declared)	**248**

Fall: 1st inns 1/90, 2/136, 3/162.

J.Knowles, R.J.Giles, W.Voce, †A.B.Wheat, H.J.Butler and A.Jepson did not bat.

SURREY

R.J.Gregory	not out	42
L.B.Fishlock	b Butler	13
E.W.Whitfield	lbw b Butler	0
H.S.Squires	b Voce	35
J.F.Parker	c & b Jepson	10
Mr F.R.Brown	c Jepson b Butler	24
Mr P.J.Dickinson	c Wheat b Butler	0
†G.S.Mobey	not out	9
Extras	(B 2, LB 2, NB 1)	5
Total	(6 wickets)	**138**

Fall: 1st inns 1/19, 2/19, 3/67, 4/89, 5/120, 6/120.

*Mr H.M.Garland.Wells, A.R.Gover and E.A.Watts did not bat.

SURREY	O	M	R	W
Gover	17	1	57	1
Watts	8	0	41	1
Brown	15	1	66	0
Dickinson	3	0	8	0
Squires	4	1	9	0
Gregory	3	0	12	0
Parker	8	0	37	1

NOTTINGHAMSHIRE	O	M	R	W
Voce	17	2	58	1
Butler	12.7	4	31	4
Heane	1	0	2	0
Gunn	6	0	33	0
Jepson	3	1	9	1

Umpires: F.Chester and E.Robinson.

Close of play scores. First day: No play.
Second day: Nottinghamshire 147/2 (W.W.Keeton 78*, J.Hardstaff 9*).

Comments: Rain was responsible for an interrupted first day, no play on the second and a curtailed last day.

SUSSEX v MIDDLESEX

Played at Hove, August 5, 7, 8, 1939.
Match drawn.

MIDDLESEX

J.D.B.Robertson ..... c J.Parks b Nye 4
Mr B.D.Carris .... lbw b J.Cornford 10
W.J.Edrich .... b J.Parks 161
D.C.S.Compton ..... c W.Cornford b J.Parks ...4
Mr F.G.Mann .... c Hammond b Nye 88
G.E.Hart .... c J.Cornford b Nye 5
Mr R.W.V.Robins ... st W.Cornford b J.Parks 16
†W.F.F.Price .... b Hammond 20
C.I.J.Smith .... c Cox b Hammond 0
J.M.Sims .... not out 5
*Mr I.A.R.Peebles ... c & b J.Parks 0
    Extras .... (B 8, LB 5, NB 2) 15
    Total **328**
Fall: 1st inns 1/10, 2/18, 3/32, 4/255, 5/263, 6/282, 7/321, 8/323, 9/232.

SUSSEX

John G. Langridge   b Peebles 21
J.H.Parks .... c Sims b Smith 18
H.W.Parks .... c Price b Smith 15
G.Cox .... c Price b Peebles 16
Jas.Langridge........ lbw b Compton 4
Mr H.T.Bartlett ..... c Robertson b Compton 23
*Flt-Lt A.J.Holmes   b Mann 79
H.E.Hammond .... b Compton 12
†W.L.Cornford ...... not out 44
J.K.Nye .... st Price b Mann 5
    Extras .... (B 11, LB 1, W 2, NB 2) 16
    Total .... (9 wickets, declared) **253**
Fall: 1st inns 1/33, 2/53, 3/66, 4/78, 5/80, 6/118, 7/143, 8/238, 9/253.
J.H.Cornford did not bat.

SUSSEX	O	M	R	W
Nye	23	2	77	3
J.H.Cornford	14	2	53	1
J.H.Parks	17.2	1	78	4
Hammond	8	0	36	2
Jas.Langridge	6	0	50	0
Cox	4	0	19	0

MIDDLESEX	O	M	R	W
Smith	12	1	30	2
Edrich	5	1	19	0
Robins	7	0	35	0
Peebles	8	0	36	2
Compton	8	1	34	3
Carris	10	1	49	0
Sims	2	0	18	0
Mann	1.6	0	16	2

Umpires: J.J.Hills and C.W.L.Parker.

Close of play scores. First day: Middlesex 41/3 (W.J.Edrich 17, F.G.Mann 3*).
Second day: Middlesex 234/3 (W.J.Edrich 125*, F.G.Mann 79*).

Comments: There was only three and a quarter hours play possible on the first two days.
Middlesex were put in to bat.
W.J.Edrich hit a 6 and 16 4's in his 161.
He and F.G.Mann added 223 for the 4th wicket in under three hours.
Middlesex made little attempt to dismiss their opponents, resting their regular bowlers, when the possibility of bowling out Sussex seemed likely. They needed to avoid taking 1st innings points, which would have worsened their position in the Championship table under the points system operating at that time.

WORCESTERSHIRE v ESSEX

Played at Worcester, August 5, 7, 8, 1939.
Toss won by Worcestershire.
Match drawn.

WORCESTERSHIRE

*Hon C.J.Lyttelton   c Nichols b P.Smith 26
E.Cooper .... c & b P.Smith 28
Mr J.Stanning .... P.Smith 30
Mr C.H.Palmer .... b P.Smith 0
H.H.I.Gibbons ...... st Wade b P.Smith 46
S.H.Martin.......... lbw b Nichols 24
Mr R.H.C.Human .... st Wade b P.Smith 7
Mr A.P.Singleton.... lbw b Stephenson 14
R.O.Jenkins .... run out 5
R.T.D.Perks .... not out 54
†J.S.Buller .... lbw b P.Smith 22
    Extras .... (B 2, LB 5, W 1) 8
    Total **264**
Fall: 1st inns 1/47, 2/70, 3/80, 4/91, 5/127, 6/138, 7/163, 8/171, 9/213.

ESSEX

L.C.Eastman......... c Lyttelton b Martin 11
A.V.Avery .... c Buller b Martin 4
*Mr D.R.Wilcox ..... b Martin 46
J.O'Connor .... c Buller b Martin.........58
M.S.Nichols .... c Gibbons b Singleton 6
T.P.B.Smith .... c Martin b Perks 17
Mr F.St.G.Unwin ... b Perks 9
Capt J.W.A.Stephenson not out 16
R.M.Taylor .... lbw b Perks 1
R.Smith .... not out 10
    Extras .... (B 4, LB 5, NB 2) 11
    Total .... (8 wickets) **189**
Fall: 1st inns 1/17, 2/22, 3/90, 4/103, 5/136, 6/152, 7/170, 8/171.

Wicketkeeper T.H.Wade did not bat.

ESSEX	O	M	R	W
Nichols	13	0	61	1
R.Smith	4	0	16	0
Taylor	6	0	36	0
T.P.B.Smith	21.3	2	85	7
Eastman	2	0	12	0
Avery	4	1	15	0
Stephenson	7	1	31	1

WORCESTERSHIRE	O	M	R	W
Perks	17	1	57	3
Martin	20	7	39	4
Human	5	1	15	0
Jenkins	6	2	17	0
Singleton	10	1	42	1
Palmer	3	0	8	0

Umpires: H.Cruice and G.M.Lee.

Close of play scores. First day: Worcestershire 85/3 (J.Stanning 30*, H.H.I.Gibbons 1*). **Second day:** Essex 189/8 (J.W.A.Stephenson 16*, R.Smith 10*).

Comments: There was no play on the third day and only two hours on the first. R.T.D.Perks and J.S.Buller hit 51 in 20 minutes for Worcester's 10th wicket. It was Buller's first appearance since his motoring accident earlier in the season.

YORKSHIRE v LANCASHIRE

Played at Headingley, Leeds, August 5, 7, 8, 1939.
Toss won by Lancashire.
Yorkshire won by five wickets.

LANCASHIRE

E.Paynter	c Wood b Robinson	23	st Wood b Robinson		25
C.Washbrook	b Robinson	30	b Verity		12
J.L.Hopwood	c Verity b Robinson	8	b Robinson		4
N.Oldfield	c Mitchell b Verity	77	b Robinson		4
J.Iddon	c Turner b Robinson	35	b Robinson		23
W.E.Phillipson	c Mitchell b Verity	28	c Mitchell b Robinson		0
†W.Farrimond	c Wood b Bowes	5	b Robinson		1
*Mr T.A.Higson	c Robinson b Verity	0	c Verity b Robinson		0
R.Pollard	b Robinson	0	not out		5
R.G.Garlick	not out	0	c Bowes b Verity		11
Mr J.M.Brocklebank	b Verity	4	lbw b Robinson		0
Extras	(B 1, LB 6)	7	(LB 7)		7
Total		**217**			**92**

Fall: 1st inns 1/47, 2/58, 3/65, 4/133, 5/163, 6/200, 7/200, 8/213, 9/213.
2nd inns 1/19, 2/30, 3/42, 4/75, 5/75, 6/76, 7/76, 8/77, 9/92.

YORKSHIRE

A.Mitchell	c Pollard b Garlick	27	b Garlick		4
L.Hutton	b Garlick	3	not out		105
W.Barber	c Phillipson b Garlick	52	c Farrimond b Pollard		6
M.Leyland	c Oldfield b Phillipson	17	b Garlick		13
C.Turner	lbw b Phillipson	4	c Paynter b Garlick		0
Mr N.W.D.Yardley	b Garlick	14	c Farrimond b Pollard		8
*Mr A.B.Sellers	b Hopwood	10	not out		9
†A.Wood	c Pollard b Hopwood	4			
E.P.Robinson	b Hopwood	0			
H.Verity	b Pollard	2			
W.E.Bowes	not out	15			
Extras	(B 9, LB 5, NB 1)	15	(LB 2)		2
Total		**163**	(5 wickets)		**147**

Fall: 1st inns 1/21, 2/54, 3/100, 4/110, 5/126, 6/134, 7/139, 8/139, 9/146.
2nd inns 1/9, 2/20, 3/83, 4/83, 5/106.

YORKSHIRE	O	M	R	W	O	M	R	W
Bowes	28	9	32	1	2	0	4	0
Turner	5	0	14	0				
Yardley	3	1	5	0				
Robinson	39	12	80	5	21.1	9	35	8
Verity	24	9	43	4	20	8	46	2
Leyland	9	3	27	0				
Hutton	3	0	9	0				

LANCASHIRE	O	M	R	W	O	M	R	W
Phillipson	4	0	15	2	2	0	11	0
Pollard	8.2	3	23	1	18.7	3	43	2
Garlick	20	5	52	4	23	5	66	3
Brocklebank	6	0	31	0	2	0	9	0
Hopwood	7	0	27	3	4	1	10	0
Iddon	-	-	-	-	1	0	6	0

Umpires: J.Hardstaff and E.J.Smith.

Close of play scores. First day: Lancashire 171/5 (N.Oldfield 48*, W.E.Phillipson 16*). **Second day:** Lancashire 23/1 (E.Paynter 10*, J.L.Hopwood 1*).

Comments: E.P.Robinson took 8 for 22 on the third morning of the match. The last six Lancashire wickets fell for 17 runs in 30 minutes. L.Hutton with 105* (including 13 4's) in the 147 needed for victory in 195 minutes, was dropped by Washbrook in making the winning hit. This was the first century versus Lancashire. Immediately the game was over, a thunderstorm broke out, flooding the ground. J.M.Brocklebank made his debut for Lancashire.

GLOUCESTERSHIRE v GLAMORGAN

Played at Bristol, August 9, 10, 11, 1939.
Toss won by Gloucestershire.
Glamorgan won by six wickets.

GLOUCESTERSHIRE

C.J.Barnett	c & b Smart	20	c Judge b Evans		20
G.M.Emmett	c Turnbull b Mercer	11	not out		24
R.A.Sinfield	b Matthews	69			
*Mr W.R.Hammond	c H.Davies b Smart	36	(5) not out		73
J.F.Crapp	c H.Davies b Judge	47			
Mr E.D.R.Eagar	c H.Davies b Matthews	29			
Mr A.H.Brodhurst	b Matthews	5			
†E.A.Wilson	not out	9			
C.J.Scott	not out	6	(3) b Matthews		3
T.W.J.Goddard	(did not bat)		(4) b Matthews		6
Extras	(B 1)	1	(NB 2)		2
Total	(7 wickets, declared)	**223**	(3 wickets, declared)		**128**

Fall: 1st inns 1/4, 2/34, 3/96, 4/145, 5/203, 6/205, 7/213.
2nd inns 1/10, 2/51, 3/38.

G.E.E.Lambert did not bat.

GLAMORGAN

A.H.Dyson	lbw b Scott	15			
T.L.Brierley	lbw b Goddard	12	b Scott		8
E.C.Jones	c Wilson b Emmett	21			
D.Davies	c Scott b Goddard	3			
*Mr M.J.L.Turnbull	c Emmett b Lambert	24	(1) b Scott		18
C.C.Smart	not out	101	(3) not out		67
Mr G.Evans	b Sinfield	14	(5) b Scott		8
†H.G.Davies	b Scott	34	(4) c Crapp b Goddard		5
A.D.G.Matthews	not out	4			
J.Mercer	(did not bat)		(6) not out		13
Extras	(B 1, LB 5, NB 1)	7	(NB 1)		1
Total	(7 wickets, declared)	**235**	(4 wickets)		**120**

Fall: 1st inns 1/26, 2/28, 3/35, 4/65, 5/111, 6/152, 7/152, 8/212.
2nd inns 1/10, 2/51, 3/64, 4/86.

P.F.Judge did not bat.

GLAMORGAN	O	M	R	W	O	M	R	W
Matthews	8	1	48	3	8	1	33	2
Mercer	15	2	57	1	2	0	7	0
Smart	7	1	40	2	1	0	11	0
Jones	5	0	19	0				
Judge	8	0	30	1	3	0	32	0
D.Davies	4	0	19	0				
Evans	4	0	9	0	5	0	43	1

GLOUCESTERSHIRE	O	M	R	W	O	M	R	W
Scott	14.4	2	57	2	9	0	54	3
Lambert	12	1	56	1	2	0	15	0
Goddard	19	3	60	2	6.2	0	50	1
Sinfield	16	4	44	1				
Emmett	1	0	11	1				

Umpires: H.Cruice and G.M.Lee.

Close of play scores. First day: Gloucestershire 223/7 (E.A.Wilson 9*, C.J.Scott 6*). **Second day:** No play.

Comments: Glamorgan won with only four minutes of the extra half-hour remaining, after three declarations on the final day.
C.C.Smart was the only visiting player to score a century (101*, including 14 4's) against Gloucestershire in 1939.
Glamorgan were set to make 117 to win in 70 minutes, after W.R.Hammond had scored an undefeated 73 in 45 minutes.

KENT v MIDDLESEX

Played at Canterbury, August 9, 10, 11, 1939.
Toss won by Middlesex.
Middlesex won by an innings and 64 runs.

MIDDLESEX

J.D.B.Robertson	b Wright	14
Mr B.D.Carris	b Watt	0
W.J.Edrich	c Fagg b Davies	91
D.C.S.Compton	lbw b Davies	11
Mr F.G.Mann	c Davies b Lewis	45
Mr G.O.B.Allen	lbw b Watt	32
G.E.Hart	lbw b Todd	26
†W.F.F.Price	b Todd	6
J.M.Sims	b Todd	3
C.I.J.Smith	not out	101
*Mr I.A.R.Peebles	b Todd	14
Extras	(B 11, LB 2, NB 2)	15
Total		**358**

Fall: 1st inns 1/2, 2/31, 3/55, 4/158, 5/179, 6/226, 7/232, 8/237, 9/242.

KENT

A.E.Fagg	run out	27	lbw b Allen	7
*Mr F.G.H.Chalk	c Edrich b Allen	0	b Sims	14
L.E.G.Ames	c Edrich b Allen	15	c Hart b Sims	89
Mr B.H.Valentine	c Edrich b Allen	40	c Price b Compton	7
L.J.Todd	c Mann b Allen	16	c Edrich b Peebles	1
†Mr W.H.V.Levett	not out	20	(9) c Allen b Sims	0
Mr P.G.Foster	b Allen	0	(6) lbw b Peebles	3
Mr J.G.W.Davies	c Allen b Peebles	1	(7) b Peebles	6
D.V.P.Wright	c Peebles b Sims	6	(8) c Carris b Peebles	0
A.E.Watt	b Allen	5	run out	16
C.Lewis	b Sims	0	not out	5
Extras	(B 2, LB 3, W 1, NB 2)	8	(B 3, LB 5)	8
Total		**138**		**156**

Fall: 1st inns 1/1, 2/37, 3/74, 4/93, 5/108, 6/108, 7/115, 8/122, 9/129.
2nd inns 1/12, 2/49, 3/74, 4/75, 5/79, 6/97, 7/97, 8/135, 9/136.

KENT	O	M	R	W
Todd	21.7	4	93	4
Watt	15	4	55	2
Wright	21	0	59	1
Davies	22	3	86	2
Lewis	13	2	50	1

MIDDLESEX	O	M	R	W	O	M	R	W
Allen	15	1	46	6	7	0	39	1
Smith	7	0	18	0	4	0	7	0
Sims	12.1	2	47	2	7.5	0	35	3
Peebles	5	0	19	1	11	2	46	4
Compton	-	-	-	-	6	1	21	1

Umpires: F.Chester and E.Robinson.

Close of play scores. First day: Middlesex 276/9 (C.I.J.Smith 32*, I.A.R.Peebles 5*). **Second day:** Kent 108/6 (W.H.V.Levett 5*, P.G.Foster 0*).

Comments: C.I.J.Smith and I.A.R.Peebles added 116 for the Middlesex 10th wicket. Smith making 98 of them.
It was Smith's first century in first-class cricket. He came in at 237/8 and scored his 101* out of 121, hitting seven 6's and five 4's. He batted in three spells for a total of 81 minutes.
Kent followed on 220 behind.
In Kent's 2nd innings, L.E.G.Ames scored 89 in 113 minutes out of 123, hitting one 6 and nine 4's.

LANCASHIRE v ESSEX

Played at Old Trafford, Manchester, August 9, 10, 11, 1939.
Toss won by Essex.
Match drawn.

ESSEX

L.C.Eastman	lbw b Phillipson	20
A.V.Avery	lbw b Brocklebank	30
*Mr D.R.Wilcox	c Farrimond b Garlick	10
J.O'Connor	b Phillipson	25
M.S.Nichols	b Pollard	69
T.P.B.Smith	c Paynter b Phillipson	50
Capt J.W.A.Stephenson	b Pollard	18
R.Smith	c Phillipson b Pollard	0
R.M.Taylor	not out	45
†T.H.Wade	not out	17
Extras	(LB 4, NB 1)	5
Total	(8 wickets, declared)	**289**

Fall: 1st inns 1/28, 2/53, 3/61, 4/102, 5/207, 6/211, 7/211, 8/254.

Mr K.Farnes did not bat.

LANCASHIRE

W.Place	c P.Smith b Farnes	2
C.Washbrook	not out	43
E.Paynter	c Wade b Nichols	4
N.Oldfield	not out	27
Extras	(B 5, LB 2)	7
Total	(2 wickets)	**83**

Fall: 1st inns 1/4, 2/23.

*Mr T.A.Higson, Mr J.M.Brocklebank, J.Iddon, W.E.Phillipson, †W.Farrimond, R.Pollard and R.G.Garlick did not bat.

LANCASHIRE	O	M	R	W
Phillipson	19	0	94	3
Pollard	21	3	66	3
Garlick	20	6	46	1
Brocklebank	14	1	60	1
Higson	4	2	9	0
Paynter	2	0	8	0
Iddon	1	0	1	0

ESSEX	O	M	R	W
Farnes	7	2	20	1
Nichols	8	1	27	1
Stephenson	3	0	13	0
Avery	3	2	2	0
R.Smith	1	0	2	0
O'Connor	1	0	12	0

Umpires: E.J.Smith and A.Skelding.

Close of play scores. First day: Essex 289/8 (R.M.Taylor 45*, T.H.Wade 17*).
Second day: No play.

Comments: M.S.Nichols and T.P.B.Smith added 105 for the 5th wicket.
On the third day, play did not commence until 4.30pm.
It was the seventh occasion in the last eight games that rain prevented even the completion of the 1st innings of both sides in a match in which Lancashire had been involved.

LEICESTERSHIRE v YORKSHIRE

Played at Grace Road, Leicester, August 9, 10, 11, 1939.
Toss won by Leicestershire.
Yorkshire won by 97 runs.

YORKSHIRE

A.Mitchell	lbw b Walsh ...21	lbw b Walsh ...42
L.Hutton	b Sperry ...4	not out ...56
W.Barber	c Dawkes b Walsh ...47	lbw b Smith ...0
C.Turner	b Walsh ...10	
W.Watson	b Drake ...30	
Mr N.W.D.Yardley	c & b Drake ...0	
*Mr A.B.Sellers	c Dawkes b Drake ...8	
†A.Wood	c Prentice b Drake ...16	(4) b Smith ...30
E.P.Robinson	c & b Walsh ...3	
J.Johnson	b Walsh ...1	
J.Smurthwaite	not out ...0	
Extras	(B 10, LB 4, NB 1) ...15	(LB 3, NB 3) ...6
Total	**155**	**(3 wickets, declared) 134**

Fall: 1st inns 1/7, 2/32, 3/62, 4/97, 5/100, 6/131, 7/148, 8/151, 9/154.
2nd inns 1/93, 2/94, 3/134.

LEICESTERSHIRE

Mr C.S.Dempster	b Robinson ...21	c Smurthwaite b Turner 12
G.L.Berry	lbw b Robinson ...44	c Sellers b Turner ...0
N.F.Armstrong	c Mitchell b Robinson ...3	b Johnson ...12
F.T.Prentice	c Robinson b Turner ...5	lbw b Robinson ...0
M.Tompkin	c Barber b Robinson ...2	c Smurthwaite b Yardley 14
*Mr M.St.J.Packe	c Wood b Turner ...0	b Johnson ...44
†G.O.Dawkes	run out ...4	c Hutton b Johnson ...2
Mr J.E.Walsh	c Yardley b Robinson ...1	b Hutton ...10
E.J.Smith	b Smurthwaite ...1	not out ...5
C.H.Drake	lbw b Robinson ...0	st Wood b Johnson ...0
J.Sperry	not out ...0	b Johnson ...0
Extras	(B 8) ...8	(B 1, LB 3) ...4
Total	**89**	**103**

Fall: 1st inns 1/48, 2/54, 3/59, 4/68, 5/69, 6/78, 7/88, 8/89, 9/89.
2nd inns 1/8, 2/12, 3/13, 4/32, 5/61, 6/63, 7/87, 8/103, 9/103.

LEICESTERSHIRE	O	M	R	W	O	M	R	W
Sperry	5	0	12	1	4	1	18	0
Drake	16	4	43	4	6	0	32	0
Walsh	19.1	2	56	5	8	0	43	1
Smith	8	0	29	0	6	0	35	2

YORKSHIRE	O	M	R	W	O	M	R	W
Yardley	4	0	20	0	1	1	7	1
Smurthwaite	4.2	2	4	1	4	0	13	0
Robinson	14	2	34	6	11	0	40	1
Hutton	5	4	1	0	2	0	11	1
Turner	10	1	22	2	5	2	12	2
Johnson	-	-	-	-	5.6	0	16	5

Umpires: D.Hendren and H.Elliott.

Close of play scores. First day: Leicestershire 89 all out. **Second day:** No play (rain).

Comments: Yorkshire were put in to bat.
Leicestershire, after an opening partnership of 48, lost their remaining nine wickets for 41 runs in their 1st innings, with E.P.Robinson having a bowling spell of six wickets for 23 runs.
Leicester were set to make 201 to win.
J.Johnson took 5 wickets for 16, finishing the match with three wickets for no runs in one over. It was only Johnson's third match for Yorkshire, since his debut in 1936.

NORTHAMPTONSHIRE v DERBYSHIRE

Played at Northampton, August 9, 10, 11, 1939.
Toss won by Northants.
Match drawn.

NORTHAMPTONSHIRE

Mr E.J.H.Dixon	b G.H.Pope ...13	lbw b A.V.Pope ...0
H.W.Greenwood	c Copson ...5	c Elliott b Copson ...0
D.Brookes	c Mitchell b G.H.Pope ...22	not out ...101
J.E.Timms	lbw b Copson ...16	b Copson ...1
P.Davis	lbw b Mitchell ...2	(6) lbw b Mitchell ...13
*Mr R.P.Nelson	b Copson ...6	(7) c Elliott b Mitchell ...19
†K.C.James	b G.H.Pope ...13	(8) c Elliott b Mitchell ...7
F.P.O'Brien	c Mitchell b G.H.Pope ...29	(5) b G.H.Pope ...16
W.E.Merritt	b G.H.Pope ...40	lbw b Smith ...38
R.J.Partridge	b G.H.Pope ...2	not out ...2
E.J.Herbert	not out ...7	
Extras	(B 6, LB 8) ...14	(B 6, LB 5) ...11
Total	**169**	**(8 wickets) 208**

Fall: 1st inns 1/6, 2/37, 3/52, 4/55, 5/75, 6/80, 7/111, 8/144, 9/146.
2nd inns 1/0, 2/0, 3/3, 4/28, 5/68, 6/86, 7/119, 8/205.

DERBYSHIRE

D.Smith	lbw b O'Brien ...63
A.F.Townsend	c & b Timms ...18
A.E.Alderman	b Partridge ...6
T.S.Worthington	b Partridge ...8
G.H.Pope	not out ...50
L.F.Townsend	b Partridge ...4
A.V.Pope	c Greenwood b Merritt ...41
Extras	(B 6, LB 1, NB 2) ...9
Total	**(6 wickets, declared) 199**

Fall: 1st inns 1/44, 2/57, 3/82, 4/111, 5/115, 6/199.

*Mr R.H.R.Buckston, †H.Elliott,
T.B.Mitchell and W.H.Copson did not bat.

DERBYSHIRE	O	M	R	W	O	M	R	W
Copson	11	3	19	3	11	6	25	2
A.V.Pope	10	3	38	0	3	1	4	1
G.H.Pope	14.2	1	38	6	7	1	13	1
Mitchell	15	0	60	1	22	1	115	3
L.F.Townsend	-	-	-	-	11	2	30	0
Smith	-	-	-	-	3	1	10	1

NORTHANTS	O	M	R	W
Partridge	16	3	66	3
Herbert	8	0	26	0
Timms	8	0	23	1
Merritt	13.5	0	56	1
O'Brien	1	0	3	1
Nelson	7	2	16	0

Umpires: F.J.Durston and C.V.Tarbox.

Close of play scores. First day: Derbyshire 126/5 (G.H.Pope 10*, A.V.Pope 9*).
Second day: No play.

Comments: D.Brookes scored the only century of the match, hitting eight 4's in his undefeated 101 made in 210 minutes.

SOMERSET v NOTTINGHAMSHIRE

Played at Weston-super-Mare, August 9, 10, 11, 1939.
Toss won by Nottinghamshire.
Nottinghamshire won by 97 runs.

NOTTINGHAMSHIRE

W.W.Keeton	c Hazell b Andrews	9	run out	4
C.B.Harris	lbw b Andrews	11	c Burrough b Buse	36
*Mr G.F.H.Heane	c Luckes b Meyer	3	(4) c Luckes b Andrews	7
J.Hardstaff	b Meyer	6	(5) b Andrews	75
G.V.Gunn	c Longrigg b Andrews	9	(6) not out	15
J.Knowles	c Hazell b Andrews	5		
R.J.Giles	b Meyer	1	(3) c Luckes b Andrews	10
W.Voce	b Meyer	0		
†A.B.Wheat	lbw b Andrews	16		
H.J.Butler	b Andrews	0		
A.Jepson	not out	31		
Extras	(B 8, LB 10, W 2)	20	(B 3, LB 3, W 1)	7
Total		**111**	(5 wickets, declared)	**154**

Fall: 1st inns 1/24, 2/28, 3/32, 4/36, 5/48, 6/49, 7/49, 8/53, 9/53.
2nd inns 1/4, 2/20, 3/30, 4/119, 5/154.

SOMERSET

F.S.Lee	b Voce	6	c Voce b Jepson	9
H.Gimblett	lbw b Voce	1	c & b Jepson	19
H.T.F.Buse	c Wheat b Voce	18	c Knowles b Butler	11
Mr R.J.O.Meyer	b Voce	0	c Knowles b Butler	9
Mr H.D.Burrough	b Voce	0	b Jepson	14
Mr F.M.McRae	c Wheat b Butler	6	c Jepson b Voce	6
*Mr E.F.Longrigg	c Hardstaff b Voce	11	b Butler	7
†W.T.Luckes	b Voce	9	not out	11
Mr J.Priddy	b Voce	10	c Wheat b Butler	0
W.H.R.Andrews	c Gunn b Jepson	5	c Wheat b Butler	0
H.L.Hazell	not out	0	b Butler	4
Extras	(B 2, LB 4)	6	(B 1, LB 3, W 1, NB 1)	6
Total		**72**		**96**

Fall: 1st inns 1/2, 2/13, 3/15, 4/15, 5/26, 6/45, 7/50, 8/59, 9/70.
2nd inns 1/25, 2/30, 3/45, 4/50, 5/72, 6/74, 7/87, 8/87, 9/87.

SOMERSET	O	M	R	W	O	M	R	W
Andrews	13	1	47	6	10.6	0	80	3
Buse	6	1	16	0	11	4	18	1
Meyer	8	1	28	4	3	0	25	0
Hazell	-	-	-	-	5	1	10	0
Priddy	-	-	-	-	3	0	14	0

NOTTINGHAMSHIRE	O	M	R	W	O	M	R	W
Voce	13.6	2	30	8	11	2	25	1
Butler	11	2	34	1	8	3	17	6
Jepson	2	0	2	1	16	4	32	3
Heane	-	-	-	-	2	0	16	0

Umpires: C.N.Woolley and G.Beet.

Close of play scores. First day: Nottinghamshire (2) 14/1 (C.B.Harris 5*, R.J.Giles 5*). **Second day:** No play.

Comments: In a bowler's match, J.Hardstaff was the only player to score over 50. His 75 was made in 60 minutes and included one 6 and nine 4's.
Somerset were set to make 194 in even time, were dismissed in 135 minutes, H.J.Butler taking three wickets in one over.

SURREY v HAMPSHIRE

Played at Kennington Oval, August 9, 10, 11, 1939.
Toss won by Hampshire.
Match drawn.

HAMPSHIRE

†N.T.McCorkell	c Dickinson b Parker	30
J.Bailey	b Gover	94
W.L.C.Creese	c Fishlock b Gover	11
J.Arnold	c Watts b Berry	28
D.F.Walker	c Watts b Parker	4
Mr R.B.Proud	b Watts	33
A.E.Pothecary	c Berry b Gover	6
P.A.Mackenzie	lbw b Gover	1
G.S.Boyes	not out	7
*Mr A.E.G.Baring	lbw b Gover	0
G.E.Heath	run out	3
Extras	(B 10, NB 6)	16
Total		**233**

Fall: 1st inns 1/54, 2/75, 3/125, 4/153, 5/208, 6/218, 7/220, 8/222, 9/224.

SURREY

R.J.Gregory	lbw b Heath	8
L.B.Fishlock	c McCorkell b Baring	4
E.W.Whitfield	not out	49
H.S.Squires	not out	32
Extras	(B 4, NB 2)	6
Total	(2 wickets)	**99**

Fall: 1st inns 1/13, 2/15.

*Mr H.M.Garland-Wells, Mr P.J.Dickinson, E.A.Watts, J.F.Parker, †G.S.Mobey, A.R.Gover and F.Berry did not bat.

SURREY	O	M	R	W
Gover	17.6	6	41	5
Watts	9	0	33	1
Berry	9	1	28	1
Parker	11	3	33	2
Garland-Wells	10	3	30	0
Squires	9	3	32	0
Gregory	7	3	17	0
Dickinson	4	2	3	0

HAMPSHIRE	O	M	R	W
Baring	12	3	48	1
Heath	10	3	33	1
Boyes	3	0	7	0
Bailey	1	0	5	0

Umpires: J.J.Hills and C.W.L.Parker.

Close of play scores. First day: Surrey 9/0 (R.B.Gregory 4*, L.B.Fishlock 4*).
Second day: Surrey 99/2 (E.W.Whitfield 49*, H.S.Squires 32*).

Comments: A.R.Gover after taking the new ball, claimed four Hampshire wickets for six runs.
There were only 50 minutes of play on the second day and nine on the third.

WORCESTERSHIRE v SUSSEX

Played at Worcester, August 9, 10, 11, 1939.
Toss won by Sussex.
Worcestershire won by an innings and 63 runs.

SUSSEX

John G.Langridge	lbw b Martin	27	st Buller b Howorth	13
J.H.Parks	c Howorth b Martin	9	lbw b Howorth	7
H.W.Parks	c Cooper b Martin	1	lbw b Perks	20
G.Cox	c Singleton b Martin	2	lbw b Martin	33
Mr H.T.Bartlett	c Singleton b Martin	6	c Buller b Martin	10
*Flt-Lt A.J.Holmes	b Perks	1	b Martin	2
†Mr S.C.Griffith	b Martin	1	b Howorth	57
H.E.Hammond	c Gibbons b Martin	5	b Martin	9
J.K.Nye	b Martin	1	b Martin	8
D.J.Wood	b Perks	1	not out	5
J.H.Cornford	not out	2	b Howorth	3
Extras	(B 1, LB 3, NB 2)	6	(LB 2, NB 3)	5
Total		**62**		**172**

Fall: 1st inns 1/21, 2/27, 3/34, 4/45, 5/48, 6/53, 7/57, 8/59, 9/60.
2nd inns 1/21, 2/24, 3/68, 4/84, 5/88, 6/89, 7/109, 8/155, 9/166.

WORCESTERSHIRE

R.Howorth	b Wood	69
E.Cooper	b Hammond	34
Mr R.H.C.Human	c Langridge b Wood	0
Mr C.H.Palmer	b Wood	4
H.H.I.Gibbons	b Nye	40
S.H.Martin	c Holmes b Cornford	13
Mr A.P.Singleton	c Langridge b Cornford	57
*Hon C.J.Lyttelton	b Wood	24
R.O.Jenkins	not out	18
R.T.D.Perks	not out	15
Extras	(B 10, LB 10, W 1, NB 2)	23
Total	(8 wickets, declared)	**297**

Fall: 1st inns 1/108, 2/108, 3/113, 4/115, 5/142, 6/234, 7/238, 8/265.

†J.S.Buller did not bat.

WORCESTERSHIRE	O	M	R	W	O	M	R	W
Martin	13	6	24	8	20	4	64	5
Perks	13	1	32	2	12	1	38	1
Howorth	1	1	0	0	12.4	1	58	4
Singleton	-	-	-	-	3	1	7	0

SUSSEX	O	M	R	W
Nye	15	1	56	1
Cornford	15	0	78	2
Wood	16	1	57	4
J.Parks	8	0	36	0
Hammond	10	1	38	1
Langridge	1	0	9	0

Umpires: H.W.Lee and A.Dolphin.

Close of play scores. First day: Worcestershire 218/5 (H.H.I.Gibbons 32*, A.P.Singleton 50*). **Second day:** Sussex 40/2 (H.W.Parks 11*, G.Cox 8*).

Comments: Sussex were dismissed before lunch on the first day.
S.H.Martin bowling unchanged in the first innings, achieved a career-best of eight wickets for 24 runs. He took all eight wickets before lunch on the first day.
R.Howorth and E.Cooper achieved Worcester's first century opening partnership of the season.
D.J.Wood claimed three wickets in an over in Worcester's 1st innings. Play was delayed until 4.15pm on the second day.
S.C.Griffith with one 6 and ten 4's hit 46 of his 57 in boundaries.

ESSEX v DERBYSHIRE

Played at Southend-on-Sea, August 12, 14, 1939.
Toss won by Derbyshire.
Essex won by an innings and 31 runs.

DERBYSHIRE

D.Smith	lbw b Nichols	14	b Nichols	16
A.F.Townsend	b R.Smith	30	b Nichols	6
A.E.Alderman	b Nichols	10	b Nichols	0
T.S.Worthington	lbw b R.Smith	6	c R.Smith b Farnes	14
G.H.Pope	b Nichols	1	c Wade b Farnes	5
A.E.G.Rhodes	c Stephenson b R.Smith	0	b Farnes	8
A.V.Pope	c P.Smith b Nichols	0	not out	12
*Mr R.H.R.Buckston	not out	5	c Taylor b Farnes	2
†H.Elliott	run out	0	b Nichols	8
T.B.Mitchell	b Nichols	0	b Farnes	7
W.H.Copson	b Nichols	1	b Nichols	0
Extras	(B 1, LB 2)	3	(B 1)	1
Total		**70**		**79**

Fall: 1st inns 1/21, 2/47, 3/56, 4/57, 5/58, 6/59, 7/63, 8/66, 9/68.
2nd inns 1/12, 2/12, 3/37, 4/49, 5/52, 6/54, 7/54, 8/67, 9/78.

ESSEX

L.C.Eastman	c Elliott b Copson	0
A.V.Avery	not out	84
*Mr D.R.Wilcox	c Smith b Copson	9
J.O'Connor	b A.V.Pope	5
M.S.Nichols	c Smith b A.V.Pope	2
T.P.B.Smith	c A.V.Pope b Copson	36
R.M.Taylor	lbw b A.V.Pope	18
Capt J.W.A.Stephenson	st Elliott b Mitchell	10
R.Smith	b Mitchell	7
†T.H.Wade	c Townsend b Mitchell	0
Mr K.Farnes	b A.V.Pope	5
Extras	(LB 4)	4
Total		**180**

Fall: 1st inns 1/0, 2/13, 3/20, 4/24, 5/104, 6/136, 7/153, 8/167, 9/167.

ESSEX	O	M	R	W	O	M	R	W
Farnes	6	0	34	0	10	1	52	5
Nichols	12.1	4	18	6	9.2	2	26	5
R.Smith	7	1	15	3				

DERBYSHIRE	O	M	R	W
Copson	14	2	35	3
A.V.Pope	15.7	2	40	4
G.H.Pope	7	0	24	0
Rhodes	9	2	29	0
Mitchell	10	1	48	3

Umpires: H.G.Baldwin and F.J.Durston.

Close of play scores. First day: Derbyshire 26/2 (D.Smith 12*, T.S.Worthington 7*).

Comments: Southend cricket week. The match was over by lunch on the second day.
Twenty-two wickets fell on the first day, Derbyshire losing 12 of them for only 96 runs.
M.S.Nichols had a spell of five wickets for five runs in Derbyshire's 1st innings. Both he and K.Farnes bowled unchanged in the 2nd innings.
A.V.Avery carried his bat for 84 in 225 minutes, hitting only one four.

HAMPSHIRE v LEICESTERSHIRE

Played at Southampton, August 12, 14, 15, 1939.
Toss won by Leicestershire.
Hampshire won by 177 runs.

HAMPSHIRE

†N.T.McCorkell	b Sperry	14	c Dawkes b Lester	24
J.Bailey	c West b Drake	13	c Tompkin b Drake	44
Mr R.B.Proud	c Watson b West	6	(6) b Lester	8
J.Arnold	b Tompkin b Lester	82	c Watson b Drake	5
W.L.C.Creese	b West	7	lbw b Lester	30
D.F.Walker	lbw b Lester	44	(3) lbw b Lester	66
A.E.Pothecary	c Dawkes b Sperry	21	not out	23
G.S.Boyes	not out	59	c Knew b Sperry	26
*Mr A.E.G.Baring	b Sperry	2		
Mr C.H.Knott	c Armstrong b Sperry	9		
G.E.M.Heath	c Dawkes b Sperry	12		
Extras	(B 14, NB 2)	16	(B 16, LB 2, NB 1)	19
Total		**285**	(7 wickets, declared)	**245**

Fall: 1st inns 1/24, 2/32, 3/60, 4/84, 5/168, 6/175, 7/212, 8/222, 9/232.
2nd inns 1/55, 2/101, 3/116, 4/176, 5/183, 6/198, 7/245.

LEICESTERSHIRE

G.Lester	c Creese b Knott	17	c Creese b Baring	2
G.L.Berry	b Bailey	16	c Walker b Knott	14
N.F.Armstrong	b Heath	17	not out	72
G.S.Watson	c McCorkell b Boyes	37	lbw b Knott	1
M.Tompkin	lbw b Boyes	53	c Walker b Knott	13
G.F.Knew	c Walker b Boyes	1	b Heath	1
†G.O.Dawkes	b Baring	8	c Creese b Bailey	19
A.R.West	c McCorkell b Baring	0	(9) lbw b Boyes	22
*W.E.Astill	not out	6	(8) b Bailey	0
C.H.Drake	b Heath	13	lbw b Baring	2
J.Sperry	run out	7	c McCorkell b Knott	17
Extras	(B 5, NB 9)	14	(NB 1)	1
Total		**189**		**164**

Fall: 1st inns 1/24, 2/50, 3/58, 4/134, 5/146, 6/155, 7/157, 8/165, 9/181.
2nd inns 1/15, 2/17, 3/213, 4/53, 5/54, 6/88, 7/88, 8/128, 9/131.

LEICESTERSHIRE	O	M	R	W	O	M	R	W
Sperry	24.4	1	83	5	21.5	1	51	1
Drake	22	2	77	1	15	0	84	2
Astill	6	0	23	0	5	1	22	0
West	15	3	46	2	11	3	29	0
Lester	13	1	40	2	11	2	28	4
Knew	-	-	-	-	4	0	12	0

HAMPSHIRE	O	M	R	W	O	M	R	W
Baring	16	2	52	2	14	3	55	2
Heath	12	2	44	2	5	0	31	1
Knott	12.6	2	46	1	12.2	1	44	4
Bailey	5	0	20	1	7	1	17	2
Boyes	10	4	13	3	3	0	16	1

Umpires: D.Hendren and J.J.Hills.

Close of play scores. First day: Leicestershire 55/2 (G.L.Berry 16*, G.S.Watson 1*). **Second day:** Leicestershire 11/0 (G.Lester 1*, G.L.Berry 10*).

Comments: Hampshire were put in to bat.
G.S.Boyes and G.E.M.Heath added 53 for Hampshire's 10th wicket.
Leicestershire were set to make 342.
A.R.West, aged 17, was making his championship debut for Leicestershire.

NOTTINGHAMSHIRE v LANCASHIRE

Played at Trent Bridge, Nottingham, August 12, 14, 15, 1939.
Toss won by Nottinghamshire.
Lancashire won by six wickets.

NOTTINGHAMSHIRE

W.W.Keeton	c Higson b Iddon	73	c Farrimond b Phillipson	4
C.B.Harris	b Higson	6	b Phillipson	0
*Mr G.F.H.Heane	run out	4	c Iddon b Phillipson	45
J.Hardstaff	b Brocklebank	70	c Pollard b Iddon	67
G.V.Gunn	c & b Brocklebank	5	c & b Pollard	63
J.Knowles	c Paynter b Iddon	1	c Paynter b Pollard	32
R.J.Giles	b Brocklebank	5	not out	6
W.Voce	c Brocklebank b Pollard	7	c Farrimond b Phillipson	2
†A.B.Wheat	not out	32	b Phillipson	0
H.J.Butler	c Higson b Phillipson	25	b Phillipson	0
A.Jepson	c Pollard b Phillipson	2	c Farrimond b Phillipson	6
Extras	(B 6, NB 1)	7	(B 3, LB 2, NB 4)	9
Total		**237**		**234**

Fall: 1st inns 1/29, 2/41, 3/138, 4/153, 5/154, 6/168, 7/175, 8/187, 9/235.
2nd inns 1/4, 2/11, 3/85, 4/144, 5/220, 6/221, 7/224, 8/224, 9/228.

LANCASHIRE

C.Washbrook	lbw b Voce	5	lbw b Voce	81
W.Place	c Wheat b Butler	8	(3) c Wheat b Jepson	17
E.Paynter	lbw b Butler	41	(2) c Hardstaff b Giles	154
N.Oldfield	b Voce	42	c Giles b Voce	2
J.Iddon	b Jepson	1	not out	26
W.E.Phillipson	b Jepson	19	not out	38
†W.Farrimond	lbw b Giles	9		
*Mr T.A.Higson	c Wheat b Butler	6		
R.Pollard	b Butler	7		
R.G.Garlick	c Wheat b Voce	1		
Mr J.M.Brocklebank	not out	0		
Extras	(LB 7, NB 3)	10	(B 2, LB 2, NB 1)	5
Total		**149**	(4 wickets)	**323**

Fall: 1st inns 1/5, 2/36, 3/75, 4/81, 5/114, 6/128, 7/137, 8/144, 9/149.
2nd inns 1/215, 2/251, 3/255, 4/258.

LANCASHIRE	O	M	R	W	O	M	R	W
Phillipson	9.2	1	29	2	15.7	1	55	7
Pollard	19	4	50	1	12	1	57	2
Higson	7	2	14	1	5	0	12	0
Garlick	12	2	48	0	10	2	40	0
Brocklebank	16	2	61	3	10	0	36	0
Iddon	9	1	28	2	8	2	25	1

NOTTINGHAMSHIRE	O	M	R	W	O	M	R	W
Voce	17	4	39	3	21	1	100	2
Butler	19.2	2	61	4	18	0	70	0
Jepson	13	2	25	2	16	0	68	1
Giles	6	1	14	1	9	0	45	1
Gunn	-	-	-	-	8	0	28	0
Harris	-	-	-	-	3	0	7	0

Umpires: C.V.Tarbox and J.A.Newman.

Close of play scores. First day: Lancashire 58/2 (E.Paynter 31*, N.Oldfield 8*). **Second day:** Nottinghamshire 205/4 (G.V.Gunn 54*, J.Knowles 26*).

Comments: Nottinghamshire collapsed on the third morning, their last six wickets falling for 25 runs in 35 minutes.
E.Paynter and C.Washbrook added 215 for the 1st wicket in Lancashire's 2nd innings.
E.Paynter hit two 6's and 19 4's in his 154 which lasted 225 minutes.
Lancashire won with ten minutes play remaining, having claimed the extra half-hour.

NORTHAMPTONSHIRE v WARWICKSHIRE

Played at Northampton, August 12, 14, 15, 1939.
Toss won by Warwickshire.
Match drawn.

WARWICKSHIRE

A.J.W.Croom ....c James b Robinson 0	not out 110	
Mr R.Sale ....c Dixon b Merritt 19	c James b Partridge 2	
W.A.Hill ....c Brookes b Merritt 138		
Mr R.E.S.Wyatt ......c James b Robinson 151	(5) c & b Robinson 30	
H.E.Dollery..........not out.................35		
F.R.Santall...........not out.................13	(4) c Dixon b Nelson 26	
*Mr P.Cranmer ......(did not bat)	(3) b Partridge 19	
†J.Buckingham ......(did not bat)	(6) not out 5	
Extras ....(B 7, LB 6, W 2) 15	(B 6, LB 2) 8	
Total ....(4 wickets, declared) **371**	(4 wickets) **200**	

Fall: 1st inns 1/3, 2/30, 3/307, 4/330.
2nd inns 1/15, 2/39, 3/77, 4/174.
J.H.Mayer, W.E.Hollies and C.W.Grove did not bat.

NORTHAMPTONSHIRE

Mr E.J.H.Dixon .....c Hollies b Mayer 5	
P.Davis..............st Buckingham b Hollies 21	
D.Brookes ....b Hollies 23	
J.E.Timms ....b Hollies 15	
H.W.Greenwood ....run out...................4	
*Mr R.P.Nelson .....c Buckingham b Hollies 93	
†K.C.James ....c Hollies b Santall 50	
F.P.O'Brien ....lbw b Hollies.............48	
W.E.Merritt ....not out...................53	
R.J.Partridge ....b Hollies 22	
A.G.Robinson ......b Hollies 0	
Extras.............(B 11, LB 11, W 1) 23	
Total **357**	

Fall: 1st inns 1/9, 2/51, 3/58, 4/64, 5/89, 6/175, 7/274, 8/301, 9/357.

NORTHANTS	O	M	R	W	O	M	R	W
Partridge 21	5	33	0	8	0	37	2
Robinson 22	4	75	2	16	3	55	1
Merritt.......................27	2	132	2	6	0	26	0
Nelson 21	11	22	0	13	1	30	1
Timms 10	0	34	0				
O'Brien 12	2	56	0	5	1	11	0
Dixon 1	0	4	0	2	0	16	0
Davis ....-	-	-	-	3	0	8	0
Greenwood ....-	-	-	-	2	0	9	0

WARWICKSHIRE	O	M	R	W
Mayer.........................25	4	81	1
Grove 21	6	61	0
Hollies........................48.4	15	119	7
Wyatt 15	1	38	0
Croom 7	0	24	0
Cranmer 5	3	5	0
Santall 2	0	6	1

Umpires: G.M.Lee and A.Dolphin.

SOMERSET v GLAMORGAN

Played at Weston-super-Mare, August 12, 14, 15, 1939.
Toss won by Somerset.
Glamorgan won by two wickets.

SOMERSET

F.S.Lee ....b Judge 2	b Smart 32	
H.Gimblett ....lbw b Matthews 15	c Dyson b Judge 45	
H.T.F.Buse ....b Judge 2	b Smart 53	
Mr R.J.O.Meyer ....b Matthews 0	b Matthews 6	
Mr H.D.Burrough ..c D.Davies b Judge...10	b Judge 9	
Mr F.M.McRae .....c H.Davies b Matthews ..0	c & b Smart 20	
*Mr E.F.Longrigg ..b Judge 47	c Smart b Jones 16	
Mr R.A.Ingle ....c Judge b Matthews 3	c Turnbull b Smart 8	
†W.T.Luckes ....lbw b Matthews 21	c Judge b Jones 4	
W.H.R.Andrews ....c Turnbull b Matthews 14	c H.Davies b Smart 0	
H.L.Hazell ....not out.................3	not out...................0	
Extras ....(B 4, LB 5, NB 1) 10	(B 1, LB 6, NB 1) 8	
Total **127**	............................**201**	

Fall: 1st inns 1/7, 2/11, 3/20, 4/25, 5/25, 6/37, 7/46, 8/105, 9/113.
2nd inns 1/65, 2/96, 3/119, 4/132, 5/164, 6/189, 7/193, 8/201, 9/201.

GLAMORGAN

A.H.Dyson ....c Meyer b Buse 25	not out 90	
T.L.Brierley ....c Luckes b Buse 1	c Luckes b Andrews 6	
E.C.Jones ....c & b Meyer 7	st Luckes b Hazell 16	
D.Davies ....lbw b Buse 5	(5) c Luckes b Andrews ..10	
*Mr M.J.L.Turnbull c Longrigg b Buse 6	(4) b Andrews 39	
C.C.Smart............c Hazell b Meyer 62	b Andrews 0	
Mr G.Evans ....st Luckes b Meyer 20	c & b Andrews 3	
†H.G.Davies ....b Hazell 0	c Andrews b Hazell 4	
P.B.Clift ....b Meyer 0	b Hazell 0	
A.D.G.Matthews.....c Luckes b Hazell 0	not out 5	
P.F.Judge ....not out...................10		
Extras ....(B 8, LB 7) 15	(B 2, LB 1, W 1, NB 2) 6	
Total **151**	(8 wickets) **179**	

Fall: 1st inns 1/10, 2/29, 3/40, 4/56, 5/79, 6/130, 7/131, 8/132, 9/133.
2nd inns 1/13, 2/47, 3/104, 4/116, 5/122, 6/138, 7/143, 8/145.

GLAMORGAN	O	M	R	W	O	M	R	W
Matthews 21.1	5	40	6	18	2	62	1
Judge 18	2	66	4	17	5	39	2
Evans 3	0	11	0	9	0	49	0
Smart ....-	-	-	-	14	2	39	5
Jones ....-	-	-	-	2.3	1	4	2

SOMERSET	O	M	R	W	O	M	R	W
Andrews 11	1	46	0	16	1	64	5
Buse 16	3	30	4	12	3	33	0
Meyer 12.6	0	52	4	7	2	38	0
Hazell.........................7	1	8	2	15.3	5	38	3

Umpires: F.I.Walden and C.N.Woolley.

Close of play scores. First day: Warwickshire 371/4 (H.E.Dollery 35*, F.R.Santall 13*). **Second day:** Northants 301/8 (W.E.Merritt 20*).

Comments: R.E.S.Wyatt and W.A.Hill added 277 in 300 minutes for the 3rd wicket. It was the second highest score for this wicket by the county.
W.A.Hill scored 138 in 330 minutes, hitting 14 4's.
R.E.S.Wyatt's 151 was made in 320 minutes and included 16 4's
A.J.W.Croom hit ten 4's in his undefeated 110 in Warwickshire's 2nd innings.

Close of play scores. First day: Glamorgan 151 all out. **Second day:** Glamorgan 158/7 (A.H.Dyson 72*, A.D.G.Matthews 1*).

Comments:: A.W.Wellard's benefit match. He was unable to play due to a knee injury. The match receipts were £426, a record benefit for a Somerset player. The match was extended until 7.30pm on the second day in an unsuccessful attempt to finish the game. It took 20 minutes of the final morning for Glamorgan to secure victory.

GLAMORGAN COUNTY CRICKET CLUB

Standing (left to right): P.B.Clift, C.C.Smart, H.G.Davies, P.F.Judge, E.C.Jones, T.L.Brierley, A.J.Watkins. Seated: A.H.Dyson, D.Davies, M.J.L.Turnbull (captain), J.Mercer, D.E.Davies.

SURREY v MIDDLESEX

Played at Kennington Oval, August 12, 14, 15, 1939.
Toss won by Surrey.
Surrey won by eight wickets.

MIDDLESEX

Mr B.D.Carris	b Parker 14	lbw b Watts	5
J.D.B.Robertson	c Dickinson b Parker ..22	b Watts	19
W.J.Edrich	b Gover 54	b Watts	62
D.C.S.Compton	c & b Parker ..52	c Gover b Brown	68
Mr F.G.Mann	lbw b Parker 11	c Gregory b Parker	12
Mr G.O.B.Allen	b Brown 3	(7) lbw b Watts	7
Mr R.W.V.Robins	b Brown 15	(8) b Watts	0
†W.F.F.Price	b Gover 14	(10) c Mobey b Gover	23
J.M.Sims	st Mobey b Brown ..13	(11) not out	1
C.I.J.Smith	b Brown 1	(9) c Fishlock b Brown	1
*Mr I.A.R.Peebles	not out 0	(6) lbw b Gover	19
Extras	(B 6, LB 9, NB 3) 18	(B 4, LB 1, NB 1)	6
Total	**217**		**223**

Fall: 1st inns 1/42, 2/47, 3/139, 4/157, 5/166, 6/174, 7/193, 8/213, 9/217.
2nd inns 1/9, 2/38, 3/131, 4/164, 5/168, 6/182, 7/182, 8/193, 9/222.

SURREY

R.J.Gregory	c Price b Smith 47	lbw b Peebles	72
L.B.Fishlock	c Smith b Allen 6	c Peebles b Sims	71
E.W.Whitfield	c Price b Robins 81	not out	11
H.S.Squires	b Sims 12	not out	6
J.F.Parker	lbw b Peebles 8		
†G.S.Mobey	lbw b Robins 30		
Mr F.R.Brown	c Allen b Robins 17		
Mr P.J.Dickinson	st Price b Robins 10		
*Mr H.M.Garland-Wells	c Price b Robins 9		
E.A.Watts	not out 15		
A.R.Gover	st Price b Robins 19		
Extras	(B 5, LB 11, NB 2) 18	(B 3, LB 5, W 1, NB 2)	11
Total	**272**	**(2 wickets)**	**171**

Fall: 1st inns 1/18, 2/90, 3/117, 4/134, 5/180, 6/202, 7/220, 8/231, 9/236.
2nd inns 1/145, 2/155.

SURREY	O	M	R	W	O	M	R	W
Gover	20.1	3	60	2	8.4	0	48	2
Watts	9	1	35	0	17	2	70	5
Parker	18	4	34	4	5	0	26	1
Brown	27	9	70	4	17	2	61	2
Gregory	-	-	-	-	3	1	12	0

MIDDLESEX	O	M	R	W	O	M	R	W
Allen	11	1	38	1	3	1	5	0
Smith	18	6	28	1	8	1	29	0
Sims	18	2	66	1	10	2	46	1
Robins	18.7	0	86	6	10	0	40	0
Peebles	12	2	36	1	8	1	28	1
Compton	-	-	-	-	2	0	12	0

Umpires: W.Reeves and H.Cruice.

Close of play scores. First day: Surrey 83/1 (R.J.Gregory 44*, E.W.Whitfield 25*). **Second day:** Middlesex 168/5 (I.A.R.Peebles 0*).

Comments: Middlesex were put in to bat.
R.J.Gregory and L.B.Fishlock were involved in the only century stand of the match, putting on 145 for Surrey's 1st wicket in the 2nd innings. Surrey hit off their target of 169 in 135 minutes.

SUSSEX v KENT

Played at Hastings, August 12, 14, 15, 1939.
Toss won by Kent.
Kent won by 108 runs.

KENT

A.E.Fagg	b Wood 25	not out	131
*Mr F.G.H.Chalk	c Cornford b J.Parks 124		
L.E.G.Ames	b Wood 6	c Langridge b Wood	56
Mr B.H.Valentine	c Griffith b Wood 104	lbw b J.Parks	12
L.J.Todd	c H.Parks b Wood 63	(6) not out	5
Mr P.G.Foster	b Wood 25	(2) c Langridge b Wood	12
T.G.Evans	b Nye 8	(5) c H.Parks b J.Parks	1
D.V.P.Wright	not out 56		
A.E.Watt	b J.Parks 9		
N.W.Harding	not out .....-		
Extras	(B 6, LB 3, NB 5) 14	(B 4, LB 1, NB 1)	6
Total	**(8 wickets, declared) 440**	**(4 wickets, declared)**	**223**

Fall: 1st inns 1/36, 2/52, 3/267, 4/267, 5/315, 6/336, 7/405, 8/429.
2nd inns 1/41, 2/167, 3/182, 4/200.
†Mr W.H.V.Levett did not bat.

SUSSEX

Mr R.G.Stainton	b Wright 12	run out	46
John G.Langridge	c Levett b Watt 26	c Levett b Harding	141
H.W.Parks	c & b Watt 28	lbw b Wright	25
J.H.Parks	b Wright 36	(8) not out	18
Mr H.T.Bartlett	b Harding 1	b Todd	10
G.Cox	b Wright 0	(4) c Fagg b Watt	82
*Flt-Lt A.J.Holmes	lbw b Wright 29	(6) c Evans b Wright	7
†Mr S.C.Griffith	b Wright 6	(7) b Wright	8
J.K.Nye	not out 23	b Wright	1
D.J.Wood	c Watt b Wright 15	c Fagg b Watt	6
J.H.Cornford	lbw b Watt 0	b Watt	3
Extras	(B 5, LB 5, NB 5) 15	(B 4, LB 8, NB 5)	17
Total	**191**		**364**

Fall: 1st inns 1/25, 2/47, 3/80, 4/86, 5/95, 6/135, 7/148, 8/155, 9/191.
2nd inns 1/92, 2/167, 3/276, 4/287, 5/306, 6/327, 7/339, 8/342, 9/360.

SUSSEX	O	M	R	W	O	M	R	W
Nye	24	0	112	1	10	3	40	0
Cornford	16	3	69	0	8	0	55	0
J.H.Parks	37	10	116	2	8	0	54	2
Wood	30	4	90	5	10	0	68	2
Langridge	2	0	13	0				
Holmes	1	0	9	0				
Cox	3	0	17	0				

KENT	O	M	R	W	O	M	R	W
Harding	12	1	52	1	13	0	77	1
Todd	5	1	14	0	18	2	58	1
Wright	14	2	69	6	21	0	125	4
Watt	11.1	0	41	3	20.7	0	87	3

Umpires: F.Chester and E.Robinson.

Close of play scores. First day: Kent 440/8 (D.V.P.Wright 56, N.W.Harding 6*). **Second day:** Sussex 62/0 (R.G.Stainton 34*, John G.Langridge 28*).

Comments: F.G.H.Chalk and B.H.Valentine added 215 for the 3rd wicket.
F.G.H.Chalk hit 14 4's in his 124, made in 240 minutes.
B.H.Valentine hit 14 4's in his 104.
Kent did not enforce the follow-on.
A.Fagg and L.E.G.Ames added 126 for the 2nd wicket in Kent's 2nd innings.
Sussex were set to make 473 to win.
John G.Langridge hit 141, including two 6's and 13 4's.
He and G.Cox added 109 for the 3rd wicket.

YORKSHIRE v WORCESTERSHIRE

Played at Bradford, August 12, 14, 15, 1939.
Toss won by Yorkshire.
Yorkshire won by 89 runs.

YORKSHIRE

A.Mitchell	c Gibbons b Perks 0	c Gibbons b Martin 20
L.Hutton	b Perks 14	b Howorth................109
W.Barber	lbw b Perks 34	lbw b Jenkins............12
C.Turner	c Singleton b Howorth ...2	c Gibbons b Singleton......1
W.Watson	c Singleton b Howorth ...5	lbw b Singleton............3
Mr N.W.D.Yardley	lbw b Perks 9	lbw b Howorth 20
*Mr A.B.Sellers	st Buller b Martin 36	c Cooper b Howorth 12
†A.Wood	lbw b Howorth 33	lbw b Perks 50
E.P.Robinson	c & b Perks 36	b Singleton 5
H.Verity	c & b Martin 1	c Jenkins b Howorth 54
J.Smurthwaite	not out 0	not out 20
Extras	(LB 1) 1	(B 1, LB 1, NB 1) 3
Total		**171** ... **309**

Fall: 1st inns 1/0, 2/47, 3/50, 4/50, 5/56, 6/64, 7/128, 8/170, 9/170.
2nd inns 1/36, 2/58, 3/63, 4/85, 5/137, 6/165, 7/191, 8/200, 9/247.

WORCESTERSHIRE

R.Howorth	b Verity 11	c & b Turner 31
E.Cooper	c Robinson b Yardley 0	c Wood b Robinson 5
Mr R.H.C.Human	lbw b Robinson 11	c Wood b Verity 21
H.H.I.Gibbons	b Robinson 15	lbw b Hutton 3
Mr C.H.Palmer	c Robinson b Hutton 29	b Hutton 4
S.H.Martin	lbw b Hutton 1	c Hutton b Verity 9
Mr A.P.Singleton	lbw b Robinson 36	c sub b Hutton 36
*Hon C.J.Lyttelton	c Wood b Verity 16	b Smurthwaite 56
R.O.Jenkins	c Robinson b Verity 9	not out 17
R.T.D.Perks	c sub b Verity 17	c sub b Hutton 0
†J.S.Buller	not out 31	c Robinson b Hutton 5
Extras	(B 4, LB 14) 18	(B 4) 4
Total	**194**	**197**

Fall: 1st inns 1/0, 2/26, 3/28, 4/45, 5/46, 6/103, 7/126, 8/132, 9/149.
2nd inns 1/35, 2/39, 3/66, 4/66, 5/70, 6/90, 7/173, 8/181, 9/181.

WORCESTERSHIRE	O	M	R	W	O	M	R	W
Perks	18	5	65	5	16	5	58	1
Martin	9.1	1	46	2	25	5	94	1
Singleton	2	0	9	0	16	3	50	3
Howorth	12	1	50	3	20.4	4	88	4
Jenkins	-	-	-	-	9	3	16	1
Palmer	-	-	-	-	1	1	0	0

YORKSHIRE	O	M	R	W	O	M	R	W
Yardley	2	0	12	1	7	0	38	0
Smurthwaite	2	0	5	0	6	1	16	1
Robinson	24	3	92	3	9	1	30	1
Verity	24.1	7	48	4	18	5	38	2
Hutton	6	1	19	2	19.6	5	58	5
Turner	-	-	-	-	6	1	13	1

Umpires: E.Cooke and A.Skelding.

Close of play scores. First day: Yorkshire 11/0 (A.Mitchell 8*, L.Hutton 3*).
Second day: Worcestershire 83/5 (S.H.Martin 8*, A.P.Singleton 5*).

Comments: L.Hutton scored 109 in 225 minutes in Yorkshire's 2nd innings. His ninth hundred of the season, his 109 took 225 minutes and included 13 4's. He also rounded off a fine all-round performance, by taking five wickets in Worcester's 2nd innings to finish with match figures of 7 for 77. In Yorkshire's 1st innings, E.P.Robinson hit three 6's and three 4's in his 36.

ESSEX v MIDDLESEX

Played at Southend-on-Sea, August 16, 17, 18, 1939.
Toss won by Middlesex.
Middlesex won by five runs.

MIDDLESEX

Mr B.D.Carris	b Nichols 53	lbw b Nichols 5
J.D.B.Robertson	lbw b Nichols 50	b Farnes 8
W.J.Edrich	b Nichols 3	b Farnes 26
D.C.S.Compton	c & b R.Smith 12	b Nichols 8
Mr F.G.Mann	c Wilcox b Nichols.......46	lbw b Farnes 9
G.E.Hart	c Taylor b Farnes.........7	c Avery b P.Smith 34
†W.F.F.Price	c & b R.Smith 10	c Wade b R.Smith 55
J.M.Sims	c & b P.Smith 17	b R.Smith 17
C.I.J.Smith	c R.Smith b Farnes 5	c R.Smith b P.Smith 9
*Mr I.A.R.Peebles	c Stephenson b Farnes 3	b P.Smith 0
L.H.Gray	not out 0	not out 1
Extras	(LB 8, NB 1) 9	(B 5, LB 6) 11
Total	**183**	**215**

Fall: 1st inns 1/69, 2/88, 3/102, 4/121, 5/166, 6/186, 7/203, 8/208, 9/213.
2nd inns 1/11, 2/15, 3/25, 4/60, 5/61, 6/123, 7/162, 8/181, 9/181.

ESSEX

L.C.Eastman	lbw b Smith 2	(11)lbw b Smith..............4
A.V.Avery	c Edrich b Smith 21	(1) lbw b Sims 11
*Mr D.R.Wilcox	c Edrich b Gray 0	(6) c Price b Sims 33
J.O'Connor	b Gray 20	c Carris b Sims 4
T.P.B.Smith	b Gray 12	(7) c Edrich b Sims 2
M.S.Nichols	c Price b Gray 6	(5) c Price b Peebles 52
R.H.Taylor	lbw b Smith 42	(3) c Price b Simms 0
Capt J.W.A.Stephenson	c Price b Sims 40	st Price b Sims 10
R.Smith	b Smith 0	not out 34
†T.H.Wade	c Price b Smith 28	(2) c Gray b Sims 24
Mr K.Farnes	not out 8	(11) c Carris b Sims 8
Extras	(B 12, NB 5) 17	(B 8, W 1, NB 6) 15
Total	**196**	**197**

Fall: 1st inns 1/13, 2/14, 3/47, 4/51, 5/63, 6/74, 7/151, 8/151, 9/176.
2nd inns 1/23, 2/23, 3/35, 4/78, 5/136, 6/139, 7/144, 8/158, 9/182.

ESSEX	O	M	R	W	O	M	R	W
Farnes	16.5	2	62	3	15	3	59	3
Nichols	19	1	102	4	11	0	53	2
R.Smith	6	1	22	2	4	0	28	2
Stephenson	3	1	3	0				
T.P.B.Smith	4	1	17	1	7.5	0	32	3

MIDDLESEX	O	M	R	W	O	M	R	W
Smith	21.4	4	48	5	16.4	0	71	1
Gray	23	2	74	4	3	0	16	0
Sims	6	1	23	1	21	1	62	8
Peebles	10	3	34	0	10	4	22	1
Robertson	-	-	-	-	6	2	11	0

Umpires: A.Dolphin and G.M.Lee.

Close of play scores. First day: Essex 146/6 (R.H.Taylor 39*, J.W.A.Stephenson 32*). **Second day:** Essex 137/5 (D.R.Wilcox 32*, T.P.B.Smith 0*).
Comments: Southend cricket week.
L.C.Eastman's benefit match. He received almost £600 from the match.
J.D.M.Robertson retired hurt in the 1st innings, resuming at the fall of the 4th wicket.
M.S.Nichols, for the fifth year in succession, became the first player to complete the double of 1,000 runs and 100 wickets, when he dismissed F.G.Mann in the Middlesex 1st innings. It was the eighth occasion he had achieved this feat.
On the third day, Essex required 66 runs to win with five wickets in hand but still needed another 21 when the 9th wicket fell.
L.C.Eastman, lamed by water on the knee, came in as the number 11 with K.Farnes as his runner.
Receipts for Eastman's benefit yielded nearly £600.

GLOUCESTERSHIRE v DERBYSHIRE

Played at Cheltenham, August 16, 17, 18, 1939.
Toss won by Derbyshire.
Derbyshire won by one run.

DERBYSHIRE

D.Smith	lbw b Barnett 30	b Lambert	8
A.F.Townsend	c Crapp b Lambert 1	c Wilson b Lambert	5
A.E.Alderman	lbw b Scott 3	b Scott	2
T.S.Worthington	c Hammond b Lambert 31	lbw b Lambert	13
G.H.Pope	b Scott 29	(6) b Scott	57
A.E.G.Rhodes	c Barnett b Lambert 45	(7) b Scott	0
A.V.Pope	c Goddard b Lambert 7	(8) c Wilson b Lambert	9
*Mr T.D.Hounsfield	c Wilson b Scott 36	(9) c Crapp b Scott	4
†H.Elliott	not out 10	(10) not out	9
T.B.Mitchell	lbw b Scott 0	(5) c Barnett b Lambert	11
W.H.Copson	run out 0	c Crapp b Lambert	23
Extras	(LB 1) 1	(B 2, LB 5)	7
Total	**193**		**148**

Fall: 1st inns 1/10, 2/15, 3/55, 4/86, 5/96, 6/117, 7/152, 8/192, 9/192.
2nd inns 1/12, 2/15, 3/17, 4/39, 5/44, 6/48, 7/65, 8/81, 9/123.

GLOUCESTERSHIRE

C.J.Barnett	c Alderman b Copson....24	c G.H.Pope b A.V.Pope...16	
G.M.Emmett	c Hounsfield b Copson 13	b Mitchell	58
W.L.Neale	b A.V.Pope 0	(7) c Smith b Mitchell	27
*Mr W.R.Hammond	lbw b A.V.Pope 10	c Hounsfield b Rhodes....87	
J.F.Crapp	b Copson 6	c Alderman b G.H.Pope	40
Mr A.H.Brodhurst	c Copson 0	b Rhodes	0
R.A.Sinfield	not out 19	(3) b Mitchell	5
†E.A.Wilson	c Copson 1	c & b Mitchell	1
C.J.Scott	b A.V.Pope 0	c & b Mitchell	4
T.W.J.Goddard	c Hounsfield b A.V.Pope 3	c Townsend b Copson	4
G.E.E.Lambert	b A.V.Pope 2	not out	1
Extras	(LB 3) 3	(B 12, LB 4)	16
Total	**81**		**259**

Fall: 1st inns 1/23, 2/24, 3/48, 4/52, 5/52, 6/63, 7/65, 8/66, 9/76.
2nd inns 1/26, 2/44, 3/125, 4/199, 5/199, 6/246, 7/247, 8/253, 9/257.

GLOUCESTERSHIRE	O	M	R	W	O	M	R	W
Scott	16	3	68	4	17	2	52	4
Lambert	16.3	1	79	4	14.2	1	69	6
Barnett	5	1	8	1	1	1	0	0
Goddard	8	0	32	0	5	1	20	0
Sinfield	2	0	5	0				

DERBYSHIRE	O	M	R	W	O	M	R	W
Copson	13	1	45	5	17	1	74	1
A.V.Pope	13.3	4	25	6	13	1	25	1
G.H.Pope	1	0	8	0	12	1	38	1
Mitchell	-	-	-	-	20.5	2	75	5
Rhodes	-	-	-	-	10	1	31	2

Umpires: H.Elliott and E.J.Smith.

Close of play scores. First day: Derbyshire 29/3 (T.S.Worthington 9*). **Second day:** Gloucestershire 247/7 (W.L.Neale 24*).

Comments: Cheltenham Cricket Festival
On the first day 23 wickets fell for 303 runs.
Gloucestershire claimed the extra half-hour on the second day, requiring 39 to win with five wickets in hand. At the close they were still 14 short with three wickets remaining.
The last pair at the wicket, W.L.Neale and G.E.E.Lambert, required four runs to win but failed by one run to secure victory for the home side.
C.J.Scott took his 100th wicket of the season.

LANCASHIRE v GLAMORGAN

Played at Preston, August 16, 17, 18, 1939.
Toss won by Glamorgan.
Lancashire won by ten wickets.

GLAMORGAN

A.H.Dyson	run out 41	c Lister b Roberts	19
D.E.Davies	lbw b Pollard............22	c & b Phillipson	43
E.C.Jones	c Place b Pollard 1	st Farrimond b Roberts	0
T.L.Brierley	c Iddon b Phillipson 8	c Pollard b Phillipson	45
*Mr M.J.L.Turnbull	c Place b Pollard 17	b Pollard	4
C.C.Smart	b Pollard 20	b Phillipson	2
D.Davies	not out 37	c & b Phillipson	1
Mr G.Evans	c Paynter b Pollard........0	c Paynter b Pollard	17
†H.G.Davies	c Paynter b Pollard........3	b Pollard	1
A.D.G.Matthews	c Lister b Roberts 12	not out	0
P.F.Judge	st Farrimond b Roberts 0	absent hurt	0
Extras	(B 1, LB 4, NB 10) 15	(B 2, LB 2, W 1, NB 2)	7
Total	**176**		**139**

Fall: 1st inns 1/48, 2/55, 3/77, 4/81, 5/110, 6/119, 7/119, 8/132, 9/176.
2nd inns 1/44, 2/56, 3/72, 4/79, 5/84, 6/90, 7/133, 8/139, 9/139.

LANCASHIRE

C.Washbrook	lbw b Matthews 1	not out	1
E.Paynter	c H.Davies b Matthews 12	not out	31
W.Place	st H.Davies b Judge 3		
N.Oldfield	lbw b Judge 31		
J.Iddon	c H.Davies b Evans 23		
W.E.Phillipson	lbw b E.Davies 113		
*Mr W.H.L.Lister	c Evans b Smart 53		
†W.Farrimond	b Judge 12		
R.G.Garlick	c D.Davies b Judge 3		
R.Pollard	b Judge 0		
W.B.Roberts	not out 18		
Extras	(B 10, LB 4, W 1)........15		
Total	**284**	(No wicket)	**32**

Fall: 1st inns 1/5, 2/8, 3/28, 4/61, 5/95, 6/175, 7/207, 8/215, 9/215.

LANCASHIRE	O	M	R	W	O	M	R	W
Phillipson	21	8	48	1	15	5	19	4
Pollard	17	5	34	6	15.2	1	53	3
Garlick	17	3	41	0	13	3	32	0
Roberts	16.3	1	38	2	17	9	18	2
Paynter	-	-	-	-	5	2	10	0

GLAMORGAN	O	M	R	W	O	M	R	W
Matthews	26	3	83	2				
Judge	19.6	1	61	5				
Evans	14	1	46	1				
Smart	14	2	49	1				
E.Davies	5.1	1	30	1				
Turnbull	-	-	-	-	1	0	21	0
Brierley	-	-	-	-	1	0	11	0

Umpires: H.W.Lee and C.N.Woolley.

Close of play scores. First day: Lancashire 78/4 (N.Oldfield 24*, W.E.Phillipson 8*). **Second day:** Glamorgan 72/2 (D.E.Davies 43*, T.L.Brierley 5*).

Comments: R.Pollard performed the hat-trick in Glamorgan's 1st innings, dismissing C.C.Smart, M.J.L.Turnbull and G.Evans with successive deliveries. It was the first by a Lancashire bowler against Glamorgan. W.E.Phillipson made 113 (which included six 4's), the highest score of his career. On the third day, after Glamorgan lost their last 7 wickets for 67 runs, with P.F.Judge unable to bat, Lancashire hit the 32 runs required to win off two overs.
Glamorgan had four injured players, two Lancashire players, J.L.Hopwood and R.G.Garlick acting as substitute fielders in the 2nd innings.

GLOUCESTERSHIRE COUNTY CRICKET CLUB

Standing (left to right): G.M.Emmett, V.J.Hopkins, C.J.Scott, R.W.Haynes, G.E.E.Lambert, E.A.Wilson. Seated: T.W.J.Goddard, B.O.Allen, R.A.Sinfield, W.L.Neale. Absent is W.R.Hammond, who missed several games through Test and other representative cricket. In his absence, the side was led by B.O.Allen.

NOTTINGHAMSHIRE v HAMPSHIRE

Played at Trent Bridge, Nottingham, August 16, 17, 18, 1939.
Toss won by Hampshire.
Nottinghamshire won by an innings and 97 runs.

HAMPSHIRE

†N.T.McCorkell	run out	2	c Meads b Voce	2
P.A.Mackenzie	lbw b Heane	58	c Voce b Butler	8
D.F.Walker	st Meads b Heane	147	b Voce	2
J.Arnold	c Meads b Butler	26	b Butler	27
W.L.C.Creese	lbw b Heane	5	c Meads b Heane	25
Mr R.B.Proud	b Heane	20	b Butler	1
A.E.Pothecary	lbw b Heane	3	b Butler	0
G.S.Boyes	c & b Jepson	0	lbw b Butler	0
*Mr A.E.G.Baring	b Jepson	8	c Meads b Voce	0
Mr C.H.Knott	c & b Heane	8	run out	1
G.E.M.Heath	not out	0	not out	2
Extras	(B 5, LB 11, W 1, NB 2)	19	(LB 3, NB 1)	4
Total		**296**		**72**

Fall: 1st inns 1/7, 2/164, 3/227, 4/238, 5/267, 6/274, 7/275, 8/279, 9/296.
2nd inns 1/10, 2/14, 3/14, 4/66, 5/66, 6/66, 7/66, 8/69, 9/70.

NOTTINGHAMSHIRE

W.W.Keeton	lbw b Baring	23
C.B.Harris	c Pothecary b Knott	60
*Mr G.F.H.Heane	b Mackenzie	50
J.Hardstaff	c & b Creese	159
G.V.Gunn	b Boyes	45
J.Knowles	c Baring b Knott	50
R.J.Giles	c Knott b Creese	25
W.Voce	c Baring b Knott	25
H.J.Butler	not out	15
A.Jepson	b Creese	1
†E.A.Meads	not out	3
Extras	(B 5, LB 4)	9
Total	(9 wickets, declared)	465

Fall: 1st inns 1/34, 2/122, 3/140, 4/280, 5/372, 6/418, 7/436, 8/447, 9/448.

NOTTINGHAMSHIRE	O	M	R	W	O	M	R	W
Voce	15	2	43	0	7	1	11	3
Butler	20	3	70	1	7.5	2	23	5
Jepson	15.2	5	28	2	5	0	21	0
Harris	3	0	13	0				
Gunn	3	0	29	0				
Giles	6	0	42	0				
Heane	14	2	52	6	6	1	13	1

HAMPSHIRE	O	M	R	W
Baring	15	0	72	1
Knott	26	2	127	3
Heath	12	0	61	0
Mackenzie	5	0	40	1
Boyes	17	2	74	1
Creese	25	5	82	3

Umpires: W.Reeves and A.Skelding.

Close of play scores. First day: Nottinghamshire 22/0 (W.W.Keeton 12*, C.B.Harris 10*). **Second day:** Nottinghamshire 465/9 (H.J.Butler 15*, E.A.Meads 3*).

Comments: D.F.Walker's 147 was his highest score for Hampshire. He hit 20 4's. He and P.A.MacKenzie added 157 for the 2nd wicket.
J.Hardstaff hit 22 4's in his 159 made in 210 minutes.
He and G.V.Gunn added 140 for the 4th wicket.
G.V.Gunn completed his 1,000 runs for the season.
H.J.Butler performed the hat-trick in Hampshire's 2nd innings. His victims were J.Arnold, A.E.Potecary and G.S.Boyes in a spell of four wickets for six runs. It was his third hat-trick.
Hampshire were dismissed in the pre-lunch session of the third day.

SOMERSET v SURREY

Played at Weston-super-Mare, August 16, 17, 18, 1939.
Toss won by Surrey.
Surrey won by ten wickets.

SURREY

R.J.Gregory	b Buse	74	not out	21
L.B.Fishlock	b Andrews	1	not out	26
E.W.Whitfield	lbw b Buse	0		
H.S.Squires	b Gimblett	40		
J.F.Parker	c Longrigg b Andrews	76		
†G.S.Mobey	lbw b Hazell	9		
Mr F.R.Brown	c McRae b Meyer	50		
*Mr H.M.Garland-Wells	b Buse	64		
Mr P.J.Dickinson	c Burrough b Buse	6		
E.A.Watts	c Buse b Andrews	29		
A.R.Gover	not out	41		
Extras	(B 5, LB 17, W 1, NB 1)	24	(LB 1)	1
Total		**414**	(No wicket)	**48**

Fall: 1st inns 1/13, 2/14, 3/85 4/161, 5/202, 6/220, 7/299, 8/328, 9/352.

SOMERSET

F.S.Lee	b Brown	53	b Watts	6
H.Gimblett	lbw b Gover	6	c Fishlock b Watts	79
H.T.F.Buse	c Gregory b Brown	11	b Watts	5
Mr R.J.O.Meyer	c Watts b Brown	7	b Gover	34
Mr H.D.Burrough	c Gover b Brown	16	c Mobey b Gover	0
Mr F.M.McRae	c Mobey b Gover	9	b Watts	94
*Mr E.F.Longrigg	c Garland-Wells b Brown	20	c Gregory b Watts	27
Mr R.A.Ingle	c Gregory b Brown	3	c Watts b Gover	2
†W.T.Luckes	lbw b Brown	6	c Mobey b Brown	31
W.H.R.Andrews	c Garland-Wells b Brown	8	c Gregory b Brown	15
H.L.Hazell	not out	2	not out	0
Extras	(B 2, LB 4)	6	(B 11, LB 6, NB 3)	20
Total		**147**		**313**

Fall: 1st inns 1/23, 2/41, 3/55, 4/82, 5/94, 6/126, 7/127, 8/130, 9/144.
2nd inns 1/20, 2/36, 3/117, 4/137, 5/137, 6/211, 7/220, 8/287, 9/313.

SOMERSET	O	M	R	W	O	M	R	W
Andrews	18.2	1	89	3	6	1	12	0
Buse	31	2	142	4	4	1	15	0
Meyer	23	4	96	1	2	0	8	0
Gimblett	3	0	8	1				
Hazell	13	3	55	1				
Lee	-	-	-	-	7	0	12	0

SURREY	O	M	R	W	O	M	R	W
Gover	14	1	50	2	20	1	89	3
Watts	10	2	22	0	14.1	1	59	5
Parker	4	1	12	0	3	0	10	0
Brown	17.2	3	34	8	21	3	91	2
Garland-Wells	10	4	23	0				
Squires	2	2	0	0	4	1	3	0
Dickinson	-	-	-	-	3	0	17	0
Gregory					9	2	24	0

Umpires: H.Cruice and J.Hardstaff.

Close of play scores. First day: Somerset 8/0 (F.S.Lee 6*, H.Gimblett 2*). **Second day:** Somerset (2) 187/5 (F.M.Mcrae 41*, E.F.Longrigg 16*).
Comments: Somerset followed on 267 behind.
F.R.Brown achieved career best bowling figures of 8 for 34 in the 1st innings.
He took the final five wickets for 12 runs in 28 balls.

SUSSEX v LEICESTERSHIRE

Played at Hastings, August 16, 17, 1939.
Toss won by Sussex.
Sussex won by an innings and 106 runs.

SUSSEX

Mr R.G.Stainton	....b Drake	45
John G.Langridge	...c Packe b Sperry	202
H.W.Parks	..........c Dawkes b Armstrong	28
G.Cox	...........b Packe b Drake	49
Jas.Langridge	........c Packe b Knew	80
J.H.Parks	...........not out	72
Mr H.T.Bartlett	.....not out	9
Extras	.............(B 10, LB 1, W 5)	25
Total	...............(5 wickets, declared)	**501**

Fall: 1st inns 1/117, 2/235, 3/308, 4/336, 5/476.

*Flt-Lt A.J.Holmes, †Mr S.C.Griffith, J.K.Nye and D.J.Wood did not bat.

LEICESTERSHIRE

G.Lester	..............c Griffith b Nye 2	(7) lbw b Jas.Langridge	0
G.L.Berry	.........c Griffith b Nye 7	(1) c Jas.Langridge b J.Parks	37
N.F.Armstrong	......c Jas.Langridge b J.Parks 5	b Nye	84
G.S.Watson	.........lbw b J.Parks 0	c Holmes b Jas.Langridge	35
M.Tompkin	........lbw b Wood 19	c Stainton b John Langridge	13
*Mr M.St.J.Packe	....b J.Parks 1	b Jas.Langridge	25
†G.O.Dawkes	.......not out 61	(2) lbw b J.Parks	27
G.F.Knew	...........c Holmes b Wood 10	b Nye	18
A.R.West	...........lbw b Wood 0	run out	21
C.H.Drake	...........st Griffith b Jas.Langridge 4	b Jas.Langridge	7
J.Sperry	...........c Stainton b Jas.Langridge 1	not out	4
Extras	.............(B 4) 4	(B 3, LB 7)	10
Total	...................**114**		**281**

Fall: 1st inns 1/3, 2/14, 3/14, 4/18, 5/25, 6/71, 7/89, 8/89, 9/112.
2nd inns 1/44, 2/65, 3/129, 4/150, 5/196, 6/214, 7/240, 8/249, 9/276.

LEICESTERSHIRE	O	M	R	W
Sperry	27	5	92	1
Drake	20	3	61	2
West	22	5	130	0
Lester	11	0	71	0
Armstrong	10	0	50	1
Knew	12	0	58	1
Berry	3	0	23	0

SUSSEX	O	M	R	W	O	M	R	W
Nye	6	0	33	2	17.6	0	83	2
J.Parks	8	1	31	3	15	3	64	2
Wood	6	0	31	3	14	0	58	0
Jas.Langridge	4	0	15	2	17	1	55	4
John Langridge	-	-	-	-	4	2	9	1
Holmes	-	-	-	-	1	0	2	0

Umpires: H.G.Baldwin and E.Robinson.

Close of play scores. First day: Sussex 501/5 (J.H.Parks 72*, H.T.Bartlett 9*).

Comments: The match finished in two days.
John G.Langridge hit 30 4's in his 202. It was his second century in successive days. He batted for 225 minutes.
He shared an opening partnership of 117 with R.G.Stainton. It was the first century opening partnership for Sussex in 1939.
He also added 118 with H.W.Parks for the 2nd wicket.
Leicestershire followed on 387 behind, after being bowled out in their 1st innings in the pre-lunch session of the 2nd day.

WORCESTERSHIRE v KENT

Played at Worcester, August 16, 17, 18, 1939.
Toss won by Worcestershire.
Kent won by an innings and 109 runs.

KENT

A.E.Fagg	b Jenkins	32
*Mr F.G.H.Chalk	..c Buller b Jenkins	57
L.E.G.Ames	..........b Perks	201
Mr B.H.Valentine	...c Singleton b L Perks	113
L.J.Todd	...........c Singleton b Perks	19
Mr P.G.Foster	.......b Perks	0
D.V.P.Wright	........run out	16
N.W.Harding	..........c Buller b Howorth	3
†Mr W.H.V.Levett	....not out	25
A.E.Watt	...........b Perks	0
C.Lewis	.............c Howorth b Martin	1
Extras	..............(B 9, LB 7, W 1, NB 8)	25
Total	....	**492**

Fall: 1st inns 1/71, 2/98, 3/300, 4/331, 5/331, 6/400, 7/417, 8/484, 9/484.

WORCESTERSHIRE

R.Howorth	..........c Chalk b Wright 19	c Lewis b Wright	41
E.Cooper	..........lbw b Harding 1	c Fagg b Wright	68
Mr R.H.Human	......b Wright 15	c Levett b Lewis	9
H.H.I.Gibbons	......not out 45	st Levett b Lewis	57
Mr C.H.Palmer	......b Wright 9	b Wright	13
S.H.Martin	..........lbw b Wright 6	b Wright	4
Mr A.P.Singleton	......lbw b Wright 0	c Watt b Lewis	2
*Hon C.J.Lyttelton	c Fagg b Harding 10	lbw b Wright	8
R.O.Jenkins	..........b Lewis 23	b Lewis	6
R.T.D.Perks	.........c Valentine b Wright 3	b Wright	20
†J.S.Buller	...........b Wright 2	not out	4
Extras	.............(B 2, LB 3, NB 4) 9	(B 7, LB 1, W 1)	9
Total	...................**142**		**241**

Fall: 1st inns 1/2, 2/33, 3/40, 4/58, 5/68, 6/68, 7/82, 8/130, 9/133.
2nd inns 1/72, 2/85, 3/161, 4/187, 5/195, 6/202, 7/203, 8/217, 9/219.

WORCESTERSHIRE	O	M	R	W
Perks	19	2	75	5
Martin	24.1	3	119	1
Howorth	15	0	98	1
Singleton	14	1	67	0
Jenkins	12	0	88	2
Palmer	2	0	20	0

KENT	O	M	R	W	O	M	R	W
Wright	16.2	4	46	7	16.2	3	77	6
Harding	10	0	40	2	5	0	23	0
Lewis	7	0	30	1	22	3	77	4
Todd	4	1	9	0	3	0	23	0
Watt	4	1	8	0	15	6	32	0

Umpires: C.W.L.Parker and F.I.Walden.

Close of play scores. First day: Kent 492 all out. **Second day:** Worcestershire 186/3 (H.H.I.Gibbons 47*, C.H.Palmer 13*).

Comments. This game was in aid of C.H.Bull's testimonial.
Kent were put in to bat.
L.E.G.Ames and B.H.Valentine added 202 in 135 minutes for Kent's 3rd wicket.
L.E.G.Ames hit 25 fours in his 201. He reached his century in just under three hours.
B.H.Valentine hit 113 in 135 minutes, scoring 15 4's.
Worcestershire followed on 350 runs behind. Kent required only an hour on the third day to win the match.

YORKSHIRE v WARWICKSHIRE

Played at Scarborough, August 16, 17, 18, 1939.
Toss won by Yorkshire.
Yorkshire won by 106 runs.

YORKSHIRE

L.Hutton	c & b Santall	28	lbw b Grove	0
A.Mitchell	lbw b Grove	4	c Buckingham b Mayer	4
W.Barber	c Croom b Santall	25	b Hollies	35
M.Leyland	c & b Grove	64		
Mr N.W.D.Yardley	c Mayer b Grove	108	not out	83
C.Turner	c Buckingham b Grove	2	not out	33
*Mr A.B.Sellers	lbw b Mayer	46		
†A.Wood	run out	14		
G.Cawthray	c Wyatt b Mayer	29		
E.P.Robinson	c Shortland b Grove	57	(4) c Buckingham b Mayer	9
H.Verity	not out	15		
Extras	(B 1, LB 10)	11	(B 4, LB 3)	7
Total		**403**	(4 wickets, declared)	**171**

Fall: 1st inns 1/7, 2/58, 3/59, 4/222, 5/228, 6/253, 7/286, 8/317, 9/340.
2nd inns 1/0, 2/20, 3/34, 4/85.

WARWICKSHIRE

A.J.W.Croom	c Turner b Verity	31	lbw b Robinson	56
W.A.Hill	lbw b Verity	22	b Robinson	40
F.R.Santall	c & b Cawthray	32	lbw b Hutton	2
Mr R.E.S.Wyatt	c Sellers b Verity	12	b Verity	138
H.E.Dollery	not out	38	c Wood b Hutton	8
N.A.Shortland	b Verity	0	st Wood b Robinson	4
†J.Buckingham	run out	10	lbw b Robinson	6
*Mr P.Cranmer	c sub b Hutton	4	c & b Hutton	16
C.W.Grove	c & b Verity	0	b Hutton	0
J.H.Mayer	lbw b Verity	0	c Verity b Hutton	8
W.E.Hollies	st Wood b Verity	2	not out	15
Extras	(LB 7)	7	(B 2, LB 15)	17
Total		**158**		**310**

Fall: 1st inns 1/38, 2/87, 3/92, 4/126, 5/127, 6/144, 7/151, 8/152, 9/152.
2nd inns 1/73, 2/81, 3/144, 4/163, 5/170, 6/196, 7/222, 8/222, 9/238.

WARWICKSHIRE	O	M	R	W	O	M	R	W
Mayer	23	2	99	2	6	2	22	2
Grove	16.1	0	102	5	4	0	17	1
Wyatt	12	1	70	0	10	2	44	0
Santall	7	0	33	2	3	0	15	0
Hollies	19	2	88	0	10	0	66	0

YORKSHIRE	O	M	R	W	O	M	R	W
Cawthray	11	1	37	1	15	4	48	0
Yardley	2	0	8	0	4	3	2	0
Turner	6	2	28	0	6	2	7	0
Verity	19.2	8	35	7	31.3	11	61	1
Robinson	6	2	11	0	32	6	85	4
Hutton	11	1	32	1	26	9	70	5
Sellers	-	-	-	-	4	1	20	0

Umpires: J.A.Newman and E.Cooke.

Close of play scores. First day: Warwickshire 50/1 (A.J.W.Croom 24*, F.R.Santall 1*). **Second day:** Warwickshire 113/2 (A.J.W.Croom 46*, R.E.S.Wyatt 16*).

Comments: M.Leyland and N.W.D.Yardley added 173 in 120 minutes for Yorkshire's 4th wicket.
N.W.D.Yardley's 108 included 18 4's. Altogether in the match he hit one 6 and 31 4's.
On the second day, Warwickshire lost nine wickets for 108 runs in 135 minutes. Yorkshire did not enforce the follow-on, eventually setting Warwickshire 417 to win. R.E.S.Wyatt batted nearly five hours for his 138, which included 15 4's in the 2nd innings. He scored 122 out of the 197 runs made on the third day, adding 72 for the last wicket with W.E.Hollies in 80 minutes. The first-day crowd of 15,000 was a Scarborough record. It was Yorkshire's fifth consecutive victory. G.Cawthray was making his debut for Yorkshire.

DERBYSHIRE v NOTTINGHAMSHIRE

Played at Rutland Ground, Ilkeston, August 19, 21, 22, 1939.
Toss won by Derbyshire.
Derbyshire won by 147 runs.

DERBYSHIRE

D.Smith	run out	44	c Wheat b Butler	35
A.F.Townsend	c Wheat b Butler	10	c & b Heane	23
A.E.Alderman	b Boce	26	lbw b Heane	0
T.S.Worthington	c Heane b Voce	0	c Wheat b Jepson	29
G.H.Pope	c Jones b Heane	121	b Butler	31
A.E.G.Rhodes	c Harris b Butler	8	c Jones b Butler	2
A.V.Pope	b Voce	43	c Butler b Voce	6
*Mr T.D.Hounsfield	b Heane	11	lbw b Heane b Voce	0
†H.Elliott	c Jepson b Heane	25	not out	10
T.B.Mitchell	c & b Heane	7	c Gunn b Voce	0
W.H.Copson	not out	14	b Voce	4
Extras	(B 4, LB 3, NB 3)	10	(B 2, LB 5, W 1)	8
Total		**319**		**148**

Fall: 1st inns 1/26, 2/65, 3/66, 4/102, 5/117, 6/225, 7/247, 8/290, 9/302.
2nd inns 1/52, 2/57, 3/74, 4/114, 5/125, 6/130, 7/131, 8/144, 9/144.

NOTTINGHAMSHIRE

C.B.Harris	c Elliott b Copson	26	c Worthington b A.V.Pope	3
D.Jones	lbw b Mitchell	41	c G.H.Pope b A.V.Pope	0
F.H.Winrow	c Alderman b A.V.Pope	6	(5) c Alderman b G.H.Pope	5
*Mr G.F.H.Heane	c G.H.Pope b Mitchell	16	(3) c Mitchell b Copson	22
G.V.Gunn	st Elliott b Mitchell	23	(4) c Elliott b Rhodes	12
J.Knowles	c Elliott b Rhodes	7	b G.H.Pope	1
R.J.Giles	st Elliott b Mitchell	37	c Copson b Mitchell	40
W.Voce	c Smith b Rhodes	2	b G.H.Pope	1
†A.B.Wheat	c Elliott b Rhodes	0	c Elliott b Mitchell	7
H.J.Butler	c Smith b Copson	18	not out	39
A.Jepson	not out	1	b G.H.Pope	0
Extras	(B 1, LB 6, NB 1)	8	(B 2, LB 3)	5
Total		**185**		**135**

Fall: 1st inns 1/56, 2/65, 3/85, 4/104, 5/126, 6/128, 7/132, 8/132, 9/183.
2nd inns 1/0, 2/7, 3/31, 4/42, 5/44, 6/46, 7/47, 8/64, 9/127.

NOTTINGHAMSHIRE	O	M	R	W	O	M	R	W
Voce	21	2	90	3	14	2	41	4
Butler	21	3	59	2	10	0	46	3
Jepson	19	5	59	0	8	0	25	1
Heane	17.4	4	64	4	8	2	28	2
Giles	3	0	18	0				
Harris	5	0	19	0				

DERBYSHIRE	O	M	R	W	O	M	R	W
Copson	18.7	3	40	2	10	2	22	1
A.V.Pope	14	2	34	1	7	2	17	2
G.H.Pope	8	2	16	0	11.4	5	21	4
Rhodes	6	1	14	3	3	1	6	1
Mitchell	14	1	73	4	6	0	64	2

Umpires: A.Skelding and C.N.Woolley.

Close of play scores. First day: Nottinghamshire 15/0 (C.B.Harris 7*, D.Jones 4*). **Second day:** Derbyshire 112/3 (T.S.Worthington 28*, G.H.Pope 18*).

Comments: G.H.Pope scored his first century since 1937. His 121, made in 240 minutes, included one 6 and 17 4's.
He and A.V.Pope put on 108 for the 6th wicket in 100 minutes, their first century partnership together.
On the third day 17 wickets fell for 171 runs in less than three and a half hours. W.Voce dismissed A.V.Pope, T.B.Mitchell and W.H.Copson in his final over to end the Derbyshire 2nd innings. His last ten balls yielded four wickets for eight runs.

GLAMORGAN v NORTHAMPTONSHIRE

Played at Cardiff, August 19, 21, 22, 1939.
Toss won by Northamptonshire.
Match drawn.

NORTHAMPTONSHIRE

*Mr E.J.H.Dixon	c H.Davies b Jones	88	b Matthews	11
C.P.Davis	lbw b Smart	18	b Matthews	9
D.Brookes	c H.Davies b Evans	5	b Matthews	4
J.E.Timms	lbw b E.Davies	45	b Watkins	15
F.P.O'Brien	c & b Smart	90	c D.Davies b Jones	36
†K.C.James	st H.Davies b Jones	59	(7) b Matthews	27
W.E.Merritt	c Jones b Smart	41	(6) run out	34
Mr S.I.Philips	not out	8	not out	8
R.J.Partridge	not out	1		
V.Broderick	(did not bat)		b Matthews	0
Extras	(B 8, W 2, NB 4)	14	(B 5, LB 7)	12
Total	**(7 wickets, declared)**	**369**	**(8 wickets, declared)**	**156**

Fall: 1st inns 1/41, 2/49, 3/147, 4/186, 5/300, 6/360, 7/363.
2nd inns 1/18, 2/26, 3/39, 4/55, 5/115, 6/124, 7/156, 8/156.

A.Robinson did not bat.

GLAMORGAN

A.H.Dyson	c Robinson b Merritt	19	(8) not out	7
D.E.Davies	c James b Robinson	4	(1) c Dixon b Partridge	85
T.L.Brierley	b Partridge	2	(2) b Partridge	4
*Mr M.J.L.Turnbull	c O'Brien b Robinson	37	(3) c James b Partridge	41
E.C.Jones	c Timms b Broderick	10		
C.C.Smart	c Timms b Merritt	79	(4) c O'Brien b Timms	12
D.Davies	run out	42	c Brookes b Robinson	0
Mr G.Evans	c James b Broderick	1	(6) run out	22
†H.G.Davies	c James b Merritt	68	(5) c James b Robinson	28
A.J.Watkins	not out	23		
A.D.G.Matthews	lbw b Merritt	5		
Extras	(B 4, LB 2)	6	(B 9, LB 10, W 4)	23
Total		**296**	**(7 wickets)**	**222**

Fall: 1st inns 1/8, 2/11, 3/55, 4/69, 5/87, 6/194, 7/195, 8/201, 9/288.
2nd inns 1/23, 2/129, 3/152, 4/172, 5/200, 6/200, 7/222.

GLAMORGAN	O	M	R	W	O	M	R	W
Matthews	22	3	87	0	13.5	2	37	5
Evans	19	1	64	1	5	1	17	0
Watkins	15	0	47	0	6	0	34	1
Smart	17	2	56	3	4	0	23	0
D.E.Davies	7	1	36	1	9	1	24	0
Jones	14	3	56	2	4	1	9	1
D.Davies	2	0	9	0				

NORTHANTS	O	M	R	W	O	M	R	W
Partridge	17	3	48	2	12	2	61	3
Robinson	12	2	43	2	9.2	1	60	2
Merritt	22.4	1	122	4				
Broderick	3	0	46	1				
Timms	6	0	31	0	9	0	78	1

Umpires: E.J.Smith and H.Elliott.

Close of play scores. First day: Northants 305/5 (F.P.O'Brien 74*, W.E.Merritt 3*). **Second day:** Northants 6/0 (E.J.H.Dixon 2*, C.P.Davis 4*).

Comments: E.J.H.Dixon captained Northants for the first time.
L.P.O'Brien and K.C.James added 114 for the 5th wicket in 90 minutes.
D.Davies and C.C.Smart put on 107 in 80 minutes for the 6th wicket (1st innings).
D.E.Davies and M.J.L.Turnbull put on 106 for the 2nd wicket in 60 minutes after Glamorgan had been set 230 to win in 135 minutes.
Ten runs were need off the final over but with G.Evans run out off the second ball, there was no time for another man to bat.
H.G.Davies achieved a new record of dismissals by a wicketkeeper for Glamorgan, his 64 passing Brierley's 62 of 1936.

GLOUCESTERSHIRE v MIDDLESEX

Played at Cheltenham, August 19, 21, 22, 1939.
Toss won by Gloucestershire.
Gloucestershire won by 186 runs.

GLOUCESTERSHIRE

C.J.Barnett	lbw b Peebles	47	lbw b Smith	45
G.M.Emmett	c price b Smith	0	(3) c Edrich b Peebles	3
W.L.Neale	c Edrich b Peebles	26	(4) c Price b Peebles	76
J.F.Crapp	c Smith b Sims	76	(5) st Price b Sims	101
V.Hopkins	lbw b Sims	9	(6) lbw b Smith	5
R.A.Sinfield	b Sims	7	(7) retired hurt	11
*Mr B.H.Lyon	b Sims	1	(2) c Collinson b Peebles	44
†E.A.Wilson	not out	26	not out	19
C.J.Scott	lbw b Sims	2	c Price b Smith	0
L.M.Cranfield	c Edrich b Sims	0	not out	17
G.E.E.Lambert	b Sims	9		
Extras	(B 9, LB 2)	11	(B 3, LB 1, NB 2)	6
Total		**214**	**(7 wickets, declared)**	**327**

Fall: 1st inns 1/0, 2/60, 3/89, 4/110, 5/132, 6/134, 7/195, 8/204, 9/204.
2nd inns 1/82, 2/87, 3/96, 4/273, 5/277, 6/285, 7/297.

MIDDLESEX

Mr B.D.Carris	run out	33	b Scott	1
J.D.B.Robertson	lbw b Sinfield	87	c Wilson b Lambert	5
W.J.Edrich	lbw b Sinfield	17	b Scott	4
Mr J.Collinson	c Hopkins b Scott	34	c Hopkins b Sinfield	13
Mr F.G.Mann	b Cranfield	4	st Wilson b Sinfield	27
G.E.Hart	b Scott	17	c Hopkins b Sinfield	0
†W.F.F.Price	c Hopkins b Sinfield	2	c Hopkins b Sinfield	17
J.M.Sims	b Cranfield	13	(9) st Wilson b Cranfield	23
C.I.J.Smith	b Scott	21	(8) c Neale b Sinfield	9
*Mr I.A.R.Peebles	b Sinfield	14	c Lyon b Sinfield	1
L.H.Gray	not out	2	not out	5
Extras	(B 1, LB 2)	3	(LB 3)	3
Total		**247**		**108**

Fall: 1st inns 1/46, 2/92, 3/148, 4/165, 5/188, 6/192, 7/195, 8/218, 9/245.
2nd inns 1/2, 2/10, 3/15, 4/29, 5/29, 6/55, 7/65, 8/97, 9/99.

MIDDLESEX	O	M	R	W	O	M	R	W
Smith	8	2	20	1	29	4	69	3
Gray	7	1	20	0	13	2	41	0
Sims	23.4	3	109	7	29	4	119	1
Peebles	19	4	54	2	16	1	74	3
Robertson	-	-	-	-	6	0	18	0

GLOUCESTERSHIRE	O	M	R	W	O	M	R	W
Scott	14	1	55	3	6	1	29	2
Lambert	4	0	32	0	3	1	4	1
Barnett	4	1	21	0				
Sinfield	16.4	2	78	4	7	0	48	6
Cranfield	11	0	58	2	4.3	0	24	1

Umpires: C.V.Tarbox and E.Cooke.

Close of play scores. First day: Middlesex 195/7 (J.M.Sims 0*). **Second day:** Gloucs 285/5 (V.Hopkins 5*, R.A.Sinfield 6*).

Comments: Cheltenham Festival.
J.F.Crapp scored his first century of the season in Gloucester's 2nd innings in 190 minutes. With W.L.Neale he added 177 for the 4th wicket. Middlesex were set to make 295 to win at a run a minute.

HAMPSHIRE v SOMERSET

Played at Bournemouth, August 19, 21, 22, 1939.
Toss won by Somerset.
Somerset won by an innings and 62 runs.

SOMERSET

F.S.Lee	c Arnold b Heath	22
H.Gimblett	c Walker b Boyes	83
H.T.F.Buse	c Creese b Boyes	79
Mr R.J.O.Meyer	c Baring b Heath	47
Mr T.R.Garnett	c & b Dean	30
Mr F.M.McRae	c Mackenzie b Creese	96
W.H.R.Andrews	run out	50
*Mr R.A.Ingle	b Heath	22
Mr H.E.Watts	not out	7
Extras	(B 6, LB 6, NB 5)	17
Total	(8 wickets, declared)	**453**

Fall: 1st inns 1/31, 2/138, 3/212, 4/252, 5/287, 6/382, 7/482, 8/453.

†W.T.Luckes and H.L.Hazell did not bat.

HAMPSHIRE

†N.T.McCorkell	c Hazell b Andrews	2	c Watts b Buse	107
P.A.Mackenzie	c Buse b Hazell	23	c Luckes b Meyer	26
D.F.Walker	c & b Buse	1	c Watts b Meyer	13
J.Arnold	c Garnett b Hazell	29	c Lee b Meyer	6
W.L.C.Creese	lbw b Hazell	15	c Watts b Buse	10
A.E.Pothecary	lbw b Hazell	5	c Meyer b Buse	5
G.Hill	st Luckes b Hazell	6	c Buse b Meyer	14
G.S.Boyes	c Gimblett b Hazell	0	lbw b Meyer	18
*Mr A.E.G.Baring	c Garnett b Andrews	46	c Hazell b Andrews	2
T.A.Dean	not out	20	not out	8
G.E.M.Heath	c Garnett b Buse	6	b Meyer	1
Extras	(B 5, LB 3)	8	(B 13, LB 5, NB 2)	20
Total		**161**		**230**

Fall: 1st inns 1/2, 2/3, 3/49, 4/73, 5/79, 6/80, 7/80, 8/87, 9/139.
2nd inns 1/96, 2/120, 3/141, 4/165, 5/170, 6/173, 7/206, 8/211, 9/215.

HAMPSHIRE	O	M	R	W
Baring	25	4	105	0
Heath	26	4	79	3
Hill	13	0	59	0
Dean	14	0	90	1
Creese	16.2	1	57	1
Boyes	12	2	46	2

SOMERSET	O	M	R	W	O	M	R	W
Andrews	11	2	35	2	18	3	85	1
Buse	6.4	1	12	2	22	3	51	3
Hazell	22	4	60	6	13	2	26	0
Meyer	11	1	46	0	19	7	48	6

Umpires: C.C.Smart and H.Cruice.

Close of play scores. First day: Somerset 381/5 (F.M.McRae 55*, W.H.R.Andrews 49*). **Second day:** Hampshire 77/0 (N.T.McCorkell 53*, P.A.MacKenzie 22*).

Comments: H.Gimblett and H.T.F.Buse added 107 for the 2nd wicket.
H.L.Hazell took the first six Hampshire wickets to fall for 33 runs.
Hampshire followed on 292 behind.
N.T.McCorkell scored his first century of the season. His 107 included 14 4's in an innings lasting 205 minutes.

LANCASHIRE v KENT

Played at Old Trafford, Manchester, August 19, 21, 22, 1939.
Toss won by Kent.
Lancashire won by four wickets.

KENT

A.E.Fagg	c Washbrook b Phillipson	15	c Farrimond b Phillipson	13
*Mr F.G.H.Chalk	c Farrimond b Phillipson	8	c Pollard b Phillipson	0
L.E.G.Ames	c Ikin b Phillipson	108	c Pollard b Phillipson	0
Mr B.H.Valentine	b Pollard	52	b Pollard	119
Mr P.G.Foster	b Pollard	1	c Pollard b Phillipson	10
L.J.Todd	b Phillipson	0	c Place b Ikin	59
T.G.Evans	lbw b Brocklebank	2	(8) c & b Pollard	22
†Mr W.H.V.Levett	c Place b Phillipson	20	(7) c Place b Phillipson	11
N.W.Harding	c Place b Phillipson	1	c Place b Phillipson	5
A.E.Watt	b Pollard	1	absent hurt	0
C.Lewis	not out	0	(10) not out	0
Extras	(B 4, NB 3)	7	(B 2, LB 7, W 1, NB 5)	15
Total		**215**		**254**

Fall: 1st inns 1/16, 2/34, 3/145, 4/155, 5/156, 6/173, 7/203, 8/212, 9/215.
2nd inns 1/0, 2/0, 3/17, 4/38, 5/174, 6/211, 7/245, 8/250, 9/254.

LANCASHIRE

C.Washbrook	c Levett b Harding	79	c Levett b Todd	38
E.Paynter	c Valentine b Todd	14	b Todd	12
W.Place	c Fagg b Lewis	22	c Foster b Ames	86
J.T.Ikin	c Levett b Todd	5	c Harding b Lewis	30
J.Iddon	not out	73	not out	39
W.E.Phillipson	b Harding	28	run out	0
*Mr W.H.L.Lister	c Levett b Harding	0	c Lewis b Todd	2
†W.Farrimond	c Levett b Harding	13	not out	7
R.Pollard	c Ames b Lewis	2		
W.B.Roberts	c Levett b Harding	0		
Mr J.M.Brocklebank	run out	1		
Extras	(B 7, LB 5, NB 3)	15	(LB 1, NB 3)	4
Total		**252**	(6 wickets)	**218**

Fall: 1st inns 1/21, 2/78, 3/83, 4/170, 5/211, 6/211, 7/238, 8/247, 9/247.
2nd inns 1/76, 2/98, 3/163, 4/187, 5/188, 6/201.

LANCASHIRE	O	M	R	W	O	M	R	W
Phillipson	14	0	70	6	21	2	76	6
Pollard	11.1	2	32	3	15.4	1	87	2
Roberts	9	0	18	0	5	1	31	0
Brocklebank	11	0	62	1	6	0	20	0
Ikin	4	0	19	0	5	2	15	1
Iddon	2	0	7	0				
Paynter	-	-	-	-	4	1	10	0

KENT	O	M	R	W	O	M	R	W
Harding	23	0	100	5	14.5	0	86	0
Todd	23	2	76	2	15	0	46	3
Watt	2	0	6	0				
Lewis	14	2	55	2	11	0	48	1
Ames	-	-	-	-	9	0	34	1

Umpires: J.A.Newman and F.I.Walden.

Close of play scores. First day: Lancashire 149/3 (C.Washbrook 72*, J.Iddon 27*). **Second day:** Kent 180/5 (B.H.Valentine 86*, W.H.V.Levett 1*).

Comments: L.E.G.Ames made 108 in 170 minutes out of 187. He hit nine 4's. In doing so, he completed the sequence of scoring a century against every first-class county. His first was against Hampshire in 1927.
He and B.H.Valentine added 111 for the 3rd wicket in 80 minutes.
B.H.Valentine's 119 was his third century in consecutive matches. He hit 14 4's in an innings of 240 minutes. He and L.J.Todd added 136 for the 5th wicket in Kent's 2nd innings.

SUSSEX v WORCESTERSHIRE

Played at Eastbourne, August 19, 21, 22, 1939.
Toss won by Worcestershire.
Sussex won by eight wickets.

WORCESTERSHIRE

R.Howorth .... c Griffith b Nye 4	c Griffith b Nye 0
E.Cooper............. b Nye 0	c John Langridge b Jas.Langridge 30
B.P.King .... c Griffith b Nye 56	lbw b Nye 118
Mr C.H.Palmer ...... c Jas.Langridge b Wood 25	st Griffith b Jas.Langridge 1
H.H.I.Gibbons ...... c John Langridge b Wood 51	c Griffith b Holmes 45
S.H.Martin .... run out 60	not out 50
Mr A.P.Singleton.... lbw b J.Parks 61	c Griffith b Nye 33
R.O.Jenkins .... b Wood 48	
*Hon C.J.Lyttelton c Hammond b J.Parks ...33	(8) not out 12
†J.S.Buller .... not out 19	
P.F.Jackson .... c & b Jas.Langridge 8	
Extras............. (B 1, LB 2, NB 4) 7	(LB 5, NB 8) 13
Total **372**	(6 wickets, declared)......**302**

Fall: 1st inns 1/4, 2/5, 3/54, 4/132, 5/142, 6/247, 7/281, 8/336, 9/351.
2nd inns 1/1, 2/82, 3/89, 4/196, 5/207, 6/280.

SUSSEX

Mr R.G.Stainton .... c & b Howorth 37	c sub b Martin 27
John G.Langridge... st Buller b Jenkins 48	c Buller b Singleton 65
G.Cox .... lbw b Jenkins 17	not out 44
*Flt-Lt A.J.Holmes c and Howorth 29	
Jas.Langridge....... lbw b Howorth 43	
J.H.Parks .... not out 115	
Mr H.T.Bartlett ..... c Palmer b Martin 89	(4) not out 59
†Mr S.C.Griffith..... lbw b Jenkins 2	
H.E.Hammond .... c Lyttelton b Jenkins ...14	
J.K.Nye .... b Jackson 55	
D.J.Wood .... not out 19	
Extras............. (LB 6, NB 1) 7	(LB 5) 5
Total .... (9 wickets, declared) **475**	(2 wickets) **200**

Fall: 1st inns 1/73, 2/99, 3/105, 4/150, 5/213, 6/332, 7/337, 8/357, 9/448.
2nd inns 1/58, 2/124.

SUSSEX	O	M	R	W	O	M	R	W
Nye	23	2	98	3	19	0	98	3
Hammond	12	2	63	0	16	1	77	0
Wood	21	1	93	3	6	0	19	0
J.Parks	19	5	58	2	10	2	26	0
Jas.Langridge...........	14.2	1	40	1	19	3	54	2
John Langridge	4	0	13	0	2	0	13	0
Holmes	-	-	-	-	1	0	2	1

WORCESTERSHIRE	O	M	R	W	O	M	R	W
Martin....................	22	2	75	1	12	0	94	1
Jackson	23	2	87	1	2	0	11	0
Singleton................	4	0	22	0	8	0	62	1
Jenkins	24	1	161	4	2	0	28	0
Howorth	26	1	123	3				

Umpires: H.G.Baldwin and A.Dolphin.

Close of play scores. First day: Sussex 25/0 (R.G.Stainton 15*, John G.Langridge 10*). **Second day:** Worcestershire 53/1 (E.Cooper 20*, B.P.King 31*).

Comments: Eastbourne Festival match.
S.H.Martin and A.P.Singleton added 105 for the 6th wicket.
In the Sussex 1st innings, H.T.Bartlett scored his 89 in 44 minutes, hitting four 6's and 11 4's.
J.H.Parks hit his first century of the season, making an undefeated 115. It took 180 minutes and included 14 4's.
B.P.King hit 17 4's in his 118 in Worcester's 2nd innings. He and H.H.I.Gibbons put on 107 for the 4th wicket. Sussex knocked off their target of 200 in less than 100 minutes, having been set to make 200 in 105 minutes. John G.Langridge reached 2,000 runs for the season on 48 in Sussex's 2nd innings.
H.T.Bartlett again scored at a rapid rate, his undefeated 59 coming in 30 minutes out of the last 76 runs scored. He had scored 148 in the match in 74 minutes.
J.K.Nye scored his first 50 for Sussex, also taking a 100 wickets in a season for the first time.

WARWICKSHIRE v SURREY

Played at Edgbaston, Birmingham, August 19, 21, 22, 1939
Toss won by Surrey.
Surrey won by an innings and one run.

SURREY

R.J.Gregory.......... c Croom b Wyatt 30
L.B.Fishlock .... c Buckingham b Croom 91
E.W.Whitfield .... c Wyatt b Hollies..........7
H.S.Squires .... lbw b Hollies............29
J.F.Parker .... b Hollies................28
Mr F.R.Brown .... lbw b Mayer 46
†G.S.Mobey .... not out 55
*Mr H.M.Garland- Wells .... c Cranmer b Wyatt.......17
Mr P.J.Dickinson.... c Croom b Hollies........2
E.A.Watts .... st Buckingham b Croom 21
A.R.Gover .... b Croom 0
Extras............. (B 3, LB 7)...............10
Total **336**

Fall: 1st inns 1/51, 2/74, 3/136, 4/173, 5/192, 6/249, 7/286, 8/295, 9/336.

WARWICKSHIRE

A.J.W.Croom .... c Fishlock b Gover 13	c Gregory b Watts 12
W.A.Hill .... c Gregory b Gover 10	c Gregory b Watts 31
F.R.Santall.......... c Gover b Brown 13	c Squires b Watts 2
Mr R.E.S.Wyatt..... c Gregory b Brown 12	c Mobey b Watts...........59
H.E.Dollery .... c Garland-Wells b Parker 25	c Garland-Wells b Watts 41
*Mr P.Cranmer..... c Garland-Wells b Brown 3	c Dickinson b Watts 3
N.A.Shortland ...... b Brown 4	c Fishlock b Watts 3
†J.Buckingham...... c Mobey b Parker 5	lbw b Watts 22
W.E.Hollies......... c Parker b Brown 3	c Mobey b Watts 1
J.H.Mayer .... c Gover b Brown 7	lbw b Watts 13
C.W.Grove .... not out 11	not out 13
Extras............. (B 5, NB 4)...............9	(B 12, LB 3, W 2, NB 3) ...20
Total **115**	....................**220**

Fall: 1st inns 1/20, 2/32, 3/50, 4/63, 5/71, 6/83, 7/91, 8/96, 9/98.
2nd inns 1/24, 2/33, 3/62, 4/147, 5/153, 6/161, 7/162, 8/166, 9/190.

WARWICKSHIRE	O	M	R	W
Mayer........................	16	2	65	1
Grove........................	16	0	65	0
Wyatt........................	20	7	49	2
Hollies........................	32	2	118	4
Santall........................	4	0	7	0
Croom........................	3.4	0	22	3

SURREY	O	M	R	W	O	M	R	W
Gover........................	11	0	32	2	12	0	36	0
Watts........................	4	0	15	0	24.1	8	67	10
Brown........................	13.6	1	46	6	17	2	78	0
Parker	7	2	13	2	5	2	7	0
Squires					4	1	12	0

Umpires: J.Hardstaff and C.W.L.Parker.

Close of play scores. First day: Surrey 336 all out. **Second day:** Warwickshire 123/3 (R.E.S.Wyatt 39*, H.E.Dollery 28*).

Comments: E.A.Watts became the third Surrey bowler to take all ten wickets in an innings. It was the first time the feat had been accomplished by a Surrey bowler since 1921. The two other Surrey bowlers were T.Richardson and T.Rushby. In one eight-over spell Watts took six wickets for four runs. Warwickshire followed on 221 behind.
W.E.Hollies became the first Warwickshire bowler to take 100 wickets in 1939.

YORKSHIRE v ESSEX

Played at Bramall Lane, Sheffield, August 19, 21, 22, 1939.
Toss won by Essex.
Essex won by an innings and 4 runs.

ESSEX

A.V.Avery	b Yardley	49
†T.H.Wade	c Verity b Robinson	84
T.P.B.Smith	lbw b Robinson	40
J.O'Connor	lbw b Robinson	13
*Capt J.W.A.Stephenson	c Robinson b Verity	5
R.Smith	c & b Verity	91
R.M.Taylor	st Fidding b Verity	6
S.J.Cray	c Robinson b Verity	31
R.M.Heaven	not out	5
Mr K.Farnes	b Verity	0
H.Daer	b Robinson	7
Extras	(B 9, LB 3)	12
Total		**343**

Fall: 1st inns 1/106 2/166, 3/188, 4/194, 5/202, 6/212, 7/321, 8/336, 9/336.

YORKSHIRE

H.Sutcliffe	c Heaven b Farnes	40	c Taylor b R.Smith	12
C.Turner	b R.Smith	9	c & b Taylor	66
W.Barber	c Wade b Farnes	48	c Taylor b Farnes	17
W.Watson	b Taylor	0	c Wade b Taylor	4
Mr N.W.D.Yardley	c Cray b Farnes	6	c Heaven b P.Smith	13
*Mr A.B.Sellers	c Cray b Taylor	4	c Cray b Taylor	30
G.Cawthray	c R.Smith b Taylor	0	c Heaven b Stephenson	28
H.Verity	c Wade b P.Smith	0	c Avery b Taylor	16
E.P.Robinson	c Cray b P.Smith	0	b Stephenson	9
†K.Fiddling	c Heaven b P.Smith	11	c Wade b Stephenson	1
J.Smurthwaite	not out	2	not out	1
Extras	(B 4, LB 5, NB 2)	11	(B 3, LB 5, W 2, NB 1)	11
Total		**131**		**208**

Fall: 1st inns 1/32, 2/89, 3/102, 4/113, 5/113, 6/116, 7/117, 8/117, 9/129.
2nd inns 1/13, 2/42, 3/53, 4/77, 5/125, 6/173, 7/196, 8/205, 9/207.

YORKSHIRE	O	M	R	W
Cawthray	15	2	54	0
Smurthwaite	16	2	64	0
Turner	19	8	37	0
Yardley	12	2	24	1
Verity	30	16	40	5
Robinson	32.7	7	112	4

ESSEX	O	M	R	W	O	M	R	W
Farnes	12	1	55	3	17	1	61	1
R.Smith	7	2	26	1	5	0	22	1
Taylor	10.2	0	35	3	14	0	75	4
P.Smith	3	0	4	3	5	0	21	1
Stephenson	-	-	-	-	7.6	1	18	3

Umpires: G.Beet and H.W.Lee.

ESSEX v NOTTINGHAMSHIRE

Played at Clacton-on-Sea, August 23, 24, 1939.
Toss won by Nottinghamshire.
Essex won by seven wickets.

NOTTINGHAMSHIRE

W.W.Keeton	retired hurt	15	absent hurt	0
C.B.Harris	c Wade b Farnes	0	(1) c Wade b Farnes	13
*Mr G.F.H.Heane	c P.Smith b R.Smith	48	c Nichols b Farnes	4
J.Hardstaff	b Nichols	117	c Taylor b Farnes	0
G.V.Gunn	c R.Smith b Nichols	40	b Farnes	0
R.J.Giles	c Vigar b Farnes	7	lbw b Nichols	1
J.Knowles	b Farnes	0	(2) c Wade b Nichols	23
W.Voce	c Vigar b Nichols	0	(7) run out	11
†A.B.Wheat	c Wade b Nichols	3	(8) b Farnes	9
H.J.Butler	b Nichols	6	(9) b Nichols	1
A.Jepson	not out	11	(10) not out	6
Extras	(B 20, LB 4)	24	(B 1, LB 1, NB 4)	6
Total		**271**		**74**

Fall: 1st inns 1/5, 2/108, 3/213, 4/230, 5/230, 6/237, 7/240, 8/248, 9/271.
2nd inns 1/30, 2/42, 3/42, 4/42, 5/43, 6/48, 7/66, 8/68, 9/74.

ESSEX

A.V.Avery	lbw b Voce	9	b Voce	0
†T.H.Wade	c Harris b Butler	50	c Wheat b Voce	21
T.P.B.Smith	b Voce	102	not out	49
J.O'Connor	c Gunn b Butler	4	c Voce b Heane	15
M.S.Nichols	lbw b Jepson	26	not out	17
R.Smith	b Heane	1		
S.J.Cray	b Heane	1		
*Capt J.W.A.Stephenson	b Voce	13		
R.M.Taylor	not out	10		
F.H.Vigar	c Harris b Voce	4		
Mr K.Farnes	b Voce	0		
Extras	(B 8, LB 2, NB 3)	13	(B 8, LB 3)	11
Total		**233**	(3 wickets)	**113**

Fall: 1st inns 1/25, 2/111, 3/115, 4/170, 5/175, 6/177, 7/214, 8/215, 9/233.
2nd inns 1/1, 2/36, 3/67.

ESSEX	O	M	R	W	O	M	R	W
Farnes	19	0	90	3	10.3	2	30	5
Nichols	12.2	2	34	5	11	2	38	3
Taylor	8	0	46	0				
R.Smith	6	0	25	1				
Stephenson	5	0	18	0	1	1	0	0
T.P.B.Smith	8	0	34	0				

NOTTINGHAMSHIRE	O	M	R	W	O	M	R	W
Voce	16.3	1	70	5	7	0	20	2
Butler	19	2	61	2	7	0	24	0
Heane	12	2	44	2	9	1	30	1
Jepson	11	2	35	1	6	1	28	0
Giles	4	1	10	0				

Umpires: J.J.Hills and E.Robinson.

Close of play scores. First day: Essex 336/8 (R.Heaven 5*). **Second day:**
Yorkshire 167/5 (C.Turner 58*, G.Cawthray 25*).

Comments: A.V.Avery and T.H.Wade began the match with an opening
partnerships of 106.
R.Smith and S.J.Cray added 109 for the 7th wicket in 85 minutes. Yorkshire
followed on 212 runs behind. On the final day, the county lost its last five
wickets in the first hour's play.
Yorkshire were without a number of their regular players, such as L.Hutton,
A.Wood, M.Leyland, W.E.Bowes, T.F.Smailes and A.Mitchell, unavailable
through either injury or Test calls.
It was Yorkshire's heaviest defeat since June 1937, against Middlesex.

Close of play scores. First day: Essex 156/3 (T.P.B.Smith 69*, M.S.Nichols 16*).

Comments: The game was completed in two days.
W.W.Keeton retired hurt with a broken finger, after being hit by Farnes.
J.Hardstaff's 117 included 13 4's and took 180 minutes. He and G.V.Gunn
added 105 runs for the 3rd wicket.
In Nottinghamshire's 1st innings, M.S.Nicholls took five wickets for 24 runs
in 66 balls.
P.Smith hit his first century of the season. He hit 13 4's in his 102.
K.Farnes performed a hat-trick in Notts' 2nd innings, dismissing G.F.H.Heane,
J.Hardstaff and G.V.Gunn in a spell of four wickets for six runs in two overs.
It was his maiden hat-trick and was to be the only one of his career.

GLAMORGAN v SURREY

Played at Swansea, August 23, 24, 1939.
Toss won by Glamorgan.
Surrey won by six wickets.

GLAMORGAN

A.H.Dyson	lbw b Gover	17	b Gover	0
D.E.Davies	lbw b Brown	40	b Parker	20
D.Davies	lbw b Garland-Wells	21	c Gregory b Brown	21
E.C.Jones	b Garland-Wells	0	(7) c Watts b Parker	10
*Mr M.J.L.Turnbull	b Gover	15	(4) b Brown	9
C.C.Smart	c Gover b Brown	0	c Garland-Wells b Brown	1
Mr G.Evans	run out	36	(5) lbw b Brown	1
P.B.Clift	c Whitfield b Gregory	32	not out	11
†H.G.Davies	c Watts b Gregory	10	c & b Parker	7
A.D.G.Matthews	not out	12	c Garland-Wells b Brown	0
P.F.Judge	c Parker b Brown	1	b Parker	0
Extras	(B 4, LB 5, NB 2)	11	(B 6, LB 4, NB 3)	13
Total		195		93

Fall: 1st inns 1/40, 2/82, 3/82, 4/92, 5/92, 6/102, 7/164, 8/173, 9/193.
2nd inns 1/3, 2/40, 3/57, 4/57, 5/58, 6/69, 7/75, 8/91, 9/92.

SURREY

R.J.Gregory	b Matthews	14	not out	37
L.B.Fishlock	b Judge	1	c & b Matthews	0
E.W.Whitfield	b Matthews	7	c Dyson b Judge	2
H.S.Squires	c E.Davies b Judge	51	c Evans b Judge	2
J.F.Parker	run out	12	c Evans b Jones	18
Mr F.R.Brown	c Evans b Judge	69	not out	19
†G.S.Mobey	b Matthews	0		
*Mr H.M.Garland-Wells	b Matthews	12		
Mr P.J.Dickinson	c Evans b Matthews	9		
E.A.Watts	c Clift b Matthews	20		
A.R.Gover	not out	2		
Extras	(B 2, LB 7, W 1)	10	(B 4)	4
Total		207	(4 wickets)	82

Fall: 1st inns 1/6, 2/8, 3/27, 4/50, 5/153, 6/153, 7/173, 8/183, 9/192.
2nd inns 1/5, 2/12, 3/28, 4/61.

SURREY	O	M	R	W	O	M	R	W
Gover	13	3	39	2	7	1	11	1
Watts	3	0	15	0	6	1	13	0
Parker	3	0	10	0	7.3	4	7	4
Brown	20.1	3	64	3	12	3	48	5
Garland-Wells	13	6	32	2				
Gregory	8	0	24	2				
Squires	-	-	-	-	1	0	1	0

GLAMORGAN	O	M	R	W	O	M	R	W
Matthews	21.2	7	56	6	5	0	31	1
Judge	21	5	84	3	7	1	26	2
D.E.Davies	1	0	11	0				
Smart	3	0	18	0				
Evans	2	0	14	0				
Jones	2	0	14	0	3	1	7	1
Clift	-	-	-	-	0.6	0	14	0

Umpires: E.J.Smith and C.V.Tarbox.

Close of play scores. First day: Surrey 153/6 (H.S.Squires 42*). **Second day:** Surrey 82/4 (R.J.Gregory 37*, F.R.Brown 19*).

Comments: The game was completed in two days.
Only two batsmen scored over 50 in this game.
H.S.Squires hit 46 out of his 51 in boundaries (one 6 and ten 4's)
He added 103 in 70 minutes with F.R.Brown for Surrey's 5th wicket.
F.R.Brown finished the game with one 6 and three 4's.

HAMPSHIRE v WORCESTERSHIRE

Played at Bournemouth, August 23, 24, 25, 1939.
Toss won by Worcestershire.
Worcestershire won by 32 runs.

WORCESTERSHIRE

R.Howorth	b Boyes	64	b Heath	5
E.Cooper	c Pothecary b Baring	12	c Boyes b Heath	3
B.P.King	run out	5	c Walker b Hill	90
Mr C.H.Palmer	c Walker b Dean	35	lbw b Hill	11
*H.H.I.Gibbons	not out	17	b Hill	0
S.H.Martin	c Walker b Dean	0	c Pothecary b Hill	15
*Mr A.P.Singleton	b Dean	0	c Hill b Baring	36
R.O.Jenkins	st McCorkell b Dean	0	c McCorkell b Hill	13
†J.S.Buller	c Boyes b Baring	6	b Creese	6
R.T.D.Perks	b Baring	23	st McCorkell b Hill	4
P.F.Jackson	b Baring	0	not out	0
Extras	(LB 1, NB 1)	2	(LB 7)	7
Total		164		190

Fall: 1st inns 1/27, 2/50, 3/103, 4/121, 5/121, 6/121, 7/121, 8/123, 9/155.
2nd inns 1/7, 2/14, 3/56, 4/56, 5/72, 6/140, 7/175,.

HAMPSHIRE

†N.T.McCorkell	b Perks	74	c Jackson b Perks	17
P.A.Mackenzie	c & b Jenkins	19	b Perks	1
D.F.Walker	run out	10	c Singleton b Martin	39
A.E.Pothecary	b Singleton	13	b Singleton	8
W.L.C.Creese	c Cooper b Howorth	18	c Singleton b Martin	22
G.Hill	c Howorth b Jenkins	6	b Martin	2
L.Harrison	c King b Jenkins	9	c Jenkins b Martin	12
G.S.Boyes	lbw b Singleton	22	c Howorth b Martin	24
*Mr A.E.G.Baring	c Buller b Howorth	8	lbw b Jackson	4
T.A.Dean	not out	2	c Singleton b Martin	0
G.E.M.Heath	st Buller b Howorth	6	not out	0
Extras	(B 2, NB 2)	4	(B 2)	2
Total		191		131

Fall: 1st inns 5/114, 8/178, 9/182.
2nd inns 1/11, 2/27, 3/40, 4/72, 5/84, 6/93, 7/118, 8/131, 9/131.

HAMPSHIRE	O	M	R	W	O	M	R	W
Baring	11.3	1	52	4	10	0	33	1
Heath	6	0	37	0	5	2	30	2
Hill	5	0	18	0	10.1	0	38	6
Boyes	8	2	17	1	7	3	27	0
Dean	8	1	38	4	4	0	36	0
Creese	-	-	-	-	3	0	19	1

WORCESTERSHIRE	O	M	R	W	O	M	R	W
Perks	14	2	43	1	14	3	43	2
Martin	12	2	30	0	17.5	3	38	6
Jenkins	11	0	42	3				
Howorth	16.5	7	46	3	7	0	26	0
Jackson	1	1	0	0	7	2	8	1
Singleton	9	3	26	2	4	1	14	1

Umpires: J.A.Smart and H.Cruice.

Close of play scores. First day: Hampshire 176/7 (N.T.McCorkell 67*, A.E.G.Baring 8*). **Second day:** Hampshire 70/3 (D.F.Walker 37*, W.L.C.Creese 5*).

Comments: T.A.Dean aged 18, took four wickets in five balls, including the hat-trick in Worcestershire's 1st innings. It was his second appearance for his county.
S.H.Martin completed the double of 1,000 runs and 100 wickets, the second player to do so, when he took his 6th wicket in Hampshire's 2nd innings.
Fall of wickets in Hampshire scorebook are incomplete.
There is no 1939 Worcestershire scorebook

KENT v YORKSHIRE

Played at Dover, August 23, 24, 1939.
Toss won by Kent.
Yorkshire won by an innings and 14 runs.

YORKSHIRE

H.Sutcliffe	b Martin	9
L.Hutton	c Foster b Wright	100
W.Barber	c Fagg b Lewis	32
C.Turner	b Wright	41
Mr N.W.D.Yardley	b Wright	1
*Mr A.B.Sellers	c & b Wright	52
†A.Wood	b Harding	21
T.F.Smailes	c & b Wright	47
E.P.Robinson	c & b Martin	2
H.Verity	not out	12
W.E.Bowes	b Harding	9
Extras	(B 1, LB 10, NB 1)	12
Total		**338**

Fall: 1st inns 1/18, 2/112, 3/174, 4/178, 5/203, 6/250, 7/104, 8/306, 9/321.

KENT

A.E.Fagg	c Sutcliffe b Bowes	42	c Barber b Robinson	13
*Mr F.G.H.Chalk	b Smailes	4	not out	115
L.E.G.Ames	c Barber b Smailes	26	b Robinson	0
Mr B.H.Valentine	c Robinson b Bowes	2	c Robinson b Verity	3
L.J.Todd	c Wood b Bowes	21	b Verity	19
Mr P.G.Foster	c Robinson b Verity	1	st Wood b Verity	9
D.V.P.Wright	c Sellers b Verity	2	st Wood b Hutton	34
N.W.Harding	c Yardley b Verity	8	c Hutton b Bowes	6
†Mr W.H.V.Levett	c & b Verity	0	c & b Bowes	0
Mr J.W.Martin	c Barber b Robinson	2	c Hutton b Verity	0
C.Lewis	not out	0	c Robinson b Verity	3
Extras	(B 1)	1	(B 12, LB 1)	13
Total		**109**		**215**

Fall: 1st inns 1/4, 2/50, 3/59, 4/95, 5/96, 6/98, 7/104, 8/104, 9/107.
2nd inns 1/22, 2/22, 3/25, 4/61, 5/75, 6/129, 7/182, 8/182, 9/183.

KENT	O	M	R	W
Martin	20	4	69	2
Todd	10	1	46	0
Harding	12.2	2	77	2
Wright	25	0	97	5
Lewis	11	2	37	1

YORKSHIRE	O	M	R	W	O	M	R	W
Bowes	11	2	38	3	7	2	38	2
Smailes	7	0	36	2	4	0	23	0
Verity	7.4	1	32	4	16.3	4	48	5
Robinson	2	1	2	1	15	3	62	2
Hutton	-	-	-	-	5	0	31	1

Umpires: H.G.Baldwin and D.Hendren.

Close of play scores. First day: Kent 17/1 (A.E.Fagg 3*, L.E.G.Ames 10*).

Comments: The match was completed in two days.
Kent put Yorkshire in to bat.
Hutton hit his 11th century of the season. His 100, made in 160 minutes, included 13 4's.
Kent followed on 229 behind
F.G.H.Chalk carried his bat for 115 in Kent's 2nd innings. He hit 13 4's.

MIDDLESEX v SOMERSET

Played at Lord's, August 23, 24, 25, 1939.
Toss won by Middlesex.
Middlesex won by 225 runs.

MIDDLESEX

J.D.B.Robertson	c Luckes b Andrews	23	b Buse	92
Mr J.H.Collinson	run out	19	c Lee b Andrews	19
W.J.Edrich	st Luckes b Meyer	14	c Meyer b Hazell	36
D.C.S.Compton	c Mayer b Buse	4	c Watts b Meyer	48
Mr F.G.Mann	c McRae b Andrews	38	c Andrews b Meyer	18
*Mr R.W.V.Robins	c Luckes b Buse	7	c Meyer b Hazell	84
B.L.Muncer	b Buse	18	c & b Buse	6
†W.F.F.Price	c Luckes b Hazell	13	not out	28
J.M.Sims	not out	29	(10) not out	1
C.I.J.Smith	c Hazell b Andrews	36	(9) c Gimblett b Hazell	16
L.H.Gray	c & b Meyer	0		
Extras	(B 4, LB 6)	10	(B 6, LB 2, NB 2)	10
Total		**211**	(8 wickets, declared)	**359**

Fall: 1st inns 1/34, 2/59, 3/62, 4/69, 5/81, 6/115, 7/144, 8/150, 9/207.
2nd inns 1/48, 2/121, 3/193, 4/202, 5/263, 6/287, 7/317, 8/335.

SOMERSET

F.S.Lee	b Smith	0	c Price b Gray	8
H.Gimblett	b Gray	4	c Sims b Compton	69
H.T.F.Buse	c Price b Smith	0	c Price b Gray	48
Mr R.J.O.Meyer	lbw b Smith	24	b Sims	1
Mr T.R.Garnett	b Smith	0	st Price b Sims	24
Mr F.M.McRae	b Muncer	33	b Muncer	14
*Mr E.F.Longrigg	run out	2	c Edrich b Sims	1
Mr H.E.Watts	c Smith b Muncer	22	st Price b Sims	0
†W.T.Luckes	not out	5	not out	18
W.H.R.Andrews	c Smith b Robins	7	c sub b Sims	43
H.L.Hazell	b Muncer	4	c Edrich b Sims	6
Extras	(B 3, LB 1, NB 1)	5	(B 3, LB 4)	7
Total		**106**		**239**

Fall: 1st inns 1/1, 2/1, 3/9, 4/10, 5/34, 6/53, 7/85, 8/92, 9/100.
2nd inns 1/35, 2/91, 3/92, 4/146, 5/160, 6/171, 7/171, 8/174, 9/232.

SOMERSET	O	M	R	W	O	M	R	W
Andrews	14	1	68	3	10	1	62	1
Buse	21	6	50	3	21	1	112	2
Meyer	19.6	3	63	2	19	2	90	2
Hazell	7	3	20	1	18	1	85	3

MIDDLESEX	O	M	R	W	O	M	R	W
Smith	11	2	28	4	11	2	30	0
Gray	4	1	22	1	17	7	39	2
Sims	5	1	26	0	23.2	1	106	6
Robins	5	1	14	1	4	1	13	0
Muncer	3.6	0	11	3	4	0	24	1
Robertson	-	-	-	-	1	0	2	0
Compton	-	-	-	-	4	0	18	1

Umpires: F.Chester and E.Cooke.

Close of play scores. First day: Middlesex 18/0 (J.D.M.Robertson 14*, J.H.Collinson 4*). **Second day:** Somerset 108/3 (H.T.F.Buse 19*, T.R.Garnett 11*).

Comments: Twenty wickets fell on the first day. Somerset were dismissed for 106 in two hours in their 1st innings.
Somerset were set 465 to win. They were dismissed before lunch on the third day.
W.F.F.Price took over as acting captain on the third day, in the absence through injury of R.W.V.Robins.

NORTHAMPTONSHIRE v LANCASHIRE

Played at Northampton, August 23, 24, 25, 1939.
Toss won by Northamptonshire.
Lancashire won by 95 runs.

LANCASHIRE

C.Washbrook	st James b Merritt	46	b Partridge	3
E.Paynter	c Merritt b Nelson	41	c sub b Timms	22
W.Place	st James b Merritt	0	c O'Brien b Merritt	71
N.Oldfield	lbw b Merritt	27	c James b Timms	0
J.Iddon	c Nelson b Merritt	19	lbw b Nelson	63
W.E.Phillipson	hit wkt b Nelson	3	lbw b Merritt	0
*Mr W.H.L.Lister	b Merritt	31	absent	0
†W.Farrimond	lbw b Lubbock	8	(7) b Merritt	7
R.G.Garlick	b Merritt	11	(8) c James b Partridge	7
R.Pollard	b Merritt	4	(9) c Phillips b Merritt	12
W.B.Roberts	not out	0	(10) not out	1
Extras	(B 1, LB 4)	5	(LB 2)	2
Total		**195**	**(9 wickets)**	**188**

Fall: 1st inns 1/65, 2/68, 3/122, 4/122, 5/125, 6/153, 7/178, 8/184, 9/195.
2nd inns 1/3, 2/29, 3/29, 4/144, 5/145, 6/153, 7/164, 8/182, 9/188.

NORTHAMPTONSHIRE

Mr E.J.H.Dixon	b Pollard	8	c Iddon b Garlick	26
Mr A.W.Snowden	run out	8	c Farrimond b Phillipson	6
D.Brookes	b Garlick	7	not out	47
J.E.Timms	c Pollard b Roberts	27	(5) c Roberts b Phillipson	1
F.P.O'Brien	c Pollard b Roberts	51	(6) c Iddon b Garlick	8
*Mr R.P.Nelson	c Roberts b Garlick	4	(7) b Phillipson	3
†K.C.James	b Pollard	22	(8) c Iddon b Roberts	3
W.E.Merritt	st Farrimond b Roberts	0	(9) b Garlick	7
Mr S.I.Philips	st Farrimond b Roberts	1	(10) c Iddon b Roberts	22
Mr C.W.S.Lubbock	not out	10	absent hurt	0
R.J.Partridge	b Garlick	4	(4) b Garlick	1
Extras	(B 6, LB 8)	14	(B 4, LB 3, NB 1)	8
Total		**156**	**(9 wickets)**	**132**

Fall: 1st inns 1/14, 2/16, 3/59, 4/61, 5/70, 6/127, 7/132, 8/136, 9/145.
2nd inns 1/19, 2/46, 3/48, 4/49, 5/62, 6/65, 7/73, 8/86, 9/132.

NORTHANTS	O	M	R	W	O	M	R	W
Partridge	14	6	25	0	18	2	59	2
Lubbock	9	1	29	1	3	0	7	0
Timms	4	0	16	0	14	6	25	2
Nelson	15	1	37	2	10	3	18	1
Merritt	20.3	4	83	7	15.1	0	62	4
O'Brien	-	-	-	-	3	1	15	0

LANCASHIRE	O	M	R	W	O	M	R	W
Phillipson	3	0	19	0	14	3	34	3
Pollard	12	2	43	2	7	1	23	0
Roberts	21	6	47	4	12.6	5	18	2
Garlick	13	3	33	3	18	2	49	4

Umpires: J.Hardstaff and G.M.Lee.

Close of play scores. First day: Northants 139/8 (F.P.O'Brien 47*, C.W.S.Lubbock 2*). **Second day:** Northants 48/3 (D.Brookes 13*, J.E.Timms 0*).

Comments: Lancashire were put in to bat.
W.Place and J.Iddon added 115 for the 4th wicket in Lancashire's 2nd innings.
J.Iddon took over the captaincy of Lancashire, when W.H.Lister left to join his Territorial regiment in the 2nd innings.
W.E.Merritt achieved his best bowling figures in a championship match with 7 for 83.

SUSSEX v DERBYSHIRE

Played at Eastbourne, August 23, 24, 25, 1939.
Toss won by Derbyshire.
Sussex won by an innings and 39 runs.

DERBYSHIRE

D.Smith	lbw b Nye	7	b Nye	7
A.F.Townsend	c Holmes b J.Parks	3	b J.Parks	0
†A.E.Alderman	b Nye	35	c John Langridge b Jas.Langridge	48
T.S.Worthington	st Griffith b Wood	46	c J.Parks b Nye	0
G.H.Pope	c John Langridge b J.Parks	71	c John Langridge b Nye	39
A.E.G.Rhodes	c Griffith b Nye	2	c Griffith b Jas.Langridge	9
A.V.Pope	c J.Parks b Wood	31	not out	30
C.Gladwin	b J.Parks	16	run out	3
*Mr R.H.R.Buckston	c Griffith b Nye	6	b Nye	0
T.B.Mitchell	c Nye b J.Parks	0	c Griffith b Jas.Langridge	1
W.H.Copson	not out	6	b Nye	15
Extras	(LB 2, W 1, NB 1)	4	(B 4, LB 1)	5
Total		**227**		**157**

Fall: 1st inns 1/6, 2/10, 3/73, 4/114, 5/116, 6/185, 7/209, 8/221, 9/221.
2nd inns 1/6, 2/8, 3/8, 4/94, 5/102, 6/114, 7/127, 8/351, 9/128.

SUSSEX

Mr R.G.Stainton	B Mitchell	72
John G.Langridge	b G.H.Pope	26
H.W.Parks	c & b Mitchell	53
G.Cox	lbw b Mitchell	8
*FLt-Lt A.J.Holmes	b Copson	94
†Mr S.C.Griffith	c A.V.Pope b Mitchell	6
Mr H.T.Bartlett	c Townsend b Mitchell	0
J.H.Parks	lbw b Mitchell	73
Jas.Langridge	not out	41
J.K.Nye	b Mitchell	27
D.J.Wood	b Mitchell	8
Extras	(B 9, LB 6)	15
Total		**423**

Fall: 1st inns 1/41, 2/157, 3/160, 4/169, 5/194, 6/194, 7/326, 8/351, 9/411.

SUSSEX	O	M	R	W	O	M	R	W
Nye	15.2	1	72	4	14	2	49	5
J.Parks	15	1	53	4	11	1	36	1
Jas.Langridge	15	1	45	0	6	0	44	3
Wood	10	1	43	2	5	1	19	0
John Langridge	1	0	4	0				
Holmes	1	0	6	0				
Cox	-	-	-	-	1	0	4	0

DERBYSHIRE	O	M	R	W
Copson	27	1	118	1
A.V.Pope	15	2	49	0
G.H.Pope	12	0	60	1
Mitchell	30.6	4	149	8
Rhodes	5	1	24	0
Gladwin	4	0	8	0

Umpires: W.Reeves and A.Dolphin.

Close of play scores. First day: Sussex 179/4 (A.J.Holmes 8*, S.C.Griffith 2*). **Second day:** Derbyshire 92/3 (A.E.Alderman 47*, G.H.Pope 34*).

Comments: H.W.Parks and R.G.Stainton added 116 for the 2nd wicket in 90 minutes. A.J.Holmes and J.H.Parks put on 132 in 105 minutes for the 7th Sussex wicket.
Derbyshire lost their last seven 2nd innings wickets for 65 runs in only 50 minutes on the third day.

WARWICKSHIRE v GLOUCESTERSHIRE

Played at Birmingham, August 23, 24, 25, 1939.
Toss won by Warwickshire.
Warwickshire won by 110 runs.

WARWICKSHIRE

A.J.W.Croom	c Scott b Lambert	12	b Scott	3
W.A.Hill	lbw b Goddard	70	b Scott	58
F.R.Santall	lbw b Scott	12	lbw b Scott	2
Mr R.E.S.Wyatt	c Hopkins b Lambert	3	b Lambert	1
H.E.Dollery	lbw b Scott	3	b Lambert	108
J.S.Ord	b Scott	0	b Lambert	44
*Mr P.Cranmer	c Wilson b Scott	15	c Wilson b Scott	2
C.W.Grove	b Sinfield	17	b Scott	4
W.E.Hollies	c Wilson b Sinfield	22	not out	1
J.H.Mayer	not out	6	b Lambert	0
†Mr C.C.Goodway	lbw b Sinfield	0	run out	15
Extras	(B 1, LB 3, NB 1)	5	(B 3, LB 5, W 1)	9
Total		165		247

Fall: 1st inns 1/21, 2/35, 3/40, 4/52, 5/52, 6/78, 7/110, 8/150, 9/165.
2nd inns 1/10, 2/12, 3/14, 4/125, 5/213, 6/222, 7/227, 8/231, 9/231.

GLOUCESTERSHIRE

C.J.Barnett	c Hollies b Grove	9	(3) c Hollies b Mayer	0
G.M.Emmett	run out	49	b Grove	14
V.Hopkins	c Goodway b Mayer	22	(1) lbw b Mayer	12
*Mr W.R.Hammond	c Goodway b Mayer	17	c & b Mayer	16
J.F.Crapp	st Goodway b Hollies	48	c Goodway b Mayer	0
R.A.Sinfield	c Hollies b Grove	1	(7) b Mayer	0
W.L.Neale	c Goodway b Grove	11	(6) lbw b Hollies	13
†E.A.Wilson	c Mayer b Wyatt	14	c Goodway b Mayer	2
C.J.Scott	lbw b Hollies	0	c Dollery b Hollies	55
T.W.J.Goddard	not out	7	c Cranmer b Hollies	0
G.E.E.Lambert	b Hollies	4	not out	1
Extras	(B 4, LB 1)	5	(B 2)	2
Total		187		115

Fall: 1st inns 1/24, 2/72, 3/97, 4/99, 5/103, 6/129, 7/169, 8/170, 9/179.
2nd inns 1/19, 2/19, 3/33, 4/34, 5/43, 6/43, 7/49, 8/113, 9/114.

GLOUCESTERSHIRE	O	M	R	W	O	M	R	W
Scott	21	1	87	4	21.5	2	87	5
Lambert	14	3	42	2	14	0	57	4
Barnett	1	0	2	0	3	0	9	0
Goddard	12	3	28	1	15	4	51	0
Sinfield	6	5	1	3	11	1	34	0

WARWICKSHIRE	O	M	R	W	O	M	R	W
Mayer	17	3	52	2	15	4	40	6
Grove	16	1	52	3	11	3	23	1
Wyatt	13	1	57	1	2	1	9	0
Hollies	4.6	1	21	3	4.7	0	41	3

Umpires: A.Skelding and G.Beet.

Close of play scores. First day: Glos 133/6 (J.F.Crapp 22*, E.A.Wilson 2*).
Second day: Gloucestershire 15/0 (G.M.Emmett 2*, V.Hopkins 12*).

Comments: W.A.Hill and H.E.Dollery added 110 for the 4th wicket in Warwickshire's 2nd innings.
H.E.Dollery batted for 180 minutes for his 108. It included one 6 and nine 4's.
Gloucestershire began the last day, needing 211 to win with nine wickets in hand.
J.H.Mayer first spell of seven overs on the third morning claimed six wickets for 14 runs.
C.J.Scott hit 44 of his 55 in boundaries (two 6's, eight 4's) in 35 minutes.
W.E.Hollies finished the game with three wickets in 15 balls for four runs.
C.C.Goodway was awarded his county cap.

ESSEX v NORTHAMPTONSHIRE

Played at Clacton-on-Sea, August 26, 28, 29, 1939.
Toss won by Essex.
Essex won by 210 runs.

ESSEX

A.V.Avery	b Partridge	13	c & b Nelson	90
†T.H.Wade	c Herbert b Partridge	13	c Greenwood b Nelson	61
T.P.B.Smith	c Greenwood b Timms	50	c & b Herbert	13
J.O'Connor	c James b Timms	5	not out	54
M.S.Nichols	c James b Partridge	30	c Merritt b Partridge	50
R.Smith	c James b Timms	21	b Herbert	13
*Capt J.W.A.Stephenson	c & b Merritt	43	not out	7
R.M.Taylor	st James b Merritt	8		
S.J.Cray	hit wkt b Merritt	5		
F.H.Vigar	not out	6		
Mr K.Farnes	st James b Herbert	2		
Extras	(B 3, LB 7)	10	(B 5, LB 9, NB 2)	16
Total		206	(5 wickets, declared)	304

Fall: 1st inns 1/21, 2/34, 3/47, 4/114, 5/118, 6/165, 7/180, 8/192, 9/199.
2nd inns 1/138, 2/162, 3/174, 4/245, 5/286.

NORTHAMPTONSHIRE

P.Davis	b Nichols	7	b Farnes	13
H.W.Greenwood	b Nichols	32	c Cray b Farnes	8
D.Brookes	b Nichols	23	b Farnes	8
J.E.Timms	lbw b Nichols	45	b Farnes	0
F.P.O'Brien	c Taylor b Nichols	6	(10) b Nichols	3
*Mr R.P.Nelson	c Taylor b Farnes	29	b P.Smith	39
†K.C.James	c Vigar b Nichols	3	(5) c Vigar b Farnes	21
W.E.Merritt	c Avery b Farnes	3	(7) c Wade b Farnes	23
Mr S.I.Philips	run out	4	c P.Smith b Nichols	0
R.J.Partridge	not out	10	(8) c Taylor b Nichols	4
E.J.Herbert	b P.Smith	5	not out	0
Extras	(B 1, LB 5)	6	(LB 7, NB 1)	8
Total		173		127

Fall: 1st inns 1/25, 2/51, 3/75, 4/81, 5/140, 6/148, 7/151, 8/159, 9/158.
2nd inns 1/18, 2/24, 3/24, 4/47, 5/54, 6/96, 7/110, 8/116, 9/127.

NORTHANTS	O	M	R	W	O	M	R	W
Partridge	16	1	63	3	15	3	54	1
Herbert	10.7	2	24	1	15	5	50	2
Timms	21	6	51	3	14	1	69	0
Merritt	11	0	46	3	7	0	30	0
Nelson	7	1	12	0	13	2	55	2
O'Brien	-	-	-	-	4	0	18	0
Phillips	-	-	-	-	1	0	12	0

ESSEX	O	M	R	W	O	M	R	W
Farnes	17	2	79	2	12	0	47	6
Nichols	18	3	38	6	8.1	2	26	3
Stephenson	5	0	16	0				
R.Smith	3	0	23	0				
T.P.B.Smith	3.6	0	11	1	10	1	46	1

Umpires: F.Chester and J.A.Newman.

Close of play scores. First day: Northants 148/6 (K.C.James 3*). **Second day:** Northants 47/4 (K.C.James 16*).

Comments: A.V.Avery and T.W.Wade put on 138 for the 1st wicket, the highest opening partnership for Essex in 1939.

HAMPSHIRE v YORKSHIRE

Played at Bournemouth, August 26, 28, 1939.
Toss won by Yorkshire.
Yorkshire won by an innings and 11 runs.

HAMPSHIRE

†N.T.McCorkell	lbw b Smailes	13	c Hutton b Bowes	5
P.A.Mackenzie	c Mitchell b Verity	51	lbw b Bowes	2
D.F.Walker	c Wood b Smailes	0	b Smailes	6
A.E.Pothecary	c Mitchell b Robinson	17	c Mitchell b Hutton	61
W.L.C.Creese	c Mitchell b Verity	2	c & b Verity	8
G.S.Boyes	c Turner b Verity	7	lbw b Bowes	6
L.Harrison	c Robinson b Bowes	0	c Mitchell b Robinson	16
G.Hill	c Mitchell b Verity	12	c & b Hutton	1
*Mr A.E.G.Baring	not out	9	c Verity b Robinson	1
T.A.Dean	st Wood b Verity	0	not out	7
G.E.M.Heath	st Wood b Verity	3	lbw b Hutton	1
Extras	(LB 2)	2	(LB 2)	2
Total		**116**		**116**

Fall: 1st inns 1/15, 2/15, 3/47, 4/54, 5/74, 6/76, 7/103, 8/108, 9/108.
2nd inns 1/7, 2/10, 3/23, 4/46, 5/67, 6/98, 7/105, 8/108, 9/108.

YORKSHIRE

H.Sutcliffe	lbw b Heath	51
L.Hutton	c McCorkell b Boyes	37
A.Mitchell	lbw b Dean	65
M.Leyland	b Baring	18
C.Turner	lbw b Dean	28
*Mr A.B.Sellers	c Boyes b Dean	8
T.F.Smailes	lbw b Dean	0
†A.Wood	lbw b Creese	13
E.P.Robinson	b Dean	0
H.Verity	not out	17
W.E.Bowes	b Creese	0
Extras	(LB 3, W 1, NB 2)	6
Total		**243**

Fall: 1st inns 1/56, 2/117, 3/143, 4/196, 5/210, 6/210, 7/213, 8/213, 9/243.

YORKSHIRE	O	M	R	W	O	M	R	W
Bowes	11	6	14	1	9	0	29	3
Smailes	10	0	40	2	7	0	23	1
Verity	14.1	5	22	6	6	0	29	1
Robinson	8	0	26	1	6	1	20	2
Hutton	3	0	12	0	5.7	2	13	3

HAMPSHIRE	O	M	R	W
Baring	8	0	35	1
Heath	8	1	38	1
Boyes	15	4	40	1
Hill	17	2	46	0
Dean	14	1	58	5
Creese	9	3	20	2

Umpires: D.Hendren and C.W.L.Parker.

Close of play scores. First day: Yorkshire 135/2 (A.Mitchell 30*, M.Leyland 13*).

Comments: The match was completed in under two days.
T.A.Dean took five Yorkshire wickets for eight runs in one spell of 25 deliveries. Twice in the innings, he took two wickets in two balls.
A.Mitchell held six catches in the match, the best fielding performance of the 1939 season.

KENT v LANCASHIRE

Played at Dover, August 26, 28, 29, 1939.
Toss won by Lancashire.
Kent won by five wickets.

LANCASHIRE

E.Paynter	b Wright	22	lbw b Wright	56
C.Washbrook	lbw b Wright	33	c Evans b Watt	73
W.Place	lbw b Watt	0	(11) not out	0
N.Oldfield	c Wright b Harding	68	(3) c Harding b Wright	34
J.Iddon	run out	47	(4) b Harding	38
W.E.Phillipson	c Davies b Harding	44	(5) c Foster b Todd	30
†W.Farrimond	b Harding	3	(6) not out	36
*Mr T.A.Higson	b Wright	7	(7) c Evans b Wright	4
R.Pollard	c Watt b Harding	18	(8) run out	1
W.B.Roberts	c Fagg b Harding	8	(9) run out	5
L.L.Wilkinson	not out	5	(10) c Todd b Wright	0
Extras	(LB 5, NB 2)	7	(B 12, LB 8, NB 4)	24
Total		**262**	(9 wickets, declared)	**301**

Fall: 1st inns 1/46, 2/47, 3/59, 4/148, 5/219, 6/222, 7/223, 8/233, 9/255.
2nd inns 1/87, 2/155, 3/194, 4/244, 5/253, 6/258, 7/267, 8/280, 9/283.

KENT

A.E.Fagg	c Iddon b Phillipson	19	c & b Roberts	138
Mr P.G.Foster	c Roberts b Wilkinson	36	(6) not out	49
L.E.G.Ames	c Wilkinson b Pollard	58	c & b Wilkinson	4
Mr B.H.Valentine	c & b Wilkinson	0	c Farrimond b Higson	68
*Mr F.G.H.Chalk	b Pollard	8	(2) b Wilkinson	94
Mr J.G.W.Davies	lbw b Wilkinson	1	(5) b Wilkinson	12
L.J.Todd	run out	23	not out	2
†T.G.Evans	c Farrimond b Pollard	9		
D.V.P.Wright	b Wilkinson	8		
N.W.Harding	b Wilkinson	1		
A.E.Watt	not out	9		
Extras	(B 3, LB 6, W 1)	10	(LB 13, W 1, NB 1)	15
Total		**182**	(5 wickets)	**382**

Fall: 1st inns 1/22, 2/87, 3/88, 4/107, 5/108, 6/142, 7/152, 8/171, 9/173.
2nd inns 1/181, 2/189, 3/285, 4/327, 5/351.

KENT	O	M	R	W	O	M	R	W
Harding	15.2	2	54	5	13	2	56	1
Todd	6	3	23	0	13	0	67	1
Watt	19	1	62	1	14	1	60	1
Wright	19	2	95	3	17	1	80	4
Davies	5	0	21	0	3	0	14	0

LANCASHIRE	O	M	R	W	O	M	R	W
Phillipson	14	1	56	1	11	0	79	0
Pollard	12	1	57	3	10	2	56	0
Higson	3	1	5	0	3	0	24	1
Wilkinson	13	1	54	5	20	1	128	3
Roberts	-	-	-	-	16	3	50	1
Paynter	-	-	-	-	5	0	30	0

Umpires: W.Reeves and H.W.Lee.

Close of play scores. First day: Kent 43/1 (P.G.Foster 12*, L.E.G.Ames 9*).
Second day: Lancashire 283/9 (W.Farrimond).

Comments: W.Place, having broken a finger, batted at number-11 in Lancashire's 2nd innings. He helped W.Farrimond add 18 runs for the last wicket before Lancashire declared leaving Kent 382 to win. Kent hit off the runs with an hour to spare.
A.E.Fagg and F.G.H.Chalk put on 181 for the 1st wicket. Fagg's 138 included 19 4's.

LEICESTERSHIRE v GLAMORGAN

Played at Grace Road, Leicester, August 26, 28, 29, 1939.
Toss won by Glamorgan.
Match drawn.

GLAMORGAN

A.H.Dyson	b Sperry	10	c Smith b Lester	59
D.E.Davies	b Sperry	42	lbw b Flamson	10
D.Davies	b Lester	10	c Dawkes b Sperry	2
*Mr M.J.L.Turnbull	c Berry b Sperry	156	(9) not out	0
T.L.Brierley	b Sperry	0	(4) c Dawkes b Sperry	17
C.C.Smart	run out	70	c Flamson b Armstrong	4
Mr G.Evans	lbw b Lester	0	not out	17
P.B.Clift	not out	20	(5) c Watson b Lester	20
†H.G.Davies	b Lester	1	(8) b Sperry	8
A.D.G.Matthews	b Lester	10		
P.F.Judge	c Sperry b Smith	9		
Extras	(B 1, LB 4, W 1)	6	(B 13, LB 3)	16
Total		**334**	(7 wickets, declared)	**153**

Fall: 1st inns 1/18, 2/43, 3/109, 4/109, 5/284, 6/294, 7/294, 8/295, 9/319.
2nd inns 1/22, 2/25, 3/65, 4/104, 5/136, 6/145, 7/153.

LEICESTERSHIRE

G.L.Berry	c H.Davies b Matthews	6
G.Lester	b Matthews	21
N.F.Armstrong	c H.Davies b Matthews	70
G.S.Watson	b Smart	145
M.Tompkin	c H.Davies b Matthews	0
*Mr M.St.J.Packe	c H.Davies b Matthews	9
†G.O.Dawkes	b Evans	7
L.D.Thursting	c H.Davies b E.Davies	5
H.A.Smith	run out	3
J.Sperry	st H.Davies b Smart	7
W.H.Flamson	not out	8
Extras	(B 2, LB 7, W 1, NB 1)	11
Total		**292**

Fall: 1st innings 1/12, 2/66, 3/139, 4/141, 5/169, 7/217, 8/281, 9/281.

LEICESTERSHIRE	O	M	R	W	O	M	R	W
Sperry	24	1	92	4	17	5	38	3
Flamson	15	2	63	0	10	2	23	1
Lester	24	3	88	4	17	1	50	2
Smith	11.1	0	47	1	10	3	23	0
Armstrong	6	0	25	0	2	1	3	1
Thursting	2	0	13	0				

GLAMORGAN	O	M	R	W
Matthews	27	2	111	5
Judge	18	2	66	0
Smart	10.3	0	33	2
Evans	8	0	41	1
Clift	2	0	7	0
E.Davies	6	1	23	1

Umpires: G.M.Lee and H.Elliott.

Close of play scores. First day: Leicestershire 12/1 (G.Lester 6*, N.F.Armstrong 0*). **Second day:** Leicestershire 253/8 (G.S.Watson 121*, J.Sperry 0*).

Comments: Rain interfered with play on the second and third days.
M.J.L.Turnbull and C.C.Smart put on 175 for Glamorgan's 5th wicket in under two hours.
M.J.L.Turnbull made 156, his highest score of the season, hitting two 6's and 18 4's. He reached his 100 in 135 minutes in his final appearance for Glamorgan. G.S.Watson scored 145 in Leicester's 1st innings. He hit one 6 and 15 4's in a stay of 210 minutes, making his highest score of the season.
H.G.Davies created a new wicketkeeping record for Glamorgan, when he dismissed six batsmen in an innings, five catches and one stumping.

MIDDLESEX v SURREY

Played at Lord's, August 26, 28, 29, 1939.
Toss won by Surrey.
Match drawn.

SURREY

R.J.Gregory	b Gray	20	c Smith b Gray	4
L.B.Fishlock	c Price b Peebles	37	c Edrich b Smith	37
E.W.Whitfield	c Robertson b Sims	4	c Sims b Compton	69
H.S.Squires	c Edrich b Sims	4	b Gray	142
J.F.Parker	lbw b Gray	43	(6) c Robertson b Gray	34
Mr F.R.Brown	c Price b Smith	38	(5) b Gray	12
G.J.Whittaker	b Sims	45	not out	10
*Mr H.M.Garland-Wells	lbw b Compton	10	b Gray	2
E.A.Watts	st Price b Compton	2	not out	41
†G.S.Mobey	b Sims	20		
A.R.Gover	not out	2		
Extras	(B 3, LB 6)	9	(B 16, LB 9)	25
Total		**234**	(7 wickets, declared)	**376**

Fall: 1st inns 1/29, 2/41, 3/47, 4/67, 5/139, 6/152, 7/181, 8/183, 9/231.
2nd inns 1/24, 2/185, 3/242, 4/255, 5/311, 6/326, 7/328.

MIDDLESEX

G.E.Hart	c Mobey b Gover	14	c & b Watts	0
J.D.B.Robertson	b Watts	15	lbw b Squires	140
W.J.Edrich	not out	110	c Gregory b Gover	79
D.C.S.Compton	c Garland-Wells b Gover	5	b Brown	14
Mr F.G.Mann	c Squires b Gover	2	not out	55
J.H.A.Hulme	c Mobey b Gover	4	not out	29
†W.F.F.Price	lbw b Brown	4		
J.M.Sims	c Watts b Parker	16		
C.I.J.Smith	b Parker	0		
*Mr I.A.R.Peebles	run out	3		
L.H.Gray	b Brown	1		
Extras	(B 1, LB 7, NB 3)	11	(B 4, LB 7)	11
Total		**185**	(4 wickets)	**328**

Fall: 1st inns 1/28, 2/30, 3/36, 4/38, 5/52, 6/57, 7/117, 8/117, 9/135.
2nd inns 1/10, 2/165, 3/201, 4/279.

MIDDLESEX	O	M	R	W	O	M	R	W
Smith	17	3	45	1	18	2	89	1
Gray	13	0	51	2	29	1	108	5
Sims	19.2	1	75	4	9	1	43	0
Peebles	15	2	38	1	15	1	54	0
Compton	7	2	16	2	7	4	51	1
Robertson	-	-	-	-	3	1	6	0

SURREY	O	M	R	W	O	M	R	W
Gover	16	2	68	4	15	1	64	1
Watts	11	2	43	1	12	0	75	1
Brown	13.2	4	38	2	21	2	81	1
Parker	3	0	16	2	5	2	15	0
Gregory	2	0	9	0	4	0	24	0
Garland-Wells	-	-	-	-	4	1	16	0
Squires	-	-	-	-	4	0	42	1

Umpires: A.Skelding and E.J.Smith.

Close of play scores. First day: Middlesex 66/6 (W.J.Edrich 20*, J.M.Sims 0*). **Second day:** Surrey 283/4 (H.S.Squires 123*, J.F.Parker 17*).

Comments: A joint benefit match for G.E.Hart and J.H.A.Hulme of Middlesex. W.J.Edrich made 110* hitting 16 4's. He scored these runs out of 130 whilst at the wicket. Resuming his innings on the second day, he scored 90 out of the 119 added by Middlesex to their overnight total. Fifty were added for the 10th wicket between Edrich and L.H.Gray, of which Gray scored one and Edrich 49. H.S.Squires and E.W.Whitfield added 161 for the 3rd wicket in Surrey's 2nd innings. H.S.Squires hit 15 4's in his 142. Middlesex were set to make 426, after Surrey had declared at midday on the final day. J.D.B.Robertson made 140 in nearly four hours and hit 18 4's. He and W.J.Edrich added 155 for the 2nd wicket. This result ended Middlesex's hopes of winning the title.

Bill Edrich on-drives Surrey's Parker during his great innings of 110 out of 157 made while he was at the wicket. In only his third regular season in first-class cricket, Edrich had yet again passed the 2,000-run mark

The end of a brave last-wicket partnership. Gray, who made a single whilst Edrich made 49, is bowled by Freddie Brown of Surrey to end the Middlesex first innings

NOTTINGHAMSHIRE v GLOUCESTERSHIRE

Played at Trent Bridge, Nottingham, August 26, 28, 29, 1939.
Toss won by Gloucestershire.
Gloucestershire won by an innings and 56 runs.

GLOUCESTERSHIRE

C.J.Barnett	c Wheat b Woodhead	81
G.M.Emmett	c Voce b Butler	16
W.L.Neale	c Voce b Butler	15
*Mr W.R.Hammond	c Butler b Voce	153
J.F.Crapp	c & b Woodhead	76
Mr E.D.R.Eagar	c Gunn b Woodhead	5
R.A.Sinfield	c Wheat b Woodhead	24
C.J.Scott	b Butler	1
†E.A.Wilson	not out	14
T.W.J.Goddard	c Harris b Woodhead	0
G.E.E.Lambert	not out	5
Extras	(B 1, LB 2, NB 2)	5
Total	(9 wickets, declared)	**395**

Fall: 1st inns 1/48, 2/101, 3/169, 4/316, 5/345, 6/357, 7/358, 8/390, 9/390.

NOTTINGHAMSHIRE

C.B.Harris	c Wilson b Lambert	10	c Hammond b Goddard	23
F.H.Winrow	b Goddard	39	c Goddard b Scott	38
*Mr G.F.H.Heane	b Lambert	14	c Eagar b Scott	16
J.Hardstaff	c Hammond b Goddard	22	c Barnett b Goddard	13
G.V.Gunn	c Hammond b Goddard	33	c Barnett b Goddard	5
R.J.Giles	c Scott b Goddard	7	run out	6
Mr W.A.Sime	b Goddard	0	c Wilson b Scott	0
W.Voce	c Wilson b Scott	10	not out	12
†A.B.Wheat	run out	21	run out	4
H.J.Butler	c Hammond b Goddard	32	b Goddard	8
F.G.Woodhead	not out	11	c Emmett b Goddard	0
Extras		0	(B 11, LB 3, NB 1)	15
Total		**199**		**140**

Fall: 1st inns 1/19, 2/45, 3/84, 4/87, 5/111, 6/111, 7/122, 8/151, 9/186.
2nd inns 1/44, 2/83, 3/90, 4/101, 5/110, 6/112, 7/113, 8/130, 9/140.

NOTTINGHAMSHIRE	O	M	R	W
Voce	19	0	137	1
Butler	22	1	104	3
Woodhead	24	1	97	5
Heane	8	1	29	0
Gunn	3	0	13	0
Sime	2	0	10	0

GLOUCESTERSHIRE	O	M	R	W	O	M	R	W
Scott	18	2	79	1	9	1	25	3
Lambert	9	0	43	2	2	0	12	0
Goddard	10.5	1	77	6	14.7	1	70	5
Sinfield	-	-	-	-	7	2	18	0

Umpires: E.Robinson and G.Beet.

Close of play scores. First day: Gloucestershire 280/3 (W.R.Hammond 128*, J.F.Crapp 36*). **Second day:** Nottinghamshire 67/1 (F.H.Winrow 25*, G.F.H.Heane 10*).

Comments: Play was delayed until 2.30pm on the first day.
C.L.Barnett made 81 out of the first 101. He hit three 6's and ten 4's in 52 minutes.
W.R.Hammond made 153 in 180 minutes, hitting three 6's and 18 4's. He made his runs out of 215 whilst at the wicket. He reached his 100 out of 131 in 110 minutes.
W.R.Hammond and J.F.Crapp added 147 for the 4th wicket.
W.Voce conceded 77 runs in his first six overs.
Notts followed on 196 behind.
T.W.J.Goddard took his 200th wicket of the season.
The game finished before lunch on the final day.

SOMERSET v DERBYSHIRE

Played at Taunton, August 26, 28, 29, 1939.
Toss won by Somerset.
Derbyshire won by seven wickets.

SOMERSET

F.S.Lee	b Copson	52	c G.H.Pope b A.V.Pope 8
H.Gimblett	lbw b A.V.Pope	5	lbw b A.V.Pope 9
H.T.F.Buse	b Mitchell	16	c G.H.Pope b Copson....41
Mr T.R.Garnett	hit wkt b Rhodes	23	b A.V.Pope................0
*Mr E.F.Longrigg	c Copson b Mitchell	21	b G.H.Pope..............14
Mr F.M.McRae	c A.V.Pope b G.H.Pope	17	b Mitchell................44
Mr H.E.Watts	b G.H.Pope	0	st Alderman b Mitchell ..11
†W.T.Luckes	b G.H.Pope	5	b Mitchell................13
W.H.R.Andrews	b A.V.Pope	15	b Rhodes 7
A.W.Wellard	c Alderman b A.V.Pope	44	c A.V.Pope b G.H.Pope...19
H.L.Hazell	not out	2	not out 0
Extras	(B 5, LB 6)	11	(B 4, LB 11, W 1) 16
Total		**211**	**182**

Fall: 1st inns 1/7, 2/39, 3/82, 4/103, 5/127, 6/127, 7/141, 8/143, 9/204.
2nd inns 1/9, 2/26, 3/32, 4/63, 5/92, 6/123, 7/150, 8/153, 9/177.

DERBYSHIRE

D.Smith	c Watts b Andrews	52	c Luckes b Andrews 27
A.F.Townsend	b Buse	17	not out....................142
†A.E.Alderman	lbw b Andrews	5	c Garnett b Andrews 55
T.S.Worthington	c Luckes b Buse	3	c Luckes b Andrews 1
G.H.Pope	lbw b Buse	0	not out 24
A.E.G.Rhodes	c Andrews b Buse	12	
A.V.Pope	st Luckes b Buse	15	
C.Gladwin	b Buse	7	
*Mr R.H.R.Buckston	not out	7	
T.B.Mitchell	c Hazell b Buse	5	
W.H.Copson	b Buse	0	
Extras	(B 8, LB 3)	11	(B 8, LB 3, NB 3) 13
Total		**134**	**(3 wickets) 262**

Fall: 1st inns 1/73, 2/81, 3/81, 4/93, 5/99, 6/117, 8/128, 9/134.
2nd inns 1/35, 2/223, 3/225.

DERBYSHIRE	O	M	R	W	O	M	R	W
Copson	15	2	43	1	13	1	41	1
A.V.Pope	14.1	4	31	3	14	2	34	3
G.H.Pope	14	4	28	3	9	0	27	2
Mitchell	15	1	80	2	10	0	55	3
Gladwin	2	0	7	0				
Rhodes	3	0	11	1	4.3	1	9	1

SOMERSET	O	M	R	W	O	M	R	W
Wellard	6	1	26	0	16	3	48	0
Andrews	13	0	56	2	19	1	78	3
Buse	10.7	1	41	8	12	0	40	0
Hazell	-	-	-	-	10	0	45	0
Gimblett	-	-	-	-	1.6	0	22	0
Watts	-	-	-	-	1	0	16	0

Umpires: E.Cooke and C.V.Tarbox.

Close of play scores. First day: Somerset 184/8 (W.H.R.Andrews 7*, A.W.Wellard 29*). **Second day:** Somerset 182 all out.

Comments: Play did not commence until after lunch on the first day.
A.F.Townsend scored his maiden century in first-class cricket, beating his previous best score of 49. His undefeated 142 included 17 4's and took 240 minutes.
He and A.E.Alderman put on 188 in 170 minutes for the 2nd wicket in the 2nd innings.
H.F.T.Buse achieved his best bowling analysis of 8 for 41.
W.T.Luckes took over the captaincy of the Somerset side on the third day, due to the illness of E.F.Longrigg.

WORCESTERSHIRE v WARWICKSHIRE

Played at Dudley, August 26, 28, 29, 1939.
Toss won by Worcestershire.
Match drawn.

WORCESTERSHIRE

E.Cooper	lbw b Hollies	66	c Wyatt b Hollies..........75
R.Howorth	c Dollery b Grove	43	lbw b Hollies 36
B.P.King	c Wyatt b Mayer	29	lbw b Wyatt 3
Mr C.H.Palmer	c Hill b Hollies	20	c Cranmer b Wyatt 51
H.H.I.Gibbons	b Grove	17	not out 75
S.H.Martin	st Buckingham b Hollies	88	b Wyatt 2
Mr A.P.Singleton	run out	69	lbw b Hollies 22
*Hon C.J.Lyttelton	b Santall	2	not out 23
R.T.D.Perks	b Hollies	14	
R.O.Jenkins	b Hollies	7	
†J.S.Buller	not out	4	
Extras	(B 4, LB 5)	9	(B 5, LB 7) 12
Total		**368**	**(6 wickets, declared).....299**

Fall: 1st inns 1/82, 2/134, 3/151, 4/162, 5/205, 6/315, 7/324, 8/353, 9/363.
2nd inns 1/78, 2/87, 3/145, 4/187, 5/201, 6/140.

WARWICKSHIRE

A.J.W.Croom	lbw b Perks	1	not out 7
W.A.Hill	c Palmer b Perks	9	c Singleton b Perks 14
F.R.Santall	c Buller b Perks	2	c Buller b Martin 2
Mr R.E.S.Wyatt	c Singleton b Perks	18	not out 10
H.E.Dollery	b Singleton	75	
Mr J.R.Thompson	b Martin	91	
*Mr P.Cranmer	c Cooper b Martin	68	
†J.Buckingham	c Martin b Howorth	0	
W.E.Hollies	b Perks	12	
J.H.Mayer	st Buller b Martin	17	
C.W.Grove	not out	6	
Extras	(LB 8, W 4, NB 6)	18	(LB 1, NB 1) 2
Total		**317**	**(2 wickets) 35**

Fall: 1st inns 1/6, 2/14, 3/17, 4/53, 5/169, 6/278, 7/281, 8/284, 9/297.
2nd inns 1/15, 2/20.

WARWICKSHIRE	O	M	R	W	O	M	R	W
Mayer	15	0	48	1	4	0	23	0
Grove	13	0	76	2	8	0	26	0
Wyatt	20.3	6	85	0	29	4	114	3
Hollies	29	7	84	5	24	2	79	3
Cranmer	2	0	18	0				
Santall	9	0	48	1	3	0	12	0
Croom	-	-	-	-	3	0	22	0
Dollery	-	-	-	-	1	0	11	0

WORCESTERSHIRE	O	M	R	W	O	M	R	W
Perks	21	4	82	5	6	1	26	1
Martin	18.7	1	84	3	6	4	7	1
Howorth	7	0	31	1				
Singleton	13	4	54	1				
Lyttelton	3	0	12	0				
Jenkins	5	0	36	0				

Umpires: H.Cruice and C.N.Woolley.

Close of play scores. First day: Warwickshire 14/2 (F.R.Santall 1*). **Second day:** Worcestershire 58/0 (E.Cooper 32*, R.Howorth 24*).

Comments: S.H.Martin and A.P.Singleton put on 110 for the 6th wicket in 70 minutes.
H.E.Dollery and J.R.Thompson added 116 for Warwickshire's 5th wicket.
Then Thompson and P.Cranmer hit 109 in 50 minutes for the 6th. P.Cranmer made 50 of his 68 in boundaries, five 6's and five 4's. A thunderstorm brought the game to a premature end after Warwickshire had been set to make 351 in 155 minutes.

WORCESTERSHIRE COUNTY CRICKET CLUB

Standing (left to right): H.Yarnold, B.P.King, E.Cooper, S.H.Martin, J.S.Buller, R.O.Jenkins, H.H.I.Gibbons. Seated: R.Howorth, A.F.T.White, Hon C.J.Lyttelton (captain), R.T.D.Perks, C.H.Bull.

LEICESTERSHIRE v DERBYSHIRE

Played at Grace Road, Leicester, August 30, 31, September 1, 1939.
Toss won by Derbyshire.
Match drawn.

DERBYSHIRE

D.Smith	c Armstrong b Sperry	0	c Sperry b Drake	81
A.F.Townsend	b Walsh	32	c Walsh b Sperry	10
†A.E.Alderman	c Packe b Sperry	91	c Walsh b Lester	61
T.S.Worthington	b Walsh	0	b Walsh	0
G.H.Pope	c Armstrong b Sperry	48	c Dawkes b Sperry	34
A.E.G.Rhodes	c Packe b Sperry	12	b Prentice	6
A.V.Pope	c Walsh b Sperry	0	c Packe b Spery	6
C.Gladwin	c Dawkes b Sperry	14	run out	13
*Mr R.H.R.Buckston	not out	3	c Armstrong b Prentice	0
T.B.Mitchell	c Armstrong b Sperry	4	st Dawkes b Sperry	1
W.H.Copson	c Packe b Walsh	2	not out	8
Extras	(B 18, LB 2)	20	(B 14)	14
Total		**226**		**234**

Fall: 1st inns 1/0, 2/75, 3/77, 4/165, 5/191, 6/191, 7/216, 8/217, 9/221.
2nd inns 1/35, 2/137, 3/137, 4/179, 5/190, 6/205, 7/222, 8/225, 9/225.

LEICESTERSHIRE

G.L.Berry	c Smith b A.V.Pope	36	c Worthington b Rhodes	20
G.Lester	c Worthington b A.V.Pope	0	not out	24
N.F.Armstrong	c Gladwin b Copson	3	not out	5
G.S.Watson	c Buckston b Copson	62		
F.T.Prentice	c & b A.V.Pope	10		
Mr C.S.Dempster	c Smith b Copson	5		
*Mr M.St.J.Packe	c G.H.Pope b Copson	20		
†G.O.Dawkes	lbw b Copson	1		
Mr J.E.Walsh	c G.H.Pope b A.V.Pope	0		
C.H.Drake	not out	0		
J.Sperry	b Copson	10		
Extras	(B 17, LB 3, W 2)	22	(B 2)	2
Total		**174**	(1 wicket)	**51**

Fall: 1st inns 1/0, 2/7, 3/70, 4/124, 5/128, 6/140, 7/148, 8/151, 9/159.
2nd inns 1/45.

LEICESTERSHIRE	O	M	R	W	O	M	R	W
Sperry	15	3	48	7	17	1	72	4
Drake	10	1	33	0	10	0	39	1
Walsh	19.3	3	79	3	12	1	65	1
Lester	8	0	27	0	4	0	18	1
Armstrong	1	0	7	0				
Prentice	4	0	12	0	8	0	26	2

DERBYSHIRE	O	M	R	W	O	M	R	W
Copson	14.6	3	39	6	8	1	19	0
A.V.Pope	19	1	72	4	5	0	9	0
Mitchell	3	0	13	0	4	0	10	0
G.H.Pope	3	2	1	0	3	1	9	0
Gladwin	4	0	27	0				
Rhodes	-	-	-	-	3	1	2	1

Umpires: C.N.Woolley and A.Dolphin.

Close of play scores. First day: Leicestershire 119/3 (G.S.Watson 57*, F.T.Prentice 7*). **Second day:** Leicestershire 51/1 (G.Lester 24*, N.F.Armstrong 5*).

Comments: D.Smith was dismissed by the first ball of the match.
On the second day, Leicestershire lost their remaining seven 1st innings wickets for 55 runs in 60 minutes, W.H.Copson taking five of them for 21 runs.
In the 2nd innings D.Smith and A.E.Alderman added 102 in 60 minutes for the 2nd wicket.
There was no play on the third day, due to rain.

MIDDLESEX v WARWICKSHIRE

Played at Lord's, August 30, 31, 1939.
Toss won by Middlesex.
Middlesex won by an innings and 200 runs.

MIDDLESEX

J.D.B.Robertson	c Grove b Wilmot	154
S.M.Brown	lbw b Hollies	50
W.J.Edrich	c & b Hollies	101
D.C.S.Compton	b Grove	86
P.W.Brooks	not out	44
*Mr F.G.Mann	c Buckingham b Grove	29
C.I.J.Smith	c Dollery b Wilmot	45
B.L.Muncer	lbw b Hollies	4
Extras	(B 8, LB 4)	12
Total	(7 wickets, declared)	**525**

Fall: 1st inns 1/171, 2/247, 3/384, 4/411, 5/465, 6/519, 7/525.

†W.F.F.Price, J.M.Sims and L.H.Gray did not bat.

WARWICKSHIRE

A.J.W.Croom	b Smith	12	retired hurt	3
W.A.Hill	b Gray	11	b Sims	23
Mr J.R.Thompson	b Gray	4	c Price b Smith	0
Mr R.E.S.Wyatt	run out	11	c Sims b Gray	6
H.E.Dollery	lbw b Smith	5	c & b Sims	32
F.R.Santall	c Edrich b Sims	43	c Edrich b Sims	3
*Mr P.Cranmer	c Edrich b Sims	8	b Smith	15
†J.Buckingham	not out	47	lbw b Muncer	13
K.Wilmot	c Brown b Muncer	23	st Price b Sims	17
C.W.Grove	c Compton b Sims	14	st Price b Sims	12
W.E.Hollies	run out	2	not out	5
Extras	(B 12, LB 1, NB 1)	14	(B 1, NB 1)	2
Total		**194**		**131**

Fall: 1st inns 1/14, 2/24, 3/35, 4/51, 5/53, 6/64, 7/138, 8/162, 9/186.
2nd inns 1/8, 2/20, 3/65, 4/68, 5/83, 6/85, 7/107, 8/125, 9/131.

WARWICKSHIRE	O	M	R	W
Grove	17	1	91	2
Wyatt	20	2	112	0
Wilmot	16	3	56	2
Hollies	26.6	1	145	3
Santall	9	0	61	0
Cranmer	1	0	11	0
Croom	5	0	37	0

MIDDLESEX	O	M	R	W	O	M	R	W
Smith	14	2	45	2	13	2	53	2
Gray	9	2	35	2	8	2	24	1
Sims	17	3	81	3	13	1	45	5
Muncer	7	2	19	1	2	1	3	1
Robertson	-	-	-	-	3	1	4	0

Umpires: E.Robertson and H.G.Baldwin.

Close of play scores. First day: Middlesex 525/7 (P.W.Brooks 44*).

Comments: The match finished in two days, Warwickshire being dismissed twice on the second day.
J.D.B.Robertson madd 154, his highest score in county cricket. He hit 20 4's.
He and S.M.Brown put on 171 for the 1st Middlesex wicket. Robertson made 102 before lunch on the first day.
W.J.Edrich made 101, including 15 4's.
He and D.C.S.Compton added 137 for the 3rd wicket.
Warwickshire followed on 331 behind.
A.J.W.Croom retired hurt, after a blow on the elbow, after batting for only seven minutes in the 2nd innings.

SUSSEX v YORKSHIRE

Played at Hove, August 30, 31, September 1, 1939.
Toss won by Sussex.
Yorkshire won by nine wickets.

SUSSEX

Mr R.G.Stainton	.... c Wood b Bowes..........14	absent hurt..................0	
John G.Langridge	...run out 60	(1) c Sellers b Robinson 3	
H.W.Parks	...........c Wood b Smailes........35	c Hutton b Verity...........9	
G.Cox	................c Mitchell b Robinson 198	c Wood b Verity.............9	
Jas.Langridge	........c Mitchell b Bowes.......17	c Mitchell b Verity.........0	
J.H.Parks	.........c Robinson b Smailes....2	(2) lbw b Verity............0	
Mr H.T.Bartlett	.....b Robinson...............24	(6) b Verity................3	
*Flt-Lt A.J.Holmes	b Verity...................11	(7) b Verity................4	
†Mr S.C.Griffith	.....c Smailes b Verity.......17	(8) b Verity................1	
J.K.Nye	...............not out 2	(9) not out 3	
D.J.Wood	...........lbw b Robinson 0	(10) run out 0	
Extras	..............(B 3, LB 4)...............7	(B 1)........................1	
Total	..................................**387**	..................................**33**	

Fall: 1st inns 1/26, 2/89, 3/133, 4/202, 5/205, 6/266, 7/321, 8/361, 9/387.
2nd inns 1/0, 2/12, 3/12, 4/13, 5/19, 6/23, 7/377, 8/30, 9/33.

YORKSHIRE

L.Hutton	............lbw b Cox 103	c Griffith b Jas.Langridge 1	
W.Barber	............c Griffith b Nye 22	not out 18	
A.Mitchell	..........c Jas.Langridge b Holmes 67	not out 11	
M.Leyland	..........c sub b J.Parks 64		
Mr N.W.D.Yardley	c & b Jas.Langridge.....108		
†Mr A.B.Sellers	......c Bartlett b J.Parks.......12		
T.F.Smailes	.........b J.Parks...................0		
†A.Wood	............c Wood b Jas.Langridge 2		
E.P.Robinson	........b Jas.Langridge 0		
H.Verity	...............not out 7		
W.E.Bowes	..........c J.Parks b Jas.Langridge 2		
Extras	..............(B 3, LB 1, W 1) 5		
Total	..................................**392**	(1 wicket) **30**	

Fall: 1st inns 1/52, 2/175, 3/204, 4/342, 5/363, 6/364, 7/377, 8/377, 9/386.
2nd inns 1/4.

YORKSHIRE	O	M	R	W	O	M	R	W
Bowes	17	0	71	2				
Smailes	12	0	48	2				
Yardley	9	0	48	0				
Verity	18	1	108	2	6	1	9	7
Robinson	15	2	87	3	5.3	0	23	1
Hutton	4	0	18	0				

SUSSEX	O	M	R	W	O	M	R	W
Nye	19	1	104	1				
J.Parks	33	3	120	3	6.6	1	21	0
Wood	10	1	30	0				
Jas.Langridge	20.4	5	84	4	6	0	9	1
Cox	10	2	34	1				
Holmes	3	0	15	1				

Umpires: J.J.Hills and C.W.L.Parker.

Close of play scores. First day: Yorkshire 112/1 (L.Hutton 55*, A.Mitchell 35*).
Second day: Yorkshire 330/3 (M.Leyland 62*, N.W.D.Yardley 72*).
Comments. J.H.Parks benefit match. This match was the only first-class fixture to be played after 31 August. Despite the extremely difficult travelling conditions, the Yorkshire players being unable to travel back to Yorkshire by car due to the travelling restrictions imposed by the impending wartime situation, the players agreed to continue the game into its third day, as it was Park's benefit match. Despite this gesture, the game produced only £734.10.6. G.Cox batted 200 minutes for his 198, hitting one six and 28 4's. L.Hutton hit 14 4's in his 103, made in about 150 minutes. He and A.Mitchell added 123 for the 2nd wicket. N.W.D.Yardley hit 108, including one 6 and seven 4's. He and M.Leyland and put on 138 in 120 minutes for the 4th wicket. H.Verity, in what proved to be his last game for Yorkshire, took seven wickets for nine runs in only 48 balls, as Sussex were bowled out for 33 in a mere 91 deliveries on a rain-affected wicket (R.G.Stainton did not bat, absent hurt). There was no play on the second day until 3.30pm.

Yorkshire's Norman Yardley pulls a ball to the boundary at Hove, on his way to 108.

Maurice Leyland in the course of his 64 against Sussex. The fielder with outstretched arm is George Cox, who earlier made 198 against the County Champions.

Two fine Yorkshire bowlers. *Left:* Bill Bowes, who finished the season with 122 wickets at 14.48 apiece. *Right:* Hedley Verity, topped the national averages with 191 wickets at 13.13 each. Four years later, Verity was to die in Italy of wounds.

SOMERSET v NORTHAMPTONSHIRE

Played at Taunton, August 30, 31, 1939.
Toss won by Northamptonshire.
Somerset won by an innings and 92 runs.

NORTHAMPTONSHIRE

Mr E.J.H.Dixon	b Andrews 2	c Wellard b Andrews 5
P.Davis	b Wellard 0	b Andrews 10
D.Brookes	b Wellard 22	c Meyer b Andrews 6
J.E.Timms	c Gimblett b Andrews ..46	b Wellard 4
F.P.O'Brien	c Wellerd b Buse 9	c Buse b Wellard............1
W.E.Merritt	c Meyer b Buse 0	(8) lbw b Wellard 2
*Mr R.P.Nelson	c Luckes b Andrews 1	(6) c Garnett b Buse 42
†K.C.James	b Wellard 12	(7) lbw b Meyer 14
Mr S.I.Philips	run out 20	c Luckes b Meyer 17
R.J.Partridge	b Andrews 0	c Luckes b Wellard 22
E.J.Herbert	not out 17	not out 16
Extras	(B 5, LB 4) 9	(LB 9, W 2) 11
Total	**138**	**150**

Fall: 1st inns 1/0, 2/4, 3/32, 4/49, 5/49, 6/67, 7/93, 8/99, 9/99.
2nd inns 1/13, 2/21, 3/24, 4/26, 5/33, 6/68, 7/73, 8/106, 9/112.

SOMERSET

F.S.Lee	st James b Merritt 36
H.Gimblett	b Timms 67
H.T.F.Buse	c James b Timms 9
*Mr R.J.O.Meyer	c Dixon b Merritt 22
Mr T.R.Garnett	b Timms 75
W.H.R.Andrews	st James b Merritt 12
Mr F.M.McRae	lbw b Timms 50
Mr H.E.Watts	b Merritt 36
†W.T.Luckes	not out 33
A.W.Wellard	b Merritt 21
H.L.Hazell	not out 4
Extras	(B 8, LB 2, W 5) 15
Total	(9 wickets, declared) **380**

Fall: 1st inns 1/105, 2/111, 3/116, 4/151, 5/164, 6/265, 7/286, 8/342, 9/370.

SOMERSET	O	M	R	W	O	M	R	W
Wellard	15	0	56	3	13.4	3	46	4
Andrews	9	1	23	4	9	0	29	3
Buse	7	0	33	2	5	0	21	1
Meyer	5	1	17	0	8	0	30	2
Hazell	4	0	0	0	1	0	13	0

NORTHANTS	O	M	R	W
Partridge	20	1	96	0
Herbert	9	1	43	0
Timms	12	0	63	4
Merritt	12.7	0	149	5
Nelson	5	2	14	0

Umpires: H.Elliott and J.Hardstaff.

189/5 (T.R.Garnett 29*, F.M.McRae 10*).

Comments: The game finished in two days.
H.Gimblett and F.S.Lee put on 105 for the 1st Somerset wicket in 55 minutes.
T.R.Garnett and F.M.McRae added 101 for the 6th wicket.

SURREY v LANCASHIRE

Played at Old Trafford, Manchester, August 30, 31, 1939.
Toss won by Surrey.
Match drawn.

SURREY

R.J.Gregory	c Paynter b Pollard 7	c Roberts b Pollard 27
L.B.Fishlock	c Pollard b Roberts 70	b Pollard 4
E.W.Whitfield	c Phillipson b Pollard ...28	lbw b Pollard 1
H.S.Squires	c Paynter b Phillipson ..64	c Washbrook b Higson ...49
J.F.Parker	c Wilkinson b Nutter 79	not out 77
G.J.Whittaker	lbw b Pollard 19	c & b Iddon 16
*Mr H.M.Garland-Wells	c Farrimond b Pollard 0	b Nutter 1
†G.S.Mobey	b Phillipson 38	b Pollard 15
E.A.Watts	not out 32	b Pollard 0
B.Constable	not out 5	b Pollard 6
A.R.Gover	(did not bat)	b Roberts 1
Extras	(B 1, LB 7) 8	(B 6, LB 6, NB 3) 15
Total	(8 wickets, declared) ...**350**	**212**

Fall: 1st inns 1/19, 2/107, 3/109, 4/208, 5/253, 6/253, 7/290, 8/343.
2nd inns 1/12, 2/23, 3/56, 4/124, 5/150, 6/153, 7/187, 8/191, 9/205.

LANCASHIRE

C.Washbrook	c Fishlock b Parker 37
E.Paynter	c Mobey b Watts 7
A.E.Nutter	c Mobey b Gover 16
N.Oldfield	lbw b Garland-Wells 91
J.Iddon	c Watts b Parker 0
W.E.Phillipson	c Parker b Watts 25
†W.Farrimond	lbw b Watts 6
*Mr T.A.Higson	c Mobey b Watts 3
R.Pollard	c Constable b Garland-Wells 6
W.B.Roberts	not out 3
L.L.Wilkinson	b Watts 10
Extras	(B 4, LB 1, NB 2) 7
Total	**211**

Fall: 1st inns 1/9, 2/37, 3/77, 4/77, 5/141, 6/153, 7/165, 8/188, 9/198.

LANCASHIRE	O	M	R	W	O	M	R	W
Phillipson	19	0	86	2	8	0	40	0
Pollard	26	2	72	4	15	1	65	6
Nutter	10	0	64	1	5	0	22	1
Wilkinson	8	0	41	0				
Higson	5	0	21	0	3	0	15	1
Roberts	23	5	58	1	7.2	1	29	1
Iddon	-	-	-	-	4	0	26	1

SURREY	O	M	R	W
Gover	8	0	49	1
Watts	16.4	1	60	5
Parker	10	0	38	2
Garland-Wells	9	1	35	2
Constable	3	0	22	0

Umpires: D.Hendren and W.Reeves.

Close of play scores. First day: Surrey 350/8 (E.A.Watts 32*, B.Constable 5*).
Second day: Surrey 212 all out.
Comments: The Oval being occupied by the Military, this match was transferred to Manchester. The Surrey team arrived in Manchester at 4am, several players sleeping in the pavilion. No play took place on the third day, due to the deteriorating international situation, with Lancashire requiring 352 to win.

Denis Compton (left) and brother Leslie look smart in the new police uniforms but wicketkeeper Fred Price has yet to be kitted out for his new role.

WORCESTERSHIRE v NOTTINGHAMSHIRE

Played at Worcester, August 30, 31, 1939.
Toss won by Nottinghamshire.
Worcestershire won by an innings and 31 runs.

NOTTINGHAMSHIRE

C.B.Harris	c Gibbons b Perks	0	b Perks		6
G.V.Gunn	c Singleton b Martin	4	c Singleton b Perks		11
*Mr G.F.H.Heane	b Howorth	91	c Perks b Howorth		25
J.Hardstaff	lbw b Perks	9	b Perks		11
R.J.Giles	b Howorth	3	b Perks		0
Mr W.A.Sime	c & b Martin	9	b Perks		4
W.Voce	c & b Howorth	18	c Cooper b Perks		5
Mr J.B.Hall	c Howorth b Singleton	14	c Buller b Perks		0
†A.B.Wheat	run out	1	lbw b Howorth		1
H.J.Butler	lbw b Singleton	1	c Lyttelton b Howorth		10
F.G.Woodhead	not out	1	not out		4
Extras	(B 10, LB 5)	15	(LB 4, W 3)		7
Total		**166**			**84**

Fall: 1st inns 1/0, 2/12, 3/35, 4/59, 5/90, 6/114, 7/143, 8/144, 9/152.
2nd inns 1/15, 2/20, 3/36, 4/38, 5/58, 6/60, 7/67, 8/68, 9/78.

WORCESTERSHIRE

R.Howorth	b Hall	7
E.Cooper	lbw b Voce	37
B.P.King	c Wheat b Voce	8
Mr C.H.Palmer	b Voce	0
H.H.I.Gibbons	lbw b Hall	23
S.H.Martin	c Butler b Woodhead	38
Mr A.P.Singleton	not out	102
*Hon C.J.Lyttelton	run out	31
R.O.Jenkins	c Wheat b Voce	11
†J.S.Buller	b Voce	1
R.T.D.Perks	b Voce	9
Extras	(B 12, W 1, NB 1)	14
Total		**281**

Fall: 1st inns 1/11, 2/22, 3/22, 4/81, 5/85, 6/177, 7/242, 8/265, 9/271.

WORCESTERSHIRE	O	M	R	W	O	M	R	W
Perks	19	1	55	2	12	1	30	7
Martin	12	1	34	2	4	0	13	0
Singleton	9	1	29	2				
Howorth	12.6	2	31	3	7.2	0	34	3
Jenkins	1	0	2	0				

NOTTINGHAMSHIRE	O	M	R	W
Voce	21.6	0	106	6
Hall	12	0	56	2
Butler	17	4	44	0
Woodhead	14	3	61	1

Umpires: J.A.Smart and F.I.Walden.

Close of play scores. First day: Worcestershire 138/5 (S.H.Martin 20*).

Comments: A.P.Singleton made an undefeated 102, his first century for Worcester, in about 150 minutes. It included 14 4's.
Only 115 behind, Notts collapsed to 84 all out, R.T.D.Perks claiming 7 for 30.
R.Howorth completed the double for the first time in his career, when he dismissed the last Nottinghamshire batsman in the 2nd innings.

THE UNIVERSITY MATCHES

The Varsity captains of 1939 apparently had the world at their feet, but each had vastly differing futures. Yorkshire-born Oxford skipper and right-hand batsman Eric J.H.Dixon *(left)* also made nine first-class appearances for Northants in 1939 after having earlier been a member of the combined Oxford and Cambridge side which toured Jamaica. In 1941, Dixon was reported missing, presumed killed in action, during World War Two. The Cambridge skipper, P.M.Studd *(right)*, also a right-hand batsman, was born in Dublin and educated at Harrow before going up to Cambridge, who were his only first-class side. In 1970-71, as Sir Peter Malden Studd, he was Lord Mayor of London.

CAMBRIDGE UNIVERSITY v NORTHAMPTONSHIRE

Played at Cambridge, May 3, 4, 5, 1939.
Toss won by Northamptonshire.
Northampton won by 78 runs.

NORTHAMPTONSHIRE

Mr A.W.Snowden	...hit wkt b Carris 72	c & b Shirreff 63	
H.W.Greenwood	....c Shirreff b Wilson 49	b Ruane 8	
D.Brookes	........c & b Carris 114	b Ruane 3	
J.E.Timms	..........c Shirreff b Singh 20	not out 103	
*Mr R.P.Nelson	....b Shirreff 23		
†K.C.James	..........b Shirreff 4		
F.P.O'Brien	........not out 53		
Mr S.M.Nasiruddin	b Wilson 0		
W.E.Merritt	........b Wilson 1	(5) not out 32	
R.J.Partridge	.......b Wilson 3		
J.E.Buswell	..........c Blake b Shirreff 7		
Extras	............(B 11, LB 4) 15	(B 4, LB 2) 6	
Total	..........................**361**	(3 wickets, declared).....**215**	

Fall: 1st inns 1/108, 2/156, 3/189, 4/248, 5/260, 6/321, 7/322, 8/324, 9/350.
2nd inns 1/18, 2/22, 3/164.

CAMBRIDGE UNIVERSITY

Mr B.D.Carris	.......c James b Timms 16	b Merritt 40	
Mr J.R.Thompson	st James b Merritt 21	b Nelson 21	
†Mr M.S.Glennie	....c James b Merritt.......11	(8) b Timms 1	
Mr A.H.Brodhurst	...c James b Merritt.........42	c Greenwood b Merritt 26	
Mr F.G.Mann	.......st James b Merritt 8	b Timms 29	
*Mr P.M.Studd	......b Partridge................27	lbw b Merritt 27	
Mr A.C.Shirreff	......c & b Nelson 47	lbw b Merritt 8	
Mr D.C.Wilson	......lbw b Merritt 0	(9) not out 17	
M.K.B.Singh	........c Greenwood b Merritt 2	(10) c James b Timms 7	
Mr J.P.Blake	.........not out 82	(3) c Greenwood b Nelson 60	
Mr J.D.Ruane	.......c Greenwood b Merritt....19	c & b Merritt 7	
Extras	..............(B 3, LB 3) 6	(B 1) 1	
Total	.............................**254**		**244**

Fall: 1st inns 1/36, 2/45, 3/54, 4/74, 5/87, 6/125, 7/127, 8/141, 9/179.
2nd inns 1/39, 2/101, 3/131, 4/155, 5/195, 6/205, 7/208, 8/215, 9/229.

CAMBRIDGE	O	M	R	W	O	M	R	W
Ruane	15	1	67	0	12	1	41	2
Shirreff	26.7	7	98	3	13	1	60	1
Singh	18	2	86	1	3	0	25	0
Wilson	18	2	50	4	13	0	53	0
Carris	15	3	45	2	6	0	25	0
Mann	-	-	-	-	1	0	5	0

NORTHANTS	O	M	R	W	O	M	R	W
Buswell	6	0	28	0	7	2	35	0
Partridge	16	0	87	1	6	1	18	0
Timms	9	1	41	1	13	0	51	3
Merritt	17	2	69	7	21.2	1	92	5
Nelson	7	1	23	1	7	2	30	2
O'Brien	-	-	-	-	4	0	17	0

Umpires: W.Wainwright and J.J.Hills.

Close of play scores. First day: Northants 356/9 (F.P.O'Brien 52*, J.E.Buswell 3*). **Second day:** Northants 131/2 (A.W.Snowden 43*, J.E.Timms 74*).
Comments: A.W.Snowden and H.W.Greenwood put on 108 for Northants 1st wicket.
D.Brookes made 114 in 180 minutes, hitting 11 4's.
In Northants 2nd innings, A.W.Snowden and J.E.Timms added 142 for the 3rd wicket.
K.C.James the Northamptonshire 'keeper, was involved in the dismissal of the first five Cambridge batsmen.
It was Northamptonshire's first victory in over 100 consecutive matches. Their last victory was in May 1935.
J.P.Blake and J.D.Ruane put on 75 for the tenth wicket in the University's 1st innings.

CAMBRIDGE UNIVERSITY v NOTTINGHAMSHIRE

At Cambridge, May 10, 11, 12, 1939.
Toss won by Cambridge University.
Nottinghamshire won by ten wickets.

CAMBRIDGE UNIVERSITY

Mr B.D.Carris	.......b Butler 12	(4) c Woodhead b Butler	26
Mr J.R.Thompson	b Voce 9	(1) b Heane 42	
Mr J.P.Blake	.........c Wheat b Voce 80	c Heane b Woodhead.......5	
Mr J.D.A.Langley	...b Butler 0	(6) c Knowles b Woodhead	25
Mr P.J.Dickinson	....b Butler 1	(7) b Woodhead............28	
*Mr P.M.Studd	......c Voce b Heane 62	(5) c Gunn b Heane 6	
Mr F.G.Mann	.......c Butler b Bradley 38	(2) lbw b Voce 10	
†Mr D.M.Witherington (9)	c & b Voce 18	b Gunn 27	
Mr A.C.Shirreff	......c Harris b Bradley 13	(8) b Gunn 18	
Mr D.W.Gillespie	....b Butler 0	lbw b Bradley 7	
Mr D.C.Wilson	......not out 0	not out 13	
Extras	............(B 3, LB 1, NB 2) 6	(B 8, LB 4, NB 2) 14	
Total	...........................**239**		**221**

Fall: 1st inns 1/16, 2/39, 3/39, 4/45, 5/165, 6/173, 7/223, 8/238, 9/239.
2nd inns 1/21, 2/38, 3/86, 4/86, 5/101, 6/144, 7/151, 8/184, 9/125.

NOTTINGHAMSHIRE

C.B.Harris	..........c Witherington b Dickinson 67	not out 23	
J.Knowles	............lbw b Shirreff 24	not out 16	
*Mr G.F.H.Heane	... run out 0		
J.Hardstaff	..........c Witherington b Gillespie 9		
G.V.Gunn	............c Dickinson b Carris 71		
Mr G.L.Willatt	......b Carris 59		
W.Voce	...............c & b Shirreff 104		
†A.B.Wheat	...........c Mann b Dickinson 5		
F.G.Woodhead	.......b Shirreff 24		
H.J.Butler	..........not out 23		
J.Bradley	...........not out 3		
Extras	..............(B 21, LB 5, NB 3) 29	(B 6, W 1) 7	
Total	..............(9 wickets, declared) **418**	(No wicket) **46**	

Fall: 1st inns 1/29, 2/38, 3/56, 4/151, 5/189, 6/288, 7/309, 8/369, 9/394.

NOTTINGHAMSHIRE	O	M	R	W	O	M	R	W
Voce	23	3	77	3	12	3	38	1
Butler	18	2	66	4	15	2	47	1
Woodhead	12	3	26	0	13	5	27	3
Bradley	13.4	1	43	2	14	1	41	1
Heane	9	2	21	1	10	0	38	2
Gunn	-	-	-	-	6	1	16	2

CAMBRIDGE	O	M	R	W	O	M	R	W
Gillespie	15	1	51	1				
Shirreff	30	2	131	3				
Dickinson	22	4	86	2	4.5	0	18	0
Wilson	24	4	65	0				
Carris	18	4	56	2				
Mann	-	-	-	-	5	0	21	0

Umpires: W.Wainwright and J.J.Hills.

Close of play scores. First day: Nottinghamshire 38/2 (C.B.Harris 8*, J.Hardstaff 0*). **Second day:** Nottinghamshire 418/9 (H.J.Butler 23*, J.Bradley 3*).

Comments: J.P.Blake and P.M.Studd added 120 for the 5th Cambridge wicket in their 1st innings.
W.Voce, although eventually making 104 in 195 minutes, was unfortunate to run four to reach his 100, only to discover that the umpire had called 'one short'. His century included one 6 and ten 4's.
J.P.Blake was awarded his blue.

161

CAMBRIDGE UNIVERSITY v MIDDLESEX

Played at Cambridge, May 13, 15, 16, 1939.
Toss won by Middlesex.
Match drawn.

MIDDLESEX

J.D.B.Robertson	b Carris	106
S.M.Brown	b Dickinson	28
Rev E.T.Killick	lbw b Dickinson	19
Mr N.S.Hotchkin	c Glennie b Gaekwar	11
Mr J.P.Mann	c Glennie b Carris	62
†W.F.F.Price	b Dickinson	80
Mr F.F.T.Barnardo	b Dickinson	0
J.H.A.Hulme	c Thompson b Dickinson	59
A.Thompson	b Shirreff	18
L.H.Gray	not out	2
*Mr I.A.R.Peebles	lbw b Shirreff	0
Extras	(LB 10, W 1, NB 2)	13
Total		**398**

Fall: 1st inns 1/64, 2/105, 3/141, 4/187, 5/306, 6/306.

CAMBRIDGE UNIVERSITY

Mr B.D.Carris	lbw b Robertson	7
Mr F.G.Mann	c Brown b Gray	36
Mr J.R.Thompson	not out	133
Mr J.P.Blake	lbw b Peebles	2
Mr G.L.Willatt	st Price b Peebles	34
*Mr P.M.Studd	lbw b Gray	1
Mr P.J.Dickinson	st Price b Peebles	8
Mr A.C.Shirreff	b Peebles	0
†Mr M.S.Glennie	c Brown b Mann	0
K.S.Gaekwar	not out	13
Extras	(B 3, LB 7)	10
Total	(8 wickets)	**244**

Fall: 1st inns 1/11, 2/70, 3/90, 4/170, 8/194.
Mr S.M.A.Banister did not bat.

CAMBRIDGE	O	M	R	W
Gaekwar	15	0	79	1
Shirreff	19.6	2	92	2
Dickinson	27	5	95	5
Banister	4	0	22	0
Carris	14	1	84	2
Mann	1	0	13	0

MIDDLESEX	O	M	R	W
Gray	16	4	42	2
Robertson	11	1	56	1
Hulme	6	0	31	0
Peebles	13	2	49	4
Thompson	4	0	14	0
Mann	8	0	42	1

Umpires: W.Wainwright and J.J.Hills.

Close of play scores. First day: Middlesex 398 all out. **Second day:** Cambridge University 244/8 (J.R.Thompson 133*, K.S.Gaekwar 13*).

Comments: J.D.M.Robertson scored a maiden century for Middlesex. He hit 13 4's in his 106, made in 135 minutes.
J.P.Mann and W.F.F.Price added 119 in 80 minutes for the 5th wicket.
J.R.Thompson scored 133 out of 233 whilst at the wicket. He scored ten 4's.
Play ended 45 minutes early on the second day due to rain and there was no play on the final day.

CAMBRIDGE UNIVERSITY v YORKSHIRE

At Fenners, Cambridge, May 24, 25, 26, 1939.
Toss won by Cambridge University.
Yorkshire won by nine wickets.

CAMBRIDGE UNIVERSITY

*Mr B.D.Carris	c Mitchell b Turner	11	b Robinson	44
Mr F.G.Mann	b Bowes	7	c & b Hutton	51
Mr J.P.Blake	b Bowes	3	b Bowes	61
Mr F.F.T.Barnardo	b Turner	0	lbw b Hutton	75
Mr A.H.Brodhurst	c Wood b Bowes	5	not out	106
Mr D.M.Witherington	run out	24	b Turner	0
†Mr K.D.Downes	b Bowes	5	c Turner b Hutton	1
Mr A.C.Shirreff	b Yardley	7	st Wood b Robinson	20
Mr D.C.Wilson	c & b Hutton	9	b Robinson	0
Mr J.Webster	not out	3	b Robinson	0
Mr J.L.Richards	st Wood b Hutton	0	b Robinson	0
Extras	(B 2, LB 6, NB 2)	10	(B 7, LB 1, NB 3)	11
Total		**84**		**369**

Fall: 1st inns 1/14, 2/23, 3/23, 4/28, 5/30, 6/40, 7/56, 8/68, 9/84.
2nd inns 1/96, 2/104, 3/227, 4/251, 5/252, 6/265, 7/346, 8/361, 9/361.

YORKSHIRE

W.Barber	lbw b Webster	29	(3) not out	5
L.Hutton	b Webster	102		
Mr N.W.D.Yardley	not out	140		
C.Turner	not out	62		
†A.Wood	(did not bat)		(1) run out	54
T.F.Smailes	(did not bat)		(2) not out	40
Extras	(B 14, LB 3)	17	(B 4, NB 1)	5
Total	(2 wickets, declared)	**350**	(1 wicket)	**104**

Fall: 1st inns 1/92, 2/217.
2nd inns 1/96.
*Mr A.B.Sellers, A.Mitchell, H.Verity, W.E.Bowes and E.P.Robinson did not bat.

YORKSHIRE	O	M	R	W	O	M	R	W
Bowes	11	3	31	4	20	5	51	1
Smailes	6	3	9	0	16	2	77	0
Turner	6	0	14	2	8	3	11	1
Yardley	7	1	15	1	4	1	12	0
Robinson	3	1	4	0	19.5	4	80	5
Hutton	1.6	0	1	2	16	6	62	3
Verity	-	-	-	-	26	6	64	0
Barber	-	-	-	-	2	1	1	0

CAMBRIDGE	O	M	R	W	O	M	R	W
Webster	22	1	96	2	7	0	36	0
Richards	9	0	32	0	4	1	18	0
Shirreff	13	1	58	0	3.6	1	21	0
Wilson	17	3	53	0	6	1	24	0
Mann	5	0	46	0				
Carris	6	0	48	0				

Umpires: J.J.Hills and W.Wainwright.

Close of play scores. First day: Yorkshire 252/2 (N.W.D.Yardley 81*, C.Turner 25).
Second day: Cambridge University 252/5 (A.H.Brodhurst 12*, K.D.Downes 0*).

Comments: L.Hutton scored 102 in about 150 minutes, hitting 12 4's. He and N.W.D.Yardley put on 125 for the 2nd wicket.
N.W.D.Yardley and C.Turner added an unbroken 133 for the 3rd wicket.
N.W.D.Yardley's 140* contained 24 4's.
J.P.Blake and F.F.T.Barnardo made 123 for the 3rd Cambridge wicket in their 2nd innings.
A.H.Brodhurst hit his first century for Cambridge, making 106* in 150 minutes, hitting 17 4's.

CAMBRIDGE UNIVERSITY v LEICESTERSHIRE

At Cambridge, June 3, 5, 6, 1939.
Toss won by Leicestershire.
Match drawn.

LEICESTERSHIRE

G.L.Berry	b Dickinson 4	b Dickinson 17	
G.S.Watson	c Blake b Webster 9	(3) c Shirreff b J.P.Mann 0	
N.F.Armstrong	st Witherington b J.P.Mann 131	(7) not out 16	
G.Lester	c Studd b Shirreff 11	(9) not out 7	
F.T.Prentice	not out 163	(2) c Witherington b Webster 65	
M.Tompkin	b Shirreff 7	(5) lbw b Broadhurst 44	
*Mr M.St.J.Packe	c Thompson b Shirreff 14	(6) c Blake b Webster 1	
Mr J.A.T.Sharp	c & b Broadhurst 16	(4) c & b J.P.Mann 0	
†G.O.Dawkes	b Dickinson 18	(8) c Shirreff b J.P.Mann 23	
C.H.Drake	b Webster 8		
W.H.Flamson	c Witherington b Dickinson 0		
Extras	(B 24, LB 5) 29	(B 10, LB 3, W 1) 14	
Total	.................**410**	(7 wickets) **187**	

Fall: 1st inns 1/19, 2/19, 3/47, 4/289, 5/298, 6/322, 7/348, 8/376, 9/403.
2nd inns 1/23, 2/29, 3/29, 4/129, 5/138, 6/139, 7/175.

CAMBRIDGE UNIVERSITY

Mr F.G.Mann	c Dawkes b Drake 128
Mr J.R.Thompson	c Drake b Flamson 130
Mr J.P.Blake	lbw b Flamson 26
Mr A.H.Brodhurst	lbw b Sharp 111
Mr J.D.A.Langley	c Lester b Prentice 13
*Mr P.M.Studd	c Dawkes b Sharp 16
Mr J.P.Mann	lbw b Sharp 9
†Mr D.M.Witherington	b Armstrong 17
Mr A.C.Shirreff	not out 19
Mr P.J.Dickinson	lbw b Sharp 40
Mr J.Webster	run out 0
Extras	(B 13, LB 9) 22
Total	.................**531**

Fall: 1st inns 1/262, 2/276, 3/303, 4/345, 5/393, 6/419, 7/456, 8/476, 9/531.

CAMBRIDGE	O	M	R	W	O	M	R	W
Webster	36	10	128	2	12	6	23	2
Dickinson	26.5	5	82	3	14	3	42	1
Shirreff	29	10	78	3	6	2	7	0
J.P.Mann	11	0	55	1	16	2	71	3
Brodhurst	9	0	38	1	12	1	30	1

LEICESTERSHIRE	O	M	R	W
Flamson	20	0	91	2
Drake	25.6	2	99	1
Armstrong	20	1	77	1
Prentice	19	1	95	1
Lester	16	1	84	0
Sharp	17	2	63	4

Umpires: J.J.Hills and W.Wainwright.

Close of play scores. First day: Leicestershire 367/7 (F.T.Prentice 139*, G.O.Dawkes 14*). **Second day:** Cambridge University 427/6 (A.H.Brodhurst 88*, D.M.Witherington 0*).
Comments: M.St.J.Packe captained Leicester for the first time. He was the youngest player to do so, aged 22 years, 286 days. N.F.Armstrong and F.T.Prentice put on 242 for Leicestershire's 4th wicket. Both completed their centuries in the same over and both innings contained 17 4's. Prentice was at the wicket for six hours for his 163*.
Cambridge had a record 1st-wicket partnership of 262 between F.G.Mann and J.R.Thompson, made in about 200 minutes.
F.G.Mann hit his maiden first-class century, his 128 containing 11 4's. J.R.Thompson hit 13 boundaries in his 130.
A.H.Brodhurst made it a third hundred for Cambridge, hitting 14 4's in an innings which lasted only 110 minutes. His 111 was his second consecutive century.
In Leicester's 2nd innings, F.T.Prentice and M.Tompkin put on a 100 for the 4th wicket. P.J.Dickinson and A.C.Shirreff were awarded their blues.
C.H.Drake, aged 17, made his debut for Leicestershire.

CAMBRIDGE UNIVERSITY v THE ARMY

At Cambridge, June 7, 8, 9, 1939.
Toss won by Cambridge University.
Match drawn.

CAMBRIDGE UNIVERSITY

Mr B.D.Carris	c White b Steele 1	b Steele 2	
Mr F.G.Mann	c Steele b Straubenzee ...51	b White 21	
Mr J.R.Thompson	c Cokayne-Frith b Straubenzee 45	lbw b Steele 23	
Mr J.P.Blake	c Hayles b Packe 68	c Packe b Nelson 46	
Mr A.H.Brodhurst	c Southby b Packe 11	c Manners b Steele 5	
*Mr P.M.Studd	c Nelson b Straubenzee 62	c Nelson b Straubenzee ...21	
Mr J.P.Mann	c Hayles b Straubenzee 39	not out 10	
†Mr D.M.Witherington	not out 52	not out 9	
Mr P.J.Dickinson	c Packe b Manners 40	lbw b Straubenzee 4	
Mr D.C.Wilson	not out 23		
Extras	(B 3, LB 12, W 3, NB 1) 19	(B 1, LB 4, NB 3) 8	
Total	(8 wickets, declared) **411**	(7 wickets) **149**	

Fall: 1st inns 8/395.

K.S.Gaekwar did not bat.

THE ARMY

Mr A.R.C.Southby	lbw b Dickinson 8
Mr M.D.P.Magill	lbw b Carris 11
Mr P.M.Nelson	c Thompson b Dickinson 62
Mr C.Cokayne-Frith	c F.G.Mann b J.P.Mann 54
Mr G.S.Grimston	c Blake b Wilson 104
*Mr C.W.C.Packe	c Wilson b Brodhurst ...145
Revd J.W.J.Steele	c Witherington b Brodhurst 6
Mr H.H.Van Straubenzee	b Brodhurst 38
Mr W.M.E.White	b Brodhurst 18
Mr D.C.J.Manners	not out 33
†Mr B.R.M.Hayles	c & b Carris 40
Extras	(B 9, LB 7, W 2) 18
Total	.................**537**

Fall: 1st inns 3/73, 8/426, 9/487.

THE ARMY	O	M	R	W	O	M	R	W
Steele	24	3	86	1	15	3	33	3
Magill	16	3	57	0				
Straubenzee	32	9	96	4	7	1	18	2
White	4	1	26	0	7	1	27	1
Manners	20	2	83	1				
Grimston	1	0	11	0				
Packe	9	1	33	2				
Nelson	-	-	-	-	15	1	63	1

CAMBRIDGE	O	M	R	W
Gaekwar	13	2	48	0
Dickinson	30	5	96	2
Carris	22	4	80	2
J.P.Mann	26	2	150	1
Wilson	13	1	62	1
Brodhurst	20	1	83	4

Umpires: W.Wainwright and G.H.Watts.

Close of play scores. First day: Cambridge University 333/7 (D.M.Witherington 13*, P.J.Dickinson 24*). **Second day:** The Army 326/4 (G.S.Grimston 81*, C.W.C.Packe 99*).
Comments: P.M.Studd and J.P.Mann added 102 in 90 minutes for the 6th wicket in 90 minutes.
G.S.Grimston and C.W.C.Packe put on 220 in two hours for the Army's 5th wicket. They scored 173 runs between tea and the close of the second day.
C.W.C.Packe hit 20 4's in his 145, which took 170 minutes.
G.S.Grimston's 104 was made in 210 minutes. It was his maiden century in first-class cricket.

CAMBRIDGE UNIVERSITY v FREE FORESTERS

At Cambridge, June 10, 12, 13, 1939.
Toss won by Free Foresters.
Match drawn.

FREE FORESTERS

Mr C.P.Johnstone	lbw b Webster	15	not out	49
Mr W.H.Webster	b Webster	24	c F.G.Mann b Webster	4
M.J.H.Pawle	c & b Shirreff	20	c Thompson b Gillespie	34
Mr B.H.Valentine	c Downes b Gillespie	10	c Brodhurst b F.G.Mann	39
Mr F.R.Brown	c J.P.Mann b Shirreff	16	not out	67
Mr S.A.Block	c & b Shirreff	52		
Mr W.M.Welch	c J.P.Mann b Gillespie	104		
Mr M.A.C.P.Kaye	c Studd b Shirreff	1		
†Mr N.B.Sherwell	c Studd b Shirreff	32		
Mr A.D.Baxter	b Carris	6		
Mr J.M.Brocklebank	not out	0		
Extras	(B 4, LB 1, W 2)	7	(B 8, NB 1)	9
Total		**287**	(3 wickets)	**202**

CAMBRIDGE UNIVERSITY

Mr F.G.Mann	c Valentine b Brocklebank	8
Mr J.R.Thompson	b Baxter	0
Mr J.P.Blake	lbw b Brocklebank	37
Mr B.D.Carris	c Pawle b Brown	63
Mr D.W.Gillespie	st Sherwell b Kaye	60
Mr A.H.Brodhurst	c Brown b Baxter	26
*Mr P.M.Studd	c Pawle b Brown	56
Mr J.P.Mann	b Kaye	15
†Mr K.D.Downes	st Sherwell b Brown	27
Mr A.C.Shirreff	b Brocklebank	11
Mr J.Webster	not out	2
Extras	(B 24, LB 3, W 2, NB 5)	34
Total		**339**

CAMBRIDGE	O	M	R	W	O	M	R	W
Webster	21	9	104	2	9	1	45	1
Shirreff	17	3	58	5	7	1	31	0
Gillespie	19	0	82	2	5	1	18	1
Brodhurst	2	0	12	0	5	0	34	0
Carris	4.1	1	9	1	2	0	14	0
J.P.Mann	3	0	15	0	3	0	20	0
F.G.Mann	-	-	-	-	3	0	31	1

FREE FORESTERS	O	M	R	W
Baxter	21	1	97	2
Kaye	13	2	62	2
Brown	27	10	48	3
Brocklebank	16.6	5	40	3
Welch	10	0	58	0

Umpires: W.Wainwright and G.H.Watts.

Close of play scores. First day: Cambridge University 57/3 (B.D.Carris 5*, D.W.Gillespie 2*). **Second day:** Cambridge University 236/6 (P.M.Studd 17*, J.P.Mann 6*).

Comments: Rain curtailed play on the second day. There was no play after 3.45pm.
W.M.Welch hit 15 4's in his 104, which took him 165 minutes. It was his maiden first-class century.
B.D.Carris and D.W.Gillespie added 114 for Cambridge's 4th wicket.

WARWICKSHIRE v CAMBRIDGE UNIVERSITY

Played at Birmingham, June 14, 15, 16, 1939.
Toss won by Cambridge University.
Match drawn.

CAMBRIDGE UNIVERSITY

Mr B.D.Carris	c Croom b Wilmot	7	(4) not out	46
Mr F.G.Mann	c Cranmer b Hollies	51	(1) not out	53
Mr J.R.Thompson	c Hollies b Taylor	0	(2) c Cranmer b Taylor	2
Mr J.P.Blake	c Goodway b Hollies	2	(3) b Cranmer	16
Mr A.H.Brodhurst	c & b Taylor	17		
*Mr P.M.Studd	c Goodway b Hollies	0		
Mr P.J.Dickinson	st Goodway b Hollies	61		
†Mr K.D.Downes	c Buckingham b Wilmot	23		
Mr D.W.Gillespie	c Goodway b Wilmot	0		
Mr A.C.Shirreff	st Goodway b Hollies	1		
Mr J.Webster	not out	0		
Extras	(W 1, NB 1)	2	(NB 1)	1
Total		**164**	(2 wickets)	**118**

Fall: 1st inns 1/16, 2/25, 3/42, 4/71, 5/71, 6/101, 7/159, 8/163, 9/164.
2nd inns 1/8, 2/45.

WARWICKSHIRE

A.J.W.Croom	c Brodhurst b Gillespie	32
W.A.Hill	c Dickinson b Gillespie	56
J.Buckingham	c Downes b Webster	69
H.E.Dollery	b Gillespie	63
Mr J.J.Hossell	c Webster b Gillespie	1
N.A.Shortland	c Thompson b Webster	6
*Mr P.Cranmer	c Mann b Webster	4
K.Wilmot	c Brodhurst b Shirreff	12
†Mr C.C.Goodway	not out	8
F.Taylor	c Studd b Webster	0
W.E.Hollies	c Brodhurst b Webster	1
Extras	(B 1, LB 1)	2
Total		**254**

Fall: 1st inns 1/67, 2/110, 3/206, 4/208, 5/219, 6/223, 7/237, 8/247, 9/248.

WARWICKSHIRE	O	M	R	W	O	M	R	W
Wilmot	12	4	21	3	10	0	31	0
Taylor	12	2	56	2	8	3	15	1
Cranmer	5	1	24	0	7	1	23	1
Hollies	16	6	61	5	12	3	32	0
Hossell	-	-	-	-	3	0	16	0

CAMBRIDGE	O	M	R	W
Webster	20.4	3	64	5
Dickinson	10	2	38	0
Shirreff	8	0	46	1
Gillespie	15	1	48	4
Brodhurst	8	1	31	0
Carris	3	0	17	0
Mann	2	0	8	0

Umpires: N.Kilner and E.J.Smith.

Close of play scores. First day: Warwickshire 81/1 (W.A.Hill 45, J.Buckingham 3). **Second day:** Cambridge University 118/2 (B.D.Carris 46*, F.G.Mann 53*).

Comments: Play ended at 5.30pm on the first day due to rain and there was no play on the third day.
A.H.Brodhurst and J.Webster were awarded their blues.
C.C.Goodway dislocated his thumb in the University's 2nd innings.
J.Buckingham taking over his accustomed role behind the stumps.

M.C.C. v CAMBRIDGE UNIVERSITY

Played at Lord's, June 17, 19, 20, 1939.
Toss won by M.C.C.
Match drawn.

M.C.C.

Mr A.Ratcliffe	b Webster	0	c Shirreff b Webster 10
Mr C.P.Johnstone	not out 78		c Blake b Carris 23
Mr W.H.Webster	c Carris b Gillespie 28		lbw b Dickinson 0
W.R.Watkins	c Downes b Shirreff 2		c Shirreff b Gillespie 21
Mr L.G.Crawley	b Gillespie 5		c Webster b Carris 17
†Mr G.E.B.Abell	c Thompson b Shirreff 15		c Gillespie b Carris 7
Mr Jahangir Khan	c Blake b Webster 42		c Studd b Carris 6
*Mr A.P.F.Chapman	c Blake b Carris 5		b Gillespie 35
C.I.J.Smith	c Shirreff b Webster 15		c F.G.Mann b Gillespie 3
Mr H.F.Benka	c Thompson b Gillespie 4		c Dickinson b Gillespie ... 59
Mr J.M.Brocklebank	b Dickinson 2		not out 6
Extras	(B 2, LB 7, W 1) 10		(B 3, LB 3) 6
Total		**193**	

Fall: 1st inns 1/0, 2/44, 3/49, 4/54, 5/81, 6/151, 7/159, 8/174, 9/194.
2nd inns 1/12, 2/13, 3/54, 4/54, 5/64, 6/80, 7/86, 8/90, 9/163.

CAMBRIDGE UNIVERSITY

Mr F.G.Mann	b Benka 22	(2) b Smith 18
Mr B.D.Carris	c Abell b Smith 1	(5) b Benka 33
Mr J.R.Thompson	b Smith 17	b Jahangir Khan 20
Mr J.P.Blake	lbw b Watkins 88	c Abell b Smith 0
Mr J.P.Mann	b Brocklebank 14	
*Mr P.M.Studd	b Watkins 34	(6) c & b Benka 22
Mr P.J.Dickinson	b Watkins 6	(1) c Abell b Watkins 16
†Mr K.D.Downes	c Abell b Jahangir Khan 0	(7) not out 10
Mr D.W.Gillespie	c Chapman b Watkins 1	(8) not out 8
Mr A.C.Shirreff	c Chapman b Watkins 1	
Mr J.Webster	not out 0	
Extras	(B 7, LB 6) 13	(LB 5, NB 1) 6
Total	**197**	(6 wickets) **133**

Fall: 1st inns 1/9, 2/37, 3/42, 4/83, 5/151, 6/161, 7/162, 8/178, 9/192.
2nd inns 1/35, 2/37, 3/37, 4/71, 5/112, 6/115.

CAMBRIDGE	O	M	R	W	O	M	R	W
Webster	10	4	53	3	5	2	17	1
Dickinson	10	2	21	1	14	1	37	1
Gillespie	21	4	65	3	16.2	3	50	4
Shirreff	15	5	40	2	6	2	24	0
Carris	4	0	17	1	17	4	59	4

M.C.C.	O	M	R	W	O	M	R	W
Smith	17	5	33	2	12	4	23	2
Jahangir Khan	13	2	34	1	5	0	17	1
Brocklebank	21	4	55	1	7	1	46	0
Benka	7	1	31	1	40		22	2
Watkins	9.4	2	31	5	10	3	19	1

Umpires: H.W.Lee and G.Beet.

Close of play scores. First day: Cambridge University 101/4 (J.P.Blake 35*, P.M.Studd 10*). **Second day:** Cambridge University 27/0 (F.G.Mann 16*, P.J.Dickinson 10*).

Comments: Rain prevented any further play after lunch on the third day with Cambridge needing 70 to win with four wickets in hand.
A.Ratcliffe was bowled by the first ball of the game.
His opening partner, C.P.Johnstone carried his bat throughout the innings for 78, made in just under four hours.

Cambridge University's fielding against M.C.C. at Lord's was of a very high standard and B.D.Carris (top left of picture), who has just caught W.H.Webster, was repeatedly applauded for his smart work close to the wicket.

GLOUCESTERSHIRE v CAMBRIDGE UNIVERSITY

Played at Bristol, June 21, 22, 1939.
Toss won by Cambridge University.
Gloucestershire won by ten wickets.

CAMBRIDGE UNIVERSITY

Mr F.G.Mann.......b Lambert 8	b Cranfield.................17
Mr B.D.Carris ......lbw b Cranfield 12	c & b Sinfield 11
*Mr J.R.Thompson b Cranfield 19	lbw b Cranfield...........7
Mr J.P.Blake ....lbw b Cranfield............0	lbw b Sinfield..............9
Mr A.H.Brodhurst...b Mills 35	c Mills b Sinfield 35
Mr P.J.Dickinson....c Hopkins b Sinfield.....25	lbw b Sinfield.............51
†Mr K.D.Downes ...c Allen b Mills.............0	c & b Cranfield.............7
Mr D.W.Gillespie ...c Haynes b Cranfield......4	not out.....................9
Mr A.C.Shirreff ......c & b Sinfield............5	b Sinfield..................4
Mr J.Webster ....lbw b Cranfield............2	b Cranfield................4
HH Prince	
U.S.Gaekwar ......not out.....................1	st Hopkins b Cranfield 0
Extras..............(B 7, LB 3)...............10	(B 9, LB 3) 12
Total **121**	...........**166**

Fall: 1st inns 1/17, 2/39, 3/39, 4/56, 5/95, 6/95, 7/109, 8/115, 9/120.
    2nd inns 1/62, 2/69, 3/80, 4/88, 5/130, 6/137, 7/148, 8/161, 9/166.

GLOUCESTERSHIRE

C.J.Barnett...........b Gaekwar.................71	not out.....................54
R.A.Sinfield ....b Webster 1	
†V.Hopkins..........c Carris b Webster 0	
*Mr B.O.Allen ....c Downes b Webster......12	(2) not out 50
J.F.Crapp ....b Dickinson 6	
G.M.Emmett........c Dickinson b Gillespie 12	
Mr A.G.S.Wilcox ....c Thompson b Shirreff 39	
R.W.Haynes ....c & b Webster 9	
A.H.Mills ....b Webster 1	
L.M.Cranfield ....not out.....................28	
G.E.E.Lambert ......b Shirreff 0	
Extras..............(LB 4) 4	(B 3) 3
Total **183**	(No wicket) **107**

Fall: 1st inns 1/4, 2/4, 3/32, 4/64, 5/93, 6/109, 7/121, 8/127, 9/183.

GLOUCESTERSHIRE	O	M	R	W	O	M	R	W
Barnett.....................5	3	10	0		7	2	26	0
Lambert....................7	1	19	1		4	0	29	0
Cranfield..................15.4	4	33	5		14.5	1	55	5
Sinfield....................17	9	21	2		17	5	44	5
Mills 4	0	28	2					

CAMBRIDGE	O	M	R	W	O	M	R	W
Webster 12	0	62	5		5	0	18	0
Dickinson....................13	1	43	1		3	0	39	0
Shirreff 5	1	12	2		3	0	31	0
Gillespie 9	0	29	1				,	
Gaekwar.....................6	2	12	1		1.3	0	16	0
Carris 5	2	14	0					
Brodhurst 2	0	7	0					

Umpires: W.H.Hale and W.M.Jones.

Close of play scores. First day: Gloucestershire 121/6 (A.G.S.Wilcox 9*, R.W.Haynes 9*).

Comments: The match finished in two days. The match began 30 minutes late on the first day, strong winds blowing the sight screens over.
Gloucestershire were without W.R.Hammond and T.W.J.Goddard.
LM.Cranfield had his best match-bowling analysis for Gloucestershire with ten wickets for 88.
C.J.Barnett and B.O.Allen hit 105 in 48 minutes to win the game by ten wickets.

ESSEX v CAMBRIDGE UNIVERSITY

Played at Brentwood, June 24, 26, 1939.
Toss won by Cambridge University.
Essex won by an innings and six runs.

CAMBRIDGE UNIVERSITY

Mr B.D.Carris ....b R.Smith 25	c Nichols b Vigar..........15
Mr F.G.Mann........c P.Smith b Nichols......3	b R.Smith 4
Mr J.R.Thompson lbw b R.Smith.............1	st Wade b Vigar 24
Mr J.P.Blake ....lbw b R.Smith.............2	lbw b R.Smith 2
Mr A.H.Brodhurst...b R.Smith.................1	st Wade b Vigar 5
*Mr P.M.Studd ....c Wade b Nichols 16	b R.Smith 2
Mr P.J.Dickinson....c Nichols b R.Smith 0	c P.Smith b Vigar 6
Mr J.A.T.Sharp......lbw b P.Smith 36	b R.Smith 0
†Mr K.D.Downes ...st Wade b Vigar 8	b R.Smith 0
Mr D.W.Gillespie ...lbw b P.Smith 15	b Unwin b R.Smith 10
Mr J.Webster ....not out 4	not out 6
Extras..............(B 3, NB 1)...............4	(LB 3) 3
Total **115**	.........**77**

Fall: 1st inns 1/16, 2/17, 3/24, 4/26, 5/45, 6/49, 7/49, 8/61, 9/104.
    2nd inns 1/14, 2/28, 3/33, 4/40, 5/47, 6/54, 7/55, 8/55, 9/61.

ESSEX

L.C.Eastman.........c Gillespie b Dickinson	17
R.Smith ....c Webster b Dickinson 7
†T.H.Wade ....c Webster b Dickinson 0
J.O'Connor ....lbw b Webster 92
M.S.Nichols ....c Downes b Webster 1
Mr H.Ashton ....c Stodd b Webster 0
Mr D.F.Cock ....c Downes b Webster 6
*Mr F.St.G.Unwin   c Brodhurst b Webster ...10
Mr A.B.Lavers ......b Webster 6
T.P.B.Smith ....c & b Webster.............26
F.H.Vigar ....not out.....................21
Extras..............(B 6, LB 4, W 2)..........12
Total **198**

Fall: 1st inns 1/21, 2/26, 3/26, 4/27, 5/27, 6/49, 7/69, 8/82, 9/134.

ESSEX	O	M	R	W	O	M	R	W
Nichols.....................12	4	20	2		5	1	12	0
R.Smith....................12	3	31	5		12.5	2	42	6
T.P.B.Smith 11.5	3	34	2					
Vigar 11	3	26	1		8	0	20	4

CAMBRIDGE	O	M	R	W
Webster 21	5	78	7
Dickinson...................17	1	71	3
Brodhurst 3	0	8	0
Gillespie 7	0	29	0

Umpires: W.Mead and C.A.G.Russell.

Close of play scores. First day: Essex 173/9 (J.O'Connor 75*, F.H.Vigar 13*).

Comments: The game was completed in two days, 19 wickets fell on the first day for 288 runs.
J.O'Connor and F.H.Vigar put on 64 for Essex's 10th wicket.
R.Smith had match figures of 11 for 73.

Surrey's H.M. ('Monty') Garland-Wells, who was also an England amateur international goalkeeper.

SURREY v CAMBRIDGE UNIVERSITY

Played at Kennington Oval, June 28, 29, 1939.
Toss won by Surrey.
Match drawn.

SURREY

†G.S.Mobey	b Webster	75
E.A.Bedser	b Webster	1
H.S.Squires	lbw b Dickinson	1
T.McMurray	lbw b Webster	1
E.W.Whitfield	st Downes b Shirreff	19
G.J.Whittaker	c Blake b Webster	65
*Mr H.M.Garland-Wells	lbw b Webster	6
F.Berry	c Brodhurst b Dickinson	51
E.A.Watts	b Dickinson	22
A.V.Bedser	not out	12
W.T.Nevell	c Webster b Dickinson	5
Extras	(B 14, LB 4)	18
Total		**276**

Fall: 1st inns 1/7, 2/8, 3/9, 4/46, 5/156, 6/162, 7/219, 8/250, 9/263.

CAMBRIDGE UNIVERSITY

Mr B.D.Carris	lbw b Berry	87
Mr F.G.Mann	lbw b E.A.Bedser	64
Mr J.R.Thompson	c & b Watts	45
Mr J.P.Blake	c A.V.Bedser b Berry	0
Mr A.H.Brodhurst	c E.A.Bedser b Watts	5
*Mr P.M.Studd	c & b Whitfield	59
Mr P.J.Dickinson	c Squires b Berry	5
†Mr K.D.Downes	b Watts	11
Mr D.W.Gillespie	lbw b Watts	2
Mr A.C.Shirreff	not out	51
Mr J.Webster	c A.V.Bedser b McMurray	20
Extras	(B 12, LB 3)	15
Total		**364**

Fall: 1st inns 1/104, 2/205, 3/205, 4/207, 5/213, 6/220, 7/243, 8/247, 9/323.

CAMBRIDGE	O	M	R	W
Webster	19	4	71	5
Dickinson	23.4	7	70	4
Shirreff	17	3	58	1
Gillespie	15	4	37	0
Carris	5	2	19	0
Brodhurst	2	0	3	0

SURREY	O	M	R	W
Watts	21	3	59	4
Berry	18	3	48	3
Nevell	13	2	35	0
A.V.Bedser	12	1	38	0
Squires	14	3	46	0
Garland-Wells	10	2	35	0
E.A.Bedser	10	0	48	1
Whitfield	7	0	34	1
Whittaker	1	0	3	0
McMurray	6	0	3	1

Umpires: A.Peach and A.E.Street.

Close of play scores. First day: Cambridge University 8/0 (B.D.Carris 3*, F.G.Mann 5*). **Second day:** Cambridge University 364 all out.

Comments: G.S.Mobey and G.J.Whittaker added 110 for the 5th wicket.
B.D.Carris and F.G.Mann shared an opening partnership of 104.
B.D.Carris and J.R.Thompson then added 101 for the 2nd Cambridge wicket.

OXFORD UNIVERSITY v GLOUCESTERSHIRE

At Oxford, April 29, May 1, 2, 1939.
Toss won by Oxford University.
Gloucestershire won by five wickets.

OXFORD UNIVERSITY

*Mr E.J.H.Dixon	c Crapp b Goddard	43	lbw b Sinfield	39
Mr R.Sale	lbw b Goddard	28	lbw b Goddard	41
Mr J.M.Lomas	lbw b Neale	5	run out	18
Mr E.D.R.Eagar	lbw b Neale	74	c Emmett b Goddard	4
Mr W.R.H.Joynson	c Lyon b Neale	11	b Sinfield	4
Mr G.Evans	b Goddard	45	(7) b Goddard	10
†Mr C.M.H.Clark	c Wilson b Lambert	19	(6) c Emmett b Sinfield	12
Mr D.E.Young	b Scott	36	not out	3
Mr D.E.Warburton	b Goddard	4	c Scott b Goddard	0
Mr C.W.S.Lubbock	c Neale b Goddard	7		
Mr D.R.Hayward	not out	0		
Extras	(B 6, LB 8)	14	(LB 1)	1
Total		**286**	(8 wickets, declared)	**132**

Fall: 1st inns 1/48, 2/54, 3/111, 4/171, 5/172, 6/210, 7/260, 8/268, 9/284.
2nd inns 1/46, 2/98, 3/102, 4/106, 5/108, 6/129, 7/131, 8/132.

GLOUCESTERSHIRE

C.J.Barnett	b Young	49	c Hayward b Lubbock	23
R.A.Sinfield	lbw b Lubbock	6		
V.Hopkins	b Evans	4	(2) c Evans b Lubbock	5
*Mr B.H.Lyon	c Eagar b Lubbock	18	(5) not out	83
J.F.Crapp	c Sale b Evans	27	(4) c Dixon b Evans	53
G.M.Emmett	b Evans	0	b Evans	16
W.L.Neale	not out	42		
†E.A.Wilson	st Clark b Young	59	(3) lbw b Young	5
T.W.J.Goddard	c Dixon b Evans	4	(7) not out	11
Extras	(B 2, NB 2)	4	(B 2, LB 7, NB 1)	10
Total	(8 wickets, declared)	**213**	(5 wickets)	**206**

Fall: 1st inns 1/10, 2/15, 3/40, 4/102, 5/102, 6/106, 7/206, 8/213.
2nd inns 1/27, 2/33, 3/64, 4/146, 5/185.

C.J.Scott and G.E.E.Lambert did not bat.

GLOUCESTERSHIRE	O	M	R	W	O	M	R	W
Scott	20	4	68	1	3	0	12	0
Lambert	14	0	50	1	4	0	12	0
Barnett	10	1	31	0	3	0	11	0
Sinfield	15	5	33	0	10	1	38	3
Goddard	17.6	5	42	5	11.4	1	58	4
Neale	8	0	48	3				

OXFORD	O	M	R	W	O	M	R	W
Evans	13.7	2	71	4	11	0	78	2
Lubbock	7	2	25	2	3	0	23	2
Hayward	7	0	56	0				
Warburton	4	0	14	0	4	0	25	0
Young	11	0	43	2	11.3	0	70	1

Umpires: C.V.Tarbox and D.Hendren.

Close of play scores. First day: Oxford University 286 all out. **Second day:** No play.

Comments: C.J.Scott bowled the first eight-ball over in first-class cricket in England.
Both captains agreed that each side should bat for 110 minutes in their second innings after Gloucestershire had declared after lunch on the third day. Gloucestershire won with seven minutes to spare.
A.E.Wilson and W.L.Neale added 100 for the 7th wicket in Gloucester's 1st innings.

OXFORD UNIVERSITY v YORKSHIRE

At Oxford, May 3, 4, 1939.
Toss won by Oxford University.
Yorkshire won by ten wickets.

YORKSHIRE

H.Sutcliffe	not out	125		
L.Hutton	c Sale b Young	12		
A.Mitchell	run out	82		
M.Leyland	c Sale b Pether	16		
W.Barber	c Proud b Lubbock	14	(1) not out	9
C.Turner	c Clark b Evans	19		
*Mr A.B.Sellers	c & b Lubbock	3		
T.F.Smailes	c Eagar b Lubbock	6		
†A.Wood	c Dixon b Evans	12	(2) not out	0
H.Verity	c Sale b Young	11		
W.E.Bowes	c Dixon b Pether	13		
Extras	(B 6, LB 2, NB 1)	9		
Total		**322**	(No wicket)	**9**

Fall: 1st inns 1/18, 2/145, 3/180, 4/209, 5/240, 6/243, 7/256, 8/58, 9/297.

OXFORD UNIVERSITY

*Mr E.J.H.Dixon	c Wood b Bowes	3	lbw b Bowes	3
Mr R.Sale	lbw b Verity	3	sat Wood b Leyland	46
Mr G.Evans	b Leyland	11	c Hutton b Verity	14
Mr E.D.R.Eagar	b Bowes	0	c Smailes b Verity	67
Mr W.R.H.Joynson	c Turner b Bowes	0	lbw b Leyland	6
Mr R.B.Proud	lbw b Smailes	6	c Smailes b Verity	54
†Mr C.M.H.Clark	b Leyland	12	b Verity	10
Mr D.E.Young	run out	5	c Mitchell b Verity	4
Mr S.Pether	b Hutton	10	lbw b Bowes	5
Mr C.W.S.Lubbock	b Leyland	26	lbw b Verity	1
Mr D.R.Hayward	not out	5	not out	4
Extras	(B 5 LB 3, NB 4)	12	(B 9, LB 3, NB 2)	14
Total		**102**		**228**

Fall: 1st inns 1/5, 2/8, 3/10, 4/30, 5/39, 6/50, 7/58, 8/58, 9/82.
2nd inns 1/5, 2/33, 3/143, 4/143, 5/150, 6/189, 7/218, 8/218, 9/220.

OXFORD	O	M	R	W	O	M	R	W
Evans	17	3	63	2				
Lubbock	10	0	35	3				
Young	27	1	112	2				
Pether	19.2	5	55	2				
Eagar	5	0	16	0				
Hayward	6	0	32	0				
Dixon	-	-	-	-	0.7	0	9	0

YORKSHIRE	O	M	R	W	O	M	R	W
Bowes	12	6	16	3	13.4	4	26	2
Smailes	7	0	16	1	10	3	18	0
Verity	10	5	17	1	22	4	73	6
Leyland	8	1	29	3	15	3	71	2
Hutton	4	1	12	1	1	1	21	0
Turner	-	-	-	-	3	1	4	0
Barber	-	-	-	-	1	0	1	0

Umpires: D.Hendren and C.V.Tarbox.

Close of play scores. First day: Oxford University 21/3 (G.Evans 1*, W.R.H.Joynson 6*).

Comments: Yorkshire were put in to bat.
H.Sutcliffe scored the first 100 of the season, the first time he had achieved this feat. It was his 144th century, his 107th for Yorkshire, and was made in 270 minutes. He hit two 6's and ten 4's. It was also Sutcliffe's first century at The Parks. It was the sixth time he had carried his bat. He scored a century against every first-class side Yorkshire had played. He and A.Mitchell put on 127 for the 2nd wicket in 100 minutes. Oxford followed on. In the University's 2nd innings, R.Sale and E.D.R.Eager added 110 for the 3rd wicket. The Oxford captain agreed to Yorkshire beginning their 2nd innings on the 2nd day in order to finish the game, which was completed by 6.41pm. In the event there would have been no play on the third day due to rain.

OXFORD UNIVERSITY v MIDDLESEX

Played at Oxford, May 6, 8, 9, 1939.
Toss won by Oxford University.
Middlesex won by seven wickets.

OXFORD UNIVERSITY

*Mr E.J.H.Dixon	b Gray	47	(5) st Price b Peebles	23
Mr R.Sale	c Ingram b Peebles	26	(1) c Robertson b Gray	4
Mr J.M.Lomas	b Gray	3	(2) lbw b Peebles	10
Mr E.D.R.Eagar	b Ingram	44	(3) b Peebles	70
†Mr C.M.H.Clark	c Robertson b Ingram	12	(6) c Robertson b Peebles	22
Mr R.B.Proud	c Gray b Thompson	28	(7) run out	24
Mr G.Evans	not out	14	(8) b Ingram	4
Mr D.E.Young	lbw b Thompson		(4) c Price b Gray	29
Mr C.W.S.Lubbock	c Peebles b Connaughton	7	c Robertson b Ingram	1
Mr S.Pether	c Robertson b Connaughton	0	c Thompson b Peebles	6
Mr D.R.Hayward	c Thompson b Connaughton	3	not out	0
Extras	(B 6, LB 2, W 1)	9	(B 20, LB 8, W 2)	30
Total		**195**		**223**

Fall: 1st inns 1/51, 2/111, 3/128.
2nd inns 3/80, 4/150.

MIDDLESEX

J.D.B.Robertson	b Lubbock	17	b Lubbock	1
G.E.Hart	run out	34	c Dixon b Lubbock	9
Revd E.T.Killick	c Evans b Eagar	19	run out	49
J.H.A.Hulme	b Evans	43	not out	18
A.Thompson	c & b Evans	29	not out	4
Mr R.Felton	b Pether	60		
†W.F.F.Price	b Hayward	60		
Mr E.Ingram	c Young b Pether	1		
*Mr I.A.R.Peebles	b Pether	21		
L.H.Gray	b Evans	22		
Mr J.M.F.Connaughton	not out	16		
Extras	(B 4, LB 4, NB 4)	12	(B 2, LB 2)	4
Total		**334**	(3 wickets)	**85**

Fall: 1st inns 1/30, 2/75, 3/75.

MIDDLESEX	O	M	R	W	O	M	R	W
Gray	17	4	35	2	20	4	45	2
Felton	3	1	4	0	2	0	5	0
Thompson	14	2	58	2	3	0	13	0
Ingram	28	13	36	2	18	6	37	2
Peebles	17	6	34	1	20.2	3	69	5
Connaughton	5.3	2	19	3	11	4	20	0
Robertson	-	-	-	-	2	1	1	0
Hulme	-	-	-	-	1	0	3	0

OXFORD	O	M	R	W	O	M	R	W
Evans	15.5	1	84	3	4.6	0	23	0
Lubbock	7	0	32	1	3	0	18	2
Young	13	0	69	0	5	1	10	0
Pether	10	0	57	3	3	0	12	0
Eagar	2	0	12	1	2	0	8	0
Hayward	12	0	68	1	2	0	10	0

Umpires: D.Hendren and C.V.Tarbox.
Close of play scores. First day: Oxford University 160/4 (C.M.H.Clark 9*, R.B.Proud 23*). **Second day:** Oxford University 80/3 (E.D.R.Eager 24*).

Comments: Play began on an unprepared pitch, the original one being too wet. Middlesex put out a weakened side, as four of their regular players were representing M.C.C. against Yorkshire.
E.D.R.Eager was awarded his blue.
R.Felton and W.F.F.Price added 111 in 55 minutes for the 6th Middlesex wicket.

OXFORD UNIVERSITY v DERBYSHIRE

Played at Oxford, on May 10, 11, 1939.
Toss won by Derbyshire.
Derbyshire won by 163 runs.

DERBYSHIRE

A.E.Alderman	b Hayward	22	b Macindoe	0
*Mr R.H.R.Buckston	c McLean b Macindoe	14	b Evans	8
D.Smith	c Fletcher b Evans	15	c Blagg b Pether	36
T.S.Worthington	b Hayward	5	c McLean b Macindoe	4
L.F.Townsend	c Fletcher b Macindoe	11	b Evans	7
G.H.Pope	c Hayward b Macindoe	20	c Young b Evans	4
A.E.G.Rhodes	c Guy b Pether	80	c Blagg b Pether	2
A.V.Pope	run out	3	b Pether	0
†H.Elliott	lbw b Evans	12	c Macindoe b Pether	4
T.B.Mitchell	c Evans b Macindoe	4	not out	0
W.H.Copson	not out	15	st Blagg b Pether	0
Extras	(B 4, LB 4, NB 1)	9	(B 5, LB 2)	7
Total		**210**		**72**

Fall: 1st inns 1/14, 2/53, 3/53, 4/62, 5/77, 6/92, 7/104, 8/143, 9/160.
2nd inns 1/0, 2/36, 3/41, 4/64, 5/68, 6/68, 7/68, 8/72, 9/72.

OXFORD UNIVERSITY

Mr J.M.Lomas	b Copson	0	b A.V.Pope	4
Mr J.B.Guy	c Smith b Copson	5	c Elliott b Copson	5
Mr L.E.McLean	b Copson	8	b A.V.Pope	1
Mr G.E.Fletcher	c Alderman b G.H.Pope	13	(4) b A.V.Pope	3
Mr E.D.R.Eagar	c Alderman b A.V.Pope	0	(5) b A.V.Pope	2
Mr D.E.Young	lbw b Mitchell	34	c Elliott b Copson	26
Mr G.Evans	lbw b Copson	0	lbw b A.V.Pope	0
†Mr P.H.Blagg	b Copson	0	b Copson	1
Mr S.Pether	c Elliott b G.H.Pope	3	b Copson	0
*Mr D.H.Macindoe	c & b Mitchell	3	b Copson	0
Mr D.R.Hayward	not out	2	not out	3
Extras	(B 3, NB 1)	4	(LB 2)	2
Total		**72**		**47**

Fall: 1st inns 1/0, 2/13, 3/14, 4/15, 5/50, 6/53, 7/53, 8/60, 9/68.
2nd inns 1/9, 2/10, 3/13, 4/14, 5/19, 6/19, 7/44, 8/44, 9/44.

OXFORD	O	M	R	W	O	M	R	W
Macindoe	18	2	65	4	7	1	27	2
Evans	16	5	59	2	10	0	31	3
Pether	8.4	2	20	1	5.2	3	7	5
Hayward	10	0	36	2				
Young	7	1	21	0				

DERBYSHIRE	O	M	R	W	O	M	R	W
Copson	6	2	12	5	4.7	2	9	5
A.V.Pope	5	0	24	1	6	0	30	5
G.H.Pope	7	3	11	2	2	0	6	0
Mitchell	5	0	21	2				

Umpires: D.Hendren and C.V.Tarbox.

Close of play scores. First day: Derbyshire 33/1 (R.H.R.Buckston 8*, D.Smith 19*).

Comments: There were three extraordinary bowling performances in this game. W.H.Copson finished the match with four wickets in five balls, including the hat-trick. He dismissed P.H.Blagg, S.Pether and D.H.MacIndoe in successive balls, then ended the University's 2nd innings with the wicket of D.E.Young. It was Copson's third hat-trick.
S.Pether took 5 for 7 in 34 balls in Derbyshire's 2nd innings, in which the last nine wickets fell for 39 runs. He also took four wickets in five balls in his 5th and 6th overs.
For Derbyshire, Copson had figures of 5 for 12 and 5 for 9, of which two runs came from overthrows.
On the second day 19 wickets fell for 86 runs, the match finishing at 2.45pm.

OXFORD UNIVERSITY v LANCASHIRE

Played at Oxford, May 17, 18, 19, 1939.
Toss won by Oxford University.
Match drawn.

OXFORD UNIVERSITY

Mr J.M.Lomas	b Phillipson	10	b Phillipson	18
Mr J.B.Guy	c Farrimond b Phillipson	7	c Farrimond b Phillipson	0
Mr L.E.McLean	run out	10	b Pollard	9
Mr E.D.R.Eagar	c Pollard b Iddon	35	c Phillipson b Birtwell	30
Mr G.E.Fletcher	c Nutter b Pollard	10	c Pollard b Hopwood	65
Mr R.B.Proud	c & b Iddon	6	c Nutter b Hopwood	63
Mr D.E.Young	not out	14	run out	1
†Mr P.H.Blagg	c Iddon b Pollard	0		
Mr S.Pether	lbw b Pollard	7	(8) not out	20
*Mr D.H.Macindoe	c Farrimond b Pollard	16	(9) not out	10
Mr D.R.Hayward	c Phillipson b Pollard	0		
Extras	(NB 2)	2	(B 1, LB 8, NB 2)	11
Total		**117**	(7 wickets)	**227**

Fall: 1st inns 1/8, 2/25, 3/35, 4/73, 5/79, 6/79, 7/80, 8/90, 9/117.
2nd inns 1/0, 2/32, 3/34, 4/78, 5/175, 6/181, 7/208.

LANCASHIRE

E.Paynter	b Pether	11
C.Washbrook	c Blagg b Macindoe	0
J.Iddon	c & b Young	16
N.Oldfield	c Pether b Eagar	41
J.L.Hopwood	c Eagar b Hayward	50
A.E.Nutter	st Blagg b Hayward	43
W.E.Phillipson	c Lomas b Macindoe	4
*Mr T.A.Higson	c Guy b Haywood	6
†W.Farrimond	b Hayward	16
R.Pollard	c McLean b Macindoe	1
Mr A.J.Birtwell	not out	0
Extras	(B 4, LB 8)	12
Total		**200**

Fall: 1st inns 1/1, 2/13, 3/44, 4/89, 5/156, 6/163, 7/176, 8/186, 9/189.

LANCASHIRE	O	M	R	W	O	M	R	W
Phillipson	11	1	24	2	10	2	57	2
Pollard	12.6	4	39	5	12	4	29	1
Hopwood	7	1	19	0	10	1	27	2
Nutter	4	0	9	0	5	1	18	0
Iddon	71		24	2	3	0	12	0
Birtwell	-	-	-	-	12	1	60	1
Higson	-	-	-	-	1	0	4	0
Oldfield	-	-	-	-	1	0	9	0

OXFORD	O	M	R	W
Macindoe	23	3	68	3
Pether	15	4	42	1
Young	9	1	28	1
Hayward	12.6	1	37	4
Eagar	6	2	13	1

Umpires: D.Hendren and C.V.Tarbox.

Close of play scores. First day: No play (rain). **Second day:** Lancashire 115/4 (J.L.Hopwood 33, A.E.Nutter 6*).

OXFORD UNIVERSITY v FREE FORESTERS

Played at Oxford, May 27, 29, 30, 1939.
Toss won by Oxford University.
Oxford won by nine runs.

OXFORD UNIVERSITY

Mr R.Sale	c Griffith b Baring	24	c & b Scott	55
Mr J.M.Lomas	c Griffith b Allen	0	(4) lbw b Brocklebank	24
Mr W.S.P.Lithgow	b Allen	0	c Mitchell-Innes b Brocklebank	27
Mr R.B.Proud	c Mitchell-Innes b Scott	21	(5) c Griffith b Allen	11
Mr L.E.McLean	b Brocklebank	51	(2) c Griffith b Allen	0
Mr E.D.R.Eagar	b Allen	92	b Allen	134
Mr D.E.Young	retired hurt	21	Absent hurt	0
Mr A.J.B.Marsham	b Baring	7	(7) c Enthoven b Baring	11
*Mr D.H.Macindoe	not out	50	(8) b Baring	26
Mr S.Pether	c Allen b Baring	3	(9) not out	17
†Mr P.H.Blagg	b Brocklebank	8	(10) st Griffith b Brocklebank	1
Extras	(B 4, NB 2)	6	(B 5, LB 7, NB 11)	23
Total		**283**		**329**

Fall: 1st inns 1/1, 2/1, 3/35, 4/91, 5/201, 8/247, 9/283.
2nd inns 1/0, 2/74, 3/105, 9/329.

FREE FORESTERS

Mr N.S.Mitchell-Innes	c Macindoe b Pether	27	b Pether	143
Mr W.A.C.Wilkinson	c Eager b Macindoe	9	lbw b Eagar	53
Mr M.Howell	c & b Pether	53	(4) b Marsham	41
Mr R.S.G.Scott	c Blagg c Pether	14	(5) b Marsham b Pether	22
Mr H.J.Enthoven	run out	0	(6) c & b Marsham	0
*Mr E.R.T.Holmes	c Sale b Eagar	49	(3) c Sale b Macindoe	32
Mr G.O.B.Allen	c Blagg b Macindoe	49	b Marsham	14
Mr A.P.F.Chapman	b Pether	6	c Eagar b Marsham	14
†Mr S.C.Griffith	b Manindoe	2	c sub b Marsham	45
Mr A.E.G.Baring	not out	6	run out	5
Mr J.M.Brocklebank	c Eagar b Pether	1	not out	5
Extras	(B 1, LB 3)	4	(B 8, LB 1)	9
Total		**220**		**383**

Fall: 4/66, 6/159.
2nd inns 1/169.

FREE FORESTERS	O	M	R	W	O	M	R	W
Allen	20	1	85	3	22	2	100	3
Baring	14	0	53	3	15	1	73	2
Enthoven	9	1	57	0	5	0	30	0
Brocklebank	12.6	0	67	2	18.2	1	81	3
Scott	4	0	15	1	3	0	17	1
Holmes	-	-	-	-	2	0	5	0

OXFORD	O	M	R	W	O	M	R	W
Macindoe	18	4	68	3	20	1	109	1
Pether	21.3	4	76	5	19	0	89	2
Marsham	3	0	34	0	25.7	1	136	5
Eagar	9	0	38	1	4	0	40	1

Umpires: E.Rushbridge and Scott.

Close of play scores. First day: Free Foresters 92/4 (M.Howell 39*, E.R.T.Holmes 3*). **Second day:** Oxford University 248/6 (E.D.R.Eagar 100*, D.H.Macindoe 4*).
Comments: E.D.R.Eager's 134 was the first century of the season by an Oxford batsman. In the 1st innings, he and D.E.Young added 110 for the 5th wicket, Young retired hurt, after being hit over the heart by G.O.B.Allen and the partnership was continued by R.B.Proud, who had been forced to retire earlier with a split finger, when he had made 12.
The Free Foresters needed 393 to win and began with N.S.Mitchell-Innes and W.A.C.Wilkinson putting on 169 for the 1st wicket. N.S.Mitchell-Innes hit two 6's and 19 4's in his 143, exactly the same number of boundaries as Eagar in his 134. He reached his 100 in 95 minutes. His 143 was made in even time. It was the University's first victory of the season.

OXFORD UNIVERSITY v MINOR COUNTIES

Played at Oxford, June 7, 8, 9, 1939.
Toss won by Oxford University.
Minor Counties won by four wickets.

OXFORD UNIVERSITY

Mr J.M.Lomas	b Wilkinson ...0	lbw b Appleyard ...12
Mr W.S.P.Lithgow	c Appleyard b Surridge ...6	b Rought-Rought ...14
Mr R.B.Proud	c & b Appleyard ...71	b Rought-Rought ...33
Mr J.Stanning	lbw b Dennis ...39	b Appleyard ...9
*Mr E.J.H.Dixon	c Appleyard b Surridge ...53	lbw b Appleyard ...10
Mr G.R.de Soysa	lbw b Surridge ...4	c Roberts b Dennis ...67
†Mr R.M.England	b Appleyard ...5	not out ...43
Mr A.J.B.Marsham	c Appleyard b Rought-Rought ...51	st Mobey b Rought-Rought 5
Mr D.H.Macindoe	not out ...43	c Mobey b Surridge ...51
Mr M.H.Farebrother	b Surridge ...0	c Rought-Rought b Surridge ...1
Mr J.M.F.Connaughton	b Surridge ...6	b Surridge ...0
Extras	(B 1, NB 2) ...3	(B 1, LB 5, NB 5) ...11
Total	**281**	**256**

Fall: 1st inns 1/0, 2/12, 3/117, 4/120, 5/133, 6/146, 7/210, 8/253, 9/253.
2nd inns 1/14, 2/38, 3/49, 4/61, 5/124, 6/158, 7/167, 8/246, 9/254.

MINOR COUNTIES

†G.S.Mobey	c Farebrother b Macindoe ...15	b Marsham ...29
F.Dennis	c & b Farebrother ...29	c Stanning b Macindoe ...0
Mr A.H.Parnaby	c Connaughton b Macindoe ...29	c Lithgow b Farebrother 101
E.A.Roberts	b Macindoe ...20	
Mr D.J.F.Watson	c England b Farebrother ...33	(4) lbw b Farebrother ...35
Mr H.W.F.Taylor	c Macindoe b Marsham ...1	not out ...19
G.Rogers	b Marsham ...0	c Dixon b Marsham ...8
Mr D.C.Rought-Rought	c England b Marsham ...5	not out ...10
*Mr W.Lovell-Hewitt	run out ...69	(5) c & b Marsham ...92
Mr W.S.Surridge	c Proud b Marsham ...20	
Mr F.Appleyard	not out ...0	
Extras	(B 9, LB 1, W 5) ...15	(B 7, LB 2, NB 1) ...10
Total	**236**	**(6 wickets) 304**

Fall: 1st inns 1/24, 2/72, 3/91, 4/110, 5/113, 6/113, 7/121, 8/178, 9/236.
2nd inns 1/2, 2/41, 3/142, 4/234, 5/275, 6/287.

MINOR COUNTIES	O	M	R	W	O	M	R	W
Wilkinson	9	1	24	1				
Rought-Rought	12	2	52	1	21	2	67	3
Surridge	11.5	1	41	5	15.3	3	59	3
Appleyard	19	2	79	2	24	7	80	3
Roberts	5	0	45	0				
Dennis	9	1	37	1	12	2	39	1
OXFORD	O	M	R	W	O	M	R	W
Macindoe	17	7	42	3	22	3	92	1
Farebrother	11	1	49	2	17	3	79	2
Marsham	20.2	1	102	4	24.7	3	105	3
Connaughton	8	2	28	0	6	2	18	0

Umpires: E.Rushbridge and R.Richards.

Close of play scores. First day: Minor Counties 83/2 (A.H.Parnaby 22*, E.Roberts 7*). **Second day:** Oxford University 179/7 (R.M.England 21*, D.H.Macindoe 4*).
Comments: J.M.Lomas was dismissed by the first ball of the match, whilst the Oxford captain arrived late, after taking examinations.
F.W.Wilkinson was injured early in the game after bowling eight overs and the Oxford captain agreed to him being replaced by D.J.F.Watson, an Oxford freshman. It proved to be Wilkinson's only first-class match.
Blues were awarded to R.B.Proud and A.J.B.Marsham.
R.B.Proud and J.Stanning added 105 for Oxford's 3rd wicket.
The Minor Counties were set to make 302 in 280 minutes, D.J.F.Watson and A.H.Parnaby added 101 for the Minor Counties 3rd wicket.
A.H.Parnaby's 101 was his maiden first-class century.
The Minor Counties won with 20 minutes to spare.

OXFORD UNIVERSITY v LEICESTERSHIRE

Played at Oxford, June 14, 15, 16, 1939.
Toss won by Oxford University.
Match drawn.

OXFORD UNIVERSITY

*Mr E.J.H.Dixon	c Dawkes b Jackson ...6	c Dawkes b Smith ...20
Mr R.Sale	b Sperry ...3	b Jackson ...9
Mr D.J.F.Watson	b Jackson ...7	(7) not out ...8
Mr R.B.Proud	b Smith ...30	c Smith b Sperry ...3
Mr J.Stanning	c Watson b Sperry ...32	retired hurt ...26
Mr E.D.R.Eagar	not out ...50	not out ...14
Mr D.E.Young	c Watson b Sperry ...0	(3) c Dawkes b Sperry ...8
Mr A.J.B.Marsham	c Dawkes b Smith ...2	
Mr G.Evans	c Dawkes b Smith ...0	
Mr S.Pether	c Dawkes b Sperry ...15	
†Mr P.B.Blagg	c Dawkes b Sperry ...1	
Extras	(B 1) ...1	(B 1, LB 1) ...2
Total	**147**	**(4 wickets) 90**

Fall: 1st inns 1/5, 2/14, 3/19, 4/64, 5/88, 6/89, 7/92, 8/92, 9/117.
2nd inns 1/26, 2/35, 3/36, 4/50.

LEICESTERSHIRE

G.L.Berry	c Young b Evans ...0
G.S.Watson	lbw b Young ...29
N.F.Armstrong	not out ...105
F.T.Prentice	b Evans ...8
Mr V.E.Jackson	c Young b Evans ...23
*Mr M.St.J.Packe	c Stanning b Marsham ...2
†G.O.Dawkes	c Sale b Evans ...0
G.F.Knew	c Blagg b Evans ...42
A.R.West	run out ...7
H.A.Smith	st Blagg b Evans ...1
J.Sperry	st Blagg b Marsham ...2
Extras	(B 9, LB 7, NB 2) ...18
Total	**237**

Fall: 1st inns 1/0, 2/50, 3/75, 4/103, 5/110, 6/113, 7/203, 8/225, 9/234.

LEICESTERSHIRE	O	M	R	W	O	M	R	W
Sperry	19.7	3	65	5	15.2	4	52	2
Jackson	13	7	19	2	6	2	11	1
Smith	14	1	62	3	9	0	25	1
OXFORD	O	M	R	W				
Evans	26	9	80	6				
Pether	15	2	39	0				
Young	11	0	44	1				
Marsham	9.4	0	45	2				
Eagar	2	0	11	0				

Umpires: E.Rushbridge and R.Richards.

Close of play scores. First day: Leicestershire 50/1 (G.Watson 29*, N.F.Armstrong 16*). **Second day:** Oxford University 90/4 (D.J.F.Watson 14*, E.D.R.Eagar 8*).

Comments: The first day's play was interrupted by rain and bad light.
There was also no play on the third day.
N.F.Armstrong made 105 in 230 minutes. It included 13 4's.
G.F.Knew, aged 18, made his debut for Leicestershire.
G.O.Dawkes equalled the Leicestershire wicketkeeping record of seven catches in a match.

SOMERSET v OXFORD UNIVERSITY

Played at Bath, June 17, 19, 20, 1939.
Toss won by Somerset.
Somerset won by 219 runs.

SOMERSET

F.S.Lee	c Blagg b Hayward 33	st Blagg b Hayward 7	
H.Gimblett	c Eagar b Macindoe 0	b Young 32	
H.T.F.Buse	c Macindoe b Evans 9	c Macindoe b Hayward ...63	
Mr C.J.P.Barnwell	b Macindoe 28	c Eagar b Hayward 17	
*Mr E.F.Longrigg	c Sale b Hayward 82	absent hurt..................0	
Mr R.A.Ingle	c Eagar b Hayward 26	not out 38	
W.H.R.Andrews	c Evans b Hayward.......6	lbw b Macindoe............0	
Mr G.M.Bennett	c Sale b Hayward 6	b Evans 2	
A.W.Wellard	c Sale b Macindoe 1	c Fletcher b Evans 11	
†W.T.Luckes	not out...................10	(5) st Blagg b Evans 59	
H.L.Hazell	b Hayward.................8	(10) c Blagg b Evans 6	
Extras	(B 14, LB 1, NB 2) 17	(B 15, LB 6, NB 1).........22	
Total	.........................**226**	..........................**257**	

Fall: 1st inns 1/0, 2/11, 3/57, 4/105, 5/157, 6/163, 7/196, 8/207, 9/211.
2nd inns 1/40, 2/42, 3/114, 4/136, 5/226, 6/231, 7/234, 8/257, 9/257.

OXFORD UNIVERSITY

Mr R.Sale	b Wellard 5	b Wellard 0	
Mr J.M.Lomas	b Wellard 20	lbw b Andrews............32	
Mr J.B.Guy	b Andrews 10	b Wellard 7	
Mr J.S.Stanning	b Wellard 25	c Gimblett b Buse 18	
Mr G.E.Fletcher	c Gimblett b Wellard 14	st Luckes b Buse 0	
Mr E.D.R.Eagar	c & b Wellard 14	c Luckes b Wellard 9	
Mr D.E.Young	b Buse 4	lbw b Andrews.............15	
*Mr D.H.Macindoe	b Hazell 11	c Luckes b Andrews 0	
Mr G.Evans	c Buse b Wellard 3	b Andrews 23	
†Mr P.H.Blagg	not out 7	not out 28	
Mr D.R.Hayward	lbw b Wellard 0	b Andrews 2	
Extras	(B 3, LB 3, NB 1) 7	(B 3, LB 4, NB 3) 10	
Total	.........................**120**	..........................**144**	

Fall: 1st inns 1/14, 2/31, 3/59, 4/68, 5/84, 6/93, 7/109, 8/113, 9/116.
2nd inns 1/0, 2/15, 3/35, 4/35, 5/46, 6/90, 7/90, 8/93, 9/128.

OXFORD	O	M	R	W	O	M	R	W
Macindoe	22	7	50	3	21	4	68	1
Evans	10	1	39	1	13.1	2	27	4
Young	9	3	36	0	15	2	50	1
Hayward	33.3	3	79	6	19	3	71	3
Eagar	3	1	5	0	3	0	19	0

SOMERSET	O	M	R	W	O	M	R	W
Wellard	16.7	1	57	7	14	3	38	3
Andrews	8	3	15	1	16.7	3	43	5
Hazell	12	5	31	1	4	0	30	0
Buse	3	0	10	1	13	4	23	2

Umpires: W.Parry and A.Bezer.

SURREY v OXFORD UNIVERSITY

Played at Kennington Oval, June 21, 22, 23, 1939.
Toss won by Oxford University.
Match drawn.

SURREY

L.B.Fishlock	c Young b Pether..........7
E.A.Bedser	b Hayward 14
H.S.Squires	c Lithgow b Young 15
T.H.Barling	c Blagg b Macindoe 45
E.W.Whitfield	b Macindoe 44
†G.S.Mobey	lbw b Hayward 6
A.J.W.McIntyre	c Blagg b Macindoe 1
*Mr H.M.Garland-Wells	b Hayward 20
E.A.Watts	c Eagar b Pether..........43
F.Berry	not out 31
A.V.Bedser	b Macindoe 0
Extras	(B 5, LB 3) 8
Total	.........................**234**

Fall: 1st inns 1/11, 2/21, 3/45, 4/112, 5/130, 6/135, 7/136, 8/168, 9/232.

OXFORD UNIVERSITY

Mr J.M.Lomas	lbw b Garland-Wells.....36
Mr R.Sale	not out....................71
Mr W.S.P.Lithgow	not out...................22
Extras	(B 2, LB 2) 4
Total	(1 wicket)...............**133**

Fall: 1st inns 1/60.

*Mr E.J.H.Dixon, Mr J.Stanning, Mr E.D.R.Eagar, Mr D.H.Macindoe, Mr D.E.Young, Mr S.Pether, †Mr P.H.Blagg and Mr D.R.Hayward did not bat.

OXFORD	O	M	R	W
Macindoe	19.2	3	64	4
Pether	16	1	34	2
Hayward	22	2	86	3
Young	8	0	19	1
Eagar	5	0	23	0

SURREY	O	M	R	W
Watts	8	1	23	0
A.V.Bedser	6	1	21	0
Berry	6	1	11	0
Squires	3	0	13	0
E.A.Bedser	8	1	19	0
Garland-Wells	9	5	19	1
McIntyre	4	0	21	0
Whitfield	1	0	2	0

Umpires: A.Peach and Carpenter.

Close of play scores. First day: Oxford University 106/6 (G.E.Fletcher 13*, D.H.Macindoe 11*). **Second day:** Oxford University 46/5 (J.M.Lomas 11*).

Comments. The match was finished before lunch at 1.10pm on the third day. W.H.R.Andrews took the last five Oxford wickets to fall on the last morning in 8.7 overs for 22.
H.Gimblett completed his 1,000 runs for the season.
R.A.Ingle took over the Somerset captaincy after E.F.Longrigg pulled a leg muscle during the first day's play.

Close of play scores. First day: No play. **Second day:** Oxford University 133/1 (R.Sale 71*, W.S.P.Lithgow 22*).

Comments: There was no play on the first and third days.
Surrey were put in to bat.
A.V. and E.A.Bedser, the Surrey twins, aged 20, made their first appearance in first-class cricket, Wisden later commented that Surrey officials predicted a great future for them.

SUSSEX v OXFORD UNIVERSITY

Played at Eastbourne, June 24, 26, 27, 1939.
Toss won by Oxford University.
Oxford University won by 56 runs.

OXFORD UNIVERSITY

Mr J.M.Lomas	lbw b Wood	2	lbw b Smith 13
Mr R.Sale	c C.Oakes b Duffield 6		b Wood 66
*Mr E.J.H.Dixon	c Smith b Duffield 67		(4) c Cox b Wood 58
Mr J.Stanning	run out 1		(6) c Collins b Smith 30
Mr E.D.R.Eagar	c J.Oakes b Duffield......4		(5) c Smith b Cox.........21
Mr G.Evans	lbw b Duffield............57		(7) b Wood 48
Mr D.H.Macindoe	c Bartlett b Cox 6		(9) not out 23
Mr R.B.Proud	b Cox 4		(3) b Smith 0
Mr A.J.B.Marsham	c J.Oakes b Cox 4		(8) c C.Oakes b Wood 41
Mr S.Pether	c Wood b Cox 10		b Wood......................1
†Mr P.H.Blagg	not out 0		b Wood 2
Extras	(B 13, LB 2, NB 2)	17	(B 9, LB 8, W 1, NB 3) 21
Total		**178**	**324**

Fall: 1st inns 1/12, 2/22, 3/23, 4/47, 5/128, 6/149, 7/159, 8/159, 9/168.
2nd inns 1/30, 2/30, 3/80, 4/130, 5/172, 6/245, 7/270, 8/314, 9/322.

SUSSEX

†V.J.Eaton	c Blagg b Marsham 27		lbw b Eagar 44
G.A.Collins	b Macindoe 2		c Lomas b Macindoe 17
Mr R.G.Grevett	b Macindoe 0		lbw b Marsham 0
G.Cox	c Blagg b Marsham 39		c Blagg b Marsham........43
Sir William Becher	st Blagg b Marsham 20		b Eagar 0
C.Oakes	c & b Macindoe 5		b Eagar 29
*Mr H.T.Bartlett	c Stanning b Macindoe 41		c & b Eagar 3
J.Y.Oakes	b Pether 22		st Blagg b Eagar 7
D.J.Wood	c Blagg b Pether..........4		c Dixon b Eagar 31
J.Duffield	lbw b Pether 0		not out 60
D.M.Smith	not out 1		b Macindoe 34
Extras	(LB 2, NB 6)	8	(B 6, LB 2, NB 1) 9
Total		**169**	**277**

Fall: 1st inns 1/3, 2/3, 3/61, 4/92, 5/93, 6/97, 7/164, 8/164, 9/164.
2nd inns 1/21, 2/22, 3/107, 4/107, 5/107, 6/112, 7/132, 8/157, 9/206.

SUSSEX	O	M	R	W	O	M	R	W
Smith	7	2	9	0	15	2	56	3
Duffield	18	3	62	4	23	1	68	0
Wood	11	2	28	1	23	5	77	6
C.Oakes	10	2	18	0	6	0	30	0
J.Oakes	5	0	38	0	3	0	13	0
Cox	4.6	1	6	4	18	4	59	1

OXFORD	O	M	R	W	O	M	R	W
Macindoe	14	0	51	4	13	1	65	2
Evans	11	2	34	0	3	0	14	0
Pether	7.6	2	28	3	4	1	8	0
Marsham	9	0	44	3	16	0	115	2
Eagar	1	0	4	0	9	0	66	6

Umpires: Stoneham and Kingswell.

Close of play scores. First day: Sussex 3/2 (V.J.Eaton 1*). **Second day:** Oxford University 192/5 (E.J.H.Dixon 41*, G.Evans 9*).

Comments: Play was delayed on the first day and bad light also brought a premature close.
J.Duffield and D.M.Smith added 71 for the last Sussex wicket in 30 minutes.

M.C.C. v OXFORD UNIVERSITY

Played at Lord's, June 28, 29, 1939.
Toss won by M.C.C.
Match drawn.

M.C.C.

Maj W.A.C.Wilkinson	st Blagg b Marsham......60		st Blagg b Evans 6
J.M.Sims	c Dixon b Marsham 33		c Proud b Pether 6
W.J.Edrich	c Eagar b Pether 91		(4) c Proud b Pether 7
D.C.S.Compton	st Blagg b Marsham 34		(5) b Young 73
†Mr G.E.B.Abell	b Pether 19		(6) b Young 6
M.Jahangir Khan	not out 7		(11) b Young 5
Mr W.W.Hill-Wood	b Young 1		(3) st Blagg b Marsham ...31
C.I.J.Smith	b Young 0		(10) c Sale b Eagar 7
*Mr A.P.F.Chapman	not out 12		(8) c Sale b Eagar 0
Mr O.G.Battcock	(did not bat)		(7) c Proud b Young 27
Mr C.H.Gibson	(did not bat)		(9) not out 23
Extras	(B 10, W 1, NB 1)	12	(B 8) 8
Total	(7 wickets, declared) ...**269**		**199**

Fall: 1st inns 1/76, 2/148, 3/196, 4/238, 5/246, 6/247, 7/251.
2nd inns 1/7, 2/31, 3/39, 4/61, 5/112, 6/139, 7/140, 8/186, 9/194.

OXFORD UNIVERSITY

Mr J.M.Lomas	c Chapman b Hillwood	138
Mr R.Sale	c Hill-Wood b Compton	24
Mr R.B.Proud	b Compton	0
Mr J.Stanning	c Abell b Smith	19
*Mr E.J.H.Dixon	c Abell b Sims	46
Mr E.D.R.Eagar	b Sims	0
Mr G.Evans	not out	63
Mr A.J.B.Marsham	not out	39
Extras	(B 3, LB 5, NB 2)	10
Total	(6 wickets, declared) **339**	

Fall: 1st inns 1/47, 2/47, 3/96, 4/190, 5/190, 6/291.
Mr D.E.Young, Mr S.Pether and †Mr P.H.Blagg did not bat.

OXFORD	O	M	R	W	O	M	R	W
Evans	19	4	70	0	3	0	16	1
Pether	12	1	67	2	5	0	26	2
Young	13	3	34	2	10.3	0	41	4
Marsham	14	0	86	3	3	0	37	1
Eagar	1	1	0	0	6	0	71	2

M.C.C.	O	M	R	W
Smith	20	3	52	1
Gibson	12	1	40	0
Battcock	11	1	36	0
Sims	22	3	78	2
Compton	12	2	40	2
Jahangir Khan	9	1	19	0
Edrich	3	1	20	0
Hill-Wood	5	0	35	1
Wilkinson	1	0	9	0

Umpires: G.H.Beet and H.W.Lee.

Close of play scores. First day: Oxford University 58/2 (J.M.Lomas 25*, J.Stanning 9*).

Comments: J.M.Lomas made his 138 in five hours, hitting 13 4's.
With G.Evans he added 101 for the 6th wicket.
D.C.S.Compton hit 52 out of his 73 in boundaries (two 6's and ten 4's), batting for only 50 minutes.

The bespectacled B.D.Carris bowling his slow left-armers over the wicket in the Oxford first innings.

At second slip, J.R.Thompson makes a fine effort to catch Oxford's J.Stanning after the ball had rebounded off the wicketkeeper's gloves. Stanning hit Webster's next delivery for four, but was then bowled off the next.

OXFORD UNIVERSITY v CAMBRIDGE UNIVERSITY

Played at Lord's, July 1, 3, 4, 1939.
Toss won by Oxford University.
Oxford University won by 45 runs.

OXFORD UNIVERSITY

Mr J.M.Lomas	lbw b Webster 8	c Blake b Gillespie	91
Mr R.Sale	c Studd b Gillespie.......65	lbw b Webster	19
Mr R.B.Proud	c & b Shirreff 19	run out	87
Mr J.Stanning	b Webster 38	not out	39
*Mr E.J.H.Dixon	b Shirreff 75		
Mr E.D.R.Eager	c Mann b Webster 31	(5) not out	27
Mr G.Evans	c Studd b Shirreff 59		
Mr A.J.B.Marsham	c Carris b Shirreff 0		
Mr D.H.Macindoe	c Studd b Shirreff 0		
Mr S.Pether	lbw b Dickinson...........6		
†Mr P.H.Blagg	not out 0		
Extras	(B 12) 12	(B 9, W 1)	10
Total	...........**313**	(3 wickets, declared).....**273**	

Fall: 1st inns 1/28, 2/100, 3/114, 4/158, 5/208, 6/298, 7/298, 8/300, 9/311.
2nd inns 1/24, 2/193, 3/218.

CAMBRIDGE UNIVERSITY

Mr B.D.Carris	lbw b Macindoe 44	b Pether	36
Mr F.G.Mann	b Evans 13	c Sale b Pether	57
Mr J.R.Thompson	b Evans 2	b Evans	22
Mr J.P.Blake	lbw b Macindoe 1	c Stanning b Macindoe	...23
Mr A.H.Brodhurst	c Macindoe b Marsham 34	b Evans	45
*Mr P.M.Studd	b Marsham 7	c Blagg b Macindoe	0
Mr P.J.Dickinson	run out 26	c Pether b Evans	100
†Mr K.D.Downes	b Evans 3	(11) not out	7
Mr A.C.Shirreff	c Lomas b Evans 2	(8) c Stanning b Evans	0
Mr D.W.Gillespie	not out 16	(9) c & b Evans	8
Mr J.Webster	c Blagg b Macindoe 4	(10) b Pether	60
Extras	(LB 3, NB 2) 5	(B 15, LB 7, NB 4)	26
Total	.............**157**		.............**384**

Fall: 1st inns 1/41, 2/43, 3/44, 4/73, 5/93, 6/122, 7/129, 8/136, 9/147.
2nd inns 1/53, 2/106, 3/149, 4/155, 5/155, 6/239, 7/239, 8/249, 9/344.

CAMBRIDGE	O	M	R	W	O	M	R	W
Webster	19	2	73	3	11	0	50	1
Dickinson	18	2	65	1	8	1	36	0
Shirreff	25.6	9	64	5	17	4	66	0
Gillespie	13	1	52	1	12	0	50	1
Carris	11	4	24	0	19	5	61	0
Brodhurst	4	1	23	0				

OXFORD	O	M	R	W	O	M	R	W
Macindoe	16.2	4	32	3	28	6	81	2
Evans	18	2	55	4	33	8	127	5
Pether	8	3	23	0	22.3	6	39	3
Marsham	9	2	42	2	20	2	106	0
Eagar	-	-	-	-	2	1	5	0

Umpires: J.Hardstaff and J.A.Newman

Close of play scores. First day: Cambridge 26/0 (B.D.Carris F.G.Mann). **Second day:** Oxford 273/3 (J.Stanning 39*, E.D.R.Eagar 27*).
Comments: J.M.Lomas and R.B.Proud added 169 for the 2nd Oxford wicket in the 2nd innings.
Play was delayed for 15 minutes on the third day because of rain. Cambridge were set 430 to win, after Oxford had declared at their overnight score.
P.J.Dickinson made 100 in Cambridge 2nd innings, hitting 12 4's. Cambridge made the highest score for the 4th innings by a University side in the University match.
Oxford won the match with only 25 minutes to spare, winning by 45 runs after the last two Cambridge wickets had added 135 runs.

Top: Oxford's R.B.Proud nearly plays on. ***Bottom:*** R.Sale hits a short-pitched delivery from Cambridge's Dickinson away on the leg side.

Surrey wicketkeeper Brooks and first slip Garland-Wells look on as Parker is tested at second slip during the game against MCC. The other Surrey fielders are Whitfield (left) and Squires.

M.C.C. v SURREY

At Lord's, May 3, 4, 1939.
Toss won by Surrey.
Surrey won by 99 runs.

SURREY

L.B.Fishlock	c & b Compton	44	c Paris b Smith	20
R.J.Gregory	c Stephenson b Smith	23	c Valentine b Stephenson	9
H.S.Squires	c Wyatt b Sims	67	lbw b Smith	25
T.H.Barling	c Valentine b Compton	4	b Sims	3
E.W.Whitfield	c Stephenson b Smith	2	b Sims	32
J.F.Parker	c Smith b Sims	4	c Compton b Sims	6
*Mr H.M.Garland-Wells	b Sims	18	c & b Stephenson	0
F.Berry	c Mitchell-Innes b Sims	25	not out	27
E.A.Watts	c & b Stephenson	1	b Sims	9
†E.W.J.Brooks	not out	5	lbw b Sims	0
A.R.Gover	st Van der Gucht b Stephenson	9	lbw b Stephenson	0
Extras	(B 13, LB 5, NB 1)	19	(B 5, LB 3)	8
Total		**221**		**139**

Fall: 1st inns 1/65, 2/80, 3/89, 4/96, 5/115, 6/158, 7/195, 8/196, 9/212.
2nd inns 1/18, 2/52, 3/61, 4/65, 5/91, 6/94, 7/110, 8/124, 9/124.

M.C.C.

Mr N.S.Mitchell-Innes	c Brooks b Gover	10	c Brooks b Watts	1
*Mr R.E.S.Wyatt	lbw b Watts	11	lbw b Gover	11
D.C.S.Compton	c Fishlock b Gover	2	c Gregory b Watts	5
Mr N.W.D.Yardley	c Squires b Gover	50	b Watts	4
Mr F.G.H.Chalk	c Brooks b Gover	5	absent hurt	0
Mr B.H.Valentine	c Fishlock b Squires	33	(5) c Squires b Parker	2
Mr C.G.A.Paris	c Brooks b Squires	1	(6) c Fishlock b Squires	15
Capt J.W.A.Stephenson	b Squires	3	(7) not out	36
†Mr P.I.Van der Gucht	not out	14	(8) c & b Parker	5
J.M.Sims	c Fishlock b Squires	0	(9) b Watts	25
C.I.J.Smith	c Garland-Wells b Gover	0	(10) c Fishlock b Squires	8
Extras	(B 4, LB 7)	11	(B 3, LB 6)	9
Total		**140**		**121**

Fall: 1st inns 1/15, 2/21, 3/33, 4/49, 5/110, 6/114, 7/126, 8/140, 9/140.
2nd inns 1/10, 2/18, 3/22, 4/22, 5/33, 6/43, 7/58, 8/112, 9/121.

M.C.C.	O	M	R	W	O	M	R	W
Smith	15	4	35	2	14	3	18	2
Stephenson	15.6	4	46	2	15	3	47	3
Sims	17	3	80	4	15	3	61	5
Compton	12	1	41	2	1	0	5	0

SURREY	O	M	R	W	O	M	R	W
Gover	14.2	2	43	5	8	0	21	1
Watts	4	0	30	1	7	0	21	4
Berry	5	1	21	0	2	1	1	0
Parker	5	2	10	0	5	0	22	2
Garland-Wells	2	0	14	0	2	0	6	0
Squires	8	3	11	4	4.4	0	41	2

Umpires: H.W.Lee and J.A.Newman.

Close of play scores. First day: MCC 114/6 (N.W.D.Yardley 43*).

Comments: The game was completed in two days.

M.C.C. v YORKSHIRE

Played at Lord's, May 6, 8, 1939.
Toss won by Yorkshire.
Yorkshire won by nine wickets.

M.C.C.

S.M.Brown	lbw b Verity	21	st Wood b Verity	8
W.R.Watkins	lbw b Verity	12	c & b Verity	3
W.J.Edrich	b Robinson	16	c Bowes b Verity	55
D.C.S.Compton	st Wood b Robinson	21	lbw b Verity	9
*Mr N.W.D.Yardley	c Smailes b Robinson	4	lbw b Verity	0
Mr R.Aird	c sub b Verity	3	c sub b Verity	1
†Mr P.I.Van der Gucht	b Robinson	0	lbw b Bowes	22
Mr R.E.C.Butterworth	b Robinson	11	c Wood b Verity	2
J.M.Sims	not out	1	c Smailes b Verity	0
C.I.J.Smith	c Sellers b Robinson	0	c Barber b Verity	12
E.A.Roberts	b Robinson	3	not out	1
Extras		0	(LB 1)	1
Total		**92**		**114**

Fall: 1st inns 1/30, 2/33, 3/58, 4/68, 5/75, 6/75, 7/81, 8/89, 9/89.
2nd inns 1/9, 2/12, 3/32, 4/34, 5/40, 6/74, 7/76, 8/76, 9/88.

YORKSHIRE

H.Sutcliffe	c Compton b Roberts	49	c Van der Gucht b Watkins	12
L.Hutton	b Smith	4	not out	31
W.Barber	b Sims	18		
M.Leyland	b Sims	27		
A.Mitchell	run out	1	(3) not out	16
*Mr A.B.Sellers	c Butterworth b Roberts	8		
T.F.Smailes	c Edrich b Roberts	21		
†T.Wood	lbw b Sims	1		
E.P.Robinson	b Sims	8		
H.Verity	not out	2		
W.E.Bowes	c Yardley b Sims	0		
Extras	(B 8, LB 1)	9		
Total		**148**	(1 wicket)	**59**

Fall: 1st inns 1/5, 2/60, 3/98, 4/98, 5/99, 6/124, 7/127, 8/143, 9/148.
2nd inns 1/25.

YORKSHIRE	O	M	R	W	O	M	R	W
Bowes	3	0	11	0	8	2	8	1
Smailes	6	0	25	0	7	1	15	0
Verity	10	4	23	3	16.1	3	62	9
Robinson	6.1	0	33	7	9	1	28	0

M.C.C.	O	M	R	W	O	M	R	W
Smith	6	0	29	1	4	1	13	0
Watkins	2	1	4	0	7	1	20	1
Sims	16.6	1	70	5				
Roberts	13	2	36	3	3.7	1	26	0

Umpires: J.Hardstaff and J.A.Newman.

Close of play scores. First day: MCC 70/5 (W.J.Edrich 29*, P.I.Van der Gucht 19*).

Comments: MCC were put into bat.
25 wickets fell for 310 on the first day.
In a bowler's match, only W.J.Edrich achieved a score of over 50. The game was completed by lunch on the second day. L.Hutton won the match for Yorkshire with two successive 6's off E.A.Roberts.

The Gentlemen. Standing (left to right): F.G.H.Chalk, F.R.Brown, J.M.Brocklebank, H.T.Bartlett, G.F.H.Heane, G.C.Griffith. Seated: B.H.Valentine, R.E.S.Wyatt, W.R.Hammond (captain), K.Farnes, Capt J.W.A.Stephenson.

The Players. Standing (left to right): L.Hutton, H.E.Dollery, W.H.Copson, D.C.S.Compton, H.Gimblett, D.V.P.Wright. Seated: W.F.Price, W.E.Bowes, E.Paynter (captain), J.Hardstaff, G.H.Pope.

Joe Hardstaff hooks Ken Farnes to the boundary, but Farnes soon had his revenge, bowling Hardstaff for 23.

G.F.H.Heane plays over the top of a ball from Bill Bowes and is bowled for 24. Heane and R.E.S.Wyatt batted bravely in dreadful light.

GENTLEMEN v PLAYERS

Played at Lord's, July 5, 6, 7, 1939.
Toss won by Players.
Players won by 160 runs.

PLAYERS

H.Gimblett	b Farnes	52	b Brocklebank	14
L.Hutton	lbw b Stephenson	1	b Stephenson	86
*E.Paynter	lbw b Stephenson	4	b Stephenson	18
D.C.S.Compton	b Stephenson	58	c Brocklebank b Stephenson	70
J.Hardstaff	b Farnes	23	not out	3
H.E.Dollery	c Chalk b Farnes	70		
G.H.Pope	st Griffith b Brocklebank	7		
†W.F.F.Price	lbw b Brocklebank	38		
D.V.P.Wright	hit wkt b Farnes	0		
W.H.Copson	b Farnes	0		
W.E.Bowes	not out	1		
Extras	(B 9, LB 5, W 2)	16	(B 7, LB 4)	11
Total		**270**	(4 wickets, declared)	**202**

Fall: 1st inns 1/12, 2/24, 3/97, 4/147, 5/158, 6/165, 7/254, 8/269, 9/269.
2nd inns 1/27, 2/56, 3/197, 4/202.

GENTLEMEN

Mr F.G.H.Chalk	c Hutton b Bowes	5	c Wright b Copson	8
Mr R.E.S.Wyatt	c Price b Bowes	35	retired hurt	16
Mr G.F.H.Heane	b Bowes	24	b Wright	25
*Mr W.R.Hammond	b Pope	20	c Wright b Copson	4
Mr B.H.Valentine	c Price b Copson	10	c Price b Bowes	8
Mr H.T.Bartlett	c Hutton b Copson	15	b Wright	60
Mr F.R.Brown	c Dollery b Copson	0	c Paynter b Wright	22
†Mr S.C.Griffith	not out	15	c Bowes b Wright	10
Capt J.W.A.Stephenson	not out	16	absent hurt	0
Mr K.Farnes	(did not bat)		(9) not out	1
Mr J.M.Brocklebank	(did not bat)		(10) b Pope	0
Extras	(B 11, LB 2, NB 5)	18		
Total	(7 wickets, declared)	**158**		**154**

Fall: 1st inns 1/25, 2/58, 3/91, 4/93, 5/117, 6/117, 7/124.
2nd inns 1/24, 2/31, 3/53, 4/87, 5/129, 6/153, 7/153, 8/154.

GENTLEMEN	O	M	R	W	O	M	R	W
Farnes	19.6	2	78	5	11	2	35	0
Stephenson	22	5	63	3	12.6	0	78	3
Wyatt	4	0	20	0	1	0	1	0
Brown	5	0	29	0	4	0	32	0
Brocklebank	16	3	64	2	9	2	45	1

PLAYERS	O	M	R	W	O	M	R	W
Bowes	17	0	34	3	8	1	25	1
Copson	20	5	49	3	9	0	35	2
Pope	14	4	23	1	4.2	0	22	1
Wright	7	0	34	0	9	0	72	4

Umpires: J.Hardstaff and E.J.Smith.

Close of play scores. First day: Gentlemen 59/1 (R.E.S.Wyatt 35*, G.F.H.Heane 12*). **Second day:** Gentlemen 158/7 (S.C.Griffith 15*, J.W.A.Stephenson 16*).

Comments: K.Farnes was making his first appearance of the season. He brought the Players innings to a close with three wickets in one over. Play was abandoned on the second day at 3.50pm, after several interruptions for rain.
L.Hutton and D.C.S.Compton put on 141 in 80 minutes for the 3rd wicket in the Players' 2nd innings.
The Gentlemen were set 315 runs to make in 210 minutes.
The Gentlemen were without both R.E.S.Wyatt, who retired hurt on 16 and J.W.A.Stephenson, who did not bat, in their second innings, both being injured.
At the request of the Australian Board of Control, M.C.C. used balls made in Australia for this match.

IRELAND v SCOTLAND

At College Park, Dublin, June 24, 26, 27, 1939.
Toss won by Scotland.
Scotland won by 162 runs.

SCOTLAND

Mr J.F.Jones	c & b Boucher	91	c Williams b Ward	0
Mr F.W.Ramsden	lbw b Boucher	26	lbw b Boucher	29
Mr A.K.McTavish	c Graham b Boucher	37	st Cuffe b M'Donald	39
Mr W.Nichol	st Cuffe b Graham	34	st Cuffre b Boucher	43
*Mr B.R.Tod	c Williams b Graham	10	run out	0
Mr R.M.M'Farland	c M'Murray b M'Donald	48	b Boucher	22
Mr W.K.Laidlaw	b M'Donald	23	b Boucher	0
Mr R.S.Hodge	c Boucher b M'Donald	11	b Boucher	31
†Mr J.S.Brand	b M'Donald	12	b Boucher	0
Mr W.R.H.Dippie	not out	7	b Boucher	0
Mr J.S.Farquhar	c Reddy b Williams	3	not out	3
Extras		8		7
Total		**310**		**174**

Fall: 1st inns 1/63, 2/113, 3/187, 4/199, 5/203, 6/256, 7/272, 8/287, 9/301.
2nd inns 1/0, 2/64, 3/95, 4/103, 5/129, 6/129, 7/165, 8/169, 9/169.

IRELAND

Mr D.R.Pigot	b Farquhar	1	b Hodge	40
Mr F.J.Reddy	c Brand b Hodge	12	b Hodge	0
*Mr J.MacDonald	b Hodge	31	c Jones b Dippie	33
Mr F.A.Blaney	lbw b Farquhar	1	c & b Hodge	13
Mr T.C.Williams	b Laidlaw	23	lbw b Dippie	2
Mr J.S.Pollock	c Jones b Laidlaw	38	c Dippie b Farquhar	25
Mr J.C.Boucher	b Hodge	0	b Hodge	4
Mr A.MacMurray	b Farquhar	5	b Dippie	4
†Mr C.R.Cuffe	lbw b Laidlaw	8	not out	17
Mr J.R.Graham	c Nichol b Laidlaw	4	st Brand b Farquhar	5
Mr J.F.Ward	not out	3	b Farquhar	3
Extras		17		33
Total		**143**		**179**

Fall: 1st inns 1/14, 2/14, 3/16, 4/63, 5/88, 6/88, 7/105, 8/120, 9/128.
2nd inns 1/3, 2/77, 3/93, 4/101, 5/111, 6/129, 7/136, 8/162, 9/168.

IRELAND	O	M	R	W	O	M	R	W
Ward	15	2	47	0	6	1	22	1
Graham	22	4	57	2	8	2	43	0
Boucher	38	9	105	3	17	2	53	7
MacDonald	29	8	57	4	12	3	35	1
Williams	21	2	36	1	3	0	14	0

SCOTLAND	O	M	R	W	O	M	R	W
Hodge	18	7	28	3	18	8	26	4
Farquhar	22	7	40	3	19.5	8	32	3
Laidlaw	17	6	28	4	15	3	47	0
Dippie	12	3	30	0	13	1	41	3

Close of play scores. First day: Ireland 9/0 (D.R.Pigot 1*, F.J.Reddy 7*).
Second day: Scotland 174 all out.

Comments: Scotland did not enforce the follow-on.

The West Indies in England, 1939

SINCE the previous encounter between the two sides in 1934-35, when an understrength England side had lost by two Tests to one in the Caribbean, the West Indians had not participated in any subsequent Test series against any other country. This was reflected in the composition of their sixth side to visit England, for only seven of the 16-strong party had Test experience. Even if those seven had taken part in the victorious series of 1934-35, it was not expected that they would either win the series or even register their first Test victory in England on this trip.

The 16 players chosen for the West Indies sixth tour of England were:

	Island	Age	Caps
R.S.Grant (capt)	Trinidad	29	4
I.Barrow	Jamaica	28	10
H.P.Bayley	B Guiana	23	0
J.H.Cameron	Jamaica	25	0
C.B.Clarke	Barbados	21	0
L.N.Constantine	Trinidad	37	15
G.E.Gomez	Trinidad	19	0
T.F.Johnson	Trinidad	22	0
G.A.Headley	Jamaica	29	16
E.A.Martindale	Barbados	29	7
J.E.D.Sealy	Barbados	26	8
V.H.Stollmeyer	Trinidad	23	0
J.B.Stollmeyer	Trinidad	18	0
K.H.Weekes	Jamaica	26	0
E.A.V.Williams	Barbados	25	0
J.M.Kidney(manager)			

Only 15 players were originally chosen but L.G.Hylton of Jamaica, a fast bowler aged 34 and with four previous Test appearances, was later added to the party after his fellow Jamaicans paid for his fare by public subscription.

The party contained a number of faces well known to English cricket followers and three at least were regarded as players of the highest class. George Headley was acknowledged as one of the world's great Test batsman, whilst Learie Constantine, even at 37 years of age, was recognized as one of the greatest all-rounders in the game. Ernie Martindale was still remembered as a fast, fiery bowler, who had given the England batsmen in 1933 a taste of West Indian 'bodyline'. One other player had survived from that last tour of England, I.Barrow, the first-choice wicketkeeper and

opening batsman, who had made a century in the Second Test at Old Trafford.

Only two other members of the party had experience of English conditions. R.S.Grant and J.H.Cameron had both played for Cambridge University, the latter also turning out for Somerset. Much would depend on the experience of these players, for the majority of the party clearly lacked knowledge of English conditions. The omission of experienced players such as C.A.Merry, who many in the West Indies felt should have made the trip, seemed to indicate that a major objective of the West Indian selectors on this tour was to lay the foundation for a future side, which would soon have to survive without the fine talents of world-class players such as Constantine and Headley.

If the primary objective was to give their younger players a taste of Test cricket, it could be claimed that on these grounds alone the tour was a successful one, for of the nine players lacking any Test experience, only H.P.Bayley failed to represent his country in the series. There were grounds for even greater satisfaction with the manner in which the tourists fared both in the Test series and against the counties. The side was to win more matches in England than any previous West Indian touring side and had not the tour been curtailed by the rapidly worsening international situation, it was possible they would have claimed even more victories.

This performance was even more praiseworthy if other factors are taken into account. The tour began badly with a defeat by Worcestershire in their opening first-class fixture, followed by two further defeats against Surrey and Glamorgan before the First Test. By the end of May, only one victory, that against Oxford University, had been recorded in seven first-class matches. It said much for the resilience of the West Indians that these early set-backs, which could have undermined the confidence of the side, were overcome, when after a close victory against Essex, their batsmen began to find their form, beginning with a record-breaking 665 against Middlesex at Lords, which made evident the potential of their batting. After their defeat in the First Test, only two more defeats were recorded against the counties during the remainder of the tour.

Their record of eight victories was also highly creditable as several of their more experienced players failed to do themselves justice. Martindale was a shadow of his

former self, having lost both pace and accuracy, whilst Barrow had a poor tour both as batsman and wicketkeeper, being replaced in the final two Tests by the talented Sealy. This additional burden may have contributed in turn to Sealy's poor showing with the bat in the Test series. Cameron also failed to live up to expectations and had an indifferent tour with the bat, being omitted from the side for the Third Test.

Much therefore depended on the success or otherwise of Headley and Constantine and both rose to the challenge. Headley headed the batting averages, scoring six hundreds and averaging over 70. The highlight of the tour was undoubtedly his two centuries in the First Test at Lords, when he became only the second Test player to accomplish this feat twice in Tests, and a magnificent undefeated 234 against Nottinghamshire, his second double-century of the tour, Constantine supported Headley's batting contribution by being the only West Indian bowler to take 100 wickets on the tour, as well as capturing most wickets in the Test series. His ability to bowl either fast or slow, his still energetic fielding and his aggressive approach to batting all made him both a major factor in the success of the West Indies and a player who could fill cricket grounds throughout the country.

Although these two players provided the main ingredients for the success of the West Indian side, a number of other players also played their part. Grant captained the side well, was an outstanding fielder close to the wicket and as a temporary opening batsman contributed a number of aggressive innings. Both the Stollmeyers had highly satisfactory tours, the younger Jeffrey having the distinction of scoring a century on his first appearance at Lord's, whilst Victor narrowly missed a hundred on his Test debut in the Third Test. K.H.Weekes finished his tour in a grand manner, taking only 110 minutes to score his maiden Test hundred in the same match.

If the batting, although often inconsistent, showed indications of future potential, similar claims could not be made for the bowling. With Martindale, Constantine and Hylton all reaching the end of their Test careers, only Clarke of the younger bowlerslooked to have a future. He emerged as the stock bowler of the side, achieving highly creditable figures throughout the tour, if doing little in the Tests. Both E.A.V.Williams and T.F.Johnson had limited Test opportunities but the latter showed some promise in his Test debut at The Oval, having the rare distinction of taking a wicket with his first ball in first-class cricket in England and also in Test cricket.

The Test series saw a growing improvement in the fortunes of the tourists. Well beaten at Lord's in the opening Test, they showed improved form in the rain-affected Second Test and made their best showing in a Test in England when, at The Oval, they amassed their highest Test score in England, with Weekes and Constantine putting a weakened England attack to the sword.

In conclusion, the West Indies gained confidence and experience from this tour and from their improved showing against England in the Test series. Although it is clear that their greatest players were nearing the end of their Test careers, a number of their younger players gained valuable experience of English playing conditions and Test cricket, all of which could prove extremely valuable for the future of West Indian Test cricket.

TOUR RESULTS

	Pld	W	L	D
Test Matches	3	0	1	2
Other First-Class matches	22	8	5	9
Other matches	6	1	0	5
Total	31	9	6	16

The following matches were not played by the West Indies owing to the worsening international situation, which cut short their tour: v Sussex, Kent, W.E.Butlin's XI, an England XI, Mr H.D.G.Leveson-Gower's XI, Ireland (2 matches).

Denis Compton scored 120 in the First Test against the West Indies to add to his 115 for MCC against the tourists.

West Indies spin bowler C.B.Clarke surveys his shattered wicket after being bowled by Bill Bowes in the First Test. Fielders, from left to right, are Wright, Hutton, Hammond and Wood.

Jeff Stollmeyer glances Bowes to fine leg on his way to 59 in the West Indies' first innings at Lord's.

ENGLAND v WEST INDIES (First Test)

Played at Lord's, London, June 24, 26, 27, 1939.
Toss won by West Indies.
England won by eight wickets.

WEST INDIES

*R.S.Grant	c Compton b Copson 22	b Bowes 23
J.B.Stollmeyer	b Bowes 59	c Verity b Copson 0
G.A.Headley	c Wood b Copson 106	c Hutton b Wright 107
J.E.D.Sealy	c Wood b Wright.........13	c Wood b Copson 29
K.H.Weekes	c Gimblett b Copson....20	c Wood b Verity 16
L.N.Constantine	lbw b Copson 14	c Hammond b Verity......17
J.H.Cameron	c Hutton b Bowes 1	c & b Wright 0
†I.Barrow	lbw b Copson 2	not out 6
E.A.Martindale	lbw b Wright..........22	c Bowes b Wright...........3
L.G.Hylton	not out.....................2	c Hardstaff b Copson......13
C.B.Clarke	b Bowes...................1	c & b Copson................0
Extras	(B 3, LB 9, NB 3)........15	(B 6, LB 4, W 1) 11
Total	..................**277**	**225**

Fall: 1st inns 1/29, 2/147, 3/180, 4/226, 5/245, 6/250, 7/250, 8/261, 9/276.
2nd inns 1/0, 2/42, 3/105, 4/154, 5/190, 6/199, 7/200, 8/204, 9/225.

ENGLAND

L.Hutton	c Grant b Hylton 196	b Hylton 16
H.Gimblett	b Cameron 22	b Martindale 20
E.Paynter	c Barrow b Cameron 34	not out 32
*W.R.Hammond	c Grant b Cameron 14	not out 30
D.C.S.Compton	c Stollmeyer b Clarke ...120	
J.Hardstaff, jnr	not out 3	
†A.Wood	not out 0	
Extras	(B 8, LB 6, W 1) 15	(LB 2) 2
Total	(5 wickets, declared) ...**404**	(2 wickets) **100**

Fall: 1st inns 1/49, 2/119, 3/147, 4/395, 5/402.
2nd inns 1/35, 2/39.

D.V.P.Wright, H.Verity, W.H.Copson, W.E.Bowes did not bat

ENGLAND	O	M	R	W	O	M	R	W
Bowes	28.4	5	86	3	19	7	44	1
Copson	24	2	85	5	16.4	2	67	4
Wright	13	1	57	2	17	0	75	3
Verity	16	3	34	0	14	4	20	2
Compton	-	-	-	-	3	0	8	0
WEST INDIES	O	M	R	W	O	M	R	W
Martindale	20	2	86	0	7.7	0	51	1
Hylton	24	4	98	1	7	1	36	1
Constantine	13	0	67	0	3	0	11	0
Cameron	26	6	66	3				
Clarke	6	0	28	1				
Sealy	3	0	21	0				
Grant	3	0	23	0				

Umpires: E.J.Smith and F.I.Walden.

Close of play scores. First day: England 11/0 (L.Hutton 4*, H.Gimblett 5*).
Second day: England 404/5 (J.Hardstaff 3*, A.Wood 0*).
Comments: It was the first Test match played in England, which featured the use of the eight-ball over.
West Indies: J.H.Cameron, C.B.Clarke, J.B.Stollmeyer and K.H.Weekes were making their Test debuts.
J.B.Stollmeyer and G.A.Headley added 118 for the 2nd wicket in 140 minutes.
G.A.Headley became the first batsman to score 100 in each innings in a Test at Lord's. It was the second occasion Headley had accomplished this feat in Tests. It brought his total of centuries against England to eight. It was also his third consecutive Test century.
Headley's 1st innings score of 106 was made in 250 minutes and included 13 4's. His second 100 included eight 4's and lasted 230 minutes.
J.H.Cameron took a wicket with his second ball in Test cricket.
England: W.H.Copson was making his Test debut.
L.Hutton and D.C.S.Compton added 248 for the 4th wicket in only 140 minutes.
L.Hutton reached his 1,000 runs in Test Cricket on the second day's play. He made 196 in 335 minutes, hitting 21 4's. England, requiring 99 to win in 110 minutes, hit off the runs in 75 minutes.

Top and bottom: George Headley, scorer of two centuries in the First Test, plays some flashing shots.

183

Above: England skipper Wally Hammond has regained his ground too late. Sealy whips off the bails and Hammond is out, stumped off Clarke for 22 in the Second Test at Old Trafford.

Right: Derbyshire's Bill Copson (bowling right) did not fare as well as his teammate, Bill Bowes, and even had the misfortune to drop Headley off his own bowling.

ENGLAND v WEST INDIES (Second Test)

Played at Old Trafford, Manchester, July 22, 24, 25, 1939.
Toss won by West Indies.
Match drawn.

ENGLAND

L.Hutton	c Martindale b Grant 13	c Sealy b Martindale 17
A.E.Fagg	b Hylton 7	b Constantine 32
E.Paynter	c Sealy b Clarke 9	c Gomez b Martindale 0
*W.R.Hammond	st Sealy b Clarke 22	b Constantine 32
D.C.S.Compton	hit wkt b Clarke 4	not out 34
J.Hardstaff, jnr	c Williams b Grant 76	c Grant b Constantine......1
†A.Wood	c & b Constantine 26	b Constantine................1
D.V.P.Wright	not out 1	not out 0
Extras	(B 3, LB 2, NB 1) 6	(B 8, LB 2, NB 1) 11
Total	(7 wickets, declared) **164**	(6 wickets, declared)......**128**

Fall: 1st inns 1/21, 2/34, 3/34, 4/53, 5/62, 6/150, 7/164.
     2nd inns 1/26, 2/30, 3/74, 4/89, 5/113, 6/126.
W.E.Bowes, W.H.Copson, T.W.J.Goddard did not bat

WEST INDIES

*R.S.Grant	c Fagg b Goddard 47	c Hardstaff b Bowes 0
J.B.Stollmeyer	c & b Goddard 5	lbw Wright 10
G.A.Headley	c Wood b Bowes..........51	c Hammond b Copson 5
G.E.Gomez	c Wood b Bowes 0	b Goddard 11
†J.E.D.Sealy	c Hammond b Bowes ...16	not out 13
J.H.Cameron	c Hutton b Bowes 5	
E.A.V.Williams	b Copson 1	
L.N.Constantine	b Bowes 0	
E.A.Martindale	c Hammond b Copson....0	
L.G.Hylton	lbw b Bowes 2	
C.B.Clarke	not out 0	
Extras	(LB 6) 6	(LB 3, NB 1) 4
Total	133	(4 wickets) 43

Fall: 1st inns 1/35, 2/56, 3/56, 4/96, 5/108, 6/113, 7/124, 8/125, 9/132.
     2nd inns 1/0, 2/11, 3/27, 4/43.

WEST INDIES	O	M	R	W	O	M	R	W
Martindale	8	2	10	0	12	2	34	2
Hylton	11	3	15	1	6	1	18	0
Clarke	13	1	59	3				
Grant	13.2	4	16	2				
Cameron	3	0	22	0				
Constantine	7	2	36	1	11	1	42	4
Williams	-	-	-	-	9	1	23	0
ENGLAND								
Bowes	17.4	4	33	6	5	0	13	1
Copson	9	2	31	2	3	1	2	1
Goddard	4	0	43	2	4.6	1	15	1
Wright	5	1	20	0	3	0	9	1

Umpires: F.Chester and E.J.Smith.

Close of play scores. First day: England 11/0 (L.Hutton 6*, A.E.Fagg 2*). **Second day:** West Indies 85/3 (G.A.Headley 16* J.E.D.Sealy 13*).
Comments: England were put in to bat. The game was constantly interrupted by rain and bad light. Play began at 2.15pm on the first day but there was only 35 minutes play. On the second day play was delayed until 12.15pm, there were two breaks for bad light and rain and stumps were drawn at 6.10pm. On the third day, England declared, leaving the West Indies to make 160 in 70 minutes. For the second time in England, a team declared twice in a Test match.
England: W.R.Hammond became the first fielder to hold a 100 catches in Test cricket, when he caught G.A.Headley off W.Copson in the West Indies 2nd innings. It was his 76th Test.
West Indies: G.E.Gomez and E.A.V.Williams were making their Test debuts. L.H.Constantine became the first West Indian to capture 50 Test wickets.

In the second innings, Hammond offers no stroke to a ball from Constantine and can only look down as he is bowled.

Bill Bowes took 6-33 in the first innings and bagged the wickets of Headley, Sealy, Cameron, Constantine and Hylton on the last morning of a rain-affected match.

ENGLAND v WEST INDIES (Third Test)

Played at Kennington Oval, London, August 19, 21, 22, 1939.
Toss won by England.
Match drawn.

ENGLAND

L.Hutton	c & b Johnson	73	not out	165
W.W.Keeton	b Johnson	0	b Constantine	20
N.Oldfield	c Sealy b Constantine	80	c Sealy b Johnson	19
*W.R.Hammond	c Grant b Constantine	43	b Clarke	138
D.C.S.Compton	c Gomez b Martindale	21	not out	10
J.Hardstaff, jnr	b Constantine	94		
M.S.Nichols	run out	24		
†A.Wood	b Constantine	0		
D.V.P.Wright	lbw b Constantine	6		
T.W.J.Goddard	b Clarke	0		
R.T.D.Perks	not out	1		
Extras	(B 4, LB 5, NB 1)	10	(B 4, LB 5, W 4, NB 1)	14
Total		**352**	(3 wickets, declared)	**366**

Fall: 1st inns 1/2, 2/133, 3/168, 4/215, 5/244, 6/333, 7/333, 8/345, 9/346.
2nd inns 1/39, 2/77, 3/341.

WEST INDIES

*R.S.Grant	c Goddard b Perks	6
J.B.Stollmeyer	c Perks b Hutton	59
G.A.Headley	run out	65
V.H.Stollmeyer	st Wood b Goddard	96
G.E.Gomez	b Perks	11
K.H.Weekes	c Hammond b Nichols	137
†J.E.D.Sealy	c Wright b Nichols	24
L.N.Constantine	c Wood b Perks	79
E.A.Martindale	b Perks	3
C.B.Clarke	b Perks	2
T.F.Johnson	not out	9
Extras	(LB 6, NB 1)	7
Total		**498**

Fall: 1st inns 1/15, 2/128, 3/134, 4/164, 5/327, 6/389, 7/434, 8/451, 9/475.

WEST INDIES	O	M	R	W	O	M	R	W
Martindale	13	0	87	1	10	2	46	0
Johnson	16	1	53	2	14	2	76	1
Constantine	17.3	2	75	5	20	3	97	1
Clarke	21	0	96	1	17	1	78	1
Grant	6	0	31	0	11	1	38	0
Headley	-	-	-	-	4	0	17	0

ENGLAND	O	M	R	W
Nichols	34	4	161	2
Perks	30.5	6	156	5
Wright	13	2	53	0
Goddard	12	1	56	1
Hutton	7	0	45	1
Compton	5	1	20	0

Umpires: F.Chester and W.Reeves.

Close of play scores. First day: West Indies 27/1 (J.B.Stollmeyer 14*, G.A.Headley 7*). **Second day:** West Indies 395/6 (J.E.D.Sealy 17*, L.N.Constantine 1*).
Comments: England: N.Oldfield was making his Test Debut. L.Hutton scored his 165* in 310 minutes. It included 17 4's. W.R.Hammond hit 21 4's in his 138. L.Hutton and N.Oldfield put on 131 for England's 2nd wicket. L.Hutton and W.R.Hammond put on 264 in 180 minutes for the 3rd wicket in England's 2nd innings, a record for all Test matches, beating the 262 made by D.R.Jardine and W.R.Hammond against Australia at Adelaide in 1929-30. It was made in 180 minutes.
West Indies: T.F.Johnson and V.H.Stollmeyer were making their Test debuts. T.Johnson took a wicket with his first ball in Test cricket, when he bowled W.W.Keeton. K.H.Weekes scored his first Test 100 in only 110 minutes. His 137 was made in 135 minutes out of 225. He hit one 6 and 18 4's. L.H.Constantine made 78 out of the last 103 of the first innings scored on the third day. He hit one 6 and 11 4's in 60 minutes. G.A.Headley and J.B.Stollmeyer added 113 for the 2nd wicket. Stollmeyer and K.H.Weekes then put on 163 for the 5th wicket in a 100 minutes. The aggregate attendance was 42,252; the largest crowd was on the second day, approximately 23,500.

Len Hutton the bowler. In the West Indies second innings at The Oval, one of England's master batsmen captured the wicket of Jeff Stollmeyer, caught by Perks.

AVERAGES ~ TEST MATCHES

WEST INDIES — BATTING & FIELDING
(15 players)

	Pld	In	NO	Runs	HS	Ave	100	50	Ct/St
V.H.Stollmeyer	1	1	0	96	96	96.00	-	1	0
G.A.Headley	3	5	0	334	107	66.80	2	2	0
K.H.Weekes	2	3	0	173	137	57.66	1	-	0
L.N.Constantine	3	4	0	110	79	27.50	-	1	1
J.B.Stollmeyer	3	5	0	133	59	26.60	-	2	1
J.E.D.Sealy	3	5	1	95	29	23.75	-	-	4/1
R.S.Grant	3	5	0	98	47	19.60	-	-	4
L.G.Hylton	2	3	1	17	13	8.50	-	-	0
I.Barrow	1	2	1	8	*6	8.00	-	-	1
G.E.Gomez	2	3	0	22	11	7.33	-	-	2
E.A.Martindale	3	4	0	28	22	7.00	-	-	1
J.H.Cameron	2	3	0	6	5	2.00	-	-	0
C.B.Clarke	3	4	1	3	2	1.00	-	-	0
E.A.V.Williams	1	1	0	1	1	1.00	-	-	1
T.F.Johnson	1	1	1	9	*9	-	-	-	1

ENGLAND — BATTING & FIELDING
(17 players)

	Pld	In	NO	Runs	HS	Ave	100	50	Ct/St
L.Hutton	3	6	1	480	196	96.00	2	1	3
D.C.S.Compton	3	5	2	189	120	63.00	1	-	1
J.Hardstaff	3	4	1	174	94	58.00	-	2	2
W.R.Hammond	3	6	1	279	138	55.80	1	-	5
N.Oldfield	1	2	0	99	80	49.50	-	1	0
E.Paynter	2	4	1	75	34	25.00	-	-	0
M.S.Nichols	1	1	0	24	24	24.00	-	-	0
H.Gimblett	1	2	0	42	22	21.00	-	-	1
A.E.Fagg	1	2	0	39	32	19.50	-	-	1
W.W.Keeton	1	2	0	20	20	10.00	-	-	0
A.Wood	3	4	1	27	26	9.00	-	-	7/1
D.V.P.Wright	3	3	2	7	6	7.00	-	-	2
R.T.D.Perks	1	1	1	1	*1	-	-	-	1
T.W.J.Goddard	2	1	0	0	0	-	-	-	2
W.E.Bowes	2			did not bat					1
W.H.Copson	2			did not bat					1
H.Verity	1			did not bat					1

WEST INDIES — BOWLING

	Overs	Mds	Runs	Wkts	Ave	Best	5wI	10wM	SRate
J.H.Cameron	29	6	88	3	29.33	3-66	-	-	77.33
L.N.Constantine	71.3	8	328	11	29.81	5-75	1	-	51.90
T.F.Johnson	30	3	129	3	43.00	2-53	-	-	80.00
C.B.Clarke	57	2	261	6	43.50	3-59	-	-	76.00
R.S.Grant	33.2	5	108	2	54.00	2-16	-	-	133.00
L.G.Hylton	48	9	167	3	55.66	1-15	-	-	128.00
E.A.Martindale	70.7	8	314	4	78.50	2-34	-	-	141.75
G.A.Headley	4	0	17	0	-	0-17	-	-	-
J.E.D.Sealy	3	0	21	0	-	0-21	-	-	-
E.A.V.Williams	9	1	23	0	-	0-23	-	-	-

ENGLAND — BOWLING

	Overs	Mds	Runs	Wkts	Ave	Best	5wI	10wM	SRate
W.H.Copson	52.4	7	185	12	15.41	5-85	1	-	35.00
W.E.Bowes	70	18	176	11	16.00	6-33	1	-	50.90
H.Verity	30	7	54	2	27.00	2-20	-	-	120.00
T.W.J.Goddard	20.6	2	114	4	28.50	2-43	-	-	41.50
R.T.D.Perks	30.5	6	156	5	31.20	5-165	1	-	49.00
D.V.P.Wright	51	4	214	6	35.66	3-75	-	-	68.00
L.Hutton	7	0	45	1	45.00	1-45	-	-	56.00
M.S.Nichols	34	4	161	2	80.50	2-161	-	-	136.00
D.C.S.Compton	8	1	28	0	-	0-8	-	-	-

AVERAGES ~ FIRST-CLASS MATCHES

WEST INDIES — BATTING & FIELDING

	Pld	In	NO	Runs	HS	Ave	100	50	Ct/St
G.A.Headley	20	30	6	1745	*234	72.70	6	9	10
E.A.V.Williams	11	15	3	370	*126	30.83	1	1	6
J.B.Stollmeyer	18	31	1	916	117	30.53	1	7	6
V.H.Stollmeyer	13	22	4	542	96	30.11	-	4	3
K.H.Weekes	19	28	1	803	146	29.74	2	5	6
R.S.Grant	21	32	4	785	95	28.03	-	3	23
J.E.D.Sealy	23	35	1	948	181	27.88	2	5	16/3
G.E.Gomez	19	30	2	719	90	25.67	-	6	10
L.N.Constantine	22	32	3	614	79	21.17	-	4	17
J.H.Cameron	17	23	2	438	106	20.85	1	1	5
H.P.Bayley	10	15	2	266	104	20.46	1	1	2
L.G.Hylton	15	19	4	215	55	14.33	-	1	10
I.Barrow	16	25	2	304	41	13.21	-	-	20/6
E.A.Martindale	20	30	7	286	39	12.43	-	-	5
C.B.Clarke	22	25	10	162	45	10.80	-	-	5
T.F.Johnson	9	9	4	30	12	6.00	-	-	4

WEST INDIES — BOWLING

	Overs	Mds	Runs	Wkts	Ave	Best	5wI	10wM	SRate
L.N.Constantine	488.4	67	1831	103	17.77	7-49	9	1	37.94
J.H.Cameron	222.6	40	664	31	21.41	6-57	2	-	57.48
C.B.Clarke	458.2	46	1898	87	21.81	7-75	6	1	42.14
R.S.Grant	211.5	33	676	25	27.04	4-41	-	-	67.72
L.G.Hylton	301	32	1081	39	27.71	5-35	1	-	61.74
G.A.Headley	10	1	30	1	30.00	1-5	-	-	80.00
T.F.Johnson	154.1	26	520	16	32.50	4-37	-	-	77.06
E.A.V.Williams	119.4	14	461	14	32.92	3-37	-	-	68.28
V.H.Stollmeyer	6	1	33	1	33.00	1-8	-	-	48.00
E.A.Martindale	397.7	41	1587	46	34.50	5-57	1	-	69.19
J.E.D.Sealy	47	4	174	5	34.80	1-8	-	-	75.20
J.B.Stollmeyer	34	2	182	3	60.66	2-58	-	-	90.66

WORCESTERSHIRE v WEST INDIES

Played at Worcester, May 6, 8, 1939.
Toss won by West Indies.
Worcestershire won by 85 runs.

WORCESTERSHIRE

C.H.Bull	b Martindale	4	c Barrow b Martindale	3
B.P.King	c Grant b Johnson	3	c Weekes b Martindale	20
E.Cooper	c Constantine b Martindale	1	b Cameron	92
H.H.I.Gibbons	c Grant b Johnson	21	b Constantine	1
S.H.Martin	c Grant b Martindale	1	b Constantine	94
*Hon C.J.Lyttelton	lbw b Constantine	7	b Stollmeyer	4
P/O J.M.H.Jewell	c Barrow b Martindale	4	c Constantine b Martindale	24
R.Howorth	b Constantine	0	c Barrow b Cameron	29
†J.S.Buller	b Johnson	10	hit wkt b Cameron	0
R.T.D.Perks	run out	13	not out	1
R.O.Jenkins	not out	9	b Constantine	1
Extras	(B 6, LB 3, NB 1)	10	(B 13, LB 8, NB 1)	22
Total		**83**		**291**

Fall: 1st inns 1/3, 2/9, 3/12, 4/18, 5/33, 6/43, 7/44, 8/58, 9/69.
2nd inns 1/8, 2/42, 3/47, 4/169, 5/192, 6/227, 7/283, 8/284, 9/287.

WEST INDIES

†I.Barrow	st Buller b Howorth	22	c & b Martin	9
J.B.Stollmeyer	c Gibbons b Perks	13	b Perks	13
G.A.Headley	lbw b Perks	50	c Jewell b Perks	7
J.E.D.Sealy	lbw b Jenkins	1	lbw b Perks	0
G.E.Gomez	c Buller b Howorth	28	c Lyttelton b Perks	30
K.H.Weekes	st Buller b Howorth	6	c & b Howorth	4
L.N.Constantine	c Jewell b Perks	3	c Gibbons b Perks	47
J.H.Cameron	c Buller b Perks	4	c & b Howorth	3
*R.S.Grant	b Perks	7	c Bull b Howorth	2
E.A.Martindale	not out	0	b Howorth	24
T.F.Johnson	b Perks	2	not out	2
Extras	(B 6)	6	(B 6)	6
Total		**142**		**147**

Fall: 1st inns 1/17, 2/45, 3/52, 4/95, 5/111, 6/118, 7/122, 8/135, 9/140.
2nd inns 1/25, 2/27, 3/27, 4/36, 5/43, 6/55, 7/112, 8/119, 9/119.

WEST INDIES	O	M	R	W	O	M	R	W
Martindale	10	2	27	4	14	2	42	3
Johnson	10.2	2	28	3	11	1	50	0
Constantine	9	0	18	2	12.6	3	49	3
Stollmeyer	-	-	-	-	9	0	53	1
Grant	-	-	-	-	4	0	27	0
Cameron	-	-	-	-	14	2	48	3
Headley	-	-	-	-	1	1	0	0

WORCESTERSHIRE	O	M	R	W	O	M	R	W
Perks	10	2	27	6	13	1	48	5
Martin	18	3	47	0	9	2	24	1
Jenkins	9	3	15	1	4	0	27	0
Howorth	20	4	47	3	7.1	2	42	4

Umpires: E.J.Smith and A.Skelding.

Close of play scores. First day: West Indies 142 all out.

Comments: The match was completed in two days.
Worcestershire were put in to bat, being bowled out in 140 minutes.
T.F.Johnson took a wicket with his first ball in first-class cricket in England.
R.T.D.Perks had match figures of 11 wickets for 75. Coming on at 118-5 in the West Indies 1st innings, he took five wickets for 13 in 3 overs.
E.Cooper and S.H.Martin added 122 for the 4th wicket in Worcester's 2nd innings.
According to *The Times*, on the second day stumps should have been drawn on the fall of the West Indies 8th wicket. However, both captains agreed that the game should continue to secure a finish, the West Indies losing their last two wickets by 6.45pm.

Jeff Stollmeyer (left) and Ivan Barrow open the West Indies innings in the first match of the tour at Worcester. Wicketkeeper Barrow played in the First Test but then lost his place to Derek Sealy.

LANCASHIRE v WEST INDIES

Played at Aigburth, Liverpool, May 10, 11, 12, 1939.
Toss won by Lancashire.
Match drawn.

LANCASHIRE

C.Washbrook	c Barrow b Constantine 64	lbw b Hylton 42
E.Paynter	b Martindale 29	b Constantine 40
J.Iddon	b Hylton 6	b Constantine 12
N.Oldfield	b Hylton 2	c Constantine b Hylton ...71
J.L.Hopwood	b Williams................5	c sub b Hylton............33
A.E.Nutter	c Constantine b Martindale 27	c Hylton b Cameron........4
R.H.Parkin	run out 10	not out 23
*Mr W.H.L.Lister	c Bayley b Martindale 35	st Barrow b Cameron.......1
W.E.Phillipson	c Barrow b Sealy 17	c Bayley b Cameron 4
†W.Farrimond	c Barrow b Hylton 9	c sub b Cameron............5
R.Pollard	not out....................15	c Constantine b Cameron 11
Extras	(B 2, LB 3, W 1, NB 1) 7	(B 6, LB 3, NB 1) 10
Total	...........................**226**	...........................**256**

Fall: 1st inns 1/45, 2/60, 3/64, 4/76, 5/130, 6/138, 7/154, 8/192, 9/206.
2nd inns 1/70, 2/96, 3/102, 4/184, 5/211, 6/213, 7/217, 8/221, 9/237.

WEST INDIES

†I.Barrow	b Pollard 26	c Pollard b Phillipson......3
E.A.Martindale	c Farrimond b Phillipson 27	c Farrimond b Phillipson 39
G.A.Headley	c Phillipson b Pollard 3	not out 76
G.E.Gomez	c Pollard b Phillipson 3	b Pollard 12
H.P.Bayley	c Farrimond b Phillipson 2	not out 7
J.E.D.Sealy	c Farrimond b Phillipson 67	
L.N.Constantine	st Farrimond b Parkin ...37	
J.H.Cameron	c Paynter b Phillipson ...45	
L.G.Hylton	c Farrimond b Pollard ...13	
E.A.V.Williams	not out 3	
*R.S.Grant	absent hurt 0	
Extras	(LB 4, NB 6)..............10	(LB 5) 5
Total	..........................**236**	(3 wickets) **142**

Fall: 1st inns 1/51, 2/58, 3/61, 4/66, 5/73, 6/129, 7/208, 8/232, 9/236.
2nd inns 1/4, 2/69, 3/94.

WEST INDIES	O	M	R	W	O	M	R	W
Martindale	17	0	73	3	9	1	52	0
Williams	12	1	43	1	10	1	57	0
Hylton	14.4	3	44	3	18	2	65	3
Constantine	11	3	26	1	11	3	49	2
Cameron	10	1	22	0	8.5	3	23	5
Sealy	5	0	11	1				

LANCASHIRE	O	M	R	W	O	M	R	W
Phillipson	25	5	48	5	11	2	18	2
Pollard	20	1	74	3	11	1	34	1
Nutter	12	2	37	0	3	1	23	0
Parkin	8	1	33	1	15	2	43	0
Hopwood	6	2	34	0	8	1	19	0

Umpires: A.Dolphin and G.M.Lee.

Two fine West Indies slip fielders, Learie Constantine (left) and John Cameron, both miss this high chance. Cameron, a Cambridge blue, was the tourists' vice captain in 1939.

Close of play scores. First day: West Indies 46/0 (I.Barrow 19*, E.A.Martindale 23*). **Second day:** Lancashire 142/3 (N.Oldfield 22*, J.L.Hopwood 21*).

Comments: The start of the first day was delayed and there was an interruption for bad light before lunch.
The West Indies were left to make 247 runs to win in 195 minutes.
The West Indies captain, R.S.Grant, was forced to retire from the match after being struck on the knee whilst fielding.

M.C.C. v WEST INDIES

Played at Lord's, May 13, 15, 16, 1939.
Toss won by M.C.C.
Match drawn.

M.C.C.

Mr B.O.Allen .... st Barrow b Hylton 85
W.J.Edrich .... lbw b Constantine 17
D.C.S.Compton ..... c Barrow b Johnson 115
Mr N.W.D.Yardley   run out....................0
*Mr B.H.Valentine   lbw b Sealey 73
Mr H.T.Bartlett .....b Johnson 12
Mr F.R.Brown ......b Constantine 14
†Mr C.R.N.Maxwell not out....................64
Capt J.W.A.Stephenson not out...................46
   Extras.............. (B 6, LB 2, NB 1) 9
   Total .... (7 wickets) **435**
Fall: 1st inns 1/59, 2/166, 3/166, 4/253, 5/283, 6/305, 7/331.
C.I.J.Smith and J.M.Sims did not bat.

WEST INDIES

*J.H.Cameron, †I.Barrow, E.A.Martindale, G.A.Headley, G.F.Gomez, L.N.Constantine, J.E.D.Sealy, K.H.Weekes, J.B.Stollmeyer, L.G.Hylton and T.F.Johnson.

WEST INDIES	O	M	R	W
Martindale	19	0	91	0
Johnson	15	2	78	2
Constantine	22	0	102	2
Hylton	15	0	69	1
Cameron	5	0	18	0
Sealy	9	2	38	1
Stollmeyer	3	0	30	0

Umpires: G.Beet and J.Hardstaff.

Close of play scores. First day: MCC 435/7 (C.R.N.Maxwell 64*, Capt J.W.A.Stephenson 46*). **Second day:** No play.

Comments: There was no play on the second and third days.
D.C.S.Compton made 115 in 168 minutes, scoring 13 4's.
He and B.O.Allen put on 107 for MCC's 2nd wicket.
Capt J.W.A.Stephenson and C.R.N.Maxwell were involved in an unbroken partnership of 107 in 30 minutes for the 8th wicket.

CAMBRIDGE UNIVERSITY v WEST INDIES

Played at Fenner's, Cambridge, May 17, 18, 19, 1939.
Toss won by West Indies.
Match drawn.

WEST INDIES

V.H.Stollmeyer ......lbw b Shirreff 36
†I.Barrow .... c J.P.Mann b Dickinson 22
G.A.Headley .... c Newton-Thompson
                   b Dickinson 103
G.E.Gomez .... c Wilson b Shirreff 3
J.H.Cameron .... c & b Shirreff 14
L.N.Constantine ....lbw b Shirreff 31
J.E.D.Sealy.......... b Dickinson 42
K.H.Weekes.......... b Dickinson 14
*R.S.Grant .... c Studd b Carris 16
C.B.Clarke .... lbw b Carris 0
T.F.Johnson .... not out 0
   Extras.............. (B 11, LB 3, NB 1) 15
   Total **296**
Fall: 1st inns 1/39, 2/70, 4/127.

CAMBRIDGE UNIVERSITY

Mr B.D.Carris ....lbw b Constantine 37	b Sealey 6
Mr F.G.Mann........ c Clarke b Johnson 29	c Grant b Constantine......9
Mr J.R.Thompson b Johnson 3	c Stollmeyer b Constantine 24
Mr J.P.Blake .... b Constantine 28	c & b Clarke...............11
*Mr P.M.Studd ......lbw b Constantine........9	(6) b Headley 26
Mr J.P.Mann .... st Barrow b Clarke 22	(5) not out 59
†Mr C.L.Newton-Thompson ......b Constantine 8	b Clarke.....................8
Mr A.C.Shirreff ......c Grant b Johnson 11	lbw b Clarke 1
Mr P.J.Dickinson....b Johnson 3	c Cameron b Constantine 22
Mr D.C.Wilson ......not out 0	c Grant b Stollmeyer 8
K.S.Gaekwar ....b Clarke 0	not out 2
Extras.............. (B 2, LB 1) 3	(B 6, LB 8, NB 2) 16
Total **153**	(9 wickets) **192**

Fall: 1st inns 2/48, 3/91, 4/104, 5/113, 8/153, 9/153.
     2nd inns 1/7, 2/35, 3/48, 4/52, 5/92, 7/110.

CAMBRIDGE	O	M	R	W
Gaekwar	9	0	33	0
Dickinson	27.3	6	78	4
Shirreff	23	1	119	4
Wilson	11	2	25	0
Carris	6	2	13	2
J.P.Mann	3	0	13	0

WEST INDIES	O	M	R	W	O	M	R	W
Johnson	14	3	37	4	7	1	28	0
Constantine	13	3	44	4	15	4	50	3
Sealy	2	0	9	0	6	2	8	1
Clarke	14.3	2	51	2	17	2	58	3
Cameron	4	1	9	0	1	0	2	0
Grant	1	1	0	0	4	1	17	0
Headley	-	-	-	-	2	0	5	1
Stollmeyer	-	-	-	-	3	1	8	1

Umpires: W.Wainwright and J.J.Hills.

Close of play scores. First day: No play. **Second day:** Cambridge University 34/0 (B.D.Carris 9*, F.G.Mann 25*).

Comments: Cambridge followed on 143 behind.
G.A.Headley scored the first century for the tourists. His 103, made in three hours, included ten 4's.

SURREY v WEST INDIES

Played at Kennington Oval, May 20, 22, 23, 1939.
Toss won by Surrey.
Surrey won by seven wickets.

WEST INDIES

†I.Barrow	c Garland-Wells b Parker 6	c Parker b Gover 7
V.H.Stollmeyer	b Brown 11	c Garland-Wells b Parker 36
G.A.Headley	c & b Brown 52	lbw b Watts 0
J.E.D.Sealy	c Garland-Wells b Brown 58	lbw b Parker 41
K.H.Weekes	lbw b Brown 20	run out 0
L.N.Constantine	not out 52	c Garland-Wells b Brown 8
J.H.Cameron	c Gover b Brown 6	c Watts b Parker 4
E.A.Martindale	st Brooks b Brown 1	b Parker 5
*R.S.Grant	b Gover 6	not out 34
L.G.Hylton	c Watts b Brown 5	c Gregory b Parker 4
C.B.Clarke	c Garland-Wells b Brown 1	st Brooks b Garland-Wells 45
Extras	(B 5, NB 1) 6	(B 1, LB 5, NB 1) 7
Total	**224**	**191**

Fall: 1st inns 1/12, 2/35, 3/108, 4/145, 5/168, 6/192, 7/198, 8/209, 9/214.
2nd inns 1/7, 2/8, 3/83, 4/86, 5/89, 6/100, 7/16, 8/109, 9/113.

SURREY

R.J.Gregory	lbw b Grant 19	b Constantine 79
L.B.Fishlock	lbw b Clarke 48	c Headley b Clarke 60
†E.W.J.Brooks	b Martindale 3	
H.S.Squires	c Constantine b Clarke 26	not out 14
T.H.Barling	c Hylton b Clarke 28	not out 3
E.A.Whitfield	b Martindale 10	
J.F.Parker	b Constantine 21	
*Mr H.M.Garland-Wells	c Grant b Clarke 22	
Mr F.R.Brown	c Headley b Constantine 24	
E.A.Watts	b Martindale 0	(3) b Hylton 45
A.R.Gover	not out 0	
Extras	(B 4, LB 5) 9	(B 1, LB 2) 3
Total	**215**	(3 wickets) **204**

Fall: 1st inns 1/38, 2/48, 3/98, 4/99, 5/138, 6/150, 7/186, 8/188, 9/215.
2nd inns 1/114, 2/181, 3/193.

SURREY	O	M	R	W	O	M	R	W
Gover	18	2	52	1	10	0	48	1
Watts	8	0	28	0	5	1	15	1
Parker	10	1	25	1	11	1	36	5
Brown	16.3	1	94	8	15	2	66	1
Gregory	4	0	10	0	3	0	13	0
Squires	3	0	9	0				
Garland-Wells	-	-	-	-	2.4	1	6	1

WEST INDIES	O	M	R	W	O	M	R	W
Martindale	15	4	42	3	11	0	54	0
Hylton	10	4	27	0	9	0	55	1
Grant	7	2	19	1				
Clarke	21	4	93	4	11	0	58	1
Constantine	10.1	1	25	2	8.3	2	18	1
Stollmeyer	-	-	-	-	1	0	11	0
Cameron	-	-	-	-	1	0	5	0

Umpires: H.W.Lee and A.Skelding.

Close of play scores. First day: Surrey 43/1 (L.B.Fishlock 21*, E.W.J.Brooks 1*). **Second day:** West Indies 158/9 (R.S.Grant 19*, C.B.Clarke 28*).
Comments: The West Indies were put in on a rain-affected wicket and suffered their second defeat of the tour.
R.J.Gregory and L.B.Fishlock put on 114 for Surrey's 1st wicket in their 2nd innings.

OXFORD UNIVERSITY v WEST INDIES

Played at Oxford, May 24, 25, 26, 1939.
Toss won by West Indies.
West Indies won by an innings and 5 runs.

WEST INDIES

V.H.Stollmeyer	b Macindoe 0
J.B.Stollmeyer	run out 44
H.P.Bayley	c Eagar b Macindoe 104
†J.E.D.Sealy	b Evans 26
G.E.Gomez	b Evans 0
†K.H.Weekes	b Evans 42
*J.H.Cameron	run out 106
E.A.V.Williams	not out 126
L.G.Hylton	not out 1
Extras	(B 22, LB 9) 31
Total	(7 wickets, declared) **480**

Fall: 1st inns 1/0, 2/87, 3/136, 4/136, 5/220, 6/238, 7/456.
C.B.Clarke and T.F.Johnson did not bat.

OXFORD UNIVERSITY

Mr R.Sale	b Hylton 23	c Sealy b Hylton 7
*Mr E.J.H.Dixon	c Sealy b Hylton 36	c Sealy b Johnson 6
Mr J.M.Lomas	c & b Cameron 49	c Weekes b Williams 59
Mr E.D.R.Eagar	c Williams b Clarke 17	b Williams 57
Mr G.E.Fletcher	b Cameron 12	b Williams 14
Mr R.B.Proud	c Hylton b Clarke 0	c Johnson b Cameron 28
Mr D.E.Young	c Johnson b Cameron 16	b Clarke 9
Mr G.Evans	c Johnson b Cameron 1	lbw b Clarke 13
Mr D.H.Macindoe	c Johnson b Sealy 47	c & b Cameron 10
†Mr P.H.Blagg	b Sealy 11	not out 8
Mr D.R.Hayward	not out 1	b Clarke 14
Extras	(B 11, LB 8) 19	(B 8, LB 8, NB 2) 18
Total	**232**	**243**

Fall: 1st inns 1/56, 2/69, 3/116, 4/150, 5/151, 6/151, 7/152, 8/202.
2nd inns 1/8, 2/44, 3/133, 4/155.

OXFORD	O	M	R	W
Macindoe	28	4	111	2
Evans	21	2	77	3
Haywood	23	3	111	0
Young	20	4	65	0
Egar	13	0	70	0
Fletcher	1	0	15	0

WEST INDIES	O	M	R	W	O	M	R	W
Johnson	9	1	24	0	14	2	34	1
Williams	3	0	14	0	10	1	37	3
Sealy	6	0	28	2				
Hylton	13	0	44	2	4	0	17	1
Clarke	23	2	70	3	19.6	2	81	3
Cameron	10	1	33	3	18	2	42	2
V.H.Stollmeyer	-	-	-	-	2	0	14	0

Umpires: D.Hendren and C.V.Tarbox.

Close of play scores. First day: West Indies 480/7 (E.A.V.Williams 126*, L.G.Hylton 1*). **Second day:** Oxford University 125/2 (J.M.Lomas 50*, E.D.R.Eager 52*).

Comments: The captain, J.H.Cameron, H.P.Bayley on only his second appearance of the tour and E.A.V.Williams all scored centuries on the first day's play. E.A.V.Williams made an undefeated 126, which included one 6 and 15 4's.
J.H.Cameron and E.A.V.Williams added 218 in 140 minutes for the 7th wicket.
Oxford followed on 248 runs behind.
L.G.Hylton was absent on the third day, due to a toe injury.
It was the West Indies first victory of the tour in their sixth first-class fixture.

GLAMORGAN v WEST INDIES

Played at Cardiff, May 27, 29 and 30 1939.
Toss won by Glamorgan.
Glamorgan won by 73 runs.

GLAMORGAN

A.H.Dyson	lbw b Williams	1	c Barrow b Constantine	34
D.E.Davies	b Cameron	25	c & b Cameron	5
T.L.Brierley	b Williams	9	c Grant b Martindale	8
*Mr M.J.L.Turnbull	lbw b Constantine	60	(8) c Stollmeyer b Constantine	36
D.Davies	b Williams	23	c Grant b Cameron	26
C.C.Smart	c Barrow b Martindale	27	b Cameron	10
Mr W.Wooller	c Headley b Grant	111	c Sealy b Constantine	14
E.C.Jones	c & b Martindale	39	(9) lbw b Constantine	0
†H.G.Davies	c Grant b Clarke	64	(4) b Martindale	3
Mr J.C.Clay	not out	2	not out	11
P.F.Judge	c Williams b Grant	2	b Constantine	3
Extras	(B 5, LB 7, W 1, NB 1)	14	(B 4, LB 2, NB 1)	7
Total		**377**		**157**

Fall: 1st inns 1/3, 2/25, 3/71, 4/103, 5/44, 6/77, 7/263, 8/366, 9/374.
2nd inns 1/14, 2/24, 3/73, 4/73, 5/83, 6/103, 7/103, 8/138, 9/142.

WEST INDIES

†I.Barrow	c Dyson b Clay	8	b Judge	0
V.H.Stollmeyer	c Dyson b Judge	2	lbw b Wooller	8
H.P.Bayley	run out	12	(5) b Wooller	1
E.A.V.Williams	b Judge	96	(8) b Clay	3
C.B.Clarke	c Judge b Clay	0	(11) not out	4
J.E.D.Sealy	b Wooller	14	(4) c Jones b D.E.Davies	58
J.H.Cameron	lbw b Clay	16	c Judge b Wooller	46
G.A.Headley	c H.Davies b D.E.Davies	20	(3) c H.Davies b Wooller	19
L.N.Constantine	c D.E.Davies b Judge	63	(6) b D.E.Davies	19
*R.S.Grant	not out	6	(9) c Smart b Judge	43
E.A.Martindale	c D.Davies b Judge	5	(10) lbw b Wooller	2
Extras	(B 6, LB 5)	11	(LB 4, W 1)	5
Total		**253**		**208**

Fall: 1st inns 1/7, 2/23, 3/23, 4/23, 5/44, 6/77, 7/134, 8/235, 9/247.
2nd inns 1/0, 2/20, 3/41, 4/49, 5/86, 6/114, 7/119, 8/201, 9/202.

WEST INDIES	O	M	R	W	O	M	R	W
Martindale	17	0	84	2	11	2	26	2
Williams	15	2	44	3	4	1	19	0
Constantine	13	0	74	1	16.1	3	49	5
Sealy	3	0	10	0	1	0	1	0
Cameron	9	1	38	1	18	5	41	3
Clarke	15	0	97	1				
Grant	2.3	0	16	2	4	0	14	0

GLAMORGAN	O	M	R	W	O	M	R	W
Judge	13.3	0	57	4	10	1	52	2
Wooller	18	4	57	1	13.1	0	69	5
Clay	16	4	59	3	12	0	53	1
D.E.Davies	10	1	46	1	9	1	26	2
Smart	4	0	23	0	1	0	3	0

Umpires: A.Dolphin and H.Elliott.

Close of play scores. First day: West Indies 47/5 (E.A.V.Williams 8*, J.H.Cameron 2*). **Second day:** Glamorgan 142/8 (D.E.Davies 5*, J.C.Clay 3*).

Comments: W.Wooller hit his maiden first-class century for Glamorgan. His 111, made in 135 minutes, included two 6's and 13 4's. He also claimed five wickets in the West Indies 2nd innings and was involved in two century partnerships. He added 107 in 80 minutes with E.C.Jones for the 7th wicket and with H.G.Davies he put on 103 in 50 minutes for Glamorgan's 8th wicket.
E.A.V.Williams and L.N.Constantine put on 101 for the 8th wicket in West Indies' 1st innings.
D.E.Davies retired hurt in the 2nd innings after being struck on the arm by E.A.Martindale. He resumed his innings at the fall of the 7th wicket. It was the West Indies' third defeat of the tour.

ESSEX v WEST INDIES

Played at Chelmsford, May 31, June 1, 1939.
Toss won by Essex.
West Indies won by two wickets.

ESSEX

L.C.Eastman	b Martindale	32	c Williams b Martindale	17
A.V.Avery	lbw b Constantine	24	lbw b Williams	55
†T.H.Wade	lbw b Constantine	12	b Clarke	55
J.O'Connor	b Constantine	2	lbw b Constantine	9
M.S.Nichols	c Barrow b Constantine	42	lbw b Constantine	6
R.M.Taylor	b Constantine	1	lbw b Constantine	2
*Capt J.W.A.Stephenson	c Williams b Cameron	3	not out	18
Mr J.N.Dennis	b Constantine	2	b Constantine	0
Mr D.F.Cock	not out	26	b Clark	25
T.P.B.Smith	c Barrow b Constantine	0	c Headley b Constantine	0
R.Smith	c Grant b Cameron	8	c Grant b Constantine	3
Extras	(LB 6)	6	(B 1, LB 2, NB 1)	4
Total		**158**		**194**

Fall: 1st inns 1/51, 2/66, 3/68, 4/75, 5/79, 6/88, 7/90, 8/145, 9/145.
2nd inns 1/33, 2/127, 3/131, 4/144, 5/147, 6/148, 7/148, 8/189, 9/190.

WEST INDIES

J.B.Stollmeyer	lbw b P.Smith	41	b Taylor	34
H.P.Bayley	lbw b R.Smith	3	lbw b R.Smith	3
G.A.Headley	not out	116	not out	48
J.E.D.Sealy	run out	1	lbw b P.Smith	9
*R.S.Grant	run out	1	b P.Smith	2
L.N.Constantine	st Wade b Taylor	8	b Nichols	14
J.H.Cameron	lbw b P.Smith	8	(8) lbw b Nichols	0
†I.Barrow	b Taylor	12	(9) run out	12
E.A.V.Williams	b P.Smith	21	(7) c Wade b P.Smith	0
E.A.Martindale	lbw b Eastman	1	not out	8
C.B.Clarke	b P.Smith	0		
Extras	(B 2, LB 4, NB 1)	7	(B 4)	4
Total		**219**	(8 wickets)	**134**

Fall: 1st inns 1/12, 2/103, 3/104, 4/112, 5/120, 6/129, 7/166, 8/215, 9/216.
2nd inns 1/3, 2/55, 3/66, 4/70, 5/91, 6/91, 7/115, 8/115.

WEST INDIES	O	M	R	W	O	M	R	W
Martindale	11	1	49	1	9	1	42	1
Williams	4	0	27	0	6	1	28	1
Cameron	13.2	3	23	2	13	4	35	0
Constantine	14	0	49	7	14.3	2	42	6
Grant	1	0	4	0				
Clarke	-	-	-	-	8	0	43	2

ESSEX	O	M	R	W	O	M	R	W
Nichols	5	0	14	0	15	3	50	2
R.Smith	8	3	32	1	2	1	4	1
Stephenson	5	1	16	0	2	0	7	0
P.Smith	19.7	0	78	4	14.7	1	41	3
Taylor	8	0	59	2	4	0	28	1
Eastman	4	1	13	1				

Umpires: D.Hendren and C.V.Tarbox.

Close of play scores. First day: West Indies 219 all out.

Comments: The second game of the Chelmsford week. The match was completed in two days.
L.N.Constantine had match figures of 13 wickets for 91 runs.
G.A.Headley's 116 not out included 16 4's.
Thirteen batsmen were adjudged lbw in the match.
It was the West Indies' first victory of the tour against a county side.

MIDDLESEX v WEST INDIES

Played at Lord's, June 3, 5, 6, 1939.
Toss won by West Indies.
West Indies won by an innings and 228 runs.

WEST INDIES

Player	Dismissal	Runs
H.P.Bayley	c Compton b Smith	19
J.B.Stollmeyer	lbw b Smith	117
G.A.Headley	c Hulme b Edrich	227
J.E.D.Sealy	c Price b Compton	181
†I.Barrow	c Price b Sims	25
L.N.Constantine	c Killick b Compton	4
E.A.Martindale	c Price b Compton	10
E.A.V.Williams	run out	12
*R.S.Grant	c Sims b Gray	40
J.H.Cameron	run out	5
C.B.Clarke	not out	8
Extras	(B 7, LB 9, NB 1)	17
Total		**665**

Fall: 1st inns 1/46, 2/262, 3/480, 4/580, 5/580, 6/589, 7/600, 8/610, 9/624.

MIDDLESEX

Player	Dismissal 1	Runs	Dismissal 2	Runs
J.D.B.Robertson	lbw b Constantine	33	c Grant b Clarke	36
S.M.Brown	st Barrow b Cameron	47	lbw b Martindale	0
W.J.Edrich	b Constantine	1	lbw b Constantine	51
D.C.S.Compton	lbw b Constantine	13	c Headley b Clarke	26
*Revd E.T.Killick	c Sealy b Cameron	2	not out	74
J.H.A.Hulme	st Barrow b Cameron	0	b Constantine	8
†W.F.F.Price	not out	59	b Cameron	1
J.M.Sims	b Constantine	8	c Cameron b Clarke	15
Mr E.Ingram	b Cameron	6	run out	21
C.I.J.Smith	b Cameron	3	b Williams	0
L.H.Gray	c Sealy b Cameron	1	c Barrow b Williams	2
Extras	(B 5, LB 5)	10	(B 12, LB 6, W 1, NB 1)	20
Total		**183**		**254**

Fall: 1st inns 1/89, 2/89, 3/91, 4/94, 5/96, 6/124, 7/136, 8/153, 9/159.
2nd inns 1/5, 2/78, 3/116, 4/127, 5/147, 6/148, 7/180, 8/240, 9/240.

MIDDLESEX	O	M	R	W
Smith	34	3	140	2
Gray	20.6	1	137	1
Sims	32	0	151	1
Ingram	19	1	103	0
Edrich	5	0	24	1
Compton	12	1	67	3
Robertson	5	1	26	0

WEST INDIES	O	M	R	W	O	M	R	W
Martindale	8	1	29	0	8	0	26	1
Williams	5	1	19	0	5.4	1	29	2
Constantine	12	0	68	4	12	3	39	2
Cameron	14.7	2	57	6	13	2	46	1
Grant	-	-	-	-	4	0	14	0
Clarke	-	-	-	-	12	0	58	3
Headley	-	-	-	-	2	0	7	0
Sealy	-	-	-	-	4	0	15	0

Umpires: F.I.Walden and C.W.L.Parker.

Close of play scores. First day: West Indies 491/3 (J.E.D.Sealy 115*, I.Barrow 3*). **Second day:** Middlesex 127/3 (W.J.Edrich 51*, E.T.Killick 7*).

Comments: West Indies 1st innings total of 665 was the highest score made at Lord's by the West Indies and the second highest ever made at Lords, the highest being Australia's 729 for 6 in 1930 against England. It was also the highest total made against Middlesex.
J.B.Stollmeyer scored a century (117) on his first appearance at Lord's. It was made in 190 minutes. J.E.D.Sealy batted 210 minutes for his 181. He reached his 100 in 120 minutes, hitting one 6 and 23 4's. G.A.Headley scored 227 in 310 minutes, hitting 23 4's. He reached his 100 in 165 minutes, which included ten 4's.
J.B.Stollmeyer and G.A.Headley added 216 for the 2nd wicket. Headley and J.E.D.Sealey then added 218 for the 3rd wicket. J.E.D.Sealey and I.Barrow put on 100 for the 4th wicket in 70 minutes. Middlesex followed on 482 behind and were dismissed before lunch on the 3rd day.
There were 16,000 present on the first day.

NORTHAMPTONSHIRE v WEST INDIES

Played at Northampton, June 7, 8, 1939.
Toss won by Northamptonshire.
West Indies won by nine wickets.

NORTHAMPTONSHIRE

Player	Dismissal 1	Runs	Dismissal 2	Runs
H.W.Greenwood	c Martindale b Hylton	3	c Weekes b Martindale	0
P.Davis	b Hylton	2	c Headley b Martindale	21
D.Brookes	c Headley b Constantine	30	c Hylton b Clarke	93
J.E.Timms	lbw b Constantine	12	c Headley b Martindale	5
*Mr R.P.Nelson	b Martindale	18	(6) c Hylton b Cameron	48
†K.C.James	b Constantine	0	(7) lbw b Constantine	10
F.P.O'Brien	b Hylton	19	(8) lbw b Hylton	14
W.E.Merritt	lbw b Martindale	18	(5) b Constantine	0
M.E.F.Dunkley	lbw b Hylton	1	c Constantine b Hylton	56
R.J.Partridge	b Hylton	0	c Gomez b Clarke	20
J.E.Buswell	not out	2	not out	1
Extras	(B 1, LB 1)	2	(B 22, LB 5, W 1, NB 3)	31
Total		**107**		**299**

Fall: 1st inns 1/5, 2/6, 3/37, 4/50, 5/54, 6/75, 7/97, 8/105, 9/105.
2nd inns 1/0, 2/71, 3/81, 4/82, 5/153, 6/200, 7/201, 8/235, 9/293.

WEST INDIES

Player	Dismissal 1	Runs	Dismissal 2	Runs
J.B.Stollmeyer	b Merritt	21	c & b Timms	6
H.P.Bayley	b Merritt	31	not out	11
G.A.Headley	b Timms	63		
†J.E.D.Sealy	b Merritt	4		
G.E.Gomez	run out	27	(3) not out	8
K.H.Weekes	c Timms b Partridge	64		
L.N.Constantine	c Nelson b O'Brien	20		
*J.H.Cameron	b Nelson	73		
E.A.Martindale	c Davis b Partridge	0		
L.G.Hylton	st James b Nelson	55		
C.B.Clarke	not out	1		
Extras	(B 16, LB 6, NB 1)	23		
Total		**382**	(1 wicket)	**25**

Fall: 1st inns 1/38, 2/73, 3/85, 4/155, 5/163, 6/205, 7/275, 8/290, 9/381.
2nd inns 1/11.

WEST INDIES	O	M	R	W	O	M	R	W
Martindale	9.6	1	37	2	14	0	72	3
Hylton	13	1	35	5	18	1	69	2
Constantine	8	2	17	3	15	1	48	2
Cameron	4	0	16	0	4	0	22	1
Clarke	-	-	-	-	7.5	0	57	2

NORTHANTS	O	M	R	W	O	M	R	W
Buswell	14	1	76	0				
Partridge	20	2	61	2	4	1	10	0
Nelson	11.6	1	34	2	1	0	3	0
Merritt	20	1	118	3				
Timms	8	0	55	1	4.2	1	12	1
O'Brien	6	1	15	1				

Umpires: J.A.Newman and D.Hendren.

Close of play scores. First day: West Indies 232/6 (K.H.Weekes 47*, J.H.Cameron 6*).

Comments: The tourists secured victory in two days, winning during the extra half-hour. It was their third consecutive victory.
L.G.Hylton returned his best bowling figures of the tour in Northamptonshire's 1st innings.

DERBYSHIRE v WEST INDIES

Played at Derby, June 10, 12, 13, 1939.
Toss won by Derbyshire.
Match drawn.

DERBYSHIRE

D.Smith	lbw b Clarke 64	lbw b Hylton 14
*Mr R.H.R.Buckston	b Martindale 18	b Martindale 12
A.E.Alderman	lbw b Constantine........2	c Constantine b Martindale 1
A.E.Alderman	b Constantine 90	c Constantine b Hylton ...25
L.F.Townsend	lbw b Clarke 0	b Hylton 3
G.H.Pope	c Barrow b Grant 35	c Constantine b Martindale 1
A.E.G.Rhodes	c Constantine b Martindale 21	b Clarke 18
Mr T.D.Hounsfield	b Clarke 56	b Clarke 7
†H.Elliott	b Martindale 1	not out 8
W.H.Copson	run out 8	c Grant b Clarke 0
H.Pope	not out 5	c Gomez b Hylton 5
Extras	(B 2, LB 3, W 2, NB 2) ...9	(B 8, LB 2) 10
Total	**309**	**104**

Fall: 1st inns 1/48, 2/53, 3/116, 4/116, 5/175, 6/221, 7/254, 8/267, 9/279.
2nd inns 1/20, 2/23, 3/30, 4/35, 5/36, 6/66, 7/79, 8/88, 9/88.

WEST INDIES

V.H.Stollmeyer	lbw b Copson............1	b Copson 0
H.P.Bayley	c Smith b Copson 44	b Copson 5
G.A.Headley	lbw b Copson 38	
K.H.Weekes	c Elliott b A.V.Pope....31	(3) c Elliott b G.H.Pope....6
G.E.Gomez	b H.Pope 55	(4) lbw b Copson 6
L.N.Constantine	c Townsend b A.V.Pope 16	(5) c Alderman b Copson....1
†I.Barrow	c & b H.Pope 18	(6) run out 15
*R.S.Grant	b Copson 19	(7) not out 15
E.A.Martindale	b Copson 18	
L.G.Hylton	b Copson 10	
C.B.Clarke	not out 3	
Extras	(B 6, LB 5) 11	(B 2, LB 4) 6
Total	**264**	(6 wickets) **54**

Fall: 1st inns 1/2, 2/83, 3/96, 4/155, 5/175, 6/199, 7/224, 8/242, 9/259.
2nd inns 1/2, 2/8, 3/18, 4/18, 5/20, 6/54.

WEST INDIES	O	M	R	W	O	M	R	W
Martindale	18	1	86	3	11	2	38	3
Hylton	11	0	54	0	14.5	0	46	4
Constantine	11	2	91	2				
Grant	9	0	27	1				
Clarke	8.2	0	42	3	4	0	10	3

DERBYSHIRE	O	M	R	W	O	M	R	W
Copson	19.4	1	73	6	6	1	19	4
G.H.Pope	25	2	92	0	8	3	12	1
A.V.Pope	15	0	66	2	4	0	8	0
H.Pope	7	0	22	2	2.7	1	7	0
Rhodes	-	-	-	-	1	0	2	0

Umpires: J.J.Hills and D.Hendren.

Close of play scores. First day: West Indies 14/1 (H.P.Bayley 7*, G.A.Headley 6*). **Second day:** West Indies 251/8 (E.H.Martindale 13*, L.G.Hylton 5*).

Comments: Each of the three day's play was reduced by bad light.
On the third day, W.H.Copson dismissed four batsmen for 13 runs in 29 balls. He took 6 for 24 on the third day.
H.Pope made his debut for Derbyshire, the three Pope brothers playing in the county side.

MINOR COUNTIES v WEST INDIES

Played at Lord's, June 14, 15, 16, 1939.
Toss won by West Indies.
Match drawn.

WEST INDIES

V.H.Stollmeyer	lbw b Robson 27	c Mobey b Appleyard 24
J.B.Stollmeyer	lbw b Robson 73	run out....................63
G.E.Gomez	b Robson 8	run out....................29
†J.E.D.Sealy	c Mobey b Edge 79	lbw b Dennis...............9
K.H.Weekes	c Taylor b Edge 55	not out 5
L.N.Constantine	c Cutler b Edge 55	
J.H.Cameron	c Baker b Edge 10	
*R.S.Grant	b Dennis 31	
E.A.V.Williams	lbw b Robson 8	
C.B.Clarke	c Taylor b Dennis 9	
T.F.Johnson	not out 0	
Extras	(B 6, LB 5, NB 4)........15	(B 6, NB 2) 8
Total	**370**	(4 wickets) **138**

Fall: 1st inns 1/60, 2/81, 3/159, 4/239, 5/280, 6/301, 7/326, 8/359, 9/367.
2nd inns 1/62, 2/105, 3/130, 4/138.

MINOR COUNTIES

Mr G.S.Butler	c Grant b Constantine 4
Mr L.G.Baker	b Williams 6
Mr H.W.F.Taylor	b Constantine 38
†G.S.Mobey	b Williams 28
F.Dennis	c J.B.Stollmeyer b Grant 95
*Mr W.Lovell-Hewitt	b Constantine 6
R.Parkin	c Weekes b Williams 55
Mr R.Eglington	c Gomez b Constantine 23
Mr F.Appleyard	b Constantine 11
H.Robson	b Grant 3
C.A.Edge	not out 15
Extras	(B 11, LB 6, NB 5) 22
Total	**306**

Fall: 1st inns 1/7, 2/14, 3/68, 4/107, 5/117, 6/241, 7/261, 8/285, 9/288.

MINOR COUNTIES	O	M	R	W	O	M	R	W
Edge	16	0	97	4	5	0	17	0
Appleyard	19	2	77	0	7	1	17	1
Parkin	4	0	19	0	5	0	16	0
Robson	16.4	2	80	4	9	0	44	0
Dennis	12	0	82	2	8	1	36	1

WEST INDIES	O	M	R	W
Johnson	11	3	22	0
Williams	14	3	33	3
Constantine	20	7	52	5
Sealy	6	0	20	0
Grant	10.2	1	34	2
Clarke	17	3	79	0
Cameron	11	1	44	0

Umpires: G.H.Watts and J.C.Hubble.

Close of play scores. First day: Minor Counties 54/2 (H.W.F.Taylor 21*, G.S.Mobey 21*). **Second day:** West Indies 138/4 (K.H.Weekes 5*).

Comments: There was no play on the third day due to rain.
F.Dennis and R.Parkin put on 124 for the 6th wicket.

Constantine on his way to 59 against the Minor Counties at Lord's. The wicketkeeper is Surrey 2nd XI player, G.S.Mobey.

LEICESTERSHIRE v WEST INDIES

Played at Leicester, June 17, 19, 20, 1939.
Toss won by Leicestershire.
Match drawn.

WEST INDIES

H.P.Bayley	lbw b Sperry	0	c Smith b Sperry	16
J.B.Stollmeyer	c Sperry b Smith	59	c Dawkes b Sperry	50
L.G.Hylton	c Armstrong b Sperry	0	(10) not out	17
J.E.D.Sealy	c Dawkes b Smith	4	c Tomkin b Smith	4
K.H.Weekes	b Sperry	0	b Sperry	62
G.E.Gomez	lbw b Smith	58	(3) lbw b Smith	37
J.H.Cameron	c Dawkes b Sperry	5	lbw b Smith	5
†I.Barrow	c Tomkin b Prentice	7	(6) run out	14
*R.S.Grant	c Knew b Smith	19	not out	45
E.A.Martindale	not out	10	(8) c Tompkin b Sperry	35
C.B.Clarke	c Armstrong b Smith	2		
Extras	(B 11, LB 4, W 3)	18	(B 15, LB 8, W 5, NB 1)	29
Total		**182**	(8 wickets)	**314**

Fall: 1st inns 1/0, 2/1, 3/8, 4/9, 5/113, 6/130, 7/145, 8/153, 9/172.
2nd inns 1/34, 2/90, 3/111, 4/120, 5/157, 6/184, 7/224, 8/282.

LEICESTERSHIRE

G.L.Berry	c Grant b Martindale	51
G.S.Watson	c Sealy b Clarke	33
N.F.Armstrong	c Stollmeyer b Hylton	7
F.T.Prentice	b Martindale	5
M.Tompkin	not out	48
Mr C.S.Dempster	c Hylton b Clarke	9
*Mr M.St.J.Packe	c Barrow b Martindale	9
G.F.Knew	b Hylton	5
†G.O.Dawkes	c Hylton b Martindale	38
H.A.Smith	run out	2
J.Sperry	b Martindale	3
Extras	(B 2, LB 4)	6
Total		**216**

Fall: 1st inns 1/84, 2/92, 3/96, 4/100, 5/115, 6/126, 7/138, 8/207, 9/209.

LEICESTERSHIRE	O	M	R	W	O	M	R	W
Sperry	19	3	42	4	27	4	111	4
Smith	21.3	5	53	5	27	1	121	3
Knew	6	1	19	0	3	0	11	0
Prentice	18	1	50	1	11	1	32	0
Armstrong	-	-	-	-	1	0	10	0

WEST INDIES	O	M	R	W
Martindale	19.2	4	57	5
Hylton	22	3	73	2
Grant	5	1	19	0
Clarke	13	1	46	2
Cameron	7	1	15	0

Umpires: G.M.Lee and W.Reeves

Close of play scores. First day: Leicestershire 90/1 (G.L.Berry 51*, N.F.Armstrong 4*). **Second day:** West Indies 193/6 (K.H.Weekes 44*, R.S.Grant 4*).

Comments: West Indies were put in to bat.
H.P.Bayley was dismissed by the first ball of the match.
J.B.Stollmeyer and G.E.Gomez added 104 for the 5th wicket in about two hours.
E.A.Martindale took five wickets in an innings for the only time on the tour.
There was only 80 minutes play on the third day, due to rain.

'Manny' Martindale of Barbados, bowling in a sweater on a cool English summer's day. Martindale had enjoyed a fine Test career but in 1939 he fell away in both pace and accuracy and endured a poor tour. For some years he was a professional with Burnley in the Lancashire League.

NOTTINGHAMSHIRE v WEST INDIES

Played at Trent Bridge, Nottingham, July 1, 3, 4, 1939.
Toss won by Nottinghamshire.
West Indies won by an innings and 94 runs.

NOTTINGHAMSHIRE

W.W.Keeton	b Hylton ...19	lbw b Grant ...82
C.B.Harris	b Constantine ...17	c Headley b Hylton ...11
*Mr G.F.H.Heane	c Sealy b Hylton ...9	b Grant ...39
J.Hardstaff	not out ...73	b Martindale ...29
G.V.Gunn	b Constantine ...0	c Sealy b Constantine ...6
J.Knowles	lbw b Constantine ...9	c Headley b Constantine ...2
R.J.Giles	b Constantine ...0	b Hylton ...52
W.Voce	c Constantine b Hylton ...17	c & b Constantine ...14
D.Watkin	b Constantine ...0	lbw b Clarke ...14
†A.B.Wheat	c & b Constantine ...0	not out ...3
A.Jepson	run out ...0	b Clarke ...7
Extras	(B 1, LB 2, W 1, NB 1) ...5	(B 6, LB 2) ...8
Total	**149**	**267**

Fall: 1st inns 1/26, 2/43, 3/57, 4/57, 5/97, 6/97, 7/140, 8/141, 9/149.
2nd inns 1/26, 2/106, 3/158, 4/173, 5/175, 6/177, 7/192, 8/256, 9/258.

WEST INDIES

*R.S.Grant	b Jepson	36
V.H.Stollmeyer	retired ill	73
G.A.Headley	not out	234
G.E.Gomez	c Voce b Giles	40
†J.E.D.Sealy	st Wheat b Watkin	115
L.N.Constantine	not out	4
Extras	(B 4, LB 4)	8
Total	(3 wickets, declared)	**510**

Fall: 1st inns 1/57, 2/276, 3/506.
K.H.Weekes, H.P.Bayley, E.A.Martindale, L.G.Hylton and C.B.Clarke did not bat.

WEST INDIES	O	M	R	W	O	M	R	W
Martindale	6	1	19	0	18	3	66	1
Hylton	13	0	50	3	13	0	67	2
Constantine	14.6	2	50	6	17	2	67	3
Clarke	7	1	25	0	9	0	31	2
Grant	-	-	-	-	8	1	28	2

NOTTINGHAMSHIRE	O	M	R	W
Voce	29	3	113	0
Jepson	26	1	95	1
Watkin	23	0	145	1
Giles	16	2	57	1
Gunn	17	2	64	0
Harris	7	1	28	0

Umpires: G.Beet and H.Elliott.

Close of play scores. First day: West Indies 169/1 (V.H.Stollmeyer 73*, G.A.Headley 59*). **Second day:** Nottinghamshire 132/2 (W.W.Keeton 65*, J.Hardstaff 10*).

Comments: G.A.Headley made an undefeated 234* in 345 minutes, hitting 23 4's. It followed his two centuries in the Lord's test and was his second double century of the tour.
V.H.Stollmeyer was unable to continue batting on the second day, after an attack of tonsilitis. The 2nd wicket partnership of 112 was continued by G.A.Headley and G.Gomez, who added a further 107 runs to realise a 2nd wicket partnership of 219.
G.A.Headley and J.E.D.Sealy added 230 for the 3rd wicket in 170 minutes, J.E.D.Sealy making 115 in that time, hitting 14 4's.

YORKSHIRE v WEST INDIES

Played at Harrogate, July 5, 6, 7, 1939.
Toss won by West Indies.
Match drawn.

WEST INDIES

*R.S.Grant	c Barber b Verity	72	b Robinson	26
J.B.Stollmeyer	lbw b Verity	19	lbw b Robinson	8
G.A.Headley	c Leyland b Verity	61	not out	44
G.E.Gomez	b Robinson	13	c Mitchell b Robinson	0
†J.E.D.Sealy	c Wood b Robinson	9	c Sellers b Verity	8
K.H.Weekes	c Sellers b Verity	0	b Leyland	17
L.N.Constantine	lbw b Leyland	7	lbw b Leyland	0
J.H.Cameron	not out	28	not out	7
E.A.V.Williams	c Verity b Smurthwaite	13		
L.G.Hylton	c Mitchell b Smurthwaite	2		
C.B.Clarke	b Robinson	4		
Extras	(B 4, LB 2)	6	(B 3, LB 3)	6
Total		**234**	(6 wickets)	**116**

Fall: 1st inns 1/58, 2/127, 3/155, 4/164, 5/169, 6/183, 7/183, 8/227, 9/229.
2nd inns 1/33, 2/40, 3/40, 4/63, 5/96.

YORKSHIRE

A.Mitchell	lbw b Clarke	33
W.Barber	b Clarke	38
Mr N.W.D.Yardley	b Constantine	13
M.Leyland	c Stollmeyer b Constantine	4
Mr G.A.Wilson	c & b Clarke	0
*Mr A.B.Sellers	b Clarke	1
†A.Wood	c Hylton b Constantine	15
E.P.Robinson	b Clarke	0
H.Verity	not out	2
F.Wilkinson	b Constantine	0
J.Smurthwaite	st Sealy b Constantine	0
Extras	(B 5, LB 3)	8
Total		**114**

Fall: 1st inns 1/59, 2/90, 3/95, 4/96, 5/96, 6/98, 7/98, 8/114, 9/114.

YORKSHIRE	O	M	R	W	O	M	R	W
Wilkinson	10	1	35	0				
Smurthwaite	11	2	33	2	3	0	11	0
Verity	14	5	77	4	11	0	44	1
Yardley	8	2	22	0				
Robinson	13	3	57	3	9	0	48	3
Leyland	2	1	4	1	5	3	7	2

WEST INDIES	O	M	R	W
Hylton	4	1	17	0
Williams	4	0	12	0
Clarke	13	1	49	5
Constantine	13	2	28	5

Umpires: C.N.Woolley and C.W.L.Parker.

Close of play scores. First day: West Indies 187/7 (J.H.Cameron 4*, E.A.V.Williams 0*). **Second day:** West Indies 116/6 (G.A.Headley 44*, J.H.Cameron 7*).

Comments: Yorkshire fielded a weakened side, with L.Hutton and W.E.Bowes appearing for the Players at Lord's and H.Sutcliffe and T.F.Smailes absent injured. Only two and a half hours play was possible on the first day and there was no play on the third day.
Of the 234 runs in West Indies' 1st innings, 148 came in boundaries.
L.N.Constantine took the last three Yorkshire wickets in one over.

LANCASHIRE v WEST INDIES

Played at Old Trafford, Manchester, July 8, 10, 11, 1939.
Toss won by West Indies.
Match drawn.

WEST INDIES

*R.S.Grant	b Nutter	95	b Nutter	21
J.B.Stollmeyer	b Phillipson	0	run out	17
G.A.Headley	hit wkt b Ikin	32	not out	43
G.E.Gomez	lbw b Pollard	65	not out	31
†J.E.D.Sealy	c Banham b Phillipson	4		
H.P.Bayley	b Ikin	8		
L.N.Constantine	lbw b Phillipson	1		
J.H.Cameron	c Ikin b Pollard	30		
E.A.Martindale	b Ikin	1		
L.G.Hylton	c Place b Pollard	22		
C.B.Clarke	not out	2		
Extras	(B 11, LB 9, NB 4)	24	(LB 2)	2
Total		**284**	(2 wickets)	**114**

Fall: 1st inns 1/5, 2/92, 3/176, 4/199, 5/221, 6/222, 7/234, 8/238, 9/279.
2nd inns 1/32, 2/49.

LANCASHIRE

C.Washbrook	lbw b Martindale	12
W.Place	b Constantine	164
J.L.Hopwood	b Constantine	91
N.Oldfield	c Sealy b Cameron	42
J.T.Ikin	not out	8
A.E.Nutter	not out	8
Extras	(B 6, LB 1, NB 1)	8
Total	(4 wickets, declared)	**325**

Fall: 1st inns 1/24, 2/220, 3/313, 4/313.
*Mr W.H.L.Lister, W.E.Phillipson, W.B.Roberts, R.Pollard and †S.T.Banham did not bat.

LANCASHIRE	O	M	R	W	O	M	R	W
Phillipson	20	2	56	3	2	0	11	0
Pollard	12.2	1	37	3	3	0	15	0
Nutter	14	1	44	1	3	0	11	1
Roberts	15	0	57	0	9	1	37	0
Ikin	14	0	66	3	10	1	38	0

WEST INDIES	O	M	R	W
Martindale	14	1	70	1
Hylton	14	1	53	0
Constantine	16	2	79	2
Clarke	14	2	53	0
Cameron	15	5	37	1
Grant	6	0	25	0

Umpires: A.Dolphin and J.J.Hills.

Close of play scores. First day: No play (rain). **Second day:** Lancashire 76/1 (W.Place 35*, J.L.Hopwood 25*).

Comments: There was no play on the first day.
J.B.Stollmeyer was dismissed by the first ball of the match.
W.Place and J.L.Hopwood put on 196 for the 2nd wicket in 180 minutes.
W.Place made 164 in 270 minutes. He hit 19 4's. It was his highest score, beating his 137 v Notts in 1937.
J.T.Ikin was making his first appearance for Lancashire.

Above: West Indies captain Ralph Grant meets King George VI at The Oval during the second game against Surrey. A Cambridge blue at cricket and soccer, Grant kept goal for the England amateur side and was also Trinidad's heavyweight boxing champion.

Left, top: Barrow is bowled by Surrey all-rounder Parker. *Left, bottom:* Jamaica's 'Bam Bam' Weekes on his way to a career-best 146 for the West Indies against Surrey. Wicketkeeper Mobey wears his 2nd XI cap but he was soon entitled to 'the full chocolate covering'.

SURREY v WEST INDIES

Played at Kennington Oval, July 26, 27, 28, 1939.
Toss won by West Indies.
West Indies won by seven wickets.

WEST INDIES

V.H.Stollmeyer ...... b Constable 73	not out 22
J.B.Stollmeyer ...... c Dickinson b Gover 6	c Mobey b Watts 1
G.A.Headley .... lbw b Gregory 93	
G.E.Gomez ...... c Dickinson b Watts 45	(3) c Gover b Watts 5
K.H.Weekes ...... c Parker b Gover 146	(4) lbw b Watts 4
†I.Barrow .... b Parker 41	
*R.S.Grant......... c Garland-Wells b Gover 9	
L.N.Constantine .... c Whitefield b Watts 20	
E.A.Martindale ... c Gover b Constable......1	(5) not out 14
C.B.Clarke .... not out..............25	
T.F.Johnson .... lbw b Garland-Wells 3	
Extras .... (B 8, LB 12, W 1, NB 4) 25	(NB 3) 3
Total **487**	(3 wickets) **49**

Fall: 1st inns 1/19, 2/177, 3/204, 4/241, 5/342, 6/357, 7/385, 8/390, 9/484.
2nd inns 1/14, 2/26, 3/30.

SURREY

L.B.Fishlock .... c V.H.Stollmeyer	lbw b Clarke 24
b Martindale 17	
R.J.Gregory......... c Barrow b Johnson ..14	not out 21
E.W.Whitfield .... lbw b Grant 30	b Clarke 49
H.S.Squires .... lbw b Grant 28	c sub b J.B.Stollmeyer....58
J.F.Parker .... b Clarke 100	c & b J.B.Stollmeyer 5
†G.S.Mobey .... lbw b Martindale 36	run out 12
Mr P.J.Dickinson.... c & b Clarke 11	b Clarke 29
*Mr H.M.Garland-	
Wells .... c Gomez b Clarke 7	b Clarke 24
E.A.Watts .... c sub b Clarke 0	c Weekes b Constantine ...16
B.Constable .... not out 13	b Constantine 0
A.R.Gover .... b Clarke 2	b Johnson 8
Extras .... (B 13, LB 3) 16	(B 11, LB 4) 15
Total **274**	....................**261**

Fall: 1st inns 1/20, 2/37, 3/94, 4/101, 5/206, 6/238, 7/252, 8/253, 9/260.
2nd inns 1/52, 2/129, 3/143, 4/159, 5/191, 6/209, 7/226, 8/252, 9/252.

SURREY	O	M	R	W	O	M	R	W
Gover 23	3	99	3	4	0	26	0
Watts 19	1	66	2	3.5	1	20	3
Parker 23	3	73	1				
Dickinson 3	0	11	0				
Constable 19	2	94	2				
Squires 12	2	38	0				
Garland-Wells 9.1	1	42	1				
Gregory 11	1	39	1				

WEST INDIES	O	M	R	W	O	M	R	W
Martindale 11	1	46	2	4	0	16	0
Johnson 11	3	28	1	5.7	1	20	1
Constantine 15	3	31	0	11	1	50	2
Clarke 16.2	3	64	5	21	3	80	4
Grant 16	2	63	2	8	1	22	0
J.B.Stollmeyer 5	0	26	0	14	2	58	2

Umpires: G.M.Lee and F.Chester.

Close of play scores. First day: West Indies 331/4 (K.H.Weekes 59*, I.Barrow 38*). **Second day:** Surrey 237/5 (J.F.Parker 85*, P.J.Dickinson 11*).
Comments: K.H.Weekes scored his first century of the tour. His 146 included 17 4's. V.H.Stollmeyer and G.A.Headley put on 158 for the 2nd wicket. G.E.Gomez and K.H.Weekes added 101 for the 5th wicket. J.F.Parker and G.S.Mobey added 105 for the 5th wicket on Surrey's 1st innings. Surrey followed on 213 behind after C.B.Clarke had taken their last five wickets for 22 runs. R.J.Gregory retired hurt with the Surrey 2nd innings score at 14/0, resuming at 226/7. West Indies won with 15 minutes of the match remaining. Both teams were presented to the King during lunch on the first day. B.Constable was making his debut for Surrey.

HAMPSHIRE v WEST INDIES

Played at Bournemouth, July 29, 31 and August 1, 1939.
Toss won by Hampshire.
West Indies won by ten wickets.

HAMPSHIRE

Mr R.H.Moore....... c Gomez b Clarke 17	b Martindale 0
J.Bailey .... c Gomez b Clarke 16	not out 70
Mr J.P.Blake .... lbw b Grant 8	(7) b Clarke 5
J.Arnold .... lbw b Clarke 14	lbw b Clarke 12
W.L.C.Creese .... b Clarke 0	lbw b Clarke 3
†D.F.Walker .... b Clarke 11	(3) b Clarke 21
*Mr G.R.Taylor ..... c Barrow b Grant 1	(9) b Clarke 0
G.S.Boyes .... b Grant 25	lbw b Grant 10
Mr A.E.G.Baring .... c Clarke b Grant 4	(6) c Barrow b Clarke 0
J.F.Godfrey .... b Clarke 1	b Clarke 1
G.E.M.Heath .... not out 0	lbw b Grant 2
Extras .... (B 6, LB 3) 9	(B 8, LB 4, NB 3) 15
Total **106**	...................**139**

Fall: 1st inns 1/27, 2/33, 3/55, 4/55, 5/56, 6/58, 7/77, 8/100, 9/105.
2nd inns 1/2, 2/40, 3/74, 4/78, 5/86, 6/98, 7/98, 8/116, 9/124.

WEST INDIES

*R.S.Grant........... c Blake b Boyes...........54	
V.H.Stollmeyer ..... lbw b Heath 0	(1) not out 16
G.A.Headley .... c Baring b Heath 6	
G.E.Gomez .... c Arnold b Baring 24	
J.E.D.Sealy........ lbw b Creese 26	
K.H.Weekes .... lbw b Creese 11	
†I.Barrow .... lbw b Baring 0	
E.A.V.Williams ...... b Bailey 28	
E.A.Martindale ...... c Blake b Heath 16	(2) not out...............7
C.B.Clarke .... not out 20	
T.F.Johnson .... b Bailey 12	
Extras .... (B 8, LB 11, NB 6) 25	(B 2) 2
Total **222**	(No wicket) **25**

Fall: 1st inns 1/1, 2/15, 3/80, 4/121, 5/125, 6/125.

WEST INDIES	O	M	R	W	O	M	R	W
Martindale 4	1	8	0	5	1	19	1
Johnson 3	1	3	0	2	1	1	0
Grant.......................19.2	4	41	4	22.4	11	24	2
Williams 2	0	13	0	2	0	5	0
Clarke 17	5	32	6	22	3	75	7

HAMPSHIRE	O	M	R	W	O	M	R	W
Baring 9	3	28	2	1	0	10	0
Heath 9	0	44	3	1	0	2	0
Godfrey 7	0	37	0				
Boyes 5	0	26	1				
Creese 11	0	44	2				
Bailey 5.6	0	18	2				
Taylor.......................-	-	-	-	1	0	11	0

Umpires: F.J.Durston and E.Robinson.

Close of play scores. First day: Hampshire 74/6 (D.F.Walker 10*, G.S.Boyes 6*). **Second day:** Hampshire 86/5 (J.Bailey 39*, J.P.Blake 0*).

Comments: Rain and bad light severely curtailed play on the first day. Only 140 minutes play was possible.
C.B.Clarke returned his best match figures of the tour, taking 13 wickets for 109 runs.
J.Bailey carried his bat for 70 in Hampshire's 2nd innings, also completing his 1,000 runs for the season.
Hampshire's best gate of the season, 7,000, watched the game on Monday. J.F.Godfrey made his debut for Hampshire.

SOMERSET v WEST INDIES

Played at Taunton, August 2, 3, 1939.
Toss won by West Indies.
Somerset won by an innings and 72 runs.

WEST INDIES

J.B.Stollmeyer	not out	45	c Gimblett b Meyer	8
V.H.Stollmeyer	lbw b Andrews	2	b Wellard	14
G.A.Headley	lbw b Wellard	0	(4) lbw b Wellard	31
K.H.Weekes	b Andrews	4	(5) c & b Hazell	54
J.E.D.Sealy	b Andrews	0	(3) c Bennett b Meyer	1
L.N.Constantine	c Buse b Andrews	4	b Hazell	10
*J.H.Cameron	b Wellard	17	absent hurt	0
†I.Barrow	c Lukes b Andrews	4	(7) c Hazell b Meyer	29
E.A.V.Williams	b Wellard	3	(8) not out	29
C.B.Clarke	b Wellard	4	(9) c Gimblett b Hazell	4
T.F.Johnson	b Andrews	0	(10) b Hazell	2
Extras	(NB 1)	1	(B 4, LB 3)	7
Total		**84**		**189**

Fall: 1st inns 1/11, 2/12, 3/19, 4/25, 5/29, 6/50, 7/55, 8/68, 9/81.
2nd inns 1/22, 2/22, 3/24, 4/88, 5/119, 6/124, 7/170, 8/175, 9/189.

SOMERSET

F.S.Lee	b Johnson	7
H.Gimblett	lbw b Williams	11
H.T.F.Buse	lbw b Clarke	21
Mr R.J.O.Meyer	c Barrow b Clarke	78
*Mr E.F.Longrigg	c Williams b Clarke	16
Mr F.M.McRae	lbw b Constantine	34
†W.T.Luckes	not out	71
Mr G.M.Bennett	c Barrow b Clarke	56
W.H.R.Andrews	c sub b Clarke	18
A.W.Wellard	c Sealy b Constantine	18
H.L.Hazell	b Clarke	1
Extras	(B 11, LB 3)	14
Total		**345**

Fall: 1st inns 1/7, 2/33, 3/49, 4/97, 5/164, 6/176, 7/289, 8/321, 9/343.

SOMERSET	O	M	R	W	O	M	R	W
Wellard	16	3	43	4	22	3	78	2
Andrews	16	4	40	6	4	0	10	0
Meyer					12	5	20	3
Hazell	-	-	-	-	15.4	1	74	4

WEST INDIES	O	M	R	W
Constantine	23	2	98	2
Johnson	11	2	38	1
Williams	11	1	44	1
Clarke	24.2	4	138	6
Sealy	2	0	13	0

Umpires: G.Beet and J.A.Newman.

Close of play scores. First day: Somerset 255/6 (W.T.Luckes 40*, G.M.Bennett 39*).

Comments: The match was completed in two days. It was the first defeat of the tourists since the Lord's Test. Their 1st innings score of 84 was their lowest of the tour.
J.H.Cameron, who had previously appeared for Somerset, was unable to bat in the West Indies 2nd innings, after injuring his hand whilst fielding.
J.B.Stollmeyer, batting for 135 minutes, carried his bat for an undefeated 45 in the 1st innings.
W.H.R.Andrews and A.W.Wellard bowled unchanged throughout the West Indies 1st innings.
G.M.Bennett and W.T.Luckes added 113 for the 7th wicket.
K.H.Weekes hit 48 of his 2nd innings score of 54 in boundaries, striking 12 4's.

GLAMORGAN v WEST INDIES

Played at Swansea, August 5, 7, 1939.
Toss won by Glamorgan.
West Indies won by two wickets.

GLAMORGAN

A.H.Dyson	lbw b Constantine	33	b Hylton	8
D.E.Davies	b Clarke	29	c Gomez b Hylton	27
T.L.Brierley	run out	1	lbw b Constantine	0
*Mr M.J.L.Turnbull	lbw b Constantine	0	(7) run out	0
Mr W.Wooller	b Clarke	0	(4) c Hylton b Constantine	1
C.C.Smart	b Constantine	4	c Weekes b Hylton	7
Mr G.Evans	c Martindale b Grant	17	(5) b Constantine	8
E.C.Jones	b Clarke	17	st Barrow b Constantine	30
†H.G.Davies	b Clarke	13	b Clarke	58
A.D.G.Matthews	lbw b Constantine	8	not out	8
P.F.Judge	not out	0	b Constantine	0
Extras	(B 1, LB 4)	5	(LB 4)	4
Total		**127**		**159**

Fall: 1st inns 1/61, 2/63, 3/63, 4/64, 5/70, 6/77, 7/102, 8/108, 9/123.
2nd inns 1/30, 2/31, 3/35, 4/38, 5/50, 6/59, 7/59, 8/139, 9/159.

WEST INDIES

*R.S.Grant	b Matthews	21	c H.Davies b Judge	46
J.B.Stollmeyer	c H.Davies b Matthews	11	lbw b Wooller	57
G.E.Gomez	lbw b Matthews	26	c H.Davies b Judge	1
J.E.D.Sealy	c H.Davies b Matthews	3	b Matthews	35
†I.Barrow	c Judge b Matthews	0	c Brierley b Smart	12
K.H.Weekes	b Matthews	0	b Matthews	2
E.A.V.Williams	c H.Davies b Wooller	9	b Matthews	18
L.N.Constantine	b Evans	7	not out	19
L.G.Hylton	run out	13	c H.Davies b Smart	1
E.A.Martindale	c H.Davies b Matthews	1	not out	3
C.B.Clarke	not out	1		
Extras	(LB 2, NB 2)	4		0
Total		**96**	**(8 wickets)**	**194**

Fall: 1st inns 1/29, 2/34, 3/38, 4/38, 5/38, 6/59, 7/59, 8/88, 9/95
2nd inns 1/70, 2/76, 3/138, 4/140, 5/142, 6/168, 7/180, 8/181.

WEST INDIES	O	M	R	W	O	M	R	W
Martindale	4	0	13	0	4	0	15	0
Hylton	6	1	18	0	11	1	31	3
Williams	3	0	14	0				
Constantine	12.3	2	33	4	12.2	2	52	5
Clarke	13	2	42	4	8	1	36	1
Grant	1	0	2	1	5	0	21	0

GLAMORGAN	O	M	R	W	O	M	R	W
Matthews	9.6	4	21	7	14	0	55	3
Wooller	12	1	44	1	13	1	42	1
Evans	4	0	27	1	1	0	10	0
Jones	-	-	-	-	2	0	16	0
D.E.Davies	-	-	-	-	2	0	12	0
Judge	-	-	-	-	7	1	41	2
Smart	-	-	-	-	2.6	0	18	2

Umpires: J.A.Smart and G.Beet.

Close of play scores. First day: Glamorgan 50/5 (G.Evans 7*).

Comments: The game was completed in two days.
On the first day 25 wickets fell for 273 runs.
Glamorgan collapsed in their 1st innings, losing their last nine wickets for 66. A.D.G.Matthews took the wickets of J.E.D.Sealy, I.Barrow and K.H.Weekes in four balls in West Indies 1st innings. He achieved career best figures of 7/21. L.N.Constantine hit C.C.Smart for six and four to secure victory for the West Indies.
H.G.Davies created a new Glamorgan wicketkeeping record with seven dismissals in the match.

WARWICKSHIRE v WEST INDIES

Played at Edgbaston, Birmingham, August 9, 10, 11, 1939.
Toss won by West Indies.
Match drawn.

WEST INDIES

*R.S.Grant	b Mayer	1		
J.B.Stollmeyer	b Mayer	16	c & b Wyatt	7
V.H.Stollmeyer	lbw b Mayer	5	(1) b Hollies	25
G.E.Gomez	c Goodway b Grove	90		
†J.E.D.Sealy	c Croom b Wyatt	22	(3) run out	8
K.H.Weekes	c & b Mayer	67		
I.Barrow	not out	4		
L.N.Constantine	c Santall b Mayer	0	(4) b Hollies	32
L.G.Hylton	b Mayer	9	(5) not out	12
E.A.Martindale	b Grove	0	(6) not out	22
C.B.Clarke	b Grove	0		
Extras	(B 5, LB 6)	11	(LB 6)	6
Total		**225**	(4 wickets, declared)	**112**

Fall: 1st inns 1/6, 2/23, 3/28, 4/57, 5/208, 6/212, 7/212, 8/222, 9/225.
2nd inns 1/34, 2/20, 3/20, 4/54, 5/82.

WARWICKSHIRE

A.J.W.Croom	b Hylton	5	c Sealy b Hylton	4
Mr R.Sale	c Martindale b Grant	25	run out	12
W.A.Hill	b Grant	21	(7) not out	10
Mr R.E.S.Wyatt	c Hylton b Clarke	2	not out	31
H.E.Dollery	lbw b Grant	8	b Clarke	16
F.R.Santall	not out	54	(3) b Hylton	3
*Mr P.Cranmer	b Clarke	3	(6) c Constantine b Clarke	21
C.W.Grove	c & b Grant	2		
†Mr C.C.Goodway	b Clarke	0		
J.H.Mayer	b Clarke	5		
W.E.Hollies	b Clarke	4		
Extras	(LB 1)	1	(B 1, LB 2)	3
Total		**130**	(5 wickets)	**100**

Fall: 1st inns 1/9, 2/51, 3/54, 4/54, 5/102, 6/109, 7/112, 8/113, 9/119.
2nd inns 1/15, 2/20, 3/20, 4/54, 5/82.

WARWICKSHIRE	O	M	R	W	O	M	R	W
Mayer	16	1	54	6	3	0	11	0
Grove	14.5	1	55	3	3	0	15	0
Wyatt	16	5	47	1	7	1	51	1
Hollies	11	0	42	0	8	2	29	2
Croom	4	0	16	0				

WEST INDIES	O	M	R	W	O	M	R	W
Martindale	5	1	9	0	3	1	6	0
Hylton	8	2	18	1	6	1	13	2
Constantine	1	0	2	0	7	0	22	0
Clarke	18.7	1	57	5	6	0	31	2
Grant	15	2	43	4	3	0	21	0
J.B.Stollmeyer	-	-	-	-	1	0	4	0

Umpires: F.I.Walden and J.A.Newman.

Close of play scores. First day: Warwickshire 18/1 (R.Sale 8*, W.A.Hill 4*). **Second day:** Warwickshire 33/1 (R.Sale 20*, W.A.Hill 7*).

Comments: Rain interrupted play on the first day and only 26 balls were bowled on the second.
G.E.Gomez and K.H.Weekes put on 151 for the West Indies' 5th wicket. R.Sale and W.A.Hill were at the wicket on all three days for their 2nd wicket partnership of 42.

GLOUCESTERSHIRE v WEST INDIES

Played at Cheltenham, August 12, 14, 15, 1939.
Toss won by West Indies.
Gloucestershire won by seven wickets.

WEST INDIES

*R.S.Grant	b Scott	12	b Lambert	8
J.B.Stollmeyer	st Wilson b Barnett	25	c & b Barnett	29
G.A.Headley	hit wkt b Barnett	5	b Scott	40
G.E.Gomez	b Scott	3	(5) c & b Goddard	50
†J.E.D.Sealy	b Scott	18	(7) c Neale b Lambert	6
K.H.Weekes	c Barnett b Goddard	5	lbw b Scott	11
V.H.Stollmeyer	not out	43	(4) lbw b Goddard	28
L.N.Constantine	c Emmett b Scott	9	c Scott b Lambert	13
L.G.Hylton	b Goddard	14	(6) c & b Scott	20
E.A.Martindale	c & b Goddard	0	b Goddard	8
C.B.Clarke	c Eagar b Lambert	26	not out	0
Extras	(LB 1, NB 1)	2	(LB 5, W 1, NB 1)	7
Total		**162**		**220**

Fall: 1st inns 1/32, 2/43, 3/44, 4/50, 5/65, 6/69, 7/78, 8/106, 9/110.
2nd inns 1/15, 2/52, 3/93, 4/134, 5/150, 6/157, 7/181, 8/205, 9/216.

GLOUCESTERSHIRE

C.J.Barnett	c Constantine b Martindale	15	b Constantine	32
G.M.Emmett	c Grant b Constantine	20	c J.B.Stollmeyer b Grant	84
W.L.Neale	lbw b Constantine	41	c Gomez b Clarke	70
*Mr W.R.Hammond	st Sealy b Clarke	22	not out	33
J.F.Crapp	b Grant	17		
Mr E.D.R.Eagar	b Constantine	15		
Mr A.H.Brodhurst	c Grant b Hylton	3	(5) not out	7
†E.A.Wilson	b Constantine	0		
C.J.Scott	c Gomez b Constantine	7		
T.W.J.Goddard	not out	3		
G.E.E.Lambert	run out	0		
Extras	(B 8, LB 1)	9	(B 3, LB 1, W 1)	5
Total		**152**	(3 wickets)	**231**

Fall: 1st inns 1/28, 2/42, 3/88, 4/116, 5/138, 6/141, 7/141, 8/149, 9/151.
2nd inns 1/59, 2/191, 3/195.

GLOUCESTERSHIRE	O	M	R	W	O	M	R	W
Scott	16	1	66	4	22	1	58	3
Lambert	9.6	1	39	1	23	1	73	3
Barnett	4	0	10	2	10	3	22	1
Goddard	10	0	45	3	17.3	3	60	3

WEST INDIES	O	M	R	W	O	M	R	W
Martindale	10	1	33	1	8	1	26	0
Hylton	5.7	1	19	1	9	1	30	0
Constantine	13	0	40	5	14	2	41	1
Headley	1	0	1	0				
Clarke	7	1	29	1	14	1	52	1
Grant	7	0	21	1	16	1	66	1
J.B.Stollmeyer	-	-	-	-	2	0	11	0

Umpires: J.Hardstaff and J.A.Smart.

Close of play scores. First day: Gloucestershire 149/8 (A.H.Brodhurst 3*). **Second day:** Gloucestershire 48/0 (C.J.Barnett 26*, G.M.Emmett 20*).

Comments: The only century partnership of the match was between G.M.Emmett and W.L.Neale who added 132 for the 2nd wicket in Gloucestershire's 2nd innings.
W.R.Hammond completed his 2,000 runs for the season winning the game for Gloucestershire with one 6 and four 4's off R.S.Grant.
The attendance was the largest on record at Cheltenham with receipts of £1,100.

The First-Class Season in the West Indies 1938-39

THE first-class season began much earlier than normal in the Caribbean, due to the visit of the Oxford and Cambridge University tourists, who had been invited to Jamaica as part of the celebrations of the 75th anniversary of Kingston Cricket Club. The touring party consisted of E.J.H.Dixon, A.H.Fabian, R.E.Whetherly, R.C.M.Kimpton, M.D.P. Magill, M.A.C.P.Kaye, M.M.Walford, G.R.De Soysa, D.C.Wilson, W.Murray-Wood, R.G.Sturdy, A.H.Brodhurst, B.H. Melle, J.W.Naylor, J.Allen, I.D.McIntosh, R.M.Hollis, N.W.Beeson, E.Hirst, J.H. Binch, J.C.N.Burrows.

The team was to play football as well as cricket and in the former sport won six out of eight matches. With regard to the cricket, the tour began with three one-day matches, all of which were drawn; these were followed by a two-day game against Kingston CC, which was won by six wickets, Walford hitting 124. In the first game against Jamaica, the tourists gained a big first-innings lead, but collapsed before Hylton and Moodie in their second innings and the game was drawn. In the next match it was agreed that each side should bat for one day, the tourists, batting second, won by two wickets. The final game was the return with Jamaica, which was lost by an innings. For the two first-class games the Universities co-opted the assistance of J.H.Cameron and he both batted and bowled well in the first match. It was a splendid tour much enjoyed by the visitors.

The annual inter-colonial tournament was staged in Barbados in January. Barbados played Trinidad in the first game and the home side was completely outplayed. On the first day the wicket took spin and Harbin and J.Stollmeyer dismissed Barbados for 208. On the second day Ben Sealey hit a brilliant hundred and Grant, after a shakey start, made 93. Harbin again bowled well in Barbados' second innings and Trinidad won by an innings. After a rest of two days, Trinidad met British Guiana in the final. It rained overnight, producing a very difficult wicket, so British Guiana lost six wickets for nine runs. Bayley managed to master the atrocious conditions and his 25 was worth a hundred. Even so, British Guiana were all out for 56. The wicket was somewhat easier when Trinidad batted and V.Stollmeyer hit out with some luck, but to good purpose, bringing his side a lead of 104. British Guiana lost five for 78 in their second innings and, though the later batsman performed better, Trinidad only needed 68 in the last innings, a task they managed without losing a wicket.

In view of the impending tour to England, it was arranged that Jamaica should go to Trinidad and play two 'Trial Matches'. Jamaica arrived on 21 January, and started the first match on 28 January. Excellent fielding and accurate slow bowling by Smith confined Trinidad's first innings to 178. Then Headley hit a chanceless 160, whilst Weekes made a hard-hit 88. Trinidad batted much better in their second innings with Gomez reaching 161 before the declaration was made. The stand of 222 between Gomez and Harbin was only 15 short of the ground record. In the final 90 minutes of play, the fast left-arm bowler, Johnson, caused all sorts of problems but Headley did not bat due to an injured hand. The Combined Team of British Guiana and Barbados met Jamaica in a second trial. In fact, Grant and Johnson of Trinidad played for the combined side, because there were only nine players from British Guiana and Barbados still in Trinidad. As in the previous game, Headley was the dominant figure, only he and Weekes could cope with the bowling of Johnson, who returned the splendid analysis of 6 for 41. When the Combined Team batted, Grant took advantage of being dropped before he had scored and hitting out, made 83, including 24 in one over off Smith. Weekes and Massado batted well for Jamaica in their second innings. A declaration was made at tea, when Weekes reached his hundred, but it was purely academic and the Combined Team batted out time.

Immediately after the game, the West Indies Cricket Board announced the team to tour England. The surprise selections were J.H.Cameron and J.B.Stollmeyer and the surprise omission, C.A.Merry.

Derek Sealy, who became the youngest player ever to appear in a Test Match when he played against England at Bridgetown in 1929-30, aged 17 years and 122 days. Playing for R.S.Grant's XI in 1938-9, Sealy hit centuries in two games against British Guiana.

JAMAICA v OXFORD & CAMBRIDGE UNIVERSITIES

Played at Sabina Park, Kingston, on August 10, 11, 12, 13, 1938.
Toss won by Oxford & Cambridge.
Match drawn.

OXFORD & CAMBRIDGE

M.M.Walford	c Hylton b Johnson	51	c Johnson b Moodie	0
*E.J.H.Dixon	b Hylton	32	c Abrahams b Hylton	14
A.H.Brodhurst	lbw b Moodie	36	b Moodie	0
G.R.J.De Soysa	b Johnson	0	(9) c & b Johnson	13
J.H.Cameron	run out	62	(7) not out	44
R.C.M.Kimpton	c Stephenson b Beckford	113	(4) b Hylton	6
B.H.Belle	c Stephenson b Beckford	12	(10) b Moodie	4
W.Murray-Wood	b Weekes	0	(5) c Weekes b Hylton	0
M.D.P.Magill	b Meikle	15	(11) b Moodie	1
M.A.C.P.Kaye	not out	21	(6) b Moodie	3
†R.E.Whetherly	lbw b Johnson	6	(8) c & b Hylton	7
Extras		7		7
Total		**355**		**99**

Fall: 1st inns 1/82, 2/94, 3/98, 4/132, 5/257, 6/294, 7/295, 8/321, 9/333.
2nd inns 1/1, 2/4, 3/20, 4/20, 5/23, 6/24, 7/52, 8/96, 9/99.

JAMAICA

†I.Barrow	c Kaye b Walford	11	(3) run out	1
O.C.Stephenson	c Kimpton b Cameron	76	(1) c Belle b Kimpton	57
S.M.Abrahams	c Kimpton b Walford	49	(4) run out	6
K.H.Weekes	c & b Murray-Wood	12	(2) c Whetherly b Cameron	106
R.C.Marley	lbw b Cameron	1	b Cameron	4
G.H.Moodie	c Magill b Murray-Wood	26	c Kimpton b Cameron	5
L.G.Hylton	b Walford	31	run out	3
D.P.Beckford	lbw b Walford	2		
*N.N.Nethersole	lbw b Walford	2	(8) c Walford b Kimpton	12
H.H.Johnson	not out	9	(9) not out	0
H.I.Meikle	c & b Walford	4		
Extras		4		10
Total		**227**	(8 wickets)	**204**

Fall: 1st inns 1/33, 2/108, 3/123, 4/124, 5/156, 6/209, 7/210, 8/211, 9/219.
2nd inns 1/122, 2/124, 3/141, 4/149, 5/173, 6/178.

JAMAICA	O	M	R	W	O	M	R	W
Johnson	17.3	2	73	3	2	1	2	1
Hylton	16	2	66	1	8	0	41	4
Beckford	16	0	52	2	6	1	17	0
Abrahams	2	0	8	0				
Moodie	12	0	67	1	8.4	2	32	5
Meikle	14	2	62	1				
Weekes	3	0	20	1				

UNIVERSITIES	O	M	R	W	O	M	R	W
Kaye	8	3	37	0				
Magill	5	0	16	0				
Cameron	20	1	69	2	16.3	0	51	3
Walford	9.4	0	49	6	6	0	34	0
Murray-Wood	16	4	38	2	9	0	37	0
Kimpton	3	0	14	0	14	0	72	2

Close of play scores. First day: Oxford and Cambridge 355 all out. **Second day:** Jamaica 37/1 (O.C.Stephenson 24*, S.M.Abrahams 1*). **Third day:** Jamaica 169/5 (S.M.Abrahams 38*, L.G.Hylton 2*).
Comments: This match was part of the celebrations of the 75th anniversary of the Kingston Cricket Club.
R.C.M.Kimpton scored 113 in 120 minutes, hitting two 6's and nine 4's. He and J.H.Cameron added 125 in 95 minutes for the 5th wicket.
There was only 30 minutes play before lunch on the second day.
Play did not begin on the third day until 3.40pm
In Jamaica's 2nd innings, O.C.Stephenson and K.H.Weekes put on 122 for the 1st wicket in Jamaica's 2nd innings.
K.H.Weekes made 106 in 141 minutes, hitting 11 4's.

BRITISH GUIANA v R.S.GRANT'S XI

Played at Bourda, Georgetown, on August 13, 15, 16, 17, 18, 19, 1938.
Toss won by R.S.Grant's XI.
Match drawn.

R.S.GRANT'S XI

*R.S.Grant	c Dunnett b Fraser	70	run out	57
J.B.Stollmeyer	lbw b Jones	118		
L.S.Birkett	c & b Fraser	0	(7) not out	9
J.E.D.Sealy	c Jones b Hill	141	(6) c Bayley b Fraser	7
G.E.Gomez	not out	84	(4) st Reece b Fraser	24
J.D.C.Goddard	b Neblett	22		
B.J.Sealey	c sub b Fraser	0	(3) c Fraser b Neblett	15
R.W.Mitchell	c Jones b Neblett	6	(5) st Reece b Fraser	13
A.S.Kelshall	c Neblett b Fraser	2	(2) lbw b Fraser	10
†D.A.Galt	run out	20	(8) c de Caires b Fraser	0
C.L.Pouchet	c Reece b Fraser	1		
Extras	(B 2, LB 4, NB 1)	7	(B 1, LB 1)	2
Total		**471**	(7 wickets, declared)	**137**

Fall: 1st inns 1/129, 2/129, 3/306, 4/356, 5/388, 6/389 7/399 8/410 9/469.
2nd inns 1/50, 2/79, 3/85, 4/116, 5/125, 6/136, 7/137.

BRITISH GUIANA

C.L.De Freitas	b Pouchet	133	c J.E.D.Sealy b B.J.Sealey	4
C.E.L.Jones	b Pouchet	13	c Grant b Pouchet	51
H.P.Bayley	c Gomez b Stollmeyer	77	b Grant	45
C.S.Persaud	c sub b Pouchet	116	not out	27
F.I.de Caires	c Galt b Pouchet	0	c & b Grant	21
*C.V.Wight	c sub b Pouchet	10		
J.M.Neblett	lbw b Pouchet	36	c sub b Gomez	9
H.A.Fraser	c J.E.D.Sealy b B.J.Sealey	9	not out	1
D.F.Hill	c & b Pouchet	1		
H.A.Dunnett	c Grant b Pouchet	0		
†C.C.Reece	not out	0		
Extras	(B 8, LB 6)	14	(B 1)	1
Total		**409**	(5 wickets)	**159**

Fall: 1st inns 1/28, 2/151, 3/339, 4/339, 5/361, 6/366, 7/385, 8/388, 9/388.
2nd inns 1/47, 2/59, 3/108, 4/146, 5/157. *Substitute fielder was Tang Choon.*

BRITISH GUIANA	O	M	R	W	O	M	R	W
Dunnett	27	3	122	0	5	1	20	0
Hill	27	3	66	1	6	0	10	0
Neblett	36	7	86	2	8	2	18	1
Persaud	16	1	44	0	2	0	22	0
Fraser	23.3	2	98	5	12	2	43	5
Jones	8	1	17	1	6	2	18	0
de Caires	2	0	10	0				
Wight	2	0	8	0	1	0	4	0
De Freitas	3	1	13	0				

R.S.GRANT'S XI	O	M	R	W	O	M	R	W
Grant	25	7	68	0	10	2	33	2
Goddard	9	3	15	0				
B.J.Sealey	46	11	101	1	17	2	52	1
Pouchet	53.1	15	120	8	11	1	61	1
Stollmeyer	20	2	69	1				
Birkett	5	2	8	0				
J.E.D.Sealy	1	0	3	0				
Gomez	4	1	11	0	3	0	12	1

Umpires: J.E.Blackman & H.Armstrong. Eight balls per over.

Close of play scores. First day: R.S.Grant's XI 369/4 (G.E.Gomez 28*, J.D.C.Goddard 7*). **Second day:** British Guiana 214/2 (C.L.De Freitas 81*, C.S.Persaud 34*). **Third day:** British Guiana 249/2 (C.L.De Freitas 91*, C.S.Persaud 59*). **Fourth day:** No play. **Fifth day:** R.S.Grant's XI 108/3 (G.E.Gomez 21*, R.W.Mitchell 3*).
Comments: Only 30 minutes play was possible on the third day, there was no play on the fourth day and play did not commence until 3.30pm on the final day. Originally the game was to be played to a finish but this was prevented by the poor weather. R.S.Grant and J.B.Stollmeyer put on 129 in 145 minutes for the 1st wicket. J.B.Stollmeyer and J.E.D.Sealy added 177 for the 3rd wicket. J.B.Stollmeyer made 118 in 285 minutes. He scored seven 4's. J.E.D.Sealy scored 141 in 160 minutes, hitting 16 4's. C.L.De Freitas and H.P.Bayley added 123 for British Guiana's 2nd wicket. C.L.De Freitas and C.Persaud put on 188 for the 3rd wicket, C.L.De Freitas making 133 and C.S.Persaud hitting 13 4's in his 116. British Guiana were set to make 200 in 120 minutes.

JAMAICA v OXFORD & CAMBRIDGE UNIVERSITIES

Played at Sabina Park, Kingston, on August 20, 22, 23, 24, 1938.
Toss won by Jamaica.
Jamaica won by an innings and 74 runs.

OXFORD & CAMBRIDGE

M.M.Walford	lbw b Smith	14	lbw b Valentine ... 5
*E.J.H.Dixon	c Stephenson b Beckford	18	c Cunningham b Moodie 37
B.H.Belle	lbw b Beckford	8	b Moodie ... 19
†R.C.M.Kimpton	c Stephenson b Smith	18	c Moodie b Weekes ... 18
J.H.Cameron	lbw b Smith	2	lbw b Moodie ... 8
G.R.J.De Soysa	b Beckford	4	c Moodie b Weekes ... 0
W.Murray-Wood	b Johnson	1	st Barrow b Cawley ... 24
R.G.Sturdy	b Moodie	42	st Barrow b Moodie ... 13
M.A.C.P.Kaye	b Johnson	0	c Beckford b Moodie ... 0
M.D.P.Magill	c Moodie b Beckford	3	c Stephenson b Cawley ... 10
D.C.Wilson	not out	5	not out ... 0
Extras		13	7
Total		**128**	**141**

Fall: 1st inns 1/33, 2/33, 3/57, 4/59, 5/65, 6/74, 7/80, 8/81, 9/98.
2nd inns 1/6, 2/42, 3/56, 4/61, 5/89, 6/95, 7/110, 8/110, 9/141.

JAMAICA

*†I.Barrow	lbw b Walford	65
K.H.Weekes	b Kaye	58
O.C.Stephenson	lbw b Wilson	45
S.M.Abrahams	c Kaye b Wilson	110
O.J.Cunningham	lbw b Murray-Wood	23
G.H.Moodie	c Sturdy b De Soysa	16
D.P.Beckford	b Wilson	0
C.L.Cawley	c Murray-Wood b Wilson	2
V.A.Valentine	c Kaye b De Soysa	11
H.H.Johnson	not out	1
F.Smith	c Magill b Wilson	8
Extras		4
Total		**343**

Fall: 1st inns 1/111, 2/113, 3/235, 4/277, 5/321, 6/321, 7/323, 8/328, 9/335.

JAMAICA	O	M	R	W	O	M	R	W
Johnson	9	0	17	2	7	0	11	0
Valentine	8	3	17	0	4	4	0	1
Beckford	11	2	29	4	1	0	1	0
Smith	12	0	48	3	9	1	23	0
Moodie	1.5	1	4	1	21	5	63	5
Weekes	-	-	-	-	9	2	33	2
Cawley	-	-	-	-	1.5	0	3	2

UNIVERSITIES	O	M	R	W
Kaye	13	0	69	1
Magill	6	0	37	0
Wilson	20.3	4	81	5
Murray-Wood	14	0	79	1
Walford	11	0	58	1
De Soysa	4	0	15	2

Umpires: E.Knibbs & H.A.Jones/H.G.MacDonald, V.G.Sasso/M.M.Walford, B.H.Belle.

Close of play scores. First day: Jamaica 86/0 (I.Barrow 53*, O.C.Stephenson 33*).
Second day: Oxford/Cambridge 23/1 (E.J.H.Dixon 8*, B.H.Belle 7*). **Third day:** Oxford/Cambridge 49/2 (E.J.H.Dixon 18*, J.H.Cameron 4*).

Comments: Rain interrupted the first day. There was no play after tea.
On the third day there was no play after lunch.
S.M.Abrahams scored his maiden first-class 100. His 110 was made in about 150 minutes and included 15 4's. He and K.H.Weekes added 122 for the 3rd wicket.
Ian Barrow captained Jamaica for the first time.
Whilst Enos Knibbs umpired for the whole of the game, he had no less than five partners at the other end, including two University players, M.M.Walford and B.H.Belle. *The Daily Gleaner* believed this could be a world record for a first class-match?

BRITISH GUIANA v R.S.GRANTS XI

Played at Bourda, Georgetown, on August 25, 26, 27, 1938.
Toss won by British Guiana.
R.S.Grant's XI won by an innings and 113 runs.

R.S.GRANT'S XI

*R.S.Grant	c De Freitas b Persaud	70
C.E.L.Jones	b Fraser	14
L.S.Birkett	run out	14
J.E.D.Sealy	lbw b Fraser	133
G.E.Gomez	c sub b Williams	119
B.J.Sealey	b Williams	24
R.W.Mitchell	not out	30
R.P.Tang Choon	c Dare b Williams	4
J.D.C.Goddard	b Griffith	10
†D.A.Galt	lbw b Persaud	0
C.L.Pouchet	c De Freitas b Griffith	2
Extras	(B 5, LB 4, NB 2)	11
Total		**431**

Fall: 1st inns 1/27, 2/63, 3/142, 4/318, 5/358, 6/393, 7/400, 8/423, 9/428.

BRITISH GUIANA

C.L.De Freitas	lbw b J.E.D.Sealy	8	b Grant ... 0
C.V.Wight	c Galt b B.J.Sealey	40	(9) c Galt b Grant ... 28
H.P.Bayley	b Pouchet	13	(8) c Galt b Tang Choon ... 62
C.S.Persaud	c Tang Choon b Pouchet	2	(5) c sub b Tang Choon ... 41
H.A.Fraser	c Tang Choon b Pouchet	4	(4) b Tang Choon ... 2
*O.S.Wight	c J.E.D.Sealy b Pouchet	3	b Grant ... 9
J.St F.Dare	run out	4	(2) b B.J.Sealey ... 11
C.R.Browne	b Tang Choon	17	(10) run out ... 34
†R.J.Christiani	not out	14	(3) b Tang Choon ... 3
J.Williams	b Tang Choon	0	(11) not out ... 4
W.G.Griffith	c Goddard b Tang Choon	0	(7) c Pouchet b Tang Choon ... 13
Extras	(LB 3)	3	(B 3) ... 3
Total		**108**	**210**

Fall: 1st inns 1/10, 2/47, 3/61, 4/67, 5/72, 6/77, 7/77, 8/100, 9/100.
2nd inns 1/2, 2/8, 3/12, 4/20, 5/54, 6/79, 7/83, 8/164, 9/190.

BRITISH GUIANA	O	M	R	W
Griffith	19.6	2	73	2
Williams	24	1	76	3
Browne	9	2	22	0
Fraser	24	1	140	2
Persaud	9	0	25	2
De Freitas	6	0	38	0
Dare	4	0	22	0
C.V.Wight	3	1	3	0
O.S.Wight	2	0	21	0

R.S.GRANT'S XI	O	M	R	W	O	M	R	W
J.E.D.Sealy	5	0	24	1	5	1	13	0
Grant	2	0	11	0	8	2	28	3
Tang Choon	5.2	0	13	3	16.6	3	81	5
B.J.Sealey	11	1	31	1	16	2	53	1
Pouchet	9	0	26	4	7	0	32	0

Umpires: J.Neblett & H.Armstrong.
Eight balls per over.

Close of play scores. First day: No play. **Second day:** R.S.Grant's XI 347/4 (F.E.Gomez 85*, B.J.Sealey 22*). **Third day:** British Guiana 55/5 (2) C.S.Persaud 28*, W.G.Griffith 0*).

Comments: R.S.Grant's XI were put in to bat.
J.E.D.Sealy and G.E.Gomez added 176 for the 4th wicket.
J.E.D.Sealy 133 included nine 4's.
G.E.Gomez scored his maiden first-class 100.
It was the first occasion that the eight-ball over was used in British Guiana, according to the *Daily Argosy*.

BARBADOS v TRINIDAD

Played at Kensington Oval, Bridgetown, Barbados, on January 7, 9, 10, 1939.
Toss won by Barbados.
Trinidad won by an innings and 19 runs.

BARBADOS

†C.E.L.Bourne	c Galt b Tang Choon	19	c Galt b Merry	8
G.McD.Carew	c J.Stollmeyer b Johnson	1	lbw b Merry	5
G.Waithe	c Birkett b Harbin	77	c & b Tang Choon	17
J.E.D.Sealy	c Galt b Harbin	9	c Grant b Harbin	19
*C. de L.Inniss	c Harbin b Johnson	5	c & b Tang Choon	18
E.L.Bartlett	lbw b J.Stollmeyer	24	run out	44
R.C.Wood	c & b J.Stollmeyer	25	c Johnson b Harbin	16
E.A.V.Williams	b J.Stollmeyer	4	c & b Harbin	23
J.L.Parris	lbw b Harbin	6	(10) b Harbin	7
C.A.Medford	c Galt b Johnson	21	(9) c Grant b Tang Choon	14
C.B.Clarke	not out	17	not out	4
Extras		0		11
Total		**208**		**186**

Fall: 1st inns 1/3, 2/30, 3/41, 4/52, 5/136, 6/160, 7/160, 8/170, 9/170.
2nd inns 1/14, 2/23, 3/43, 4/67, 5/92, 6/111, 7/147, 8/175, 9/176.

TRINIDAD

V.H.Stollmeyer	lbw b Williams	86
J.B.Stollmeyer	c Waithe b Medford	11
C.A.Merry	c Bourne b Williams	23
L.S.Birkett	lbw b Clarke	40
G.E.Gomez	lbw b Williams	0
B.J.Sealey	b Parris	116
L.Harbin	lbw b Parris	37
*R.S.Grant	b Williams	93
R.P.Tang Choon	st Bourne b Parris	0
†D.A.Galt	lbw b Clarke	0
T.F.Johnson	not out	1
Extras		6
Total		**413**

Fall: 1st inns 1/15, 2/69, 3/134, 4/139, 5/212, 6/274, 7/373, 8/373, 9/380.

TRINIDAD	O	M	R	W	O	M	R	W
Johnson	9.6	2	24	3	3	1	20	0
Grant	5	1	14	0	1	0	7	0
Sealey	3	1	3	0	3	0	7	0
Tang Choon	12	1	50	1	9	0	44	3
Harbin	20	2	85	3	15	0	73	4
J.Stollmeyer	7	0	32	3				
Merry	-	-	-	-	6	1	7	2
V.Stollmeyer	-	-	-	-	2	0	17	0

BARBADOS	O	M	R	W
Williams	22.6	1	92	4
Medford	10	1	52	1
Parris	21	1	108	3
Clarke	26	3	108	2
Sealy	12	1	25	0
Wood	5	0	22	0

Umpires: H.C.Griffith and E.L.Ward.

Close of play scores. First day: Trinidad 60/1 (V.H.Stollmeyer 29*, C.A.Merry 17*). **Second day:** Trinidad 356/6 (B.J.Sealey 104*, R.S.Grant 49*).
Comments: The winners of this game would play the cup-holders, British Guiana, in the final of the Annual Inter-Colonial Cricket Tournament.
T.F.Johnson had figures of two wickets for four runs off five overs before lunch on the first morning.
E.L.Bartlett retired hurt with the score on 79/4, returning at the fall of the 5th wicket.
B.J.Sealey scored 116 in 225 minutes, hitting 13 4's. He reached his century in 175 minutes.
R.S.Grant hit 93 in a 100 minutes, hitting 23 off an over (8 ball) from J.L.Parris during his last-wicket partnership of 33 with T.F.Johnson.

BRITISH GUIANA v TRINIDAD

Played on January 13, 14, 1939.
Toss won by Trinidad.
Trinidad won by 10 wickets.

BRITISH GUIANA

C.E.L.Jones	c Grant b Sealey	2	(3) b Harbin	7
C.L.De Freitas	c Merry b Johnson	0	(1) lbw b Grant	0
H.P.Bayley	c Sealey b Constantine	25	(4) b Harbin	10
B.M.Gaskin	c Constantine b Sealey	0	(11) not out	6
C.S.Persaud	c Galt b Constantine	0	b Johnson	36
*K.L.Wishart	c sub b Constantine	6	b Johnson	35
U.B.McKenzie	c Galt b Constantine	0	(8) c Tang Choon b Harbin	28
H.A.Fraser	c Sealey b Merry	11	(7) c Grant b Johnson	1
†R.J.Christiani	c Merry b Johnson	0	b Tang Choon	23
B.Thomas	not out	6	lbw b Johnson	10
W.G.Griffith	c Gomez b Johnson	0	(2) c Stollmeyer b Johnson	5
Extras		6		10
Total		**56**		**171**

Fall: 1st inns 1/3, 2/3, 3/3, 4/3, 5/9, 6/9, 7/36, 8/36, 9/56.
2nd inns 1/3, 2/7, 3/22, 4/41, 5/78, 6/80, 7/117, 8/137, 9/159.
Substitute fielder was Pouchet.

TRINIDAD

C.A.Merry	lbw b Griffith	20	not out	43
V.H.Stollmeyer	b Griffith	83	not out	24
L.S.Birkett	lbw b Persaud	9		
B.J.Sealey	c Christiani b Fraser	2		
E.Constantine	st Christiani b Persaud	27		
R.P.Tang Choon	c Wishart b Persaud	0		
G.E.Gomez	st Christiani b Gaskin	1		
L.Harbin	lbw b Gaskin	1		
*R.S.Grant	c Jones b Persaud	5		
†D.A.Galt	b Gaskin	1		
T.F.Johnson	not out	2		
Extras		9		1
Total		**160**	(no wickets)	**68**

Fall: 1st inns 1/23, 2/44, 3/47, 4/92, 5/92, 6/93, 7/107, 8/125, 9/131.

TRINIDAD	O	M	R	W	O	M	R	W
Johnson	9.3	5	17	3	14	3	29	4
Grant	2	1	2	0	6	2	17	1
Sealey	5	2	11	2				
Constantine	6	1	14	4	3	0	8	0
Merry	4	1	6	1				
Tang Choon					19.3	2	68	1
Harbin					15	3	39	4

BRITISH GUIANA	O	M	R	W	O	M	R	W
Griffith	4.6	1	28	2	3	0	11	0
Gaskin	21	2	38	3	2	0	8	0
Persaud	14	2	49	4	3.6	0	24	0
Fraser	5	0	30	1				
McKenzie	2	0	6	0				
Thomas					2	0	24	0

Umpires: H.C.Griffith and E.L.Ward

Close of play scores. First day: Trinidad 160 all out.

Comments: The final of the Annual Inter-Colonial Cricket Tournament.
The match was completed in two days.
British Guiana were put into bat on a rain-affected wicket. They were all out in 110 minutes, scoring only two runs more than the lowest score in the tournament, 54 by Barbados against Trinidad in 1906.
Trinidad were the winners for the 11th time.

BARBADOS v BRITISH GUIANA

Played at Kensington Oval, Bridgetown, on January 17, 18, 19, 1939.
Toss won by British Guiana.
Match drawn.

BRITISH GUIANA

C.L.De Freitas	lbw b Constantine	8	run out	87
U.B.McKenzie	c Sealy b Clarke	89	absent hurt	
H.P.Bayley	lbw b Constantine	3	c Williams b Clarke	15
C.S.Persaud	c Goddard b Clarke	18	c Cumberbatch b Williams	21
†R.J.Christiani	lbw b Constantine	1	(2) c Carew b Williams	30
B.Thomas	hit wkt b Clarke	15	c & b Burke	5
*K.L.Wishart	c Sealy b Constantine	38	(7) c Cumberbatch b Burke	14
H.A.Fraser	b Williams	17	(5) c Bourne b Clarke	8
D.F.Hill	lbw b Clarke	9	(9) b Clarke	0
B.B.McG.Gaskin	st Bourne b Clarke	4	(8) c & b Burke	5
W.G.Griffith	not out	11	(10) not out	
Extras	(B 2, NB 1)	3	(B 6, LB 1, NB 5)	12
Total		**216**		**197**

Fall: 1st inns 1/9, 2/15, 3/54, 4/58, 5/99, 6/144, 7/176, 8/194, 9/198.
2nd inns 1/89, 2/133, 3/150, 4/167, 5/171, 6/188, 7/197, 8/197, 9/197.

BARBADOS

†C.L.C.Bourne	lbw b Griffith	4	c De Freitas b Gaskin	4
G.McD.Carew	lbw b Griffith	7	(7) not out	24
E.L.Bartlett	b Griffith	5	(2) c Christiani b Griffith	0
J.E.D.Sealy	lbw b Thomas	71	c Griffith b Persaud	13
J.D.C.Goddard	b Persaud	19	(3) c Thomas b Gaskin	30
C.St C.Cumberbatch	b Persaud	59		
*L.N.Constantine	c Bayley b Fraser	1	(8) lbw b Hill	11
E.A.V.Williams	c Wishart b Fraser	26	(6) c Christiani b Griffith	34
J.L.Parris	not out	36	(5) c Bayley b Persaud	13
C.B.Clarke	c Christiani b Persaud	14		
I.Burke	c Thomas b Persaud	0		
Extras	(B 3, LB 3)	6	(LB 6)	6
Total		**248**	(7 wickets)	**135**

Fall: 1st inns 1/4, 2/13, 3/20, 4/62, 5/142, 6/145, 7/193, 8/197, 9/244.
2nd inns 1/0, 2/16, 3/53, 4/53, 5/75, 6/81, 7/135.

BARBADOS	O	M	R	W	O	M	R	W
Williams	12	0	58	1	15	2	50	2
Sealy	4	0	10	0	4	1	10	0
Constantine	11	4	41	4	8	2	28	0
Clarke	12.6	2	62	5	11.3	1	46	3
Parris	6	1	28	0	2	0	13	0
Burke	3	0	13	0	8	3	24	3
Goddard	1	0	1	0	4	0	14	0

BRITISH GUIANA	O	M	R	W	O	M	R	W
Griffith	15	3	53	3	2.3	0	8	2
Gaskin	12	1	38	0	12	0	58	2
Persaud	13	1	46	4	11	0	46	2
Fraser	9	0	52	2	2	0	16	0
Thomas	10	1	46	1				
Hill	2	0	7	0	2	1	1	1

Umpires: G.N.Francis and E.Parker.
Eight balls per over.

Close of play scores. First day: Barbados 27/3 (J.E.D.Sealy 8*, J.D.C.Goddard 3*). **Second day:** British Guiana 87/0 (C.L.De Freitas 54*, R.J.Christiani 30*).

Comments: A friendly fixture, arranged to improve relations between British Guiana and the other islands, according to the local newspaper the *Daily Argosy*. U.B.McKenzie, opening for British Guiana, was the last man out in the 1st innings.

TRINIDAD v JAMAICA

Played January 28, 30, 31 and February 1, 1939.
Toss won by Jamaica.
Match drawn.

TRINIDAD

V.H.Stollmeyer	run out	66		
J.B.Stollmeyer	c Weekes b Johnson	12	(1) st Messado b Hylton	28
C.A.Merry	b Hylton	32	(2) c & b Beckford	25
G.E.Gomez	c Messado b Hylton	2	(3) not out	161
B.J.Sealey	c Messado b Smith	8	(4) lbw b Hylton	2
L.Harbin	c Headley b Moodie	18	(5) lbw b Beckford	89
*R.S.Grant	b Beckford	0		
†D.A.Galt	b Hylton	8	(7) not out	1
R.P.Tang Choon	c Headley b Johnson	13	(6) c Beckford b Smith	0
T.F.Johnson	not out	9		
C.L.Pouchet	c Headley b Moodie	0		
Extras		10		18
Total		**178**	(5 wickets, declared)	**324**

Fall: 1st inns 1/26, 2/101, 3/105, 4/114, 5/142, 6/143, 7/144, 8/162, 9/173.
2nd inns 1/41, 2/88, 3/92, 4/314, 5/315.

JAMAICA

O.C.Stephenson	run out	8	c Grant b Johnson	2
S.M.Abrahams	b Johnson	0	run out	8
*G.A.Headley	c Tang Choon b Grant	160		
K.H.Weekes	c Tang Choon b V.Stollmeyer	88	(8) not out	2
C.C.Passalaigue	b Sealey	65	not out	6
D.P.Beckford	c Merry b Sealey	14	(3) c sub b Johnson	0
G.H.Moodie	not out	5	(4) c Galt b Johnson	6
L.G.Hylton	c Tang Choon b Grant	0	(6) lbw b Johnson	0
†L.Messado	run out	1	(7) lbw b Grant	7
H.H.Johnson	b Sealey	0		
F.Smith	b Sealey	9		
Extras	(B6, LB2, NB3)	11		0
Total		**361**	(6 wickets)	**31**

Fall: 1st inns 1/7, 2/8, 3/159, 4/292, 5/340, 6/346, 7/346, 8/351, 9/351.
2nd inns 1/8, 2/8, 3/14, 4/16, 5/16, 6/26.
Substitute fielder was E.Constantine.

JAMAICA	O	M	R	W	O	M	R	W
Hylton	16	3	49	3	22	3	82	2
Johnson	11	0	37	2	16	3	48	0
Moodie	13.7	1	34	2	10	0	47	0
Smith	21	6	33	1	17	5	33	1
Stephenson	1	0	7	0				
Beckford	3	0	8	1	18	1	55	2
Abrahams	-	-	-	-	6	0	41	0

TRINIDAD	O	M	R	W	O	M	R	W
Johnson	14	3	40	1	7	2	15	4
Merry	6	1	21	0	3	2	4	0
Harbin	8	0	54	0				
Pouchet	16	2	59	0				
J.Stollmeyer	15	0	48	0				
Tang Choon	6	0	39	0	2	0	4	0
V.Stollmeyer	6	0	22	1				
Sealey	10.1	2	29	4	6	3	3	0
Grant	12	2	38	2	3	1	5	1

Close of play scores. First day: Trinidad 162/8 (R.P.Tang Choon 11*, T.F.Johnson 0*). **Second day:** Jamaica 302/4 (G.A.Headley 128*, D.P.Beckford). **Third day:** Trinidad 103/3 (G.E.Gomez 40*, L.Harbin 5*).

Comments: The first of the two trial matches, played to decide the composition of the West Indian touring party for England in 1939. Trinidad were put in to bat. On the second day, Jamaica scored 302 in 255 minutes. G.A.Headley hit 14 4's in his 160, which took 297 minutes. He reached his 100 in 196 minutes. He and K.H.Weekes added 151 for the 3rd wicket. Headley and C.C.Passalaigue put on 133 for the 4th wicket. G.E.Gomez scored 161* in Trinidad's 2nd innings in about 400 minutes. He reached his century in 251 minutes. G.Gomez and L.Harbin put on 222 for the 4th wicket (2nd innings). The third day was interrupted by rain, there being no further play after 5.00pm. On the last day, Trinidad declared at tea, leaving Jamaica to get 142 to win in 84 minutes.

JAMAICA v COMBINED TEAM

Played February 4, 6, 7, 1939.
Toss won by Jamaica.
Match drawn.

JAMAICA

O.C.Stephenson	c Grant b Williams	2	b Johnson ... 0
S.M.Abrahams	c Sealy b Johnson	34	
*G.A.Headley	c Gaskin b Johnson	103	
G.H.Moodie	lbw b Williams	53	
D.P.Beckford	c Sealy b Williams	5	(4) not out ... 29
C.C.Passalaigue	b Johnson	1	
†K.H.Weekes	c & b Clarke	18	(3) not out ... 100
L.G.Hylton	lbw b Johnson	22	
L.Messado	b Johnson	0	(2) c Gaskin b Williams ... 60
H.H.Johnson	not out	0	
F.Smith	b Johnson	0	
Extras		18	... 8
Total		**256**	(2 wickets, declared) ... **197**

Fall: 1st inns 1/5, 2/79, 3/204, 4/213, 5/215, 6/215, 7/254, 8/255, 9/256.
2nd inns 1/0, 2/140.

COMBINED TEAM

*R.S.Grant	c Smith b Beckford	83	
G.McD.Carew	c Messado b Hylton	3	c Passalaigue b Johnson ... 0
H.P.Bayley	c Weekes b Hylton	16	b Passalaigue ... 17
J.E.D.Sealy	c Weekes b Johnson	2	not out ... 9
C.S.Persaud	c Weekes b Hylton	0	not out ... 5
†R.J.Christiani	c Johnson b Beckford	6	(1) c Weekes b Smith ... 58
R.C.Wood	st Weekes b Smith	35	
E.A.V.Williams	c Passalaigue b Smith	28	
C.B.Clarke	not out	6	
T.F.Johnson	b Smith	0	
B.McG.Gaskin	lbw b Moodie	1	
Extras		1	... 9
Total		**181**	(3 wickets) ... **98**

Fall: 1st inns 1/9, 2/47, 3/50, 4/53, 5/80, 6/117, 7/173, 8/176, 9/176.
2nd inns 1/0, 2/48, 3/93.

COMBINED TEAM	O	M	R	W	O	M	R	W
Johnson	16	4	41	6	7	1	25	1
Gaskin	8	0	19	0	10	1	31	0
Williams	16	0	64	3	11	1	42	1
Clarke	17	1	62	1	15	2	61	0
Grant	5	2	6	0	4	0	7	0
Persaud	6	1	17	0	10	4	21	0
Wood	1	0	2	0				
Carew	1	0	5	0				
Sealy	3	0	22	0	1	0	2	0
JAMAICA	O	M	R	W	O	M	R	W
Hylton	12	2	33	3	3	0	5	0
Johnson	10	1	38	1	3	1	6	1
Beckford	7	1	28	2	5	0	24	0
Smith	8	0	67	3	2	0	10	1
Moodie	4.2	0	14	1	4	0	15	0
Stephenson	-	-	-	-	3	0	7	0
Passalaigue	-	-	-	-	2	0	22	1

Close of play scores. First day: Jamaica 230/6 (K.H.Weekes 4*, L.G.Hylton 11*). **Second day:** Jamaica 32/1 (K.H.Weekes 11*, L.Massado 21*).
Comments: Second trial match for the forthcoming West Indian tour of England in 1939. The Combined side comprised a mixture of players from Barbados, British Guiana and two representatives from Trinidad. G.A.Headley scored 103 in 182 minutes, hitting ten 4's. He and G.H.Moodie added 125 for the 3rd wicket. F.Smith conceded 24 runs in one over, all scored by R.S.Grant. K.H.Weekes scored an undefeated 100 in 211 minutes. He and L.Messado added 140 for the 2nd wicket. On the last day, J.E.D.Sealy captained the Combined Team in the place of R.S.Grant, who was assisting in the selection of the West Indian touring party to England.

George Headley of Jamaica, the so-called 'Black Bradman' and the dominant figure in West Indies cricket before the war. He scored centuries against the Combined Team (twice) in the 1938-9 domestic West Indies season and was a natural choice for the forthcoming tour to England.

MCC in South Africa, 1938-39

AS THE South African cricket authorities decided to suspend the Currie Cup competition for 1938-39, in view of the forthcoming visit of the MCC team, the season in South Africa consisted of only 17 first-class matches, made up of the 12 games played between MCC and the various provincial sides and the five Test matches between England and South Africa.

MCC, making their first visit to South Africa for eight years and, perhaps mindful of losing their last two series against the South Africans in 1930-31 and 1935, selected what was considered by many to be the most representative side ever to tour South Africa. The touring party, managed by Flight-Lieutenant A.J.Holmes, consisted of the following 15 players.

Batsmen

	County	Age	Caps
W.R.Hammond (capt)	Glos	35	69
H.T.Bartlett	Sussex	24	0
W.J.Edrich	Middx	22	4
L.Hutton	Yorks	22	6
E.Paynter	Lancs	37	13
B.H.Valentine	Kent	30	2
N.W.D.Yardley	Yorks	23	0

Wicketkeepers

	County	Age	Caps
L.E.G.Ames	Kent	33	42
P.A.Gibb	Yorks	25	0

Bowlers

	County	Age	Caps
K.Farnes	Essex	27	10
T.W.J.Goddard	Glos	38	3
R.T.D.Perks	Worcs	27	0
L.L.Wilkinson	Lancs	22	0
D.V.P.Wright	Kent	24	3
H.Verity	Yorks	33	34

The decision to send such a powerful side was to prove a wise one. MCC remained undefeated throughout the tour, victory was achieved in the five-match Test series and the record crowds who turned out to watch many of the games made the trip a financial success. The latter was, to a considerable degree, the consequence of the positive and enterprising cricket played by the tourists against the provincial sides. It was unfortunate that the more pedestrian and rather negative approach adopted by both sides in the Test series, culminating in the 'Timeless Test' at Durban, should have overshadowed the brighter cricket played in the majority of the other matches.

The major strength of the tourists lay in their batting and, helped by a succession of perfect pitches and some moderate South African bowling, MCC ran up a number of formidable totals against many of the provincial sides. Only once in the 12 provincial games did MCC side find themselves behind after the first innings. Even the rare collapse was prevented from becoming a disaster by a large innings from one of the batsmen. Every recognized batsman in the side scored at least one century on tour, with Hutton and Paynter leading the way with five apiece. A total of 28 centuries was scored by nine batsmen, all of whom averaged over 40 runs an innings on the tour. These figures give a clear indication of the strength and depth of the England batting, even without players of the calibre of Compton, who had decided to play football for Arsenal in the winter, Barnett and Hardstaff. More impressive, however, was the consistently rapid rate of scoring in many of the matches. The positive approach adopted by all the England batsmen in the provincial games was one of the most pleasing and encouraging features of the trip.

It was not altogether surprising that this consistent level of performance by all the major batsmen gave little opportunity at Test level for the hard-hitting middle-order batsmen, Yardley and Bartlett, both of whom had excellent tours. Yardley was to make only a single Test appearance, whilst Bartlett was the only member of the party not to appear in a Test. Both could have felt somewhat aggrieved at their inability to force their way into the England side, for Edrich had a wretched run of scores in the first four Tests. Despite calls for his replacement, Edrich belatedly repaid his captain's faith in his ability with a double century in the Fifth Test, an innings which brought his side to the brink of victory.

Hutton, after scoring three centuries in his previous six Tests, including his record 364 against the Australians in 1938, failed to do himself justice in this series, being the only leading England batsman not to score a hundred in the Tests, in sharp contrast to his prolific scoring against the provincial sides. It can, however, only be termed a failure within the context of a high-scoring series, for he still managed to maintain a Test average in the mid-40s.

Whilst Hammond, Paynter, Valentine and Ames all made their expected contributions in the Tests, an additional source of runs was to come from the reserve wicketkeeper P.A.Gibb, who had probably envisaged a tour of only provincial appearances. Coming into the First Test as a replacement opening batsman for Hutton, who was ruled out through injury, Gibb was to retain his place by a succession of determined innings, admirably filling the role of sheet-anchor in the team.

The bowlers found themselves with a much harder task. After a number of early successes in the opening matches, they began to run up against some fine South African batting, which was also to take full advantage of the excellent wickets, especially in the Tests. Despite this, Farnes, the only experienced specialist pace bowler in the England side, was to take 16 Test wickets and play a decisive role in England's only victory in the series. Verity was once again the best of the slow bowlers, claiming the most Test wickets as well as being the most accurate of the four spinners. Wright, Goddard and Wilkinson never quite did enough to guarantee themselves a regular Test place, the trio being constantly permutated in the Test matches as partners to the reliable Verity. Wright was both the most erratic and the most dangerous of the spinners, whilst the steadier Goddard had the satisfaction of claiming two hat-tricks during the tour. Wilkinson was also steady rather than penetrative, but had the additional asset of being an outstanding fielder. He also had the satisfaction of heading the tour's bowling averages, a fine performance after only one full season in first-class cricket. Perks could also feel pleased with his five wickets on his Test debut in the final match of the tour. The fielding remained consistently of a high standard, with Ames maintaining his usual reliable standard behind the stumps and Gibb proving a competent understudy.

If the matches against the various provincial sides were often marked by aggressive batting and fast scoring, the same, unfortunately, could not be said of the Test series, which was dominated, with a few exceptions, by safety first tactics and slow batting by both sides. P.A.Gibb's 93 in 276 minutes in the First Test and B.Mitchell's 42 in 270 minutes in the Second were good examples of the over cautious approach by some of the batsmen in the early part of the series, whilst Hammond's decision to continue batting into the third day of the Second Test seemed to some observers to have been an ultra-cautious one.

The Third Test was to be the only match to produce a result. England put themselves into a strong position with an inspiring and aggressive batting display by Paynter and Hammond, one of the rare moments during the series when the batsmen freed themselves from their cautious approach. A fine bowling display from Farnes, who was able to disconcert the South African batsmen with a number of rising deliveries on a wicket which gave a little help, saw South Africa easily defeated by an innings within three days. The following Test, restricted by rain — the third day being completely washed out — produced yet another draw but, significantly, for the first time in the series, South Africa led on the first innings, with the experiment of using Melville as an opener giving his side its first century opening partnership of the series.

It had earlier been decided that if neither side had conclusively won the rubber by the final match, the Fifth Test was to be played to a finish. A combination of a perfect wicket, twice restored to its earlier pristine condition by the heavy roller after interruptions for rain, and a determination by both sides to bat for as long as possible, produced the longest-ever first-class match in the history of the game. Records were created daily until, ironically, the onset of rain and the necessity of MCC to catch the boat home resulted in the game being abandoned with no definite result. It had been a magnificent performance by an England side, who had come within 42 runs of what seemed an impossible winning target of 696 runs but it also raised the important question of whether limitless matches were in cricket's best interests.

If losing the Test series at home was a disappointment to the South African public, there was no doubt that both South African domestic and Test cricket had benefited from the tour. By the end of the series, Melville had established himself not only as the recognised first choice as captain of his country but also as a formidable opening bat. His partner, P.G.V.van der Bijl, a newcomer to Test cricket, also made a number of useful contributions and was unfortunate to just miss becoming the first South African cricketer to make a hundred in each innings of a Test. B.Mitchell, A.D.Nourse, E.L.Dalton and K.G.Viljoen all proved they had learnt from their previous trip to England in 1935 and were capable of making runs at Test level. Three players new to Test cricket, the opener P.G.V.van der Bijl, the wicketkeeper R.E.Grieveson and the medium-pacer N.Gordon all gave evidence of successful Test futures. It was evident that a nucleus of a settled South African Test side was created in the series, although it also underlined the dearth of a quality spinner and pace bowler.

For England, the tour reinforced the view that their batting was strong both in depth and talent and with players of the calibre of Compton, Hardstaff and Barnett all challenging for places, future competition would be fierce. It was difficult to be too critical of the bowlers, who were not assisted by the almost complete change-over to turf wickets in South Africa, a move which the local groundsman saw as a test of their competence to produce batting wickets of the highest quality. Whether the introduction of the eight-ball over also proved a handicap to the bowlers was debatable and was certainly never mentioned as a problem during the tour. On their performance both in the Tests and against the provincial sides, none of the bowlers could be ruled out of contention for the forthcoming series against the West Indies in England.

It was a pity that the 'Timeless Test' came to overshadow all else that had taken place on the tour. The MCC side proved popular wherever they played and provided a boost to the game in South Africa. The Test series, if not always inspiring, was free from controversy and unpleasantness. It had provided useful experience for the many young cricketers, who were in the early stages of what could be long and fruitful Test careers. All the members of the MCC party were able to look back on this tour with some degree of satisfaction. The future of both English and South African cricket looked to be one of exciting possibilities with every indication that the next series between the two sides, scheduled to be played in England in 1940, would be keenly contested.

TOUR RESULTS

	Pld	W	L	D
Test Matches	5	1	0	4
Other First-Class matches	12	7	0	5
Other match	1	1	0	0
Total	18	9	0	9

A prolific scorer for Transvaal in Currie Cup cricket, 'Dooley' Briscoe could not reproduce that form in his limited international career of two Tests, one of them against England in December 1938. As Captain A.W.Briscoe MC, he was killed in action in Abyssinia in 1941.

ENGLAND — BATTING & FIELDING
(14 players)

	Pld	In	NO	Runs	HS	Ave	100	50	Ct/St
W.R.Hammond	5	8	1	609	181	87.00	3	2	6
E.Paynter	5	8	0	653	243	81.62	3	2	3
B.H.Valentine	5	6	2	275	112	68.75	1	1	1
L.E.G.Ames	5	8	3	339	115	67.80	1	1	8/2
P.A.Gibb	5	8	0	473	120	59.12	2	2	0
L.Hutton	4	6	0	265	92	44.16	0	2	3
W.J.Edrich	5	6	0	240	219	40.00	1	0	4
D.V.P.Wright	3	2	0	59	33	29.50	-	-	1
H.Verity	5	4	0	66	29	16.50	-	-	3
K.Farnes	5	4	1	25	20	8.33	-	-	0
T.W.J.Goddard	3	2	1	8	8	8.00	-	-	1
N.W.D.Yardley	1	1	0	7	7	7.00	-	-	0
L.L.Wilkinson	3	2	1	3	2	3.00	-	-	0
R.T.D.Perks	1	1	1	2	*2	-	-	-	0

SOUTH AFRICA — BATTING & FIELDING
(16 players)

	Pld	In	NO	Runs	HS	Ave	100	50	Ct/St
A.D.Nourse	5	9	2	422	120	60.28	2	1	1
B.Mitchell	5	9	1	466	109	58.25	1	3	5
R.E.Grieveson	2	2	0	114	75	57.00	-	1	7/3
P.G.V.van der Bijl	5	9	0	460	125	51.11	2	1	-
A.Melville	5	7	1	286	103	47.66	1	2	1
E.A.B.Rowan	4	7	1	284	*89	47.33	-	3	2
E.L.Dalton	4	6	1	220	102	44.00	1	1	1
K.G.Viljoen	4	6	0	192	74	32.00	-	3	-
X.C.Balaskas	1	1	0	29	29	29.00	-	-	-
A.B.C.Langton	5	7	1	115	*64	19.16	-	1	2
W.W.Wade	3	4	0	52	28	13.00	-	-	4/0
E.S.Newson	2	3	0	20	16	6.66	-	-	2
A.W.Briscoe	1	1	0	2	2	2.00	-	-	-
E.Q.Davies	3	4	2	4	*2	2.00	-	-	-
N.Gordon	5	6	2	8	*7	2.00	-	-	1
G.E.Bond	1	1	0	0	0	-	-	-	-

ENGLAND — BOWLING

	Overs	Mds	Runs	Wkts	Ave	Best	5wI	10wM	SRate
H.Verity	283.2	89	552	19	29.05	5-70	1	-	119.26
K.Farnes	186.3	35	519	16	32.43	4-29	-	-	93.18
R.T.D.Perks	73	11	199	6	33.16	5-100	1	-	97-33
T.W.J.Goddard	105	26	282	8	35.25	3-54	-	-	105.00
L.L.Wilkinson	71.5	9	271	7	38.71	2-12	-	-	81.85
W.R.Hammond	60	13	161	3	53.66	1-11	-	-	160.00
D.V.P.Wright	134	19	526	9	58.44	3-146	-	-	119.11
W.J.Edrich	50	7	154	2	77.00	1-9	-	-	200.00
L.Hutton	1	0	10	0	-	0-10	-	-	-

SOUTH AFRICA — BOWLING

	Overs	Mds	Runs	Wkts	Ave	Best	5wI	10wM	SRate
E.L.Dalton	77.5	5	347	9	38.55	4-59	-	-	69.00
N.Gordon	245.6	28	807	20	40.35	5-103	2	-	98.30
A.B.C.Langton	219.6	37	672	13	51.69	5-58	1	-	135.23
E.S.Neson	92.6	11	224	4	56.00	2-58	-	-	185.50
B.Mitchell	129	11	491	6	81.33	3-75	-	-	172.00
E.Q.Davies	64	3	352	3	117.33	1-77	-	-	170.66
G.E.Bond	2	0	16	0	-	0-16	-	-	-
X.C.Balaskas	24	0	115	0	-	0-115	-	-	-

AVERAGES - FIRST-CLASS MATCHES

MCC — BATTING & FIELDING

	Pld	In	NO	Runs	HS	Ave	100	50	Ct/St
E.Paynter	12	14	0	1072	243	76.57	5	4	5
L.Hutton	14	19	1	1168	202	64.88	5	4	7
W.J.Edrich	15	20	5	914	219	60.93	4	2	12
W.R.Hammond	15	18	1	1025	181	60.29	4	4	15
N.W.D.Yardley	11	12	2	577	*182	57.70	3	-	2
L.E.G.Ames	13	16	3	683	115	52.53	2	2	14/7
H.T.Bartlett	10	10	3	358	100	51.14	1	1	5
B.H.Valentine	13	16	3	590	112	45.38	2	2	6
P.A.Gibb	12	17	0	738	120	43.41	2	3	10/1
D.V.P.Wright	13	10	2	248	61	31.00	-	1	6
H.Verity	12	12	2	245	39	24.50	-	-	7
K.Farnes	14	11	4	146	*33	20.85	-	-	5
R.T.D.Perks	10	7	3	57	22	14.25	-	-	2
T.W.J.Goddard	10	8	2	76	33	12.66	-	-	2
L.L.Wilkinson	12	6	2	25	*13	6.25	-	-	4

Played in one match: Flight-Lieutenant A.J.Holmes 3*

MCC — BOWLING

	Overs	Mds	Runs	Wkts	Ave	Best	5wI	10wM	SRate
L.L.Wilkinson	231.3	31	830	44	18.86	5-10	2	-	42.06
H.Verity	428	132	937	47	19.93	7-22	3	1	72.85
T.W.J.Goddard	311	72	817	31	26.35	6-38	1	-	80.26
K.Farnes	384.7	59	1207	44	27.43	7-38	2	1	69.97
D.V.P.Wright	343.4	35	1453	51	28.49	6-55	2	-	53.88
R.T.D.Perks	244.5	29	788	25	31.52	5-100	1	-	78.28
W.J.Edrich	143	16	458	13	35.23	4-10	-	-	88.00
W.R.Hammond	97	23	260	7	37.14	1-3	-	-	110.85
L.Hutton	24	1	108	2	54.00	1-20	-	-	96.00

Also bowled: B.H.Valentine 3-1-12-0; N.W.D.Yardley 3-0-15-0; E.Paynter 2-0-7-0.

SOUTH AFRICA v ENGLAND (First Test)

Played at Old Wanderers, Johannesburg, December 24, 26, 27, 28, 1938.
Toss won by England.
Match drawn.

ENGLAND

W.J.Edrich	c Mitchell b Davies	4	c Mitchell b Gordon	10
P.A.Gibb	c Melville b Mitchell	93	b Dalton	106
E.Paynter	b Mitchell	117	c Langton b Gordon	100
*W.R.Hammond	lbw b Gordon	24	lbw b Dalton	58
†L.E.G.Ames	c Wade b Gordon	42	not out	3
N.W.D.Yardley	c & b Mitchell	7		
B.H.Valentine	c Wade b Gordon	97		
H.Verity	b Dalton	26		
L.L.Wilkinson	lbw b Gordon	2		
K.Farnes	b Gordon	0		
T.W.J.Goddard	not out	0		
Extras	(B3, LB 6, NB 1)	10	(B 7, LB 2, W 2, NB 3)	14
Total		**422**	(4 wickets, declared)	291

Fall: 1st inns 1/4, 2/188, 3/234, 4/278, 5/292, 6/294, 7/378, 8/389, 9/415.
2nd inns 1/38, 2/206, 3/281, 4/291.

SOUTH AFRICA

B.Mitchell	b Farnes	73	not out	48
P.G.V.van der Bijl	lbw b Verity	4	b Hammond	38
*A.Melville	c & b Verity	0		
A.D.Nourse	c & b Goddard	73	(3) not out	17
N.Gordon	st Ames b Goddard	0		
†W.W.Wade	b Goddard	0		
K.G.Viljoen	b Wilkinson	50		
E.L.Dalton	c Edrich b Verity	102		
G.E.Bond	lbw b Wilkinson	0		
A.B.C.Langton	not out	64		
E.Q.Davies	b Verity	0		
Extras	(B 5, LB 18, NB 1)	24	(LB 5)	5
Total		**390**	(1 wicket)	108

Fall: 1st inns 1/42, 2/44, 3/160, 4/160, 5/160, 6/173, 7/281, 8/281, 9/378.
2nd inns 1/67.

SOUTH AFRICA	O	M	R	W	O	M	R	W
Davies	19	0	102	1	14	2	67	0
Langton	27	5	74	0	16	3	64	0
Gordon	33.4	3	103	5	14	0	59	2
Mitchell	22	2	75	3	11	1	58	0
Dalton	10	1	42	1	6.5	0	29	2
Bond	2	0	16	0				

ENGLAND	O	M	R	W	O	M	R	W
Farnes	23	1	87	1	7	3	17	0
Edrich	9	0	44	0	3	0	7	0
Verity	44.1	16	61	4	16	8	17	0
Hammond	10	3	27	0	6	3	13	1
Wilkinson	22	0	93	2	8	3	18	0
Goddard	27	5	54	3	11	3	31	0

Umpires: R.G.A.Ashman and G.L.Sickler

Close of play scores. First day: England 326/6 (B.H.Valentine 12*, H.Verity 19*). **Second day:** South Africa 166/5 (B.Mitchell 72*, K.G.Viljoen 0*). **Third day:** England 103/1 (P.A.Gibb 53*, E.Paynter 32*).
Comments: Test debuts South Africa: G.E.Bond, N.Gordon, A.Melville, P.G.V. van der Bijl, W.W.Wade. England: P.A.Gibb, L.L.Wilkinson, N.W.D.Yardley.
Batting, England: E.Paynter was the sixth batsman in Tests to score 100 in each innings. His 117 was scored in 176 minutes, with one 6 and eight 4's and his 100 in 189 minutes, including ten 4's. P.A.Gibb scored a century on his Test debut. He reached his century in 184 minutes and his final score of 106 lasted 192 minutes and included seven 4's. He failed by seven runs to become the first player in Tests to make 100 in each innings on their Test debut. P.A.Gibb and E.Paynter put on 184 in 276 minutes and 168 in 141 minutes for the 2nd wicket in England's two innings. W.R.Hammond became the first batsman to score 6,000 runs in Tests. England's match aggregate of 713 was a record against South Africa, beating the 620 also made at Johannesburg in 1923.
Batting, South Africa: E.L.Dalton made 102 in 209 minutes, hitting nine 4's. B.Mitchell and A.D.Nourse added 116 in 135 minutes for the 3rd wicket. E.L.Dalton and K.Viljoen put on 108 in 142 minutes for the 7th wicket.
Bowling, England: T.W.J.Goddard became the second bowler in England/South Africa Tests to perform the hat-trick, when he dismissed A.D.Nourse, N.Gordon and W.W.Wade in South Africa's first innings. The England declaration left South Africa to make 324 in 168 minutes. On the third day, there was a record attendance of 22,000, the highest for any Test in South Africa.

SOUTH AFRICA v ENGLAND (Second Test)

Played at Newlands, Cape Town, December 31, 1938, January 2, 3, 4, 1939.
Toss won by England.
Match drawn.

ENGLAND

L.Hutton	b Gordon	17
P.A.Gibb	c Wade b Gordon	58
E.Paynter	lbw b Langton	1
*W.R.Hammond	b Davies	181
†L.E.G.Ames	b Gordon	115
W.J.Edrich	b Gordon	0
B.H.Valentine	lbw b Gordon	112
H.Verity	b Langton	29
D.V.P.Wright	c Nourse b Langton	33
K.Farnes	not out	1
T.W.J.Goddard	did not bat	
Extras	(LB 9, NB 3)	12
Total	(9 wickets, declared)	**559**

Fall: 1st inns 1/29, 2/20, 3/139, 4/336, 5/338, 6/410, 7/504, 8/537, 9/559.

SOUTH AFRICA

B.Mitchell	b Wright	42	c Ames b Farnes	1
P.G.V.van der Bijl	c Valentine b Verity	37	hit wkt b Goddard	87
E.A.B.Rowan	b Wright	6	not out	89
A.D.Nourse	lbw b Verity	120	not out	19
A.W.Briscoe	lbw b Goddard	2		
†W.W.Wade	c Edrich b Verity	10		
A.B.C.Langton	lbw b Goddard	0		
X.C.Balaskas	c Paynter b Verity	29		
*A.Melville	b Verity	23		
N.Gordon	st Ames b Goddard	0		
E.Q.Davies	not out	0		
Extras	(B2, LB 7, NB 8)	17	(B 1, LB 3, NB 1)	5
Total		**286**	(2 wickets)	**201**

Fall: 1st inns 1/66, 2/79, 3/151, 4/160, 5/176, 6/177, 7/214, 8/283, 9/286.
2nd inns 1/2, 2/149.

SOUTH AFRICA	O	M	R	W
Davies	16	1	77	1
Langton	30.7	3	117	3
Gordon	40	3	157	5
Balaskas	24	0	115	0
Mitchell	20	0	81	0

ENGLAND	O	M	R	W	O	M	R	W
Farnes	13	3	37	0	8	1	23	1
Edrich	5	1	15	0	3	1	5	0
Goddard	38	15	64	3	11	1	68	1
Wright	26	3	83	2	12	0	62	0
Verity	36.6	13	70	5	10	5	13	0
Hammond					9	0	25	0

Umpires: R.G.A.Ashman and G.L.Sickler

Close of play scores. First day: Gibb 56*, W.R.Hammond 54*. **Second day:** England 553/8 (D.V.P.Wright 27*, K.Farnes 1*). **Third day:** South Africa 213/6 (X.C.Balaskas 28*, A.D.Nourse 74*).
Comments: There was no play before 3.30pm on the first day.
Batting, England: England's total of 559/9 was the highest score by England against South Africa. It was the first occasion on which three England batsmen scored hundreds in the same innings against South Africa in South Africa. W.R.Hammond's 181, made in 337 minutes, included 16 4's. He reached his century in 211 minutes. L.E.G.Ames made 115 in 145 minutes, hitting 13 4's. His 100 came up in 127 minutes. B.H.Valentine made his 112 in 160 minutes with one 6 and 12 4's in his total. His 100 took 150 minutes. P.A.Gibb and W.R.Hammond put on 109 in 126 minutes for the 3rd wicket. W.R.Hammond and L.E.G.Ames added 197 in 145 minutes for the 4th wicket, an England record for this wicket against South Africa.
Batting, South Africa: A.D.Nourse made his maiden century against England. His 120, which took 268 minutes, included one 6 and 12 4's. His 100 was made in 242 minutes.
South Africa followed on 273 runs behind.
E.A.B.Rowan and P.G.V.van der Bijl added 147 in 129 minutes for the 2nd wicket in South Africa's 2nd innings.

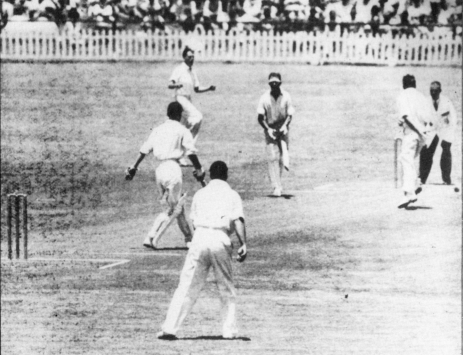

SOUTH AFRICA v ENGLAND (Third Test)

Played at Kingsmead, Durban, January 20, 21, 23, 1939.
Toss won by England.
England won by an innings and 13 runs.

ENGLAND

L.Hutton	lbw b Gordon	31
P.A.Gibb	c Wade b Davies	38
E.Paynter	c Melville b Langton	243
*W.R.Hammond	c Mitchell b Gordon	120
†L.E.G.Ames	not out	27
W.J.Edrich	)	
B.H.Valentine	)	
H.Verity	) ....did not bat	
D.V.P.Wright	)	
K.Farnes	)	
L.L.Wilkinson	)	
Extras	(B 5, LB 4, NB 1)	10
Total	(4 wickets, declared)	**469**

Fall: 1st inns 1/38, 2/153, 3/395, 4/469.

SOUTH AFRICA

B.Mitchell	c Ames b Edrich	30	c Ames b Farnes		109
P.G.V.van der Bijl	run out	28	b Verity		13
E.A.B.Rowan	lbw b Wright	4	c Ames b Hammond		67
A.D.Nourse	c Hammond b Farnes	0	c Ames b Edrich		27
K.G.Viljoen	c Hammond b Wright	2	c Hammond b Farnes		61
E.L.Dalton	b Wilkinson	12	(7) c Hammond b Verity		8
†W.W.Wade	c Hammond b Farnes	14	(8) lbw b Farnes		28
*A.Melville	not out	5	(6) b Wilkinson		10
A.B.C.Langton	c Hutton b Farnes	0	b Wilkinson		12
N.Gordon	b Farnes	1	c Edrich b Verity		0
E.Q.Davies	lbw b Wilkinson	2	not out		2
Extras	(B 1, LB 3, W 1)	5	(B 7, LB 9)		16
Total		**103**			**353**

Fall: 1st inns 1/60, 2/61, 3/65, 4/65, 5/79, 6/87, 7/98, 8/98, 9/100.
2nd inns 1/46, 2/165, 3/223, 4/247, 5/282, 6/306, 7/308, 8/345, 9/346.

SOUTH AFRICA	O	M	R	W
Davies	15	0	106	1
Langton	23.4	0	107	1
Gordon	29	0	127	2
Mitchell	8	0	45	0
Dalton	13	0	74	0

ENGLAND	O	M	R	W	O	M	R	W
Farnes	13	1	29	4	28.2	8	80	3
Hammond	2	1	2	0	3	0	11	1
Wright	12	1	37	2	15	2	56	0
Verity	8	4	9	0	35	10	71	3
Edrich	4	0	9	1	7	2	16	1
Wilkinson	6.5	2	12	2	26	4	103	2

Umpires: R.G.A.Ashman and G.L.Sickler.

Close of play scores. First day: England 373/2 (E.Paynter 197*, W.R.Hammond 99*). **Second Day:** South Africa (2nd inns) 73/1 (B.Mitchell 53*, E.A.B.Rowan 7*).
Batting, England: E.Paynter's 243, which took 334 minutes, included 24 4's and was the highest individual score in Tests between England and South Africa, beating the 211 by J.B.Hobbs at Lord's in 1924. He was the first batsman to score double centuries against both South Africa and Australia. It was his highest Test score, beating his 216, made at Trent Bridge the previous summer against Australia. It was the highest Test score made in South Africa by any batsman. He had now scored most 100's in this series. W.R.Hammond's 120 was scored in 178 minutes and included 16 4's. His 100 came in 169 minutes. P.A.Gibb and E.Paynter added 115 in 110 minutes for the 2nd wicket. E.Paynter and W.R.Hammond put on 242 in 178 minutes for the 3rd wicket. For the second time in Tests, no maidens were bowled during an innings which exceeded one 100 runs. England's eight centuries in the series was a new record for any side in a series against South Africa.
Batting, South Africa: First innings: South Africa followed-on 366 behind. Second innings: B.Mitchell scored 109 in 190 minutes, hitting 14 4's. His 100 came in 156 minutes. B.Mitchell and E.A.B.Rowan put on 119 in 137 minutes for the 2nd wicket. E.A.B.Rowan 67 was the highest score in Test cricket to contain no boundaries.

Eric Dalton dives in vain as Paul Gibb cuts the ball down towards the slips at Kingsmead. South African skipper Alan Melville is to Dalton's right.

Eddie Paynter slams Dalton to leg for four during his third-wicket partnership with Wally Hammond that produced 242 runs, only three short of the record held by Frank Woolley and Bob Wyatt. Hammond's eventual score of 120 followed his century in the Second Test.

SOUTH AFRICA v ENGLAND (Fourth Test)

Played at Old Wanderers, Johannesburg, February 18, 20, 21 (no play), 22, 1939.
Toss won by England.
Match drawn.

ENGLAND

L.Hutton	b Mitchell 92	c Grieveson b Gordon 32
P.A.Gibb	c Mitchell b Langton 9	c Grieveson b Gordon 45
E.Paynter	c Newson b Langton ...40	c Grieveson b Newson 15
*W.R.Hammond	c Newson b Gordon 1	not out 61
†L.E.G.Ames	b Langton 34	b Gordon 17
B.H.Valentine	c Grieveson b Gordon ...11	not out 25
W.J.Edrich	lbw b Langton 6	
H.Verity	c Rowan b Mitchell 8	
K.Farnes	c Grieveson b Newson 4	
T.W.J.Goddard	c van der Bijl b Langton 8	
L.L.Wilkinson	not out 1	
Extras	(W 1) 1	(B 2, LB 6) 8
Total	**215**	(4 wickets) **203**

Fall: 1st inns 1/18, 2/96, 3/99, 4/159, 5/187, 6/187, 7/197, 8/201, 9/205.
2nd inns 1/64, 2/91, 3/103, 4/145.

SOUTH AFRICA

P.G.V.van der Bijl	lbw b Goddard 31
*A.Melville	c Verity b Wilkinson 67
E.A.B.Rowan	b Farnes 85
B.Mitchell	c Ames b Farnes 63
A.D.Nourse	hit wkt b Verity 38
A.B.C.Langton	c Hutton b Verity 6
E.L.Dalton	not out 20
E.S.Newson	b Hammond 16
K.G.Viljoen	lbw b Verity 5
†R.E.Grieveson	)
N.Gordon	) ....did not bat
Extras	(B 5, LB 12, NB 1) 18
Total	(8 wickets, declared) ...**349**

Fall: 1st inns 1/108, 2/108, 3/224, 4/280, 5/294, 6/311, 7/340, 8/349.

SOUTH AFRICA	O	M	R	W	O	M	R	W
Newson	13	0	53	1	11	2	22	1
Langton	19.2	1	58	5	12	1	49	0
Gordon	15	1	47	2	22	4	58	3
Mitchell	12	3	37	2	12	1	42	0
Dalton	5	0	19	0	3	0	24	0

ENGLAND	O	M	R	W
Farnes	26	7	64	2
Edrich	4	0	11	0
Verity	37.5	10	127	3
Goddard	18	2	65	1
Wilkinson	9	0	45	1
Hammond	7	1	19	1

Umpires: R.G.A.Ashman and G.L.Sickler

Close of play scores. First day: South Africa 11/0 (P.G.V.van der Bijl 2*, A.Melville 9*). **Second day:** South Africa 249/3 (E.A.B.Rowan 53*, A.D.Nourse 20*). **Third day:** No play.

Comments: There was no play on the third day and no play before 2pm on the second. W.R.Hammond won the toss for the eighth successive time. L.E.G.Ames established a new England wicketkeeping record, when he overtook A.F.A.Lilley's 92 Test dismissals, leaving only W.A.Oldfield ahead with 130 Test victims. P.G.V.van der Bijl and A.Melville put on 108 in 99 minutes for the 1st wicket. E.A.B.Rowan and B.Mitchell added 116 in 112 minutes for the 3rd wicket. South Africa declared at lunch on the last day.

SOUTH AFRICA v ENGLAND (Fifth Test)

Played at Kingsmead, Durban, March 3, 4, 6, 7, 8, 9, 10, 11 (no play), 13, 14, 1939.
Toss won by South Africa.
Match drawn.

SOUTH AFRICA

*A.Melville	hit wkt b Wright 78	(6) b Farnes 103
P.G.V.van der Bijl	b Perks 125	c Paynter b Wright 97
E.A.B.Rowan	lbw b Perks 33	c Edrich b Verity 0
B.Mitchell	b Wright 11	(1) hit wkt b Verity 89
A.D.Nourse	b Perks 103	(4) c Hutton b Farnes 25
K.G.Viljoen	c Ames b Perks 0	(5) b Perks 74
E.L.Dalton	c Ames b Farnes 57	c & b Wright 21
†R.E.Grieveson	b Perks 75	b Farnes 39
A.B.C.Langton	c Paynter b Verity 27	c Hammond b Farnes 6
E.S.Newson	c & b Verity 1	b Wright 3
N.Gordon	not out 0	not out 7
Extras	(B 2, LB 12, NB 6) 20	(B 5, LB 8, NB 4) 17
Total	**530**	**481**

Fall: 1st inns 1/131, 2/219, 3/236, 4/274, 5/278, 6/368, 7/475, 8/522, 9/523.
2nd inns 1/191, 2/191, 3/191, 4/242, 5/346, 6/382, 7/434, 8/450, 9/462.

ENGLAND

L.Hutton	run out 38	b Mitchell 55
P.A.Gibb	c Grieveson b Newson 4	b Dalton 120
E.Paynter	lbw b Langton 62	(5) c Grieveson b Gordon 75
*W.R.Hammond	st Grieveson b Dalton ...24	st Grieveson b Dalton 140
†L.E.G.Ames	c Dalton b Langton 84	(6) not out 17
W.J.Edrich	c Rowan b Langton 1	(3) c Gordon b Langton 219
B.H.Valentine	st Grieveson b Dalton ...26	not out 4
H.Verity	b Dalton 3	
D.V.P.Wright	c Langton b Dalton 26	
K.Farnes	b Newson 20	
R.T.D.Perks	not out 2	
Extras	(B 7, LB 17, W 1, NB 1) 26	(B 8, LB 12, W 1, NB 3) ..24
Total	**316**	(5 wickets) **654**

Fall: 1st inns 1/9, 2/64, 3/125, 4/169, 5/171, 6/229, 7/245, 8/276, 9/305.
2nd inns 1/78, 2/358, 3/447, 4/611, 5/650.

ENGLAND	O	M	R	W	O	M	R	W
Farnes	46	9	108	1	22.2	2	74	4
Perks	41	5	100	5	32	6	99	1
Wright	37	6	142	2	32	7	146	3
Verity	55.6	14	97	2	40	9	87	2
Hammond	14	4	34	0	9	1	30	0
Edrich	9	2	29	0	6	1	18	0
Hutton	-	-	-	-	1	0	10	0

SOUTH AFRICA	O	M	R	W	O	M	R	W
Newson	25.6	5	58	2	43	4	91	0
Langton	35	12	71	3	56	12	132	1
Gordon	37	7	82	0	55.2	10	174	1
Mitchell	7	0	20	0	37	4	133	1
Dalton	13	1	59	4	27	3	100	2

Umpires: R.G.A.Ashman and G.L.Sickler

Close of play scores. First day: South Africa 229/2 (P.G.V.van der Bijl 105*, B.Mitchell 4*). **Second day:** South Africa 423/6 (A.D.Nourse, 77*, R.E.Grieveson 26*). **Third day:** England 35/1 (L.Hutton 24*, E.Paynter 6*). **Fourth day:** England 268/7 (L.E.G.Ames 82*, D.V.P.Wright 5*). **Fifth day:** South Africa 193/3 (A.D.Nourse 1*, K.G.Viljoen 1*). **Sixth day:** England 0-0 (L.Hutton 0*, P.A.Gibb 0*). **Seventh day:** England 253/1 (P.A.Gibb 78*, W.J.Edrich 107*). **Eighth day:** No play (rain). **Ninth day:** England 496/3 (W.R.Hammond 58*, E.Paynter 24*).

Comments. Test debut: England R.T.D.Perks.

New Records:

It was the longest first-class match played. The 'Timeless Test' lasted 43 hours and 16 minutes. Rain after tea on the tenth day finally caused the game to be abandoned as a draw with the M.C.C. party due to leave for England from Cape Town on 17 March.

The run aggregate of 1,981 runs was the highest in a first-class match. South Africa's run aggregate of 1,011 was a record for South Africa in any Test. England's 970 runs was their highest run aggregate for a Test in South Africa. It was the first occasion in Tests that each side had a match aggregate of over 900 runs.

The match contained 16 individual scores of over 50, a new Test record. South Africa's nine 50's in the match was a new South African Test record.

England's 2nd-innings total of 654-5 was the highest 4th-innings total in first-class cricket. It was the highest innings by either side in Tests between England and South Africa.

South Africa was the second Test side to score over 450 in each innings. A record number of deliveries, 5,447, were bowled in this Test.

Match details:

South Africa, First Innings:

South Africa's 530 was their highest Test score. It was the longest innings in any Test between England and South Africa, lasting 13 hours.

P.G.V.van der Bijl scored 125 in 438 minutes, hitting one 6 and 11 4's. He reached his century in 287 minutes. It was the longest Test innings played by a South African batsman.

A.D.Nourse made 103 in 364 minutes, hitting six 4's. He reached his 100 in 356 minutes, the slowest Test century by a South African batsman.

R.E.Grieveson's 75 was the highest score made by a wicketkeeper on his debut innings in Tests. He had not batted on his previous Test appearance.

A.Melville and P.G.V.van der Bijl put on 131 in 200 minutes for the 7th wicket.

South Africa, Second Innings:

A.Melville scored 103 in 210 minutes, including ten 4's. His 100 was made in 199 minutes.

P.G.V.van der Bijl became the first South African to make a century and 90 in the same Test.

P.G.V.van der Bijl and B.Mitchell put on 191 in 222 minutes for the 1st wicket.

A.Melville and K.G.Viljoen added 104 in 124 minutes for the 5th wicket. A.D.Nourse in the 1st innings and K.G.Viljoen in the 2nd completed 1,000

runs in Test cricket. H.Verity had bowled 766 balls in the match, the most balls bowled by any bowler in a Test match, beating the previous record of 749, held by J.C.White against Australia at Adelaide in 1929.

P.A.Gibb took over as 'keeper with the score on 387-6.

England, Second Innings:

England needed 696 runs to win.

P.A.Gibb scored 120 in 451 minutes, hitting two 4's. His 100 was reached in 362 minutes, the slowest Test century by an England batsman.

W.J.Edrich made 219 in 436 minutes, hitting 25 4's. His 100 came up in 193 minutes and included 12 4's.

W.R.Hammond scored 140 in 349 minutes, hitting seven 4's. His 100 was made in 273 minutes.

P.A.Gibb and W.J.Edrich put on 280 in 343 minutes for the 2nd wicket. This was the highest partnership for any wicket in Tests between England and South Africa.

W.R.Hammond and E.Paynter added 164 in 213 minutes for the 4th wicket. England were only 42 runs short, when the match was abandoned as a draw.

Series records:

There were 17 centuries scored in the series. This equalled the record achieved in the 1928-9 series between England and Australia. W.R.Hammond hit his 25th Test hundred, equalling D.G.Bradman's record of most centuries in Tests.

South African batsmen made six hundreds in the series, a new South African Test record.

Six batsmen scored over 400 runs in the same series, a new Test record for this series.

E.Paynter's aggregate of 653 runs in this series was the highest in Tests between England and South Africa.

E.Paynter and W.R.Hammond each scored over 600 runs in the series, the first time two England batsmen had achieved this feat in the same series against South Africa.

South Africa's aggregate of 2,801 runs in the series was the highest by a South African Test side in any series.

England's run aggregate of 3,129 in the series was a new England record against South Africa.

The total aggregate of 5,930 runs in the series was a new record for a series between the two countries.

M.C.C. TEAM v ORANGE FREE STATE

Played at Bloemfontein, on November 26, 28, 1938.
Toss won by Orange Free State.
M.C.C. Team won by an innings and 24 runs.

ORANGE FREE STATE

C.J.Kaplan	c Gibb b Wright	30	b Wilkinson	35
J.C.Newton	b Wright	12	b Verity	16
*E.W.Warner	b Wright	2	c Verity b Wright	15
S.K.Coen	lbw b Wilkinson	29	c Bartlett b Verity	61
M.G.Francis	lbw b Wright	17	c Wilkinson b Verity	35
R.T.Dick	c Bartlett b Wright	4	b Verity	2
L.Tuckett	b Wilkinson	5	c sub b Verity	0
†J.Robins	b Wilkinson	17	lbw b Verity	0
H.A.Sparks	not out	4	b Wilkinson	16
T.W.Fraser	c Hammond b Wilkinson	0	c Perks b Verity	0
D.A.Sparks	lbw b Wilkinson	0	not out	57
Extras		8		23
Total		**128**		**260**

Fall: 1st inns 1/35, 2/45, 3/46, 4/64, 5/76, 6/83, 7/115, 8/128, 9/128.
2nd inns 1/43, 2/71, 3/75, 4/151, 5/166, 6/167, 7/172, 8/185, 9/192.

M.C.C. TEAM

H.Verity	c & b H.Sparks	14
†Mr P.A.Gibb	c & b Fraser	16
E.Paynter	c Robins b H.Sparks	2
*Mr W.R.Hammond	c Newton b Dick	48
Mr N.W.D.Yardley	not out	182
Mr B.H.Valentine	b H.Sparks	26
Mr H.T.Bartlett	b H.Sparks	100
Flt-Lt A.J.Holmes	not out	3
Extras		21
Total	**(6 wickets, declared)**	**412**

Fall: 1st inns 1/27, 2/33, 3/39, 4/100, 5/169, 6/397
R.T.D.Perks, L.L.Wilkinson and D.V.P.Wright did not bat.

M.C.C. TEAM	O	M	R	W	O	M	R	W
Perks	6	1	10	0	7	0	28	0
Hammond	3	1	10	0	3	0	3	0
Wright	11	0	81	5	10	0	65	1
Verity	3	0	9	0	17	4	75	7
Wilkinson	6	2	10	5	15.7	2	66	2

ORANGE FREE STATE	O	M	R	W
D.Sparks	14	1	70	0
H.Sparks	18	3	89	4
Fraser	10	0	78	1
Tuckett	19	3	66	0
Dick	12	2	55	1
Francis	3	0	33	0

Close of play scores. First day: M.C.C. 228/5 (N.W.D.Yardley 87*, H.T.Bartlett 22*).
Comments: The game was completed in two days.
N.W.D.Yardley made 182* in 227 minutes, which included two 6's and 25 4's. His 100 was reached in 150 minutes.
H.T.Bartlett also hit an undefeated 100, with three 6's and eight 4's.
N.W.D.Yardley and H.T.Bartlett added 227 in 120 minutes for the 6th wicket.
M.C.C. declared at lunch on the second day.
The game ended with the Orange Free State last-wicket pair adding 68 in 24 minutes, with the last man, D.A.Sparks hitting seven 6's and three 4's in an innings of 57 not out, which lasted a mere 24 minutes. His 50 came up in 17 minutes.
The manager of the M.C.C. party, A.J.Holmes, made his only appearance of the tour.

M.C.C. TEAM v NATAL

Played at Kingsmead, Durban, on December 3, 5, 6, 1938.
Toss won by Natal.
Match drawn.

NATAL

K.C.Collins	c Farnes b Wright	10	not out	13
D.R.Fell	c Ames b Edrich	18	not out	14
*R.L.Harvey	b Wilkinson	92		
A.D.Nourse (jnr)	b Wilkinson	13		
W.W.Wade	b Edrich	56		
E.L.Dalton	lbw b Verity	47		
O.C.Dawson	c Verity b Wright	19		
†R.J.Williams	c Ames b Verity	21		
R.H.Henderson	b Verity	0		
A.P.Murray	lbw b Wright	15		
I.D.E.Anderson	not out	0		
Extras		16		3
Total		**307**	**(No wicket)**	**30**

Fall: 1st inns 1/16, 2/43, 3/72, 4/199, 5/218, 6/270, 7/280, 8/282, 9/307.

M.C.C. TEAM

L.Hutton	run out	108
W.J.Edrich	c Harvey b Dalton	98
H.Verity	c Anderson b Dawson	24
*Mr W.R.Hammond	c & b Dalton	122
†L.E.G.Ames	c & b Dalton	44
Mr N.W.D.Yardley	c Dalton b Henderson	10
Mr H.T.Bartlett	c Murray b Dalton	0
Mr B.H.Valentine	c Williams b Dalton	2
D.V.P.Wright	b Dalton	7
Mr K.Farnes	not out	33
L.L.Wilkinson	b Henderson	6
Extras		4
Total		**458**

Fall: 1st inns 1/207, 2/207, 3/247, 4/344, 5/367, 6/367, 7/375, 8/416, 9/421.

M.C.C. TEAM	O	M	R	W	O	M	R	W
Farnes	26	5	59	0				
Edrich	14	2	42	2				
Verity	26	10	49	3				
Wright	21.4	2	81	3				
Wilkinson	22	2	57	2				
Hammond	1	0	3	0				
Yardley	-	-	-	-	3	0	15	0
Valentine	-	-	-	-	3	1	12	0

NATAL	O	M	R	W
Dawson	24	4	57	1
Harvey	10	1	27	0
Anderson	14	0	73	0
Murray	22	2	84	0
Dalton	26	3	116	6
Henderson	20.2	0	97	2

Close of play scores. First day: Natal 157/3 (R.L.Harvey 76*, W.W.Wade 33*).
Second day: M.C.C. 105/0 (L.Hutton 65*, W.J.Edrich 39*).

Comments: The game was constantly interrupted by rain.
R.L.Harvey and W.W.Wade put on 127 in even time for the 4th wicket.
L.Hutton and W.J.Edrich had an opening partnership of 207 in 148 minutes.
L.Hutton's 108 was made in 148 minutes and included 13 4's. He reached his century in 130 minutes.
W.R.Hammond scored 122 in 156 minutes, hitting one 6 and nine 4's. His century took 107 minutes.

M.C.C. TEAM v WESTERN PROVINCE

Played at Newlands, Cape Town, on November 12, 14, 15, 1938.
Toss won by Western Province.
M.C.C. Team won by eight wickets.

WESTERN PROVINCE

*P.G.V.van der Bijl	lwb b Edrich 19	b Wright 14
K.G.Dimbleby	c Hammond b Goddard 20	b Farnes 0
G.E.Bond	b Farnes 13	c Bartlett b Farnes 23
W.B.H.Foley	b Farnes 37	b Wright 25
A.R.M.Ralph	lbw b Hammond 23	not out 61
H.van der Spuy	not out 31	c Hammond b Farnes 31
G.Georgeu	c & b Farnes 5	lbw b Wright 2
D.Price	b Edrich 3	b Farnes 0
B.K.Roscoe........	lbw b Edrich 4	b Farnes 7
†A.B.Glantz........	lbw b Edrich 0	c Ames b Farnes 0
G.Brinkhaus........	b Wright 2	b Farnes 4
Extras........	17	12
Total	174	169

Fall: 1st inns 1/41, 2/41, 3/58, 4/107, 5/138, 6/154, 7/166, 8/170, 9/170.
2nd inns 1/1, 2/15, 3/45, 4/66, 5/135, 6/146, 7/147, 8/159, 9/159.

M.C.C. TEAM

W.J.Edrich	lbw b Brinkhaus 7	not out 15
L.Hutton	c Price b Brinkhaus 14	c Glantz b Brinkhaus 0
*Mr W.R.Hammond	b Bond 7	
†Mr P.A.Gibb	c Glantz b Brinkhaus 19	
L.E.G.Ames	b Price 45	
Mr B.H.Valentine ...	c Glantz b Bond 13	(3) lbw b Roscoe 28
Mr H.T.Bartlett	not out 91	(4) not out 19
D.V.P.Wright	st Glantz b Roscoe 22	
Mr K.Farnes	c Price b Roscoe 6	
T.W.Goddard.......	c Brinkhaus b Roscoe 16	
R.T.D.Perks	c Ralph b Price 6	
Extras........	30	7
Total	276	(2 wickets) 69

Fall: 1st inns 1/19, 2/26, 3/47, 4/78, 5/99, 6/147, 7/217, 8/225, 9/270.
2nd inns 1/0, 2/39.

M.C.C. TEAM	O	M	R	W	O	M	R	W
Farnes 12	12	3	32	3	12.4	2	38	7
Perks 9	9	1	22	0	2	1	1	0
Wright 13.3	13.3	1	52	1	12	0	64	3
Goddard 17	17	7	38	1	12	2	26	0
Edrich 7	7	3	10	4	3	0	16	0
Hammond 2	2	1	3	0	6	2	12	0

W PROVINCE	O	M	R	W	O	M	R	W
Brinkhaus....................19	19	0	69	3	5.5	0	33	1
Bond....................16	16	1	56	2				
Price....................14.7	14.7	0	80	2	2	0	13	0
Roscoe....................9	9	1	41	3	3	0	16	1

Close of play scores. First day: M.C.C. 70/3 (P.A.Gibb 15*, L.E.G.Ames 12*).
Second day: M.C.C. 198/6 (H.T.Bartlett 55*, D.V.P.Wright 14*).

Comments: There was only two hours play on the second day.
K.Farnes brought Western Province's second innings to a close with a spell of four wickets for 16 runs in 28 balls after tea on the final day.

M.C.C. TEAM v GRIQUALAND WEST

Played at Kimberley, on November 19, 21, 22, 1938.
Toss won by M.C.C.
M.C.C. Team won by an innings and 289 runs.

M.C.C. TEAM

L.Hutton	c & b McNally 149
W.J.Edrich	c Macnamara b McNally 109
E.Paynter	c Boggan b Franz 158
*Mr W.R.Hammond	lbw b McNally 12
†L.E.G.Ames	c Steyn b Franz 28
Mr N.W.D.Yardley	c Nicholson b McNally 142
Mr H.T.Bartlett	b Franz 5
H.Verity	c & b Franz 31
Mr K.Farnes	not out 8
T.W.J.Goddard	b Franz 1
R.T.D.Perks	b McNally 22
Extras........	11
Total	676

Fall: 1st inns 1/263, 2/265, 3/285, 4/392, 5/499, 6/521, 7/645, 8/645, 9/647.

GRIQUALAND WEST

F.W.Whelan	b Perks 9	b Verity 10
A.P.Steyn	c Hutton b Verity 24	b Goddard 65
A.Dunn	c Edrich b Verity 11	b Edrich 13
T.H.Boggan	lbw b Verity 0	st Ames b Hammond 17
*†F.Nicholson	st Ames b Verity 5	c sub b Goddard 61
A.H.Gyngell	b Verity 0	c Edrich b Hutton 16
L.E.Macnamara	b Goddard 13	c Hammond b Goddard...20
J.Waddington	lbw b Verity 0	st Ames b Verity 5
J.P.McNally	st Ames b Edrich 17	c Edrich b Verity 27
E.V.Franz	b Verity 21	not out 7
A.Waddington	not out 7	c Goddard b Verity 11
Extras........	7	21
Total	114	273

Fall: 1st inns 1/14, 2/39, 3/39, 4/51, 5/51, 6/68, 7/68, 8/68, 9/102.
2nd inns 1/27, 2/34, 3/94, 4/118, 5/144, 6/178, 7/243, 8/246, 9/253.

GRIQUALAND WEST	O	M	R	W
A.Waddington 24	24	0	154	0
Dunn....................17	17	0	96	0
J.Waddington 16	16	1	118	0
McNally....................24	24	1	154	5
Franz 20	20	1	105	5
Gyngell 4	4	0	38	0

M.C.C. TEAM	O	M	R	W	O	M	R	W
Farnes 5	5	1	34	0	9	1	29	0
Perks 6	6	1	22	1	11	1	30	0
Verity....................13.7	13.7	6	22	7	26.2	13	44	4
Goddard 10	10	2	26	1	24	6	66	3
Edrich 1	1	0	3	1	8	0	28	1
Hammond ....-	-				5	0	28	1
Hutton ....-	-				10	1	27	1

Close of play scores. First day: M.C.C. 569/6 (N.W.D.Yardley 86*, H.Verity 12*). Second day: Griqualand West 116/3 (A.P.Steyn 63*, F.Nicholson 6*).
Comments: England's total of 676 was the highest first-class score in South Africa and was made in only 368 minutes. It was the first occasion in South Africa that four hundreds were scored in one innings. L.Hutton and W.J.Edrich put on 263 for the 1st wicket in just over 156 minutes. E.Paynter and L.E.G.Ames added 107 in 62 minutes for the 4th wicket. E.Paynter and N.W.D.Yardley put on 107 in 62 minutes for the 5th wicket in 89 minutes. N.W.D.Yardley and H.Verity then added 124 runs in 58 minutes for the 7th wicket. L.Hutton's 149 included one 6 and 14 4's. He reached his century in 110 minutes, his innings in all lasting 159 minutes. W.J.Edrich hit two 6's and six 4's in his 109, which took 156 minutes. E.Paynter scored 158, hitting eight 6's and 12 4's in a stay of 125 minutes. He reached his 100 in 92 minutes. N.W.D.Yardley hit three 6's and 21 4's in his 142, made in 108 minutes. His 100 was made in 90 minutes. Griqualand West followed-on 562 runs behind after being dismissed in only 127 minutes in their first innings.

M.C.C. TEAM v NORTH-EASTERN TRANSVAAL

Played at Pretoria, on December 10, 12, 13, 1938.
Toss won by North-Eastern Transvaal.
M.C.C. Team won by an innings and 76 runs.

NORTH-EASTERN TRANSVAAL

D.G.Helfrich	c Valentine b Perks	13	c Gibb b Edrich	2
M.A.Wright	c Gibb b Goddard	11	b Edrich	0
N.J.Rein	c Gibb b Goddard	12	b Wilkinson	25
R.Martin	c Gibb b Goddard	3	b Perks	2
T.E.Cook	c Perks b Wilkinson	8	st Gibb b Goddard	5
L.O.Waller	lbw b Wilkinson	20	c Wilkinson b Verity	32
X.C.Balaskas	run out	11	lbw b Wright	12
L.S.Brown	b Wilkinson	75	c Valentine b Verity	35
H.H.Watt	lbw b Wilkinson	0	(11) b Verity	0
P.Lance	lbw b Wilkinson	0	(9) c Wilkinson b Verity	20
*†J.D.Lindsay	not out	4	(10) not out	4
Extras		4		5
Total		**161**		**142**

Fall: 1st inns 1/20, 2/30, 3/34, 4/49, 5/51, 6/63, 7/128, 8/136, 9/136.
2nd inns 1/2, 2/5, 3/14, 4/22, 5/54, 6/69, 7/113, 8/124, 9/142.

M.C.C. TEAM

L.Hutton	lbw b Watt	66
W.J.Edrich	lbw b Lance	6
E.Paynter	lbw b Watt	102
Mr B.H.Valentine	st Lindsay b Cook	100
*Mr N.W.D.Yardley	b Brown	42
†Mr P.A.Gibb	c Brown b Balaskas	28
H.Verity	not out	25
D.V.P.Wright	not out	4
Extras		6
Total	(6 wickets, declared)	**379**

Fall: 1st inns 1/16, 2/109, 3/237, 4/322, 5/322, 6/367.

T.W.J.Goddard, R.T.D.Perks and L.L.Wilkinson did not bat.

M.C.C. TEAM	O	M	R	W	O	M	R	W
Perks	10	3	28	1	8	1	23	1
Edrich	3	0	5	0	8	2	17	2
Wright	6	2	16	0	6	0	20	1
Goddard	14	3	49	3	5	1	11	1
Wilkinson	10.2	1	24	5	7	0	46	1
Verity	6	0	35	0	5.5	1	20	4

NE TRANSVAAL	O	M	R	W
Watt	6	1	59	2
Lance	19	1	59	1
Brown	25	2	108	1
Cook	7	0	27	1
Balaskas	23	1	120	1

Close of play scores. First day: M.C.C. 109/2 (E.Paynter 36*). **Second day:** M.C.C. 379/6 (H.Verity 25*, D.V.P.Wright 4*).

Comments: L.S.Brown hit 52 out of his 75 in boundaries with four 6's and seven 4's.
B.H.Valentine and E.Paynter added 128 for the 3rd wicket.
E.Paynter scored 102 in 192 minutes, hitting two 6's and three 4's.
B.H.Valentine's 100 took 162 minutes and included one 6 and four 4's.

M.C.C. TEAM v TRANSVAAL

Played at The Wanderers, Johannesburg, on December 16, 18, 19, 1938.
Toss won by Transvaal.
Match drawn.

TRANSVAAL

B.Mitchell	lbw b Wilkinson	133	c Farnes b Wilkinson	38
S.H.Curnow	lbw b Wilkinson	34	lbw b Wilkinson	51
*A.Melville	c Ames b Farnes	14	not out	40
†R.E.Grieveson	b Wilkinson	8		
A.W.Briscoe	c Wright b Farnes	42	(4) not out	38
D.W.Begbie	c Wright b Farnes	10		
K.G.Viljoen	b Wilkinson	97		
A.B.C.Langton	c Hutton b Farnes	58		
E.S.Newson	not out	13		
N.Gordon	not out	1		
Extras		18		7
Total	(8 wickets, declared)	**428**	(2 wickets)	**174**

Fall: 1st inns 1/93, 2/117, 3/135, 4/209, 5/251, 6/262, 7/402, 8/420.
2nd inns 1/86, 2/97.

E.Q.Davies did not bat.

M.C.C. TEAM

L.Hutton	b Davies	0
W.J.Edrich	b Langton	38
E.Paynter	b Newson	5
*Mr W.R.Hammond	c Langton b Gordon	24
†L.E.G.Ames	b Davies	109
Mr N.W.D.Yardley	b Davies	13
Mr H.T.Bartlett	c sub b Langton	26
D.V.P.Wright	c Langton b Davies	28
Mr K.Farnes	c Grieveson b Davies	0
L.L.Wilkinson	not out	13
T.W.J.Goddard	c Briscoe b Davies	3
Extras		9
Total		**268**

Fall: 1st inns 1/0, 2/5, 3/50, 4/75, 5/106, 6/173, 7/249, 8/249, 9/256.

M.C.C. TEAM	O	M	R	W	O	M	R	W
Farnes	23	2	93	4	5	0	17	0
Edrich	14	0	68	0	5	1	24	0
Wright	17	1	95	0	10	0	52	0
Goddard	30	4	67	0	10	1	28	0
Wilkinson	21	4	78	4	8	1	39	2
Hammond	5	3	9	0				
Paynter	-	-	-	-	2	0	7	0

TRANSVAAL	O	M	R	W
Davies	13.7	0	82	6
Newson	4	3	2	1
Gordon	15	0	43	1
Langton	17	1	81	2
Mitchell	13	1	51	0

Close of play scores. First day: Transvaal 300/6 (K.G.Viljoen 25*, A.B.C.Langton 17*). **Second day:** M.C.C. 238/6 (L.E.G.Ames 104*, D.V.P.Wright 20*).

Comments: B.Mitchell made 133 in 250 minutes, hitting one 6 and 14 4's. His century, the first against the tourists, was scored in 185 minutes.
K.G.Viljoen and A.B.C.Langton added 140 in 120 minutes for the 7th wicket.
L.Hutton took no further part in the game, after being struck on the head by the third ball of the M.C.C. innings. He was doubly unfortunate as the ball then rolled against the stumps, dismissing him for nought. L.E.G.Ames hit 109 in 145 minutes, hitting two 6's and five 4's. His century took 137 minutes.
Transvaal did not enforce the follow-on.
There were a number of interruptions, caused by rain on the third day.
B.H.Valentine acted as substitute for L.Hutton in the second innings.

M.C.C. TEAM v EASTERN PROVINCE

Played at Port Elizabeth, on January 7, 9, 1939.
Toss won by Eastern Province.
M.C.C. Team won by an innings and 235 runs.

EASTERN PROVINCE

J.Gorton	b Farnes	0	b Perks	12
R.W.Robson	c Wright b Farnes	6	c Wright b Farnes	5
F.Macdonald	c Hammond b Perks	0	b Farnes	1
R.Southey	c Edrich b Wright	46	(6) lbw b Edrich	16
D.E.Dimbleby	b Farnes	33	(4) c Yardley b Perks	14
B.C.Lynch	b Wright	6	(7) c Yardley b Wright	14
L.G.Randall	b Farnes	0	(5) b Wright	4
*A.H.Coy	not out	54	(10) b Wright	0
J.Buchanan	c Edrich b Wright	4	(8) c Paynter b Wright	4
N.Ferreira	b Farnes	0	(11) not out	24
W.Proctor	lbw b Wright	14	(9) b Perks	3
Extras		9		14
Total		**172**		**111**

Fall: 1st inns 1/5, 2/6, 3/6, 4/69, 5/78, 6/79, 7/122, 8/138, 9/141.
2nd inns 1/6, 2/8, 3/31, 4/36, 5/43, 6/59, 7/63, 8/74, 9/75.

M.C.C. TEAM

L.Hutton	c Buchanan b Coy	202
†Mr P.A.Gibb	b Proctor	51
E.Paynter	b Buchanan	99
*Mr W.R.Hammond	c Macdonald b Coy	52
Mr N.W.D.Yardley	c Macdonald b Proctor	18
W.J.Edrich	c Macdonald b Buchanan	31
Mr H.T.Bartlett	not out	33
D.V.P.Wright	not out	24
Extras		8
Total	(6 wickets, declared)	**518**

Fall: 1st inns 1/168, 2/345, 3/366, 4/406, 5/455, 6/462.
Mr K.Farnes, R.T.D.Perks and L.L.Wilkinson did not bat.

M.C.C. TEAM	O	M	R	W	O	M	R	W
Farnes	15	0	58	5	5	1	14	2
Perks	8	1	16	1	10	1	29	3
Wright	15.7	2	45	4	9	1	39	4
Wilkinson	7	2	17	0	1	0	9	0
Edrich	4	0	27	0	6	0	6	1

E PROVINCE	O	M	R	W
Ferreira	15	0	97	0
Lynch	13	0	71	0
Coy	18	1	104	2
Buchanan	16	0	117	2
Proctor	13	1	114	2
Macdonald	1	0	7	0

Close of play scores. First day: M.C.C. 237/1 (L.Hutton 152*, E.Paynter 27*).

Comments: The match was completed in two days.
L.Hutton's 202 included two 6's and 23 4's. He scored his first 100 in 80 minutes, and his 202 in 167 minutes.
L.Hutton and P.A.Gibb put on 168 in 88 minutes for the 1st wicket.
L.Hutton and E.Paynter then added 177 in 79 minutes for the 2nd wicket.
E.Paynter made 99 in 87 minutes, whilst H.T.Bartlett hit N.Ferreira for 20 runs (five 4's) off his 15th and last over.

M.C.C. TEAM v BORDER

Played at East London, on January 13, 14, 16, 1939.
Toss won by Border.
M.C.C. Team won by nine wickets.

BORDER

C.White	b Goddard	12	c Verity b Wilkinson	18
†G.G.L.Mandy	b Perks	18	b Wilkinson	6
S.L.White	lbw b Wright	4	lbw b Wilkinson	10
H.L.Whitfield	lbw b Wright	0	lbw b Wilkinson	10
D.F.Dowling	c Edrich b Wright	0	c Valentine b Perks	61
R.J.Evans	lbw b Wilkinson	11	c Edrich b Perks	88
*H.W.Bowley	c Wilkinson b Verity	23	b Wright	26
R.Chapman	b Wright	14	(9) run out	25
R.Richter	not out	20	(8) b Perks	0
R.E.B.Morkel	c Verity b Wilkinson	0	c Valentine b Wright	6
R.Beesley	b Wilkinson	6	not out	1
Extras		13		24
Total		**121**		**275**

Fall: 1st inns 1/27, 2/31, 3/45, 4/45, 5/45, 6/45, 7/76, 8/115, 9/115.
2nd inns 1/22, 2/43, 3/44, 4/130, 5/168, 6/225, 7/225, 8/258, 9/264.

M.C.C. TEAM

L.Hutton	c Morkel b Beesley	3	lbw b Morkel	0
H.Verity	lbw b Morkel	9	not out	28
W.J.Edrich	c & b Beesley	8	not out	50
†L.E.G.Ames	run out	3		
*Mr N.W.D.Yardley	st Mandy b Chapman	126		
Mr H.T.Bartlett	lbw b Chapman	46		
Mr B.H.Valentine	c Mandy b Evans	39		
D.V.P.Wright	c Richter b Dowling	61		
L.L.Wilkinson	c Morkel b Chapman	1		
R.T.D.Perks	lbw b Chapman	1		
T.W.J.Goddard	not out	14		
Extras		9		1
Total		**320**	(1 wicket)	**79**

Fall: 1st inns 1/3, 2/13, 3/17, 4/34, 5/114, 6/199, 7/281, 8/291, 9/296.
2nd inns 1/0.

M.C.C. TEAM	O	M	R	W	O	M	R	W
Perks	7	0	30	1	17	1	86	3
Edrich	2	0	4	0	5	0	9	0
Wright	10	2	32	4	13	0	53	2
Wilkinson	7.1	0	15	3	21.5	3	63	4
Verity	2	0	8	1	11	1	26	0
Goddard	9	5	19	1	9	5	14	0

BORDER	O	M	R	W	O	M	R	W
Morkel	16	0	57	1	5.4	0	15	1
Beesley	18	1	82	2	3	0	10	0
Evans	15	0	103	1	4	0	25	0
Chapman	10	0	60	4	4	0	23	0
Richter	2	0	6	0	2	0	5	0
Dowling	5		3	1				

Close of play scores. First day: M.C.C. 191/5 (N.W.D.Yardley 76*, B.H.Valentine 37*). **Second day:** Border 222/5 (R.J.Evans 72*, D.F.Dowling 60*).

Comments: D.V.P.Wright achieved a hat-trick in the 1st innings, when he dismissed S.L.White, H.L.Whitfield and D.F.Dowling with successive deliveries.
N.W.D.Yardley scored 126 in 162 minutes, hitting one 6 and 11 4's. His century was reached in 138 minutes.
R.J.Evans' innings of 88 was the highest score by a Border player against any touring side. Border's total of 275 was also the highest total by Border against an M.C.C. side.

M.C.C. TEAM v COMBINED TRANSVAAL XI

Played at Johannesburg, on January 27, 28, 30, 1939.
Toss won by Combined Transvaal.
Match drawn.

COMBINED TRANSVAAL XI

E.A.B.Rowan	lbw b Goddard 24	(3) not out 67
D.G.Helfrich	b Farnes....................9	(1) c Gibb b Goddard 31
A.W.Briscoe	b Perks.....................2	(4) not out 12
B.Mitchell	c Bartlett b Goddard 83	
K.G.Viljoen	c Gibb b Perks............76	
*A.Melville	c Hammond b Verity......1	(2) c Gibb b Hammond 107
†R.E.Grieveson	run out 25	
S.F.Viljoen	b Goddard 28	
E.S.Newson	not out....................41	
L.S.Brown	b Goddard 3	
F.J.Wickham	b Farnes..................2	
Extras	10	3
Total	304	(2 wickets) 220

Fall: 1st inns 1/17, 2/28, 3/42, 4/184, 5/193, 6/212, 7/245, 8/280, 9/292.
2nd inns 1/70, 2/185.

M.C.C. TEAM

L.Hutton	lbw b Newson............148
†Mr P.A.Gibb	b S.F.Viljoen 40
Mr N.W.D.Yardley	st Grieveson b Mitchell ...0
*Mr W.R.Hammond	c Wickman b S.F.Viljoen 79
L.E.G.Ames	b Newson 6
Mr B.H.Valentine	b Newson...............71
Mr H.T.Bartlett	b S.F.Viljoen 17
H.Verity	c Grieveson b S.F.Viljoen 39
Mr K.Farnes	not out..................16
T.W.J.Goddard	b S.F.Viljoen 1
R.T.D.Perks	b S.F.Viljoen...............0
Extras	17
Total	434

Fall: 1st inns 1/118, 2/118, 3/247, 4/273, 5/301, 6/343, 7/388, 8/428, 9/434.

M.C.C. TEAM	O	M	R	W	O	M	R	W
Farnes	21	0	86	2	4	0	21	0
Perks	25	4	74	2	10	0	50	0
Goddard	22	2	71	4	15	2	60	1
Verity	19	4	63	1	4	0	19	0
Hutton	-	-	-	-	10	0	51	0
Hammond	-	-	-	-	6	0	16	1

COMB TRANSVAAL	O	M	R	W
Newson	24	3	78	3
S.F.Viljoen	21.7	3	91	6
Brown	12	0	80	0
Wickham	20	2	79	0
Mitchell	13	1	73	1
K.Viljoen	1	0	7	0
Melville	2	0	9	0

Close of play scores. First day: Combined Transvaal 230/6 (R.E.Grieveson 21*, S.F.Viljoen 5*). **Second day:** M.C.C. 290/4 (L.E.G.Ames 4*, B.H.Valentine 15*).
Comments: K.Viljoen and B.Mitchell put on 142 in 158 minutes for the 4th wicket (1st innings).
L.Hutton scored 148 in 209 minutes, having reached his 100 in 172 minutes. His fourth 100 of the tour, his final score included 17 4's.
L.Hutton and P.A.Gibb put on 118 in 116 minutes for the 1st wicket.
L.Hutton and W.R.Hammond added 129 in 86 minutes for the 3rd wicket.
Combined Transvaal 2nd innings:
A.Melville's 107, made in 144 minutes, included one 6 and 11 4's. He reached his century in 137 minutes.
A.Melville and E.A.B.Rowan added 115 in 92 minutes for the 2nd wicket.

M.C.C. TEAM v RHODESIA

Played at Bulawayo, on February 4, 6, 7, 1939.
Toss won by M.C.C.
Match drawn.

M.C.C. TEAM

H.Verity	c Charsley b Bell 9
L.Hutton	c Bell b Charsley 145
E.Paynter	c Evans b Tomlinson 53
*Mr W.R.Hammond	c Fuller b Bell 7
†L.E.G.Ames	st Evans b Charsley 47
W.J.Edrich	not out....................14
Mr N.W.D.Yardley	not out...................22
Extras	10
Total	(5 wickets, declared) 307

Fall: 1st inns 1/24, 2/139, 3/152, 4/270, 5/271.
Mr H.T.Bartlett, Mr K.Farnes, D.V.P.Wright and L.L.Wilkinson did not bat.

RHODESIA

D.S.Tomlinson	lbw b Wilkinson 20
J.H.F.Fuller	hit wkt b Wright 46
R.J.Noble	b Wright 0
*C.J.R.Hayward	c Hammond b Farnes 9
F.Davidson	b Wilkinson 23
A.Hyde	c & b Hutton 37
P.N.F.Mansell	lbw b Wright 62
J.H.Charsley	lbw b Wilkinson 3
T.Davidson	b Wright..................17
†H.K.S.Evans	c Hutton b Verity 0
A.J.Bell	not out.....................1
Extras	24
Total	242

Fall: 1st inns 1/39, 2/46, 3/72, 4/99, 5/105, 6/200, 7/205, 8/238, 9/239.

RHODESIA	O	M	R	W
Bell	14	0	76	2
Charsley	17	4	59	2
T.Davidson	9	0	63	0
Tomlinson	7	0	75	1
Mansell	4	1	24	0

M.C.C. TEAM	O	M	R	W
Farnes	9	0	32	1
Edrich	5	0	12	0
Wilkinson	15	2	66	3
Wright	12.6	1	64	4
Verity	11	4	15	1
Hammond	3	1	9	0
Hutton	3	0	20	1

Close of play scores. First day: M.C.C. 152/2 (L.Hutton 73*, W.R.Hammond 7*). **Second day:** No play (rain).

Comments: There was only 94 minutes play on the first day and none on the second, L.Hutton scored 145 in 160 minutes, hitting 23 4's in his first innings on a matting wicket. He reached his century in 126 minutes. With E.Paynter he added 115 in 45 minutes for the 2nd wicket. He then put on 118 for the 4th wicket with L.E.G.Ames.

M.C.C. TEAM v RHODESIA

Played at Salisbury, on February 10, 11, 13, 1939.
Toss won by M.C.C.
Match drawn.

M.C.C. TEAM

†Mr P.A.Gibb .... c Hayward b Charsley ...23	b Armstrong 37
D.V.P.Wright .... c Hayward b Charsley....3	
Mr N.W.D.Yardley c Hyde b Noble...........2	lbw b Hyde 13
*Mr W.R.Hammond c Evans b Charsley 43	
Mr B.H.Valentine ... c Charsley b Tomlinson 5	(4) not out 20
W.J.Edrich.......... lbw b Tomlinson.........2	(2) not out 101
Mr H.T.Bartlett ..... b Charsley 21	
L.L.Wilkinson ...... lbw b Tomlinson.........2	
Mr K.Farnes .... c Davidson b Charsley ...33	
T.W.J.Goddard...... c Davidson b Charsley ...33	
R.T.D.Perks .... not out 6	
Extras............................7	3
Total 180	(2 wickets, declared)......174

Fall: 1st inns 1/9, 2/21, 2/39, 3/39, 4/54, 5/76, 6/90, 7/98, 8/106, 9/157.
2nd inns 1/78, 2/129.

RHODESIA

J.H.F.Fuller .... b Goddard 22	c Hammond b Farnes 22
F.Davidson.......... c Bartlett b Wilkinson 6	(4) b Goddard 0
D.S.Tomlinson ..... lbw b Goddard 27	(2) b Perks..................6
*C.J.R.Hayward ... c Wright b Farnes 10	(5) not out 15
M.Napier .... b Goddard 0	(6) c Gibb b Wilkinson ...24
P.N.F.Mansell ...... b Goddard 0	(7) c Gibb b Wright.........7
R.J.Noble .... b Farnes 3	(8) not out 1
A.Hyde .... not out 11	(3) lbw b Goddard 3
J.H.Charsley........ c Valentine b Goddard 1	
A.Armstrong........ lbw b Wright 5	
†H.K.S.Evans....... b Goddard 5	
Extras.............................6	17
Total 96	(6 wickets) 95

Fall: 1st inns 1/35, 2/52, 3/64, 4/64, 5/64, 6/68, 7/72, 8/73, 9/87.
2nd inns 1/9, 2/17, 3/30, 4/38, 5/79, 6/92.

RHODESIA	O	M	R	W	O	M	R	W
Charsley	17	2	58	6	10	3	24	0
Noble	3	0	18	1	4	0	20	0
Tomlinson	11	0	87	3	4	0	20	0
Armstrong	3	0	10	0	13	4	31	1
Mansell	-	-	-	-	4	0	33	0
Hyde	-	-	-	-	6	0	23	1
Napier	-	-	-	-	4	0	20	0

M.C.C. TEAM	O	M	R	W	O	M	R	W
Farnes	11	0	18	2	11	4	25	1
Perks	2	0	5	0	4	0	11	1
Goddard	17	3	38	6	12	3	22	2
Wilkinson	4	0	21	1	4	2	5	1
Wright	4	2	8	1	10	2	15	1

Close of play scores. First day: M.C.C. 162/9 (T.W.J.Goddard 21*, R.T.D.Perks 0*). **Second day:** M.C.C. 174/2 (B.H.Valentine 20*, W.J.Edrich 101*).
Comments: The match was played on a matting wicket. The first day had several interruptions due to rain.
T.W.J.Goddard performed the hat-trick in Rhodesia's 1st innings in his tenth over, claiming the wickets of D.S.Tomlinson, M.Napier and P.N.F.Mansell. It was his second hat-trick of the tour.
W.J.Edrich scored an undefeated 101 in 140 minutes, hitting two 6's and 11 4's.
Rhodesia, helped by a delayed start to the third day, were able to draw the game.

M.C.C TEAM v NATAL

Played at Pietermaritzburg, on February 25, 27, 28, 1939.
Toss won by M.C.C.
M.C.C. Team won by nine wickets.

NATAL

D.R.Fell............. c Paynter b Wright.......22	c Farnes b Perks 20
J.H.L.Randles ...... c Wright b Perks 3	lbw b Wright 42
*R.L.Harvey .... lbw b Hammond 21	c Hammond b Wright......7
A.D.Nourse (jnr) .... st Ames b Wright 67	(5) c Farnes b Perks 8
W.W.Wade.......... c Ames b Perks 17	(4) b Wright 32
E.L.Dalton .... c sub b Wilkinson 110	b Farnes 18
†R.R.Yuill .... b Wilkinson 6	b Wright 11
O.C.Dawson .... b Wilkinson 20	run out 45
H.E.Dalton .... b Perks 9	(10) c Ames b Wright 4
R.S.K.Rose.......... lbw b Wilkinson 0	(11) not out 5
J.R.Ellis .... not out 5	(9) c Edrich b Wright......11
Extras.............................15	16
Total 295	219

Fall: 1st inns 1/6, 2/39, 3/53, 4/106, 5/177, 6/199, 7/280, 8/285, 9/292.
2nd inns 1/43, 2/62, 3/97, 4/112, 5/133, 6/135, 7/165, 8/197, 9/201.

M.C.C.TEAM

L.Hutton .... hit wkt b Ellis 15	not out 53
Mr P.A.Gibb .... c Nourse b E.L.Dalton...48	lbw b Dawson 3
W.J.Edrich.......... st Yuill b Harvey 150	not out 45
*Mr W.R.Hammond c Rose b Ellis 22	
†L.E.G.Ames ...... c Wade b H.E.Dalton ...62	
Mr B.H.Valentine ... st Yuill b Ellis 11	
D.V.P.Wright ...... st Yuill b H.E.Dalton ...40	
Mr K.Farnes .... c Yuill b Rose 25	
R.T.D.Perks .... not out 20	
E.Paynter .... absent hurt 0	
L.L.Wilkinson...... absent hurt 0	
Extras......................14	9
Total 407	(1 wicket) 110

Fall: 1st inns 1/48, 2/99, 3/148, 4/262, 5/287, 6/362, 7/362, 8/407.
2nd inns 1/7.

M.C.C. TEAM	O	M	R	W	O	M	R	W
Farnes	17	2	61	0	13	3	71	1
Perks	16	2	56	3	13.5	0	68	2
Edrich	7	1	24	0	1	0	9	0
Wright	16	0	90	2	12	0	55	6
Hammond	3	2	6	1				
Wilkinson	9.7	0	43	4				

NATAL	O	M	R	W	O	M	R	W
Dawson	9	0	31	0	6	0	17	1
Harvey	9	1	47	1				
Rose	28.3	5	111	1	8	1	23	0
Ellis	19	2	93	3	3	0	23	0
H.E.Dalton	20	4	62	2	7	2	25	0
E.L.Dalton	10	2	49	1	1.2	0	13	0

Close of play scores. First day: Natal 295 all out. **Second day:** Natal 28/0 (D.R.Fell 19*, J.K.L.Randles 8*).

Comments: Natal were put into bat.
E.L.Dalton scored 110 in 136 minutes, hitting one 6 and 12 4's.
W.J.Edrich's 150 came in 229 minutes and included one 6 and 24 4's.
W.J.Edrich and L.E.G.Ames added 114 in 67 minutes for the 4th wicket.
L.Hutton and W.J.Edrich won the match for M.C.C. with an unfinished 2nd wicket partnership of 103.

The First-Class Season in New Zealand 1938-39

THE major tour to New Zealand during the season was organized by Sir Julien Cahn. The touring side consisted of Sir Julien Cahn, C.S.Dempster, H.Mudge, C.R.N.Maxwell, C.C.Goodway, G.F.H.Heane, V.E.Jackson, T.P.B.Smith, W.E.Astill, J.E.Walsh, J.G.Lush, A.H.Dyson, W.E.Phillipson, J.Hardstaff, N.Oldfield, E.A.Watts and G.Wolfe (secretary).

A series of ten matches were played and the strong touring side returned home undefeated. The major fixture was against a representative New Zealand side at Wellington, but unfortunately rain ruined the match. The tourists played three provincial teams. In the match against Canterbury, Hardstaff played a splendidly defiant innings of 180, after Canterbury had made 464 in the first innings and the match was drawn. Otago were overwhelmed by an innings, Dempster hitting exactly 200 in 337 minutes and the bowling of Peter Smith being too good for the home side. Against Auckland the tourists gained a first-innings lead of nearly 200, but Whitelaw and Weir defied all attempts to force a victory. Whitelaw made 100 and Weir 96. The matches against the provincial sides were included as first-class, but the New Zealand Board later decided that they should not have such status as they were 12-a-side.

On the domestic front, Auckland gained 20 points in the Plunket Shield competition and therefore took the trophy, the detailed table reads:

	W	W 1st inn	L 1st inn	L	Pts
Auckland	2	1	0	0	20
Canterbury	2	0	1	0	18
Wellington	1	0	0	2	8
Otago	0	0	0	3	0

Under the captaincy of A.J.Postles, Auckland began the season with an even draw against Canterbury, bad light and rain reducing the playing time. Canterbury slumped to 117 for 6 — only 112 ahead in their second innings at the close of the third day, but Cromb, batting at number-eight, hit an undefeated 126 and Auckland found themselves batting out time on the last evening, rather than cruising to a win. In Auckland's second match, Otago gained

first-innings lead, but then fell apart in their second innings, Vivian taking five for 46. Auckland were left 155 minutes to make 203 — Sale hit 43 in 42 minutes and the runs were made with time in hand.

Vivian played a major part in Auckland's third and final match, taking ten wickets as Wellington were all out for 239 and 215, giving Auckland an innings victory. The main feature of Auckland's total was an eighth-wicket stand of 189 between Carson and Matheson, the former made 136 and the latter 90.

Canterbury, like Auckland, claimed two victories. Against Wellington they began poorly when Pritchard, the fast bowler who in later years did yeoman service for Warwickshire, dismissed Walter Hadlee in the first over, but later Menzies took control, making 163 in 152 minutes. Canterbury gained a first-innings lead of 140 and on the last day, Wellington needed 449 to win, a task they never looked like achieving, Mulcock taking five wickets and Cromb four.

In their third match, Canterbury started their reply to Otago's 266 with an impressive first-wicket stand of 102, but then seven wickets went down for 24 runs. Otago gained a first innings lead of 64, but 80 not out by Menzies on the final day meant that Otago were defeated.

Wellington's single victory came at the expense of Otago. Playing at home, Wellington made 379 for 7 on the opening day, Ongley and Rainbird each reaching three figures and the pair added 180 for the sixth wicket. Pritchard's fast bowling skittled out Otago for 188, Pritchard taking seven for 32. The follow-on was enforced and this time Pritchard's opening partner, Ashenden did the damage with six for 44, victory being by an innings.

There is little to be said for Otago, the province losing all three of their matches, as well as the game against Sir Julien Cahn's team. 121 by Mills was the only Plunket Shield hundred made for the side during a rather depressing year.

Martin Donnelly had a quiet time in the 1938-9 Plunket Shield for Canterbury, despite being quite outstanding on New Zealand's 1937 tour to England when he scored 1,414 runs (average 37.21). After the war, however, he was to develop into the best left-handed batsman of that era. Donnelly, who played for Taranaki and Wellington before Canterbury, and after the war for Oxford University, Middlesex and Warwickshire, was also a brilliant close fielder.

CANTERBURY v AUCKLAND

Played at Lancaster Park, Christchurch on December 24, 26, 27, 28, 1938.
Toss won by Canterbury.
Auckland won by five runs on first innings.

CANTERBURY

*W.A.Hadlee	lbw b Weir 92	st Jackman b Vivian 21
F.W.J.Bellamy	c Wallace b Cowie.....0	b Cowie 10
D.N.Stokes	b Vivian 23	b Cowie 3
J.L.Kerr	c & b Weir 12	b Matheson 22
A.W.Roberts	b Matheson 57	(6) b Cowie 26
M.P.Donnelly	lbw b Cowie 25	(5) c Matheson b Vivian 1
R.E.J.Menzies	b Matheson 8	lbw b Matheson 33
I.B.Cromb	b Cowie 5	not out 126
†R.C.Webb	c Jackman b Cowie.....3	b Matheson 7
H.Davis	lbw b Cowie 8	b Vivian 19
E.T.Mulcock	not out 5	b Weir b Vivian 7
Extras	(B 13, LB 3) 16	(B 8, LB 9) 17
Total	**.....254**	**.....292**

Fall: 1st inns 1/1, 2/62, 3/92, 4/174, 5/216, 6/220, 7/234, 8/236, 9/243.
2nd inns 1/23, 2/35, 3/37, 4/40, 5/76, 6/98, 7/178, 8/212, 9/280.

AUCKLAND

P.E.Whitelaw	lbw b Bellamy 36	c Webb b Davis 0
*A.J.Postles	c Mulcock b Donnelly 21	lbw b Roberts 9
W.M.Wallace	b Donnelly 105	b Mulcock 32
V.J.Scott	c Bellamy b Roberts 9	not out 48
H.G.Vivian	c & b Roberts 6	not out 67
G.L.Weir	run out 23	
H.T.Pearson	lbw b Roberts 5	
A.M.Matheson	lbw b Roberts 33	
†C.K.Q.Jackman	run out 0	
J.Cowie	run out 0	
C.A.Snedden	not out 0	
Extras	(B 10, LB 11) 21	(B 3, LB 6, NB 1) 10
Total	**.....259**	**(3 wickets) 166**

Fall: 1st inns 1/34, 2/70, 3/98, 4/108, 5/156, 6/162, 7/254, 8/254, 9/259.
2nd inns 1/0, 2/31, 3/44.

AUCKLAND	O	M	R	W	O	M	R	W
Cowie	23.6	3	60	5	32	6	76	3
Matheson	22	2	71	2	24	3	76	3
Vivian	20	6	56	1	31.2	7	85	4
Snedden	7	0	36	0	3	0	15	0
Weir	6	0	15	2	10	3	23	0

CANTERBURY	O	M	R	W	O	M	R	W
Davis	19	8	40	0	9	0	38	1
Mulcock	21	10	23	0	15	2	43	1
Bellamy	23	2	52	1	4	0	15	0
Donnelly	32.3	13	69	2	2.6	0	24	0
Cromb	2	0	5	0				
Roberts	26	11	49	4	12	1	36	1

Umpires: T.W.Burgess and J.Young.

Close of play scores. First day: Auckland 13/0. **Second day:** Auckland 156/5. **Third day:** Canterbury 117/6.

Comments: Bad light ended play early on the first day; rain delayed play on the second day.
W.M.Wallace scored 105 in 302 minutes, hitting ten 4's.
I.B.Cromb's 126*included ten 4's and took 201 minutes.
V.J.Scott and H.G.Vivian shared an undefeated partnership of 122 for the 4th wicket.
Rain interfered with play on the final day.

WELLINGTON v OTAGO

Played at Basin Reserve, Wellington on December 24, 26, 27, 1938.
Toss won by Wellington.
Wellington won by an innings and 130 runs.

WELLINGTON

†*E.W.T.Tindill	b Silver 46
H.F.Rice	b Elmes 13
J.R.Sheffield	c Uttley b Elmes 18
T.A.Harpur	b Robertson 12
J.Ell	c Uttley b Silver 10
J.A.Ongley	c Fraser b Groves 110
W.G.Rainbird	c Cutler b Purdue 102
N.Gallichan	c Knight b Elmes 50
T.L.Pritchard	c Mills b Elmes 35
J.A.McKeown	st Mills b Groves 1
J.G.Ashenden	not out 1
Extras	(B 9, LB 1, NB 1) 11
Total	**.....409**

Fall: 1st inns 1/35, 2/75, 3/77, 4/87, 5/116, 6/296, 7/350, 8/400, 9/407.

OTAGO

*K.F.M.Uttley	b Pritchard 15	c Rainbird b Ashenden 4
G.J.Robertson	b Pritchard 15	b Ashenden 3
V.J.Leader	b Pritchard 0	(7) c Ell b Ashenden 24
A.R.Knight	b Rice 0	(3) c Ashenden b Pritchard 29
A.S.H.Cutler	c & b Rice 2	(6) c Rice b Gallichan 4
C.J.Elmes	b Pritchard 23	(5) lbw b Ashenden 40
T.C.Fraser	b Pritchard 2	(8) b Rice 1
†G.H.Mills	lbw b Gallichan 37	(4) c Tindill b Gallichan 20
L.J.Groves	not out 9	b Ashenden 16
J.W.Purdue	b Pritchard 1	(11) not out 1
R.Silver	c Sheffield b Pritchard 6	(10) b Ashenden 4
Extras	(B 1, LB 7) 8	(B 7, LB 3, NB 1, W 4) 15
Total	**.....118**	**.....161**

Fall: 1st inns 1/34, 2/34, 3/35, 4/35, 5/39, 6/42, 7/81, 8/109, 9/110.
2nd inns 1/6, 2/17, 3/56, 4/58, 5/67, 6/72, 7/125, 8/142, 9/146.

OTAGO	O	M	R	W
Silver	18	2	63	2
Purdue	22	1	93	1
Elmes	18.4	1	97	4
Leader	19	1	53	0
Groves	19	1	78	2
Robertson	3	0	14	1

WELLINGTON	O	M	R	W	O	M	R	W
Pritchard	15.7	2	32	7	17	2	48	1
Ashenden	12	0	42	0	14.1	3	44	6
Rice	6	1	11	2	6	4	5	1
McKeown	4	0	20	0				
Gallichan	4	0	5	1	14	6	31	2
Harpur	-	-	-	-	30	18	0	

Umpires: C.W.Moore and J.H.Watson.

Close of play scores. First day: Wellington 379/7. **Second day:** Otago 23/2.

Comments: J.A.Ongley scored 110 in 154 minutes, hitting 11 4's.
W.G.Rainbird scored 102 in 166 minutes, hitting five 4's.
Ongley and Rainbird added 180 for the 6th wicket.
Otago followed on 291 behind.

CANTERBURY v WELLINGTON

Played at Lancaster Park, Christchurch, on December 30, 31 1938 and January 2, 1939.
Toss won by Canterbury.
Canterbury won by 236 runs.

CANTERBURY

*W.A.Hadlee	c Tindill b Pritchard......0	b Ashenden	0
F.W.J.Bellamy	c Pritchard b Ashenden 29	st Tindill b McKeown	69
J.L.Kerr	c Ell b Wilson...........24	c Gallichan b McKeown	66
A.W.Roberts	b Ashenden...............51	(8) c McKeown b Ashenden	5
I.B.Cromb	c Gallichan...........10	(6) c & b Ashenden	55
M.P.Donnelly	c Tindill b Pritchard.....3	(5) c Tindill b Pritchard	0
R.E.J.Menzies	c McKeown b Wilson...163	(4) c Rice b Gallichan	34
W.McD.Anderson	b Wilson...............38	(7) c Sheffield b Ashenden	37
†R.C.Webb	c Tindill b Ashenden 1	c Rice b Pritchard	21
H.Davis	c Wilson b Ashenden ...16	lbw b Pritchard	5
E.T.Mulcock	not out...............5	not out	7
Extras	(B 3, LB 6)..........9	(B 4, LB 5)	9
Total	...................**349**		**308**

Fall: 1st inns 1/0, 2/52, 3/66, 4/91, 5/104, 6/130, 7/217, 8/218, 9/325.
2nd inns 1/4, 2/131, 3/148, 4/148, 5/225, 6/239, 7/254, 8/295, 9/297.

WELLINGTON

†*E.W.T.Tindill	....lbw b Roberts 60	c Roberts b Davis	11
H.F.Rice	c Webb b Mulcock 16	c Bellamy b Mulcock	0
J.R.Sheffield	c Kerr b Donnelly 9	c Menzies b Mulcock	38
J.Ell	b Donnelly 14	c Roberts b Cromb	41
J.A.Ongley	run out 33	c Webb b Mulcock	25
W.G.Rainbird	b Davis 42	c & b Mulcock	30
N.Gallichan	c Donnelly b Cromb 2	c Davis b Mulcock	27
D.S.Wilson	b Cromb 11	c Bellamy b Cromb	4
T.L.Pritchard	c Kerr b Davis 0	b Cromb	23
J.G.Ashenden	c Kerr b Davis 11	c Kerr b Cromb	5
J.A.McKeown	not out 3	not out	0
Extras	(B 5, LB 1, NB 2)..........8	(B 4, LB 4)	8
Total	...................**209**		**212**

Fall: 1st inns 1/48, 2/73, 3/93, 4/105, 5/168, 6/172, 7/192, 8/192, 9/199.
2nd inns 1/8, 2/16, 3/87, 4/113, 5/129, 6/168, 7/178, 8/185, 9/210.

WELLINGTON	O	M	R	W	O	M	R	W
Pritchard	16	2	61	2	19	1	62	3
Ashenden	19	0	95	4	19	0	75	4
Wilson	9.7	0	78	3	7	0	38	0
Gallichan	7	1	41	1	13	1	55	1
McKeown	8	1	45	0	7	0	42	2
Rice	4	0	20	0	10	2	27	0

CANTERBURY	O	M	R	W	O	M	R	W
Davis	7.6	1	25	3	7	1	28	1
Mulcock	23	6	47	1	22	1	85	5
Roberts	11	0	32	1	3	1	8	0
Donnelly	21	5	64	2	13	2	35	0
Cromb	8	1	19	2	7.7	0	48	4
Bellamy	3	0	14	0				

Umpires: T.W.Burgess and J.McGuiness.

Close of play scores. First day: Wellington 93/3. **Second day:** Canterbury 259/7.

Comments: R.E.J.Menzies scored 163 in 152 minutes, hitting 24 4's. He and H.Davis added 107 for the 9th wicket.
In Canterbury's 2nd innings F.W.J.Bellamy and J.L.Kerr put on 127 in 120 minutes for the 2nd wicket.

OTAGO v AUCKLAND

Played at Carisbrook, Dunedin on December 31, 1938 and January 2, 3, 4, 1939.
Toss won by Otago.
Auckland won by seven wickets.

OTAGO

G.J.Robertson	c & b Matheson...........73	b Cowie	26
*K.F.M.Uttley	b Cowie...............17	b Vivian	8
C.K.Saxton	b Cowie...............0	b Postles	17
D.A.R.Moloney	run out...............48	(7) c & b Vivian	16
C.J.Elmes	lbw b Weir...............34	b Cowie	43
A.R.Knight	st Jackson b Vivian...33	(4) b Vivian	12
†G.H.Mills	c Wallace b Matheson 121	(6) lbw b Postles	1
T.C.Fraser	b Cowie...............54	c Postles b Vivian	0
V.J.Leader	b Cowie...............6	b Vivian	7
R.Silver	b Cowie...............7	run out	12
J.W.Purdue	not out...............3	not out	0
Extras	(B 20, LB 8, N 1, W 2)...31	(B 4, LB 2)	6
Total	...................**427**		**148**

Fall: 1st inns 1/37, 2/37, 3/117, 4/172, 5/178, 6/267, 7/365, 8/387, 9/397.
2nd inns 1/34, 2/42, 3/66, 4/66, 5/68, 6/113, 7/113, 8/131, 9/148.

AUCKLAND

P.E.Whitelaw	c Mills b Purdue 0	not out	72
*A.J.Postles	b Leader 51	c Moloney b Leader	11
W.M.Wallace	b Robertson 35	c Uttley b Leader	21
H.T.Pearson	b Purdue 49		
V.J.Scott	lbw b Leader 13		
H.G.Vivian	c Silver b Leader 14	(4) c Fraser b Leader	40
G.L.Weir	c Mills b Moloney 36		
V.S.Sale	lbw b Leader 106	(5) not out	43
A.M.Matheson	lbw b Leader 24		
†C.K.Q.Jackman	not out 7		
J.Cowie	b Leader 20		
Extras	(B 11, LB 6, W 1)...18	(B 10, LB 6, W 2)	...18
Total	...................**373**	(3 wickets)	...............**205**

Fall: 1st inns 1/0, 2/47, 3/137, 4/157, 5/160, 6/182, 7/275, 8/340, 9/347.
2nd inns 1/36, 2/66, 3/130.

AUCKLAND	O	M	R	W	O	M	R	W
Cowie	36	7	79	5	13.2	1	38	2
Matheson	38.3	8	94	2	6	1	11	0
Vivian	27	3	55	1	25	8	46	5
Weir	30	1	98	1	4	0	12	0
Scott	7	0	23	0				
Postles	8	1	32	2	10	0	35	2
Sale	5	1	15	0				

OTAGO	O	M	R	W	O	M	R	W
Purdue	23	4	69	2	6	0	32	0
Silves	10	2	42	0	9	0	43	0
Robertson	11	0	36	1				
Moloney	37	3	120	1	6	0	28	0
Leader	21.5	4	44	6	9	0	58	3
Elmes	12	3	44	0	3	1	26	0

Umpires: L.Diehl and G.McDonald.

Close of play scores. First day: Otago 209/5. **Second day:** Auckland 53/2. **Third day:** Otago 11/0.

Comments: V.S.Sale's 106 was made in 158 minutes and included 12 4's. Auckland required to score 203 in 155 minutes but won with time to spare.

AUCKLAND v WELLINGTON

Played at Eden Park, Auckland on February 3, 4, 6, 7, 1939.
Toss won by Auckland.
Auckland won by an innings and 35 runs.

AUCKLAND

*A.J.Postles	b Ashenden	8
P.E.Whitelaw	c & b Harpur	56
W.M.Wallace	c Ashenden b Gallichan	23
H.G.Vivian	c Rainbird b Pritchard	5
G.L.Weir	c Ell b Browne	54
V.J.Scott	c Tindill b Lamason	61
V.S.Sale	c Lamason b Pritchard	38
W.N.Carson	c Gallichan b Pritchard	136
A.M.Matheson	b Pritchard	90
†R.Skeet	not out	0
J.Cowie	b Pritchard	0
Extras	(B 8, LB 9, NB 1)	18
Total		**489**

Fall: 1st inns 1/25, 2/63, 3/68, 4/155, 5/163, 6/218, 7/295, 8/484, 9/489.

WELLINGTON

†E.W.T.Tindill	c Matheson b Cowie	4	c Vivian b Carson	32
J.R.Sheffield	c Carson b Vivian	26	c Whitelaw b Matheson	1
T.A.Harpur	c Skeet b Vivian	10	c Weir b Vivian	6
J.Ell	c Postles b Vivian	14	c Carson b Vivian	77
J.A.Ongley	c Cowie b Matheson	77	(6) c Matheson b Vivian	0
W.G.Rainbird	c Skeet b Postles	54	(7) c Cowie b Carson	52
*J.R.Lamason	b Postles	7	(8) b Sale	12
N.Gallichan	c & b Postles	20	(9) c Vivian b Cowie	9
M.G.Browne	not out	11	(5) b Vivian	13
T.L.Pritchard	c Cowie b Vivian	8	b Cowie	0
J.G.Ashenden	c Postles b Vivian	0	not out	4
Extras	(B 4, LB 3, NB 1)	8	(B 2, LB 6, NB 1)	9
Total		**239**		**215**

Fall: 1st inns 1/4, 2/39, 3/48, 4/61, 5/189, 6/197, 7/204, 8/223, 9/239.
2nd inns 1/2, 2/24, 3/66, 4/107, 5/121, 6/142, 7/177, 8/194, 9/196.

WELLINGTON	O	M	R	W
Pritchard	38.2	11	99	5
Ashenden	36	4	118	1
Gallichan	34	6	98	1
Lamason	16	3	53	1
Browne	12	0	68	1
Harpur	10	1	28	1
Ell	2	0	7	0

AUCKLAND	O	M	R	W	O	M	R	W
Cowie	13	0	72	1	19	2	73	2
Matheson	15	2	45	1	13	3	22	1
Weir	8	1	14	0				
Vivian	31.4	13	49	6	27	8	59	4
Carson	7	0	19	0	6.1	0	26	2
Postles	9	0	32	2	5	1	24	0
Sale	-	-	-	-	1	0	2	1

Umpires: O.R.Montgomery and R.H.Simmons.

Close of Play. First day: Auckland 332/7. **Second day:** Wellington 182/4. **Third day:** Wellington 180/7.

Comments: W.N.Carson and A.M.Matheson added 189 for the 8th wicket, a record 8th wicket partnership for Auckland.
J.A.Ongley and W.G.Rainbird put on 128 for Wellington's 5th wicket.
Wellington followed on 250 behind.
In Wellington's 2nd innings, R.Skeet was injured, V.S.Sale taking over behind the stumps for a time.

OTAGO v CANTERBURY

Played at Carisbrook, Dunedin on February 3, 4, 6, 7, 1939.
Toss won by Otago.
Canterbury won by five wickets.

OTAGO

K.F.M.Uttley	run out	50	b Mulcock	14
A.R.Knight	b Mulcock	6	c Donnelly b Cromb	41
G.J.Robertson	c Watt b Mulcock	5	run out	29
D.A.R.Moloney	c Bellamy b Mulcock	7	st Webb b Newton	73
C.J.Elmes	c & b Mulcock	39	c Menzies b Donnelly	3
V.J.Leader	c Webb b Davis	1	(9) b Davis	16
*V.G.Cavanagh	lbw b Mulcock	89	c Donnelly b Neton	25
†G.H.Mills	c Kerr b Newton	0	(6) c Davis b Cromb	0
T.C.Fraser	lbw b Cromb	20	(8) c Bellamy b Mulcock	10
R.Silver	c Mulcock b Davis	37	not out	7
G.Lemin	not out	8	c Webb b Mulcock	3
Extras	(B 2, NB 2)	4	(B 4, LB 6, NB 1)	11
Total		**266**		**232**

Fall: 1st inns 1/17, 2/23, 3/32, 4/96, 5/97, 6/131, 7/131, 8/176, 9/250.
2nd inns 1/49, 2/67, 3/141, 4/146, 5/146, 6/188, 7/192, 8/220, 9/220.

CANTERBURY

F.W.J.Bellamy	b Silver	38	(5) c Mills b Elmes	27
*J.L.Kerr	c Cavanagh b Moloney	73	(1) b Moloney	33
M.P.Donnelly	c Knight b Silver	1	(2) b Elmes	49
R.E.J.Menzies	b Moloney	0	(6) not out	80
I.B.Cromb	b Silver	6	(3) c Knight b Leader	12
W.McD.Andrew	run out	0	(7) not out	8
R.C.Shand	c Knight b Leader	22	(4) c Silver b Leader	70
†R.C.Webb	lbw b Moloney	40		
H.Davis	not out	11		
E.T.Mulcock	run out	1		
F.Newton	b Moloney	2		
Extras	(B 1, LB 6, NB 1)	8	(B 8, LB 10)	18
Total		**202**	(5 wickets)	**297**

Fall: 1st inns 1/102, 2/112, 3/113, 4/122, 5/124, 6/126, 7/126, 8/197, 9/198.
2nd inns 1/67, 2/94, 3/100, 4/150, 6/282.

CANTERBURY	O	M	R	W	O	M	R	W
Davis	20.2	3	75	2	21	1	59	1
Mulcock	31	7	97	5	26.7	6	57	3
Newton	14	2	49	1	13	4	29	2
Cromb	8	1	34	1	12	0	42	2
Bellamy	1	0	7	0	7	2	13	0
Donnelly	-	-	-	-	11	2	21	1

OTAGO	O	M	R	W	O	M	R	W
Silver	20	4	65	3	14	0	62	0
Lemin	4	1	15	0	7.2	0	26	0
Robertson	7	1	22	0	11	5	22	0
Leader	11	2	21	1	30	8	63	2
Moloney	19.6	1	53	4	15	1	66	1
Elmes	4	0	18	0	18	4	40	2

Umpires: L.Diehl and G.McQueen.

Close of play scores. First day: Canterbury 83/0. **Second day:** Otago 146/5. **Third day:** Canterbury 119/3.

Comments: F.W.J.Bellamy and J.L.Kerr put on 102 for Canterbury's 1st wicket.
Bad light ended play prematurely on the second day.
The last day was interrupted by rain.
R.C.Shand and R.E.J.Menzies shared a 5th wicket partnership of 132 in Canterbury's 2nd innings, which largely contributed to their victory.

NEW ZEALAND v SIR JULIEN CAHN'S XI

Played at the Basin Reserve, Wellington on March 10, 11, 13, 1939.
Toss won by New Zealand.
Match drawn.

NEW ZEALAND

P.E.Whitelaw	lbw b Smith	26
J.A.Ongley	b Walsh	35
R.E.J.Menzies	st Maxwell b Walsh	14
W.M.Wallace	not out	54
M.P.Donnelly	c Maxwell b Walsh	4
*D.A.R.Moloney	lbw b Walsh	12
W.N.Carson	not out	20
Extras	(B 4, LB 1)	5
Total	(5 wickets, declared)	**170**

Fall: 1st inns 1/57, 2/75, 3/77, 4/88, 5/145.

†E.W.T.Tindill, J.Cowie, J.G.Ashenden, T.L.Pritchard did not bat.

SIR JULIEN CAHN'S XI

C.S.Dempster	b Pritchard	44
A.H.Dyson	b Cowie	2
V.E.Jackson	c Whitelaw b Ashenden	17
J.Hardstaff	b Ashenden	1
*G.F.H.Heane	c Ongley b Cowie	3
N.Oldfield	not out	42
E.A.Watts	c Tindill b Cowie	32
†C.R.N.Maxwell	c Wallace b Carson	11
W.E.Phillipson	not out	1
Extras	(B 4, LB 4, NB 2)	10
Total	(7 wickets)	**163**

Fall: 1st inns 1/11, 2/57, 3/59, 4/66, 5/77, 6/140, 7/162.

T.P.B.Smith, J.E.Walsh did not bat.

SIR JULIEN CAHN'S XI	O	M	R	W
Phillipson	8	2	32	0
Watts	5	0	28	0
Walsh	20	5	67	4
Smith	14	3	38	1

NEW ZEALAND	O	M	R	W
Cowie	13	1	46	3
Pritchard	10	1	34	1
Ashenden	11	1	45	2
Donnelly	2	0	18	0
Carson	2	0	10	1

Umpires: C.W.Moore and J.Young.

New Zealand's team which met Sir Julien Cahn's XI at Wellington. Back row (left to right): J.G.Ashenden, W.N.Carson, J.Cowie, R.E.J.Menzies, T.L.Pritchard, P.E.Whitelaw. Front row: W.G.Rainbird (12th man), E.W.T.Tindill, D.A.R.Moloney (captain), J.H.Phillips (manager), W.M.Wallace, M.P.Donelly, J.A.Ongley.

Close of play scores. First day: No play. **Second day:** No play.

Comments: The only game of the ten matches on Sir Julien Cahn's XI tour of New Zealand to be adjudged first-class. Rain prevented any play on the first two days.
New Zealand made 170/5 in 154 minutes before declaring.
W.W.Wallace hit eight 4's in his 54, made in 70 minutes.
The attendance was about 5,000.

The First-Class Season in Australia 1938-39

WITH high scoring the order of the day, concern was shown regarding the quality of the pitches prepared for Sheffield Shield matches. The whole of the pitch was covered and it was suggested by *The Cricketer's* Australian correspondent that the game's name ought to be changed from 'cricket' to 'batting'.

The Australian public was still rather numbed by the lack of success of the 1938 touring team to England, when the tourists only had one Test Match decisively in their favour — the Headingley game. The Australian Test attack was almost totally dependent on O'Reilly and one major feature of the 1938-39 season was the fact that O'Reilly decided not to play in three of the six New South Wales matches, the reason given that he was fed up by the unresponsive pitches and the defensive methods employed by most batsmen.

So far as records were concerned the season belonged to Bradman. In his first six innings he recorded six hundreds, equalling the feat achieved by C.B.Fry. Bradman's sequence was:

118 Test XI v The Rest, Melbourne.
225 South Australia v Queensland, Adelaide.
186 South Australia v Queensland, Brisbane.
143 South Australia v New South Wales, Adelaide.
107 South Australia v Victoria, Melbourne.
135* South Australia v New South Wales, Sydney.

About 15,000 spectators came to see Bradman bat in his seventh innings and attempt to break Fry's record, but he was dismissed for five. This put his Sheffield Shield average for 1938-39 at 160.20 with 801 runs.

W.A.Brown of Queensland scored even more runs than Bradman, hitting 1,047 in the season in 11 innings with one not out. He also captained Queensland.

Three major batsmen did not play regularly, McCabe through ill health and Fingleton and Chipperfield for business reasons, but Hassett, who had been the youngest member of the 1938 touring side, produced some good innings for Victoria and had an aggregate of 830 runs.

With O'Reilly absent from many matches, the veteran Grimmett, now aged 46, took most Sheffield Shield wickets. He began with 11 in the first match for South Australia against New South Wales and then took nine in the following game against Queensland, but then failed to capture a single wicket against Victoria.

Don Tallon, the Queensland wicket-keeper, equalled two world records behind the stumps. Playing against New South Wales at Sydney he took four catches and made two stumpings in the first innings, and in the second took a further five catches and one more stumping, making a total of 12 dismissals in the match, a feat only achieved once before — by Ted Pooley of Surrey against Sussex at The Oval in 1868. Then at Brisbane, against Victoria, Tallon dismissed seven men in the first innings — four stumpings and three catches. In the second innings he added two more dismissals. However, also in the first innings, which amounted to 348, he did not allow a single bye.

The final Sheffield Shield table was as follows:

	P	W			L	D	Pts
South Australia	6	3	1	1	0	1	21
Victoria	6	3	1	0	1	1	20
Queensland	6	2	1	0	3	0	13
New South Wales	6	0	0	2	4	0	2

The winners, South Australia, last won the title in 1935-36. Outside the Sheffield Shield, five other first-class matches were played. At Melbourne in December, Bradman's Team, composed of players who had toured England, played K.E.Rigg's team to mark the centenary of Melbourne Cricket Club. Bradman and McCabe shared a stand of 163, both batsmen hitting hundreds. On the first day, Rigg's Team batted in poor conditions with a dust storm halting play for a time.

The other matches were played by Victoria, which side opposed both Western Australia and Tasmania, home and away.

Arthur Chipperfield of New South Wales went into the 1938-9 Australian season after a rather unhappy time in England, when his part in the tour there was greatly reduced by appendicitis. Chipperfield made one big score in that season's Sheffield Shield, 154 against South Australia, but his side still lost by an innings.

QUEENSLAND v NEW SOUTH WALES

Played at Brisbane, on November 25, 26, 28, 29, 1938.
Toss won by Queensland.
Match drawn; Queensland won by 330 runs on the first innings.

QUEENSLAND

*W.A.Brown	run out	84
R.E.Rogers	c Minter b James	55
T.Allen	c Barnes b McCabe	31
†D.Tallon	c Easton b Murphy	36
G.G.Cook	c James b Murphy	82
G.G.Baker	b Barnes	157
M.S.Guttormsen	b Barnes	6
C.D.Hansen	c Easton b O'Brien	24
P.L.Dixon	c Easton b Barnes	5
L.W.T.Tallon	run out	3
C.P.Christ	c McCabe b Murphy	0
Extras	(B 11, LB 4, NB 3)	18
Total		**501**

Fall: 1st inns 1/100, 2/176, 3/189, 4/228, 5/438, 6/456, 7/473, 8/495, 9/501.

NEW SOUTH WALES

J.H.Fitzpatrick	c D.Tallon b Cook	61	c Cook b Dixon		0
*S.J.McCabe	c Christ b Dixon	35	c Rogers b Dixon		1
V.M.McCaffrey	c Guttormsen b Cook	4	c Rogers b W.Tallon		27
S.G.Barnes	c Baker b Christ	38	c D.Tallon b Cook		121
E.J.Minter	c D.Tallon b Christ	0	(7) c Guttormsen b Cook		33
R.V.James	st D.Tallon b Christ	8	(8) c Brown b Christ		31
†F.A.Easton	c D.Tallon b Christ	0	(9) c Rogers b W.Tallon		16
C.G.Pepper	st D.Tallon b Christ	3	(10) not out		26
E.C.S.White	run out	12	(5) st D.Tallon b W.Tallon		13
L.J.O'Brien	st D.Tallon b W.Tallon	3	(6) b Christ		19
J.J.Murphy	not out	2	not out		8
Extras	(LB 4, NB 1)	5	(B 4, LB 2, NB 2)		8
Total		**171**	(9 wickets)		**303**

Fall: 1st inns 1/54, 2/63, 3/123, 4/123, 5/133, 6/133, 7/143, 8/165, 9/169.
2nd inns 1/1, 2/2, 3/93, 4/119, 5/161, 6/207, 7/224, 8/261, 9/277.

NEW SOUTH WALES	O	M	R	W
O'Brien	24	1	81	1
Murphy	34.3	2	143	3
White	31	6	67	0
Pepper	14	0	72	0
James	16	3	65	1
McCabe	12	1	26	1
Barnes	10	2	29	3

QUEENSLAND	O	M	R	W	O	M	R	W
Dixon	12	1	48	1	20.2	2	80	2
Cook	11	1	37	2	17	2	63	2
Christ	17	3	47	5	24	6	56	2
W.Tallon	10.2	2	34	1	18	1	84	3
Rogers	-	-	-	-	2	0	7	0
Baker					3	0	5	0

Umpires: J.A.Scott and K.Fagg

Close of play scores. First day: Queensland 288/4 (G.G.Cook 31*, G.G.Baker 41*). **Second day:** Queensland 495/8 (C.D.Hansen 21*, L.W.T.Tallon 0*). **Third day:** New South Wales (2nd inns) 122/4 (S.G.Barnes 75*, L.J.O'Brien 3*).

Comments: W.A.Brown and R.E.Rogers put on 100 for Queensland's 1st wicket.
G.G.Baker and G.G.Cook created a 5th-wicket record for Queensland with a partnership of 210 runs.
G.G.Baker hit 18 4's in his 157 S.G.Barnes scored 121, which included one 6 and 11 4's.
New South Wales followed on 330 runs behind.
Rain on the final afternoon saved New South Wales from almost certain defeat.

VICTORIA v QUEENSLAND

Played at Melbourne, on December 16, 17, 19, 20, 1938.
Toss won by Queensland.
Victoria won by three wickets.

QUEENSLAND

*W.A.Brown	lbw b Fleetwood-Smith	61	c sub b McCormick		99
R.E.Rogers	c Sievers b Fleetwood-Smith	41	lbw b Bromley		104
T.Allen	b Fleetwood-Smith	2	c Barnett b McCormick		136
†D.Tallon	b McCormick	7	b Fleetwood-Smith		19
G.G.Cook	b Bromley	12	c Hassett b McCormick		58
G.G.Baker	b Fleetwood-Smith	7	not out		51
M.S.Guttormsen	lbw b Fleetwood-Smith	4	not out		23
P.L.Dixon	c Barnett b Fleetwood-Smith	0			
L.W.T.Tallon	b McCormick	36			
J.A.Ellis	b Sievers	4			
C.P.Christ	not out	4			
Extras	(B 2, LB 4, NB 1)	6	(B 14, LB 3, W 1, NB 2)		20
Total		**184**	(5 wickets, declared)		**510**

Fall: 1st inns 1/70, 2/88, 3/105, 4/118, 5/126, 6/134, 7/138, 8/156, 9/161.
2nd inns 1/181, 2/250, 3/281, 4/423, 5/454.

VICTORIA

*K.E.Rigg	b Ellis	36	lbw b Dixon		49
I.S.Lee	run out	7	b Dixon		34
R.G.Gregory	c D.Tallon b Ellis	53	lbw b Ellis		77
A.L.Hassett	c Dixon b Ellis	104	c and b Dixon		73
J.A.Ledward	c D.Tallon b Ellis	8	c Guttormsen b Christ		44
F.W.Sides	lbw b Cook	42	b Dixon		5
E.H.Bromley	b Cook	0	run out		4
†B.A.Barnett	c & b Cook	21	not out		24
M.W.Sievers	not out	67	not out		0
L.O'B.Fleetwood-Smith	c Brown b Ellis	0			
E.L.McCormick	b Christ	29			
Extras	(B 6, LB 2, NB 1)	9	(B 5, LB 4, W 3)		12
Total		**376**	(7 wickets)		**322**

Fall: 1st inns 1/28, 2/64, 3/130, 4/142, 5/236, 6/236, 7/278, 8/281, 9/281.
2nd inns 1/77, 2/90, 3/219, 4/233, 5/242, 6/264, 7/318.

VICTORIA	O	M	R	W	O	M	R	W
McCormick	11.4	1	47	2	22	0	125	3
Sievers	15	2	44	1	28	2	92	0
Fleetwood-Smith	20	3	58	6	20	1	73	1
Bromley	8	2	29	1	24	4	114	1
Ledward	-	-	-	-	10	1	49	0
Gregory	6	0	37	0				

QUEENSLAND	O	M	R	W	O	M	R	W
Ellis	25	2	104	5	14	0	101	1
Cook	16	2	67	3	7	1	26	0
Dixon	10	1	53	0	11.3	0	67	4
Christ	29.7	12	47	1	14	1	90	1
W.Tallon	18	0	96	0				
Rogers	-	-	-	-	5	0	26	0

Umpires: A.N.Barlow and G.A.Browne

Close of play scores. First day: Victoria 55/1 (K.E.Rigg 31*, R.G.Gregory 17*). **Second day:** Queensland 35/0 (R.E.Rogers 22*, W.A.Brown 10*). **Third day:** Queensland 405/3 (T.Allen 121*, G.G.Cook 43*).

Comments: T.Allen's 136 included 18 4's and took 204 minutes.
W.A.Brown and R.Rogers put on 181 for Queensland's 1st wicket, a State record against Victoria.
T.Allen and G.G.Cook added 142 for Queensland's 4th wicket.
Victoria were set to make 319 in 245 minutes.
R.G.Gregory and A.L.Hassett put on 129 for their 3rd wicket.

SOUTH AUSTRALIA v NEW SOUTH WALES

Played at Adelaide, on December 16, 17, 19, 20, 1938.
Toss won by South Australia.
South Australia won by an innings and 55 runs.

SOUTH AUSTRALIA

K.Ridings	b O'Reilly	31
R.S.Whitington	c James b Murphy	0
*D.G.Bradman	b Murphy	143
C.L.Badcock	not out	271
R.A.Hamence	c Barnes b Fitzpatrick	90
†C.W.Walker	lbw b O'Reilly	0
M.G.Waite	run out	21
F.A.Ward	b Barnes	0
C.V.Grimmett	run out	35
Extras	(B 3, LB 4, NB 2)	9
Total	(8 wickets, declared)	**600**

M.J.Cotton & J.Scott did not bat.
Fall: 1st inns 1/0, 2/67, 3/242, 4/445, 5/446, 6/512, 7/514, 8/600.

NEW SOUTH WALES

J.H.Fitzpatrick	b Grimmett	23	b Cotton	5
A.G.Cheetham	st Walker b Grimmett	27	c Cotton b Scott	9
C.M.Solomon	c Walker b Grimmett	1	c & b Grimmett	13
S.G.Barnes	b Cotton	117	c Whitington b Ward	28
*J.H.W.Fingleton	c Walker b Scott	0	c Ward b Grimmett	3
A.G.Chipperfield	c Walker b Cotton	154	lbw b Ward	13
R.V.James	lbw b Grimmett	9	lbw b Grimmett	42
†F.A.Easton	c Walker b Grimmett	17	not out	7
E.C.S.White	lbw b Grimmett	14	c & b Ward	21
W.J.O'Reilly	lbw b Grimmett	20	c Bradman b Ward	7
J.J.Murphy	not out	3	c Badcock b Grimmett	4
Extras	(B 2, NB 3)	5	(B 1, LB 2)	3
Total		**390**		**155**

Fall: 1st inns 1/43, 2/45, 3/66, 4/67, 5/252, 6/288, 7/350, 8/356, 9/379.
2nd inns 1/8, 2/21, 3/49, 4/59, 5/74, 6/76, 7/120, 8/134, 9/149.

NEW SOUTH WALES	O	M	R	W
Murphy	32	1	126	2
Cheetham	20	1	85	0
O'Reilly	36	9	99	2
White	28	1	103	0
Chipperfield	8	0	60	0
Barnes	15	2	62	1
James	1	0	13	0
Fitzpatrick	11	0	40	1
Fingleton	5	0	3	0

SOUTH AUSTRALIA	O	M	R	W	O	M	R	W
Cotton	23	1	76	2	6	0	24	1
Waite	15	3	37	0	5	0	17	0
Ward	20	2	81	0	14	3	40	4
Scott	29	10	75	1	5	1	12	1
Grimmett	36.6	11	116	7	14.7	1	59	4

Umpires: J.D.Scott and A.G.Jenkins.

Close of play scores. First day: South Australia 353/3 (C.L.Badcock 130*, R.A.Hamence 47*). **Second day:** New South Wales 40/0 (A.G.Cheetham 16*, J.H.Fitzpatrick 22*). **Third day:** New South Wales 346/6 (A.G.Chipperfield 149*, F.A.Easton 16*).

Comments: South Australia's score of 600/7 was the highest against New South Wales.
D.G.Bradman scored 143 in 230 minutes, hitting 11 4's.
C.L.Badcock's 271*was made in 495 minutes and included two 6's and 15 4's.
Bradman and Badcock put on 175 for the 3rd wicket.
Badcock and R.A.Hamence then added 203 for the 4th wicket, a State record against New South Wales.
S.G.Barnes and A.G.Chipperfield put on 185 for the 5th NSW wicket in their 1st innings.

VICTORIA v NEW SOUTH WALES

Played at Melbourne, on December 23, 24, 26, 27, 1938 (28 in NSW year book)
Toss won by New South Wales.
Victoria won by four wickets.

NEW SOUTH WALES

*J.H.W.Fingleton	c Ledward b Fleetwood-Smith	45	lbw b McCormick	10
J.H.Fitzpatrick	c Ledward b McCormick	5	c Sides b Ring	16
A.G.Cheetham	b Fleetwood-Smith	42	b Fleetwood-Smith	8
S.G.Barnes	c Sides b Ring	16	c McCormick b F.Smith	98
A.G.Chipperfield	c & b McCormick	66	lbw b Fleetwood-Smith	73
C.M.Solomon	c Hassett b McCormick	30	st Barnett b Ring	99
V.W.McCaffrey	b McCormick	5	c Ring b Fleetwood-Smith	18
†F.A.Easton	b McCormick	7	c Ledward b Fleetwood-Smith	2
E.C.S.White	not out	14	not out	38
W.J.O'Reilly	c Sievers b Fleetwood-Smith	47	b Fleetwood-Smith	0
J.J.Murphy	st Barnett b Ring	8	c Hassett b Fleetwood-Smith	10
Extras	(B 4, LB 3, NB 2)	9	(B 10, LB 4, NB 2)	16
Total		**294**		**388**

Fall: 1st inns 1/9, 2/93, 3/112, 4/114, 5/210, 6/212, 7/220, 8/228, 9/285.
2nd inns 1/24, 2/28, 3/187, 4/221, 5/283, 6/332, 7/333, 8/338, 9/358.

VICTORIA

*K.E.Rigg	b O'Reilly	84		
I.S.Lee	c Barnes b Cheetham	121	c Easton b O'Reilly	37
R.G.Gregory	lbw b White	71	c White b Barnes	5
A.L.Hassett	c Easton b O'Reilly	56	lbw b O'Reilly	0
J.A.Ledward	c Barnes b Fitzpatrick	37	c White b O'Reilly	27
F.W.Sides	not out	53	c Cheetham b White	43
†B.A.Barnett	c Barnes b Fitzpatrick	7	not out	9
M.W.Sievers	lbw b O'Reilly	33	c Fitzpatrick b O'Reilly	48
D.T.Ring	c Chipperfield b O'Reilly	15	not out	4
E.L.McCormick	c & b O'Reilly	5		
L.O'B.Fleetwood-Smith	b O'Reilly	0		
Extras	(B 9, LB 10, NB 3)	22	(B 2, LB 3, NB 1)	6
Total		**504**	(6 wickets)	**179**

Fall: 1st inns 1/171, 2/269, 3/317, 4/385, 5/391, 6/411, 7/472, 8/498, 9/504.
2nd inns 1/86, 2/95, 3/95, 4/95, 5/150, 6/175.

VICTORIA	O	M	R	W	O	M	R	W
McCormick	17	0	62	5	15	0	71	1
Sievers	18	5	54	0	14	0	61	0
Ledward	1	0	4	0				
Fleetwood-Smith	22	0	100	3	26.4	1	144	7
Ring	14.4	1	65	2	21	2	96	2

NEW SOUTH WALES	O	M	R	W	O	M	R	W
Murphy	22	1	84	0	6	1	31	0
O'Reilly	43.2	7	152	6	13	0	60	4
Cheetham	15	0	89	1	6	0	24	0
Fitzpatrick	10	1	47	2	1	0	5	0
Barnes	17	1	50	0	5	0	32	1
White	15	4	57	1	4	0	21	1
Chipperfield	1	0	3	0				

Umpires: A.N.Barlow and G.A.Browne.

Close of play scores. First day: Victoria 9/0 (K.E.Rigg 8*, I.S.Lee 0*). **Second day:** Victoria 348/3. **Third day:** New South Wales 215/3 (A.G.Chipperfield 72*, C.M.Solomon 17*).

Comments: K.E.Rigg and I.Lee put on 171 for the 1st wicket.
S.G.Barnes and A.G.Chipperfield put on 159 for the NSW 3rd wicket.

SOUTH AUSTRALIA v QUEENSLAND

Played at Adelaide, on December 24, 26, 27, 28, 1938.
Toss won by Queensland.
South Australia won by an innings and 20 runs.

QUEENSLAND

*W.A.Brown	c Walker b Scott	12	not out	174
R.E.Rogers	c Walker b Waite	0	c Bradman b Cotton	2
T.Allen	b Grimmett	21	lbw b Ward	16
†D.Tallon	b Grimmett	6	b Cotton	11
G.G.Baker	lbw b Grimmett	22	st Walker b Ward	43
G.G.Cook	not out	34	b Grimmett	35
C.D.Hansen	run out	12	run out	11
M.S.Guttormsen	c K.Ridings b Ward	8	run out	7
L.W.T.Tallon	b Grimmett	6	lbw b Grimmett	0
J.A.Ellis	lbw b Grimmett	0	b Grimmett	0
C.P.Christ	st Walker b Grimmett	0	st Walker b Ward	0
Extras	(B 1, LB 3, NB 6)	10	(B 10, LB 1, W 1)	12
Total		**131**		**311**

Fall: 1st inns 1/4, 2/28, 3/41, 4/46, 5/82, 6/105, 7/118, 8/131, 9/131.
2nd inns 1/3, 2/53, 3/73, 4/98, 5/206, 6/301, 7/310, 8/310, 9/310.

SOUTH AUSTRALIA

R.S.Whitington	st D.Tallon b Cook	11
K.L.Ridings	c D Tallon b Ellis	7
*D.G.Bradman	c Baker b Christ	225
C.L.Badcock	c W.Tallon b Ellis	100
R.A.Hamence	c & b W.Tallon	17
M.G.Waite	c Guttormsen b Cook	52
†C.W.Walker	b Baker	32
F.A.Ward	run out	9
C.V.Grimmett	not out	0
H.J.Cotton	b Baker	0
J.Scott	b Baker	0
Extras	(B 5, LB 3, W 1)	9
Total		**462**

Fall: 1st inns 1/17, 2/23, 3/225, 4/274, 5/405, 6/426, 7/456, 8/462, 9/462.

SOUTH AUSTRALIA	O	M	R	W	O	M	R	W
Cotton	10	0	51	0	18	2	62	2
Waite	4	0	9	1	9	1	20	0
Scott	7	3	11	1	9	7	15	0
Grimmett	14.7	2	33	6	34	3	96	3
Ward	6	0	17	1	38.4	8	106	3

QUEENSLAND	O	M	R	W
Ellis	26	0	87	2
Cook	25	2	85	2
Christ	33	3	102	1
Baker	8.5	0	36	3
W.Tallon	18	1	90	1
Rogers	8	1	42	0
Allen	2	0	11	0

Umpires: J.D.Scott and A.G.Jenkins

Close of play scores. First day: South Australia (D.G.Bradman 83*, C.L.Badcock 79*). **Second day:** South Australia 462 all out. **Third day:** Queensland 152/4 (W.A.Brown 91*, G.G.Cook 16*).

Comments: D.G.Bradman's 225 included 14 4's and took 330 minutes.
C.L.Badcock scored a 100 in 150 minutes, hitting seven 4's.
Bradman and Badcock put on 202 in 151 minutes for the 3rd wicket.
Bradman and M.G.Waite added 131 in 112 minutes for the 5th wicket.
W.A.Brown carried his bat, making 174 in his second innings.
There was no play on the 3rd day until 2.30pm.

VICTORIA v SOUTH AUSTRALIA

Played at Melbourne, on December 30, 31, 1938, January 2, 3, 1939.
Toss won by Victoria.
Match drawn; Victoria won on first innings.

VICTORIA

*K.E.Rigg	b Waite	7	(1) b Waite	51
I.S.Lee	c Walker b Scott	6	c sub b Ward	9
R.G.Gregory	st Walker b Ward	71	st Walker b Ward	54
A.L.Hassett	not out	211	st Walker b Ward	54
J.A.Ledward	c Scott b Waite	2	c & b Ward	0
F.W.Sides	run out	44	c Scott b P.Ridings	61
†B.A.Barnett	lbw b Ward	50	(2) lbw b Ward	54
M.W.Sievers	b Ward	1	(7) not out	20
D.T.Ring	c Hamence b Waite	51	(8) st Walker b Ward	19
E.L.McCormick	b P.Riding	0	(9) not out	1
L.O'B.Fleetwood-Smith	b Ward	43		
Extras	(LB 6, NB 7)	13	(B 6, LB 2, W 1, NB 5)	14
Total		**499**	(7 wickets, declared)	**283**

Fall: 1st inns 1/12, 2/23, 3/129, 4/134, 5/219, 6/312, 7/314, 8/426, 9/427.
2nd inns 1/108, 2/112, 3/135, 4/150, 5/195, 6/255, 7/281.

SOUTH AUSTRALIA

R.S.Whitington	lbw b Sievers	100	not out	27
K.L.Ridings	c Lee b Sievers	27	not out	18
*D.G.Bradman	c Hassett b Sievers	107		
C.L.Badcock	c & b McCormick	1		
†C.W.Walker	b Sievers	14		
F.A.Ward	c Barnett b Sievers	62		
R.A.Hamence	b Sievers	84		
M.G.Waite	lbw b Ring	0		
P.Ridings	c & b Ring	33		
C.V.Grimmett	st Barnett b Ring	34		
J.Scott	not out	4		
Extras	(B 5, LB 15, NB 2)	22	(B 5)	5
Total		**488**	(No wicket)	**50**

Fall: 1st inns 1/70, 2/227, 3/230, 4/238, 5/263, 6/379, 7/380, 8/424, 9/483.

SOUTH AUSTRALIA	O	M	R	W	O	M	R	W
P.Ridings	19.2	3	73	1	9	0	37	1
Waite	32	5	123	3	24	6	63	1
Scott	17	2	67	1	13	1	43	0
Grimmett	25	0	98	0				
Ward	25	1	125	4	27	4	126	5

VICTORIA	O	M	R	W	O	M	R	W
McCormick	22	4	78	1	3	1	13	0
Sievers	43	11	95	6	3	0	9	0
Ring	31.1	2	116	3	6	1	8	0
Fleetwood-Smith	35	4	152	0	3	1	2	0
Gregory	4	0	25	0	4	3	3	0
Hassett	-	-	-	-	2	0	10	0

Umpires: A.N.Barlow and G.A.Browne

Close of play scores. First day: Victoria 363/7 (A.L.Hassett 151*, D.Ring 19*).
Second day: South Australia 240/4 (F.A.Ward 0*, C.W.Walker 4*). **Third day:** Victoria 16/0 (I.S.Lee 6*, B.A.Barnett 8*).

Comments: A.L.Hassett scored 211 in 355 minutes, hitting 17 4's. D.G.Bradman scored 107 in 106 minutes. It was his 22nd century in the calendar year.
Bradman and R.S.Whitington put on 157 for the 2nd wicket.
F.A.Ward and R.A.Hamence added 116 for the 6th wicket.

Two great Australian Test players who both scored heavily in the Sheffield Shield game between Victoria and South Australia. *Left:* Don Bradman, whose 107 in 106 minutes for South Australia was his 22nd century of the calendar year. A few days earlier, Bradman had scored 225 against Queensland. *Right:* Lindsay Hassett, whose 211 for Victoria against Bradman's team came up in 355 minutes at the MCG.

NEW SOUTH WALES v QUEENSLAND

Played at Sydney, December 31, 1938, January 2, 3, 4, 1939.
Toss won by New South Wales.
Queensland won by eight wickets.

NEW SOUTH WALES

J.H.Fitzpatrick	st D.Tallon b Christ	26	c D.Tallon b Ellis	0
A.G.Cheetham	c D.Tallon b Dixon	20	c Christ b Ellis	10
S.G.Barnes	c D.Tallon b Christ	21	c sub b Christ	51
C.M.Solomon	b Ellis	4	c Baker b Ellis	31
V.W.McCaffrey	c D.Tallon b Ellis	4	st D.Tallon b W.Tallon	40
C.G.Pepper	b Dixon	39	c D.Tallon b Dixon	17
*K.C.Gulliver	c D.Tallon b Dixon	31	c D.Tallon b Dixon	40
R.V.James	st D.Tallon b Christ	11	c Christ b W.Tallon	42
†F.A.Easton	b Dixon	0	c D.Tallon b Ellis	0
E.C.S.White	c and b Ellis	44	c D.Tallon b Ellis	17
J.J.Murphy	not out	3	not out	5
Extras	(B 2, LB 4, NB 5)	11	(LB 9, NB 2)	11
Total		**214**		**264**

Fall: 1st inns 1/31, 2/67, 3/75, 4/79, 5/79, 6/137, 7/154, 8/158, 9/175.
2nd inns 1/0, 2/27, 3/89, 4/95, 5/114, 6/191, 7/197, 8/229, 9/229.

QUEENSLAND

*W.A.Brown	c Pepper b Cheetham	95	c Cheetham b Murphy	168
R.E.Rogers	lbw b Cheetham	2		
G.G.Cook	lbw b Barnes	19	(2) run out	93
T.Allen	b Cheetham	5	(3) not out	3
C.D.Hansen	c sub b Fitzpatrick	7		
†D.Tallon	b Gulliver	28	(4) not out	9
G.G.Baker	c Gulliver b Murphy	0		
L.W.T.Tallon	b Barnes	13		
P.L.Dixon	lbw b Barnes	10		
C.P.Christ	run out	0		
J.A.Ellis	not out	7		
Extras	(B 10, LB 1, W 3)	14	(B 3, LB 3)	6
Total		**200**	(2 wickets)	**279**

Fall: 1st inns 1/5, 2/74, 3/83, 4/96, 5/140, 6/145, 7/178, 8/182, 9/184.
2nd inns 1/265, 2/268.

QUEENSLAND	O	M	R	W	O	M	R	W
Ellis	13	1	42	3	21	2	67	5
Cook	9	1	27	0	9	0	41	0
Dixon	15	1	61	4	14	1	59	2
Christ	18	3	60	3	15	1	51	1
W.Tallon	2	0	13	0	8	1	32	2
Baker	-	-	-	-	1	0	3	0

NEW SOUTH WALES	O	M	R	W	O	M	R	W
Murphy	18	5	31	1	16	2	54	1
Cheetham	18	1	52	3	20	4	71	0
White	12	5	18	0	8	3	18	0
Fitzpatrick	9	2	22	1	9	2	18	0
Pepper	3	0	16	0	8	0	38	0
Barnes	10.2	6	20	3	8	0	46	0
Gulliver	8	2	27	1	2	0	14	0
James	-	-	-	-	1	0	5	0
McCaffrey	-	-	-	-	1	0	9	0

Umpires: G.E.Borwick and F.Lyons

Close of play scores. First day: Queensland 18/1 (W.A.Brown 8*, G.G.Cook 4*). **Second day:** New South Wales 76/2 (S.G.Barnes 37*, C.M.Solomon 27*). **Third day:** Queensland 112/0 (W.A.Brown 78*, G.G.Cook 30*).
Comments: D.Tallon equalled the world record with 12 wicketkeeping dismissals, held by E.Pooley, Surrey v Sussex, Oval, 1868. It broke the Australian record of nine dismissals.
W.A.Brown and G.G.Cook created a new opening partnership record for Queensland with 265, beating the 184 made in 1911.
New South Wales continued to field in pouring rain when Queensland still needed 22 to win.

QUEENSLAND v SOUTH AUSTRALIA

Played at Brisbane, on January 7, 9, 10, 11, 1939.
Toss won by Queensland.
South Australia won by ten wickets.

QUEENSLAND

*W.A.Brown	c K.Ridings b Waite	1	lbw b K.Ridings	81
G.G.Cook	b Cotton	22	(6) b K.Ridings	2
T.Allen	c Ward b Cotton	5	(2) b Cotton	5
R.E.Rogers	run out	11	(3) c K.Ridings b Ward	45
†D.Tallon	b Cotton	115	absent hurt	0
C.G.R.Stibe	c Walker b K.Ridings	58	(4) lbw b Scott	23
G.G.Baker	b K.Ridings	78	(5) b K.Ridings	17
L.W.T.Tallon	c Walker b Ward	23	(7) not out	40
P.L.Dixon	b Cotton	2	(8) b K.Ridings	4
J.A.Ellis	b Cotton	1	c K.Ridings b Cotton	5
C.P.Christ	not out	2	(9) run out	1
Extras	(B 6, LB 9, NB 3)	18	(B 4, LB 2 W 1, NB 3)	10
Total		**336**		**233**

Fall: 1st inns 1/4, 2/11, 3/28, 4/163, 5/168, 6/301, 7/322, 8/333, 9/333.
2nd inns 1/13, 2/92, 3/138, 4/179, 5/180, 6/185, 7/189, 8/204, 9/233.

SOUTH AUSTRALIA

K.L.Riding	b Ellis	122	(2) not out	10
R.S.Whitington	c D.Tallon b W.Tallon	125		
*D.G.Bradman	c Christ b W.Tallon	186		
C.L.Badcock	c Rogers b Christ	1	(1) not out	4
R.A.Hamence	c Stibe b Christ	13		
E.J.R.Moyle	c Brown b Cook	46		
†C.W.Walker	c & b W.Tallon	20		
F.A.Ward	b Ellis	18		
H.J.Cotton	st Brown b W.Tallon	2		
J.Scott	not out	5		
M.W.Waite	absent ill	0		
Extras	(B 3, LB 9, W 5, NB 2)	19		
Total		**557**	(No wicket)	**14**

Fall: 1st inns 1/197, 2/306, 3/311, 4/337, 5/469, 6/530, 7/541, 8/551, 9/557.

SOUTH AUSTRALIA	O	M	R	W	O	M	R	W
Cotton	25	5	49	5	16.6	4	49	2
Waite	21	2	86	1				
Scott	23	6	48	0	15	1	55	1
Ward	24	1	108	1	25	6	93	1
K.Ridings	5	1	27	2	6	1	26	4

QUEENSLAND	O	M	R	W	O	M	R	W
Ellis	32.7	1	126	2				
Cook	25	0	101	1				
Dixon	19	2	93	0				
Christ	43	9	110	2				
W.Tallon	20	2	80	4				
Allen	1	0	4	0				
Baker	3	0	24	0	1	1	0	0
Stibe	-	-	-	-	10	9	0	
Rogers	-	-	-	-	0.7	0	5	0

Umpires: K.Fagg and F.J.Bartlett

Close of play scores. First day: Queensland 325/7 (W.Tallon 17*, L.P.Dixon 1*). **Second day:** South Australia 280/1 (K.Ridings 108*, D.G.Bradman 42*). **Third day:** Queensland 73/1 (W.A.Brown 21*, R.E.Rogers 41*).
Comments: D.Tallon's 115 included 12 4's and took 195 minutes.
D.Tallon and G.G.Cook added 135 for the 4th wicket, Tallon scoring 113 of them.
C.G.I.Stibe and G.G.Baker scored 133 in 90 minutes for the 6th wicket.
R.S.Whitington and K.S.Ridings shared an opening partnership of 197.
K.S.Ridings and D.G.Bradman added 109 for the 2nd wicket.
D.G.Bradman's 186 was his fifth successive hundred.
On the third day, W.A.Brown kept wicket in the absence of the injured Tallon.

NEW SOUTH WALES v SOUTH AUSTRALIA

Played at Sydney, on January 14, 16, 17, 18, 1939.
Toss won by New South Wales.
Match drawn; South Australia won on the first innings.

NEW SOUTH WALES

A.G.Cheetham	c Bradman b Grimmett	10	c Moyle b P.Ridings	25
B.V.McCauley	lbw b Grimmett	25	run out	76
S.G.Barnes	b P.Ridings	12	c Cotton b Grimmett	33
*A.G.Chipperfield	c Cotton b Waite	15	st Moyle b Waite	12
C.M.Solomon	c P.Ridings b Ward	34	c P.Ridings b Grimmett	0
C.G.Pepper	c Waite b Grimmett	17	not out	0
V.W.McCaffrey	c P.Riddings b Grimmett	6		
R.V.James	b Cotton	45	(7) not out	4
L.C.Hynes	not out	63		
†S.G.Sismey	c P.Ridings b Cotton	6		
L.J.O'Brien	b Cotton	0		
Extras	(B 8, W 1, NB 4)	13	(B3, LB 3)	6
Total		**246**	**(5 wickets)**	**156**

Fall: 1st inns 1/32, 2/46, 3/50, 4/90, 5/102, 6/118, 7/143, 8/220, 9/246.
2nd inns 1/53, 2/98, 3/133, 4/134, 5/156.

SOUTH AUSTRALIA

K.L.Ridings	lbw b Cheetham	28
R.S.Whitington	lbw b Barnes	59
*†D.G.Bradman	not out	135
F.A.Ward	c O'Brien b Hynes	18
C.L.Badcock	c & b Hynes	98
Extras	(B 1, LB 2, NB 8)	11
Total	(4 wickets, declared)	**349**

Fall: 1st inns 1/76, 2/94, 3/163, 4/349.

†E.J.R.Moyle, P.Ridings, M.G.Waite, H.J.Cotton, C.V.Grimmett and R.A.Hamence did not bat. E.J.R.Moyle was the wicketkeeper in the second innings.

SOUTH AUSTRALIA	O	M	R	W	O	M	R	W
Cotton	10.6	1	44	3	3	0	14	0
Waite	11	1	49	1	8	1	15	1
Grimmett	15	3	53	4	15	1	51	2
P.Ridings	7	1	37	1	5	0	19	1
Ward	7	0	41	1	9	0	51	0
K.Ridings	2	0	9	0				

NEW SOUTH WALES	O	M	R	W
O'Brien	15	0	76	0
Hynes	16.3	0	86	2
Cheetham	23	0	104	1
Pepper	7	0	47	0
Barnes	8	2	25	1

Umpires: G.E.Borwick and F.Lyons

Close of play scores. First day: South Australia 116/2 (D.G.Bradman 22*, F.Ward 4*). **Second day:** No play. **Third day:** No play.

Comments: D.G.Bradman's 135* took 200 minutes and included seven 4's. He equalled the world record of six consecutive centuries, held by C.B.Fry since 1901.
D.G.Bradman and C.L.Badcock put on 186 in 126 mins for the 4th wicket.
S.G.Sismey, aged 19, was making his debut for New South Wales.

NEW SOUTH WALES v VICTORIA

Played at Sydney, January 28, 30, 31, February 1, 1939.
Toss won by New South Wales.
Victoria won by eight wickets.

NEW SOUTH WALES

A.G.Cheetham	c Fleetwood-Smith b Scott	17	lbw b Fleetwood-Smith	16
B.V.McCauley	c Rigg b McCormick	6	c McCormick b Scott	22
S.G.Barnes	c Hassett b Scott	0	run out	48
*A.G.Chipperfield	c Sievers b McCormick	27	lbw b Fleetwood-Smith	25
C.M.Solomon	c Gregory b Scott	8	c Hassett b Scott	49
R.V.James	b Scott	34	b Scott	17
V.W.McCaffrey	b Scott	7	c Sievers b Scott	13
C.G.Pepper	run out	13	b Fleetwood-Smith	5
L.C.Hynes	c McCormick b Scott	0	c Barnett b Scott	6
†S.G.Sismey	b Scott	0	not out	2
F.P.J.Gilmore	not out	1	run out	1
Extras	(LB 2, NB 5)	7	(B 5, LB 4, NB 4)	13
Total		**120**		**217**

Fall: 1st inns 1/22, 2/22, 3/40, 4/52, 5/75, 6/103, 7/104, 8/105, 9/113.
2nd inns 1/41, 2/62, 3/104, 4/129, 5/165, 6/178, 7/206, 8/212, 9/215.

VICTORIA

*K.E.Rigg	b Cheetham	7	c Sismey b Gilmore	5
I.S.Lee	b Hynes	30	not out	43
R.G.Gregory	c Sismey b Gilmore	76	lbw b Pepper	25
A.L.Hassett	lbw b Pepper	82	not out	0
F.W.Sides	lbw b Gilmore	10		
H.H.Oakley	c Sismey b Cheetham	6		
†B.A.Barnett	b Gilmore	7		
M.W.Sievers	c Solomon b Cheetham	17		
R.B.Scott	c Sismey b Hynes	1		
E.L.McCormick	c Gilmore b Hynes	8		
L.O'B.Fleetwood-Smith	not out	2		
Extras	(B 3, LB 6, W 1, NB 3)	13	(B 1, LB 5)	6
Total		**259**	**(2 wickets)**	**79**

Fall: 1st inns 1/28, 2/47, 3/201, 4/214, 5/221, 6/221, 7/233, 8/237, 9/255.
2nd inns 1/16, 2/75.

VICTORIA	O	M	R	W	O	M	R	W
McCormick	6	0	26	2	6	0	37	0
Sievers	7	3	18	0	13.7	0	38	0
Scott	11.7	3	33	7	13	0	46	5
Fleetwood-Smith	10	1	36	0	15	0	83	3

NEW SOUTH WALES	O	M	R	W	O	M	R	W
Gilmore	15	0	50	3	5	0	13	1
Cheetham	18.4	1	60	3	6	0	20	0
Hynes	13	2	57	3				
Barnes	6	0	14	0	3	0	18	0
Chipperfield	4	0	24	0				
James	2	0	11	0				
Pepper	4	0	30	1	3	0	13	1
Solomon					3.2	0	9	0

Umpires: G.E.Borwick and F.Lyons

Close of play scores. First day: Victoria 176/2 (A.L.Hassett 64*, R.G.Gregory 65*). **Second day:** New South Wales 217 all out.

Comments: R.Barry-Scott took 12 wickets for 79 on his debut. This included a spell of four wickets for no runs before lunch on the first day.
A.L.Hassett and R.G.Gregory added 154 for the 3rd wicket.

QUEENSLAND v VICTORIA

Played at Brisbane, on February 4, 6, 7, 8, 1939.
Toss won by Victoria.
Queensland won by an innings and 11 runs.

VICTORIA

*K.E.Rigg	st D.Tallon b Christ 46	c Christ b W.Tallon 54
I.S.Lee	c D.Tallon b J.Ellis 9	lbw b W.Tallon 64
R.G.Gregory	b W.Tallon 27	b Cook 45
A.L.Hassett	b Christ............139	c sub b W.Tallon 9
F.W.Sides	lbw b Ellis.............40	c D.Tallon b W.Tallon 0
H.H.Oakley	st D.Tallon b Cook 40	st D.Tallon b W.Tallon 7
†B.A.Barnett	c D.Tallon b Ellis 6	b Cook 22
M.W.Sievers	st D.Tallon b W.Tallon...1	absent 0
R.B.Scott	c D.Tallon b Dixon 27	(8) lbw b Dixon 2
E.L.McCormick	not out 3	(9) b Dixon 0
L.O'B.Fleetwood-Smith	st D.Tallon b Christ.......1	(10) not out 9
Extras	(LB 6, NB 3) 9	(B 1, LB 2, NB 1) 4
Total	**348**	**216**

Fall: 1st inns 1/22, 2/61, 3/123, 4/210, 5/277, 6/288, 7/289, 8/331, 9/345.
2nd inns 1/117, 2/132, 3/152, 4/153, 5/165, 6/203, 7/206, 8/207, 9/216.

QUEENSLAND

*W.A.Brown	lbw b Fleetwood-Smith	215
G.G.Cook	b McCormick	44
†T.Allen	lbw b Gregory	79
R.E.Rogers	lbw b McCormick	30
D.Tallon	c Lee b Gregory	44
C.G.R.Stibe	b Scott	0
G.G.Baker	c Gregory b McCormick	97
L.W.T.Tallon	not out	37
Extras	(B 12, LB 6, W 4, NB 7)	29
Total	**(7 wickets, declared)**	**575**

Fall: 1st inns 1/94, 2/259, 3/326, 4/394, 5/396, 6/491, 7/575.

P.L.Dixon, C.P.Christ and J.A.Ellis did not bat.

QUEENSLAND	O	M	R	W	O	M	R	W
Ellis	23	1	64	3				
Cook	10	0	41	1	15	4	35	2
Dixon	19	0	81	1	11.5	1	38	2
Christ	21.1	6	48	3	23	3	62	0
W.Tallon	25	4	87	2	21	1	77	5
Baker	5	0	18	0				

VICTORIA	O	M	R	W
McCormick	34.3	2	105	3
Scott	33	1	161	1
Sievers	10	5	15	0
Fleetwood-Smith	34	3	146	1
Gregory	15	0	96	2
Hassett	6	0	23	0

Umpires: G.W.Given and J.A.Scott

Close of play scores. First day: Victoria 289/7 (A.L.Hassett 114*). **Second day:** Queensland 168/1 (W.A.Brown 76*, T.Allen 34*). **Third day:** Queensland 575/7 (L.W.T.Tallon 37*).

Comments: D.Tallon equalled the world record of seven dismissals in an innings by a wicketkeeper, the first Australian 'keeper to do so.
A.L.Hassett's 139 included 11 4's and took 302 minutes.
W.A.Brown was the first batsman to pass 1,000 runs for the season.
W.A.Brown and T.Allen added 165 for the 2nd wicket.
K.E.Riggs and I.S.Lee had an opening partnership of 117 in Victoria's 2nd innings.

SOUTH AUSTRALIA v VICTORIA

Played at Adelaide, on February 24, 25, 27, 28, 1939.
Toss won by South Australia.
Match drawn.

VICTORIA

*K.E.Rigg	c Horsell b P.Ridings	78
I.S.Lee	b Cotton	13
R.G.Gregory	b Cotton	33
A.L.Hassett	b Ward	102
F.W.Sides	c Cotton b Ward	10
G.E.Tamblyn	lbw b Ward	0
†B.A.Barnett	run out	51
R.B.Scott	run out	2
E.L.McCormick	c Cotton b Ward	14
F.L.O.Thorn	c Horsell b Grimmett	3
L.O'B.Fleetwood-Smith	not out	1
Extras	(B 3, LB 5, NB 6)	14
Total		**321**

Fall: 1st inns 1/32, 2/98, 3/160, 4/182, 5/182, 6/277, 7/285, 8/304, 9/313.

SOUTH AUSTRALIA

R.S.Whitington	b Scott	18
K.L.Ridings	lbw b Thorn	14
*D.G.Bradman	c Fleetwood-Smith b Thorn	5
C.L.Badcock	c Lee b Scott	14
R.A.Hamence	lbw b Fleetwood-Smith	35
M.G.Waite	not out	63
P.L.Ridings	lbw b McCormick	12
†J.A.J.Horsell	lbw b F.Smith	29
F.A.Ward	not out	2
Extras	(B 6, LB 2, NB 7)	15
Total	**(7 wickets)**	**207**

Fall: 1st inns 1/30, 2/38, 3/42, 4/78, 5/113, 6/135, 7/198.
C.V.Grimmett and H.J.Cotton did not bat.

SOUTH AUSTRALIA	O	M	R	W
Cotton	23	3	73	2
Waite	25	5	65	0
P.Ridings	12	1	55	1
Grimmett	24	4	57	1
Ward	19.4	1	57	4

VICTORIA	O	M	R	W
McCormick	16	2	45	1
Scott	15	1	49	2
Thorn	16	2	51	2
Fleetwood-Smith	14	1	34	2
Gregory	2	0	13	0

Umpires: J.D.Scott and A.G.Jenkins.

Close of play scores. First day: Victoria 284/6. **Second day:** South Australia 207/7 (M.G.Waite 63*, F.Ward 2*).

Comments: Victoria were put in to bat, rain prevented any play on the last two days, probably depriving Victoria of a first-innings lead, which would have given them the Championship.

AUSTRALIAN XI v THE REST
(D.G.Bradman's Team v K.E.Rigg's Team)

Played at Melbourne, on December 9, 10, 12, 13, 1938.
Toss won by The Rest.
Match drawn.

THE REST

*K.E.Rigg	lbw b Fleetwood-Smith	48	c Hassett b O'Reilly 71
I.S.Lee	run out	12	st Barnett b Fleetwood-Smith 27
R.G.Gregory	lbw b Fleetwood-Smith	14	lbw b Fleetwood-Smith ...32
J.A.Ledward	lbw b O'Reilly	11	c sub b Fingleton 85
S.G.Barnes	lbw b O'Reilly	63	lbw b Waite 4
†D.Tallon	c McCabe b O'Reilly	7	b Hassett 23
M.W.Sievers	lbw b O'Reilly	0	not out 44
E.H.Bromley	c Brown b Fleetwood-Smith	34	b O'Reilly 17
L.E.Nagel	b Fleetwood-Smith	6	b Bradman 11
G.Eyres	c & b O'Reilly	1	
C.P.Christ	not out	6	
Extras	(B 6, LB 2, W 4, NB 1)	13	(B 3, LB 4, NB 3) 10
Total		**215**	(8 wickets) **324**

Fall: 1st inns 1/35, 2/63, 3/79, 4/112, 5/177, 6/201, 7/201, 8/203, 9/209.
2nd inns 1/74, 2/116, 3/123, 4/178, 5/207, 6/257, 7/305, 8/324.

AUSTRALIAN XI

J.H.W.Fingleton	c Sievers b Eyres	23
W.A.Brown	c & b Christ	67
*D.G.Bradman	b Nagel	118
S.J.McCabe	c Lee b Nagel	105
A.L.Hassett	run out	12
C.L.Badcock	not out	51
M.G.Waite	b Sievers	28
†B.A.Barnett	lbw b Sievers	0
W.J.O'Reilly	c Christ b Bromley	0
L.O'B.Fleetwood-Smith	b Sievers	2
E.L.McCormick	c Gregory b Bromley	3
Extras	(B 11, LB 6)	17
Total		**426**

Fall: 1st inns 1/48, 2/138, 3/301, 4/332, 5/353, 6/409, 7/409, 8/412, 9/419.

AUSTRALIAN XI	O	M	R	W	O	M	R	W
McCormick	10	0	39	0	14	0	58	0
Waite	7	2	9	0	13	2	47	1
O'Reilly	18.5	2	75	5	18	2	54	2
Fleetwood-Smith	21	2	79	4	19	2	93	2
Hassett	-	-	-	-	3	0	26	1
Fingleton	-	-	-	-	2	0	18	1
Brown	-	-	-	-	1	0	8	0
Badcock	-	-	-	-	1	0	10	0
Bradman	-	-	-	-	0.1	0	0	1

THE REST	O	M	R	W
Eyres	23	2	81	1
Sievers	15	3	53	3
Nagel	26	4	93	2
Christ	29	4	104	1
Bromley	11.7	0	53	2
Barnes	1	1	0	0
Gregory	3	0	25	0

Umpires: A.N.Barlow and G.A.Browne

Close of play scores. First day: The Rest 151/4 (S.G.Barnes 51*, E.H.Bromley 3*). **Second day:** Australian XI 220/2 (D.G.Bradman 82*, S.J.McCabe 39*). **Third day:** The Rest 23/0 (I.S.Lee 10*, K.E.Rigg 12*).
Comments: There was only three hours play on the first day, the game being interrupted by a violent dust storm.
D.G.Bradman hit 12 4's in his 118, which took 210 minutes.
S.J.McCabe's 105 took 140 minutes and included 11 4's.
Bradman and McCabe added 163 for the 3rd wicket.
The match was to celebrate the centenary of the Melbourne Cricket Club.

TASMANIA v VICTORIA

Played at Launceston, on December 26, 27, 28, 1938.
Toss won by Victoria.
Match drawn.

VICTORIA

H.Dowsley	lbw b Murfett	16	
*H.H.Oakley	hit wkt b Putman	60	
K.R.Miller	st Gardiner b Putman	4	(2) not out 7
D.H.Fothergill	c Putman b Oakes	39	
P.J.Beames	not out	226	
I.W.Johnson	lbw b Pearsall	23	
D.J.A.Fitzmaurice	c Putman b Murfett	22	(3) not out 8
†E.A.Baker	c Putman b Jeffrey	3	(1) b Oakes 0
G.S.Meikle	lbw b Putman	28	
F.L.O.Thorn	b Oakes	0	
R.B.Scott	not out	13	
Extras	(B 1, LB 2)	3	
Total	(9 wickets, declared)	**437**	(1 wicket) **15**

Fall: 1st inns 1/61, 2/76, 3/94, 4/138, 5/188, 6/260, 7/265, 8/342, 9/347.
2nd inns 1/2.

TASMANIA

*R.O.G.Morrisby	b Scott	4
R.V.Thomas	b Scott	15
E.H.Smith	c Scott b Dowsley	7
M.J.Combes	b Johnson	28
S.W.L.Putman	c Miller b Thorn	9
C.L.Jeffrey	lbw b Scott	46
A.L.Pearsall	lbw b Thorn	43
†J.Gardiner	b Fitzmaurice	64
J.I.Murfett	hit wkt b Scott	20
D.H.Thollar	not out	8
C.J.G.Oakes	lbw b Scott	2
Extras	(B 8, LB 1, NB 3)	12
Total		**258**

Fall: 1st inns 1/5, 2/28, 33/28, 4/47, 5/90, 6/133, 7/224, 8/242, 9/255, 10/258.

TASMANIA	O	M	R	W	O	M	R	W
Oakes	15	0	102	2	2	0	6	1
Thomas	8	1	62	0	3	1	7	0
Putman	17	0	106	3				
Murfett	7	0	54	2	1	0	2	0
Thollar	8	0	44	0				
Pearsall	6	0	34	1				
Jeffrey	5	0	32	1				

VICTORIA	O	M	R	W
Scott	21	2	62	5
Dowsley	5	0	26	1
Thorn	15	2	44	2
Meikle	12	0	58	0
Johnson	8	1	21	1
Fitzmaurice	6	0	35	1

Umpires: M.Conway and Sayer.

Close of play scores. First day: Victoria 437/9 (P.J.Beames 226*, R.B.Scott 13*). **Second day:** No play (rain).

Comments: P.J.Beames' 226* was made in 215 minutes, hitting one 6 and 28 4's. He was recalled by the Tasmanian captain, when given out lbw when on 93.

TASMANIA v VICTORIA

Played at Hobart, on December 30, 31, 1939.
Toss won by Tasmania.
Victoria won by ten wickets.

VICTORIA

*R.O.G.Morrisby	c Beames b Scott	70	b Johnson	21
R.V.Thomas	c Fothergill b Scott	67	c Dowsley b Johnson	42
A.L.Pearsall	b Dempster	42	run out	27
C.L.Jeffrey	not out	80	c Baker b Meikle	53
S.W.L.Putman	b Thorn	28	b Thorn	7
G.T.H.James	b Thorn	6	c Dowsley b Thorn	15
E.H.Smith	b Thorn	9	c Oakley b Thorn	7
†J.Gardiner	c Oakley b Thorn	0	b Thorn	5
J.N.W.Nicolson	retired hurt	0	absent injured	0
J.I.Murfett	c Oakley b Thorn	1	(9) not out	11
J.Tringrove	c Beames b Scott	1	(10) c Meikle b Thorn	3
Extras	(B 3, LB 7, NB 1)	11	(B 3, LB 2)	5
Total		**315**		**196**

Fall: 1st inns 1/138, 2/144, 3/239, 4/285, 5/291, 6/312, 7/312, 8/313, 9/315.
2nd inns 1/59, 2/68, 3/126, 4/135, 5/169, 6/171, 7/181, 8/182, 9/196.

VICTORIA

*H.H.Oakley	c & b Murfett	162
H.Dowsley	c Murfett b Pearsall	64
K.R.Miller	lbw b Pearsall	3
P.J.Beames	not out	169
D.H.Fothergill	c Gardiner b James	0
I.W.Johnson	not out	88
R.A.Dempster	(1) not out	12
†E.A.Baker	(2) not out	11
Extras	(B 3, LB 2)	5
Total	(4 wickets, declared) **491**	(No wicket) **23**

Fall: 1st inns 1/157, 2/168, 3/281, 4/282.
G.S.Meikle, F.L.O.Thorn, R.B.Scott did not bat.

VICTORIA	O	M	R	W	O	M	R	W
Scott	27.1	4	79	3	10	0	60	0
Dempster	11	2	39	1	3	2	10	0
Thorn	23	1	111	5	19.7	1	74	5
Meikle	9	0	35	0	9	0	24	1
Fothergill	4	0	13	0				
Dowsley	3	0	16	0				
Johnson	4	1	11	1	7	0	14	2
Beames	-	-	-	-	2	0	9	0

TASMANIA	O	M	R	W	O	M	R	W
James	13	2	55	1	1.4	0	11	0
Murfett	17	0	96	1	2	0	12	0
Tringrove	14	0	111	0				
Putman	11	0	74	0				
Pearsall	14	1	94	2				
Thomas	8	0	56	0				

Umpires: T.W.Barnes and M.Hansen.

Close of play scores. First day: Tasmania 308/5 (C.L.Jeffrey 77*, E.H.Smith 7*). **Second day:** Victoria 491/9 (P.J.Beames 169*, I.W.Johnson 88*).

Comments: P.J.Beames scored 169*in 160 minutes, hitting one 6 and 21 4's.
H.H.Oakley scored 162 in 175 minutes, hitting 15 4's.
In Victoria's innings, H.H.Oakley and H.Dowsley made 157 for the 1st wicket.
P.J.Beames and I.W.Johnson put on 113 for the 3rd wicket.
In Tasmania's innings, R.O.G.Morrisby and R.V.Thomas scored 138 for the 1st wicket.
P.J.Beames and I.W.Johnson shared an unfinished 5th wicket partnership of 209 in 105 minutes.
J.N.W.Nicholson took no further part in the match after being struck on the head by a bouncer from R.B.Scott.

WESTERN AUSTRALIA v VICTORIA

Played at Perth, on March 9, 10, 11, 1939.
Toss won by Western Australia.
Match drawn.

WESTERN AUSTRALIA

C.W.T.MacGill	lbw b McCormick	0	retired hurt	6
A.E.Read	c Baker b Thorn	41	c Baker b Hassett	24
*W.T.Rowlands	c Baker b McCormick	18		
A.D.Watt	b McCormick	3	b Hassett	19
K.S.Jeffreys	c Miller b McCormick	1	(6) c Fleetwood-Smith b Ring	33
A.E.O.Barras	c Fleetwood-Smith b Thorn	54	(5) st Baker b Thorn	95
M.Inverarity	not out	68		
†O.I.Lovelock	b Ring	51	(7) not out	15
A.G.Zimbulis	lbw b Ring	1	(3) c Miller b McCormick	21
G.Eyres	c Miller b Ring	1		
R.L.Mills	c Baker b Thorn	3		
Extras	(B 6, LB 4, NB 6)	16	(B 5, LB 1, W 2, NB 4)	12
Total		**257**	(5 wickets, declared)	**225**

Fall: 1st inns 1/0, 2/30, 3/36, 4/44, 5/119, 6/136, 7/229, 8/231, 9/241.
2nd inns 1/40, 2/76, 3/77, 4/174, 5/225.

VICTORIA

K.E.Rigg	c MacGill b Eyres	6		
I.S.Lee	c Lovelock b MacGill	12		
A.L.Hassett	b Eyres	8		
F.W.Sides	b MacGill	121	(5) not out	13
G.E.Tamblyn	b Eyres	1	(1) b Mills	4
K.R.Miller	lbw b Eyres	1	(4) not out	17
†E.A.Baker	c Barras b Eyres	19	(2) lbw b Barras	24
D.T.Ring	b Jeffreys	1	(3) b Watt	13
E.L.McCormick	b MacGill	13		
F.L.O.Thorn	c & b MacGill	30		
L.O.Fleetwood-Smith	not out	0		
Extras	(B 9, LB 5)	14	(B 7)	7
Total		**226**	(3 wickets)	**78**

Fall: 1st inns 1/8, 2/32, 3/38, 4/40, 5/42, 6/98, 7/116, 8/137, 9/215.
2nd inns 1/9, 2/31, 3/61.

VICTORIA	O	M	R	W	O	M	R	W
McCormick	15	3	48	4	12	2	43	1
Thorn	20	1	68	3	13.2	2	46	1
Fleetwood-Smith	14	2	59	0	6	0	37	0
Ring	19	2	66	3	11	2	45	1
Hassett	-	-	-	-	9	0	42	2

WESTERN AUSTRALIA	O	M	R	W	O	M	R	W
Eyres	19	4	47	5	5	3	14	0
Mills	7	2	32	0	4	0	6	1
MacGill	14.4	2	45	4				
Zimbulis	9	0	50	0				
Jeffreys	6	0	38	1				
Watt	-	-	-	-	6	0	29	1
Barras	-	-	-	-	5	1	22	1

Umpires: F.R.Buttsworth and J.P.Robbins

Comments: G.E.Tamblyn's 100 was made in 190 minutes.
A.L.Hassett scored 103 in 87 minutes, including three 6's and 12 4's. He reached his 100 with one 6.
A.E.O.Barras scored 113 on his debut in first-class cricket, scoring ten 4's. Barras and M.Inverarity added 112 for the 6th wicket.

WESTERN AUSTRALIA v VICTORIA

Played at Perth, on March 4, 6, 7, 1939.
Toss won by Victoria.
Match drawn.

VICTORIA

*K.E.Rigg	c MacGill b Halcombe....6	c Read b Zimbulis	52
I.S.Lee	b Halcombe 1	b MacGill	1
A.L.Hassett	lbw b Halcombe 14	st Lovelock b Jeffreys	103
K.R.Miller	c Barras b Zimbulis 38	(5) lbw b Zimbulis	55
†E.A.Baker	st Lovelock b Zimbulis....7	(6) c & b Zimbulis	17
G.E.Tamblyn	b Halcombe 100	(4) b Jeffreys	9
D.T.Ring	b MacGill 26	c Zimbulis b MacGill	25
R.B.Scott	lbw b Zimbulis 49	absent injured	0
E.L.McCormick	b Halcombe 8	(8) b MacGill	4
F.L.O.Thorn	c Read b Zimbulis.........1	(9) not out	11
L.O.Fleetwood-Smith	not out.....................0	(10) c Mills b Zimbulis	23
Extras	(B 9, LB 3, W 1, NB 3)...16	(B 6, LB 3, NB 1)	10
Total	....**266**		.........**310**

Fall: 1st inns 1/5, 2/9, 3/38, 4/123, 5/146, 6/196, 7/212, 8/249, 9/250.
2nd inns 1/6, 2/87, 3/91, 4/172, 5/210, 6/268, 7/269, 8/279, 9/310.

WESTERN AUSTRALIA

C.W.T.MacGill	c Miller b Ring	48
A.E.Read	c Hassett b Ring	13
*W.T.Rowlands	c & b Ring	6
A.D.Watt	c Baker b Ring	54
K.S.Jeffreys	c Baker b McCormick	16
A.E.O.Barras	c Tamblyn b Ring	113
M.Inverarity	b Thorn	38
†O.I.Lovelock	not out	71
A.G.Zimbulis	st Baker b Ring	2
R.L.Mills	b Fleetwood-Smith	1
R.A.Halcombe	(did not bat)	
Extras	(B 27, LB 5, W 2)	34
Total	(9 wickets, declared)	....**396**

Fall: 1st inns 1/58, 2/78, 3/91, 4/128, 5/171, 6/283, 7/380, 8/393, 9/396.

WESTERN AUSTRALIA	O	M	R	W	O	M	R	W
Halcombe	17	1	40	5				
Mills	17	3	55	0	5	0	33	0
MacGill	10	2	34	1	12	1	77	3
Zimbulis	19.6	0	121	4	12.7	0	108	4
Jeffreys	-	-	-	-	11	0	56	2
Inverarity	-	-	-	-	4	0	18	0
Rowlands	-	-	-	-	3	0	8	0

VICTORIA	O	M	R	W
McCormick	18	1	60	1
Scott	9.4	0	25	0
Thorn	19	5	84	1
Ring	23	0	97	6
Fleetwood-Smith	18.7	3	96	1

Umpires: F.R.Buttsworth and J.P.Robbins.

Close of play scores. First day: Western Australia 5-0 (C.W.T.MacGill 1*, A.E.Read 2*). **Second day:** Western Australia 276/5 (A.E.O.Barras 70*, M.Inverarity 35*).

Comments: G.E.Tamblyn's 100 was made in 190 minutes.
A.L.Hassett scored 103 in 87 minutes, including three 6's and 12 4's. He reached his 100 with a 6.
A.E.O.Barras scored 113 on his debut in first-class cricket, scoring ten 4's. Barras and M.Inverarity added 112 for the 6th wicket.

The First-Class Season in India 1938-39

NO overseas touring sides visited the Indian sub-continent during the season, so cricket interest centred on the long-established Bombay Tournament and the relatively new Cricket Championship of India, known as the Ranji Trophy.

The Bombay Tournament was arranged for the first time as a Pentangular Competition. The Hindus, who had fallen out with the organizers over the question of allocation of seats at the Brabourne Stadium, had been placated and they therefore joined the Muslims, Parsees, Europeans and The Rest, the last named under the leadership of Mr De Mello, formerly the Secretary to the Board of Control.

The Rest met the Hindus and if it had not been for some brilliant batting from Lala Amarnath, they might have run the Hindus close. As it was, Amarnath hit 241 in his best style and The Rest lost by an innings. The Europeans had an unexpected victory over the Parsees when Philpot-Brookes turned the game with a second innings 143 at a run-a-minute.

In the semi-final the Europeans met the Muslims and the left-arm bowling of Orton captured seven wickets, but Mushtaq Ali batted well and the Muslims won. In the Final, the Hindus lacked both Amarnath and Merchant and the rest of their batsmen found the speed of Nissar too much. Muslims built up a commanding first-innings lead and though there was consistent batting in the Hindus second innings it was not enough to deny the Muslims the tournament.

Twenty-one sides entered the Ranji Trophy competition: Bengal & Assam, Bihar, United Provinces, Central India, Western Indian States, Maharashtra, Gujarat, Nawanagar, Baroda, Bombay, Sind, Southern Punjab, Rajputana, Delhi & District, NWFP, Army, Northern India, Hyderabad, Mysore, CP & Berar and Madras.

Bengal won the title, beating Southern Punjab in the Final. The winners owed their success to the strength of their batting and their high scoring meant that they won three out of four matches by an innings. Bihar were overwhelmed in the first round, whilst Central India fared little better in the second. Against Madras, Bengal hit 515, with Malcolm making an undefeated 181. The third game, against Southern Punjab was much closer, in that Wazir Ali hit 222 for Punjab giving a first-innings lead of 106, but Malcolm made 91 in Bengal's second innings and Miller 85, so Punjab began the last innings needing 313 for victory — they could muster only 134.

Sind played well in their matches. Captained by M.J.Mobed, they beat Bombay, who had won the title in 1935 and 1936, and then defeated Nawanagar, due to a sparkling 203 by J.Naoomal. Both these victories were, however, attained on first-innings lead. Sind met disaster in their third match against Southern Punjab, being bowled out in the second innings for 23, Nissar taking 6 for 17 and Amarnath returning the remarkable analysis of 7-5-2-4.

Southern Punjab were, by common consent, regarded as the strongest side in the Ranji Trophy, but they had never won the competition. For the 1938-39 matches the side had been reinforced by the inclusion of Nissar, Wazir Ali, Nazir Ali and Amir Elahi. Nazir hit 166 and Amir Elahi took 6 for 68 in their first win over Rajputana. Despite an excellent hundred by Holdsworth, they then defeated North West Frontier Province by an innings, Amarnath taking 10 for 53 in the match. Northern India were beaten by nine wickets and, as already pointed out, Sind were beaten, but Southern Punjab failed in the Final.

In terms of statistics, Southern Punjab had the best two bowlers, Amarnath with 26 wickets at 12.34 each and Amir Elahi with 28 at 24.00 being the only two to claim over 20 victims. Leading run scorer was J.Naoomal, with 418 at an average of 104.50; Wazir Ali came second with 370 (average 92.50) and B.W.Malcolm third with 302 (average 151.00).

The Madras Presidency match was a low-scoring affair. The outstanding performance was by J.Spitteler, who took nine wickets for the Europeans, but he was still on the losing side — the Europeans had not won since 1933-34.

The Lahore Tournament was revived after a lapse of eight years but rain washed out one game. C.S.Nayudu took 7 for 21 to dismiss the Muslims for 79 in their second innings and the Hindus went on to victory by four wickets.

The Moin-ud-Dowlah Gold Cup Tournament was not played due to the death of the Nawab — in fact it was not played again until 1948-49.

There was no first-class cricket in Ceylon in 1938-39, although the former Middlesex cricketer, Dr D.H.Gunasekera captained a Ceylon team to Malaya. Five matches were played without defeat, the principal fixture being against All-Malaya at Singapore, which was won by 127 runs.

No major touring sides visited India or Ceylon during the season.

K.A.D.Naoroji, captain of the Bihar XI and president of the Bihar Cricket Association. Naoroji, who was now in his mid-40s, played his early cricket at Cambridge University.

Shute Bannerjee was then a promising young fast bowler and useful tail-end batsman for Bihar. In 1948 he became the first Bengali to play for India when he appeared against the West Indies. Bannerjee captained Bihar from 1942 to 1958.

BOMBAY PENTANGULAR

All matches played at Brabourne Stadium, Bombay, between 23 November to 5 December 1938.

EUROPEANS v PARSEES

Played at Brabourne Stadium, November 23, 24, 25 1938.
Toss won by Europeans.
Europeans won by 19 runs.

EUROPEANS

C.E.Inder	b Kalapesi ...2	c Meherhomji b Palsetia 22
R.C.Summerhayes	c Kalapesi b Palsetia ...12	c Palsetia b Havewalla ...0
R.F.Moss	st K.Meherhomji b Havewalla...28	c Meherhomji b Palsetia 15
G.D.Chetwode	b Havewalla ...6	lbw b Palsetia ...1
A.F.Wensley	lbw b Havewalla ...23	c M.Patel b Palsetia ...59
J.E.Tew	b Palsetia ...0	b Nariman ...71
Lt.Philpot-Brookes	st Meherhomji b Jamshedji 23	b Palsetia ...143
P.M.Dowson	c Palsetia b Jamshedji 22	b Palsetia ...10
†K.S.H.Wilson	b Havewalla ...0	c Canteenwalla b Havewalla 2
*H.L.Murray	c Meherhomji b Jamshedji 13	lbw b Palsetia ...10
C.T.Orton	not out ...13	not out ...5
Extras	...0	(LB 2, NB 4, W 11) ...7
Total	**...142**	**...345**

Fall: 1st inns 1/7, 2/27, 3/42, 4/49, 5/50, 6/77, 7/105, 8/105, 9/119.
2nd inns 1/0, 2/27, 3/33, 4/44, 5/144, 6/193, 7/242, 8/249, 9/261.

PARSEES

†K.R.Meherhomji	lbw b Dowson ...14	c Summerhayes b Wensley 66
F.K.Nariman	b Wensley ...8	b Murray ...0
N.F.Canteenwalla	c Tew b Wensley ...17	c Philpot-Brookes b Wensley ...32
E.B.Aibara	c Moss b Dowson ...51	c Wilson b Murray ...29
S.M.H.Colah	lbw b Inder ...6	lbw b Murray ...37
D.R.Havewalla	c Dowson b Wensley ...0	run out ...9
J.B.Khot	b Murray ...92	not out ...34
*B.K.Kalapesi	c Summerhayes b Murray ...34	lbw b Murray ...2
J.B.Patel	c Moss b Murray ...10	c Dowson b Wensley ...1
J.Palsetia	b Murray ...0	c Orton b Murray ...4
R.J.D.Jamshedji	not out ...0	c Inder b Dowson ...10
Extras	...0	(B 7, LB 2) ...9
Total	**...235**	**...233**

Fall: 1st inns 1/19, 2/22, 3/62, 4/70, 5/71, 6/110, 7/221, 8/226, 9/226.
2nd inns 1/0, 2/91, 3/107, 4/164, 5/174, 6/174, 7/185, 8/189, 9/201.

PARSEES	O	M	R	W	O	M	R	W
Kalapesi	14	2	20	1	1	0	7	0
Palsetia	14	1	24	2	24.2	8	109	7
Havewalla	14	1	52	4	29	4	126	2
Jamshedji	9.3	3	46	3	9	0	41	0
Patel	-	-	-	-	11	4	18	0
Khot	-	-	-	-	4	1	15	0
Nariman	-	-	-	-	2	0	22	1

EUROPEANS	O	M	R	W	O	M	R	W
Murray	15.2	5	35	4	24	7	61	4
Dowson	24	4	74	1	10.2	2	33	1
Wensley	25	5	56	2	25	3	84	4
Inder	14	4	36	1	7	1	32	0
Orton	8	1	34	0	3	0	14	0

Umpires: J.Birtwistle & D.K.Naik

Close of play scores. First day: Parsees 172/6 (J.B.Khot 58*, B.K.Kalapesi 18*).
Second day: Europeans 319/9 (Lt.Philpot-Brookes 119*, C.T.Orton 3*).

Comments: Lt.Philpot-Brookes scored 143 in 104 minutes. He hit three 6's and 19 4's.
J.E.Tew and A.F.Wensley added 100 for the 5th wicket in 75 minutes.
J.B.Khot and B.K.Kalapesi put on 111 for the 7th wicket in the 1st innings.
It was the Europeans' first victory in this tournament for ten years.

HINDUS v THE REST

Played at Brabourne Stadium, November 26, 28 1938.
Toss won by Hindus.
Hindus won by an innings and 16 runs.

HINDUS

D.D.Hindlekar	b De Mello ...1
K.Bose	lbw b Harris ...21
M.H.Mankad	b J.Harris ...32
C.K.Nayudu	c Shaw b Harris ...16
L.Amarnath	lbw b Hazare ...241
V.M.Merchant	retired hurt ...71
L.P.Jai	b D'Avoine ...103
L.Amar Singh	b Harris ...6
C.S.Nayudu	not out ...42
R.B.Nimbalkar	not out ...4
Extras	(B 5, LB 9, NB 9) ...23
Total	**(7 wickets, declared) ...560**

Fall: 1st inns 1/5, 2/53, 3/58, 4/77, 5/471, 6/492, 7/547.
S.N.Banerjee did not bat.

THE REST

M.Cohen	c Hindlekar b Amar Singh 0	c Hindlekar b Bannerjee ...9
J.O.Gonsalves	lbw b Amar Singh ...6	lbw b Nimbalkar ...35
M.Bhaskar	b C.K.Nayudu ...88	c sub b Bannerjee ...6
V.S.Hazare	lbw b C.S.Nayudu ...14	c Nimbalkar b C.S.Nayudu 49
P.A.D'Avoine	b C.S.Nayudu ...0	b C.S.Nayudu ...13
P.C.D.McCarthy	b C.S.Nayudu ...37	lbw b C.S.Nayudu ...0
J.Harris	b C.S.Nayudu ...100	c C.K.Nayudu b C.S.Nayudu 43
P.P.Fernandes	b Amir Singh ...12	run out ...21
E.Shaw	c Nimbalkar b C.S.Nayudu 53	c Mankad b C.K.Nayudu ...9
A.S.De Mello	not out ...13	run out ...0
A.C.Pereira	run out ...6	not out ...0
Extras	(B 5, LB 13, NB 2) ...20	(B 1, LB 4, NB 1) ...6
Total	**...349**	**...195**

Fall: 1st inns 1/1, 2/20, 3/48, 4/48, 5/129, 6/174, 7/215, 8/330, 9/331.
2nd inns 1/12, 2/33, 3/69, 4/70, 5/94, 6/155, 7/164, 8/179, 9/179.

THE REST	O	M	R	W				
Harris	42	10	134	4				
De Mello	33	5	76	1				
Shaw	11	4	47	0				
Hazare	34	8	94	1				
Pereira	24	1	116	0				
Gonsalves	5	1	11	0				
Bhaskar	10	0	35	0				
D'Avoine	5	0	24	1				

HINDUS	O	M	R	W	O	M	R	W
Bannerjee	10	3	19	0	9	1	21	2
Amar Singh	27	6	83	3	4	0	9	0
Amarnath	6	1	28	0	9	3	16	0
C.S.Nayudu	29	5	99	5	20.4	3	73	4
C.K.Nayudu	18.3	2	82	1	9	3	35	1
M.H.Mankad	5	0	18	0				
Nimbalkar	-	-	-	-	12	2	35	1

Umpires: Vali Ahmed & N.A.Dubash

Close of play scores. First day: Hindus 336/4 (L.Amarnath 139*, L.P.Jai 42*).
Second day: The Rest 209/6 (J.Harris 42*, P.P.Fernandes 9*).

Comments: L.Amarnath scored 241 in 360 minutes, hitting 26 4's. It was the highest individual score in this tournament.
L.P.Jai scored 103 in 145 minutes, hitting seven 4's.
L.Amarnath and V.M.Merchant put on 197 for the 5th wicket.
L.Amarnath and L.P.Jai added a further 197 for the 6th wicket.
J.Harris made a 100 in 145 minutes, hitting 11 4's. J.Harris and E.Shaw put on 115 for the 8th wicket in the 1st innings.

MUSLIMS v EUROPEANS

Played at Brabourne Stadium, November 29, 30 and December 1, 1938.
Toss won by Muslims.
Muslims won by 97 runs.

MUSLIMS

S.M.Kadri	c Tew b Dowson 37	c Wilson b Dowson 19	
S.Mushtaq Ali	c Tew b Orton 157	c Philpot-Brookes b Dowson 25	
Abbas Khan	st Wilson b Wensley......8	lbw b Orton 10	
S.Wazir Ali	c Wilson b Orton..........0	lbw b Wensley..........112	
S.Nazir Ali	lbw b Orton 0	c Summerhayes b Wensley 47	
Dilwar Hussain	lbw b Orton 9	lbw b Wensley 1	
Amir Elahi	not out 23	c Summerhayes b Wensley 0	
Saeed Ahmed	lbw b Orton 3	b Orton 12	
K.C.Ibrahim	lbw b Orton 0	c Wilson b Murray 32	
S.Mubarak Ali	b Wensley...........0	b Murray 1	
Mohamed Nissar	b Orton 0	not out 2	
Extras	(B 9) 9	(B9, LB 2) 11	
Total	....................**246**	....................**272**	

Fall: 1st inns 1/155, 2/206, 3/206, 4/206, 5/214, 6/228, 7/232, 8/236, 9/241.
2nd inns 1/35, 2/56, 3/64, 4/153, 5/156, 6/156, 7/186, 8/265, 9/269.

EUROPEANS

C.E.Inder	b Nazir Ali 5	c & b Amir Elahi 11	
R.C.Summerhayes	lbw b Mubarak Ali 31	b Saeed Ahmed 54	
P.M.Dowson	c Wazir Ali b Amir Elahi 20	b Saeed Ahmed 50	
R.F.Moss	c Mubarak Ali b Amir Elahi 14	c & b Saeed Ahmed 5	
A.F.Wensley	lbw b Nissar ...50	c Wazir Ali b Mubarak Ali 9	
J.E.Tew	c D.Hussain b Mubarak Ali.........4	b Amir Elahi 43	
Lt.Philpot-Brookes	c Kadri b Amir Elahi 5	c Mushtaq Ali b Amir Elahi 14	
F.C.Kidd	run out 2	st Abbas Khan b Amir Elahi 11	
K.S.H.Wilson	b Mubarak Ali ...19	st Abbas Khan b Saeed Ahmed 34	
H.L.Murray	not out 3	c Nissar b Amir Elahi 2	
C.T.Orton	b Mubarak Ali 0	not out 4	
Extras	(B 11, LB 7, NB 1) ...19	(B 7, LB 2, NB 2, W 1) 12	
Total	..................**172**	..................**249**	

Fall: 1st inns 1/18, 2/51, 3/73, 4/84, 5/98, 6/141, 7/148, 8/154, 9/172.
2nd inns 1/22, 2/111, 3/123, 4/127, 5/143, 6/179, 7/202, 8/217, 9/227.

EUROPEANS	O	M	R	W	O	M	R	W
Dawson	15	2	40	1	24	7	54	2
Kidd	2	0	6	0				
Murray	11	2	24	0	23.2	6	64	2
Wensley	28	5	84	2	25	5	59	4
Orton	12.4	2	51	7	15	1	81	2
Inder	8	0	32	0	2	1	3	0

MUSLIMS	O	M	R	W	O	M	R	W
Nissar	17	3	39	1	11	0	50	0
Nazir Ali	7	2	19	1				
Mubarak Ali	10.1	2	25	4	18	3	52	1
Amir Elahi	17	3	57	3	18	0	82	5
Saeed Ahmed	10	5	13	0	20.3	2	48	4
Mushtaq Ali					1	0	5	0

Umpires: D.K.Naik and N.A.Dubash

Close of play scores. First day: Europeans 81/3 (R.C.Summerhayes 31*, A.F.Wensley 1*). **Second day:** Muslims 221/7 (S.Wazir Ali 91*, K.C.Ibrahim 7*).
Comments: Mushtaq Ali scored 157 in 180 minutes, hitting 17 4's.
C.T.Orton performed the hat-trick in the Muslims' 1st innings, dismissing S.Mushtaq Ali, S.Wazir Ali and S.Nazir Ali.
S.Mushtaq Ali and S.M.Kadri put on 155 for the 1st wicket in the Muslims' 1st innings.
S.Wazir Ali made 112 in the second innings, hitting eight 4's in a stay of 191 minutes.

MUSLIMS v HINDUS

Played at Brabourne Stadium, December 3, 4, 5 1938.
Toss won by Hindus.
Muslims won by six wickets.

HINDUS

†D.D.Hindlekar	b Saeed Ahmed 1	b Amir Elahi 14	
M.H.Mankad	b Nissar 2	c Amir Elahi b Mubarak Ali 32	
R.B.Nimbalkar	c Amir Elahi b Saeed Ahmed 0	c & b Amir Elahi 23	
Prithviraj	b Saeed Ahmed 1	b Nissar 65	
*C.K.Nayudu	c Amir Elahi b Nissar...25	lbw b Nissar 66	
Roshan Lal	c Shaahab-ud-Din b Nissar...........0	b Amir Elahi 13	
L.Amar Singh	b Saeed Ahmed 9	b Amir Elahi 7	
L.P.Jai	c Abbas Khan b Shahab-ud-Din...1	run out...................43	
C.S.Nayudu	b Nissar...................10	c Kadri b Amir Elahi 75	
P.J.Chury	b Nissar...................4	not out 19	
S.N.Banerjee	not out..................14	b Saeed Ahmed 8	
Extras	(LB 1, NB 1) 2	12	
Total	....................**69**	....................**377**	

Fall: 1st inns 1/3, 2/3, 3/3, 4/6, 5/7, 6/23, 7/26, 8/51, 9/52.
2nd inns 1/14, 2/79, 3/158, 4/176, 5/284, 6/286, 7/309, 8/333, 9/335.

MUSLIMS

S.Mushtaq Ali	c Mankad b C.S.Nayudu 27	c & b C.S.Nayudu 22	
S.M.Kadri	c Nimbalkar b C.S.Nayudu 65	lbw b Amar Singh 12	
K.C.Ibrahim	lbw b C.S.Nayudu 7	lbw b C.K.Nayudu 13	
*S.Wazir Ali	b C.K.Nayudu 30	not out 1	
S.Nazir Ali	c Prithviraj b C.K.Nayudu 9	not out 44	
†Abbas Khan	c Nimbalkar b C.S.Nayudu 1	b Amar Singh 8	
Saeed Ahmed	lbw b C.K.Nayudu 78		
Amir Elahi	b C.S.Nayudu 96		
S.Mubarak Ali	c Prithviraj b C.S.Nayudu 0		
Shahab-ud-Din	not out...................10		
Mohamed Nissar	c C.K.Nayudu b C.S.Nayudu 0		
Extras	(B 4, LB 11, NB 2) ...17	(B 4, LB 3) 7	
Total	..................**340**	(4 wickets) 107	

Fall: 1st inns 1/48, 2/58, 3/119, 4/129, 5/132, 6/166, 7/322, 8/322, 9/337.
2nd inns 1/17, 2/45, 3/82, 4/99.

MUSLIMS	O	M	R	W	O	M	R	W
Nissar	10	2	20	35	33	2	106	0
Saeed Ahmed	12	6	12	4	32	12	54	1
Shahab-ud-Din	4	0	14	1	10	1	40	0
Amir Elahi	2	0	21	0	35.4	5	125	5
Mubarak Ali	-	-	-	-	12	1	36	1
Nazir Ali	-	-	-	-	1	0	4	0

HINDUS	O	M	R	W	O	M	R	W
Bannerjee	10	1	30	0				
Amar Singh	17	6	44	0	18	6	47	1
Mankad	20	1	46	0	2	1	2	0
C.S.Nayudu	32.5	7	109	7	8	0	27	1
C.K.Nayudu	24	3	87	3	8.2	1	24	1
R.B.Nimbalkar	3	1	6	0				

Close of play scores. First day: Muslims 201/7 (Saeed Ahmed 31*, Amir Elahi 22*). **Second day:** Hindus 191/4 (C.S.Nayudu 17*, Prithviraj 6*).

Comments: Saeed Ahmed and Amir Elahi added 156 for the 7th wicket in the Muslims' 1st innings.
Attendance 40,000 on first day.

RANJI TROPHY

BARODA v BOMBAY

Played at College Ground, Baroda, on October 28, 29, 30 1938.
Bombay won the toss.
Bombay won on first innings.

BOMBAY

†D.D.Hindlekar	c Gupte b S.Desai	34
A.A.Hakim	lbw b H.Desai	13
S.M.Kadri	c Pradhan b S.Desai	10
V.M.Merchant	not out	143
*L.P.Jai	c S.Desai b H.Desai	59
D.R.Havewalla	st Pradhan b Nimbalkar	64
M.S.Naik	c Adhikari b Sheikh	68
J.B.Khot	not out	16
Extras	(B 22, LB 6, NB 6)	34
Total	(6 wickets, declared)	**441**

Fall: 1st inns 1/31, 2/59, 3/66, 4/154, 5/239, 6/373.
R.R.Wadkar, S.Anwar and D.V.Koppikar did not bat.

BARODA

†R.A.Pradhan	lbw b Anwar	2
Y.E.Sheikh	c Koppikar b Khot	49
H.R.Adhikari	run out	37
R.B.Nimbalkar	c Havewalla b Jai	119
*W.N.Gorpade	c Koppikar b Khot	13
A.G.Gupte	lbw b Havewalla	32
S.G.Powar	run out	16
R.G.Powar	lbw b Havewalla	22
H.Desai	b Hakim	0
J.J.Yelwande	not out	5
S.Desai	c Havewalla b Hakim	0
Extras	(B 21, LB 7, NB 3)	31
Total		**326**

Fall: 1st inns 1/4, 2/77, 3/192, 4/196, 5/242, 6/262, 7/301, 8/321, 9/322.

BARODA	O	M	R	W
Yelwande	16	6	54	0
S.Desai	36	8	96	2
Gorpade	4	0	14	0
H.Desai	21	2	58	2
Gupte	6	2	10	0
Nimbalkar	18	0	87	1
Sheikh	18	0	75	1
Adhikari	3	0	13	0

BOMBAY	O	M	R	W
Anwar	14	6	10	1
Hakim	13	3	30	2
Havewalla	17	6	28	2
Wadkar	20	3	40	0
Koppikar	34	7	95	0
Merchant	13	5	31	0
Khot	16	3	37	2
Jai	4	0	24	1

Close of play scores. First day: Bombay 277/5 (V.M.Merchant 57*, M.S.Naik 15*). **Second day:** Baroda 97/2 (Y.E.Sheikh 39*, R.B.Nimbalkar 11*).

Comments: Ranji Trophy, West Zone match.
V.M.Merchant scored an undefeated 143 in 343 minutes. He reached his 100 in 313 minutes. He and M.S.Naik added 134 for the 6th wicket. R.B.Nimbalkar scored 119 in 150 minutes for Baroda.
Bombay secured the final Baroda wicket in the closing minutes of the third day.
Y.E.Sheikh and R.B.Nimbalkar put on 115 for Baroda's 3rd wicket.

WESTERN INDIA v MAHARASHTRA

Played at Rajkot, on November 4, 5, 1938.
Western India won the toss.
Western India won by 110 runs.

WESTERN INDIA

Pratap Rai	lbw b Jadhav	3	(2) b Sohoni	10
†Faiz Ahmed	b Sohoni	24	(4) b Sohoni	2
M.E.Sheikh Dina	lbw b Patwardhan	0	(11) lbw b Sohoni	20
*K.S.Abdul Khaliq	b Patwardhan	2	(6) lbw b Ayub	0
Shantilal Gandi	lbw b Ayub	38	b Sohoni	7
Saeed Ahmed	lbw b Ayub	13	(7) lbw b Sohoni	9
Sukhvantrai	b Jadhav	23	(8) run out	29
Akbar Khan	b Jadhav	21	(9) not out	40
K.S.Pradyumansinhji	lbw b Patwardhan	0	(10) b Jadhav	15
C.Purshottam	not out	7	(3) b Ubheykar	33
Dhirubha	lbw b Patwardhan	5	(1) b Patwardhan	6
Extras	(LB 2)	2	(B1, LB 8)	9
Total		**138**		**180**

Fall: 1st inns 1/15, 2/20, 3/24, 4/30, 5/80, 6/81, 7/121, 8/124, 9/124
2nd inns 1/13, 2/38, 3/40, 4/58, 5/59, 6/74, 7/75, 8/112, 9/146

MAHARASHTRA

B.B.Mullick	run out	13	b Saeed Ahmed	0
M.M.Naidu	lbw b Akbar Khan	23	c Akbar Khan b Saeed Ahmed	18
S.Nazir Ali	lbw b Shantilal	7	(5) c sub b Shantilal	2
†Y.N.Gokhale	lbw b Akbar Khan	10	(7) lbw b Saeed Ahmed	9
*D.B.Deodhar	b Shantilal	0	(6) c Saeed Ahmed b Shantilal	0
K.M.Jadhav	b Akbar Khan	30	(8) lbw b Shantilal	17
K.P.Ubhaykar	b Shantilal	6	(3) b Saeed Ahmed	5
M.Ayub	b Akbar Khan	28	(4) c Akbar Khan b Shantilal	8
S.W.Sohoni	lbw b Shantilal	2	(10) c Dhirubha b Shantilal	10
B.J.Mohoni	not out	6	(9) b Saeed Ahmed	5
M.K.Patwardhan	b Shantilal	3	not out	2
Extras	(LB 3)	3	(LB 1)	1
Total		**131**		**77**

Fall: 1st inns 1/25, 2/41, 3/57, 4/51, 5/63, 6/85, 7/97, 8/100, 9/128
2nd inns 1/12, 2/23, 3/26, 4/33, 5/34, 6,/40, 7/53, 8/64, 9/66.

MAHARASHTRA	O	M	R	W	O	M	R	W
Jadhav	15	3	27	3	13	6	31	1
Patwardhan	17.1	1	51	4	13	1	43	1
Sohoni	10	1	20	1	16.1	1	58	5
Ayub	4	0	20	2	6	1	12	1
Mohoni	5	1	18	0	4	0	15	0
Ubhaykar	-	-	-	-	7	3	12	1

WESTERN INDIA	O	M	R	W	O	M	R	W
Shantilal	16.5	2	53	5	13.5	0	51	5
Akbar Khan	15	0	52	4				
Saeed Ahmed	3	0	17	0	14	4	25	5
Sukhvantrai	1	0	6	0				

Close of play scores. First day: Western India (2) 19/1 (Prataprai 6*, Purshottam 5*)

Comments: Ranji Trophy, West Zone.
The game was completed in two days.

NAWANAGAR v GUJERAT

Played at Ajitsintyi Ground, Jamnagar, on November 4, 5, 6, 1938.
Nawanagar won by eight wickets.

GUJERAT

†J.M.Sahana	c Mubarak Ali b Mankad 11	lbw b Mankad	14
U.R.Chhipa	c Yadvendrasinhji b Amar Singh	not out	5
	...8		
R.M.Patel	lbw b Amar Singh ...10	b Amar Singh	31
P.N.Cambhatta	lbw b Amar Singh ...4	c Ranvirsinhji b Amar Singh	46
C.F.Parmar	c Yadvendrasinhji b Mankad ...24	c Indravijayasinhji b Mankad	11
*M.Bhagwandas	b Mankad ...13	lbw b Amar Singh	0
M.K.Pathan	not out ...14	c Aziz b Amar Singh	3
A.Patel	c & b Amar Singh ...11	lbw b Mankad	12
M.L.Prajapati	c Mankad b Amar Singh 7	c & b Amar Singh	14
M.S.Balooch	c Jayendrasinhji b Mankad	c & b Mankad	7
	...0		
Noor Mahomed	b Mankad ...0	st Aziz b Mankad	1
Extras	...3		4
Total	**105**		**148**

Fall: 2nd inns 1/6, 2/30, 3/70, 4/107, 5/107, 6/113, 7/129, 8/135, 9/137.

NAWANAGAR

K.Ranvirsinhji	lbw b Bhagwandas ...22	b Bhagwandas	6
M.H.Mankad	c Balooch b Bhagwandas 80	st Sahana b Chhipa	3
O.Manilal	c Sahana b Chhipa ...3	not out	5
*R.K.Indravijayasinhji	c Prajapati b Chhipa 0		
S.H.M.Colah	run out ...49	not out	2
L.Amar Singh	c J.Patel b Balooch ...8		
K.Yadvendrasinhji	lbw b Balooch ...23		
R.Jayendrasinhji	b Chhipa ...9		
S.N.Banerjee	c R.Patel b Balooch ...38		
Mubarak Ali	c Balooch b Chhipa ...3		
†Abdul Aziz	not out ...1		
Extras	...2		0
Total	**238**	**(2 wickets)**	**16**

Fall: 1st inns 1/47, 2/62, 3/62, 4/138, 5/147, 6/174, 7/193, 8/215, 9/228.
2nd inns 1/9, 2/13.

NAWANAGAR	O	M	R	W	O	M	R	W
Amar Singh	22	5	56	5	27	5	56	5
Banerjee	8	1	12	0	10	2	19	0
Mubarak Ali	5	2	13	0	8	2	21	0
Mankad	12.2	3	21	5	15	3	48	5

GUJERAT	O	M	R	W	O	M	R	W
Bhagwandas	12	1	61	2	6	1	13	1
Balooch	28.3	6	65	3				
Noor Mahomed	4	0	12	0				
Chhipa	29	5	68	4	6.2	3	3	1
Patel R.M.	9	1	16	0				
Prajapati	3	0	14	0				

Close of play scores. First day: Nawanagar 188/6.

Comments:
Ranji Trophy Western Zone match.
A fine all-round performance by M.H.Mankad, who top-scored with 80 in 155 minutes, hitting nine 4's and took ten wickets in the match for 69 runs.
L.Amar Singh also took ten wickets in the match for 112.

SIND v BOMBAY

Played at Karachi, on November 5, 6, 7, 1938.
Toss won by Bombay.
Sind won on first innings.

BOMBAY

†D.D.Hindlekar	b Hyder Ali	10
A.A.Hakim	c M.J.Mobed b Hyder Ali	27
R.R.Wadkar	c Abbas Khan b Ghulam Mahomed	8
V.M.Merchant	st D.J.Mobed b Ghulam Mahomed	120
*L.P.Jai	b Hyder Ali	67
D.R.Havewalla	b Khadim Hussain	56
M.S.Naik	b M.J.Mobed	15
J.B.Khot	b Ghulam Mahomed	7
L.B.Kenny	lbw b M.J.Mobed	6
D.V.Koppikar	st D.J.Mobed b Naoomal	27
S.Anwar	not out	5
Extras	(D 11, LB 6, NB 1)	18
Total		**366**

Fall: 1st inns 1/17, 2/30, 3/49, 4/168, 5/255.

SIND

Ghulam Mahomed	b Anwar	5
J.W.Anson	run out	21
Abbas Khan	lbw b Khot	14
Naoomal Jeoomal	lbw b Havewala	149
*M.J.Mobed	c Khot b Wadkar	27
M.A.Gopaldas	lbw b Hakim	30
Daud Khan	not out	74
Hyder Ali	c Merchant b Wadkar	40
S.M.Bhickaji	not out	1
Extras	(B 7, W 2)	9
Total	(7 wickets)	**370**

Fall: 1st inns 2/28, 3/62.
†D.J.Mobed and Khadim Hussain did not bat.

SIND	O	M	R	W
Khadim Hussain	29	8	62	1
Hyder Ali	54	14	117	3
Ghulam Mahomed	35	8	64	3
M.J.Mobed	30	11	45	2
Naoomal Jeoomal	10	1	40	1
Gopaldas	7	1	20	0

BOMBAY	O	M	R	W
Merchant	9	1	26	0
Anwar	19	4	29	1
Hakim	15	3	46	1
Havewala	33	8	64	1
Khot	31	8	63	1
Wadkar	32	10	72	2
Koppikar	18	2	61	0

Close of play scores. First day: Bombay 251/4 (V.M.Merchant 74*, D.R.Havewala 52*). **Second day:** Sind 81/3 (Naoomal Jeoomal 27*, M.J.Mobed 14*).

Comments: Ranji Trophy Western Zone match.
V.M.Merchant scored 120 in 390 minutes, hitting 12 4's.
L.P.Jai and V.M.Merchant added 119 for the 4th wicket.
Naoomal Jeoomal made 149 in 300 minutes. He put on 112 for the 6th wicket with Daud Khan.

NAWANAGAR v WESTERN INDIA

Played at Ajitsintyi Ground, Jamnagar, on November 9, 10, 11, 1938.
Toss won by Western India.
Nawanagar won by four wickets.

WESTERN INDIA

Pratap Rai	b Amar Singh 9	lbw b Mankad	14
†Faiz Ahmed	c & b Banerjee 0	b Mankad	15
M.E.Sheikh Dina	lbw b Amar Singh 9	lbw b Mankad	2
*K.S.Abdul Khaliq	c Wensley b Mankad 18	(9) lbw b Mankad	15
Sukhvant Rai	lbw b Amar Singh 42	b Amar Singh	67
Saeed Ahmed	c Wensley b Mankad 6	c Aziz b Amar Singh	18
Akbar Khan	b Amar Singh 30	b Ranvirsinhji	32
Purshottam	c Indravijayasinhji b Amar Singh 16	c Amar Singh b Mubarak Ali 10
R.P.Rathod	c Indravijayasinhji b Mubarak Ali 22	(4) lbw b Amar Singh 0
K.S.Pradyumansinhji	not out 12	not out	1
Jayantilal Oza	c Amar Singh b Mubarak Ali..........0	lbw b Mankad	0
Extras	2		11
Total	**166**		**185**

Fall: 1st inns 1/4, 2/13, 3/18, 4/62, 5/84, 6/84, 7/115, 8/147, 9/162.
2nd inns 1/34, 2/36, 3/37, 4/37, 5/65, 6/132, 7/154, 8/184, 9/184.

NAWANAGAR

R.U.Ranvirsinhji	lbw b Akbar Khan 14	c Faiz Ahmed b Jayantilal	13
M.H.Mankad	c Jayantilal b Akbar Khan 54	c Faiz Ahmed b Akbar Khan	21
O.Manilal	b Saeed Ahmed 0	run out	44
Indravijayasinhji	st Faiz Ahmed b Saeed Ahmed........40	(5) lbw b Saeed Ahmed 57
S.H.M.Colah	lbw b Akbar Khan 17	(4) lbw b Akbar Khan 13
L.Amar Singh	st Faiz Ahmed b Saeed Ahmed........20	(7) c Jayantilal b Akbar Khan 4
*A.F.Wensley	c Purshottam b Saeed Ahmed.........0	(8) not out 0
Yadvendrasinhji	not out 1	(6) not out 28
S.S.Banerjee	lbw b Saeed Ahmed 3	
Mubarak Ali	lbw b Akbar Khan 7	
†Abdul Aziz	c Jayantilal b Saeed Ahmed 8	
Extras	4		4
Total	**168**	**(6 wickets)**	**184**

Fall: 1st inns 1/22, 2/25, 3/93, 4/120, 5/147, 6/149, 7/149, 8/152, 9/159.
2nd inns 1/15, 2/39, 3/61, 4/142, 5/154, 6/159.

NAWANAGAR	O	M	R	W	O	M	R	W
Amar Singh	26	7	50	4	24	4	78	3
Banerjee	9	0	31	1	3	0	16	0
Mubarak Ali	3	0	12	2	6	0	21	1
Mankad	15	1	54	2	13.3	3	32	5
Wensley	6	1	14	0	3	0	19	0
Ranvirsinhji	1	0	3	1	4	1	8	1

WESTERN INDIA	O	M	R	W	O	M	R	W
Saeed Ahmed	24.2	5	69	6	30	7	60	1
Jayantilal Oza	6	0	29	0	13	1	40	1
Akbar Khan	25	4	55	4	22.1	3	51	3
Purshottam	2	0	11	0	3	0	11	0
Rathod	-	-	-	-	4	0	18	0

Close of play scores. First day: Nawanagar 159/9 (Yadvendrasinhji 0*). **Second day:** Nawanagar 142/4 (Indravijayasinhji 48*).

Comments: Ranji Trophy, Western Zone match.

SOUTHERN PUNJAB v RAJPUTANA

Played at Rajandia Gym Club Ground, Patiala, on November 12, 13, 14, 1938.
Toss won by Southern Punjab.
Southern Punjab won by 184 runs.

SOUTHERN PUNJAB

†Joginder Singh	b Bradshaw 9	b Bradshaw	10
Abdul Rehman	c Naidoo b Bradshaw 3	c Mathur b Bradshaw	4
L.Amarnath	lbw b Bradshaw 11	c Mathur b Mahabir Dayal	0
S.Nazir Ali	c Patel b Atique Hussain 106	(8) lbw b Bradshaw	4
*Maharaja of Patiala	b Bradshaw 6	(7) c & b Atique Hussain	132
Mahomed Saeed	c McCanlis b Kesri 81	(5) lbw b Bradshaw	12
M.Surjit Singh	lbw b Bradshaw 20	b Bradshaw	23
Murrawat Hussain	b Naidoo 22	(9) c Hans Rai b Bradshaw	10
Amir Elahi	b Naidoo 11	(4) lbw b Atique Hussain	6
M.Nissar	st Mathur b Naidoo 18	b Bradshaw	1
Shahabdin	not out 1	not out	0
Extras	16		19
Total	**304**		**221**

Fall: 1st inns 1/9, 2/12, 3/23, 4/29, 5/163, 6/216, 7/263, 8/284, 9/293.
2nd inns 1/13, 2/16, 3/20, 4/21, 5/44, 6/109, 7/159, 8/190, 9/221.

RAJPUTANA

†D.Mathur	b Amir Elahi 17	c Surjit Singh b Amir Elahi	11
Mahabir Dayal	b Nissar 4	b Murrawat Hussain	0
N.P.Kesri	c Patiala b Amir Elahi ...28	(5) c Patiala b Amir Elahi	13
Hans Rai	c & b Murrawat Hussain 73	st Joginder Singh b Amir Elahi	30
Atique Hussain	b Nissar 11	(6) run out	24
W.H.Bradshaw	b Amir Elahi 2	(10) c Nazir Ali b Patiala	7
Sultan Abbas	b Nissar 5	(8) b Amir Elahi	18
K.Lakshmansingh	b Nissar 0	(9) c Saeed b Amir Elahi	0
G.R.Naidoo	lbw b Nissar 0	(3) b Nissar	25
*M.A.McCanlis	b Murrawat Hussain 22	(7) lbw b Amir Elahi	0
M.Patel	not out 3	not out	4
Extras	25	Extras	19
Total	**190**		**151**

Fall: 1st inns 1/14, 2/42, 3/85, 4/103, 5/108, 6/113, 7/119, 8/119, 9/175.
2nd inns 1/2, 2/20, 3/47, 4/69, 5/104, 6/107, 7/118, 8/120, 9/147.

RAJPUTANA	O	M	R	W	O	M	R	W
Bradshaw	22	5	69	5	22.2	6	52	7
Kesri	11	0	35	1				
Mahabir Dayal	14	1	60	0	14	1	60	1
Atique Hussain	9	0	51	1	6	2	24	2
McCanlis	5	0	36	0	1	0	12	0
Naidoo	8.5	1	26	3	7	0	36	0
Sultan Abbas	2	1	11	0	3	1	18	0

SOUTHERN PUNJAB	O	M	R	W	O	M	R	W
Nissar	19	4	54	5	11	3	19	1
Amarnath	7	2	8	0	7	4	8	0
Amir Elahi	22	0	70	3	20	2	68	6
Nazir Ali	4	0	10	0	6	3	10	0
Murrawat Hussain	6.2	1	10	2	5	2	11	1
Shahabdin	4	1	13	0	5	0	13	0
Patiala	-	-	-	-	5	2	3	1

Close of play scores. First day: Rajputana 26/1 (D.Mathur 13*, N.P.Kesri 9*).
Second day: Southern Punjab (2) 114/6 (Maharaja of Patiala 51*, Murrawat Hussain 0*).

Comments: Ranji Trophy, North Zone.
S.Nazir Ali and Mahomed Saeed put on 134 for the 5th wicket.
In Southern Punjab's 2nd innings, the Maharaja of Patiala hit two 6's and 16 4's in his 132.

HYDERABAD v MYSORE

Played at Hyderabad, on November 25, 26, 27, 1938.
Toss won by Hyderabad.
Hyderabad won on first innings.

HYDERABAD

S.R.Mehta	lbw b Vijayasarathi 35	lbw b Nicholas 15
Venkataswami	c Darashah b Rangaraj 0	lbw b Rangaraj 0
B.Zahiruddin	c Rama Rao b Murari 152	c Vijayasarathi b Ramaswami 17
Ushaq Ahmed	run out.................6	run out..................27
S.M.Hadi	c Rangaraj b Ramaswami 21	lbw b Darashah...........88
R.K.Rao	c Rangaraj b Ramaswami 10	c Ramaswami b Ramakrishnappa....40
*S.M.Hussain	c Vijayasarathi b Ramaswami........82	not out 24
Z.S.Lodi	b Murari 5	
Ibrahim Khan	c Rangaraj b Ramaswami 32	
†V.G.Mache	not out................14	(8) lbw b Ramaswami 6
Raizul Huq	c Vijayasarathi b Murari ...7	
Extras	18	19
Total	...........**382**	(7 wickets, declared).....**236**

Fall: 1st inns 1/1, 2/106, 5/182, 6/353.

MYSORE

M.B.Rama Rao	c Ushaq Ahmed b Ibrahim Khan.......17	c Mehta b Zahiruddin 26
M.B.Krishna Rao	b Zahiruddin 8	not out 49
B.V.Ramakrishnappa	b Ibrahim Khan 18	b Riazul Huq 32
*T.Murari	b Rao 27	
B.Nicholas	b Mehta 76	
M.Dayanand	c Ibrahim Khan b Mehta 12	
S.Darashah	c Hadi b Riazul Huq 49	
M.G.Vijayasarathi	b Ibrahim Khan...........66	
K.S.Rangaraj	b Mehta 2	
Y.S.Ramaswami	c & b Ibrahim Khan 5	
†E.Krishnaswami	not out 0	
Extras	5	4
Total	...........**285**	(2 wickets) **111**

MYSORE	O	M	R	W	O	M	R	W
Rangaraj	13	4	36	1	5	0	20	1
Darashah	19	3	50	0	10	4	26	1
Ramaswami	32	1	114	4	28	9	81	2
Vijayasarathi	15	0	54	1	4	1	12	0
Nicholas	11	2	47	0	10	2	33	1
Dayanand	6	1	30	0	5	2	23	0
Murari	8.3	0	33	3	5	0	24	0
Ramakrishnappa					4.1	0	18	1

HYDERABAD	O	M	R	W	O	M	R	W
Ibrahim Khan	27.5	6	66	4	6	2	14	0
Riazul Huq	16	3	52	1	4	1	11	0
Zahiruddin	8	0	33	1	5	1	10	1
Mehta	183	42		3	8	2	23	0
R.K.Rao	15	2	53	1	2	0	3	0
Ushaq Ahmed	5	0	18	0	6	1	17	0
Venkataswami	1	0	16	0	3	0	14	0
Hussain	-	-	-	-	3	0	15	0

Close of play scores. First day: Hyderabad 382 all out. **Second day:** Hyderabad 8/1.
Comments: Ranji Trophy, South Zone match. B.Zahiruddin scored 152, including 16 4's. It was the highest score by an Hyderabad batsman in the tournament. He and S.R.Mehta put on 105 for the 2nd wicket. Zahiruddin then added 171 for the 6th wicket with Mahomed Hussain — a record for this wicket in the Ranji Trophy. Mysore were set to make 343 in 120 minutes to win.

NW FRONTIER PROVINCE v DELHI & DISTRICTS

Played at Club Ground, Peshawar, November 26, 27, 28, 1938.
North West Frontier Province won by an innings and 171 runs.

DELHI AND DISTRICTS

Khallil Ahmed	lbw b Faqir Hussain 3	c Fazal Rahim b Faqir Hussain 0
Yakub	lbw b Faqir Hussain 1	c Zardad b Faqir Hussain 1
Jamilul Rehman	b Faqir Hussain 0	c Bruiski b Faqir Hussain 1
C.Evett	c Faqir Hssain b Bruiski 73	b Faqir Hussain 2
*G.M.Din	b Faqir Hussain 12	b Faqir Hussain 13
Anwar Khan	c Parmanand b Balbir ...39	c Faqir Hussain b Zardad 4
Muzaffar	c Bruiski b Sher Mahomed 9	c Holdsworth b Zardad....10
Kiran Bahadur	c Parmanand b Sher Mahomed.....48	c Karim Bux b Zardad 4
Fasihuddin	lbw b Faqir Hussain 8	c Bruiski b Zardad 0
Shamsunder	c Holdsworth b Faqir Hussain........0	not out 2
Rashid	not out..................1	b Faqir Hussain 0
Extras	13	3
Total	...........**207**	...........**40**

NORTH WEST FRONTIER PROVINCE

*R.L.Holdsworth	b Muzaffar b Shamsunder 177
†Karim Bux	b Evett 11
Mosley	b Kiran Bahadur 20
Fazal Rahim	b Kiran Bahadur 10
Bruiski	c Din b Kiran Bahadur 12
Sher Mahomed	lbw b Shamsunder 96
Harbhajan	not out 52
Parmanand	b Shamsunder 23
Balbir	c Muzaffar b Shamsunder 8
Faqir Hussain	not out 2
Extras	7
Total	(8 wickets, declared) **418**

Zardad did not bat.

NW FRONTIER	O	M	R	W	O	M	R	W
Faqir Hussain	18.2	3	38	6	7.4	1	18	6
Zardad	16	2	50	0	7	0	19	4
Balbir	12	1	35	1				
Sher Mahomed	10	0	32	2				
Bruiski	3	1	7	1				
Parmanand	9	0	32	0				

DELHI AND DISTRICT	O	M	R	W
Fasihuddin	5	1	17	0
Evett	12	1	39	1
Kiran Bahadur	26	2	93	3
Shamsunder	35	4	103	4
Din	39	6	103	0
Rashid	6	0	25	0
Zafar	7	0	31	0

Close of play scores. First day: North West Frontier 45/1. **Second day:** North West Frontier 355/6 (Harbhajan 8*, Parmanand 10*).
Comments:
Ranji Trophy, North Zone.
R.L.Holdsworth's 177 was the highest individual score by a NWFP batsman in the Ranji Trophy.
NWFP 418/8 declared was their highest total in the Ranji Trophy.

BENGAL v BIHAR

Played at Tallah Park, Calcutta, on December 3, 4, 1938.
Toss won by Bihar.
Bengal won by an innings and 185 runs.

BIHAR

A.Chowdhury	c Surita b Mitter	0	b T.Bhattacharjee	8
L.F.Coelho	b T.Bhattacharjee	5	c T.Bhattacharjee b K.Bhattacharjee	10
E.Park	b Mitter	1	b T.Bhattacharjee	9
B.Sen	b K.Bhattacharjee	20	lbw b Dutt	14
S.K.Roy	b Banerjee	19	c T.Bhattacharjee b K.Bhattacharjee	9
P.M.Kapadia	c Behrend b K.Bhattacharjee	4	c Banerjee b K.Bhattacharjee	5
S.Chakraburtty	c K.Bhattacharjee b Banerjee	0	b Dutt	0
*K.A.D.Naoroji	not out	35	b K.Bhattacharjee	13
M.Sen Gupta	b K.Bhattacharjee	1	b Dutt	0
D.Khambatta	b Banerjee	8	b Dutt	5
S.Coates	c Mitter b Banerjee	8	not out	0
Extras		4		3
Total		**105**		**76**

BENGAL

S.W.Behrend	c Coates b Khambatta	35
P.N.Miller	lbw b Khambatta	35
A.Jabbar	b Sen Gupta	108
N.Chatterjee	not out	141
G.F.Carter	not out	13
Extras		34
Total	(3 wickets, declared)	**366**

K.Bhattacharjee, T.Bhattacharjee, *J.N.Banerjee, S.Dutt, I.Surita and
B.Mitter did not bat.

BENGAL	O	M	R	W	O	M	R	W
B.Mitter	8	2	33	2	7	1	23	0
T.Bhattacharjee	4	2	4	1	6	2	11	2
J.N.Banerjee	12	2	32	4				
Behrend	4	1	7	0	4	0	10	0
K.Bhattacharjee	11	4	25	3	7	1	18	4
S.Dutt	-	-	-	-	4.2	1	11	4

BIHAR	O	M	R	W
Chakraburtty	20	2	79	0
Coelho	11	0	70	0
Khambatta	28	4	80	2
Kapadia	10	1	56	0
Sen Gupta	4	1	27	1
B.Sen	3	0	15	0
Naoroji	1	0	5	0

Close of play scores. First day: Bengal 18/2 (A.Jabbar 63*, N.Chatterjee 46*).

Comments:
Ranji Trophy, East Zone match. The game was completed in two days.
N.Chatterjee scored 141* in 153 minutes, hitting two 6's and 16 4's. He and
A.Jabbar put on 241 for the 3rd wicket, a record for this wicket in Ranji Trophy.
A.Jabbar's 108 was made on his first appearance in the competition.
J.N.Bannerjee was the first Indian to captain Bengal in the Ranji Trophy.
Bihar's 76 was their lowest total in the competition.

CENTRAL INDIA v UNITED PROVINCES

Played at Yeshwant Club Ground, Indore, December 10, 11, 12,
1938.
Toss won by Central India.
Central India won by 246 runs.

CENTRAL INDIA

Saiduddin	c Bolam b Garudachar	32	lbw b Garudachar	26
*Dilawar Hussain	b Garudachar	70	b Garudachar	41
Shahabuddin	c Phansalkar b Alexander	4		
V.S.Hazare	b Alexander	14	lbw b Alexander	19
J.N.Bhaya	b Garudachar	9	not out	82
Ziaul Hussain	b Alexander	6		
Sardar Md.Khan	lbw b Alexander	0	lbw b Narayan Raju	25
Basant Singh	c Shambu Singh b Alexander	13	not out	38
†Goodridge	c Garudachar b Alexander	4		
Ghani Khan	lbw b Garudachar	3	lbw b Alexander	27
S.R.Kalewar	not out	6		
Extras		9		21
Total		**170**	(5 wickets, declared)	**279**

UNITED PROVINCES

A.N.Murty	lbw b Ziaul Hussain	8	did not bat	
Ranjit Singh	b Shahabuddin	3	b Ziaul Hussain	7
Mahomed Hussain	c Sardar Md b Shahabuddin	11	b Ziaul Hussain	10
J.Phansalkar	lbw b Ziaul Hussain	1	b Ziaul Hussain	0
B.K.Garudachar	b Hazare	3	c Dilawar b Ziaul Hussain	8
Shambu Singh	c Hazare b Ziaul Hussain	11	b Hazare	11
Raghunatha Rao	c & b Hazare	4	run out	38
Pasha	run out	0	b Basant Singh	8
Narayan Raju	c Hazare b Ziaul Hussain	0	lbw b Basant Singh	8
*†J.Bolam	b Hazare	1	b Bhaya	18
J.E.Alexander	not out	4	not out	39
Extras		3		7
Total		**49**	(8 wickets)	**154**

UNITED PROVINCES	O	M	R	W	O	M	R	W
Alexander	20.5	5	44	6	25	4	81	2
Garudachar	20	4	63	4	27	2	84	2
Narayan Raju	7	3	11	0	15	2	54	1
Murty	11	3	36	0				
Raghunatha Rao	2	0	7	0	11	1	31	0
Ranjit	-	-	-	-	1	0	8	0

CENTRAL INDIA	O	M	R	W	O	M	R	W
Ziaul Hussain	10	3	18	4	8	3	27	4
Shahabuddin	5	1	18	2	6	0	19	0
Hazare	4.3	1	10	3	3	0	5	1
Basant Singh	-	-	-	-	9	3	19	2
Kalewar	-	-	-	-	8	2	17	0
Ghani	-	-	-	-	2	0	9	0
Sardar Mahomed	-	-	-	-	3	0	29	0
Dilawar Hussain	-	-	-	-	2	0	14	0
Bhaya	-	-	-	-	1	0	8	1

Close of play scores. First day: United Provinces 39/5 (Raghunatha Rao 10*,
Narayan Raju 0*).

Comments: Ranji Trophy, East Zone.
United Provinces made their largest total in the Ranji Trophy.

MADRAS v HYDERABAD

Played at Chepaule, Madras, December 17, 18, 19 1938.
Toss won by Hyderabad.
Madras won by six wickets.

HYDERABAD

S.R.Mehta	st Ward b Ram Singh....22	b Ram Singh	16
†G.V.Mache	lbw b Gopalan............6	b Gopalan	7
B.Zahiruddin	b Gopalan	0	not out....48
E.B.Aibara	b Parthasarathi	26	c Madhava Rao b Rangachari....19
*S.M.Hussain	b Rangachari	34	c & b Ram Singh....0
S.M.Hadi	c Ramaswami b Parthasarathi....21	lbw b Parankusam....25	
Ushaq Ahmed	c Gopalan b Parankusam....14	c Ward b Gopalan....1	
F.Toorkey	b Rangachari	0	b Rangachari....8
R.K.Rao	b Rangachari	3	c Ward b Parankusam....1
Ibrahim Khan	b Gopalan	6	c Ram Singh b Robins....21
K.Naik	not out	0	b Robins....11
Extras		7	11
Total		**139**	**168**

MADRAS

*C.P.Johnstone	c Mehta b Naik	11	c Hadi b Naik....18
A.W.Stansfeld	b Naik	40	c sub b Ibrahim Khan....25
A.G.Ram Singh	c Mehta	14	c Zahiruddin b Naik....14
†H.P.Ward	b Rao	3	not out....37
V.N.Madhava Rao	b Ibrahim Khan	6	
C.Ramaswami	lbw b Hussain	14	(5) b Ibrahim Khan....45
M.J.Gopalan	b Ibrahim Khan	4	(6) not out....7
W.V.H.Robins	not out	46	
G.Parthasarathi	b Ibrahim Khan	0	
T.S.Parankusam	lbw b Ibrahim Khan	0	
C.R.Rangachari	c Rao b Naik	10	
Extras		11	4
Total		**159**	(4 wickets) **150**

MADRAS	O	M	R	W	O	M	R	W
Rangachari	18	4	26	3	16	3	43	2
Gopalan	12	5	15	4	10	1	28	2
Parthasarathi	18	0	46	2	9	0	39	0
Parankusam	5.1	0	11	1	4	0	7	2
Ram Singh	11	1	31	1	14	2	33	2
Johnstone	1	0	3	0				
Robins	-	-	-	-	3	0	7	2

HYDERABAD	O	M	R	W	O	M	R	W
Ibrahim Khan	20	6	39	4	24	4	55	2
Mehta	10	3	19	1	10	2	30	0
Naik	16	2	38	3	22	8	48	2
Rao	8	1	38	1	2	0	5	0
Ushaq Ahmed	3	0	11	0				
Hussain	1	0	3	1	2	0	7	0
Zahiruddin	-	-	-	-	2	1	1	0

Close of play scores. First day: Madras 94/5. **Second day:** Madras (2) 57/1 (A.W.Stansfield 25*, A.G.Ram Singh 14*).

Comments: Ranji Trophy, South Zone fixture.
Ibrahim Kahn (4/39) claimed three wickets in one over.

SIND v NAWANAGAR

Played at Gym Ground, Karachi, December 24, 25, 26, 1938.
Toss won by Sind.
Sind won on first innings.

SIND

Ghulam Mahomed	b Banerjee	2	b Mubarak Ali....15
†Abbas Khan	b Mubarak Ali	6	b Banerjee....13
Daud Khan	b Mubarak Ali	5	c Ranvirsinhji b Mubarak Ali....45
J.Naoomal	not out	203	b Banerjee....49
*M.J.Mobed	c Mankad b Mubarak Ali	0	not out....54
J.Harris	b Ranvirsinhji	15	c Colah b Mubarak Ali....9
Hyder Ali	c Ranvirsinhji b Manked	3	c Banerjee b Ranvirsinhji 49
S.M.Bhicaji	c Banerjee b Mubarak Ali....38	c Mankad b Mubarak Ali 12	
D.J.Mobed	b Mubarak Ali	7	
Khadim Hussain	c Yadvendrasinhji b Mankad....32		
J.K.Irani	c Aziz b Mubarak Ali	6	not out....5
Extras		9	12
Total		**326**	(7 wickets, declared) **263**

Fall: 1st inns 1/8, 2/8, 3/15, 4/15, 5/59, 6/63, 7/128, 8/150, 9/263.
2nd inns 1/26, 2/36, 3/55, 4/126, 5/153, 6/171, 7/247.

NAWANAGAR

R.K.Ranvirsinhji	c & b Harris	4	c Hyder Ali b Khadim Hussain....1
V.M.Mankad	c D.Mobed b Khadim Hussain....56	c Naoomal b Hyder Ali...31	
O.Manilal	c Daud Khan b Harris....0		
S.H.M.Colah	b M.J.Mobed	18	not out....49
*R.K.Indravijayasinhji	not out	121	not out....40
R.K.Yadvendrasinhji	c Abbas Khan b Hyder Ali 14		
A.F.Wensley	c Abbas Khan b Ghulam Mahomed	1	
R.K.Jayendrasinhji	run out	4	
S.N.Banerjee	lbw b Khadim Hussain	41	
S.Mubarak Ali	run out	0	
†Abdul Aziz	c Hyder Ali b M.J.Mobed	0	
Extras		12	4
Total		**271**	(2 wickets) **125**

Fall: 1st inns 3/59, 4/112, 5/155, 6/160, 7/174, 8/267, 9/268.

NAWANAGAR	O	M	R	W	O	M	R	W
Banerjee	15	3	59	1	21	2	75	2
Mubarak Ali	25	7	89	6	30	9	51	4
Ranvirsinhji	20	1	72	1	11	2	43	1
Mankad	26	7	74	2	9	0	53	0
Wensley	1	0	6	0				
Manilal					16	3	29	0
Jayendrasinhji	4	1	17	0				

SIND	O	M	R	W	O	M	R	W
Harris	31	13	55	2	4	0	11	0
Khadim Hussain	22	8	45	2	7	1	25	1
Ghulam Mahomed	14	2	41	1	4	0	18	0
Hyder Ali	22	6	55	1	8	1	34	1
M.J.Mobed	19.5	7	22	2	3	0	7	0
Naoomal	9	0	37	0				
Bhicaji	1	0	4	0	5	0	26	0

Close of play scores. First day: Nawanagar 23/2 (V.M.Mankad, S.H.M.Colah). **Second day:** Sind (2) 15/0 (Ghulam Mahomed 6*, Abbas Khan 9*).

Comments: Ranji Trophy, West Zone. Game to decide which team qualified for the semi-final.
J.Naoomal scored 203* in 270 minutes, hitting 30 4's, the highest score by a Sind player in the Ranji Trophy. He added 113 for the 9th wicket with Khadim Hussain. The last two wickets of the Sind 1st innings added 176, more than doubling the side's total.
R.K.Indravijayasinhji's 121* included 14 4's.

BENGAL v CENTRAL INDIA

Played at Calcutta, on December 31, 1938 and January 1, 2, 1939.
Bengal won by an innings and 121 runs.

CENTRAL INDIA

*Dilawar Hussain ...b Longfield 9	(6) lbw b Banerjee 2
Saiduddin ....b Longfield 10	(1) run out 3
M.K.Alirajpur ....c Carter b S.Dutt 1	(9) c Longfield b S.Dutt ...10
V.S.Hazare ....c Van der Gucht b Behrend 32	b Longfield 1
J.N.Bhaya...........b Behrend 20	(7) b Longfield 89
Lt.Benbow ....b Longfield 1	(5) c Van der Gucht b Banerjee 0
A.U.Botawala ....c Van der Gucht b Behrend 5	(8) c S.Dutt b P.Dutt 11
Shahabuddin ....c S.Dutt b Behrend......14	(3) b P.Dutt...............13
Sardar Md.Khan .....b Longfield 7	(2) c S.Dutt b P.Dutt........5
Basant Singh ....b Longfield 2	c Banerjee b Longfield 2
Ziaul Hussain ....not out 0	not out 6
Extras........... 7	7
Total **108**	.........................**149**

BENGAL

†P.I.Van der Gucht   lbw b Shahabuddin 115
S.W.E.Behrend ......c Botawala b Basant Singh69
K.Bose ....c Botawala b Basant Singh 0
A.Jabbar ....c Bhaya b Hazare 44
A.G.Skinner ....c Hussain b Basant Singh 52
G.F.Carter ....lbw b Shahabuddin 6
N.Chatterjee ....c Basant Singh
b Shahabuddin........41
J.N.Banerjee .... c Bhaya b Hazare 25
*T.C.Longfield ......c Saiduddin b Hazare 14
P.D.Dutt ....not out 1
S.Dutt................not out 1
Extras......................................10
Total ....(9 wickets, declared) **378**

BENGAL	O	M	R	W	O	M	R	W
Banerjee...............13	3	19	0	16	5	36	2
P.Dutt.....................12	2	28	0	15	5	31	3
Longfield 16.3	9	27	5	6.3	1	6	3
S.Dutt.....................6	0	14	1	9	2	45	1
Behrend 8	2	13	4	7	1	24	0

CENTRAL INDIA	O	M	R	W
Ziaul Hussain 29	5	114	0
Botawala 9	1	25	0
Shahabuddin 21	1	102	3
Hazare 29	4	92	3
Basant Singh 12	3	35	3

Close of play scores. First day: Bengal 154/0 (P.I.Ven der Gucht 95*, S.W.Behrend 54*). **Second day:** Central India (2) 21/3 (Shahabuddin 8*, Lt.Benbow 0*).

Comments: Ranji Trophy East Zone, Winner to play in the semi-finals of the competition.
P.I.Van der Gucht scored 115 in 158 minutes, hitting 17 4's. He and S.W.E.Behrend put on 189 for the 1st wicket, a record for the 1st wicket in this competition.

SOUTHERN PUNJAB v NW FRONTIER PROVINCE

Played at Patiala, on January 2, 3, 4, 1939.
Toss won by North West Frontier Province.
Southern Punjab won by an innings and 37 runs.

NORTH WEST FRONTIER PROVINCE

*R.L.Holdsworth....not out 100	(5) c Shahabdin b Patiala 16
†Kareem Bux ....lbw b Amarnath 3	(1) lbw b Amarnath........4
Fazal Rahim ....c Saeed b Amarnath 0	(2) c Roshan Lal
	b Murrawat Hussain 0
Sher Mahomed ......b Amir Elahi 59	c Murrawat
	Hussain b Shahabdin 18
Amin Hassan ....st Rehman b Amir Elahi 12	(3) b Shahabdin 13
Bruiski ....c Rehman b Nazir Ali.....1	b Amarnath................12
A.Latif ....b Amarnath 34	b Amarnath................0
Buchanan ....b Amarnath 0	c Wazir Ali b Patiala 15
Parmanand ....b Amarnath 0	c Shahabdin b Amarnath 17
Balbir ....b Amarnath 2	not out 4
Zardad..............c Patiala	b Patiala 9
b Murrawat Hussain...0	
Extras..16	7
Total **227**	...........................**115**

SOUTHERN PUNJAB

†Abdul Rehman.....b Balbir 72
Prithviraj ....c Kareem Bux b Zardad ...7
L.Amarnath ....c Holdsworth
b Sher Mahomed......87
S.Wazir Ali..........c Bruiski b Zardad 52
*Maharaja of Patiala b Zardad 75
S.Nazir Ali ....c Holdsworth b Balbir ...11
Mahomed Saeed .....not out 10
Roshan Lal ....lbw b Zardad 21
Murrawat Hussain   b Zardad 7
Amir Elahi..........c Latif b Zardad 1
Shahabdin ....b Zardad 5
Extras.......................................31
Total **379**

SOUTHERN PUNJAB	O	M	R	W	O	M	R	W
Amarnath 25	10	36	6	10	5	17	4
Murrawat Hussain.........13	1	47	1	5	0	16	1
Amir Elahi 21	1	86	2	7	1	25	0
Shahabdin 5	0	22	0	4	0	14	2
Nazir Ali 15	3	20	1				
Wazir Ali ....-	-	-	-	5	0	14	0
Patiala ....-	-	-	-	6.2	0	22	3

NW FRONTIER	O	M	R	W
Abdul Latif 31	6	86	0
Zardad.....................33.3	9	99	7
Buchanan 9.5	0	31	0
Parmanand 6	2	19	0
Sher Mahomed 6	1	18	1
Balbir.......................22	6	55	2
Amin Hassan 5	0	40	0

Close of play scores. First day: Southern Punjab 75/1 (L.Amarnath 33*). **Second day:** North West Frontier 24/2 (Amin Hassan 11*, Sher Mahomed 7*).
Comments: Ranji Trophy, North Zone match.
R.L.Holdsworth carried his bat in NW Frontier's 1st innings. It was the first occasion in any game in the Ranji Trophy. L.Amarnath and Abdul Rehman added 143 for the 2nd wicket.
S.Wazir Ali and the Maharaja of Patiala added 131 for the 4th wicket.
L.Amarnath also top-scored for Bengal with 87, which contained 14 4's and took ten wickets for 43 in the match.

H.H.Shaikh Abdul Khaliq Saheb, captain of Western Indian, was a fine batsman who was coached by 'Ranji' in his early days.

The Maharaja of Patiala, captain of Southern Punjab. In November 1938 he scored 132 not out against Rajputana.

BENGAL v MADRAS (Semi-final)

Played at Calcutta, on January 21, 22, 23, 24, 1939.
Toss won by Bengal.
Bengal won by an innings and 285 runs.

BENGAL

S.W.Behrend	c Ramaswami b Rangachari	39
†P.I.Van der Gucht	b Rangachari	4
P.N.Miller	c & b Parthasarathi	83
K.Bose	run out	50
A.Jabbar	c Gopalan b Spitteler	46
N.Chatterjee	c Nailer b Gopalan	9
B.W.Malcolm	not out	181
*T.C.Longfield	run out	8
J.N.Banerjee	c Bhadradri b Parthasarathi	3
K.Bhattacharjee	lbw b Parthasarathi	23
T.Bhattacharjee	lbw b Parthasarathi	44
Extras		25
Total		**515**

MADRAS

A.V.Krishnaswami	b T.Bhattacharjee	2	b T.Bhattacharjee ... 9
A.W.Stansfeld	b T.Bhattacharjee	15	b Banerjee ... 10
A.G.Ram Singh	lbw b Banerjee	5	c Malcolm b Longfield ... 13
B.S.Bhadradri	b Longfield	29	c Jabbar b Longfield ... 16
*C.Ramaswami	b Banerjee	0	c Behrend b T.Bhattacharjee ... 3
R.Nailer	c Van der Gucht b Banerjee	0	c Van der Gucht b Malcolm ... 31
M.J.Gopalan	b K.Bhattacharjee	23	st Van der Gucht b Chatterjee ... 20
G.Parthasarathi	c Van der Gucht b Banerjee	15	c K.Bhattacharjee b Chatterjee ... 0
†T.M.Duraiswami	b T.Bhattacharjee	10	c Miller b Malcolm ... 3
C.R.Rangachari	b T.Bhattacharjee	0	b Malcolm ... 5
R.Spitteler	not out	0	not out ... 3
Extras		15	... 3
Total		**114**	**116**

MADRAS	O	M	R	W
Rangachari	29	2	111	2
Gopalan	34	9	92	1
Spitteler	14	2	56	1
Parthasarathi	26.2	3	115	4
Ram Singh	27	1	116	0

BENGAL	O	M	R	W	O	M	R	W
T.Bhattacharjee	18	4	36	4	10	3	23	2
Banerjee	20	10	29	4	7	5	7	1
Longfield	6.2	2	17	1	9	1	32	2
K.Bhattacharjee	13	3	16	1	4	0	25	0
Behrend	2	1	1	0				
Chatterjee	-	-	-	-	4	0	23	2
Malcolm	-	-	-	-	1.2	0	3	3

Close of play scores. First day: Bengal 379/8 (E.W.Malcolm 118*, K.Bhattacharjee 16*). **Second day:** Madras 114 all out.
Comments: Ranji Trophy, Semi-final tie.
Bengal's 515 was the highest team score in the history of the Ranji Trophy.
B.W.Malcolm's undefeated 181 took just over three hours. It was his first appearance in the Ranji Trophy.
He added 115 for the 10th wicket with T.Bhattacharjee. The last two Bengal wickets put on 193 runs.

SOUTHERN PUNJAB v NORTHERN INDIA

Played at Patiala, on January 21, 22, 23, 1939.
Southern Punjab won by nine wickets.

NORTHERN INDIA

Muni Lal	run out	16	c Rehman b Murrawat Hussain ... 10
Gul Mahomed	b Nissar	9	lbw b Amarnath ... 41
Ram Parkash	b Amarnath	27	(4) b Amarnath ... 16
Mahomed Gulzar	lbw b Amir Elahi	0	(5) b Amir Elahi ... 9
Kishen Ghand	b Nissar	11	(6) b Amir Elahi ... 10
*M.R.Bhide	lbw b Nissar	4	(7) st Rehman b Amir Elahi 2
†C.G.Craddock-Watson	b Nissar	1	(3) b Amir Elahi ... 33
Aftab Ahmed	b Nissar	11	run out ... 20
Habibullah	c Wazir Ali b Amir Elahi	0	c Nissar b Amarnath ... 23
Nazir Nizami	not out	7	(11) b Amarnath ... 0
Mazar Mahomed	c and b Amir Elahi	15	(10) not out ... 4
Extras		15	... 15
Total		**116**	**183**

SOUTHERN PUNJAB

†Abdul Rehman	lbw b Mazar Mahomed	0	b Habibullah ... 17
Amir Elahi	b Mazar Mahomed	8	not out ... 35
S.Wazir Ali	b Habibullah	20	not out ... 35
Mahomed Saeed	b Aftab Ahmed	10	
*Maharaja of Patiala	b Habibullah	10	
S.Nazir Ali	b Habibullah	55	
L.Amarnath	b Aftab Ahmed	4	
M.Surjit Singh	lbw b Aftab Ahmed	43	
Roshan Lal	lbw b Habibullah	5	(2) not out ... 65
Murrawat Hussain	c Bhide b Habibullah	0	
M.Nissar	not out	5	
Extras		20	... 3
Total		**180**	**(1 wicket) 120**

SOUTHERN PUNJAB	O	M	R	W	O	M	R	W
Amarnath	5	1	9	1	24	5	45	4
Nissar	15	4	36	5	12	1	36	0
Murrawat Hussain	5	1	6	0	3	0	10	1
Amir Elahi	11.2	0	50	3	11	1	65	4
Nazir Ali	-	-	-	-	5	1	12	0

NORTHERN INDIA	O	M	R	W	O	M	R	W
Mazar Mahomed	14	3	28	2	6	2	26	0
Nizami	7	1	24	0	7	0	20	0
Habibullah	29.2	3	65	5	13	4	33	1
Aftab Ahmed	14	1	39	3	10	0	22	0
Gul Mahomed	2	9	4	0	5	9	16	0

Close of play scores. First day: Southern Punjab 135/6. **Second day:** Southern Punjab 33/0 (Abdul Rehman 14*, Roshan Lal 18*).

Comments: Ranji Trophy, North Zone. Match to decide semi-final place.

SOUTHERN PUNJAB v SIND (Semi-final)

Played at Patiala, February 10, 11, 12, 1939.
Southern Punjab won by seven wickets.

SIND

B.S.Ambep	c Patiala b Amir Elahi...19	b Amarnath	7
A.Dipchand	lbw b Amir Elahi ...46	b Amarnath	0
†Abbas Khan	b Shahabdin...84	c Amir Elahi b Nissar	4
J.Naoomal	c Saeed b Amir Elahi ...12	c Amarnath b Nissar	5
M.A.Gopaldas	c Nissar b Amir Elahi...22	c Surjit Singh b Nissar	0
*M.J.Mobed	lbw b Amir Elahi...3	c Patiala b Nissar	0
Daud Khan	lbw b Murrawat Hussain 18	b Nissar	0
Hyder Ali	c Rehman b Shahabdin 18	lbw b Nissar	2
Ghulam Mahomed	lbw b Shahabdin ...0	lbw b Amarnath	0
W.Mascarenhas	not out...64	not out	1
D.J.Mobed	b Shahabdin...30	lbw b Amarnath	0
Extras	23		4
Total	**339**		**23**

Fall: 1st inns 1/39, 2/99, 3/119, 4/159, 5/1169, 6/210, 7/223, 8/223, 9/283.
2nd inns 1/9, 2/12, 3/17, 4/17, 5/17, 6/17, 7/17, 8/19, 9/21.

SOUTHERN PUNJAB

†Abdul Rehman	c Abbas Khan b Mobed 16	lbw b Ghulam Mahomed	3
Roshan Lal	lbw b Mobed ...19	b Naoomal	19
L.Amarnath	c Abbas Khan b Naoomal 8	(4) not out	95
S.Wazir Ali	lbw b Mobed ...8	(5) not out	23
*Maharaja of Patiala b Ghulam Mahomed ...19			
Mahomed Saeed	b Ghulam Mahomed 14	(3) b Naoomal	20
M.Surjit Singh	b Mobed ...33		
Amir Elahi	b Mobed ...5		
Murrawat Hussain	not out...47		
M.Nissar	c Daud Khan b Ghulam Mahomed 8		
Shahabdin	run out...1		
Extras	19		8
Total	**197**	(3 wickets)	**168**

Fall: 1st inns 1/29, 2/42, 3/54, 4/59, 5/77, 6/95, 7/143, 8/179, 9/189.
2nd inns 1/8, 2/67, 3/98.

SOUTHERN PUNJAB	O	M	R	W	O	M	R	W
Amarnath	24	6	55	0	7	5	2	4
Nissar	18	3	41	0	7	1	17	6
Shahabdin	12	2	35	4				
Amir Elahi	38	5	134	5				
Murrawat Hussain	10	5	21	1				
Wazir Ali	2	0	6	0				
Patiala	6	0	24	0				

SIND	O	M	R	W	O	M	R	W
Ghulam Mahomed	19	7	40	3	12	2	27	1
Hyder Ali	10	6	27	0	14	3	34	0
Naoomal	15	0	63	1	13	0	46	2
M.J.Mobed	21	3	48	5	6	0	25	0
Gopaldas	-	-	-	-	8	3	20	0
Mascarenhas	-	-	-	-	3	0	8	0

Close of play scores. First day: Sind 338/9. **Second Day:** Sind 17/5.

Comments: Ranji Trophy, Semi-final match.
Sind's 2nd innings total of 23 was only one run higher than the lowest ever recorded in this competition, 22 by their opponents in 1935. The last eight wickets fell for six runs and six batsmen were out for a duck.

BENGAL v SOUTHERN PUNJAB (Final)

Played at Calcutta, February 18, 19, 20, 21, 1939.
Toss won by Bengal.
Bengal won by 178 runs.

BENGAL

†P.I.Van der Gucht	c Murrawat Hussain b Amir Elahi ...35	(5) c Amir Elahi b Murrawat Hussain	65
S.W.Behrend	b Amir Elahi ...39	(1) c Saeed b Shahabdin	11
P.N.Miller	st Rehman b Amir Elahi 4	(2) b Murrawat Hussain	85
K.Bose	c Amarnath b Amir Elahi 48	run out	0
A.G.Skinner	b Amarnath ...22	(6) c Rehman b Murrawat Hussain	1
A.Jabbar	st Rehman b Amir Elahi 7	(9) lbw b Amarnath	58
B.W.Malcolm	b Amarnath ...30	b Wazir Ali	91
*T.C.Longfield	b Murrawat Hussain ...21	c Saeed b Murrawat Hussain	17
T.Bhattacharjee	b Amarnath ...2	(10) b Amarnath	9
K.Bhattacharjee	not out...4	(3) lbw b Amarnath	19
J.N.Banerjee	lbw b Amarnath ...1	not out	29
Extras	9		33
Total	**222**		**418**

Fall: 1st inns 1/52, 2/58, 3/128, 4/144, 5/154, 6/172, 7/209, 8/217, 9/217.
2nd inns 1/23, 2/54, 3/55, 4/161, 5/165, 6/278, 7/310, 8/310, 9/329.

SOUTHERN PUNJAB

†Abdul Rehman	b Banerjee ...16	c & b K.Bhattacharjee	4
Roshan Lal	lbw b K.Bhattacharjee ...8	(5) not out	35
*S.Wazir Ali	not out ...222	(6) b Longfield	10
Azmat Hyat	c Bose b Longfield ...21	(3) b Longfield	10
L.Amarnath	b K.Bhattacharjee ...8	(4) b Behrend	37
Mahomed Saeed	b Banerjee ...20	(7) c sub b Malcolm	1
Murrawat Hussain	run out...3	(2) c Jabbar b T.Bhattacharjee	0
M.Surjit Singh	b Behrned...3	c K.Bhattacharjee b Longfield	15
Abdul Hamid	c Miller b K.Bhattacharjee 1	b Longfield	1
Amir Elahi	c Longfield b K.Bhattacharjee 8	c Skinner b K.Bhattacharjee	19
Shahabdin	c Van der Gucht b K.Bhattacharjee ...13	c Van der Gucht b K.Bhattacharjee	0
Extras	5		2
Total	**328**		**134**

Fall: 1st inns 1/19, 2/25, 3/90, 4/113, 5/166, 6/173, 7/180, 8/194, 9/239.
2nd inns 1/4, 2/5, 3/18, 4/61, 5/75, 6/80, 7/105, 8/109, 9/134.

SOUTHERN PUNJAB	O	M	R	W	O	M	R	W
Shahabdin	14	1	73	0	9	0	44	1
Amarnath	29.5	12	44	4	54.3	24	97	3
Murrawat Hussain	15	5	23	1	43	16	97	4
Amir Elahi	25	5	73	5	24	1	101	0
Abdul Hamid	-	-	-	-	2	0	7	0
Wazir Ali	-	-	-	-	5	1	15	1
Mahomed Saeed	-	-	-	-	9	1	24	0

BENGAL	O	M	R	W	O	M	R	W
T.Bhattacharjee	11	2	37	0	4	2	2	1
J.N.Banerjee	19	4	49	2				
K.Bhattacharjee	24.2	1	100	5	20.4	5	57	3
Longfield	19	1	68	1	17	3	48	4
Malcolm	3	1	13	0	3	0	11	1
Skinner	5	1	20	0				
Behrend	9	1	36	1	4	0	14	1

Close of play scores. First day: Southern Punjab 29/2 (Wazir Ali 2*). **Second day:** Bengal (2) 20/0 (S.W.Behrend 11*, P.N.Miller 8*). **Third day:** Bengal (2) 310/7 (T.C.Longfield 7*).

Comments: Ranji Trophy Final.
S.Wazir Ali made the highest individual score in the tournament. His undefeated 222 took 284 minutes and included 33 4's. He reached his 100 in 171 minutes and his double-century in 251 minutes. Southern Punjab's last two wickets added 148 runs, giving them a 1st innings lead of 106.
P.I.Van der Gucht and P.N.Miller added 106 for the 4th wicket.
P.N.Miller and B.W.Malcolm added 113 for the 6th wicket.
With A.Jabbar and J.N.Banerjee putting on 89 for Bengal's 10th wicket, Southern Punjab needed 313 to win.
It was the first occasion Bengal had won the trophy.

CRICKET CLUB OF INDIA v C.P. AND BERAR

Played at Nagpur, January 14, 15, 16, 17, 1939.
Toss won by C.P. and Berar
C.P. and Berar won by 39 runs.

C.P. AND BERAR

†D.D.Hindlekar	b Naoomal	51	lbw b Mubarak Ali	1
S.Ishtiaq Ali	b Mubarak Ali	7	(7) b Naoomal	41
S.Mushtaq Ali	b Mankad	40	(2) b Harris	23
*C.K.Nayudu	c Meherhomji b Mubarak	15	(3)c Meherhomji b Havewalla	11
C.S.Nayudu	c Meherhomji b Mubarak	13	(4) c Meherhomji b Mubarak	52
E.B.Aibara	b Naoomal	11	c Meherhomji b Mubarak	0
V.S.Hazare	c Mubarak b Mankad	10	(5) lbw b Ranvirsinhji	15
P.R.Nayudu	c Mankad b Naoomal	1	(10) run out	50
J.N.Bhaya	c Mankad b Naoomal	16	st Meherhomji b Havewalla	38
S.A.Latif	c Mankad b Naoomal	2	(11) not out	6
Zahur Ahmed	not out	15	(8)c Meherhomji b Ranvirsinhji	1
Extras		8		15
Total		**189**		**253**

Fall: 1st inns 1/26, 2/75, 3/105, 4/125, 5/141.
2nd inns 3/51, 4/122, 5/123, 7/164, 8/167, 9/228.

CRICKET CLUB OF INDIA

†K.R.Meherhomji	c C.S.Nayudu b Hazare	6	(2) c & b C.S.Nayudu	24
M.H.Mankad	b Hazare	13	(1) lbw b C.S.Nayudu	7
K.S.Ranvirsinhji	st Hindlekar b C.S.Nayudu	32	lbw b C.S.Nayudu	0
V.M.Merchant	b Mushtaq Ali	7	(8) c Mushtaq Ali b Hazare	1
L.Amarnath	c Hindlekar b Hazare	32	absent ill	-
*J.Naoomal	not out	88	(4) lbw b C.S.Nayudu	11
K.S.Indravijaysinhji	c & b C.S.Nayudu	20	(5) c & b C.S.Nayudu	15
D.R.Havewalla	c Zahur Ahmed b C.K.Nayudu	52	(9) b Hazare	39
J.Harris	b Hazare	10	(6) c Zahur b C.S.Nayudu	3
S.Mubarak Ali	st Hindlekar b C.S.Nayudu	15	(7) b C.S.Nayudu	6
V.N.Raiji	c Mushtaq Ali b Hazare	0	(10) not out	1
Extras		17		4
Total		**292**		**111**

Fall: 1st inns 1/15, 2/20, 3/42, 4/88, 5/94, 6/163, 7/255, 8/266.
2nd inns 1/31, 2/31, 3/36, 4/53, 5/66, 6/77, 7/97, 8/98, 9/111.

CP AND BERAR	O	M	R	W	O	M	R	W
C.K.Nayudu	26	5	65	1	3	0	13	0
C.S.Nayudu	35	7	93	3	11	1	43	7
Mushtaq Ali	9	2	?3	1				
Hazare	42.2	9	69	5	13	3	43	2
Latif	3	0	3	0				
Zahur Ahmed	2	0	9	0	2	0	8	0
Ishtiaq Ali	1	0	3	0				

CC OF INDIA	O	M	R	W	O	M	R	W
Amarnath	13	5	31	0	20	13	14	0
Mubarak	23	5	26	3	31	8	76	3
Harris	7	5	19	0	13	1	19	1
Mankad	14	2	43	2	5	0	25	0
Havewalla	13	0	44	0	13	0	22	2
Naoomal	13.2	2	18	5	23	0	58	1
Ranvirsinhji	-	-	-	-	11	1	24	2

Close of play scores. First day: Cricket Club 25.2 (Ranvirs Singh 2*, V.M.Merchant 3*). **Second day:** Cricket Club 292 all out. **Third day:** C.P. And Berar 228/9 (P.R.Nayudu 32*, S.A.Latif 0*).

HINDUS v MUSLIMS

Played at University Ground, Lahore, on March 4, 5, 1939.
Toss won by Muslims.
Hindus won by 4 wickets.

MUSLIMS

Gul Mahomed	c Jagdish Lal b Naoomal	95	(2) b Nayudu	9
Mohammad Aslam	b Nayudu	4	(7) c Jagdish Lal b Nayudu	3
S.Mushtaq Ali	c Prithviraj b Naoomal	78	c & b Chunilal	14
Muzaffar Beg	c Nayudu b Naoomal	4	(1) lbw b Chunilal	19
*M.Baqa Jilani	run out	32	(4) b Nayudu	1
†Abbas Khan	b Naoomal	1	(5) lbw b Nayudu	0
Gulzar Mohammad	c Nayudu b Naoomal	11	(6) b Nayudu	7
Aftab Ahmed	b Nayudu	6	(9) b Nayudu	17
Habibullah	c Prithviraj b Nayudu	11	(10) not out	5
Muzaffar Khan	not out	10	(8) c Jagdish Lal b Chunilal	0
Nazir Nizami	c Hindlekar b Nayudu	2	lbw b Nayudu	0
Extras		5		4
Total		**259**		**79**

Fall: 1st inns 1/29, 2/166, 4/333.
2nd inns 1/22, 2/41, 3/42, 4/42, 5/54, 6/56, 7/56, 8/62, 9/79.

HINDUS

†D.D.Hindlekar	c & b Gul Mahomed	61	b Habibullah	1
Jagdish Lal	b Nazir Nizami	9	(3) b Aftab Ahmed	27
Munilal	c Muzaffar Beg b Gul Mahomed	30	(2) b Nazir Nizami	1
Ram Prakash	c Jilani b Gul Mahomed	14	(6) run out	2
Prithviraj	b Aftab Ahmed	1	c Muzaffar Khan b Habibullah	14
C.S.Nayudu	b Nazir Nizami	6	(7) not out	18
J.Naoomal	b Gul Mahomed	35	(4) lbw b Habibullah	14
*M.R.Bhide	c Muzaffar Beg b Habibullah	32	not out	10
G.Kischenchand	b Habibullah	31		
Hiralal	not out	3		
Chunilal	c Muzaffar Beg b Habibullah	9		
Extras		17		7
Total		**248**	(6 wickets)	**94**

Fall: 1st inns 1/17, 2/92, 3/116, 4/121, 5/121, 6/136, 7/184, 8/229, 9/237.
2nd inns 1/3, 2/3, 3/22, 4/60, 5/74, 6/78.

HINDUS	O	M	R	W	O	M	R	W
Hiralal	5	0	29	0	6	0	26	0
Chunilal	8	3	21	0	11	0	28	3
Nayudu	28	4	111	4	11	2	21	7
Kischenchand	2	0	11	0				
Naoomal	19	1	82	5				

MUSLIMS	O	M	R	W	O	M	R	W
Nazir Nizami	26	4	68	2	8	1	24	1
Habibullah	18	4	41	3	13	4	36	3
Jilani	7	1	39	0				
Mushtaq Ali	2	0	14	0				
Gul Mahomed	12	4	30	4				
Aftab Ahmed	15	4	39	1	8	0	18	1
Muzaffar Khan	-				3	0	9	0

Close of play scores. First day: Hindus 121/5 (C.S.Nayudu 0*).

Comments: Match completed in two days.
Lahore Tournament.

EUROPEANS v INDIANS

Played at Chepauk Ground, Madras, on January 13, 14, 15, 1939.
Toss won by Europeans.
Indians won by four wickets.

EUROPEANS

*C.P.Johnstone	b Rangachari	1	c Doraiswami b Rangachari	44
A.W.Stansfield	c Gopalan b Parthasarathi	13	lbw b Parthasarathi	9
C.N.Reed	b Parthasarathi	10	c Parthasarathi b Parankusam	33
R.Nailer	b Rangachari	37	b Deenan	1
H.W.Horton	run out	6	c Ram Singh b Parankusam	9
†H.P.Ward	c Ram Singh b Parankusam	0	c Doraiswami b Rangachari	1
W.V.H.Robins	st Doraiswami b Ram Singh	15	b Parankusam	39
R.H.Taite	b Parthasarathi	38	b Rangachari	0
J.P.McIver	b Gopalan	29	b Ram Singh	2
R.Spitteler	b Gopalan	0	(11) not out	1
F.F.Coldwell	not out	0	(10) b Gopalan	15
Extras		6		15
Total		**155**		**169**

Fall: 1st inns 1/1, 2/26, 3/33, 4/57, 5/57, 6/83, 7/87, 8/145, 9/145.
2nd inns 1/33, 2/80, 3/81, 4/106, 5/108, 6/112, 7/113, 8/133, 9/165.

INDIANS

A.V.Krishnaswami	lbw b Spitteler	4	(6) b Spitteler	0
†T.M.Doraiswami	b Spitteler	3	(1) b Spitteler	4
A.G.Ram Singh	c Ward b McIver	66	(5) c Ward b Spitteler	46
B.S.Bhadradi	lbw b Johnstone	30	lbw b Spitteler	26
P.V.Lakshmanan	b Spitteler	16	(3) c Johnstone b Coldwell	3
A.Jagannathan Rao	b Spitteler	41	(7) not out	15
*M.J.Gopalan	c Spitteler b Robins	23	(8) not out	15
G.Parthasarathi	c Nailer b Robins	0		
S.G.Deenan	c Spitteler b Robins	9	(2) c Ward b Spitteler	5
C.R.Rangachari	c Spitteler b Robins	7		
T.S.Parankusam	not out	0		
Extras		4		9
Total		**203**	(6 wickets)	**123**

Fall: 1st inns 1/6, 2/11, 3/65, 4/115, 5/125, 6/165, 7/165, 8/193, 9/203.
2nd inns 1/2, 2/4, 3/11, 4/13, 5/46, 6/106.

INDIANS	O	M	R	W	O	M	R	W
Rangachari	15	4	27	2	18	5	46	3
Gopalan	5.3	0	14	2	9.3	1	20	1
Deenan	3	0	12	0	2	0	7	1
Parthasarathi	13	0	53	3	4	0	25	1
Ram Singh	11	0	36	1	9	1	18	1
Parankusam	3	0	7	1	14	3	38	3

EUROPEANS	O	M	R	W	O	M	R	W
Spitteler	27	10	53	4	17	5	29	5
Coldwell	14	2	34	0	12.1	1	47	1
Taite	12	2	43	0				
Johnstone	7	1	20	1	4	1	10	0
Robins	13.4	1	36	4	3	0	18	0
McIver	6	1	13	1	4	0	10	0

Close of play scores. First day: Indians 122/4 (P.V.Lakshmanan 14*, Jagannathan Rao 1*). **Second day:** Indians 11/2 (S.G.Deenan 4*, P.V.Lakshmanan 3*).
Comments: Madras Presidency Match.

INDEX OF MATCH SCORECARDS